Qualitative Research in Action

Qualitative Research in Action

edited by
TIM MAY

SAGE Publications
London • Thousand Oaks • New Delhi

Introduction © Tim May 2002
Chapter 1 © Dorothy E. Smith 2002
Chapter 2 © Sam Porter 2002
Chapter 3 © Peter K. Manning 2002
Chapter 4 © Christian Heath and Jon Hindmarsh 2002
Chapter 5 © Malcolm Williams 2002
Chapter 6 © Martín Sánchez-Jankowski 2002
Chapter 7 © Nigel G. Fielding 2002
Chapter 8 © Valerie Walkerdine, Helen Lucey and June Melody 2002
Chapter 9 © Kathleen Gerson and Ruth Horowitz 2002
Chapter 10 © Jennifer Mason 2002
Chapter 11 © Steph Lawler 2002
Chapter 12 © Linda McKie 2002
Chapter 13 © Lynne Haney 2002
Chapter 14 © Tracey Reynolds 2002
Chapter 15 © Amanda Coffey 2002
Chapter 16 © Lisa Adkins 2002
Chapter 17 © Beverley Skeggs 2002
Chapter 18 © Sherryl Kleinman 2002

First published 2002

SAGE Publications Ltd
6 Bonhill Street
London EC2A 4PU

SAGE Publications Inc.
2455 Teller Road
Thousand Oaks, California 91320

SAGE Publications India Pvt Ltd
32, M-Block Market
Greater Kailash – I
New Delhi 110 048

British Library Cataloguing in Publication data

A catalogue record for this book is available
from the British Library

ISBN 0 7619 6067 8
ISBN 0 7619 6068 6 (pbk)

Library of Congress Control Number 2001 132949

Typeset by SIVA Math Setters, Chennai, India
Printed in Great Britain by The Cromwell Press Ltd, Trowbridge, Wiltshire

CONTENTS

Notes on Contributors   vii

Acknowledgements   xiii

Introduction: Transformation in Principles and Practice   1

Part 1   Putting the Practice into Theory   **15**

1   Institutional Ethnography   17
     Dorothy E. Smith

2   Critical Realist Ethnography   53
     Sam Porter

3   Framing the Rational in Fieldwork   73
     Peter K. Manning

4   Analysing Interaction: Video, Ethnography
     and Situated Conduct   99
     Christian Heath and Jon Hindmarsh

Part 2   Generalization, Interpretation and Analysis   **123**

5   Generalization in Interpretive Research   125
     Malcolm Williams

6   Representation, Responsibility and Reliability in
     Participant-Observation   144
     Martín Sánchez-Jankowski

7   Automating the Ineffable: Qualitative Software and the
     Meaning of Qualitative Research   161
     Nigel G. Fielding

8   Subjectivity and Qualitative Method   179
     Valerie Walkerdine, Helen Lucey and June Melody

Part 3   Choices in Context   **197**

9   Observation and Interviewing: Options and Choices
     in Qualitative Research   199
     Kathleen Gerson and Ruth Horowitz

10 Qualitative Interviewing: Asking, Listening and Interpreting 225
Jennifer Mason

11 Narrative in Social Research 242
Steph Lawler

Part 4 Power, Participation and Expertise **259**

12 Engagement and Evaluation in Qualitative Inquiry 261
Linda McKie

13 Negotiating Power and Expertise in the Field 286
Lynne Haney

14 On Relations between Black Female Researchers
and Participants 300
Tracey Reynolds

Part 5 Reflexivity, the Self and Positioning **311**

15 Ethnography and Self: Reflections and Representations 313
Amanda Coffey

16 Reflexivity and the Politics of Qualitative Research 332
Lisa Adkins

17 Techniques for Telling the Reflexive Self 349
Beverley Skeggs

18 Emotions, Fieldwork and Professional Lives 375
Sherryl Kleinman

Index 395

NOTES ON CONTRIBUTORS

Lisa Adkins is Lecturer in Sociology at the University of Manchester. Her research interests are in the areas of social theory, feminist theory, sexuality, gender and economy. Her publications include *Gendered Work* (Open University Press, 1995), *Sexualizing the Social* (with Vicki Merchant, Macmillan, 1996) and *Sex, Sensibility and the Gendered Body* (with Janet Holland, Macmillan, 1996). Recent articles have been published in *Theory, Culture and Society* and *Economy and Society*. She is currently completing a book called *Revisions: Towards a Feminist Sociology of Late Modernity* (Open University Press) which considers theories of identity transformation in relation to gender and sexuality.

Amanda Coffey is based at the School of Social Sciences, Cardiff University. She is one of the founding editors of the journal *Qualitative Research* and a co-editor of *The Handbook of Ethnography* (Sage, 2001). Her research interests include ethnographic representation and (auto)biography in qualitative method. Her publications include (with Paul Atkinson) *Making Sense of Qualitative Data* (Sage, 1996) and *The Ethnographic Self* (Sage, 1999).

Nigel G. Fielding is Professor of Sociology and Co-Director of the Institute of Social Research at the University of Surrey. He has taught field methods and criminology at Surrey since 1978. His research interests are in qualitative methods, new research technologies and criminal justice. He was editor of the *Howard Journal of Criminal Justice* from 1985 to 1998, and is co-editor of the series 'New Technologies for Social Research' (Sage). He has published twelve books and is currently working on the second edition of *Computer Programs for Qualitative Data Analysis* (with E. Weitzman and R. Lee) and a four-volume set on *Interviewing* (both for Sage).

Kathleen Gerson is Professor (and Chair) of Sociology at New York University, where she specializes in the study of gender, work, family and social change processes. She is the author of several books, including *No Man's Land: Men's Changing Commitments to Family and Work* (Basic Books, 1993) and *Hard Choices: How Women Decide about Work, Career, and Motherhood* (University of California Press, 1985). She is currently at work on a study of 'Children of the Gender Revolution', in which she is examining the experiences, responses and gender strategies of the young women and men who have grown up in non-traditional families over the last few decades of tumultuous work and family changes in American society. Additional ongoing projects include a study of trends in working time, work arrangements and gender equity in modern workplaces and an examination of how growing conflicts between family and work have created new moral dilemmas that are blurring the gender boundaries between women and men.

Lynne Haney is an Assistant Professor of Sociology at New York University. She has conducted ethnographic research on the state in both the United States and in Hungary. Her book, *Inventing the Needy: Gender and the Politics of Welfare in Hungary*, is forthcoming from the University of California Press. She is also one of the authors of *Global Ethnography: Forces, Connections, and Imaginations in a Postmodern World* (University of California Press, 2000), which lays out a framework for studying globalization ethnographically. Her current research project examines the politics of contemporary welfare reform in the United States through interviews with two generations of low-income women in Maryland and California.

Christian Heath is a Professor at King's College London and leads the Work, Interaction and Technology Research Group. He specializes in video-based field studies of social interaction. Current projects include studies of museums, of operation centres on London Underground and of medical consultations, and address such varied issues as the embodiment of suffering, the aesthetic experience of art-work and ecological perception of public behaviour. These projects also involve the design and deployment of new artefacts and technologies ranging from interactive art installations through to image recognition systems. His recent publications include *Technology in Action* (with Paul Luff, Cambridge University Press, 2000).

Jon Hindmarsh is a Research Fellow in the Work, Interaction and Technology Research Group in the Management Centre, King's College London. His principal interests concern the interactional organization of talk and embodied conduct within workplace settings, such as control centres, anaesthetic rooms and classrooms. He has also collaborated with computer scientists on studies of social interaction in virtual reality and is currently extending that work to inform the design of advanced, interactive exhibits in museums and galleries. Recent articles have appeared in the *Journal of Contemporary Ethnography*, *Journal of Pragmatics* and *Symbolic Interaction*. He is also co-editor of *Workplace Studies* (with Paul Luff and Christian Heath, Cambridge University Press, 2000).

Ruth Horowitz is Professor of Sociology at New York University and received her PhD from the University of Chicago. *Teen Mothers: Citizens or Dependents?* (University of Chicago Press, 1995) won the Charles Horton Cooley Award and *Honor and the American Dream: Culture and Identity in a Chicano Community* (Rutgers University Press, 1983) received an honourable mention for the C.W. Mills Award. She is currently working on a project about public participation on state medical licensing and disciplinary boards in the United States.

Sherryl Kleinman is Professor of Sociology at the University of North Carolina, Chapel Hill. She is the author of *Equals before God: Seminarians as Humanistic Professionals* (University of Chicago Press, 1984), *Opposing Ambitions: Gender and Identity in an Alternative Organization* (University of Chicago Press, 1996) and co-author of *Emotions and Fieldwork* (with Martha Copp, Sage, 1993). She is currently writing sociologically informed personal essays for audiences within and beyond academia.

Steph Lawler is a Lecturer in Sociology at the University of Durham, where she teaches modules in the sociology of gender, childhood and research in sociology and social policy. She spent several years researching narratives of maternal and daughterly identities and has written on the mother–daughter relationship, gender and class and relations of expertise. She is currently planning research into adult and child identities expressed through kinship narratives. Her most recent publication is *Mothering the Self: Mothers, Daughters, Subjects* (Routledge, 2000).

Linda McKie is Research Professor in Sociology at Glasgow Caledonian University. Prior to moving to Glasgow in 1999 she undertook sociological research in the Department of General Practice and Primary Care at the University of Aberdeen. Her current work includes the development of qualitative evaluation of community health work; gender, caring and citizenship, and disclosing domestic violence in primary health care. Recent publications include *Gender Power and the Household* (with Sophia Bowlby and Susan Gregory, Macmillan, 1999), *Organizing Bodies: Policy, Institutions and Work* (with Nick Watson, Macmillan, 2000) and *Constructing Gendered Bodies* (with Kathryn Backett-Milburn, Palgrave, 2001).

Peter K. Manning is Brooks Chair of Criminal Justice at Northeastern University, Boston. In 2001, he was Senior Research Scholar at Northeastern College of Criminal Justice in Boston. He has been a Fellow of Wolfson and Balliol Colleges, Oxford, and Senior Research Associate at the Centre for Socio-Legal Studies, Oxford, as well as a Visiting Professor at MIT, The University at Albany and York University, Toronto. He has been a Fellow at the Rockefeller Villa, Bellagio, in 2000, and is named in *Who's Who in America* and *Who's Who in the World*. He was awarded the Bruce Smith Award and the O.W. Wilson Award by the Academy of Criminal Justice Sciences. He has published some twelve books, numerous chapters and articles in professional journals, and has just completed *Picturing Policing* (2001). His current research is on the rationalization of policing including crime analysis and mapping, and involves fieldwork in two large US police departments.

Jennifer Mason is Senior Lecturer in Sociology and Deputy Director of the Centre for Research on Family, Kinship and Childhood, at the University of Leeds. She is author of *Qualitative Researching* (Sage, 1996) and co-author (with Janet Finch) of *Passing On: Kinship and Inheritance in England*

(Routledge, 2000), *Wills, Inheritance and Families* (Clarendon Press, 1996) and *Negotiating Family Responsibilities* (Routledge, 1993).

Tim May is Professor of Sociology at the University of Salford, having previously worked at Durham (1995–99) and Plymouth (1989–95). In addition to articles on the same subjects, he has authored and co-edited books on organizational change (1991), social research (1993, 2nd edn 1997), ethnography (1993), social theory (1996), philosophy and social research (with Malcolm Williams, 1996), work with offenders (1996) and philosophy, social theory and methodology (with Malcolm Williams, 1998). More recently he has written, with Zygmunt Bauman, *Thinking Sociologically* (Blackwell, 2001) and the third edition of *Social Research* (Open University Press, 2001). Among other projects, he is currently writing a book on reflexivity (Sage) and continuing to edit an international book series (Issues in Society, Open University Press).

Sam Porter is Professor of Nursing Research in the School of Nursing and Midwifery, Queen's University Belfast. Formerly, he held a post in the Department of Sociology in Queen's and his research activities span the disciplines of nursing and sociology. As well as engaging in substantive qualitative research, he has written extensively on research methodology, social theory and the connection between these two areas. His latest book is *Social Theory and Nursing Practice* (Macmillan, 1998).

Tracey Reynolds is Research Fellow at the Race and Ethnicity Research Unit, South Bank University, London. Her PhD doctoral thesis focused on Black mothering in Britain. Her current research interests and publications are around the areas of the Black family, mothers and paid work, and Black community activism. She also lectures in social research skills at the university.

Martín Sánchez-Jankowski is Professor of Sociology and Director of the Center for Urban Ethnography at the University of California, Berkeley. His speciality is the sociology of poverty and he has primarily used participant-observation methodology for his research since 1975. He is the author of *Islands in the Street* (University of California Press, 1991) and his recent publications include 'African American poverty and the dispersal of the working class' (1999) and 'Using computers to analyze ethnographic field data' (1998). He is finishing a book on the dynamics of social change and maintenance in long-term poverty neighbourhoods and has begun a multi-year research project on violence in inner-city schools in the United States.

Beverley Skeggs is Professor of Sociology at Manchester University. She was Co-Director of Women's Studies at Lancaster University 1994–97. She has published *Formations of Class and Gender* (Sage, 1997), *Feminist Cultural Theory* (Manchester University Press, 1995) and *Transformations: Thinking through Feminism* (with colleagues, Routledge, 2000). She has also written on postmodernism, toilets, music and sexuality. Her most recent research project is on *Violence, Sexuality and Space*.

Dorothy E. Smith is in the Department of Sociology and Equity Studies of the University of Toronto. She has been preoccupied since the late 1970s or so with developing the implications for sociology of taking women's standpoint. Her books include *The Everyday World as Problematic: A Feminist Sociology* (University of Toronto Press, 1987), *The Conceptual Practice of Power* (University of Toronto Press, 1990), *Text, Facts, and Femininity* (Routledge, 1990) and *Writing the Social: Critique, Theory and Investigations* (University of Toronto Press, 1999).

Valerie Walkerdine, Helen Lucey and June Melody worked together as the research team for the ESRC research project 'Transition to Womanhood in 1990s Britain' at Goldsmiths College, University of London. Valerie is presently Foundation Professor of Critical Psychology, Head of the Centre for Critical Psychology and regional head of the School of Psychology at the University of Western Sydney in Australia. Helen is Research Fellow in the School of Education, King's College London, and June Melody is training to be a psychoanalyst in London. Their latest book is *Growing Up Girl: Psychosocial Explorations of Gender and Class* (Palgrave, 2001).

Malcolm Williams is Principal Lecturer in Sociology at the University of Plymouth, UK. He is author of *Science and Social Science* (Routledge, 2000) and *Introduction to Philosophy of Social Research* (with Tim May, Routledge, 1996). Also (with Tim May) he is co-editor of *Knowing the Social World* (Open University Press, 1998). He has also published a number of articles in the areas of research methodology, housing need and counter-urbanization.

ACKNOWLEDGEMENTS

First, my thanks to all of the contributors. They put up with my constant requests and even my 'nudges' to get chapters completed on time and were also kind enough to comment on my introductory chapter.

Those at Sage Publications were very supportive of the project and thanks are due to Michael Carmichael, Zoe Elliott and the editorial and production teams, as well as to Malcolm Reed for compiling the index and Christine Firth for performing such excellent work on the manuscript.

My thanks to those friends who have remained so supportive and to Dee, Cian and Calum, my love and gratitude.

INTRODUCTION:

Transformation in principles and practice

Tim May

Welcome to *Qualitative Research in Action*. In the planning of this volume a particular process was adopted. The reasons for this were not only due to the geographical spread of the contributors, but also to permit chapters to be exchanged and commented upon. Overall, the purpose was to enable a thematic coherence to emerge within the volume as a whole. It was also recognized that while we talk about the links between process and product in research practice, along with the need to share experiences, this is often not the case when it comes to the production of edited collections. Given this, the idea of 'pairing' was introduced. The aim here was to make the process of writing for an edited collection more thematic, as well as pleasurable and supportive. The result is a book structured around 'issues in practice' as its main focus.

Before moving on to provide an overview of the chapters, it is necessary to situate them in terms of the issues that have informed, in various ways, thinking about the practice of qualitative research. To detail these transformations, brought about by a number of different traditions – for example, feminisms, social constructionist perspectives, critical theory, critical realism, postmodernism and post-structuralism – is not my task here. Nevertheless, it is to draw out some of the themes in order to provide a context for the chapters and part headings that appear in this volume.

PRACTICE, PROCESS AND TEXTS

We have witnessed in the latter part of the twentieth century a number of critiques concerning the status of social research in society. Although mostly aimed at positivism and empiricism, it has resulted in extensions of particular discourses into terrains that were once presumed to be clear in their demarcation points, for instance the relationships between philosophy, theory, methodology and method. We can now observe that data are produced, not collected, and it is the process of production that is fundamentally related to the product (May 2001). Whether overtly, or as a result of the presuppositions that are inevitably embedded within ways of thinking that inform practice and so often remain beyond question, the decisions that are made about theory, methods, methodology, ethics and politics are now open to routine scrutiny. Particular ideas of neutrality, such as the maintenance of objectivity through positioning the researcher as nothing but a passive instrument of data collection, are now exposed as falsehoods that seek to mask the realities of the research process. The knower (as researcher) is now implicated in the construction of the known (the dynamics and content of society and social relations).

At this point we might note that this trend is nothing new. In *The Sociological Imagination*, originally published in 1959, Mills had a chapter on 'reason and freedom'. Here he noted how social science had inherited terms which, although outdated, remain rooted in practice. He then moved on to argue that these 'standard categories of thought', if generalized to contemporary situations, 'become unwieldy, irrelevant, not convincing … so now The Modern Age is being succeeded by a *post-modern period*. Perhaps we may call it: The Fourth Epoch' (Mills 1970 [1959]: 184, added emphasis).

There are many other examples that could have been used to illustrate this point. Jürgen Habermas (1992) argues that the opening for postmodernism in western thought began in the late nineteenth century in the writings of Nietzsche, while Barry Smart (1993) finds references to the term in 1930s literary criticism. If the epoch which has given us these critiques, however, is concerned with the search for new values, identities and ways of life, perhaps it is not surprising that we can range, in reaction to these criticisms, from those who argue that nothing has changed to those for whom anything less than total embrace is an act of betrayal. As a result we find calls for a return to a 'scientific basis' for disciplines mixing with those who denounce social research in favour of other mediums of representation, for example, poetry, fiction and art. Those napping in the cosy slumbers of past scientific 'pretensions' can then find their practices being characterized as branches of literary criticism.

Here we can detect movements in opposite directions and this detracts from the productive potential that comes with engagement. Polarizations between an unproblematic science and acts of literary deconstruction do little to aid understanding. While the idea that one can, without question, claim to speak in the name of a separate and unproblematic reality should be exposed to scrutiny, so too should the claim to speak in the name of different realities as mediated by alternative modes of representation. We see the same tendencies in both claims: that is, to legislate over the constitution and nature of social reality. In the process scientism – defined as the belief that science is the *only* form of legitimate knowledge – becomes confused with science. The latter, if mixed with a sensitivity to context and a willingness to engage in an understanding of the relationship between justification and application that is not taken to be beyond question, can be moulded by considerations that lie beyond the confines of its boundaries. These include the desirability of various courses of actions, as well as recognition of different forms of life.

There is also the transmission and effect of these critiques as they become aligned with modes of scholastic communication to consider. A series of acts of demolition on so-called classic texts can assist in the process of accumulating, to deploy the tools of analysis of Pierre Bourdieu (Bourdieu and Wacquant 1992), cultural capital within academic fields. The project is to expose the presuppositions of those who were once canonized as representatives of a tradition that budding apprentices are expected to emulate in their practice. These texts may be laid bare in order to render public just how they cannot live up to their own aspirations, let alone those standards which those who charge themselves with this undertaking invoke.

The effect is to produce competing academic camps with those defending established procedures pitted against those who set themselves the task of finding tacit assumptions that represent nothing more than nostalgic yearnings for a bygone age. The search for true knowledge is the target of attack for representing the 'fantasy to seize reality' and thus the solution becomes: 'Let us wage war on totality; let us be witnesses to the unpresentable; let us activate the differences' (Lyotard 1993: 46). We then await the next stage for those thinkers subject to acts of deconstruction: the process of resurrection. At this point those same thinkers, when translated in different ways according to different influences, appear as more subtle and useful to the present age than previous interpretations might have suggested. Careers are then forged in acts of deconstruction against which another set in the intellectual class can then sharpen their pencils.

Such activity is a vital part of the vibrancy of intellectual work and functions as an instrument for sensitizing researchers to the consequences of practices and assumptions. At what point, however, does such activity become counter-productive from the point of view of research practice and understanding itself? When does it cease to inform in order to change practice and instead undermine it and so lead to paralysis and inactivity? Take, for example, methodological translations of the works of Jacques Derrida (1978). These can lead to reflexive accounts that, paradoxically, reproduce the very ego-identity that is the subject of his critical interventions (see Norris 1987). Manifest in confessions of failed attempts to discover an unproblematic reality, what then emerges is a whole new industry for textual reflections on the futility of this enterprise (May 1998). The result is that representations can be rendered so incoherent that engagement is difficult, if not impossible, for the purposes of illuminating the dynamics of social issues. We end up with accounts that can reproduce the very targets of Derrida's critiques: the closure of texts and the centrality of the subject in the production of those texts.

In the face of these trends it is possible to form the distinct impression that methodological discussions are now trapped within descending interpretative circles. With the struggle for academic capital in place, reputations may be forged via interpretations of interpretations. Yet how are the interpreters authorized to make such interpretations in the first place? Would this be something to do with the institutional authority that is bestowed upon them and that enables a distance to be maintained from the practice and products of systematic social investigation?

Of course there are clear advantages of such distance, particularly when compared with those whose practice is driven by the interests of sponsors who make specific demands according to the pursuit of narrow interests. Yet it can so easily lapse into an indulgence that misses its mark. The limits to reflexivity then inhere in a willingness to subject one's own position and what it does or does not authorize as a result, to critical scrutiny (May 1999, 2000). Add to this the fact that the world is not about to stop and listen to such debates and this tells us something about the ways in which our dominant modes of organizing social relations take their revenge on discourses. If we turn our attention to such matters we might then be able to expose what Michel Foucault (1991) called the 'limits of appropriation' of discourse. In this way we may not see it as all encompassing of social relations and begin to ask how it is that the analyst may claim a privileged vantagepoint in the face of what are taken to be overwhelming social forces?

The issue now turns to reconstruction. Engaged, theoretically informed empirical work, can be conducted in order to illuminate issues and bring to the attention of a wider audience the dynamics and consequences of social relations. From a more critical genre, this provides for the possibility of things being other than they are via a critique of what Roberto Unger (1987) has called 'false necessity'. This same genre can be captured in Foucault's work. For Foucault, to assume that the end of critique is some consensual state of affairs runs the danger of the constitution of a complacent attitude that, by default, disguises non-consensuality in a celebration of finality (Foucault 1984). A critical ethos must be seen as a necessary, but not sufficient condition, to guard against 'power as evil'. This appears as a process without end. The potential for a critical approach to research work, considered genealogically, is its ability not only to 'reveal reality', but also to 'deconstruct necessity' (Hoy 1998). What is at stake is not just how others dominate us, but also how we dominate ourselves. We find the same impulse in feminist-inspired research where reconstruction is identified alongside the need for deconstruction in order to remain sensitive to the working assumptions that inform practice (Harding and Hintikka 1983). Similarly, in order to avoid the traps of a 'false' universalism and particularism, we find Pierre Bourdieu's (2000) concern to conduct research as a contribution to a 'realpolitik of reason'.

These issues are not, contrary to the attitude of those who regard philosophical matters as detracting from the 'real' work, irrelevant. Built into assumptions are epistemological and ontological presuppositions that render the world intelligible. However, if a certain form of practice and contemplation – as that which enables research to be undertaken in the first place – is born in a double movement of reflexivity in terms of possessing a point of view on the point of view (Bourdieu and Wacquant 1992), it is because researchers have a distance from the necessity they examine in order to turn practice into an object of investigation. Practice, after all, must be indifferent to the conditions of its possibility in order to be practice *as such*. Imagine the paralysis that would come with repeated reflections upon every act prior and subsequent to its execution. Although language carries a degree of reflexivity (Garfinkel 1967; Harré 1998), continual and conscious monitoring of actions *within* actions would bring them to a halt. Further, what may be omitted from such deliberations are the conditions that enable and constrain actions. The study of the conditions of knowledge production in terms of the positioning of the researcher is thus a guard against not only the conflation of scholastic with practical reason, but also the complacency and arrogance that is born in dispositions that have the potential to accompany *all* modes of thought – whatever their claims may be concerning the constitution of social reality.

Without a gaze turned towards the continuing endeavours and positions of researchers, those who once sought something called an unproblematic 'reality' can turn their attention to past mistakes, while experimenting with new forms of writing. Again, however, the potential for further illumination of social dynamics and situations can so easily slip from being complementary, to having a substitutory role in relation to research practice. It then moves, by default, forms of representation aside from social research from having a regulatory and reflexive function, to a constitutive one. Different forms of representation are then assumed to take precedence over the results of systematic social investigation and in so doing simply reverse the scales. Fiction becomes reality, rather than having the potential to be complementary in its discovery. Yet questions will still be begged when we ask of such forms of representation: whom do they affect? Under what circumstances and for what reasons? Utilizing what resources and with what overall consequences? Systematic social investigation enables us to seek answers to such questions.

We also have to ask another question: what are the costs of these conflations to future generations of researchers? What about those who are under pressure to produce results according to the edicts of institutions and sponsors who, after all, pay their wages? In the face of this how can critical interventions provide those researchers with the resources to challenge organizations that will continue to commission research? It is they who are positioned to completely ignore such critical interventions, but not necessarily the next generation of academics who may now be doctoral students and those on temporary research contracts. Similarly, how can the policy process be informed and changed while noting, of course, that it is often the art of persuasion, rather than the results of systematic social investigation, which informs such outcomes?

Here we can detect another possible consequence in relation to engagements between social research and social life. If there is a withdrawal from fields of current endeavour there are plenty of those who are unfettered by the latest critiques concerning the quest to uncover realities that are only too happy to fill it. These are the armies of 'journalists, pundits, politicians, and pop-theorists, who are always more than willing to supply that need'

(McCarthy in Hoy and McCarthy 1994: 220). In what is taken to be a methodologically post-positivist/empiricist/modernist age, 'instrumental positivism' (Bryant 1985) still appears to find a way of marching onwards.

None of this is to suggest that neatly demarcated boundaries exist. It is to say that a failure to understand the forces which act upon the process of social research and the conditions under which it is enacted, leads to a limited understanding of its place and value in social life. Those who wish to change practice, but do not take this into account, simply miss the target. In the productive agonisms that can and should exist between social research and social life, we need to understand much more about how and under what circumstances it can be deployed without a capitulation to the power of those social forces that seek to mould its practices and findings in their name.

CONTRIBUTIONS: ISSUES, THEMES AND CONTENT

There is no doubt that there are positive benefits in the processes of rethinking the issues, processes and practices of research. Different ways of organizing research can also open up new possibilities (Gulbenkian Commission 1996). Yet it is upon qualitative research that these critiques have so often alighted and it is for these reasons that this volume was brought together to consider their implications for actual practice. In the process new terrains of inquiry have been opened up, or subjected to scrutiny in new ways. These include the relations between fieldwork and social identity, actions, emotions, narratives, reflexivity, participation, representation and generalization. Along with these we have witnessed the introduction of new technologies of data analysis, evaluation research and ways of combining methods to enhance insight into the dynamics of social life.

All of these topics and more are examined in this collection. It has been designed with the intention of assisting the process of reconstruction alongside a continued monitoring of the working assumptions of research practice. What distinguishes this volume, from other collections, is not only the focus and scope of its contributions, but also the contributors themselves. They come from different intellectual traditions and range from those well established in their disciplines, to those who have recently embarked upon their careers. What emerges is a sense of the issues that continue to arise in practice, as well as how they are addressed, under what circumstances and with what effects. The contributors are reflecting upon their experiences in terms of what it has informed them about the process of conducting qualitative research. As a result we learn about what we may *and* may not expect of the product, as well as the actual content and context of its practice. Important, but often-neglected, issues thereby emerge from within these chapters.

For the purposes of assisting the reader, the book is divided into five parts. All of them are informed by the theme of interrogating practice in terms of its potential for explaining social relations via actual research examples; bearing in mind the transformations that have taken place in thinking about the role and process of research in understanding social relations. The first part, however, is explicitly focused around this general issue. Part 2 is then organized around concerns with generalization, interpretation and analysis and Part 3 examines methodological choices in practice. Part 4 specifically focuses upon issues of power, participation and expertise in the research process. The final part is organized around the themes of reflexivity, the self and positioning. These parts cannot be exhaustive nor can there be any claim of this type. Nevertheless, they are distinctive and so it is hoped that the reader, once equipped with these accounts, will be better able to engage with issues in practice that, as noted earlier, may often be overlooked.

PUTTING THE PRACTICE INTO THEORY

Part 1 opens with a contribution by Dorothy E. Smith. In this chapter we find a detailed overview of her approach to studying social relations by taking a procedural mode of understanding to what has become a highly influential practice rooted, as it is, within the women's movement and focused upon the 'everyday world as problematic'. Using examples drawn from work with collaborators, she considers the relations between material conditions, discourses and school, home and work. The purpose of the analyst, she argues, is to map how social relations are coordinated by and contribute to activities in different sites in order to bring to people's attention how their lives and actions relate to those of others, about which they may not be aware. In the process we gain an understanding of not only the main tenets of this approach in relation to its aims and modes of engagement with the social world, but also how it addresses the relations between the conduct of research and those who are its subjects and co-producers.

In Chapter 2 Sam Porter discusses the extent to which qualitative research can be used to examine the relationship between social structures and social actions. Beginning with an overview of two classic texts – Durkheim's *Elementary Forms of Religious Life* and Weber's *Protestant Ethic and the Spirit of Capitalism* – he argues that Durkheim did not attempt to provide a methodological justification for his approach, while Weber's idea of *verstehen* was somewhat vague. He then moves on to trace the development of qualitative work, via phenomenology and postmodernist approaches and in so doing notes a gradual drift away from an examination of social structures. This provides him with an opening for an exposition of critical realism via examples drawn from his own work.

Claims to explanation often rest upon the invoking of rational action of some type. In the west we live in a system of organizing social relations that is presumed to be underpinned by actions that aim to maximize individual utility through the selection of particular means; all of which takes place in an environment which is supposed to reflect 'laws' of supply and demand.

As this is the ideological basis of a system that is so taken-for-granted in the habitual actions that inform everyday life, it would appear to be the dominant way of viewing human action. However, when it comes to utilizing such ideas in research, this story is a long way from an accurate description of human actions. Despite this, there is a frequent conflation of this normative background with the presumed neutrality of its modes of description. As a result researchers have to be aware of the assumptions they make in understanding the actions of those they study.

Taking themes from transformations in social thought, including the postmodern insight that the grounds of human action are often irrational, Peter K. Manning (Chapter 3) engages with these issues via examples taken from his work on police detectives. In the course of his account he takes various approaches to rationality to task. While any identified features of actions may be generalizable, this is an issue that requires empirical investigation. Indeed, what we find within police work is a covering, or procedural, rationality, that is orientated to working in a context where legal rules have to be taken into consideration. Nevertheless, this combines with a context-sensitive rationality that also contains what might otherwise be termed 'irrational' behaviour. Yet it is seen in these terms only if the local settings in which human action takes place are ignored.

A concern with a context-sensitive rationality, as opposed to one that is imposed by the observer, finds its expression in the work of Harold Garfinkel (1967). Garfinkel's approach is to start from the analysis of local 'experience structures' and not to generalize from social structures to personalities. Ethnomethodology was born in this move. It is this perspective, in terms of the study of institutional talk and its relationship to ethnography, that is the subject of Chapter 4 by Christian Heath and Jon Hindmarsh.

Using video and conversation data, the authors argue that the issues which arise in research between the subject and object and talk and non-verbal communication, are amenable to study from an ethnomethodological perspective. They present studies to demonstrate how there are continual and concerted efforts, on the part of social actors, to produce a social scene. These are not only context-sensitive and producing actions, but also renewing activities. It is an analysis of these, they argue, that enables the modes of sense-making in local settings and the production of intelligibility to be understood. The authors then move on to demonstrate how conversation analysis and ethnomethodology can provide data that is more usually associated with ethnographic work and this enables a greater understanding of, for example, the interactions between people and technology.

GENERALIZATION, INTERPRETATION AND ANALYSIS

In the opening chapter to Part 2, Malcolm Williams picks up on the issue of generalization that Sam Porter raises in Chapter 2. While explicitly seeking to avoid a quantitative–qualitative divide, he examines a number of epistemological and ontological themes. Taking case studies to illustrate his points, he argues that there are clearly ways in which qualitative research seeks to generalize from case studies to other circumstances, often by invoking the notion of 'typicality'. Seeking to steer a course between ideographic and nomothetic approaches, he employs *moderatum* generalizations within a pluralist approach to research practice. This is regarded as being able not only to take on board the issues that he raises and so account for the claims often made by qualitative researchers, but also to provide for a politically informed engagement which is necessary for social transformation.

Now add issues of generalization to one of the most important issues that researchers face: the movement from fieldwork to writing up. While qualitative work seeks to represent social processes, this is associated with the issues of confidentiality, sequences of thought, action and meaning and how many supporting data need to be included in field reports. A consideration of these matters often derives from a phrase that is indicative of the naturalistic underpinnings of observation-based research: that is, 'what you see is what you get!' Nevertheless, this does not relieve the researcher of some core responsibilities, including not only generalization, but also reliability.

Chapter 6 by Martín Sánchez-Jankowski seeks some practical solutions to these core issues. By examining the sequencing of actions there are ways in which an account can represent facets of observed action. At the same time, we often read accounts and ask of the observer how did they know that? Particularly when it comes to unobserved phenomena. To these questions, however, we must also add the matter of *how* observed actions should be reported. In a wide-ranging discussion he notes how errors may be reduced in observation research through attention to a set of core issues. This also has the benefit of addressing the prejudice, often reproduced by qualitative researchers themselves, that it is only survey work which is reliable.

'Solutions' to methodological and theoretical issues often appear in the form of 'techno-fixes'. In terms of a practical-political problem of representation, it is often the case that as long as the researcher can somehow become 'detached' from the production of their findings, its validity and reliability is assumed to be greater. Thus, arithmetical and graphical forms of representation still hold power over an audience *as if* the process of selectivity had not taken place. In qualitative research matters relating to selectivity for the purpose of producing accurate representations were to receive a boost with the introduction of dedicated computer software. Originally designed for the purpose of data analysis, its use has now extended to encompass collection, literature searches and the writing-up process itself. Nigel G. Fielding, while noting in Chapter 7 that 'epistemological preoccupations are more enduring than any technology', examines the history of different packages and their relationship to the qualitative research process. This history, underpinned by the story of code-and-retrieve, then provides a basis for him to move on to demystify these technological changes and examine their effects upon the practices, procedures and principles of qualitative research itself.

Aside from the role of technology in analysis, there is also the place of the researcher in the process. With this in mind, Valerie Walkerdine, Helen Lucey and June Melody (Chapter 8) examine fantasy, transference and counter-transference in relation to not only data analysis, but also production. Using examples from their work, there is an examination of subjectivity and its relation to the production of fieldnotes and how differing subjectivities inform interpretations of the same data. We thus return to an earlier theme raised by Peter K. Manning, only this time focused upon a different question: how is it that a non-rational understanding of the actions of researchers themselves affects the fieldwork process and product? The concern here is to move beyond ideas of narratives and discourses, without necessarily abandoning the insights that they have generated, to consider how people live with the contradictions and demands that are placed upon their everyday lives.

CHOICES IN CONTEXT

With choices in context in mind, Kathleen Gerson and Ruth Horowitz consider the relations between interviewing and observation-based studies. Chapter 9 compares and contrasts these two main research techniques via examples drawn from their own work. They note that observational methods provide information concerning how individuals and groups behave in a range of social settings, while interviews uncover the perceptions, motives and accounts that people offer for their actions and beliefs. Although often taken to be methods with different epistemological assumptions and theoretically at odds with one another, they are also seen to complement each other in significant ways. What we end up with, therefore, is a demonstration of how what are often maintained to be opposing positions can, when combined in practice, enrich our insights into social life.

Jennifer Mason continues in Chapter 10 with the theme of choice in methods. By asking what interviews are and what they do, in conceptual and epistemological terms, she is then in a position to explore issues associated with generalization. At this point interviewers are often faced with the act of interviewing being a static-causal snapshot when they actually seek to understand social processes. A decontextualized form of knowledge gathering thus becomes highly problematic. To overcome this tendency she argues that the interview should be seen as a process of co-participation in which both parties regard it as a site of knowledge production. To elaborate upon this idea she considers it in terms of her own work on families and kinship noting, during the course of the discussion, how some aspects of the 'social' cannot be captured through a concentration on talk alone.

Jennifer Mason's chapter raises issues associated with time, subjectivity and narratives. Just what is the significance of narratives in terms of how they are deployed in social life in order to construct accounts and social identities? It is these types of questions that Steph Lawler raises in Chapter 11 by taking narratives as accounts that bring together past and present with self and other. These are expressed in terms of transformations over time, along with actions and characters, within an overall plot. To understand narratives it is necessary to situate people within particular historical and cultural milieus in order to see how they are indicative of what may and what may not, be said. The result, to borrow a characterization from the work of Paul Ricoeur (1994), is to steer a middle course between Cartesian 'epistemic exhaltations' of the self and its apparent 'humiliation' in the hands of Nietzsche.

POWER, PARTICIPATION AND EXPERTISE

Power, participation and expertise are clearly matters that inform the conduct of research in the field. Thus, in the opening chapter to Part 4, Linda McKie notes that it is often assumed qualitative fieldwork enables the voices of respondents to be heard in ways that quantitative work does not permit. Mix this with evaluation studies and it can raise expectations among participants that may not be met by the process and its product. Add to this the flow of power and its sites of production and this will have an effect upon how researchers can engage with communities and other stakeholders in the research process. Drawing upon her own experiences in two evaluation projects in Scotland, she then notes the tensions between informing the policy process in order to improve conditions for local people and the generation of information that enhances policy-makers' 'power over' communities.

Linda McKie provides us with a very good illustration of the practical issues that arise in the conduct of evaluation work and how this affects its credibility and potential within different settings. By considering her own experiences in these contexts and how the projects unfolded and what actions were taken during the process, she highlights the importance of dialogue and deliberation. What is then required on the part of the researcher is a heightened sense of the dynamics of power in terms of how they inform the design, conduct and dissemination of the research itself. It is this theme that informs the next two chapters.

Lynne Haney (Chapter 13) examines the roles of power and negotiation in the context of two ethnographic studies – one in California and the other in Hungary – she has conducted on the state. These studies, she argues, provide critical cases for viewing the dynamics of the fieldwork process. Following the work of Dorothy E. Smith, state institutions are viewed as spaces in which 'relations of the ruling' are contested among women who, as state actors, exercise power over women as clients. As a result these conditions create particular issues for reflexive researchers. In order to consider how and under what circumstances these arise and the manner in which they may be acted upon, she discusses feminist-inspired debates about co-participation. She then turns to how a blurring between 'rulers' and 'ruled' occurred in terms of the methodological injunction to listen to the 'voices of women'. However, her own research practice did not then turn inwards, but outwards via an analysis of structural forces and 'ethnohistory'.

Lynne Haney regards an inward-looking practice as one that focuses upon the position of the researcher without due regard to wider social processes. Such thinking may be argued to have informed debates concerning the position of white female researchers researching black women. This does not suggest a balance of power, simply that the assumption of the powerful researcher and the powerless research subject requires a more nuanced understanding. Tracey Reynolds (Chapter 14) brings this to her account of being a black female researcher interviewing other black women in contemporary Britain. By taking a relational approach, she argues that power should be seen as shifting and renegotiating itself according to differing contexts in terms not only of race, but also gender and class. From this point of view, to automatically assume an imbalance of power in favour of the researcher is highly problematic when it comes to the dynamics of the fieldwork process itself.

REFLEXIVITY, THE SELF AND POSITIONING

Contributors have sought to illuminate issues surrounding representation, generalization, analysis and power in fieldwork, but how does this relate to the idea of the reflexive turn in social research, the self and positioning? The final part thus starts with Amanda Coffey considering the literary turn in ethnographic writings and its relationship to the self. While, as I noted earlier, this has sensitized us to important issues for practice, it has also had the effect of diverting attention away from what is discovered as a result of the research process itself. An understanding of social issues is thereby in danger of being abandoned in favour of introspection without engagement. To this extent the idea of producing selves within research texts should be viewed as only one part of the ways in which relations between the researcher and the social settings they seek to understand should be considered. Amanda Coffey therefore turns our attention to these issues and the limits to autoethnography for the purpose of representation.

Lisa Adkins then moves our focus to the politics of reflexivity in Chapter 16. Drawing upon her studies of gender, sexuality and work, she argues that the turn towards particular ideas on reflexivity in social research entails relations between the knower and known that permit only certain voices to be heard. A vision of the mobility of the knower, in terms of their identity, is underpinned by the assumption that they are able to move across boundaries. This raises key questions: what kind of self is required to be a reflexive researcher? What kind of narratives do research subjects/ co-producers need to perform in order to be reflexive? In asking such questions, she produces an account which questions the so-called reflexive turn in terms of its ability to amplify marginalized voices.

Beverley Skeggs picks up the idea of mobile selves in Chapter 17. In the grander claims of social theory there is often a conflation of two dimensions of action: ability and capability. The former refers to an agent's ability to monitor and account for their actions, while the latter is concerned with the power to act. This, following the work of Pierre Bourdieu, concerns dispositions and positions within fields of relations characterized by the distribution of differing forms of capital (Bourdieu 1992). With this in mind the issues surrounding and informing mobility should not be the assumption that all are mobile, as Lisa Adkins also argues in Chapter 16, but who, under what circumstances and utilizing what resources? In drawing upon her own fieldwork, Beverley Skeggs argues that attention should be turned to understanding and explaining why some people are not mobile and how their fixed positions are relied upon for the mobility of others. Without this consideration in place, calls to reflexivity become nothing more than a licence to confess, as opposed to a study of practices in relation to positioning. In the course of her discussion she thus uncovers boundaries to potentiality whose existence creates a refusal, on the part of some, to see reflexivity and mobility as privileges born of positioning.

An assumption is often made that emotions are a block to objective analysis. Such a belief is frequently perpetuated within the conditions of knowledge production itself. In university departments, for example, aloof detachment can mix with the posturing that accompanies positions informed by the accumulation of cultural capital. In these circumstances individualism may flourish and the commitment and passion to conduct research can be bracketed. This is particularly paradoxical when a discipline certainly respects and celebrates the individual, but for which individualism is a totally false description of the social world. Sherryl Kleinman (Chapter 18) thus starts with such conditions and their effects upon her identity and understandably uncertainty. Nevertheless, she charts how she took such feelings as an impetus for further understanding through her own fieldwork. The result is an insightful account of how it is that emotions can inform not only a greater understanding of ourselves, but also those who are the subjects and co-producers of qualitative research.

SUMMARY

All of the chapters in this collection constitute core insights into the perspectives, experiences and issues that inform and arise from the process and practice of qualitative research. As I noted at the beginning of this introduction, there is a tendency to regard textual critiques as somehow sufficient for the changing of practice. Without sensitivity to the pressures and experiences that inform research, however, this so easily lapses into a constructivist idealism that misses its mark. In the first instance this necessitates an understanding of the issues that arise within research practice, as well as an understanding of the conditions of knowledge production itself. The potential to inform practice may then be derived from an explanation of the relations that exist between dispositions, positions and practices. The chapters in this volume are a valuable and insightful contribution to that process.

REFERENCES

Bourdieu, P. (1992) *The Logic of Practice*, translated by R. Nice. Cambridge: Polity.

Bourdieu, P. (2000) *Pascalian Meditations*, translated by R. Nice. Cambridge: Polity.

Bourdieu, P. and Wacquant, L.J. (1992) *An Invitation to Reflexive Sociology*. Cambridge: Polity.

Bryant, C. (1985) *Positivism in Social Theory and Research*. London: Macmillan.

Derrida, J. (1978) *Writing and Difference*. London: Routledge.

Foucault, M. (1984) *The Foucault Reader*, edited by P. Rabinow. Harmondsworth: Penguin.

Foucault, M. (1991) 'Politics and the study of discourse', in G. Burchell, C. Gordon and P. Miller (eds) *The Foucault Effect: Studies in Governmentality*. London: Harvester Wheatsheaf.

Garfinkel, H. (1967) *Studies in Ethnomethodology*. Englewood Cliffs, NJ: Prentice-Hall.

Gulbenkian Commission (1996) *Open the Social Sciences: Report of the Gulbenkian Commission on the Restructuring of the Social Sciences*. Stanford, CA: Stanford University Press.

Habermas, J. (1992) *The Philosophical Discourse of Modernity: Twelve Lectures*. Cambridge: Polity.

Harding, S. and Hintikka, M.B. (eds) (1983) *Discovering Reality: Feminist Perspectives on Epistemology, Metaphysics, Methodology, and Philosophy of Science*. London: D. Reidel.

Harré, R. (1998) *The Singular Self*. London: Sage.

Hoy, D.C. (1998) 'Foucault and critical theory', in J. Moss (ed.) *The Later Foucault: Politics and Philosophy*. London: Sage.

Hoy, D.C. and McCarthy, T. (1994) *Critical Theory*. Oxford: Blackwell.

Lyotard, J-F. (1993) 'Answering the question: what is postmodernism?', in T. Docherty (ed.) *Postmodernism: A Reader*. London: Harvester Wheatsheaf.

May, T. (1998) 'Reflexivity in the age of reconstructive social science', *International Journal of Methodology: Theory and Practice* 1(1): 7–24.

May, T. (1999) 'Reflexivity and sociological practice', *Sociological Research Online* 4(3), http://www.socresonline.org.uk/socresonline/4/3/may.html

May, T. (2000) 'The future of critique? Positioning, belonging and reflexivity', *European Journal of Social Theory* 3(2): 157–173.

May, T. (2001) *Social Research: Issues, Methods and Process*, 3rd edn. Buckingham: Open University Press.

Mills, C.W. (1970 [1959]) *The Sociological Imagination*. Harmondsworth: Penguin.

Norris, C. (1987) *Derrida*. London: Fontana.

Ricoeur, P. (1994) *Oneself as Another*, translated by K. Blamey. Chicago: University of Chicago Press.

Smart, B. (1993) *Postmodernity*. London: Routledge.

Unger, R.M. (1987) *Social Theory: Its Situation and its Tasks – A Critical Introduction to Politics, a Work in Constructive Social Theory*. Cambridge: Cambridge University Press.

PART 1

PUTTING THE PRACTICE INTO THEORY

1 INSTITUTIONAL ETHNOGRAPHY

Dorothy E. Smith

Note: in this introduction to institutional ethnography as a method of inquiry, I make use of various concepts that organize that method. I have had in mind a hypertext procedure. When a concept is encountered that has a specialized use in this context, readers have the equivalent of a button to press to shift to a locale where they will find an account of how that concept is being used. In this case the equivalent of a button is a word in upper-case: 'institutional ETHNOGRAPHY' signals a concept provided with an explanation in an alphabetized list of such concepts at the end of the chapter.

The method of inquiry to be described in this chapter originates in the women's movement of the 1970s in North America. I discovered then my double life of household/mothering and the university as a daily traverse across the line of fault between a woman's life in the particularities of home and children and the impersonal, extra-local relations that the university sustains. Here, in these two work situations, were radically different modes of consciousness. The consciousness that organizes household work and childcare is highly attentive to the particularities of the local setting – the physical layout of the household, taking in the state of the floors, putting clean sheets on the beds, checking the refrigerator to see what's there for supper, calling the kids in from play to get ready for school. It is a consciousness that coordinates multiple particular details, cues and initiatives, involving relationships with particularized others – children, partner, neighbours, and so on. The consciousness that organizes and is organized in the university setting and in relation to academic work is entirely different. It participates in a DISCOURSE in which particular others appear only as their printed names in texts, or positioned as members of definite classes of others – colleagues, students, supervisors, administrators and others. Here the subject participates in relations that extend beyond the local and particular, connecting her or him with others known and unknown in an impersonal organization, both of the university and of the extra-local relations of academic discourse. Particularized relationships emerge within institutionalized forms of coordination. The two modes of consciousness cannot coexist.

In the women's movement of the 1970s I learned to take my experience as a woman as foundational to how I could know the world. From a standpoint in the everyday world, the objectified social relations of my work in the university came into view for me in a new way. I could see how the institutional order of which sociology was part was itself a production in and of people's everyday activities, but that it connected people translocally across multiple local settings. The sociology I had been trained in was written almost exclusively by men from their viewpoint. The pronouns 'he' and 'him' were treated as the universal subject. The women's movement in sociology was slowly learning how to recognize the extent to which the sociology in which we had learned to talk, write and teach and which claimed objectivity was deeply infected with assumptions that relied on excluding women and their concerns and experience from the discourse. Starting to rediscover the social from the standpoint in the everyday world of our experience was essential to a critique of the language of sociological discourse. In remaking sociology, feminists evolved a critique from that basis and also sought to remake the discipline to enable the experiential to be spoken with authority. My own work was part of this movement with the discourse (Smith 1974). I wanted to remake sociology from the ground up so that, rather than the object being to explain people's social behaviour, the discipline could be turned upside down to become a sociology *for* women (Smith 1977), in which our EVERYDAY/EVERYNIGHT WORLDS would be rediscovered as they are organized by social relations not wholly visible within them. I called this 'making the everyday world a sociological problematic' (Smith 1979, 1987).

INSTITUTIONAL ETHNOGRAPHY

The sociology that has come out of that experience has come to be called 'INSTITUTIONal ethnography'. In contrast to other sociologies, it does not take its problems or questions from one or other variant of sociological discourse – symbolic interaction, Marxism, ethnomethodology or other 'school' of sociological thinking and research. This doesn't mean that it makes no use of such theories, but the central project is one of inquiry which begins with the issues and problems of people's lives and develops inquiry from the standpoint of their experience in and of the actualities of their everyday living. It is not, however, confined to description of local social organization or to expressions of people's own experiences. Though the latter are important, indeed essential, to institutional ethnography, the sociological project is one that takes up the everyday world as a problematic for investigation. Every local setting of people's activity is permeated, organized by and contributes to social relations coordinating activities in multiple local sites. The work of the sociologist is to discover these relations and to map them so that people can begin to see how their own lives and work are hooked into the lives and work of others in relations of which most of us are not aware.

If we take the idea of being in people's everyday/everynight worlds seriously, we run into the problem that we cannot grasp how they are put together from within them as they are experienced. Our directly known worlds are not self-contained or self-explicating despite the intimacy of our knowledge of them. The everyday/everynight of our contemporary living is organized by and coordinated with what people, mostly unknown and never to be known by us, are doing elsewhere and at different times. Institutional ethnography proposes to address this as its problematic. It takes up a stance in people's experience in the local sites of their bodily being and seeks to discover what can't be grasped from within that experience, namely the social relations that are implicit in its organization. The project calls on us as sociologists to discover just how the everyday/everynight worlds we participate in are being put together in people's local activities, including, of course, our own. It conceives of the social as actually happening among people who are situated in particular places at particular times and not as 'meaning' or 'norms'. It draws on people's own good knowledge of their everyday/everynight worlds and does not substitute the expert's 'reality' for what people know in the doing. The aim is to create a sociology *for* rather than *of* people.

Institutional ethnography's radical move as a sociology is that of pulling the organization of the trans- or extra-local RULING RELATIONS (Smith 1999) – bureaucracy, the varieties of text-mediated discourse, the state, the professions, and so on – into the actual sites of people's living where we have to find them as local and temporally situated activities. Concepts, beliefs, theory, ideology – the forms of thought in general – are integral to these forms of social organization and relations and are understood as critical to their local replication. An institutional language or 'speech genre' (Bakhtin 1986b) is itself a dimension of how a given institutional language is renewed and adapted as it is entered into and coordinates the subjectivities of people at work in particular local settings. Institutional ethnography refuses to accept the terms of such genres as constitutive of the objects of its exploration. Rather, as far as is practicable within a given scope of investigation, it locates the object or objects of its exploration in the actualities of the work/activity as it is coordinated, including the concepts, theories and so forth that are implicated in that coordination.

The double dialogue of sociological inquiry

Ethnography, writing about how people live, has a long history, originating in descriptions of how 'others', people not like ourselves, live. It has been deeply embedded in imperialism. In sociology today it is largely used to describe how others live who differ from 'us', sociological readers, and who are marginalized in some way in the society. It is this relationship that creates the ambiguities of the power relationships that Tracey Reynolds (Chapter 14 in this volume) analyses. On the one hand, if ethnographers are to properly describe a people's ways of living, they have to understand the people, must become to some degree close to and be trusted by them; on the other ethnographers are committed to betraying these confidences to outsiders who may make of what is told whatever they want. Ethnographers' descriptions represent them for others 'objectively' and 'as they really are'.

Description commits an invisible mediation. The describer is supposed to vanish in the act of writing so that somehow the original of what has been written will appear directly to the reader through the text. But as we know now, from the many critics of anthropological ethnography, this is not possible (see e.g. Clifford and Marcus 1986; Abu-Lughod 1998). Indeed it looks as if the ethnographic act aimed at describing people's ways of living is an oxymoron. The project is fundamentally contradictory.

Sociology is peculiar in that it aims at understanding the same world that sociologists are part of and do their sociological work in. Classically, sociology has sought devices that would enable its accounts of the social to pretend to stand outside it. However, it confronts a fundamental difficulty in sustaining this: sociological inquiry is necessarily engaged in a dialogic relationship with those it studies. Sociologists are in dialogue, direct or indirect, of some kind or another with others in the world they share with them. In dialogue with others we are captured, changed, come to see things differently. In the view put forward here, sociology, despite its claims to objectivity, can never achieve it. It can never insulate itself from the dynamic of an object that refuses to remain an object. Nor can sociologists simply segregate the sociological from the other-than-sociological dialogues they carry on. It is in the nature of their subject matter that they are exposed to capture by perspectives and ways of thinking other than the sociological. Disciplinary concepts and theories function to regulate sociological discourse and to guard it against this essential risk (Smith 1999), always imperfectly. Out of the primary dialogue with people who constitute both the resources for the accounts to be written and their ultimate users, we fashion a secondary dialogue within the order of sociological discourse, constrained by its conventions, methodologies, rules of evidence, discursive objects and other aspects of the 'order of discourse' (Foucault 1981).

Ethnographic work is explicitly a dialogue. Or rather two intersecting dialogues, one with those who are members of the settings to be described and the other with the discourse our description is to be read in. Dialogue number one is the ethnographer's interviews with informants or observations of people's everyday lives (observation is no less dialogic though the ethnographer doesn't speak). Dialogue number two is the dialogue between ethnographers and their readers, the people they write for. Ethnographers write about their research in dialogue with the discourse in which their study originates. That discourse has already shaped the dialogue with the people whose lives they are describing in the choices of topics for their interviews or what they are attentive to in their observations. The issue of power lies in this intersection. The ethnographer's power is to take what people have to say and to reassemble it to appear in quite a different setting in a different language and with interests and purposes that are not theirs.

Part of the problem I've described comes from the difficulties created by working up what is essentially dialogic into a monologic form (Bakhtin 1981), that is, by writing over or reinterpreting the various perspectives, experiences, ways of using language, of the primary dialogue into a single overriding version in which the differences, if they are registered at all, appear only as expressions or instances of the dominant discourse. The institutional ethnographic approach to the necessarily dialogic of any ethnography is one that recognizes and works with it. Its aim is not to describe how people live or the meanings they share (Emerson *et al.* 1995). It receives people's accounts of their everyday life experiences as they tell them. They are the expert practitioners of their everyday worlds; they know how they go about doing things. The institutional ethnographer's interest is in learning from them first and then beginning to locate in their accounts the junctures between the everyday worlds as they told them and how they are hooked into relations that connect them beyond scope of experience. The aim of the enterprise is to be able to return to those who are situated as were the interlocutors in the same institutionally ordered relationships, including, of course, those who directly participated, with something like a map of how the local settings of their work are organized into the relations that rule them. The project is analogous to cartography. It should produce accounts of the social relations and organization in which the doings of the people talked to are embedded that will enlarge individuals' perspectives beyond what they can learn directly from their participation in the everyday/everynight world.

Finding the social

The social, the object of institutional ethnography's attention, is conceived of as arising in people's activities (what they do, say, write and so on) in particular local settings at particular times. Institutional ethnography's people are always embodied. They are always somewhere at some time. The social is a focus on activities as they are coordinated, neither exclusively on the activities nor detaching the coordinating as 'system' or 'structure'. The social is a focus on what is actually happening; it is to be discovered in people's doings in the actual local settings of their lives. In emphasizing the concerting of people's activities as its focus, institutional ethnography moves away, on the one hand, from concepts such as Pierre Bourdieu's concept of *habitus* (Bourdieu 1990) that reduce the social to properties of individuals or concepts such as social structure or system that reify the coordinative dimension of people's activities.

This ontology of the social includes in a single ontological realm the standard dichotomy that lays practices on the one side and forms of consciousness, beliefs, ideology, concepts, theories, and so on, on the other. Language, concepts, thinking are here all recognized as among people's activities. They occur in time and are done in the particular local settings of people's bodily being. Thought and mind may be experienced as divorced from the local and from individuals' bodily being, but the experience of separation from local actualities is itself produced right there in them as people adopt a disciplining of the body so familiar we pay no attention to it and as they take for granted the text as their medium of access to the beyond-the-local. Concepts and theories appear extra-temporal on the page but in actuality they are people's doings in their reading and thinking and in their talk in particular local settings and at particular times. All the phenomena in language, therefore, are included in the institutional ethnographer's object of study and they are indeed of special importance as coordinators or organizers of people's divergent consciousnesses. Hence the institutional ethnography relies on the language in which people speak of what they know how to do, of their experience, and of how they get things done. The language, perhaps better, the speech genre of the institutional setting carries institutional organization.

Conceiving of the social, the object of our investigations, as the ongoing coordinating or concerting of people's activities is a minimal theoretical move. It locates only a point of entry. It makes no commitment to what may be found. That remains to be discovered. Or has been discovered. Nor does it make an a priori commitment to a particular level of abstraction. Sociology provides grand resources to support the elaboration of any preliminary formulation as inquiry goes forward. Once we are free from the constraints of belonging to and subordinating our investigation to the dictates of one of its 'schools' and governing what can be found by its conventions, we can draw on what comes to hand in our cartography. Specialized theories recognize and analyse different levels or aspects of the social. Ethnomethodology's conversational analysis, for example, formulates and makes visible the concerting of people's talk in conversation. The theory of Marx's major study of Capital brings into view and analyses the peculiar properties and dynamics of the social relations among people arising in the exchange of money and commodities. And again, at a level prior to conversational analysis, George Herbert Mead's (1947) work provides an interactional theory of symbolic behaviour (language).

Institutional ethnography begins with and takes for granted that people experience, see, and conceive things differently. Each individual begins from the null point of consciousness (Schutz 1962), based in her or his body which situates consciousness in a site no one shares. The articulations of the social organize multiple layers of diverging locations that are mediated to people through their activities and people's activities themselves organize perspectives that diverge in the very process of their concerting. Since coordinating and concerting are the stuff of the social, differences of perspective, interest, and so on are expected. Social relations and organization generate difference. Divergence is primary: consensus is a chimera. Indeed coming at things differently is what makes the concerting of people's activities endlessly open-ended and productive. In institutional settings and hence of special interest to their ethnographer are those socially organized forms that generalize and objectify since these must subdue and displace the particularity of individual perspective that arises spontaneously in actual work settings. Institutions, as objectifying forms of concerting people's activities are distinctive in that they construct forms of consciousness – knowledge, information, facts, administrative and legal rules, and so on and so on – that override individuals' perspectives. Foundational to these forms of consciousness are TEXTS, printed, computerized or otherwise replicated. The architecture of institutions is through and through textual whether in print or computerized and institutional ethnography increasingly incorporates attention to texts and textuality. Objectification and generalization are themselves the local practices of people's everyday/everynight lives and are to be explored as locally achieved (Marx's conceptualization of the economic forms of social relations, for example, specifically provides for how people as individuals become both individuated and invisible in the interchange between money and commodities). In a sense the collection of data and their analysis aim at discovering just how the institutional is being produced by people at work in the particularities of their everyday/everynight lives.

In what follows, I have adopted the device of describing two studies in some detail. The first of these is research which Alison Griffith, Ann Manicom and I were doing some while back exploring the relationship of the work that mothers do in the home to the educational work of the school. In that study we relied almost entirely on open-ended interviewing as a research method. The second study to be described focuses more on the textual dimensions of institutional processes. It describes part of a study by Ellen Pence in which she introduces texts into an investigation of the work organization of the judicial processes focused on cases of domestic abuse.

DOING INSTITUTIONAL ETHNOGRAPHY

Finding a direction

Of all the possibilities of ethnographic focus, what is to be systematically recognized as relevant to the institutional ethnographic project? The lived world can never be exhaustively described or enumerated. It is always more and other than anything that can be said, written, or pictured of it. Any kind of storytelling selects from the raw material, shapes it, and creates discursive order. The storytelling is achieved in actuality whether in writing or reading, but the actuality always escapes; it is always over; it is always other. When I went out as an innocent graduate student to do an ethnographic study of a state mental hospital in California, I was sent out simply to observe. But simply observing is disorganizing. Observation without an attentional frame is anomie. It means not knowing how to look, what to select, what to ask, what to follow up, and so on. It means not knowing what part to play in the dialogue. The problem is only overcome by somehow finding a direction (and some despairing graduate students, working with this recipe, never do). The observation and interviewing that go into ethnographic study need a general formulation of what we would be attending to and recognizing and in how we analyse them and the relevant institutional texts.

Institutional ethnography begins by locating a standpoint in an institutional order that provides the guiding perspective from which it will be explored. It begins with some issues, concerns or problems that are real for people. These guide the direction of inquiry. Alison Griffith and I began with our experience as single parents. We decided we wanted to understand why we had the kinds of problems with the schools that we identified with being seen as defective parents of actually or potentially defective children. Over the period of two or three years before we decided to undertake the research, we shared confidences, complaints, miseries and guilt arising from our relationship to our children's schools. On long walks through the RAVINES IN TORONTO we shared the stories of our mothering work, of our children's struggles, of our fears about interfering, of pushing teachers too hard, of not pushing them hard enough. Our explorations opened up the social relations and organization of schooling as those in relation to which women's work as mothers is done.

On these walks, we also framed our collaborative research project on mothering for schooling. We had learned over the years how to interpret ourselves as imperfect families and we knew we were seen just so by teachers and administrators in the schools our children attended. We knew that problems our children might have in school would be and were interpreted in terms of their defective families and our experience had been that being labelled in this fashion undermined our ability to be effective in dealing with their schools. Alison had already laid the groundwork for our more systematic and sociological reflections on our experience by her research into the ideology of the single parent family and its various uses by educational psychologists, educational administrators and teachers (Griffith 1984). Now we thought we could find out more about what was so special about the 'Standard North American' family (Smith 1999) of father earning the income to support a wife and mother at home and children in school if we talked to mothers with children in elementary school about the work they were doing in relation to their children's schooling. Because our own experience had been as members of a 'deviant' category of families *vis-à-vis* the school system, we were interested in learning more about the 'normal' family against which our own had been seen as wanting.

From experience to institution

We decided to work with a procedure which would first establish a particular standpoint located in women's everyday lives in the institutional context and hence in the ways they are related to and participate in it. We would start by interviewing intensively a small number of women with children in elementary school. Their interviews would give us a standpoint from which we could open up exploration from the side of the school and school board. An institutional order doesn't offer a 'natural' focus. It is a complex of relations rather than a definite unitary form such as a corporation. Hence, in addition to whatever political interests the sociologist may have, locating a specific institutional standpoint organizes the direction of the sociological gaze and provides a framework of relevance.

The investigation itself builds from one stage of research to the next on the basis of interviews. The interviews in explicating women's EXPERIENCE of their work as mothers in relation to their children's schooling, would specify the problematic of the research beyond its tentative formulation in our own experience, Alison's and mine, of the same kind of work. What defined the textual community thus to be created was the institutional regime we and the women we would talk to participated in and were defined by. After we'd talked to the women, the second stage of research would situate their experiences in the organization of the schools attended by the children. The movement of research goes from an exploration of the everyday particularities of women's work as mothers to exploring the generalizing and generalized relations in which each individual's everyday world is embedded. We could not know the specific character of the problematic of the everyday of mothers' work until we had explored it with them. That done, we could go on to open up the institutional order to which their work contributes and with which it is coordinated.

We thought that women's mothering work would vary not only from individual to individual, but also according to different conditions of mothering. If mothering differed, so would schooling. Our interest was not in the effects of different mothering practices on the achievement of the individual child, but in different forms of the social relations set up between varying individuals at work under varying conditions and the characteristic standardizing of the institutional regime. For these reasons we decided to talk to women whose children were attending schools in middle-class and working-class school districts (Walker 1990b).[1]

Dialogue in practice

Institutional ethnography isn't about explaining people's behaviour or about testing theory-derived hypotheses by relating variables derived from individuals' responses to structured questions. The problem is not to select a sample that can properly be treated as representing a particular population, nor to be able to make statements of relations among variables that can be generalized from a sample to the population it represents. Institutions are themselves generalizers and their ethnography looks for the ways in which the particularities of people's everyday doings bring into being the distinctively generalized forms of the institutional order. Locating people to talk to involves making decisions about the perspective from which an institution is to be explored. Alison and I had a specific agenda. We began with mothers and the work of mothers in relation to their children's schooling. We were interested in how that might translate into differences in the organization of schooling. We talked to twelve women in all, six with children in an elementary school in a district largely populated with people in a low income group and six with children in a school in a largely professional-managerial population. Why six in each? We certainly did not claim to have drawn a sample of any kind. We had specifically sought to locate 'non-defective' families, i.e. families in which both parents were present. We did not think we could learn enough without being confronted with differences in the conditions under which women's work as mothers was done and hence with having to recognize the ways in which the generalized/generalizing relations worked on and organized how women managed the 'schooling' dimensions of their work under varying conditions of that work. We did not only want to explore that work in settings where it was economically supported; we wanted to see how it was done where economic conditions made it more difficult.

Institutional ethnography is sampling an institutional process rather than a population. No doubt there would be more systematic procedures than those we used in this early study. But in principle institutional ethnography might begin with one individual. The presence of institutional organization is *in* what someone has to say about her or his work (in the sense that we use the term here – see Glossary). Choosing a standpoint from which the institution will be explored is a key step in the ethnography (Smith 1987: 181–190). Others may be interviewed but those interviews will not establish a new standpoint though they will, importantly, provide a different perspective on the major themes that have emerged from interviews with those who make up what we might call the 'standpoint' sample.

Interviewing

One of the problems of sociological research in institutional settings is that interview respondents speak from the generalized and generalizing discourse. Even when they talk about their own work, they may move into their everyday competence in the ideological language of the institutional discourse. Such discourses are extraordinarily lacking descriptive content and can be largely useless to interviewers unless they are investigating the order of the institutional discourse itself. Here is where our concept of WORK kicks in. It focuses on the concrete and everyday and particularizes rather than generalizes. Hence in devising our new interview schedules Alison and I had to find a format that would anchor the interview at the descriptive level and avoid elevation into the institutional (Smith 1990a). 'Work', in our sense, has the major merit also of evading the divorce of subjective and objective that often requires the sociologist to hover unhappily between objectified description (as in ethnomethodology's conversational analysis) or concepts of meaning which are generated by methodological apotheosis (as with grounded theory). Marjorie DeVault (1991) in her study of feeding the family demonstrates how interviewing people about their work in the generous sense of the term used here elicits talk about how they think and feel about the work of feeding the family as well as about the practicalities. Meaning and subjectivity are not differentiated from accounts of people's doings.

When our initial research plans and progress were disrupted, Alison and I had to plan our next steps with greater economies of time in mind. For the very open interviewing we had used at first, we substituted a more formalized traditional approach using more or less set questions. Our interviews in the new setting opened by taking respondents through a standard school day, asking them for each step about the work they did in relation to it: what was involved for them in getting their child off to school? Did they come home for lunch and what had to be done (prepare meal, get child back to school on time, and so on)? When the child/ren came home from school, what then? And so on. Since we were not following the traditional sociological procedure of starting from disciplinary concepts or theory to specify first questions and then coding categories, our interviews did not seek to make up a collection of data we could wrap up in a box of code. We found what we had not known how to look for. It pushed us to think further than we had at the outset. The concept of SOCIAL RELATIONS proved more analytically powerful than we had anticipated in those days when institutional ethnography was still relatively undeveloped. We'd thought of the orderly parameters of the school day simply as a data-eliciting device, and, although we were aware of the problem of the assumed typicality of the day, we had discounted that in favour of the access to the concreteness of the everyday work of seeing to it that children have eaten breakfast, are dressed appropriately for school and weather, that they are pried away from television, if indeed they are allowed to watch first thing, and so on. We had not seen, as we came to see later, the school day's orderliness as an intersecting of the work of school teachers and administrators (as well as, ultimately, the law) and of mothers who sustained its scheduled character by the work they aimed at achieving it. But we also talked to women for whom achieving the regularity of the school day was not salient. And to those who expressed the strain of coordinating their own and their partner's schedule of paid work to the unaccommodating school schedulers of their children. We began in this way to see the typical schedule of the school day as a joint product and, eventually, to analyse it as a 'social relation' (discussed at greater length in the following section).

Research as discovery

In institutional ethnography, the researcher is permitted to learn, perhaps must learn, from each interview what may inform and change the subsequent (DeVault and McCoy 2000). There is progression from interview to interview, even when the same topics or questions are introduced each time. In our dialogue with our respondents, our thinking was changed and sometimes in ways that were only contingently related to the planned relevances that guided interview topics. One such moment led us to become aware of a dimension of our work and thinking that we had not recognized at the inception of our study, though it now seems obvious. Or rather it expressly recognizes a dialogic of social inquiry that is always ineluctably there. The formalized structuring of questions used in survey research and in some forms of qualitative research (though now by no means all) suppresses the effect of dialogue, aiming at the outset to produce a monologic (Bakhtin 1981) in which the respondent's part is subdued to the terms of the pre-set questions and the pre-coded responses. For the most part sociological method expressly suppresses the dialogue at work in what we call our 'data'. Dialogue is concealed either by the use of data that has suppressed dialogue before it arrives at the analytic site or by deploying theory that converts the many-voiced into the monologic (Bakhtin's term). Recognizing interviewing or observation as essentially dialogic recognizes the researcher's interests in the research as integral to the dialogue while at the same time relying on the other to teach, if you like, what the researcher must learn from him or her. Sociological research, in these terms, can be successful only if it takes advantage of what Hans-Georg Gadamer (1994) takes to be essential to dialogue, namely that the parties to it take the risk of being changed. Do respondents in an interview risk being changed by the interview? In hearing themselves focus in their talk on what they have not perhaps imagined would be of interest to anyone, are they changed? Is it something that can be made explicit? I doubt it. These are the normal risks of conversation. But institutional ethnographers are actively seeking to be changed, to discover not only what they did not know but also, as they go about their work, how to think differently about what they are learning. Furthermore, they are doing discursive work and hence their change aims at change in institutional ethnographic discourse and more generally in what we know about how institutions work.

For Alison and I, another moment of change was particularly significant, not only for the specifics of our study, but also because it introduced to us the idea that institutional ethnography did not 'naturally' confine the researcher to the planned parameters of the project. In the course of interviewing, we encountered situations that made us, as single parents, uncomfortable, even anxious. One such was that of an interview with a woman who was the wife of a professional, did not work outside the home, and had much time to spend with her children. She described her many activities with her children, at that time 7 and 8, including taking them to see Shakespeare plays at the Stratford (Ontario) Festival. She told us that her children helped choose which plays they should go to. Such amplitude of time let alone of other resources precipitated feelings of guilt, anxiety and pain in the researchers, who had not had time or other resources to do this kind of work with their children. But that did not excuse us. We were responsible whether the conditions of doing that work were present or not. Normally such responses are ignored and certainly not considered relevant to the investigation. But institutional ethnography, recognizing that researchers are in the same world as that they are investigating, can take advantage of such responses as opportunities for opening up dimensions of the institutional regime that weren't recognized at the outset of the project. So, rather than leaving things at the stage of telling and sympathetic listening, we started to question why we reacted in this way to interview experiences of this kind. Tracing this research byway, we came upon what we now call the mothering discourse (Griffith and Smith 1987). From historians we learned that this discourse emerged, in North America at least, in the early twentieth century. It was associated with the rise of the new middle class organized around education, credentials and career-structured occupations and the professions. In a sense, women in the middle classes were mobilized by the mothering discourse to commit themselves, under the guidance of professional experts, to a demanding work of child rearing, socialization and education. Mothering discourse places on mothers an undefined responsibility for their child's educational achievements, personality and general well-being. A mother's responsibility is not determined by specific tasks but by outcomes. Any problem that the child might encounter is read back into what she has done or failed to do.

In the 1932 edition of *The Normal Child*, Alan Brown reminded readers that 'the mental environment of the child is created by the mother. This is her responsibility and her opportunity.' These words were echoed in countless publications throughout the period. A 1936 article in *Chatelaine* [a Canadian women's magazine] warned mothers that 'your child mirrors you and your home: if your child is a problem child, probably you are a problem mother.' (Arnup 1994: 151)

The mothering discourse has changed over the years in its specifics, but not in the onus of responsibility it lays on mothers (today we begin to see fathers implicated too, particularly in relation to their sons). For participants in the mothering discourse, their responsibility knows no limit, either practical or emotional or of knowledge, on what she should have contributed to the child.

We discovered also, somewhat to our chagrin, that the conceptions built into our interview strategies presupposed the mothering discourse and that many of the women we talked to were also participants. They knew how to 'talk' the discourse just as we did and we have no idea how deeply our shared discursive competence went into shaping the stories we were told. There were also those, though few, who clearly were not participants. One interview I did myself returned me to a familiar experience. Some while earlier I'd interviewed my mother, then in her mid-eighties, about her experiences as a young woman in the women's suffrage movement in England. Although I was a reasonably experienced interviewer, I had the uncomfortable sense that I could not line up my questions with where she was coming from. Even though I paid due respect to what she had to say and listened carefully, I felt at each question that I was somehow interrupting her train of thought and that my questions had no continuity with the preceding responses. At a later time, after she'd died and after I'd had an opportunity of teaching an undergraduate course that I'd had to prepare for by reading extensively about the women's suffrage movement in Canada and the United Kingdom, I came to have an understanding of that period that I'd not had at the time of our interview. I knew then that it was my ignorance that structured the interview. Now in my interview with this particular respondent, I was having the same experience. I was not able to locate myself properly in the universe of discourse from which she spoke. Looking back I can see the effects of the mothering discourse in how I assumed that all mothers would be primarily oriented to a child's successful school career and hence did not attend to the possibility that for some such issues as the economic well-being of the family or a sense of the importance of local and family relationships might be given priority (these are my guesses after studying the transcribed interview many times). The mothering discourse allowed no such alternative priorities and I did not attend to that possibility. In the absence of my awareness of the problematic status of this assumption, I failed to engage with her in the kind of talk that might have opened up other ways of thinking in me.

Institutional ethnography is, in principle, never completed in a single study. Exploring an institutional regime is best done from more than one perspective. Inquiry is conceived overall as opening different windows based in how people are positioned in the institutional regime, each giving a different view of the terrain. Ann Manicom's (1988) study of the experience of elementary school teachers in the classroom opens such a window in its exploration of teachers' work in schools in differing class contexts. In a school in a low-income district, the teachers she spoke to reported that they had to put considerable classroom time into teaching children such skills as how to turn the pages of a book in the right direction and the direction in which the writing is read, or how to use pencils and crayons. While the children they taught might be skilled in 'street smarts', some had not acquired the background competences that could be taken for granted by teachers in the school in the middle-class district. Her work emphasizes the implications not for the individual child but for how teaching can proceed in the elementary classroom and hence the implications for the level at which the curriculum can be taught. Quite simply, the more time that had to be given to teaching 'background' skills, the less time to teach the curriculum. Relating her study to ours brought the social relations of mothering and schooling more clearly into focus. On the one hand there were mothers at work in their homes under whatever conditions of time and other resources available to do the supplementary work of teaching and sustaining the orderly process of the school day, and on the other, there were teachers whose conditions of work in the classroom were shaped by the time and whatever other resources were available in the home. The mothering discourse earlier described was clearly of importance in coordinating the efforts of participating mothers with those of teachers and of the school in general. Non-participating mothers did not have the same commitment to the work that would complement the teachers' work in the classroom.

Working with the data

In institutional ethnography, the concept of social relation is central to the analysis. Analysis does not work with a set of categories and concepts that are laid over the texts of our transcribed interviews but locates what we have learned from respondents about their 'work' as it is coordinated by relations connecting it with the work of others, known and unknown. As George Smith (1995) emphasizes, the concept of social relation does not identify a class of phenomena, but focuses on how what people are doing and experiencing in a given local site is hooked into sequences of action implicating and coordinating multiple local sites where others are active (Smith 1990b: 93–96). Hence analysis isn't a mock-up of a statistical procedure, but one that examines how work in one institutional site connects with the work of others in other such sites. The interviewing procedure has this analytic strategy built into it. It is also available, however, in particular interviews in the ways in which people in how they speak incorporate the socially organized relations in which their experience arises.

We take the view that social organization is built into people's ways of speaking or writing, 'speech genres' to use Bakhtin's (1986b) term (LANGUAGE AND SOCIAL ORGANIZATION). Hence social relations are already implicit in *how* people talk about their work. We can, we believe, find in their talk their particular moments of participation in social relations that hook their local experience to the work of others elsewhere, known and unknown. In the interview transcripts, therefore, we look for what people say about the 'work' they do that connects them to the work others are doing elsewhere or elsewhen.

Schools rely on the extensive supplementary educational work that many mothers do at home. It may involve such familiar tasks as helping the child with homework, tutoring the child, reading, visits to libraries, museums and zoos. It also includes less formal aspects like teaching the child to identify colours, familiarizing the child with letters using the plastic alphabet with fitted with magnets that can be stuck to the refrigerator. Mothers, sometimes both parents, but mothers in particular go on school trips and volunteer time to the school. Then there are the less visible forms of work, such as that of monitoring the child's school experience by asking her or him about what happened at school that day or scrutinizing work brought home, usually done when a child returns home from school in the afternoon. Mothers must also sometimes spend time dealing with a child's anxieties about school – perhaps a teacher's speaking to her or him sharply, perhaps a schoolmate's teasing, or the like. Such mothering work is mobilized by the mothering discourse. The generalization of the school system has come to be complemented and sustained by a generalized discourse that assigns to mothers this kind of supplementary educational work. Manicom's (1988) study has given us a stronger sense of just how important this work is for the school in general, let alone for the individual child's career at school. This is the work that the mothering discourse calls women to; it is a service to child and school that lacks specification and boundaries. It can use up all the time that is available – and still leave a mother feeling that she is wanting.

The school day is thus seen relationally. The daily scheduling of the school's work by teachers, school secretaries and school administrators is complemented by the work of family members, women, children and sometimes men. What seems to have this firm and finalized existence, the school day, comes into being as a relation that is re-created everyday on one side at home and on the other at school. The school day, from the side of the school, is the framework within which curriculum space is allocated to different parts of the curriculum.

When the school day is examined relationally, we can also see how the realization of the province's school curriculum as an allocation of daily time-slots depends on the family's commitment to the work of 'getting to school on time'. But back in the home is another hook-up. There are the schedules of paid employment that don't coordinate with the schedule of the school. The school day presupposes a parent available at home to manage the schedule of the 'home day' so as to coordinate the uncoordinated. Here was a difference between the women whose children attended the school in the middle-class district. For the most part, their husbands were in paid employment outside the home and they were not. A couple worked a few hours a week. One, who actually turned out to be a single parent, did work full time. She was the only single parent in the group of women we talked to. Apparently the school was not aware of this in giving us her name as someone willing to be approached for an interview. Families with the children in the school in the lower-income area had rather different patterns of organization. There was one in which the family organization was just the same as most of those with children attending the middle-class school in that the husband was employed full time (he was an engineer) during the daytime and the wife was not in paid employment. But in all the others, no parent was at home full time during the day; all the women, with one exception (she was in full-time training as a veterinary assistant), in various ways were engaged in earning a living, though not all are in regular jobs. So the time of the women with children in the lower-income district school was not available in the same way at the times that were fitted to the school day, nor in general for the supplementary educational work on which the middle-class school relies. Of course, these were families which were 'intact', i.e. in which both parents were present and the latter were not, according to the school board and school administrators we spoke to necessarily typical of the downtown community where there was a relatively high proportion of single parents. Single parents, as was our own experience, are likely to be less well situated in terms of time and resources than the mothering discourse model requires. It is hard for them to make the objective of a child's success in school the priority around which the household day and resources is managed.

We are talking about the work and experience of individuals, but the relations in which they are active and to which they contribute, are 'institutional', that is, they are generalized across individual situations and experiences. Though individuals and how they go about their work is individually various and unique to each, they are active in producing together objectified forms that transcend individuals and are both historical and allochronic. Institutional ethnography recognizes that the institutional forms and relations are always being produced by individuals at work and yet that they are generalized and standardized. The women we talked to each had their own way of organizing the work of schooling that is done in the home; each family's way was an idiosyncratic configuration of particular people. Yet they were all in various ways active in producing and reproducing the institutional character of the schools their children attended. It is this institutional character of the social relations coordinating the work being done by mothers and by the professionally and administratively regulated work of teachers that enters the unique and particular relationships between child, parent and teacher to the societal level of the social relations of class.

In this way, institutional ethnography opens up into larger social relations, exploring the institutional order. We can begin to locate people's everyday lives in the institutional order, in changes in it, in shifts in government policy, and in more general changes in economic organization that are taking place. It is also possible to locate specific possibilities of change (Pence 1996). The complex of the ruling relations, including the functional foci of specific institutions, is grasped from a standpoint within them and is brought into view in how these relations coordinate people's local practices. In tracing these relations, we've found that tracking the interchanges of the-time-it-takes is analytically valuable in sorting out the interconnections (we note though we have not explored the theoretical and analytic linkages to Marx's conception of labour time). In education, how time is allocated is central to how a public educational system produces inequality. Imagine a total educational work time, to be allocated to either school or home. Current assumptions (built into curriculum expectations) are that the supplemental education work mobilized by the mothering discourse will be done at home. Where time is not available at home to do this work or when that work is not done for whatever reason, the school does not expand its time to compensate. We can begin to see then how the public school system comes to operate as an 'engine of inequality' (Smith 1997). An important dimension of the availability of teachers' educational time is class size. Class size is regulated sometimes directly but always through funding. As less public money is spent in education, class size and/or the teacher–student ratio increases and teachers have less time to spend with individual children and, in particular, do not have the time to do 'repair' work with a child who may be falling behind her or his classmates in a particular area. In this situation, the tendency is for the teacher to pass the problem back into the home, as by asking parents to spend time reading with the child, or the like. We asked the teachers we interviewed how it would be if their class size was halved. All responded, almost with the same words: 'Oh, then we'd really be able to work with the children as individuals.'

We were, of course, discovering class, though in a new way. We were discovering that the public school system functions in North America as an 'engine of inequality' and we could begin to describe how people are putting together this engine in the practices of their daily lives as those practices are coordinated with one another to create social relations that the different parties may not be aware of, and do not intend. We had opened up an institutional process to discover a work of women and the conditions of its doing; we discovered how that work was mobilized and organized by a mothering discourse that claimed women's time not just as something done for her children but as something done for the school her children attend. In the economic conditions that govern the availability of time, we could see home and women's work as a kind of conduit that transmitted those conditions to the school, again not as a matter of an individual mother of a particular child but as a consequence for the school itself and how it could deliver a standardized curriculum. In a sense, we were unpicking class itself against those theory-derived conceptualizations that create virtual collections of people in a virtual structure. We were replacing this with an examination of the interlocking of work, time and economy of actual people situated differently in an institutional order, so that one aspect of the social relation (in the sense used here) in which both parents and teachers are active becomes visible.

But making visible a more extended organization of social relations is not the only or indeed the primary object of institutional ethnography. We have, through this work, been able to talk with women about how their work as mothers is located and show them something of the relations they are caught up and are active in. Our analysis shifts responsibility from women as mothers not to the teacher but to how teachers' time is allocated and to the issues of funding and class size that are consequential for the conditions of teachers' work and ability *in practice* to treat each child as an individual.

Texts as coordinators

The grand puzzle of institutions is how they generalize across many local settings of people's activities. Institutional ethnography argues that generalization is text mediated and that standardized and replicable texts coordinate the local settings of people's work. Texts as read and written in the everyday actuality of people's work coordinate what people are doing in one local setting with work done by others elsewhere or at different times. Texts bring external regulation into the immediacy of the everyday/everynight world. They can be seen in the quotation above from a historian's account of what Alison and I have called 'mothering discourse' (Griffith and Smith 1987). However they may be read, the printed text, the computer software or other textual form bring an identical set of words or images into local sites. Of course, not everybody reads a given text in the same way, but for every site into which a given text is inserted one side of the text–reader conversation is fixed and unchanging from site to site to site.

In an ethnography therefore texts are taken up as they enter into action. Their conceptual dimensions are held not as meaning, but as 'organizers' packaged for transmission to multiple sites. The tricky matter for the ethnographer is to locate texts in time and as constituents of social relations. The social act unfolds in time as well as in actual local settings. The texts that coordinate local settings and particular times, articulating them into extended social relations beyond, must be recognized as 'occurrences' at the moment of reading that enter into the reader's next doings or 'responses'. Or they are at work in talk or in writing/reading as organizers of local settings, referenced, aimed at, governing, the ongoing development and concerting of activities.

Reading is interactive. The text is both activated by the reader and interpreted in relation to the local work organization and courses of action of the setting in which it is read. The text–reader conversation is active, but it is also peculiar and unlike conversation in face-to-face talk in that the text remains the same thing no matter how many times it is read. Spoken conversation takes shape as each speaker responds to the other whereas in text–reader conversations, one side is fixed, predetermined and remains unchanged by the history of its reading. One 'party' to the conversation is fixed and non-responsive to the other; the other both takes on the text, in a sense becoming its voice, even its agent (Smith 1990a, 1999), and at the same time, responds to, interprets, and acts from it. The printed or otherwise replicated text standardizes for any reader one term of the text–reader conversation. Readers in different sites and at different times can engage with and be regulated by the 'same' text. In a sense, the words that organize may thus be spoken in just the same way to different people at different times. At the time that Alison and I did our research, we were scarcely aware of the significance of texts in the organization of institutional relations. We might have examined them at a number of points at which they coordinate parent–school relations – the report card, for example (Stock 2000), or in the texts of the mothering discourse – but we did not. Here then I draw on a study by Ellen Pence (1996) of the judicial process in cases of domestic abuse.

Ellen Pence was part of a group in Duluth, Minnesota, that had been providing advocacy support for women whose partners had been charged with domestic abuse. Those working in this way had ample experience of how little even the improved efficacy of the judicial process contributed to women's safety. Pence's study drew on that experience supplemented by rare opportunities for observation and participation, making the texts so ubiquitous in the judicial process part of her observational and analytic focus. Her study of the judicial process traces it from the moment when the dispatcher receives a 911 emergency call to sentencing. She never sees the problems as those of individuals. Rather she examines the interlocking textually coordinated sequences of action that relate the law, the work of the police, lawyers, probation officers, women's advocates, judges, social workers and so on. The work organization is not an effect of a single unit regulating the various functions within a corporate entity. The work in each site is coordinated with others through the texts that each is legally responsible for producing at various stages of the overall process. Each textual step is the basis on which the next step is taken.

The standpoint she adopted was that of women situated in (and in many ways outside) the judicial process whose partners had been charged with domestic abuse. The police responding to the 911 emergency call that initiates the process in most cases translate what they discover in the setting and the events that occur there in their presence into a report. George Smith (1990a) has made a detailed analysis of this step in his study of charges brought against gay men engaged in sexual activity in a bath-house in Toronto in the 1980s. He shows the police report as constructed to select those aspects of what the police saw and how they attended to what could be fitted to fit the law under which the men were charged. In the instance of domestic abuse, the process is initiated by someone present at the scene, sometimes one of the adult participants, sometimes a child, occa-sionally a neighbour. The work of the police in rendering the local particu-larities of events into textual form is critical in the initiation of the judicial sequence of action and their report, as Pence (1996) shows, plays a critical role in coordinating the work of others. The report standardizes for all involved what is known of the incident for the prosecuting attorney, for the lawyer for the defence, for social services (particularly if children are present), and so on. If someone is arraigned for trial, this report will have played a central part.

Pence introduces the concept of PROCESSING INTERCHANGES as part of her analysis of how texts coordinate this judicial process. Text-processing interchanges are those work sites in the institutional processes into which a given text is entered and from which it is passed on or incorporated into new texts to the next site which may also be a processing interchange. She quotes a fictional account created by a detective to illustrate the ways in which the processing of a case can be dragged out by the sequence of steps that are involved. It also illustrates a sequence of processing interchanges:

> Jan. 1, 1993, a Friday: A domestic between a co-habiting couple occurs in the city. The victim gets a black eye and bloody nose and calls the police. A sqd. [police squad] responds and finds the offender gone and is not able to locate him within the 4 hours. They go back to their business.
> Jan. 2: The sqd. [officer in charge of squad] dictates a report.
> Jan. 4: The report is transcribed and returned to the Patrol division.
> Jan. 7: The report is signed by the supervisor and taken to the traffic division where it is logged as a warrant request.
> Jan. 8: It is placed in the city attorney basket. It is Friday.
> Jan. 11: It is logged into the city attorney's office and sent to an attorney. Some time within the next couple of weeks, an attorney will review it, decide to issue, direct a clerical to fill out the neces-sary forms.
> Jan. 25: The file is returned to the DPD (Duluth Police Department) Detective Bureau clerical person with a summons attached.
> Jan. 27: The clerical types out the summons information and mails the package out, including all of the reports, the victim and witness information and statements.

Jan. 28: The victim and offender, having continued to live together, share the first day since the assault that they have not thought or argued about it.

Jan. 29: The offender opens his mail and notes that his court date is set for Feb. 22.

Feb. 22: He doesn't appear for court. At the end of the day, the court file is carried back into the Clerk of Courts offices.

Feb. 23: It is placed into a basket where it sits for the standard two week minimum grace period.

March 10: It is removed from that basket and placed into the 'return to city atty [attorney] for warrant basket.' It may sit there until a stack 'worth' picking up or mailing back over accumulates but to be charitable, let's say it goes within a couple of days.

March 12: It is received in the city atty's office and sent to the issuing attorney.

March 17: It is dictated as a warrant and returned to the DPD.

March 18: Sgt. Nichols carries it to the court, swears to it and has it signed by a Judge. He then carries it into the Clerk of Court's office. There it is placed into a basket of complaints to be filed when they have time. This may take a week.

March 24: It is placed into the warrants basket to be picked up by the Sheriff's warrants office.

March 26: It is received into the warrants office, logged in, entered into the computer and placed into the basket for service.

March 27 and 28: The couple spends first weekend since his failure to appear, not worrying and arguing about what will or should happen.

March 30: He calls and agrees to come in the next day.

March 31: He appears and pleads not guilty. A jury pretrial [jpt] is set for the first week of May (jpt's are always the first week of the month and he is now too late for April). (Pence 1996: 67–68)

This account makes vivid how the text of the original police report travels, is added to and incorporated into other texts, and how the accumulating texts coordinate the activities of people positioned differently in the institutional order. And, of course, the whole of this sequence has implicit reference to the legislation that has established domestic abuse within criminal law as well as to other like texts that regulate local practices (G.W. Smith 1995). Then, taking the standpoint of battered women in relation to the institutional process, we can see, as does the detective who wrote the memorandum, how the time the textual processing takes jeopardizes the safety of the woman involved.

Pence's (1996) work is neither simply analytic nor simply critical. Her interest in using this method of inquiry is to disclose how institutional processes are assembled in the everyday work of people implicated in them. From the standpoint of women who are abused, the outcomes of the judicial process are rarely successful in securing their safety and may even place them at greater risk. If people at work in the police and judicial process could examine, by examining the textual forms of organization, how their work is concerted so that it produces the outcomes it does, maybe they could also find ways of designing it differently. For example, the protocol for making reports is not well established and standardized across the state. There are no established instructions for what must be attended to when the police come to a situation of domestic abuse. Though domestic abuse comes under the criminal code in Minnesota, the scene is not treated as a crime scene. The degree of injury is not always established. Extraneous detail not strictly relevant to determining whether there are grounds for a charge, such as that the parties have been drinking, are included. The reports may be so sparse that they are inadequate to determine whether a charge should be laid. Where those involved are native peoples or African American, the reports may be deeply flawed by racism. And so on. One place to begin, then, is to introduce standardized procedures for writing such reports which are becoming part of police training and are also required by the supervisor who checks the report.

In this brief exposition of one part of Pence's (1996) study, we can see how the 'observation' of how texts coordinate institutional process complements rather than displaces the explication of the interlocking work of people whose local activities are bringing into being the institution's translocal and allochronic order. Alison's and my study was oriented to a social relational sequence that, at the point of interchange between mothers' work and the work of teachers and school administrators where texts were not, for the most part, directly implicated. Pence's study focuses on the significance of texts and the processing of texts in the sequential organizing of people's work. Choice of approach depends on the situation that the researcher has undertaken to explore and on the forms of coordinating people's activities that actually obtain there. The textual, however, has special significance because it allows the institutional ethnographer to locate the essential modes in which translocal and allochronic relations are coordinated and through which the institutional property of being generalized across local sites is achieved. But the analysis of textural coordinators does not mean suspending an interest in people's work in the local settings of their everyday/everynight living. Not only their work with texts, but also how their work in general is coordinated by texts, are integral features of institutional organization.

Pence (1996) suggests that those involved in institutional processes can themselves conduct a systematic investigation using institutional ethnography as a critical method for examining the actual outcomes of how their work is coordinating. Focusing on the mediated role of texts displaces focus on individuals and brings into critical consciousness aspects of how their work is coordinated that are not ordinarily examined and are, at the same time, of considerable importance in how the institutional process works. Such a critical investigation can be the basis on which changes can be designed and introduced that do not require the radical modifications of a whole that are generally beyond people's power to achieve.

CONCLUSION

Increasingly social organization as it evolves among people in direct relationships is displaced or regulated by exogenous systems of rationally designed, textually mediated forms of organization that connect people's everyday/everynight worlds into the contemporary regime of capital accumulation. Institutional ethnography aims at uncovering, from the standpoint of people located in a definite institutional site, the progressive despoiling of people's local and particularizing control over their everyday lives as the expansion of the ruling relations continually displaces and expropriates their self and mutually generated relations, their own knowledge, judgement and will. The studies that have been and are being done explore each from a different site the complex of the ruling relations. The concept of institution is not intended to confine investigation to forms of objectified organization associated with the professions. Institutional ethnogaphy's characteristic strategies reach equally effectively into the ruling relations of capital. A study by Dawn Currie and Anoja Wickramasinghe (1998) begins with the everyday experience of women garment workers in factories in a Free Trade Zone in Sri Lanka. Currie and Wickramasinghe (1998) describe the long hours, the stress, the effects on their health, job insecurity and 'the growing casualization of work' as women experience them. They go on from this account to locate such experiences in economic policies of Sri Lanka in the changed global economy and the complex of communication and management created by transnational corporations specializing in textiles. The latter locates Sri Lankan textile factories in a worldwide hierarchical division of the labour of fashion production articulated to different markets (Cheng and Gereffi 1994). From there connections can be made with the organization of design and advertising in the fashion industry that establish the perennially changing and market-differentiating norms of style, colour and so on that become a motive to buy.

Studies such as those described all too briefly above go much beyond what particular studies may have to tell us. It might seem as though institutional ethnography produces a collection of particular studies, interesting perhaps as such and possibly useful to those whose lives are shaped in the ruling relations and would like them to be different. But each study reaches into and investigates relations that are generalized beyond the particular case. Indeed that is a distinctive effect of the objectified forms of the ruling relations. Each study examines a facet of the great trajectory of ruling that has been developing and being developed both technologically and in scope and effectiveness since the nineteenth century. Each study, therefore, brings into view an aspect of the changing regime of accumulation that is assembling distinctive institutional forms evolved out of and transformative of those that have gone before. Each study therefore brings into view another piece of the complex of objectified relations and organization, mediated by texts (print and electronic) in which our daily/nightly lives are embedded and by which they are organized.

Institutional ethnographic research and analysis does not displace or reconstruct the experiences of those implicated in an institutional regime. Rather, by locating people's site of experience in the social relations of the institutional regime and explicating what we can of the relations that enter into that experience, we can create something like a map of the relations in which people's own doings and experiences are situated and by which they are shaped. When I teach institutional ethnography as a research approach, I recommend it as a skill in an analysis and explication of the form of power in which most people in our kind of societies are implicated. Nor does it explicate power as the ineluctable. Ellen Pence has developed institutional ethnography as a method that people working in institutional settings can use to explore and redesign the coordinating of their own work (Pence 1996, 2001). The ways in which power is brought into view as a mobilization of people's coordinated activities also points to ways in which change can be inserted into organization from within. And we are all insiders in one way or another.

Exploring the ruling relations from different positions discovers them in greater depth and complexity. Each new study, responding to the different properties and features of organization that come into view, has something new to say about how they are put together. New kinds of analyses are suggested, worked with and become available to the next practitioner. The products of the work of institutional ethnography not only feed into academic settings, although these are by no means neglected, but also reach into teaching, into the initiation of change and into awareness of the implications of changes that are imposed upon us.

LIST OF CONCEPTS

Discourse

My usage originates in Michel Foucault's conception which appeared originally in his *Archaeology of Knowledge* (1972) and was subsequently developed particularly in his lecture on 'the order of discourse' (Foucault 1981). I use it to designate a class of those relations that organize the local translocally. A general usage of discourse from which mine diverges is Diane Macdonnell's (1986). She describes discourse as 'The kind of speech proper to the shop-floor of a factory conflicts with that of the boardroom. Different social classes use the same words in different senses and disagree in their interpretation of events and situations' (Macdonnell 1986: 3). Gee, Hull and Lankshear's (1996) use is rather like Macdonnell's but they extend it to a range of social forms including 'different sorts of street gangs, elementary schools and classrooms, academic disciplines and their sub-specialities, police, birdwatchers, ethnic groups, genders, executives, feminists, social classes and sub-classes and so on and so forth' (Gee *et al.* 1996: 10). And they point out that 'We are all capable of being different kinds of people in different Discourses' (1996: 10) (the parallels between this concept of discourse and the ordinary sociological conceptions of role and social system are striking).

My own conception of discourse rejects this generalization of the concept to what used to be described in sociology as 'subcultures'. I want to preserve Foucault's (1981) conception of the order of discourse but to stretch it in ways that escape Foucault's paradigm. I take it up from women's standpoint as I've defined it. Hence the subject is always embodied and is located in an actual situation of activity which the discourse coordinates with others also at work. Not only is discourse taken to be practices (Foucault), but also the practices are of definite individuals located just as they are in the actualities of their everyday/everynight worlds as they/we experience them. Their 'practices' are coordinated through discourse as how what they do is made accountable to themselves and others (Garfinkel 1967). Since discourse is viewed as organized social relations among people, the order of discourse is seen as bringing into being an objectified organization of social relations that exist only in people's activities but that come to stand over against them, overpowering their lives. This indeed is a central difference between this and other concepts of discourse. This is the specific relevance of the concept to institutions when the generalization of the work that produces the institution on an everyday basis is problematized rather than taken for granted. A rule of institutional ethnography's discourse is that inquiry may not escape people's essential embodiment and hence their essentially localized (time and place) mode of being in the world. The objectification and trans-local organization of discursive relations must themselves somehow be produced and reproduced by particular people located just where they are.

Ethnography

As in 'institutional ethnography'; I quote from earlier work:

> The notion of ethnography is introduced to commit us to an exploration, description, and analysis of such a complex of relations, not conceived in the abstract but from the entry point of some particular person or persons whose everyday world of working is organized thereby. Ethnography does not here mean, as it sometimes does in sociology, restriction to methods of observation and interviewing. [It means] rather a commitment to an investigation and explication of how 'it' actually ... works, of actual practices and relations. ... Institutional ethnography explores the social relations individuals bring into being in and through their actual practices. Its methods, whether of observation, interviewing, recollection of work experience, use of archives, textual analysis, or other, are constrained by the practicalities of investigation of social relations as actual practices. Note however that the institutional ethnography as a way of investigating the problematic of the

everyday world does not involve substituting the [sociologist's] analysis, the perspectives and views [for those of the people she talks to or observes]. (Smith 1987: 160–161)

They are the expert practitioners of their own lives and the ethnographer's work learns from them and goes beyond what they know only in finding how they are connected beyond what is visible to them.

Everyday/everynight worlds

I use this expression as a reminder that women's work in the home isn't just a daytime affair.

Experience

The concept as it is used here does not refer to an authentic individual act of consciousness that gives access to a world directly known. Postmodernist feminist theory has been properly critical of feminist theory that has attempted to transpose what has been the experience of some women into generalized formulations legitimized with reference to the authenticity of women's experience. The critique asserts that there is no experience that is not already discursively structured. It is essentially spoken or written and hence is necessarily and always mediated by the structuring of the discourse in which it is uttered. This critique, however, ignores that extraordinary moment earlier in the women's movement when we (women) were discovering how to think ourselves apart from masculinized forms of thought. The latter constituted us as other, positioned, but not subjects. We had no language for speaking our condition. To speak from experience was to struggle with discourse and to appropriate terms or force them to behave as they had not behaved before. Rather therefore than the deterministic formulation of feminist postmodernism, we turn to how Mikhail Bakhtin conceives of speech genre, a concept closely parallel to that of discourse. Speech genres are laid down as people speak and write with others in the settings of their activities. Any particular utterance (particular speaker, particular time, particular place, particular others) draws on what has been laid down in the past to get something said and at the same time launches the genre into the future with whatever modifications have been introduced to realize the speaker's intentions. Her/his utterance is determined by what is already established; it depends on this utterly; using its terminology and syntactic strategies s/he reproduces the genre. At the same time s/he may refashion it to meet what s/he is trying to get said and this refashioning is projected into the future. Bakhtin's theory is dialogic. Each next speaker or writer is in dialogue with discourse.

This is how I conceive of experience. Not as an already given authentic knowledge of what is for the individual consciousness, but as a dialogue, now an actual conversation, whether in writing to an abstract reader or spoken directly to another. As a social form, it has definite conventions. One speaks of her/his experience and the other, who may question, assigns the privilege of narration to the person whose experience is uttered. Sometimes there is a struggle with the discourse within which the dialogue is engaged to get it to speak what is coming to be experience-as-uttered. Discourse does not determine; it is dialogically engaged with what the speaker or writer is trying to find a way of telling.

Institution

As in institutional ethnography: the best I can do here is to quote from an earlier work in which I first wrote about institutional ethnography:

> I am using the terms 'institutional' and 'institution' to identify a complex of relations forming part of the ruling [relations], organized around a distinctive function – education, health care, laws, and so on. In contrast to such concepts as bureaucracy, 'institution' does not identify a determinate form of social organization, but rather the intersection and coordination of more than one relational mode of [ruling]. Characteristically state agencies [and laws] are tied in with professional forms of organization, and both are interpenetrated by relations of discourse of more than one order. We might imagine institutions as nodes or knots in the [ruling] relations ... coordinating multiple strands of action into a functional complex. Integral to the coordinating process are ideologies systematically developed to provide categories and concepts expressing the relation[ship] of local courses of action to the institutional function. (Smith 1987: 160)

It is a specific capacity of institutions that they generalize. And are generalized. Hence in institutional settings, people are active in producing the generalized out of the particular.

Language and social organization

Again, I quote:

> As interviewers we persuade people to talk about the everyday worlds in which they are active. ... the social organization of our daily practices governs our choice of syntactic forms and terms when we speak them. ... It would be hard for someone to speak unmethodically in referencing social organization of which she is a competent practitioner. We speak from the known-in-practice ongoing concerting of actual activities. We speak knowing how rather than knowing that. We do not, of course, except in rare instances, speak *of* that social organization. We speak *methodically*. When we first encounter a new social organizational setting, we typically find that there is a problem of speech. It is like this: while we may be sure that we understand everything that is said, we are not at all sure that we will be able to speak correctly; we are not sure that the appropriate terms, names, titles, and so forth will fall

into place or – what is perhaps even more important – that we will know how to assemble these in the appropriate ways. But what are these appropriate forms? They are seldom as distinct as matters of protocol, of different official language uses. They are commonly the difference between how those speak who are ongoing practitioners of a world and who know how to use its language in situ as part of its ongoing concerting and how those speak who are as yet feeling their way into the properties of its everyday practices. The language of the setting observes the relations of its social organization. Its proper uses indeed preserve them. In the interview situation, the original setting is not operative, but registers as an underlying determinant of how the informant talks of the setting because it is the only way in which it makes sense to talk. (Smith 1987: 188–189, original emphasis)

Processing interchanges

No one oversees a case from its inception to its final resolution. No single person hand-carries it from one processing point to another. The case is routed. Interchanges are connected through routing instructions and procedures. Some of these connections operate quite smoothly; others do not. Some of them are critical to women's safety. The dispatcher, or in civil court, the clerk, is the first person in a long chain of responders to a domestic assault case. The station of each responder has built into its information-collecting and information-producing functions mechanisms that link the information into an overall case construction. It is neither the worker nor the woman who was beaten who moves from one point to the next in the stages of case processing; it is the case file. This file stands in for the woman who was assaulted, for her assailant, and for those who act to intervene. (Pence 1996: 53)

Processing interchanges are designed to organize the information received by intervening practitioners and to institutionally structure the kind of information that is produced at each interchange. Almost all interchanges are structured by the required use of forms, administrative procedures, regulations, or laws which screen, prioritize, shape, and filter the information the worker uses to produce accounts, reports, or documents related to a case. (Pence 1996: 55)

Ravines in Toronto

A surprising city, Toronto is riddled with ravines, many of which have not been developed. Trails have been created; the ravines are modestly but not too enthusiastically groomed; in some parts they remain quite wild and even occasionally difficult. There are a few unfortunate golf courses that bar the foot traveller and in one or two spots, the only way through is the railroad line and its insecurities, but generally it is possible to travel substantial distances with only occasional returns to the surface to find a connecting link between one part of a ravine and another where the path has been closed off by narrowing sides. Toronto's ravines play a part in Margaret Atwood's *The Edible Woman*.

Ruling relations

The ruling relations become visible when we start enquiry in the everyday worlds of people's experience. They are relations that coordinate people's activities across and beyond local sites of everyday experience. We know them variously as bureaucracy, discourse (in the Foucauldian sense), management, mass media, institutions, and so on and so on. In contrast to those forms of coordinating people's activities that are direct (moving furniture, for example, or playing soccer), they are extra- or trans-local and based in texts of various kinds (print, computer, film, television, and so on). Such concepts as information, knowledge, 'culture', science, and the like are rethought as relations among people that rely on the materiality of the text and its increasingly complex technologies. Institutions are specific functional foci within the complex of ruling relations.

Social relations

'Social relations' does not refer to relationships such as instructor–student, between lovers, parent–child, and so on. Rather it directs attention to and takes up analytically how what people are doing and experiencing in a given local site is hooked into sequences of action implicating and coordinating multiple local sites where others are active (D.E. Smith 1990b: 93–96; G.W. Smith 1995). A social 'relation is not a thing to be looked for in carrying out research, rather, it is what is used to do the looking' (G.W. Smith 1995: 24). It is a practical realization of the commitment to the discursive problematic of the everyday/everynight world (D.E. Smith 1987).

Texts

Printed or electronic or otherwise replicable texts have the extraordinary capacity of double presence: they are read or produced in the actual local settings of people's work or other activities and at the same time their replication in multiple different settings (and at different times) enters a standardized component into every settings in which the same text is read/viewed. It is, I suggest, texts that produce, in and out of the ephemerality of people's everyday activities, the stability and replicability of organization or institution.

Unlike some theorizing of 'text', the term is used here strictly to identify texts as material in a form that enables replication (paper/print, film, electronic and so on) of what is written, drawn or otherwise reproduced. Materiality is emphasized because we can then see how they are used to create a crucial join between the everyday actualities of people's activities and the social relations they coordinate.

Work

Dialogues with experience can participate in many discourses. Often it's thought that experience must refer to the subjective, the personal. The discourse of institutional ethnography selects 'work' as a metaphor that focuses the examination of experience on what people do. I do not want this notion to be shifted towards the notion of competence, though the institutional ethnographer relies on the knowhow of her or his respondents. Competence shifts the ground away from the concerting of people's activities and towards an individuating of the social. It installs people's doing in a disposition and formulated thus the social never actually happens. The concept of work as it is used here to focus the attention of both parties to the dialogue on what is done and being done, under what conditions, in relation to whom, and with what resources. Here is how I conceptualized this in my original formulation of institutional ethnography.

> We are familiar with the way in which the concept of work had not been extended in the past to women's work in the home as housewife. Our notion of work had to be expanded to include housework, and in doing so we discovered some of its presuppositions – the implicit contrast, for example, between work and leisure, which is based upon work as paid employment and does not apply to housework. Expanding the concept of work for our purposes requires its remaking in more ample and generous forms. Some wages-for-housework theorists have developed an expanded concept of housework, which I shall use as a model. They have used it to include all the work done by women [as well as by men] to sustain and service their … functioning in the wage relation and hence indirectly to sustain and service the enterprises employing their labor. This generous conception of [work] includes not only domestic labor proper but such activities as driving to one's place of employment, eating lunch in the cafeteria or making and eating sandwiches, purchasing and maintaining clothes, and so forth. All these aspects of everyday life are essential to the economy though they would not ordinarily be described as work, let alone as housework. For wages-for-housework theorists, housework becomes an economic category identifying those work processes that are in fact part of the economy but are not represented as work, being described as consumption or not at all. (Smith 1987: 165)

The concept of work as used in institutional ethnography identifies what people do that takes some effort and time, that they mean to do, that relies on definite resources, and is organized to coordinate in some way with the work of others similarly defined. The merit of this concept when inquirers enter into dialogue with their respondents is that it bridges both subjective and objective. It is both about what people do and it is also about the consciousness that necessarily goes along with doing. As George Herbert Mead (1947) said in recommending his brand of behaviourism over that of Watson, the act begins inside the individual and proceeds outside and inside and outside cannot be separated. Feeding the family, as Marjorie DeVault (1991) has described it, doesn't just mean preparing the food and putting it on the table; it also means planning the meal, thinking through what might already be in store somewhere, deciding what has to be shopped for and how to fit the shopping into the daily routine, coordinating the cooking and serving of a meal with the diverse schedules of different family members, and so on. This inside/outside disclosure anchors the ethnography in an everyday/everynight world while avoiding the divorce of subjective from objective that characterizes research oriented to 'meaning'. It also anchors the terminology in the discourse of the respondent's setting which is shared by others in the same setting and bears the social organization of their coordinated work. The trick, however, is to be able to extend this concept beyond what people might ordinarily think of as 'work' and beyond how we might ordinarily think about it, to see thinking or reading as work or the production of objectivity in science as people's concerted work. On the other hand, it's important too to keep in mind that 'work' here is a metaphor. At some point it may hamper rather than help and then sociologists need to remember that they are focused on people's doing in the most general sense and need to find some other concept.

NOTE

1 We started interviewing in one community doing interviews that sometimes lasted a couple of hours and met two or three times. We had made our contacts through the schools and after only two or three interviews and one meeting with a principal, we were rudely ejected by the superintendent of schools. We had to move to another community and there, because our time was now more restricted, we worked with a more structured interview procedure. All research has an economy that shapes it beyond methodology and theory.

REFERENCES AND BIBLIOGRAPHY OF INSTITUTIONAL ETHNOGRAPHIC STUDIES

Abu-Lughod, L. (1998) *Remaking Women: Feminism and Modernity in the Middle East*. Princeton, NJ: Princeton University Press.

Arnup, K. (1994) *Education for Motherhood: Advice for Mothers in Twentieth-Century Canada*. Toronto: University of Toronto Press.

Atwood, M. (1997) *The Edible Woman*. London: Virago.

Bakhtin, M.M. (1981) *The Dialogic Imagination: Four Essays*, edited by M. Holquist. Austin, TX: University of Texas Press.

Bakhtin, M.M. (1986a) *Speech Genres and Other Late Essays*, translated by V.W. McGee. Austin, TX: University of Texas Press.

Bakhtin, M.M. (1986b) 'The problem of speech genres', in M.M. Bakhtin, *Speech Genres and Other Late Essays*, translated by V.W. McGee. Austin, TX: University of Texas Press.

Bannerji, H. (1995) 'Beyond the ruling category to what actually happens: notes on James Mill's historiography in "The history of British India"', in M. Campbell and A. Manicom (eds) *Knowledge, Experience, and Ruling Relations: Studies in the Social Organization of Knowledge*. Toronto: University of Toronto Press.

Bourdieu, P. (1990) *The Logic of Practice*. Stanford, CA: Stanford University Press.

Bullock, A. (1990) 'Community care: ideology and experience', in R. Ng, G. Walker and J.M. Jacob (eds) *Community Organization and the Canadian State*. Toronto: Garamond Press.

Campbell, M. (1984) 'Information systems and management of hospital nursing: a study in the social organization of knowledge', PhD thesis, University of Toronto.

Campbell, M.L. (1988) 'Management as ruling: a class phenomenon in nursing', *Studies in Political Economy* 27: 29–51.

Campbell, M.L. (1994) 'The structure of stress in nurses' work', in B. Singh Bolaria and H.D. Dickinson (eds) *Health Illness and Health Care in Canada*, 2nd edn. New York: Harcourt Brace.

Campbell, M. (1995) 'Teaching accountability: what counts as nursing education?' in M. Campbell and A. Manicom (eds) *Knowledge, Experience, and Ruling Relations: Studies in the Social Organization of Knowledge*. Toronto: University of Toronto Press.

Campbell, M. (1998a) 'Institutional ethnography and experience as data', *Qualitative Sociology* 21(1): 55–73.

Campbell, M. (1998b) 'Research on health care experiences of people with disabilities: exploring the everyday problematic of service delivery', paper presented at 'Exploring the Restructuring and Transformation of Institutional Processes: Applications of Institutional Ethnography', York University, Toronto, October.

Campbell, M. and Manicom, A. (eds) (1995) *Knowledge, Experience, and Ruling Relations: Studies in the Social Organization of Knowledge*. Toronto: University of Toronto Press.

Cheng, L. and Gereffi, G. (1994) 'U./S. retailers and Asian garment production', in E. Bonacich, L. Cheng, N. Chinchilla, N. Hamilton and P. Ong (eds) *Global Production: The Apparel Industry in the Pacific Rim*. Philadelphia, PA: Temple University Press.

Clifford, J. and Marcus, G.E. (eds) (1986) *Writing Culture: The Poetics and Politics of Ethnography*. Berkeley, CA: University of California Press.

Currie, D. and Wickramasinghe, A. (1998) 'Engendering development theory from the standpoint of women, in D. Currie, G. Noga and P. Gurstein (eds) *Learning to Write: Women's Studies in Development*. Vancouver: Collective Press.

Darville, R. (1995) 'Literacy, experience, power', in M. Campbell and A. Manicom (eds) *Knowledge, Experience, and Ruling Relations: Studies in the Social Organization of Knowledge*. Toronto: University of Toronto Press.

De Montigny, G.A.J. (1995a) *Social Working: An Ethnography of Front-line Practice*. Toronto: University of Toronto Press.

De Montigny, G.A.J. (1995b) 'The power of being professional', in M. Campbell and A. Manicom. *Knowledge, Experience, and Ruling Relations: Studies in the Social Organization of Knowledge*. Toronto: University of Toronto Press.

DeVault, M.L. (1991) *Feeding the Family*. Chicago: University of Chicago Press.

DeVault, M.L. and McCoy, L. (2000) 'Institutional ethnography: using interviews to investigate ruling relations', in J.F. Gubrium and J.A. Holstein (eds) *Handbook of Interviewing*. Thousand Oaks, CA: Sage.

Diamond, T. (1986) 'Social policy and everyday life in nursing homes: a critical ethnography', *Social Science and Medicine* 23(12): 1,287–1,295.

Diamond, T. (1992) *Making Gray Gold: Narratives of Nursing Home Care*. Chicago: University of Chicago Press.

Emerson, R.M., Fretz, R.I. and Shaw, L.L. (1995) *Writing Ethnographic Fieldnotes*. Chicago: University of Chicago Press.

Foucault, M. (1970) *The Order of Things: An Archaeology of the Human Sciences*. London: Tavistock.

Foucault, M. (1972) *The Archaeology of Knowledge and the Discourse on Language*. New York: Pantheon.

Foucault, M. (1979) *Discipline and Punish: The Birth of the Prison*. New York: Vintage.

Foucault, M. (1980) *Power/Knowledge: Selected Interviews and Other Writings, 1972–1977*. New York: Pantheon.

Foucault, M. (1981) 'The order of discourse', in R. Young (ed.) *Untying the Text: A Poststructuralist Reader*. London: Routledge.

Gadamer, H-G. (1994) *Truth and Method*. New York: Continuum.

Garfinkel, H. (1967) *Studies in Ethnomethodology*. Englewood Cliffs, NJ: Prentice-Hall.

Gee, J., Hull, G. and Lankshear, C. (1996) *The New Work Order: Behind the Language of the New Capitalism*. Boulder, CO: Westview.

Grahame, K. (1999) 'State, community and Asian immigrant women's work: a study in labor market organization', PhD dissertation, University of Toronto.

Grahame, P.R. (1998) 'Ethnography, institutions, and the social organization of knowledge', *Human Studies* 21(4): 347–360.

Griffith, A.I. (1984) 'Ideology, education, and single parent families: the normative ordering of families through schooling', PhD dissertation, University of Toronto.

Griffith, A.I. (1995) 'Mothering, schooling, and children's development', in M. Campbell and A. Manicom (eds) *Experience, Knowledge, and Ruling Relations: Explorations in the Social Organization of Knowledge*. Toronto: University of Toronto Press.

Griffith, A.I. (1998) 'Educational restructuring in Ontario', paper presented at 'Exploring the Restructuring and Transformation of Institutional Processes: Applications of Institutional Ethnography', York University, Toronto, October.

Griffith, A.I. and Smith, D.E. (1987) 'Constructing cultural knowledge: mothering as discourse', in J. Gaskell and A. McLaren (eds) *Women and Education: A Canadian Perspective*. Calgary: Detselig.

Griffith, A.I. and Smith, D.E. (1990a) 'Coordinating the uncoordinated: mothering, schooling and the family wage', in G. Miller and J. Holstein (eds) *Perspectives on Social Problems*, vol. 2. Greenwich, CT: JAI Press.

Griffith, A.I. and Smith, D.E. (1990b) 'What did you do in school today? Mothering, schooling and social class', in G. Miller and J. Holstein (eds) *Perspectives on Social Problems*, vol. 2. Greenwich, CT: JAI Press.

Heap, J.L. (1995) 'Foreword', in M. Campbell and A. Manicom, *Knowledge, Experience, and Ruling Relations: Studies in the Social Organization of Knowledge*. Toronto: University of Toronto Press.

Jackson, N. (1995) '"These things just happen": talk, text, and curriculum reform', in M. Campbell and A. Manicom (eds) *Knowledge, Experience, and Ruling Relations: Studies in the Social Organization of Knowledge*. Toronto: University of Toronto Press.

Khayatt, D. (1995) 'Compulsory heterosexuality: schools and lesbian students', in M. Campbell and A. Manicom (eds) *Knowledge, Experience, and Ruling Relations: Studies in the Social Organization of Knowledge*. Toronto: University of Toronto Press.

Kinsman, G. (1995) 'The textual practices of sexual rule: sexual policing of gay men', in M. Campbell and A. Manicom (eds) *Knowledge, Experience, and Ruling Relations: Studies in the Social Organization of Knowledge*. Toronto: University of Toronto Press.

McCoy, L. (1995) 'Activating the photographic text', in M. Campbell and A. Manicom (eds) *Knowledge, Experience, and Ruling Relations: Studies in the Social Organization of Knowledge*. Toronto: University of Toronto Press.

McCoy, L. (1999) 'Accounting discourse and textual practices of ruling: a study of institutional transformation and restructuring in higher education', unpublished doctoral dissertation, University of Toronto.

Macdonnell, D. (1986) *Theories of Discourse: An Introduction*. Oxford: Basil Blackwell.

Manicom, A. (1988) 'Constituting class relations: the social organization of teachers' work', PhD thesis, University of Toronto.

Manicom, A. (1995) 'What's health got to do with it? Class, gender and teacher's work', in M. Campbell and A. Manicom (eds) *Knowledge, Experience, and Ruling Relations: Studies in the Social Organization of Knowledge*. Toronto: University of Toronto Press.

Marx, K. and Engels, F. (1976) *The German Ideology*. Moscow: Progress.

Mead, G.H. (1947) *Mind, Self and Society: From the Perspective of a Social Behaviorist*, edited by C.W. Morris. Chicago: University of Chicago Press.

Mueller, A. (1987) 'Peasants and professionals: the social organization of women in development knowledge', unpublished doctoral dissertation, University of Toronto.

Mueller, A. (1991) *In and Against Development: Feminists Confront Development on its Own Ground*. East Lansing, MI: Michigan State University.

Mueller, A. (1995) 'Beginning in the standpoint of women: an investigation of the gap between "Cholas" and "Women of Peru"', in M. Campbell and A. Manicom (eds) *Knowledge, Experience, and Ruling Relations: Studies in the Social Organization of Knowledge*. Toronto: University of Toronto Press.

Mykhaloviskiy, E. (1998) 'We do meaning: health services research, research transfer and the social organization of interpretive practices', paper presented at 'Exploring the Restructuring and Transformation of Institutional Processes: Applications of Institutional Ethnography', York University, Toronto, October.

Naples, N. and Sachs, C. (2000) 'Standpoint epistemologies and the uses of self-reflection in feminist ethnography: lessons for rural sociology', *Rural Sociology* 65(2): 194–214.

Ng, R. (1986) *Politics of Community Services: Immigrant Women, Class and State*. Toronto: Garamond Press.

Ng, R. (1990) 'Immigrant women: the construction of a labour market category', *Canadian Journal of Women and the Law* 4: 96–112.

Ng, R. (1995) 'Multiculturalism as ideology: a textual analysis', in M. Campbell and A. Manicom (eds) *Knowledge, Experience, and Ruling Relations: Studies in the Social Organization of Knowledge*. Toronto: University of Toronto Press.

Ng, R. (1998) 'Immigration policy, labour adjustment and the transformation of garment workers' lives', paper presented at 'Exploring the Restructuring and Transformation of Institutional Processes: Applications of Institutional Ethnography', York University, Toronto, October.

Pence, E. (1996) 'Safety for battered women in a textually-mediated legal system', unpublished doctoral dissertation, University of Toronto.

Pence, E. (2001) 'Safety for battered women in a textually-mediate legal system', *Studies in Societies, Cultures and Organizations*, special issue on 'Institutional Ethnography'.

Rankin, J.M. (1998) 'Health care reform and restructuring of nursing in British Columbia', paper presented at 'Exploring the Restructuring and Transformation of Institutional Processes: Applications of Institutional Ethnography', York University, Toronto.

Rankin, J. (2001) 'Texts in action: how nurses are doing the fiscal work of health care reform', *Studies in Societies, Cultures and Organizations*, special issue on 'Institutional Ethnography'.

Reimer, M. (1988) 'The social organization of the labour process: a case study of the documentary management of clerical labour in the public service', PhD dissertation, University of Toronto.

Reimer, M. (1995) 'Downgrading clerical work in a textually mediated labour process', in M. Campbell and A. Manicom (eds) *Knowledge, Experience, and Ruling Relations: Studies in the Social Organization of Knowledge*. Toronto: University of Toronto Press.

Schutz, A. (1962) 'On multiple realities', in *Collected Papers*, vol. I. The Hague: Martinus Nijhoff.

Sèchehaye, M. and Renée, P. (1969) *Autobiography of a Schizophrenic Girl, with Analytic Interpretation*, translated by G. Rubin-Rabson. New York: Grune and Stratton.

Sharma, N. (1998) 'Capitalist restructuring and the social organization of "non-immigrants" in Canada: the reformalization of non-membership', paper presented at 'Exploring the Restructuring and Transformation of Institutional Processes: Applications of Institutional Ethnography', York University, Toronto, October.

Simpson, P.E. (1998) 'An inquiry into the Canadian development worker role as a site for the reorganization of Canada's international relations', paper presented at 'Exploring the Restructuring and Transformation of Institutional Processes: Applications of Institutional Ethnography', York University, Toronto, October.

Smith, D.E. (1974) 'Women's perspective as a radical critique of sociology', *Sociological Inquiry* 4(1): 1–13 (a revised version was published in D.E. Smith 1990a).

Smith, D.E. (1977) 'Some implications of a sociology for women', in N. Glazer and H. Waehrer (eds) *Women in a Man-Made World*, revised edn. Chicago: Rand-McNally.

Smith, D.E. (1979) 'A sociology for women', in J. Sherman and F. Beck (eds) *The Prism of Sex: Essays in the Sociology of Knowledge*. Madison, WI: University of Wisconsin Press.

Smith, D.E. (1987) *The Everyday World as Problematic: A Feminist Sociology*. Boston, MA: Northeastern University Press.

Smith, D.E. (1990a) *The Conceptual Practices of Power: A Feminist Sociology of Knowledge*. Toronto: University of Toronto Press.

Smith, D.E. (1990b) *Texts, Facts, and Femininity: Exploring the Relations of Ruling*. New York: Routledge.

Smith, D.E. (1997) 'The underside of schooling: restructuring, privatization, and women's unpaid work', *Journal for a Just and Caring Education* Fall: 14–29.

Smith, D.E. (1999) *Writing the Social: Critique, Theory and Investigations*. Toronto: University of Toronto Press.

Smith, G.W. (1988) 'Occupation and skill: government discourse as problematic', occasional paper no. 2, The Nexus Project: Studies in the Job Education Nexus, Toronto.

Smith, G.W. (1990a) 'Policing the gay community', in R. Ng, G. Walker and J. Muller (eds) *Community Organization and the Canadian State*. Toronto: Garamond Press.

Smith, G.W. (1990b) 'Political activist as ethnographer', *Social Problems* 37: 401–421.

Smith, G.W. (1995) 'Accessing treatments: managing the AIDS epidemic in Ontario', in M. Campbell and A. Manicom (eds) *Knowledge, Experience, and Ruling Relations: Studies in the Social Organization of Knowledge*. Toronto: University of Toronto Press.

Smith, G.W. (1998) 'The ideology of "fag": barriers to education for gay students', *Sociological Quarterly* 39(2): 309–335.

Stock, A. (2000) 'An ethnography of assessment in elementary schools', doctoral dissertation, University of Toronto.

Turner, S.M. (1995) 'Rendering the site developable: textual organization in the planning process', in M. Campbell and A. Manicom (eds) *Experience, Knowledge, and Ruling Relations: Explorations in the Social Organization of Knowledge*. Toronto: University of Toronto Press.

Ueda, Y. (1995) 'Corporate wives: gendered education of their children', in M. Campbell and A. Manicom (eds) *Knowledge, Experience, and Ruling Relations: Studies in the Social Organization of Knowledge*. Toronto: University of Toronto Press.

Walker, G. (1990a) *Family Violence and the Women's Movement: The Conceptual Politics of Struggle*. Toronto: University of Toronto Press.

Walker, G. (1990b) 'The conceptual politics of struggle: wife battering, the women's movement and the state', *Studies in Political Economy* 33: 63–90.

Walker, G. (1995) 'Violence and the relations of ruling: lessons from the battered women's movement', in M. Campbell and A. Manicom (eds) *Knowledge, Experience, and Ruling Relations: Studies in the Social Organization of Knowledge*. Toronto: University of Toronto Press.

Walker, G. (1998) 'Internal pressures, external forces: the ongoing struggle of the battered women's movement and the state', paper presented at 'Exploring the Restructuring and Transformation of Institutional Processes: Applications of Institutional Ethnography', York University, Toronto, October.

2 CRITICAL REALIST ETHNOGRAPHY

Sam Porter

This chapter is about how ethnographers might deal with the issue of social structures. Two main questions are addressed. First, are there such things as social structures? Second (predicated upon a positive answer to the first question), is it possible to use ethnographic methods to examine those structures and their relationship with social action? The suggested answer to this is that the philosophy of science known as critical realism provides a sound basis for moving ethnography beyond the examination of specific social instances, in order to examine the general structural context of those instances.

The chapter has three main sections. The first section entails an historical review of the way (primarily sociological) ethnographers have dealt with the issue of structure. It starts by looking at the foundational work of Durkheim and Weber, and their attempts to incorporate the structuring of human action into their theories of research. Following from this baseline, there is an examination of the phenomenological and postmodernist turns in ethnographic theorizing, which concentrates on how the influence of these two movements led to the erasure of structure from the ethnographic imagination. The section concludes with a brief review of what Brewer (2000) terms post-postmodernist approaches to ethnography, which is seeking tentatively to pull back from the extremes of methodological individualism and scepticism.

The second section introduces critical realism and attempts to argue how the use of this philosophical position as a grounding for ethnography is capable of solving many of the problems raised by phenomenology and postmodernism in relation to the place of structure in our understanding of the social world.

The final section works through a practical example of the use of critical realist ethnography. This is an ethnographic study of power relations between nurses and doctors in an intensive care unit which attempts to generalize beyond the interactions observed and comments of individuals heard, in order to show how those relations are socially structured.

THE HISTORY OF STRUCTURE IN ETHNOGRAPHY

The elementary forms

Probably the most seminal attempt to understand the nature of structures using ethnographic information was that of Durkheim's *Elementary Forms of Religious Life* (1995 [1912]), which relied for empirical data upon ethnographic studies of the religious practices of Australian aboriginals. However, the point of Durkheim's use of ethnography was not simply to describe the ideographic experiences of the individuals observed. His aim was far bolder:

> I will make every effort to describe the organization of this system with all the care and precision that an ethnographer or a historian would bring to the task. But my task will not stop at description. Sociology sets itself different problems from those of history or ethnography. It does not seek to become acquainted with bygone forms of civilization for the sole purpose of being acquainted with and reconstructing them. Instead, like any positive science, its purpose above all is to explain a present reality that is near to us and thus capable of affecting our ideas and actions. That reality is man. ... I have made a very archaic religion the subject of my research because it seems better suited than any other to help us comprehend the religious nature of man, that is, to reveal a fundamental and permanent aspect of humanity. (Durkheim 1995: 1)

The latter sentence does not entail a theological statement, rather a fundamentally sociological one. As Durkheim stated elsewhere:

> Religion contains in itself from the very beginning, even in an indistinct state, all the elements which, in dissociating themselves from it, articulating themselves, and combining with one another in a thousand ways, have given rise to the various manifestations of collective life. (Durkheim 1897, cited by LaCapra 1985: 247)

Thus, Durkheim's project was to use ethnographic material on the religious life of an 'organic' society (cf. Durkheim (1984 [1893]), where, '[a]t the same time all is uniform, all is simple' (Durkheim 1995: 5), in order to uncover the elementary forms of religion which constituted one of the most fundamental structures underpinning collective life. By examining the undifferentiated components, as displayed under conditions of organic solidarity, Durkheim then argued that the significance of this 'fundamental and permanent aspect of humanity' could be traced through the development of society, allowing us to understand better how religion, or at least the transformed remnants of religion, continued to have a profound influence upon the collective life of modern society.

The purpose of this brief synopsis is not to defend Durkheim's thesis on the social structural position of religion, still less to defend his belief in the veracity of positive science. Rather, it is to note that from the era of its formulation as a distinct academic discipline, sociology approached ethnography from a particular standpoint. Namely, it aimed to use ethnographic material to tell us something wider about social life than the particular experiences of those who were the subject of ethnographic studies.

Weber's Verstehende

It might be argued that contemporary ethnography has an altogether different sociological parentage, namely the *Verstehende* sociology of Max Weber, which was based on a distinctly nominalist position, and thus would seem to place the focus of research firmly on individuals rather than structures:

> When reference is made in a sociological context to a state, a nation, a corporation, a family, or an army corps, or to similar collectivities, what is meant is ... *only* a certain kind of development of actual or possible social actions of individual persons. (Weber 1978 [1956]: 14, original emphasis)

The problem with such a position is that, whether or not it is correct, people in general tend not to adopt it, and instead regard collectivities as having a reality beyond that of individuals, and act accordingly. This is a point that Weber concedes, but to which he responds with an idealist interpretation:

> These concepts of collective entities ... have a meaning in the minds of individual persons, partly as of something actually existing, partly as something with normative authority. ... Actors thus in part orient their action to them, and in this role such ideas have a powerful, often decisive, *causal* influence on the course of action of real individuals. (Weber 1978 [1956]: 14, added emphasis)

Thus, Weber is brought to a position whereby, while denying the material reality of structures, he accepts that they have real causal effects. In doing so, he comes very close to Durkheim's position, who, while arguing for the coercive power of social facts, is perfectly prepared to accept that they 'have no existence save in and through individual consciousness' (Durkheim 1982 [1895]: 52). The significant issue here is that Weber's acceptance of the causal efficacy of social collectivities leads him further to accept that research focusing on the meanings of individuals is not sufficient on its own to gain full sociological understanding.

> A correct causal interpretation of typical action means that the process which is claimed to be typical is shown to be both adequately grasped at the level of meaning and at the same time the interpretation is to some degree causally adequate. ... even the most perfect adequacy on the level of meaning has causal significance from a sociological point of view only insofar as there is some kind of proof for the existence of a probability that action in fact normally takes the course which has been held to be meaningful. (Weber 1978 [1956]: 12)

There are ambiguities here in relation to the distinction between cause and correlation, ambiguities which were played out in Weber's own empirical analysis of the relationship between religion and socio-economic organization (see Parkin 1982). However, the point is that, like Durkheim, Weber had aspirations for sociological knowledge that went beyond the ideographic uncovering of understandings of particular individuals.

Phenomenological ethnography

While Durkheim and Weber made significant statements about the use of ethnography as a method of sociological exploration, they were less than comprehensive on ontological, epistemological and methodological details of their approaches. Despite the considerable length of *Elementary Forms*, it is almost entirely taken up with empirical information and theoretical extrapolations based on that information. Durkheim pays little heed to the methodological quandaries relating to ethnography that contemporary ethnographers would take as standard; questions such as the status of accounts of western ethnographers examining non-western social practices, or of the secondary use of ethnographies. While Weber's development of the *Verstehende* method was more comprehensive, he remained vague about key conceptual issues. This vagueness was seized upon by Alfred Schutz in his *Phenomenology of the Social World* (1972):

> The present study is based on an intensive concern of many years' duration with the theoretical writings of Max Weber. During this time I became convinced that while Weber's approach was correct and that he had determined conclusively the proper starting point of the philosophy of the social sciences, nevertheless his analyses did not go deeply enough to lay the foundations on which alone many important problems of the human sciences could be solved. Above all, Weber's central concept of subjective meaning calls for a thoroughgoing analysis. As Weber left this concept, it was little more than a heading for a number of important problems which he did not examine in detail. (Schutz 1972: xxvii)

Schutz's argument that Weber failed to state clearly the essential attributes of *Verstehen*, subjective meaning or social action allowed him the opportunity to develop Weber's methodology in his own direction. Specifically, it allowed Schutz to graft on his own interpretation of Husserlian phenomenology. The key notion that he adopted from Husserl was that what appears to be the natural ordering of the world is in fact the result of conceptual judgements of the mind.

This move meant that Weber's rather ambiguous, but essentially two-way conception of the causal flow between structures and actions was now firmly grounded in a uni-directional causal flow, with structures being reduced to the status of epiphenomena of subjectivities. For Schutz, the social world was 'essentially only something dependent upon and still within the operating intentionality of ego-consciousness' (1967: 44). The problems of this emphasis on the subjective at the cost of recognition of the causal effects of the wider social world upon the subjectivities of individuals have been identified by Giddens (1976), who has criticized Schutz's position on the grounds that it can take account neither of the unacknowledged effects of actions, nor of determining conditions that are not mediated by the consciousness of actors.

This discussion of Schutz has been confined to the level of theory. We need to ask what are the consequences of such a position being adopted by the empirical ethnographer? I wish to argue that the significance of Schutz's ideas for ethnographic sociological research lay in the tendency for many ethnographers to rely exclusively on uncovering, in an unproblematic fashion, the subjective interpretations of individuals, at the cost of examining how social structures and processes influenced those interpretations.

Let me take one example, that of Hockey's (1986) ethnographic study of British soldiers. Hockey clearly situates his study within the subjectivist tradition, noting that his research involved stressing 'the importance of interpreting the behaviour of people in terms of their subjectively intended meanings' (1986: 10). Part of the study involves an account of soldiers on combat duty in rural Ireland. In good ethnographic tradition, the soldiers' everyday lives are richly described. Unfortunately, description is as far as it goes. The simple but crucial question of *why* the soldiers were acting in the way that they were in the location in which they found themselves is beyond the remit of this subjectivist inquiry. For example, we are given a description of highly armed troops, who are psychologically on a combat footing in a foreign country, the native inhabitants of which they treat with, at best, suspicion. This information is of limited utility unless we ask why this is so, and in order to do so, we need to understand how the political, social and economic relations between Ireland and Britain have been historically structured.

The restriction of the interpretation of behaviour to the subjectively intended meanings that immediately generated it obviates the possibility of deeper analysis of the social situation encountered by the ethnographer. In short, the social phenomenological assumption that individual interactions and interpretations are all there are leads to analytic superficiality. While understanding the interpretations of the social actors is a necessary condition for sociological knowledge, it is not a sufficient one (Porter 1993).

The import of this critique of phenomenological ethnography is that if ethnography is to be an effective method of social research, it needs to be grounded in an ontological, epistemological and methodological model that can provide a deeper understanding than subjectivism is capable of; one which is able to link the subjective understandings of individuals with the structural positions within which those individuals are located.

Postmodernist ethnography

As we have seen, Durkheim, in his study of elementary forms of religious life, felt few qualms about using ethnographic data about the beliefs and practices of people in a culture radically different to his and using them to make sweeping generalizations about the nature of human society *in toto*. Thus, the intricacies and complexities of the lives of these people were subsumed into the framework of his functionalist 'meta-narrative', to use Lyotard's (1984) term.

Here we can see the ethnographer as a figure of authority, claiming the right to explain people's lives from his or her singular point of view. This issue of explanatory presumptuousness was especially acute in the discipline of anthropology, where one found western ethnographers presuming to explain various non-western cultures according to their own western lights. This academic imperialism involved an uncomfortably close affinity with the military, economic and political imperialism of western capital and nations.

The construction of the non-western 'other' within the self-serving rubric of the western paradigm has come in for severe criticism (see, for example, Said 1978). One of the results of this sort of critique has been a crisis in confidence on the part of western ethnographers. One of the responses to this crisis has been to radically undermine the authority of the ethnographic author. This involves moving from a critique of the particular meta-narratives that ethnographers adopted to frame their explanations to a generalized attack on the use of any sort of meta-narrative. Thus, for example, Crapanzano warns that the events being described by the ethnographer will be 'subverted by the transcending stories in which they are cast' (1986: 76). Here we can see a full swing across the spectrum of epistemological confidence – from the point where ethnographers assume unproblematically the validity of their authorial position, to the point where ethnographies are seen as nothing more than the inventions of their authors (see Clifford 1986).

A concomitant rejection of patriarchal meta-narratives led many feminist ethnographers to adopt a similar critique. Thus, for example, Stanley (1987) developed her radically perspectivist 'reverse archaeology'. Reverse archaeology goes beyond the traditional perspectivist tenet that different observers will have different perspectives on the same phenomenon, to asserting that the same observer will have constantly different perspectives on the social patterns that they observe. Once again, we have moved from the unreflexive certainties of patriarchal thought to the acceptance of the indeterminacy of knowledge.

From particular politico-epistemological problematics, postmodernism rapidly moved to occupy a central space in thinking about qualitative research (see, for example, Scheurich 1997; Cheek 2000). In short, pluralism, perspectivism and scepticism became the order of the day.

The rejection of authorial meta-narrational certainties and their replacement by a robust epistemological scepticism has even more profound consequences for our knowledge of the social world than that of the phenomenological turn in qualitative research. Phenomenology still held on to the anchor of subjective experience, and the possibility that the perspective of the subject was amenable to interpretation at the point of encounter between its horizon and that of the researcher's (see Gadamer 1975). With postmodernism, even this is abandoned to the kaleidoscope of changing patterns and perspectives that allow us little or no confidence to assume that one interpretation of the social world can claim epistemological superiority over any other.

The difficulty with such a position is that, if ethnographies are simply authorial inventions, rather than reflections, of greater or lesser accuracy, of social reality, then what is the point of ethnography? While the problem of intellectual arrogance is solved, it is done so at the cost of abandoning the very *raison d'être* of ethnographic research. This, I believe, is the *reductio ad absurdum* of the postmodernist position. If absolute uncertainty and relativism are accepted, there is little else for ethnographers to say about the social world, for what they say can claim no superiority in terms of adequacy over that which anyone else says.

Post-postmodernist ethnography

While it is as yet too early to tell definitively, there are indications that postmodernism has passed its high-water mark. There are good practical reasons for this, in that if ethnography is to be of any utility for our understanding of society, it has to posit some form of generalizable truth claims. This is not to say that the issues highlighted by both phenomenology and postmodernism can be rejected out of hand. From phenomenology, we can glean the importance of understanding subjective meanings as the basis of social action. From postmodernism, we are made aware of the dangers of making absolute claims about those understandings. There is now a growing acceptance that an adequate ethnographic model needs to incorporate these insights, while at the same time going beyond them, in order to take into account the patterning of social behaviour. Thus, for example, in Chapter 5 in this book, Malcolm Williams argues that while strong claims about the capacity to generalize from ethnographic data cannot be sustained, this does not obviate the need for some sort of generalization. As a consequence, he advocates '*moderatum* generalizations', whereby it is claimed that aspects of a particular situation can be seen to be instances of a broader recognizable set of features.

These moves beyond postmodernism are not confined to the realms of sociological theorizing, indeed they are far more crucial to the endeavours of practising qualitative researchers, in that it is they who are required to demonstrate the broad pertinence of their work. To take one substantive area of research, that which looks at the health behaviours of young people, it is increasingly being recognized that we cannot understand why young people behave as they do in relation to the consumption of such things as tobacco and alcohol unless we include social structure in our explanation. Thus, Pavis *et al.* (1998) state that 'Our research suggests the persistence of significant structural limitations in the pathways to adulthood, although these may be different to those experienced by previous generations' (1998: 1,412). Similarly, Denscombe (2001) puts forward the thesis that one of the primary factors in explaining adolescent smoking are the 'uncertain identities' of young people. While the notion of uncertain identity may seem in itself to be a very postmodern one, Denscombe wishes to uncover from whence such uncertainty comes. He concludes that 'the evidence from this research would still tend to support the contention … that the social/historical context of late modernity heightens the significance of uncertain identities in the lives of young people' (2001: 175).

Examples from other substantive areas of qualitative research could be used just as well to demonstrate that while researchers remain sensitized to postmodernism's attack on the arrogance of sureness, there is a drawing back from its extreme position, and an acceptance that it is both permissible and desirable to make knowledge claims which extend beyond the individual.

This leads to the question of what sort of philosophy of science can be used to ground this post-postmodernist (Brewer 2000) position. Such a model would be required to allow for the possibility of generalization, while at the same time avoiding the errors in previous models identified by phenomenology and postmodernism. In other words, it would be a model which accepts that there is a reality beyond individuals, but which does not over-extend its claims about how much we can know about that reality (in response to postmodernism) or about the degree to which external reality controls the decisions of individuals (in response to phenomenology). In short, what is needed is a realism that is not naive.

A number of attempts have been made to construct just such a realist basis for ethnography, most notably Hammersley's (1992) 'subtle realism' and Altheide and Johnson's (1998) 'analytical realism'. Critical realism differs from both of these models in that it gives less away to the phenomenological and postmodernist critiques. As such, its claims are contentious. However, I hope to argue that the use of critical realism as a basis for ethnography is both viable and useful. The first stage of this argument is to outline what the philosophical position of critical realism entails and how it relates to ethnography.

THE TENETS OF CRITICAL REALISM

At the basis of critical realism is an acceptance of the crucial importance of what Kant (1896) termed the transcendental question, which asks what must be the case, a priori, in order for events to occur as they do. Thus, in relation to society, it asks what factors lead to the patterning of human understandings and actions. The a priori answer to the question is that, because actions are patterned, rather than random, they must be structured in some way.

Already, we have got to the stage where a number of possible objections need to be answered. From a postmodernist point of view, it might be argued that this transcendental conjuring up of structures is just another example of the arrogance of modernist meta-narration. In response it is important to underline the limits of this transcendental move. The assertion that structures exist is as far as critical realist a priori reasoning goes – identification of the nature of those structures is a matter of empirical endeavour, and thus consists of fallible knowledge claims. Thus, for example, transcendental realism does not warrant the sort of vulgar Marxist argument concerning the deterministic role of economic relations. This is not to say that, in certain cases, economic factors may indeed be the primary structural influence upon the patterning of human relations, but discovering whether or not this is the case is an empirical issue.

From a Weberian point of view, critical realism might be accused to the error of reification. The argument here is that if structures do not exist as perceivable things, then they do not exist, except in the minds of individuals. In response, critical realism argues that the perceptual criterion of reality is not the only criterion, and adds to it the causal criterion, which turns on the capacity of an entity to bring about changes in material things. On this criterion, to be is not to be perceived, but to be able to do (Bhaskar 1989a). Entities in this category include gravity and magnetism. Neither of these forces can be directly perceived, but their effects upon material things can be. Thus, for example, we know that the structural mechanism of magnetism exists, because we can see its effects upon the patterning of iron filings. Similarly, belief in the reality of social structures is justified on the grounds of the perceivable effects they have upon patterns of human behaviour.

The phenomenologist in turn might point to the apparent structural determinism of such a position, arguing that human behaviour displays considerable variation, and it does so because it is grounded in the meanings of individual actors. This is the reason why positivist social scientific attempts to identify universal empirical regularities have come to naught. To treat human beings as objects whose actions are determined by extraneous factors is to misinterpret the nature of humanity.

While accepting the phenomenological point that human activity is conscious, critical realism argues that this does not warrant the further phenomenological assumption that activity can be solely explained in terms of individual consciousness. There are two related reasons for the rejection of individualist reductionism. First, the social context within which an individual lives provides the conditions for her consciousness. Second, the wider social effects of actions may not be those consciously intended by the actor. Thus Bhaskar (1989b) characterizes the relationship between society and people thus:

> people, in their conscious human activity, for the most part unconsciously reproduce (or occasionally, transform) the structures that govern their substantive activities of production. Thus people do not marry to reproduce the nuclear family, or work to reproduce the capitalist economy. But it is nevertheless the unintended consequence (and inexorable result) of, as it is also the necessary condition for, their activity. (Bhaskar 1989b: 80)

Social phenomenology's insistence that the ethnographer should concentrate exclusively on understanding the subjective meanings and actions of individuals is at least partially grounded in the traditional dichotomy in social science between the positivist and hermeneutic traditions. On the one hand, positivism adheres to naturalism, which asserts that the laws operating in the social world are essentially of the same quality as those operating in the natural world and can therefore be studied in the same manner (see Comte 1974). On the other hand, the hermeneutic tradition sees the social world and the natural world as radically different arenas, thus requiring radically different methods of study (see Winch 1959).

Critical realism seeks to overcome this dichotomy through its adoption of a modified naturalism. The commonality between the natural and social sciences lies in the connection between empirical investigation and theory construction, which in both cases involves the move from observed phenomena to generative structure (Bhaskar 1989a). However, while both the natural and social worlds are to be understood through elucidation of the relationship between structure and phenomenon, the nature of that relationship is crucially different. First, unlike natural structures, social structures do not exist independently of the activities they govern. Second, they do not exist independently of social actors' conceptions of what they are doing as they act. Third, they are only relatively enduring, so the tendencies they ground may not be invariant over space and time (Bhaskar 1989a).

This is not to say that critical realism conceives of natural structures as determining constant conjunctions of events. It is noted that within the positivist paradigm, the search for invariant cause and effect relations is, wherever possible, conducted within the closed system of experimental design, in order to exclude confounding variables. This ignores the fact that both the natural and social worlds are open systems, where constant conjunctions do not pertain. They do not pertain because events are rarely subject to a single generative structure, and it is the specific combination of structural influences that will determine the nature of events. Thus, critical realists have abandoned constant conjunction as the bedrock for the identification of causal structures, replacing it with the notion of tendencies.

But of what do the structures which generate tendencies consist? The critical realist answer to this question is 'structures of relations'. In contrast to methodological individualist models, critical realism's relational model of society argues that social relations are emergent from and irreducible to individuals. However, this does not involve the adoption of the traditional structural functionalist line, which sees groups as having a fundamental reality that can provide the bedrock of social explanation (Collier 1994). Instead, the approach taken mirrors closely that of Marx: 'Society does not consist of individuals, but expresses the sum of interrelations, the relations within which these individuals stand' (Marx 1973 [1858]: 265). Thus, one is only a wife by dint of one's relationship with a husband, or a worker because of one's relationship with an employer. The initial purpose of social science thus becomes one of uncovering how these relationships are structured.

I describe the uncovering of structural relations as the initial purpose of social science because, along with Marx, critical realism seeks to go further than this: 'The philosophers have only *interpreted* the world, in various ways, the point is to *change* it' (Marx and Engels 1970 [1847]: 123, original emphasis). In a similar fashion to critical theory, critical realism rejects the fact–value distinction. Instead, it examines the structuring of human relations using the criterion of whether they promote or constrain the human freedom and dignity of those involved in them. Thus, to use the examples cited above, the structured relations involved in the patriarchal nuclear family can be subjected to critical analysis in order to ascertain the degree to which they constrain the human freedom and dignity of female partners within those relationships. A similar analysis could be made of the effects of capitalist relationships on workers' lives.

Such a model contains within it the currently rather unfashionable notion of false consciousness. People, through their actions, such as getting married or getting a job, often reproduce oppressive structures. In fact, because structures are dependent for their existence upon actions, oppressive structures depend upon actions based upon false consciousness, or at least upon lack of consciousness of their oppressive effects, for their survival. 'A woman's place is in the home' or 'wages are fair exchange for labour' might be seen as examples of false consciousness, while 'I got married because I love him' or 'I took a job with Siemens because computers are the big thing in the twenty-first century' could be seen as examples of lack of consciousness. Here we can see a dialectical relationship between structure and action – oppressive structures promote the adoption of false consciousness by individuals, while the actions predicated upon that false consciousness are functional to the continued survival of those structures. Thus, the role of social science is not only to uncover the structuring of relations, but also to use that information as the basis for informed action to remove the sources of structural oppression.

The relationship between structure and action

It can be seen from our examination of critical realist philosophy that it adopts a position that rejects the individualist voluntarism at the core of both phenomenology and postmodernism. However, it does not base that rejection upon the collectivist reification of social entities adopted in positivist and functionalist interpretations of society:

> the existence of social structure is a necessary condition for any human activity. Society provides the means, media, rules and resources for everything we do. … It is the unmotivated condition for all our motivated productions. We do not create society – the error of voluntarism. But these structures which pre-exist us are only reproduced or transformed in our everyday activities; thus society does not exist independently of human agency – the error of reification. The social world is reproduced and transformed in daily life. (Bhaskar 1989b: 3–4)

As is indicated in the above quotation, structure and action are seen as distinct but interdependent. Their distinctness is grounded in temporal differences – the social structures in which individuals are located pre-exist those individuals. This factor is significant, in that it distinguishes critical realism from another influential conception of the relationship between structure and action – Giddens's (1984) theory of structuration. Giddens's project is similar to that of critical realism, namely to overcome the dichotomy between interpretivism and structuralism. However, the crucial difference lies in his conception of the relationship between structure and action. For Giddens, structure and action are simply two sides of the one coin (Craib 1992). Structures enjoy only a virtual reality until they are 'instantiated' through social actions. In other words, structure and action exist only in the same instance. As a result, it is argued that structuration theory 'cannot recognize that structure and agency work on different time intervals' (Archer 1995: 89). While critical realism accepts Giddens's point that structures cannot exist independently of social actions, it asks the question, 'whose actions?' and answers 'the actions of the past'. The social structures that affect our lives have not been conjured up by our own instantiation of them, but are rather the result of earlier social actions.

What contemporary actions do is either maintain or transform already developed structures. However, transformation of structures through action is rarely an instantaneous process. There are two main reasons for this. First, not everyone in society acts in the same way and there will often be groups in society who benefit from the status quo, and who will therefore have the motivation to resist change. Second, the structural conditions pertaining will often place limitations on the pace of change. Archer (1995) uses the example of the literacy campaign in revolutionary Cuba. In that case, the structural conditions of the educational system inherited from the Batista regime meant that there simply were not enough people equipped to teach literacy to make alterations to that structure anywhere near instantaneous. Thus, from a critical realist perspective, rather than being one, structure and action have distinct realities of their own which operate on different timescales.

The place of ethnography in critical realist social science

Having outlined the general tenets of critical realism's views of social science, it is now necessary to examine how the ethnographic method might fit into such a model. It will be remembered that one of the limitations of naturalism accepted by critical realism centred on the observation that social structures do not exist independently of social actors' conceptions of what they are doing when they act. Acceptance of this facet of the relationship between social action and social structure has considerable epistemological consequences, in that it points to the limits of the use of quantification in the social sciences. As Bhaskar puts it:

> the *conceptual* aspect of the subject-matter of the social sciences circumscribes the possibility of meaningful *measurement*. ... For meanings cannot be measured, only

understood. Hypotheses about them must be expressed in language, and confirmed in dialogue. Language here stands to the conceptual aspect of social science as geometry stands to physics. And precision of meaning now assumes the place of accuracy in measurement as the a posteriori arbiter of theory. (Bhaskar 1989a: 46, original emphasis)

Because the subject matter of social science is conceptual, there is a need for the qualitative testing of theories about the nature and effects of social structures upon social actions and vice versa. It is for this reason that ethnographic methods have a role to play in critical realist social science. However, the purpose of ethnographic investigation is not to ideographically illuminate the understandings and actions of individuals, but to use examination of those understandings and actions as part of the process of uncovering the relationship between agency and structure. Thus, the role of ethnography is twofold. First, it is used as a method to uncover the manifest interactions of the social world, which are then subjected to the transcendental process of theory generation to infer the structural conditioning of those interactions. Second, it is used to subsequently test the veracity of theories concerning the nature and effects of the structures pertaining.

In other words, while critical realism continues to use ethnographic techniques of data collection, it abandons many of the methodological assumptions normally associated with ethnography (cf. Brewer 1991). The advantages of such an approach is that it enables research to bring social science back into the ethnographic equation. Rather than confining its focus to individual experience, or rejecting the notion of knowledge altogether, critical realism is able to use ethnographic data to illuminate structured relations, and beyond that, to show how these relations may be oppressive, and to point to the sort of actions required to make them less oppressive.

AN EXAMPLE OF CRITICAL REALIST ETHNOGRAPHY

Thus far, the discussion has been somewhat esoteric. In this section, I wish to provide an example to show how critical realist ethnography might work in practice. The example I wish to use involves my examination of the relationships pertaining between Black and Asian doctors and White nurses in the intensive care unit of an Irish hospital (Porter 1993).

Before recounting the ethnographic data gleaned in this research, I should elucidate the assumptions upon which I was working. The most significant issue to note was my acceptance that racism, because it involves enduring relations between actors in different social positions, can be categorized as a social structure. Being Black or Asian in a White racist society often entails involvement in enduring disadvantageous relations. Moreover, racist-engendered positions predate actors currently situated within them. Looked at another way, racist beliefs and acts cannot be explained solely through elucidation of the attitudes of the individuals involved. Because such an individualist approach is unable to explain the origins of individual attitudes, it leads to their reification (Rex 1970). In order to avoid such a static conception of racism, the articulation between racist attitudes, acts and structured relations needs to be considered.

This is not to say that the existence of structural racism means that all interactions between White and Black or Asian individuals will necessarily be characterized by racism. It will be remembered that this notion of constant conjunction is rejected by critical realism both on the grounds that the relationship between generative structure and event takes place in an open system, and a fortiori in relation to human actions, that social structures are only relatively enduring and dependent upon the conceptions of actors. Individuals' actions are not determined by the structural relations within which they live. Rather, those structures, by providing the means, media, rules and resources available to enable or coerce action, will engender tendencies towards certain courses of actions. Thus individuals will enjoy more or less powerful positions in a racist relationship depending on how they are categorized in racist terms. Being White in a racist society does not necessarily mean that one will adhere to racist ideology. Nonetheless, there will be pressure to do so, in that racist attitudes can provide an ideological rationalization for the structural inequalities from which a White person may benefit.

In relation to racism in the specific context of hospitals, I had the benefit of previous ethnographic work in a British casualty unit which had discovered that a significant variable affecting relationships between nurses and doctors was geographical origin (Hughes 1988). Hughes discovered that, in their interaction with doctors who had recently immigrated from the Asian subcontinent, White nurses frequently abandoned outward shows of deference, directed doctors to perform tasks, reprimanded them for their behaviour, and openly criticized their professional competence.

Using the transcendental move, I concluded that the patterns of behaviour and attitude displayed by White nurses in Hughes's (1988) ethnography took the configurations that they did because they were influenced by the generative structure of racism. This was not the interpretation that Hughes, utilizing an interactionist model, favoured. He posited two reasons for nurses' lack of deference. First, that the doctors studied were unfamiliar with British culture and thus dependent upon nurses for cultural translation, allowing the nurses to become far more actively involved in therapy than they would otherwise have been. Second, that relations between young inexperienced Asian doctors and mature White nurses led to dilemmas in status. These reasons were synthesized in the statement that 'differential competence in utilizing relevant bodies of social knowledge is perhaps the most salient interactional manifestation of "status" characteristics' (Hughes 1988: 18).

The ethnographic observations from my study elicited considerably different characteristics from those found by Hughes (1988). The interaction between White nurses and Black or Asian doctors showed little alteration in the balance of power as compared to relationships between White nurses and doctors. Indeed, in the unit observed, the doctor most respected for his clinical knowledge was African.

With a background in medical research, this doctor was used by nurses as a font of knowledge. However, observations of his interactions with nurses indicated that he made conspicuous efforts to ensure that nurses fully appreciated just how much he knew, or, rather, just how little the nurses knew in comparison to him. A subsequent informal interview with the doctor confirmed that this flaunting of knowledge was part of a deliberate strategy on his part:

> I asked him what it was like coming to work in a place like this. He went over some of the pros and cons of his move. [One con he identified was] that every time he got a new post, he had to start all over again. People automatically assumed that because he 'wasn't from here' he wouldn't know anything. Every time, he had to go through the same old routine before they accepted that he was good at his job. He wryly concluded: 'but I think people soon get the message'.

Another strategy used by Black and Asian doctors was authoritarianism. For example, an Asian consultant had a reputation for distant superiority, which involved minimal communication with nurses beyond the issuing of instructions or castigations:

> In the process of a 'ward round', the consultant comes across a heavily stained dressing.
>
> *Consultant:* Who is looking after this patient?
> *Staff nurse:* I am.
> *Consultant:* This is a disgrace. This dressing should have been changed hours ago.
> [The staff nurse reddens but does not reply.]
> *Sister:* The wound's been giving us a lot of trouble. There's a lot of exudate and we're having to change the padding almost continually.
> *Consultant:* Hmm. Is he pyrexial?

This sort of authoritarianism was rarely openly challenged by nurses, though their relationship with this doctor was one of starched compliance rather than cooperation. Thus, encounters between doctors and nurses observed in my ethnographic study displayed considerably more deference than those encountered in Hughes (1988). However, some nurse–nurse interactions in my study revealed a different story. When 'backstage' (Goffman 1969), out of earshot of doctors and patients, nurses often used the opportunity to complain to each other about the behaviour of their medical colleagues. On occasion these complaints were observed to be expressed in racist terms. Thus, a complaint about the authoritarianism of another doctor was couched in the following terms:

Staff nurse: I think she thinks that that dot on her head makes her a maharaja or something. Someone should tell her we're not Indian peasants.

Nor was racism simply a pathological reaction to heavy-handed authoritarianism, but was on occasion adopted in relation to those doctors who were not regarded by nurses as autocratic. For example, the African clinical expert was described thus:

Staff nurse: He's the smartest Black person I've ever met.

To summarize and compare the ethnographic data recounted thus far, observations in my study uncovered a latent racism, where racist attitudes were occasionally privately expressed, but where there was little interactional evidence of a significant alteration in power relations between Black and Asian doctors and White nurses. In contrast, interactions observed by Hughes (1988) were characterized by significant alterations in power relations. Another difference between the two studies was that while Hughes reported that the Asian doctors observed tended to be unfamiliar with the cultural cues of British culture, and were therefore dependent on White nurses for cultural translation, the doctors in my study had, for the most part, lived in Ireland for a considerable time and were familiar with its culture.

From comparison of the data, it might seem that Hughes's interactionist interpretation is justified on the grounds of its parsimoniousness, in that it can explain the data without recourse to the transcendental reference to social structures. For Hughes, status differentials were manifested in differential competence in the utilization of social knowledge. My data could be accommodated in this explanation by noting that status differentials remained latent precisely because there was no differential competence in the utilization of social knowledge. Yet such an explanation, by concentrating on manifest interactions, does not address the issue of why 'dilemmas in status' between Black and Asian and White members of society exist in the first place. Moreover, there are dangers in making too close a linkage between status and cultural competence. It is certainly not the case that racism is suffered exclusively by those unattuned to British or Irish culture, as the experiences of second and third generation Black British people demonstrates (Brown 1984).

We are thus in a situation where an interactionist approach is unable to explain racism as an enduring set of social relations, but where the variable manifestations of overt racism observed belie crude structuralist explanations. It is my contention that critical realist ethnography can provide a fruitful alternative to these dichotomous approaches.

Critical realism allows us to accept that, while the agents involved thought and acted within the matrix of a racist generative structure, because that structure operated within an open system along with other structures, its effects were seen as tendencies, rather than constant conjunctions. Another structure which was influencing the nature of agents' thoughts and actions was that of occupational relations animated by professional power. While being Black or Asian in a racist society tends to reduce one's social status, the professional power entailed in being a member of the medical profession tends to enhance it.

Professional power depends upon the acceptance by others of the ideology of professionalism, which has probably been most clearly (if naively) identified by Parsons (1951), in his list of pattern variables. Because nurses hanker after a professional status that they have not fully attained and which they see so successfully adopted by medicine, they take professional ideology very seriously indeed. The professional pattern variables put forward by Parsons are largely accepted within the culture of nursing. Acceptance of universalistic-achievement values means doctors are seen as having attained their occupational status solely through their ability. Affective neutrality assumes that judgements should be made solely on the basis of scientific rationality. Functional specificity leads doctors to be judged solely according to the level of their medical skills. Given the acceptance of these values as criteria for judging professional actions, naked racism, being particularistic, ascriptive, affective and diffuse, is not a justifiable form of social interaction between nurses and doctors. To be acceptable, racism needs to take on a 'rational' form that does not appear to flout the tenets of professional ideology. This is what is happening when differential cultural competence is being married to 'race'. Criticisms of cultural incompetence can be dressed up as universalistic, achievement-oriented, affectively neutral and functionally specific to the skills of medicine. Yet, the racism is still there. From such a perspective, criticisms of cultural competence can be seen as vehicles through which racism is expressed. In cases where a doctor's cultural familiarity is such that this vehicle cannot be used, this does not mean that racism ceases to exist, but that an avenue for its expression in the public arena is closed off. Ethnographic evidence that this tension between racist and professional ideologies was experienced by some nurses comes from the following discussion between two nurses concerning a Muslim doctor carrying out his religious observances in the unit:

Staff nurse 1: Why didn't you say something to him about it?

Staff nurse 2: Well, it wouldn't be proper. It would be a bit unprofessional …

Staff nurse 1: It's not exactly professional to get down on your knees in the middle of the clinical room …

Staff nurse 2: Yea, but you couldn't say 'Listen you, you're not in Arab land now'. I suppose I could have told him that clinical areas have to be open to staff at all times.

It is not just that social structures operate in an open system. They are also dependent for their maintenance or transformation on the actions of individuals. We have already seen how nurses' acceptance of professional ideology has the effect of maintaining the professional power of doctors. This acceptance was deliberately fostered by the actions of a number of Black and Asian doctors. We have noted two strategies. One was the use of authoritarianism which relied rather crudely on the occupational status of the doctor. While this authority was rarely openly challenged by nurses, it was accepted with bad grace. A more subtle and successful strategy was adopted by the African doctor who portrayed himself as the font of medical knowledge. Because this strategy was more closely attuned to the assumptions of professional ideology, his status was both formally and conatively accepted by nurses.

SUMMARY

From the social context examined, we can see the complex relationship that exists between social actions and structures. While structures provide the context for actions, that context is itself determined by the particular combination of structures pertaining and the degree to which actions reinforce or undermine the relative strength of those structures. Furthermore, actions may be the result of taken-for-granted assumptions – or doxic experience, to use Bourdieu's (1990) term – which both promote and are promoted by pertaining structures. Here I am thinking of nurses' adherence to professional ideology. Or actions may be the result of agents' reflexively considered strategies. An example here would be the motivations underpinning the actions adopted by doctors to reinforce their professional status and thereby limit the possibility of racist interactions.

Elucidation of such a multilayered social situation requires at least two things from the researcher. First of all, it requires a clear picture of the interactions of individuals, both at the level of action and of motivation. Such a picture can emerge only through the utilization of close observational techniques. Second, it requires theoretical work to explain why individuals' interactions take the patterns that are observed using those techniques. This in turn requires acceptance of the existence of structured, but non-determining social relations.

CONCLUSIONS

Following the debunking of traditional social scientific verities by phenomenology and postmodernism, it is incumbent upon ethnographers to take into account the fact that the social world is a complex and often contradictory place, inhabited by thinking, volitional agents. Moreover, we need to recognize that gaining knowledge about that world is a far from unproblematic process. However, that does not mean that we need to abandon the notion of the social either to the methodological individualism of phenomenology or to the anti-realist scepticism of postmodernism. If ethnography has any pretensions to providing information that will be of practical use, it has no option but to claim the capacity to provide generalizable knowledge.

That claim, in turn, rests upon the assumption that human activities and relations are, at least to some degree, structured.

Indeed, as Malcolm Williams notes (Chapter 5 in this volume), while it is rarely acknowledged, the presentation of generalized claims is a common feature of contemporary ethnographies. At the same time, individualism and scepticism remain powerful forces within qualitative methodological theorizing. There would therefore seem to be a significant dissonance between theory and practice. This is not a sustainable position. Unless ethnographers are prepared to settle for claims that their work entails an activity akin to fiction writing, or, at best, one-off portraiture, then there is a need to return to the epistemology of generalization and the ontology of structure. It has been the contention of the chapter that critical realism can be used to facilitate just such a return. Hence my contention that the marriage of critical realist theory with ethnographic methods holds out such fruitful possibilities.

REFERENCES

Altheide, D. and Johnson, M. (1998) 'Criteria for assessing interpretive validity in qualitative research', in N. Denzin and Y. Lincoln (eds) *Collecting and Interpreting Qualitative Materials*. London: Sage.

Archer, M. (1995) *Realist Social Theory: The Morphogenetic Approach*. Cambridge: Cambridge University Press.

Bhaskar, R. (1989a) *The Possibility of Naturalism: A Philosophical Critique of the Contemporary Human Sciences*, 2nd edn. London: Harvester Wheatsheaf.

Bhaskar, R. (1989b) *Reclaiming Reality: A Critical Introduction to Contemporary Philosophy*. London: Verso.

Bourdieu, P. (1990) *The Logic of Practice*. Cambridge: Polity.

Brewer, J. (1991) *Inside the RUC: Routine Policing in a Divided Society*. Oxford: Clarendon.

Brewer, J. (2000) *Ethnography*. Buckingham: Open University Press.

Brown, C. (1984) *Black and White in Britain*. London: Heinemann.

Cheek, J. (2000) *Postmodern and Poststructural Approaches to Nursing Research*. London: Sage.

Clifford, J. (1986) 'Introduction: partial truths', in J. Clifford and G.E. Marcus (eds) *Writing Culture: The Poetics and Politics of Ethnography*. Berkeley, CA: University of California Press.

Collier, A. (1994) *Critical Realism: An Introduction to Roy Bhaskar's Philosophy*. London: Verso.

Comte, A. (1974) *The Essential Comte*, edited by A. Andreski. London: Croom Helm.

Craib, I. (1992) *Anthony Giddens*. London: Routledge.

Crapanzano, V. (1986) 'Hermes' dilemma: the masking of subversion in ethnographic description', in J. Clifford and G.E. Marcus (eds) *Writing Culture: The Poetics and Politics of Ethnography*. Berkeley, CA: University of California Press.

Denscombe, M. (2001) 'Uncertain identities and health-risking behaviour: the case of young people and smoking in late modernity', *British Journal of Sociology* 52(1): 157–177.

Durkheim, E. (1966 [1897]) *Suicide*. New York: Free Press.

Durkheim, E. (1982 [1895]) *The Rules of Sociological Method*, translated by W.D. Halls. London: Macmillan.

Durkheim, E. (1985 [1893]) *The Division of Labor in Society*, translated by W.D. Halls. New York: Free Press.

Durkheim, E. (1995 [1912]) *The Elementary Forms of Religious Life*, translated by K.E. Fields. New York: Free Press.

Gadamer, H-G. (1975 [1960]) *Truth and Method*, translated by W. Glyn-Doepel. New York: Seabury.

Giddens, A. (1976) *New Rules of Sociological Method*. London: Hutchinson.

Giddens, A. (1984) *The Constitution of Society*. Cambridge: Polity.

Goffman, E. (1969) *The Presentation of Self in Everyday Life*. Harmondsworth: Penguin.

Hammersley, M. (1992) *What's Wrong with Ethnography?* London: Routledge.

Hockey, J. (1986) *Squaddies: Portrait of a Subculture*. Exeter: University of Exeter Press.

Hughes, D. (1988) 'When nurse knows best: some aspects of nurse/doctor interaction in a casualty department', *Sociology of Health and Illness* 10(1): 1–22.

Kant, I. (1896) *Critique of Pure Reason*, translated by F. Müller. London: Macmillan.

LaCapra, D. (1985) *Emile Durkheim: Sociologist and Philosopher*. Chicago: University of Chicago Press.

Lyotard, J-F. (1984) *The Postmodern Condition: A Report on Knowledge*. Manchester: Manchester University Press.

Marx, K. (1973 [1858]) *Grundrisse*. Harmondsworth: Penguin.

Marx, K. and Engels, F. (1970 [1847]) *The German Ideology*. London: Lawrence and Wishart.

Parkin, F. (1982) *Max Weber*. London: Ellis Horwood/Tavistock.

Parsons, T. (1951) *The Social System*. Glencoe, IL: Free Press.

Pavis, S., Cunningham-Burley, S. and Amos, A. (1998) 'Health related behavioural change in context: young people in transition', *Social Science and Medicine* 47(10): 1,407–1,418.

Porter, S. (1993) 'Critical realist ethnography: the case of racism and professionalism in a medical setting', *Sociology* 27(4): 591–609.

Rex, J. (1970) *Race Relations and Sociological Theory*. London: Weidenfeld and Nicolson.

Said, E. (1978) *Orientalism*. New York: Pantheon.

Scheurich, J. (1997) *Research Method in the Postmodern*. London: Falmer.

Schutz, A. (1967) *Collected Papers, Volume 1*. The Hague: Nijhoff.

Schutz, A. (1972) *The Phenomenology of the Social World*. London: Heinemann.

Stanley, L. (1987) 'Biography as microscope or kaleidoscope? The case of "power" in Hannah Culwick's relationship with Arthur Munby', *Women's Studies International Forum* 10(1): 19–31.

Weber, M. (1978 [1956]) *Economy and Society*, translated by E. Fischoff, H. Gerth, A. Henderson, F. Kolegar, C. Wright Mills, T. Parsons, M. Rheinstein, G. Roth, E. Shils and C. Wittich; edited by G. Roth and C. Wittich. Berkeley, CA: University of California Press.

Williams, A. (1990) *Reflections on the Making of an Ethnographic Text*. Manchester: University of Manchester.

Winch, P. (1959) *The Idea of Social Science*. London: Routledge and Kegan Paul.

3 FRAMING THE RATIONAL IN FIELDWORK

Peter K. Manning

Sociological analysis rests fundamentally on irony: demonstrating that what appears is not what is; that surface belies depth; that the apparent irrationality of criminals, rioters, and murderers, is in fact patterned rationality. This turn, showing the workings of such mannered rationality, presumes an analytic metalanguage that recasts the concrete, the grasped, as something quite different. The synthesis of rationality performed by Weber and recast by Parsons remains the sociological touchstone. A number of interpretive approaches consistent with qualitative work are discussed below. They have built on this synthesis. Recent theorizing glossed as postmodernism (Poster 1990; Lemert 1995) reverses the enlightenment tradition reflected in sociology. This writing transforms rationality from a constant 'figure' of modernity, understood best against irrationality as a 'ground' in which the occasional appearance of rational action is notable, into a ground, a governing mode of irrationality, from which occasioned and occasional rationality emerges. Rationality, science, technology and modern civic administration, are misleading and false or at best factious. In many ways, what passes for the rational is merely the conventional wisdom, which serves those in power. These turns on rationality leave little room for focused and context-based fieldwork that begins with a context within which deciding takes place.

This chapter traces the most important consequence of such movements of thought in the emergent role of rationality in qualitative sociology. Following an overview of some of the ways in which modern social science has grappled with rationality, I present an alternative focus using framing, the field and the surround, and characterize homicide detective work as situated and situational rationality. It is argued that the situational rationality of detective work is ill suited to easy rationalization.[1] The implications of this formulation for qualitative work are examined in a final section.

THE RATIONAL

Parsons's magisterial work, *The Structure of Social Action* (1936), established a working agenda for an entire generation of sociologists, drawing upon German idealism (Kant, Dilthey, Rickert, Weber), while fashioning versions of Durkheim, Marshall and Pareto. Parsons, working in the idealist tradition, emphasized the value-bases for the three types of social action identified by

Weber. Traditional, rational and charismatic were bases of legitimization for subjective meanings attached to rules and commands. This ideal-typical construction set the stage for modern studies of rationality; it was based on the notion that means and ends were connected within sets of elaborate rules and offices that constitute modern bureaux. The idea of rationality stood on the methodical linking of efficient means to well-accepted ends, and these procedural devices were replicated in the courts, bureau and other forms of public discourse and administration. In many respects, this instrumental rationality was invisibly grounded in other assumptions about social life such as Protestant aestheticism, science, enlightenment values and a rational politics (Merelman 1998: 351). The broader context of rationality grounds the specific instances and concrete examples of it.

This Parsonian synthesis obscured Weber's very complex and subtle position (see Sica 1988; Espeland 1998; Merelman 1998). 'Rational' in his vocabulary pointed to diverse processes, meant many things, and signified complex historical developments and substantive content. It was set always in the context of deciding. Weber delineated individual irrationality, the passions, feelings, sentiments and impulses of people, from the cumulative, 'objective' rationality associated with institutionalized procedures, transcendental values and patterns of choice. Weber, furthermore, saw that given a commitment to, for example, an aesthetic cluster of values such as modern art, one could act to sustain such values rationally, as in organizing a gallery exhibition. Similarly, courts, while adhering formally to stipulated procedures, can decide cases using concrete, substantive rationality based on the offender, the offence, the victim or its symbolic importance (e.g. a 'hate crime') rather than on formal rationality based on legal procedures, precedents, guidelines, doctrine, rules and evidence.

The rational in the Weberian scheme did not stand alone. Many kinds of rationality, seen as a process of associating ends and means, with diverse histories exist, and are in tension with forces of institutionalized rationality. This formulation not only means that competition emerges between forms of rationality within organizations, but also suggests tensions between objective and substantive rationality, between situated deciding and the long-term legitimized rationality. The underlying issue was comparative analytic sociology – how can generalizations about social order be produced given the tensions between forms of rationality, individual subjectivities and collective rationality?

The diverse meanings of rationality were for Weber displayed in the tensions between culture, politics and the state administrative structure, and the forces of irrationality that constantly arose from cults, religions, antinomial movements and nihilism. As Antonio (1995) elegantly demonstrates, Weber knew of Nietzsche's profound distrust of the modern rational state and its suppression of passion, culture and personal autonomy. Concrete forms of rationality, both substantive and formal rationality, and resistance to them shape modern social life, and their tensions underlie change. The interplay of values, norms and meaning was always embedded in broader questions of legitimacy. In many respects, the modern state obscures the seething and unresolved conflicts and passions of competing groups. In many respects, Weber's grand synthesis of rationality is tenuous (Sica 1988) because it seeks to identify the governing forces that embed deciding, an ideal type that must be stretched to cover the instant case or example. This is background for the modern attempts to explicate in social research the place of rationality.

QUALITATIVE WORK AND CONCEPTIONS OF RATIONALITY

Shifting now to the application of conceptions of rationality, some six modes of constructing the rational can be demonstrated using well-known field studies.

Symbolic anthropology

Social scientists influenced by Clifford Geertz (1973) ground their arguments in detailed explications of context such that the deciding, whether concerning the self, sustaining a culture, gaming or cannibalism, has an apparent rationality. They have elevated substantive rationality to demonstrate the perverse rationality of even the most exotic, macabre and isolated cultures. As a result, the details become fascinating and self-explanatory. Science, or formal rationality, rules some matters, such as canoe building, or in modern periods, treatment of infectious and many chronic diseases (Fabrega 1998), while substantive rationality shapes the ritualistic or broadly ceremonial decisions. The weight of evidence strongly supports an emergent rationality that is grounded in sanctioned deciding that incorporates the mix of values featured in the culture. In this sense, the language games that obtain in pre-literate societies are expressive exercises in which the values are played out in known forms. For example, a healing ceremony in south-eastern Mexico among the Zinacantan (Fabrega and Silver 1973) implores the gods to heal or be propitiated, requires gift exchanges that function to integrate and bind parties, families, relatives and healers, renews belief in norms of religious piety, forgiveness and obligation, as well as requiring manipulation of religious phrases, bodily motions and gestures, and use of symbols. The expressive and the instrumental aspects of this cannot be disentangled. Furthermore, outcomes and consequences, return to health, chronic incapacitation or death cannot be easily distinguished from the belief system in which they are cast and which always contains an explanation. This system remains a cultural gloss because it explores the powerful and consistent consequences of a unified culture rather than of individual deciding.

Semiotics

The assumption here is that the appearances of the world, mainly given to us via words, are 'surface' features, which cannot be understood without reference to a code. The logic of symbols obtains, once one discovers, or uncovers, the 'code' or the means by which the messages are seen as communicating. Semiotics is not a method, but is a technique for describing the logic of symbols. The two principled kinds of semiotics differ radically in their assumptions about deciding. First, the posited rationality of semiotics found in de Saussure (1966) is the logic of mathematics, economics and Aristotelian thinking. It continues the notion of binary decisions, the law of the excluded middle, hierarchical and consistent governing principles. Given a sign composed of signifier and signified, both connected in the nature of the arbitrary meanings of a given culture, the primitive meaning connections between the signifier and the signified are assumed, not discovered. Variations exist, but are built into the analysis. If in western European societies the colour 'black' signifies reverence and a distant thoughtful mood, it is displayed at ceremonies honouring people, dead or alive. White stands as a contrast, signifying a different mood and attitude. The colours also connote 'good' and 'evil', but these poles are subsumed under the formal code as less salient than the mood they convey. In Japan, the signification is reversed. White signifies honouring and reverence. These oppositions are based on general readings of culture and have shaped structuralism's sometimes rather thin caricatures of culture. Second, pragmatic semiotics, based on the work of Pierce (1936, 1958) and more recently of Eco (1979), relies on the identification of the 'interpretant' or basis for interpretation that links X and Y. In this formulation, pragmatic deciding is the basis for the links, and the complex constructions of meaning within given domains. This connects the semiotics of Eco with the work of Mead (1934), his student, Charles Morris, and Morris's student, Thomas Sebeok. In many respects, this draws on the Meadian proposition that meaning arises in the completion of the gesture toward an object. Since the powerful device is the code rather than individual actors' sense-making activities, semiotics is a marvellous tool for simplification and disaggregating of complex materials but overlooks historical variations on usage, and overemphasizes the constraints of culture's codes.

Context-based rationality

Mannheim (1960) and Elster (1983, 1984, 1989, 1999) argue for a situated rationality. Consider Mannheim's (1960) and Garfinkel's (1967) arguments that rationality was determined by the situation, weighing the factors and deciding. The continuity in social life arose as deciders look for a pattern at the same time that they seek instances of it in events. Playing a video game or chess presents a good example, as players are both trying to develop a strategy, reflect back on their previous moves and decisions, and project them forward as a pattern to imagine how to play. The individual moves are not seen alone, but in a prospective–retrospective perspective. This argument from situational rationality is consistent with pragmatism in general because it locates the dynamics of deciding in the here and now, and the gestures and actions toward the problem. This truncates issues of the competing rationalities that may play into the deciding, and how they are resolved, and in general obviates questions of power. Although more structural in orientation, Jon Elster's approach explores the patterning of choice by context. He points out that there are occasions in which non-rational forces shape deciding almost in spite of rational 'impulses' which he explores in his *Ulysses and the Sirens* (1983) or that non-rational motivations lead us to deny things we fancy, a topic of *Sour Grapes* (1984). The time and energy one might devote to an ideal solution is inconsistent with an efficient outcome; there is often in life no guarantee that more information, greater thought, of weighing of options will increase satisfaction derived from an outcome. Conversely, Elster explores the forces of rational choice that obtain in spite of irrationality. Perhaps the most powerful of his writings explores *Solomonic Judgments* (1989) in which randomness in outcome may be preferred because of limited time or information constraints. In this sense, random processes may be the closest approximation to 'just' or fair decisions. Short-term and long-term rationality may be in conflict. We may be required to act irrationally in a market-driven society, and so not compete in a commodity race with neighbours, if we espouse long-run rationality. Often, decisions are made in line of 'indirect goods' or the 'side bets' and satisfactions we encumber almost in spite of rational deciding. Because we cannot predict outcomes, and the consequences of most decisions are situated and unfolding, abandoning an attachment to rationality is the best course of action (or non-action). The problem repeatedly is that we are unclear about how rational to be, and are wedded 'irrationally' to rationality. In many respects, Elster argues that people oscillate from normative guidance via rules to rationality or principles that reflect the ends we wish to accomplish in interaction with others. This latter, of course, requires that our others are also on the whole acting rationally! Elster's rationality is a situated and contextual rationality which might be called 'becoming rational' as situations require modes of self-understanding and 'predicting' what the other as a rational being is intending or will do. Much necessary wisdom is grasped, intuitive and situated, and is independent of discourse. Elster's brand of rational choice is based on empirical realities rather than hypothetical models or attributed motives and values. His works explores the conditions under which, rare indeed, that rationality obtains and is reasonable and rational. It is often the irrational attachment to rationality that creates paradoxes. Having said that, Elster, a logician and historian, posits rationality as a kind of working framework, which has great promise, and uses examples from literature, philosophy and history to support his claims. In sophisticated analysis of such key emotions as honour, jealousy, envy and shame, he concludes that social emotions and their expression are shaped by the social context in which they arise (Elster 1999: 203). It is the problem of fieldwork, then, to describe and analyse the social context in which emotions arise.

Higher rationalities

Following the Second World War, a reaction to the rationality of both Marxism and fascism arose in France and blossomed in due course into various versions of structuralism (Dosse 1997a [1991], 1997b [1992]). Its early thrust was to sustain humanity in light of the growing spurious rationality of modern life that suppresses feelings, emotions, and sexuality in particular. (These themes are echoed in Foucault, who is the 'son' of these luminaries of the generation before his own in French universities.) For purposes of illustration, let us take the idea of 'negative gratuity' in Kojeve (Drury 1994) adopted by members of the Collège de Sociologie – Bataille, Callois and Leiris. While enlightenment values stressed transcendental knowledge and development, the triumph of reason, and a slow developmental evolution, post-war French thought shaped by Hegel, Nietzsche and Heidegger emphasized the consequences of the death of history, and the importance of excess, the non-rational in the sense of the playful or aesthetically meaningful. Stripped of meaning and necessity, being must be constructed in light of the threat of death, or non-being. The adaptation to this existential quandary was various: playful and gamelike in the work of writers Georges Perec and Raymond Queneau, surrealists such as Breton and Dali and abstract artists such as Kandinsky. Others tried to create a dialogue to assert meaning and significance through an attack on reason and rationality itself, and counter-asserted the negative gratuity, a dark and romantic idea what might be called the joys of sex, risk and anti-rationality. This is mirrored in current preoccupation with risky experience. The underlining proposition, found in Heidegger, Kojeve and their followers, was that the denial of death, or non-being, meant that grappling with the meanings of being, being in the world, was impossible. The profundity of that proposition shapes the ideas about the nature of society, the rational and rationalizing processes. Since rationality drives the development of a more market-based society, it is only through opposition to rationality itself, in its several forms – education, corrections, policing and governance – that resistance is sustained. This position elevates feeling over thought, and has global and non-empirical echoes of grand philosophy, while its themes are quite provocative to explore in the context of organizational life.

Self-presentation as a driving social force

Goffman's (1959) form of situated rationality is shaped by existentialism, a derivative of the above French movements of thought. Goffman posited a central dilemma of the actor-being or doing – terms from Sartre's *Being and Nothingness* (1953), his reworking of Heidegger's *Being and Time* (1953). The being question was often side-stepped in favour of doing, acting, presenting an impression and sustaining a self. The inability to act, to assert a self to be validated by others, is a consequence of dread and fear. The stripped person whose self is at risk for Goffman is a pitiful and pitiable manqué. Language is a part, but only a small part, of performing convincingly because people discount what they see, and do not trust impressions that can be easily manipulated. In this existential situation, we see echoes of Heidegger's notion that man denies his being, or the nature of it, because he denies death. The self is never a thing, always becoming, caught in temporality and in opposition to the other with whom the self is easily conflated. Goffman, following Sartre, argues for a humanism in which some mutual regard and shared fate is delegated to a team, or a dyad, or a loose assemblage of performers. Goffman's rationality is that of the situation, its dynamics and forms not fully understood, long-term goals and purposes blurred, and the strategic being highly bounded. Goffman eschews a goals-purpose model of action, even in organizations, and rejects a 'pipeline theory of communication' which sorts out messages by their instrumental aim and the rest as ignorance and error. Goffman, like Elster, assumes an ironic pose, one in which actors can seek expressive fun, or 'action', rationally, yet be unclear and uncaring about the long-term consequences of their actions. While self-presentation is a fundamental drive, it is always contingent upon the validation of others and as such is a compromise formation.

Revisionist structuralists

Bourdieu (1977) and Giddens (1981, 1984, 1990, 1991) find rationality embedded in process, obscured by *habitus*, institutional rationalizations and the broader processes of sense-making. Notions like agency, or resources, and rules or means, are invisible ordering devices for these theorists as 'minds' and 'souls' disappear into the codes of action they circumscribe. There is little room for the negotiating, sense-making, actor in the scene. Giddens poses the reflexive process as the background to sustained rationality, even as a weak alternative to a formally grounded legitimate society. Reflexivity reflects weak authority and competing rationalities (Espeland and Stevens 1998) as well as irrational forces at play. Technical solutions to the tensions between rationality and irrationality as system properties have given rise to the current fascination with rational choice theories and the metrification of economists. This suggests a quest for statistical ordering, using techniques, scaling and formulae, among apparently disparate properties and entities (Espeland and Stevens 1998). These nevertheless are unsatisfactory because they begin by positing rationality, interests, choice and the evaluative act(s) of deciding prior to examining context and aims.

In summary, these approaches all remain limited as working fieldwork perspectives. I would suggest an understanding of rationality-in-the-field requires us to first describe in detail the key processes and routines that organize collective action. This then permits identification of the key deciding points and uncertainties that attend them. In such uncertain circumstances, people must decide without adequate or full (or too much) information about the consequences of their actions. This means that the values and norms that they hold and the working rules that have evolved are employed to pin down meaning. Often, this means that schemes of typification and generalization, 'profiling' are used to reduce uncertainty to manageable dimensions, and to coordinate with one's colleagues in organizations. Furthermore, since variations in individual decisions can never be fully captured in explanations (time, energy and the attention of others will not permit it) stock phrases, clichés and rules of thumb are exchanged to rationalize and account for the deciding done. These accounts in turn are only as good as the audience(s) that accepts them. In this way, organizations are arenas in which situationally justified actions are made non-problematic. That is, when decisions are complex, non-routinized and the technology is 'human', sense making requires a wait and see attitude, trust and tacit knowledge. In short, it is not possible to understand rationality outside of a particular, specified context. Having said this, it also must be said that the features of such deciding may in fact be general and generalizable, but this remains to be empirically investigated, once the features are isolated analytically in that context.

FRAME, FIELD AND SURROUND

Frame analysis

A useful approach to the investigating rationality in fieldwork is derived from later Goffman (1974). Only the bare tenets are outlined here. Let us begin at the most abstract social level, the surround, and work 'down' to the concept of a frame. All deciding is embedded or layered in social orders. Beginning at the most distant, the broadest political environment is the *surround* or that which clearly cannot be controlled or altered by those who decide. The field, a set of subjective and objective forces, is located analytically within the surround (Bourdieu 1977). The *field* is an institutional structure, or set of norms and procedures that shape careers, grant meaning to objects, and constrain dynamics. The field contains many *frames* that give rise to action and define the nature of the event or situation confronting the actor. To some degree, the situation of deciding is a given; one is thrown into life and must come to grips with its meanings. Framing is deciding 'what's going on here', given a primary face-to-face social reality. I want to use *frame* in a generic sense, as answering the question of what is going on here. In social life, actors require meaning. They encounter a situation 'primary reality' and try to see if meanings in context indicate a secondary reality emerging. Given that events are ambiguous, and can be cast as stories, little dramas, regrounding of events, rehearsing them, and so on, we often have to use cues to make sense of how realities shift. In a sense, Goffman argues that all social reality is contextual, none has a hegemonic grip on 'reality'. Goffman names five frames (drama, play, ceremonies, rehearsals and technical regroundings). These are generally consensual in nature, whereas when efforts are made to mislead someone the 'frame' is a 'fabrication'. The actor chooses among the choices available, constituted by elements that are defined in or out of the frame; those that are negative realities (those that threaten the tenacity of the frame) and those matters that break the shared frame.

Homicide framed as a technical regrounding

Consider the work of a homicide detective in framing terms. Even if the murder is cleared via confession, the police must frame it as a coherent story or narrative that will enable the case to pass through the criminal justice system. If the case becomes a 'whodunnit', the framing of the sequence of events is even more essential. Police detective work, to be discussed below, is an attempt to re-create or script dramatically previously enacted events. To some degree, this means that the police are engaged in 'technical regroundings' (Goffman 1974: 58–74) interpreting actions in terms of some new set of motives or purposes not apparent in the 'primary reality' as initially framed. This process of actually framing a case begins with the first visit to the scene and carries on to the conclusion of the case. My focus here is on explicating the form, or case-logic, that results from framing a murder as an investigation to be worked.

Detective work generally as framing

Consider further deciding in detective work in framing terms. First the *surround* of policing is the taken-for-granted aspects of society that cannot be changed, shaped or altered, such as the ecology of the city, the composition of the city's population in terms of ethnicity, class and status, the nature of crime, criminals and victims, and more immediately, the budget processes that define promotion opportunities, raises and salaries, and new hires. The media, whose meretricious eyes shape actions in advance and generate covering paperwork and accounts, increasingly constitute it. Analogously, think of the budget processes in a large city, or fluctuations in the tax base of a Midwestern university whose lifeblood is the state-allocated budget. The policing, a set of assumptions and material constraints defines 'real policing' – controlling incidents and producing face-to-face solutions to real time here and now presented problems by means of tactical manoeuvre. The surface features of an event as framed or defined against the backdrop of the field and the surround, city politics, media attention, the city's structure, and the like. Abundant evidence suggests that police use the ecological and demographic features of cities to shape their decisions to stop, question, arrest and possibly confine people (Fagan and Davies 2000) and these are largely sociological or structural features that constitute the surround within which the fate-shaping stops made by officers unfold.

Second the *field* for police is the configuration of values and routines that organize their deciding. Detectives must struggle with a configuration that includes tensions between independence and dependence; colleagues and the public; collective obligations and individual ethics and morality; and loyalty based on rank and organizational position and loyalty based on personal relations. These tensions interact in given situations or configurations, and are not static 'occupational culture' with transituational rules and norms, and binding and blinding perspectives.

The organizing social form is the object of concern within the routines of a detective. Working for detectives is working a case. As I discuss below, a detective 'catches' cases as a result of standard organizational procedures – by assignment, by rotation or special detailing or seconding (as in the UK when a senior member of the Criminal Investigation Department (CID) is seconded to another force to supervise a major case) and works it.

The case as a social form

The case is the key concept. The 'case' is a concept, itself a social creation, constituted by tradition, by unspoken and tacit knowledge, and by organizational processes. The homicide squad receives its cases. 'Homicide' defined legally is replaced by working rules that bridge everyday realities and anomalies. A standard or 'typical' homicide case involves a dead body, evidence (physical and other), a weapon, witnesses and suspect(s). The victim (a body) must be present, declared dead, suspicious circumstances confirmed by the coroner or official, death pronounced, and police notified. In this ideal-typical case, once the person is confirmed as dead, an investigation is unfolded: the case is the organizing point by which other materials (evidence, witness statements, interviews, depositions, etc.) are framed and around which an investigation is hung. Subsequent decisions follow from the case-as-focus frame. Investigative procedures, shaped by local traditions, are craftwork, viewed as highly skilled, partially intuitive, partially rational and routinized with an aim to 'clear' the crime. Clearance is an organizational definition that is context based (see below). This ideal arises in some percentage of cases because elements of the case may be missing: the body (people disappear; missing persons are reported dead; circumstances, such as an abandoned car and signs of a struggle, suggest 'foul play' but no body is found); other evidence (naked body is found floating in a river); witnesses (no one saw the event, they deny knowledge of the murder; a body is found in an alley several days after death); death has not been pronounced or remains under investigation (e.g. a coroner's jury or hearing is scheduled); or two people die and it is written off or cleared immediately as a dual homicide, or a murder-suicide. After the case is worked, suspects, if any identified, and interviewed (often a crucial turning point in investigations, and a core mini-drama for detectives), a charge may be laid, delayed, or the interview and admission used to go to trial. In general the policy in detective units is that homicides will not be bargained, that is the suspect will be given immunity, a bargain to a lesser charge, or considerations based on clearing other crimes, or testifying in other crimes. In fact, bargaining is routinely done at every point (McConville *et al.* 1993). It is a key contingency that alters the horizon of every case that is worked beyond the initial paperwork, interviews and phone calls. Anomalies are smoothed by tacit knowledge and organizational conventions, not by rational deciding. The organization clarifies the nature of the work required, not the world-at-large, the law, medicine, or conventional morality.

The work of the homicide detective illustrates situational rationality. This form of rationality is case-based, craft-like, personalistic and often stylistic, and sensitive to the changing horizon of possibilities that a case represents. The detective's 'case' is defined by the layered meanings it denotes and connotes in the subjective and objective forces in the surround (the social structure of the city) and field (the occupational values, routines and tacit knowledge) and framing or regrounding the events. The content of the *frame*, or case, more detailed aspects of work, how the elements are identified, how they are typified, and their salience within the case, will not be discussed here (see Sudnow 1965; Ericson 1982; McConville *et al.* 1993).

RATIONALIZATION AND RATIONALITY IN HOMICIDE WORK

The organization of homicide work

I want to outline the *structure and function of police investigative units* that deal with homicide and suspected homicide, and then focus more closely on the contextual or situational nature of their abiding rationality.

Homicide bureaux are considered elite units within police departments, and a move into the unit is considered a promotion regardless of rank. Detectives investigate, process prisoners and present evidence in court. Becoming a detective requires personal skill, good interpersonal networks within the organization, or 'politics', support from present detectives, and 'fit' with local traditions. Becoming a detective indicates informal power relations in the detective unit. It signifies that the person has the potential to be trusted, is loyal, a 'team player' and has investigative skills. When organizations are riven by conflict between ethnic groups, divisions exist between the top command and detectives, transfers and promotions indicate additional power relations. Transfer of black officers into the detective ranks in the 1970s, following a change in Detroit city politics, altered the previous dominance of white, catholic Irish investigators. Apprenticeship training as a probation investigator and a brief advanced course once promoted constitute training.

A homicide unit is composed of plainclothes officers, usually housed in central headquarters, who receive cases primarily from uniform officers or dispatchers who report suspicious deaths or near deaths. A detective who is 'up' 'catches' the assignment (usually on a rotated basis) and proceeds, usually with a partner, to the crime scene to investigate. Very large case files are created and maintained carefully, containing interviews, physical evidence, if any, witness statements, suspect lists and a running record of activities related to the case. These formal public records are reflected in detectives' daybooks in which they record their movements and daily activities. Cases assigned to partners are the official workload, and overtime is distributed by sergeants' or inspectors' decisions. The personnel, size of the unit, the number of homicides and the percentage 'cleared' (an organizational label) vary in urban departments. Most reported crimes, unlike homicide, are processed quickly and given little attention (Audit Commission 1993). The clearance rate for homicide varies across the country: estimates are from 60 per cent to over 90 per cent (Bureau of Justice Statistics 1998). The homicide clearance rate itself appears to have little independent association with reported crime rates in general. It is a powerful reflexive indicator used generally to assess the performance of the unit, even while it is routinely manipulated, and is insensitive to the quality of the investigation and court results.

Working a case

A detective's approach to 'working a case' is not fixed, nor determined by written procedures. Paperwork is required, but the order in which tasks are undertaken and the level and direction of effort are left to partners. Cases are created and assigned daily, and paperwork is demanded at regular intervals (these vary but includes the creation of a case and a follow-up usually within two weeks of the initial investigation). Waegel (1981) writes:

> [detectives] typically must process a steady stream of cases … under rigid time constraints . . . these agents do not generally proceed by following a set of codified rules and procedures. However, their discretion is not unlimited, nor are their decisions … individualistic. (Waegel 1981: 263)

Detectives are under pressure in general, although this varies temporally, to 'produce' outcomes, an expected volume of paper, cases processed under time limits and to cope with a constant input of cases. However, like all workers, detectives in medium-sized cities, who manage one-half to one-quarter of the workload of detectives in the New York Police Department (NYPD) and Chicago, consider themselves swamped, overworked and unable to complete the burdensome paperwork in time.

Organizational structure and the detective occupational culture interact over time in case processing. If a case is defined as politically salient or 'high profile', control over the case moves up the hierarchy and is controlled by sergeants and above. Decisions are taken collectively and in consultation with top command by those in charge. In other respects, or in the normal case, the grounds of the occupational culture would define how and when to proceed on a case (Corsiaros 1999).

Investigation is a priority job. Unlike most reported crime that becomes a detective's responsibility, a reported homicide is not disposed of without investigation. Homicide is not likely to be quickly suspended or abandoned for lack of an immediate likely solution (Waegel 1981: 267). Nevertheless, the workload is monitored and output evaluated. Detectives are expected to 'produce', although this is defined contextually and it is unclear what the 'product' of a homicide investigation is other than efforts to produce a clearance. Production norms based on bureaucratic rules about routine and timely filing of reports, and pressures to produce closures if not arrests, remain (Wilson 1978).

Once categorized as to be investigated, cases are divided according to working rules in the unit into routine and non-routine. In Baltimore (Simon 1991), this binary distinction was colourfully called 'dunkers' (easy self-cleared cases with witness, evidence and perhaps even a confession) versus 'whodunnits'. Performance is indicated traditionally by unit clearance rates. Officer and squad keep records of clearances, and sergeants and lieutenants seek to increase the clearance rate or the percentage of homicides cleared. 'Cleared' is the central thematic term in homicide units, but it is context-dependent. The criteria for clearing a homicide are neither universal, nor universally applied. While the Bureau of Justice Statistics compiles the Uniform Crime Reports, defines and sets standards for homicides and clearances, practice in individual departments varies as do the warranted processes of producing an organizationally acceptable clearance. Research (Greenwood *et al.* 1977) suggests that a few key elements – physical evidence, witnesses present, or a confession – are of critical importance in determining the probability of a clearance. These are rarely under the officer's control.

Typification is key to working a case. The social constraints resulting from the analytic features of the crime and its social organization lead homicide detectives to draw subtle yet parochial distinctions to classify and distinguish the quality of investigations and the quality of investigators' work. Evaluations do not rely entirely on the percentage of cases cleared. Such matters as 'flair', how creative the detective is in re-creating the crime scene, pursuing leads, maintaining evidence files and following hunches, is taken into account, as well as the conventional wisdom about the difficulty of the case. Clearing high-profile cases conveys lasting respect. Status accrues as a result accomplishing the possible with style, in a collegial and equalitarian organizational environment. Failure to carry the load, ducking cases, failing to clear conventional crimes and adding to others' workload decrease status. Where ethnicity divides the unit, racial stereotypes also shape prestige. Rank or formal position are rarely used to define social relations (Corsiaros 1999).

The craft and the work[2]

Having made a case for the situated rationality of homicide work, I want to discuss aspects of the work that are variable. What, given the context of homicide work, does the fieldworker want to identify, describe, measure, compare and analyse, either across organizations or variations over time within an organization? I highlight each of the clusters of variables of interest.

Resources are important and rarely assessed. Resources in detective units, while stated in the unit's budget as fixed, are actually quite flexible in their use and can be augmented or reduced very quickly by command decisions. The number of officers available, who can be assigned, those assigned to a case, the length of the assignment, and the overtime available vary across units and within them. Court time and payment for court is defined contractually by union rules and is a subtle process of gaming in which the courts, the police and individual detectives engage. That is, if a hearing or trial is scheduled when an officer is on duty no overtime is accrued; this is in general the aim of the courts; on the other hand, officers may wish to be paid time and a half or more depending on the organization, and thus prefer to have it scheduled in their off-duty time (Corsiaros 1999). Resources and their allocation are loosely coupled to the resources available in other departmental units, for example by other detective units or uniform division who can lend personnel for investigations or raids, pay for information, transfer prisoners, and shaped by alternative sources of income accessible to the unit from fines or seizures.

It is perhaps obvious that the *skills of homicide detectives* vary, but no study has detailed the relative skills of individual homicide detectives by any systematic measurement of clearances, major cases solved, or the like. Investigators' skills vary widely. The assumption of equal skill is contradicted by interviews with homicide detectives and ethnographic evidence. Poorer detectives are likely to have more cases open than others, and are teamed with other more competent officers to reduce the differential in cases cleared (Simon 1991). In most offices, cases are assigned in order to a rota of duty officers, and the person who 'catches' the case may not be competent, say, if it is a complicated case with several suspects, abundant physical evidence and legal subtleties.

Measuring *the workload of detectives* is a complex matter. The notion of rotation, intended to equalize the case-workload, is inconsistent with the assumption that equally skilled officers are assigned to every case. Complex cases are assigned to more skilled or senior officers, thus increasing their formal workload, and reducing the load of others. These officers are expected to close fewer cases and to produce results on a few. They are also allowed to carry cases longer, informally or formally, and to continue to work vexing cases. Workload (cases per officer) is not equal in homicide units because skill in clearing cases is not equal.

Knowledge is personal knowledge and often kept secret from others. Knowledge developed and synthesized on a case is rarely widely shared with others, nor written and accessible. What might be called collective or institutional memory, facts and associations possessed by individual officers that are not written down or shared, increase iniquitous practices. The occupational culture assumes that information is virtually personal property and secrecy is highly valued. This is magnified by the absence of articulated databases within departments, and (especially in homicide) the absence of data sharing, accessible informant files, records and case files of other squads such as gang, juveniles, drug and/or warrant serving squads.

The working style of detectives, meaning how one does things, varies. Detectives in general enjoy being 'out of uniform' and value style in dress, manner and approach to suspects and witnesses. Style includes self-presentation and appearance, as well as fronts and tools (radios, cell phones, guns, handcuffs and the law). Officers' approach to cases varies, as does their use of computers, records, physical evidence and informants. Seasoned detectives are more resistant to using expert systems than younger officers use with some computer literacy. A corollary orientation to computing is unwillingness to enter facts, evidence and developments into computer-based case files. The style of an officer is partially determined by workload. In South Central Los Angeles, for example (Corwin 1996), homicide detectives had so much work they rarely filled in the paperwork and ran six to nine months behind. The central character in that book, for example, preferred to pressure informants to confess as a primary tool, and rarely used physical evidence. Clearly, workload varies the likelihood of certain aspects of an investigation being followed up, and tends to increase the pressure to clear the case by means other than an arrest or outstanding warrant. Officers work from the case 'out' and develop their cases privately, thus restricting access to their cases to others, and reducing capacity of crime analysts or other officers to infer patterns of co-offending, identify multiple victims of the same murderer, or links between crimes. The individual detective is seen as the defining 'expert' in a case unless it is reassigned. 'Working' a homicide case seems to involve a combination of substantive and concrete local knowledge of offenders, settings, and types of offences, associational thinking and sometimes pursuing intuitive hunches and following 'leads', rather than linear, algorithmic and probabilistic thinking.

Motives and satisfactions of detectives vary, and their style of working is shaped in part by their values. Detective work is driven by a combination of moralization, revenge, justice and self-righteousness. Corsiaros's (1999) work, for example, shows that detectives define the moral character of suspects and their own notions of justice; bringing satisfaction in occupationally defined terms. Justice can be obtained, in their view, by failing to act as well as acting. These decisions may divide detectives, their middle management and higher command. The interconnection of racism with such moralizing is explosive, as shown in the O.J. Simpson case in Los Angeles and the Stephen Lawrence case in London. In one case sympathy and identification with the suspect (e.g. in the initial brief and cursory interview with Simpson after he was charged) in the other, vast cover-up, incompetence, perjury and failure to identify with the victim and his family (Macpherson 1999). The values and motives of the detectives investigating the case shadowed both investigations. Because the moralizing perspective defines the outlines of the case, changes in laws, procedures and policies lead to systematic resistance and avoidance of the foreshadowed consequences, including inputting and reporting information on cases.

The *indices of success* are embedded in tacit knowledge about what is 'good police work', mistakes and errors out of the control of the case officer, 'effort and style points' and current expectations in the unit. For example, the pressure to produce varies by the time of the month and the number of arrests or clearances made thus far in the month (McConville *et al.* 1993). Homicide investigation is focused primarily, but not exclusively, on an organizationally defined outcome: a 'clearance'. Some representative modes of organizational closure include closing by: shifting the case to another jurisdiction or agency (a murder of a service man is shifted to the Federal Bureau of Investigation (FBI) although he was killed in a city); issuing a warrant; knowledge that another agency has issued a warrant; arrest of a suspect or suspects; confession or subsequent plea bargain; deeming it double murder, murder-suicide or self-defence, exhausted statute of limitations. These modes for clearing vary across departments, as do the tacit practices producing given closures.

Clearance is a context-based idea. As this implies, clearances, although a standard measure of police detective work, like arrests, are not always sought. It depends. Closing a case, clearing it from organizational records, is but one of several functions of a homicide investigation. While conventional wisdom would elevate the instrumental aim, a closure, there are expressive or socio-emotional aspects of the investigation, the quality of the police work involved, or the wish to hold a case to obtain witness cooperation, confession, or to protect witnesses or victims' families. The rise of victims' rights groups, victim-compensation schemes as well as courts allowing victims and families of victims to testify before sentencing is rendered, have brought new attention to the interactional and socio-emotional support offered by police to victims. A well-done investigation may produce better evidence, it might produce good will, willingness to provide information to the police on other occasions, cooperation in future investigations. The interconnection of crimes in crime-ridden neighbourhoods, and the mutiple victim families, repeat victims as well as repeat offenders, means that the networks of cooperation that ideally homicide detectives use can be quite significant. In short, many functions are carried out by a homicide investigation, and detectives' aims vary from case to case, even given that clearing the case is very salient. Even in a matter as serious as murder, charges are laid to discipline people, force them to confess to complicity in other crimes, or to a lesser charge. Thus, the present stated case is merely background to other moral and political issues (Corsiaros 1999: 98). The bases for these charges range from framing, or planting evidence, to merely known to be weak or insubstantial cases from the court or prosecutors' perspective.

Assessment is complex and personalized. It is difficult to assess the efficacy of an investigation or of an investigator, because like all complex human-tasks, many factors out of police control affect the length and effort entailed in an investigation. Perhaps the most obvious fallacious assumption is the omission of factors other than random errors which shape practice. Craft work as well as the police occupational culture expects and rewards coping with the unexpected, events of social importance but of low statistical probability such as a child kidnapping, a mass murder or a series of rapes of elderly women. Such matters are central to policing because they are focal, raise public anxieties about police effectiveness, and produce enormous good will if cleared. The differences in the salience of cases are very important. A case will be given more time and attention depending on the status, gender and age of the victim. High-status victims, if they received media attention, are also the subject to additional police time and attention. These are 'red ball' or 'big cases'. Very young and very old victims are seen as of public concern, especially an abduction or kidnapping and murder of a child (usually female), and require special handling of the media. If the victim is a police officer or relative of a police officer, it will receive special attention, and often special task forces are assigned (Simon 1991; Corsiaros 1999). Detectives, like all officers, are especially sensitive to cases that might reveal their 'dirty laundry' – crimes involving other officers, cover ups of controversial decisions or corruption more generally (Corsiaros 1999).

The definition of a case is very subtle. It cannot be entirely captured by official figures based on 'outcome' data. Some cases, as I have mentioned, hover for days and sometimes weeks before they are an official case, yet officers are assigned to the case, may have to spend time in hearings, autopsies, emergency rooms and with witnesses, only to find that the victim lived, or was a suicide or died accidentally. Some cases that are worked for some time are transferred to another agency such as the FBI, or the state police, and they are noted as cleared but no credit occurs to a person. Cases may be worked for some time but witnesses refuse to testify, or to give depositions, or even be interviewed, and the District Attorney in the USA or the Crown Prosecutor in the UK drops the case. The weighting of such cases with respect to workload and credit is not easily resolved when comparisons across organizations are sought.

The unevenness of the workload creates a sequencing effect. The clustering of cases in a given time span varies their salience. A cluster of murders, for example, may not violate statistical norms nor affect the year-long rate, thus if a city averages eighteen murders a year, three in one day may not alter the rate, but they will alter public and police concern and activity. The surround changes, and affects the field. Routines and algorithms are designed to order and routinize case processing, but the moral and political meaning of cases is variable, and their appearance at a given time and place is not predictable. Police ideology, partially a self-protective pose, says: You never know what might happen, when, how and to whom.

The occupational culture of detectives

The culture of detectives, like the occupational culture of policing, varies by the size of the organization, by rank and gender, as well as ethnicity

(Martinez, forthcoming). Occupational culture here means the readings (interpretations) officers give to other officers' and civilians' readings. For example, detectives learn to work cases by watching other detectives work, hearing their stories about their cases, those that worked and did not (second-hand renditions or readings) and store these cues as guidelines that might configure their own choices. Much of this knowledge and learning is pre-cognitive, or indirect rather than explicit tutelage. Learning hinges on negative instances, horror stories, gallows humour and cases marked as 'how not to do it'.

There are dynamics of competition within police units. Rank, skill and social status within the unit do not always cohere. Investigative expertise and rank achievement are different. While social relations tend to be personalistic, feudal and cliquish, and not based on rank, sergeants can guide, shape and either hinder or facilitate an investigation, but seldom directly 'overrule' the decision of a colleague. In homicide, the task generally is to clear a murder case, so decisions about the case evolve forward from the incident and take on a new character once an arrest is made. Resistance to new rules, procedures and 'politics' (when higher rank officers decide not to move to indictment after an arrest) is normal because the detective views him or herself as the entrepreneur and expert in the case assigned.

While emphasis is placed on creative investigation, detective work, and its success, is fundamentally reactive – cases are worked as they arise and with the evidence presented mostly in the first instance (Greenwood *et al.* 1977). The causes of homicide, the ecological patterning of the events, social structure and the economy, even motives, fade into the background in the actual investigation. These are givens, constraints within which the investigator must work. Notions of prevention, crime management, risk reduction and even concern with repeat offenders and their patterns are of little value since homicide is generally a one-time crime for all but a very small number of offenders.

There is an irony in homicide work as in other police work; the routine and emergency are not in balance, nor are the 'whodunnits' common. The core of the work is clerical, routine and boring, such as paperwork, making phone calls or organizing evidence. While the aim is to close cases, manage prisoners (those arrested) and process them, and to investigate reported occurrences, most detective work is clerical, not investigative. Investigation is the most salient and dramatically important aspect of the work, but the time spent in the office in case processing is far greater.

There is a tension between loyalty to fellow officers and the working rules of the occupational culture (Corsiaros 1999: 117ff). Tensions arise in how to assemble personal notebooks to contain consistent stories, passive or active perjury in court, loyalty to partners, and avenging disrespect to fellow officers. Cooperation and competition subtly are interwoven in practice, because status accrues to solving big cases, and informal rankings of each other are envious and often quite invidious.

Paperwork is loathed and it is distrusted. Paper representations are salient legal and organizational reality, but they have a complex, shifting relationship to actual and reported events. Paper written is designed to influence supervisors, those 'above', attorneys in the prosecutors' office, or juries, attorneys and judges in court and peers. The paper reality created or accepted by detectives (as a result of loyalty to a partner for example) governs and is interconnected with the narrative they produce for booking, indictment or formal trials. 'Covering your ass' (CYA), it should be noted, does not always mean lying, suborning to perjury, or other illegalities: CYA can produce careful attention to legalities such as obtaining witnesses to support a story, checking with supervisors, and observing rules for taping interviews, uttering warnings and observing requirements for obtaining warrants.

These several features of the work are loosely associated as an *occupational perspective*, or way of viewing and acting upon the world. Think of these connections, roughly in order of the description above. The resources available vary over time, and officers (here I refer to homicide detectives) know that substantively, cases vary in their importance, a fact indicated by shifting resources to an important case for example. This means all cases are not equal, nor is equal credit given; this is constantly dramatized by shifting cases around and reassigning them. While homicide work is a competitive world, and skills, experience and style vary, many cases are solved on the spot, or dismissed after limited investigation. These are factors out of the control of the detective. This builds in a sense of cynicism, frustration and unfairness to the work. Abstract ideas like justice, fairness and legality are not salient features of the perspective; they tend to cling to case outcomes and examples, concrete instances and stories rather than transcendental notions so treasured by philosophers and jurisprudentialists. The competitiveness of detectives makes creating linked databases connected to case files resisted, and frustrates attempts to create expert systems, crime analysis units, or strategic crime mapping. Officers in middle management, sergeant and inspector, are dealing primarily with mistakes, errors, malfeasance, incompetence and low performance, often in response to citizens' complaints. Their time horizon is set for processing complaints; they have standard forms, and great latitude. Command officers in theory deal with 'policy', 'force mission statements and goals', but since we know very little about what chiefs and their staffs actually do, it must be assumed that they take a more Weberian approach to long-term planning, budgeting and analysis. What little evidence does exist suggests that the 'crisis' style management developed on the street to deal with the immediate incident becomes the paradigm for all kinds of 'management' decisions (Chatterton and Hougland 1996).

In summary, these several features provide the form for working cases, but they do not encompass the detailed content of 'solving' a case. The case is an object to be framed within a field and worked given a surround. The perspective is not determinant nor does it contain absolute values, although the features are valued, because they cannot always hold and are often in conflict in a given case. They are woven together in complex fashion in stories that suppress some aspects of an incident and highlight others. They are partially shared with uniformed officers, and other investigators, but some or characteristically associated with homicide work. The features shift in salience situationally and are interdigitated with the working rules of the job. They are part of the field within which the actual elements of a case are framed. They set priorities and meanings; grant prestige within the unit (and in often in society); define the boundaries of imagination and the possible, and are in constant tension with commensuration, transitive judgements, and linear thinking.

RATIONALITY IN CONTEXT[3]

All this has one central and abiding point for fieldwork: *do not trust the written case record without knowing the 'story' or context within which it was worked and by whom.* Homicide investigations present elegant and striking examples of contrasts between kinds of rationalities, rooted in different histories, developmental patterns and time. They exist as archaeological fragments within departments, not as collective, consciously articulated practices, but as semi-visible, even to experienced investigators. Let us first observe, as does Espeland (1998), that organizations are arenas of 'contested rationalities'; in other words, the social contexts in a big organization vary, and the deciding that is defined as rational also varies.

First, in the *field* or 'on the ground', uniformed police use pragmatic, here-and-now logic to decide whether to intervene and how to intervene, but the field is always subject to redefinition, surprise and the unexpected (Bayley and Bittner 1986; Mastrofski 1999). The aims of the encounter vary, and can be seen only as presenting a family of problems to the officer. The officer, in turn, cannot predict and must rely on a set of loosely related tactics by which he or she brings the situation under control and resolves (closes) it. This kind of deciding takes into account many factors that vary by neighbourhood, time of day, colour of the citizens and the officers' past experiences.

Second, a different *kind of rationality* is employed when the encounter is written up (if it is); it is based on the format in which the information is to be cast; the channels through which it is to be communicated, the expected audience for the paperwork, and the tacit expectations the officers read off about their work rate and output as well as what laws should be enforced at the current 'political environment' or surround (Meehan 2000).

Third, *detectives work with a case-oriented logic*, as we have seen. Their horizon or time perspective is somewhat longer, the information they possess once processed and often ambiguous, and the reconstructive-imaginative aspect of the work more concentrated and augmented by additional evidence, statements and depositions that are gathered after the initial event.

Fourth, *investigations vary and should be compared to other investigative forms.* Officers working in narcotics, internal affairs and special task forces must create their cases, and therefore imagine the shape of the crimes, or make them happen. They problem solve, use prospective or longer-term rationality, and have far greater flexibility in creating the problem to which they bring their attention.

Fifth, *the social world of middle management and higher command, even with investigative backgrounds, shifts toward visible conventionally defined results, and is more sensitive to external audiences.*

The current practice in these five contexts is not always verbally rationalized or explained, and if an explanation is offered, it is an exception that supports the rule of common-sense understanding. Apprentice work relies on oral didacticism. The police field, symbolized by the organization's structure, official rules and procedures, creates homogeneity where heterogeneity exists, and submerges the ongoing conflict and competition between rationalities. Current shorthand terms and *non-discursive practices* (what is done, not what is talked about) sustain the working fiction that work always proceeds as usual. The fiction of uniformity is also sustained by apparently interchangeable databases. For example, in large cities, such as Toronto and Los Angeles, databases can be accessed from any division or precinct, and detectives can note or flag the file if a query comes in (see Detective Smith concerning this . . .), if stops are made of a car or person by officers. How this database is used in enforcement or crime analysis is another matter.

Consider again the *ostensive purposes of a homicide investigation*. One might argue that it serves to deter offenders from repeating, deters potential murderers from undertaking or planning a murder, marks societal concern, that it makes an example of punishing murderers, or that victims and society are avenged. In this sense, a murder investigation could be said to entail an absolute moral imperative: murder is a fundamental wrong that should be visibly and officially punished. If murder is not punished, the argument goes, society is in danger. A society with a high rate of crime can be seen as violent and a source of fear. This moral-legal argument connects police work tightly with legality and morality, and links these two to public values, concerns and peace of mind. Formal rationality would define homicide investigation as devoted to finding the perpetrator and bringing him or her to 'justice'. Setting aside the rather complicated character of formalized justice in the courts, and bearing in mind that many social factors other than the evidence that attaches to the charged person shape it, it is clear that homicide investigation is not exclusively defined by the organization as a matter of arresting and charging a person with a homicide, or even of producing a clearance.

Substantive rationality always shapes the 'instant' or present case. Homicide investigations are matters of *substantive rationality*; rationality defined in terms of the values of the organization and of detective works more precisely. This means it is ill suited to the crude expert systems that have been proposed as a 'solution' that will make certain more efficient detective work (see Ratledge and Jacoby 1979; Cicourel 1986; Arney 1991) to homicide work. Recall that clearance rates for homicide have been declining even as the murder rate (reported homicides) has dropped since 1991 (it is still double that of 1962!). Recall also that the modes of clearing cases vary within and across organizations. Of the many ways of producing a 'clearance', only one involves arresting and charging a person with homicide. The arrested person may well not be charged by the District Attorney, or processed further by the criminal justice system, or may be found not guilty. Definitional processes at the crime scene, hospital and medical examiner's offices vary, producing different meanings of 'homicide', 'suicide', 'murder-suicide' and accidental death. Each of these modes of opening or closing a case is embedded in rational practices that produce understood and justified outcome data (Cicourel and Kitsuse 1967). The pattern of 'irrationality', defined as effort and resources devoted to functions other than arresting and bringing to justice perpetrators is well legitimized within homicide units. To push this further, if one were to use cost-effective measures to assess the production of clearances, homicide would be very ineffective, but it tops the table within police departments for effectiveness.

As high-profile cases show, those with high-status victims that have press attention and arouse political opinion and top command concern, the goodwill, prestige and perhaps public confidence associated with solving a major case, especially one which becomes media material such as the Timothy McViegh case, is highly valued and essential to maintaining the police mandate. Conversely, public and media frustration and anger, in part stimulated and created by the media, associated with the failure to convict O.J. Simpson of the murder of Nicole Brown Simpson and Ronald Goldman, and to make an arrest in the Jonbenet Ramsey case, remains active. Furthermore, it would be irrational not to attempt to expand extra resources to solve high-profile cases, given the potential police increments of goodwill, satisfying public feelings of revenge and satisfaction, and mollifying politicians demanding an arrest. Detectives link self-esteem and aesthetics (flair and quality investigations) with solutions of major cases, and with avoiding public scandal or embarrassment as a result of their errors.

Once framed, a complex situation changes its character. Consider a homicide investigation with a set of attendant facts concerning the victim, the suspects, witnesses, physical evidence, and so on. These are framed into the deciding by traditional formatting within the organization (its records and categories and classifications). Other matters are thus 'framed out' or excluded from the decision. The ways in which the elements of a decision are found within the frame. The *frame* sits within a *field* or subjective and objective factors that are organizational in large part. These are overtime, skill, assignment patterns, emphases of particular supervisors (on paperwork, closure or teamwork) and pressures to produce generally (as defined within the unit). The field in turn is shaped by the largest level of influence or the *surround*, the set of forces such as the media, high politics and ideological trends that enter and leave the field from time to time. These are not unpredictable in their arrival, but they are lurking and their potential is always ambiguous. Thus, the here and now is always shaped and constrained by the shared, collective and organizational processes of framing, field and surround.

CONCLUSIONS

In many salient respects, policing is a pre-modern occupation with sacred aspects because of its links to the law, morality and the state, isolated, and driven by a mixture of rank authority, colleagueship and feudal loyalties. It manifests many rationally articulated processes such as the processing of prisoners for court, laying of formal charges, and the social organization of reactive dispatching. Record-keeping systems for arrests are increasingly computerized and widely accessible to officers. In these processes, information technology has reduced time, simplified complexity and tightened links, that is the exchange of information between units within departments, and increased surveillance and control of uniformed officers. These formal and collective rationalizations encapsulate investigative work. They shape the operating context for transactions with uniformed officers who produce cases for all investigators except vice and narcotics. On the other hand, detective work, especially homicide work, maintains loose coupling with other units, operating on a case basis, maintaining secrecy about decisions, working with partners in loose supervision, and sensitive to a tightly knit, face-to-face group of colleagues who are their teammates. Their case-oriented, substantively rational work must also meet legal rules and procedures, a covering rationality that enables them to dispose of their cases. The situational rationality that obtains, sensitive to surround, field and frame as perspective, is functionally suited to subtle tasks, people work, and readings of trust. It also covers a pattern of choice that is apparently rational, organized around clearing cases, but subtly irrational in operation.

These features of the work, glossed as 'context', set in a surround, field and framed as 'cases', provide the phenomenological structure within which what non-police call (often incorrectly) 'murder' is seen. It is the task of the investigator to illuminate this context comparatively. The following then become working rules in the field:

- Find how cases are defined and framed.
- Discover the field within which they are given meaning: what are the subjective and objective constraints on working a case?
- Focus on what is out of sight: context, assumptions, the unspoken, the unwritten and the 'obvious'.
- Ask how things are done, not why.
- Always ask for the story 'behind' a case.
- Distrust arguments from efficiency, rationality, efficaciousness and external standards imposed on workers.
- Follow through a handful of cases to identify the key contingencies, turning points and mistakes that are possible at each stage in deciding.
- Recognize that not everything can be explained, verbalized and neatly ordered.
- Recall that making sense of a case is not the same as making sense of cases.

- Learn how to work a case yourself.
- Many stories float around an organization, not one.

NOTES

1   In what follows, I draw on fieldwork (Manning 1979, 2001), studies of detective work (Skolnick 1967; Greenwood *et al.* 1977; Waegel 1981; Ericson 1982; Simon 1991; Corwin 1996), and recent unpublished fieldwork on the social organization of detective work (Brandl 1989; Martinez 1997; Corsiaros 1999). I am presently involved in a lengthy study of crime mapping and crime analysis in a large eastern city.

2   A series of contemporary ethnographies identify the paradoxes created by 'rationalizing' craftwork (Orr 1996; Barley and Orr 1997). These studies ironically describe technologically shaped work such as xerox repair, computer designing of structures, computer programming and cat-scan operators. Deeper problems arise when such systems are expected to function flawlessly, smoothly integrate operator and machine, and avoid errors that might endanger lives.

3   Rationalization, linking considered objectives with indicators, is being forced on the police in the UK, Australia and Canada by budget constraints, pressures of the market and market rhetoric, and by governmental and executive pressures from the Home Office in the UK and the Solicitor General's office in Canada. Information-driven policing, taking into account the role of crime and fear of crime in shaping public confidence, is shaping many forces in Canada and the UK. Rationalization is a currently powerful force because it is connected tightly to the modern ideology of neo-liberalism, market efficiency and the commodification of public services. The combination of pragmatism and using market records to measure the production of 'products', when used in connection with public services, suggests that information technology can increase productivity, save time and ensure systematic record keeping. In particular, police are struggling with rationalization in the guise of setting priorities and more precisely allocating the call load, implementing career planning assistance to young officers, employing management by means of stated written objectives, accounting and budgeting, and establishing crime-management initiatives.

REFERENCES

Antonio, R. (1995) 'Nietzsche's anti-sociology', *American Journal of Sociology* 101: 1–43.

Arney, W. (1991) *Experts in the Age of Systems*. Albuquerque, NM: University of New Mexico Press.

Barley, S. and Orr, J. (eds) (1997) *Between Craft and Science: Technical Work in U.S. Settings*. Ithaca, NY: IRL Press.

Bayley, D. and Bittner, E. (1986) 'The tactical choices of police patrol officers', *Journal of Criminal Justice* 14: 329–348.

Bourdieu, P. (1977) *Outline of a Theory of Practice*. Cambridge: Cambridge University Press.

Brandl, S. (1989) 'Detective work', unpublished PhD dissertation, College of Social Science, Michigan State University.

Bureau of Justice Statistics (1998) *Homicide Report*. Washington, DC: US Government Printing Office.

Chatterton, M. and Hougland, P. (1996) 'Strategic management', unpublished report, Henry Fielding Centre, University of Manchester.

Cicourel, A. (1986) 'Expert systems ...', in R. Schweder (ed.) *Cultural Systems*. Chicago: University of Chicago Press.

Cicourel, A. and Kitsuse, J. (1967) 'A note of the uses of official statistics', *Social Problems* 11(Fall): 132–139.

Corsiaros, M. (1999) 'Detective work and high profile cases', unpublished PhD, Department of Sociology, York University, Toronto.

Corwin, R. (1996) *Homicide in LAPD*. New York: Bantam.

Dosse, F. (1997a [1991]) *The History of Structuralism: The Rising Sign, 1945–1966*, vol. 1, translated by D. Glassman. Minneapolis, MN: University of Minnesota Press.

Dosse, F. (1997b [1992]) *The History of Structuralism*, vol. 2, translated by D. Glassman. Minneapolis, MN: University of Minnesota Press.

Douglas, J. (1967) *Suicide*. Princeton, NJ: Princeton University Press.

Drury, S. (1994) *Kojeve*. New York: St Martin's Press.

Eco, U. (1979) *The Theory of Semiotics*. Bloomington, IN: University of Indiana Press.

Elster, J. (1983) *Ulysses and the Sirens*. Cambridge: Cambridge University Press.

Elster, J. (1984) *Sour Grapes*. Cambridge: Cambridge University Press.

Elster, J. (1989) *Solomonic Judgements*. Cambridge: Cambridge University Press.

Elster, J. (1999) *Alchemies of the Mind*. Cambridge: Cambridge University Press.

Ericson, R. (1982) *Making Crime*. Toronto: University of Toronto Press.

Espeland, W. (1998) *The Struggle for Water*. Chicago: University of Chicago Press.

Espeland, W. and Stevens, M. (1998) 'Commensuration as a social process', *Annual Review of Sociology* 24: 313–343.

Fabrega, H. (1998) *The Evolution of Sickness and Healing*. Berkeley, CA: University of California Press.

Fabrega, H. and Silver, D. (1973) *Illness and Curing in Zinacantan*. Palo Alto, CA: Stanford University Press.

Fagan, J. and Davies, C. (2000) 'Street stops and broken windows', *Fordham Urban Law Review* 28(4): 457–504.

Garfinkel, H. (1967) *Studies in Ethnomethodology*. Englewood Cliffs, NJ: Prentice-Hall.

Geertz, C. (1973) *The Interpretation of Cultures*. New York: Basic Books.

Giddens, A. (1981) *The Class Structure of Advanced Societies*. London: Hutchinson.

Giddens, A. (1984) *The Constitution of Society*. Berkeley, CA: University of California Press.

Giddens, A. (1990) *The Consequences of Modernity*. Stanford, CA: Stanford University Press.

Giddens, A. (1991) *Modernity and Self-Identity*. Cambridge: Polity.

Goffman, E. (1959) *The Presentation of Self in Everyday Life*. Garden City, NY: Doubleday Anchor.

Goffman, E. (1974) *Frame Analysis*. New York: Basic Books.

Greenwood, P.W., Chaiken, J.M. and Petersilia, J. (1977) *The Criminal Investigation Process*. Lexington, MA: D.C. Heath.

Heidegger, M. (1963 [1953]) *Being and Time*. Albany, NY: SUNY Press.

Lemert, C. (1995) *Sociology after the Crisis*. Boulder, CO: Westview.

McConville, M., Sanders, A. and Leng, R. (1993) *The Case for the Prosecution*. London: Routledge and Kegan Paul.

Macpherson, Sir William (1999) *Report on the Stephen Lawrence Inquiry*, Cm 4262. London: Stationery Office.

Mannheim, K. (1960) *Essays in the Sociology of Knowledge*. London: Routledge and Kegan Paul.

Manning, P.K. (1979) *Narcs' Game*. Cambridge, MA: MIT Press.

Manning, P.K. (1992a) 'Technological dramas and the police', *Criminology* 30: 327–345.

Manning, P.K. (1992b) 'Information technology and the police', in M. Tonry and N. Morris (eds) *Modern Policing*. Chicago: University of Chicago Press.

Manning, P.K. (1996) 'Dramaturgy, politics and the axial media event', *Sociological Quarterly* 37: 101–118.

Manning, P.K. (1997 [1977]) *Police Work*. Prospect Heights, NJ: Waveland.

Martinez, R. (1997) Unpublished field notes on Miami-Dade police homicide detectives.

Martinez, R. (forthcoming) *Homicide Work in Six Cities* (working title). Boulder, CO: Westview.

Mastrofski, S. (1999) *Policing for People*. Washington, DC: Police Foundation.

Mead, G.H. (1934) *Mind, Self and Society*. Chicago: University of Chicago Press.

Meehan, A.J. (2000) 'The organizational career of gang statistics', *Sociological Quarterly* 41: 337–370.

Merelman, R. (1998) 'On legitimalaise in the United States', *Sociological Quarterly* 39: 351–368.

Orr, J. (1996) *Talking about Machines*. Ithaca, NY: Cornell LIR Press.

Parsons, T. (1960 [1936]) *The Structure of Social Action*. New York: Free Press.

Pierce, C. (1936) *Collected Works*, vols I–VI. Cambridge, MA: Harvard University Press.

Pierce, C. (1958) *Collected Works*, vols VII–VII. Cambridge, MA: Harvard University Press.

Poster, M. (1990) *The Mode of Information*. Stanford, CA: Stanford University Press.

Ratledge, E. and Jacoby, J. (1979) *Artificial Intelligence and Expert Systems*. Westport, CT: Greenwood Press.

Ritzer, G. (1999) *Enchanting a Disenchanted World*. Thousand Oaks, CA: Pine Forge Press.

Sartre, J.P. (1953) *Being and Nothingness*. New York: Philosophical Library.

Saussure, F. de (1966) *Cours*, translated by C. Bally and A. Sechehaye. New York: McGraw-Hill.

Sica, A. (1988) *Weber, Irrationality and Social Order*. Berkeley, CA: University of California Press.

Simon, D. (1991) *Homicide*. Boston, MA: Little, Brown.

Skolnick, J. (1967) *Justice without Trial*. New York: John Wiley.

Sudnow, D. (1965) 'Normal crimes', *Social Problems* 12: 255–276.

Sudnow, D. (1968) *Dying*. Englewood Cliffs, NJ: Prentice-Hall.

Waegel, W. (1981) 'Case routinization in investigative police work', *Social Problems* 28: 263–275.

Wilson, J.Q. (1978) *The Investigators*. New York: Basic Books.

4 ANALYSING INTERACTION:

Video, ethnography and situated conduct

Christian Heath and Jon Hindmarsh

Some of the finest ethnographic studies of organizations emerged in Chicago following the Second World War. Due in no small way to the lectures and essays of E.C. Hughes, a substantial body of naturalistic studies of work and occupations emerged which began to chart the routines and realities involved in everyday organizational life. Hughes, his colleagues and students powerfully demonstrate, through numerous empirical studies, the ways in which work is thoroughly dependent upon and inseparable from a tacit and emergent culture which is fashioned and refashioned in the light of the problems that people face in the routine accomplishment of their day-to-day work. For Hughes, social interaction lies at the heart of organizational life. It is through social interaction that organizations emerge and are sustained; it is a consequence of social interaction that people develop routines, strategies, practices and procedures, and it is by virtue of social interaction that clients receive, and perceive, goods and services in ways defined by the organizations and its occupation(s). For example at one point Hughes suggests: 'The subject matter of sociology is interaction. Conversation of verbal and other gestures is an almost constant activity of human beings. The main business of sociology is to gain systematic knowledge of social rhetoric' (Hughes 1971: 508).

The commitment of Hughes to interaction as 'the subject matter of sociology' reflects a long-standing recognition within the discipline of the importance of social interaction to human existence and sociality. It pervades the writings of major figures such as Durkheim, Weber and Parsons; Simmel goes so far as to suggest that the 'description of the forms of this interaction is the task of the science of society in its strictest and most essential sense' (Simmel 1950: 21–22). Despite the importance that sociology ascribes to social interaction, the details of its production remain surprisingly disregarded. Interaction provides the foundation to social organization, it informs sociological theorizing, it underpins substantive contributions across a variety of fields and yet largely fails to form a topic of inquiry in its own right. It is extraordinary to consider that Goffman in his presidential address to the American Sociological Association in 1982, more than a century after the emergence of a discipline of sociology, felt it necessary to plea for the study of 'the interaction order' (Goffman 1983).

In this chapter, we consider the ways in which the social and interactional organization of everyday activities can be subject to detailed scrutiny. The discussion draws from ethnomethodology and conversation analysis. It is concerned with how we can use video recordings of everyday settings, augmented by more conventional fieldwork, to explore the ways in which participants accomplish practical activities in and through interaction with others. It is not however solely or even primarily concerned with the analysis of talk, but rather with ways in which the production and interpretation of action relies upon a variety of resources – spoken, bodily and of course material resources, such as objects, texts, tools, technologies and the like. We would also like to mention in passing the relation between more conventional ethnography and studies of 'talk-in-interaction', and explore some ways in which we might interweave one or two concerns within these very different approaches.

The example we will discuss is drawn from a medical consultation in general practice. We have chosen this example since it is a domain which has been subject to a substantial body of ethnographic or qualitative research from a range of standpoints. It is also a setting which is familiar to us all and does not require a lengthy introduction or explanation. This chapter discusses why and how we might collect video recordings of everyday activities for research purposes and proposes a number of analytic considerations or assumptions which might help inform the analysis of relatively fine details of social interaction. It then focuses on the example. To begin however it is perhaps helpful to discuss why video-based field studies may provide a distinctive contribution to our understanding of the medical consultation as well as of course a broad range of other everyday activities.

ETHNOGRAPHY AND INSTITUTIONAL TALK

The professions in medicine and medical practice formed topics of particular interest to Hughes, his colleagues and students. Consider for example the powerful study by Strauss (1964) concerned with the organization of psychiatric care, Roth's (1963) treatise on the treatment negotiation in tuberculosis clinics, and Goffman's (1961) influential analysis of the career of mental patients. These and an extraordinarily rich array of related studies (see e.g. Becker 1963; Davis 1963; Glaser and Strauss 1965) have had a profound influence on the ethnographic research, and their approach, their analytic concerns and their conceptual distinctions pervade more contemporary studies of medical practice and occupational life (see e.g. Strong 1979; Atkinson 1995). In characterizing his own work and the studies of his colleagues and students, Hughes neatly summarizes their concerns and approach to the analysis of work and interaction. He suggests that the aims are

to discover patterns of interaction and mechanisms of control, the things over
which people in a line of work seek to gain control, the sanctions which they have
or would like to have at their disposal, and the bargains which were made –
consciously or unconsciously – among a group of workers and between them and
other kinds of people in the drama of their work. (Hughes 1971: 240)

Despite their commitment to social interaction and the organization of
everyday practice, there has been a growing recognition that ethnography,
or at least studies in the genre of Hughes and related research, fails to get to
grips with the practical and concerted accomplishment of work – that is to
examine and explicate the interactional and contingent character of practice
and action. So for example in medicine, professional practice is accomplished at least in part through people talking with each other, whether it is
doctors and patients within the consultation or the members of different professions engaged in highly technical activities. The issue is not simply one of
detail, or as computer scientists sometimes say 'granularity', but rather that
the emergent, practical and contingent accomplishment of work and occupational life disappears from view – from analytic consideration – in these
fine ethnographies. Social interaction is placed at the heart of the analytic
agenda and yet the very concepts which pervade certain forms of ethnographic research, concepts such as 'negotiation', 'bargaining', 'career',
'shared understanding', 'trajectory', even 'interpretative framework', gloss
the very phenomena that they are designed to reveal.

Over the past few decades we have witnessed the emergence of a very different body of sociological research – a corpus of studies which have
attempted to examine in fine detail the social and interactional organization
of everyday activities. Emerging through ethnomethodology, research in
conversation analysis has been increasingly concerned with 'institutional
interaction' and in particular 'talk at work' (see for example Boden and
Zimmerman 1991; Drew and Heritage 1992). Medicine, medical practice and
the delivery of health care has become a particular focus of these studies,
and there is a growing body of studies of talk and interaction in such areas
as oncology, general practice, psychiatry, nursing, instruction and counselling (e.g. Heath 1986; ten Have 1991; Bergmann 1992; Maynard 1992;
Peräkylä 1998; Pilnick 1998). These studies powerfully reveal the ways in
which a broad range of activities such as investigation, diagnosis, treatment
and advice are accomplished in and through interaction, in particular talk,
and chart the practices and procedures, conventions and reasoning through
which patients and practitioners produce and make sense of their everyday
practical activities in concert with each other. Despite the analytic richness of
these studies, however, and their concern with social interaction, it is not
at all apparent that for ethnographers such studies provide a satisfactory
contribution, let alone a way forward for studies of work and interaction.

There is not the space here to discuss these issues in any detail but it is perhaps useful to mention one or two points that bear upon the following discussion. In general, the tension derives from the very different idea 'context'

found within these bodies of sociological research and ways in which particular characteristics can be said to play upon, or feature in, the organization of conduct. For ethnography, for example, the seemingly narrow focus on talk, and disregard of such potentially relevant features as the identities of the participants and their professional background, the wider organizational framework, and the physical setting appears to produce a denuded characterization of conduct. For conversation analysis, a rigorous commitment to demonstrating empirically the relevance of particular features of the context to the actual production of action by participants in interaction removes any liberal appeal to an array of potentially, *but undemonstrable,* 'broader' contextual characteristics (see Silverman 1999).

In this chapter we wish to address one or two of these tensions by discussing the ways in which we can begin to consider how bodily conduct and material features of the setting, as well as talk, feature in the practical accomplishment of social activities. In particular, we explore the ways in which talk is inextricably embedded in the material environment and the bodily conduct of the participants, and how objects and artefacts such as paper and pens become momentarily relevant within the course of particular actions and activities. We also wish to point to the critical import of undertaking fieldwork as well as collecting recordings when undertaking studies of specialized forms of activity such as medical practice. In this way we hope to illustrate how characteristics of the setting which are given some importance in many ethnographic studies may be reconsidered or respecified using a rather different analytic framework.

ANALYTIC CONSIDERATIONS

Since its inception, qualitative sociology has drawn upon field studies and in particular (non)participant-observation of naturally occurring activities in everyday settings. Fieldwork has provided the critical resource for the discovery of indigenous social organization and a whole assembly of concepts and theories have emerged which are richly suited to characterizing observations – concepts such as career, negotiation, labelling, performance, role distance and the like (see e.g. Hughes 1958; Goffman 1967). Fieldwork is critical to any research which is concerned with investigating specialized forms of social activity and settings with which researchers may be unfamiliar, but it is not clear that it provides the resources necessary for the analysis of social interaction. For example, it is not possible to recover the details of talk through field observation alone, and if it is relevant to consider how people orient bodily, point to objects, grasp artefacts, and in other ways articulate an action or produce an activity, it is unlikely that one can grasp little more than a passing sense of what happened. Moreover, to a large extent, participants themselves are unaware of the ways in which they organize their conduct in interaction; they are inevitably engaged in the topic or business at hand rather than the analysis of the ways in which it is being accomplished. Indeed, as Garfinkel (1967) and in a rather different way Goffman (1963) demonstrate, the competent accomplishment of social actions and activities is dependent upon participants glossing the very ways in which they produce and recognize conduct. So for example consider the way in which we can provide only the most cursory insights into the production of the most seemingly banal activities such as asking a question, stepping on an escalator, pointing to a picture, even though such actions are dependent upon an array of social and interactional competencies. The tacit, 'seen but unnoticed' character of human activity and social organization, coupled with the complexity of action and interaction, suggests that we need additional resources if we hope to explicate the details of human conduct in its 'naturally occurring' environments.

Video recordings help provide those resources. They allow us to capture versions of conduct and interaction in everyday settings and subject them to repeated scrutiny using slow motion facilities and the like. Thus, they provide access to the fine details of conduct, both talk and bodily comportment. They allow us for example to track the emergence of gesture, to determine where people are looking and what they are looking at, and to recover the ways in which they orient to and handle objects and artefacts. They also provide the opportunity to show the data on which observations are based to other researchers and subject their analysis to the scrutiny by members of the academic community, a problem which has long haunted more conventional ethnographic research. Unlike more conventional ethnographic data, video recordings can provide the opportunity of developing a database which can be subject to a broad range of analytic concerns and interests; they are not simply tied to particular projects, specific approaches, or the interests of a particular researcher.

For those with an interest in the material settings in which action and interaction arises, video recordings provide researchers with the opportunity to analyse the emerging characteristics of those ecologies. We can for example see people writing documents, manipulating objects, using artefacts such as telephones, computers and fax machines; we can also recover changes on screens such as computer or television monitors, additions to records, modifications to plans, and the like. Video recordings therefore provide us with a resource with which to analyse 'situated' action, as it emerges within its ordinary ecologies.

> In sum, the use of recorded data serves as a control on the limitations and fallibilities of intuition and recollection; it exposes the observer to a wide range of interactional materials and circumstances and also provides some guarantee that analytic considerations will not arise as artefacts of intuitive idiosyncrasy, selective attention or recollection, or experimental design. (Heritage and Atkinson 1984: 4)

Despite the potential opportunities afforded by video, it is still relatively rare to find video-based field studies within qualitative sociology. In social anthropology there has been a long-standing interest in using first film and more recently video as a way of presenting activities and rituals, and the documentary programme now plays an important part in both academic and popular studies of 'other' cultures. In anthropology, like sociology, however, there is not a significant tradition in using either film or video as a vehicle to actually analyse the organization of social action and interaction. This curious absence of video as an analytic resource derives perhaps more from the absence of a relevant methodological orientation than a lack of interest in exploiting sociological possibilities of video. Indeed, the conceptual and analytic commitments found within a substantial body of qualitative research, including symbolic interactionism, activity theory and so on, which richly illuminate materials generated through conventional fieldwork, do not necessarily resonate with the details of activities one confronts with video recordings of everyday settings.

Nevertheless, the resources through which we can begin to exploit video for the purposes of sociological inquiry are provided by ethnomethodology and conversation analysis. Like other forms of qualitative social science they do not involve a method *per se*, a set of clearly formulated techniques and procedures, but rather a methodological orientation from which to view naturally occurring activities and events. Before illustrating the approach, it is perhaps helpful to provide a brief overview of three of the key analytic orientations found within ethnomethodology and conversation analysis (Garfinkel 1967; Sacks 1992).

First, talk and bodily conduct are social action and are the primary vehicles through which people accomplish social activities and events. Second, the sense and significance of social actions and activities are inseparable from the immediate context; they emerge moment by moment reflexively creating the context in which they arise. Third, participants use and rely upon practices, procedures and reasoning, in short 'methodological resources', through which they produce social actions and make sense of the actions of others.

Schegloff and Sacks (1974) argue that the concern with talk in conversation analysis does not derive from an interest in language *per se*, but from the recognition that social actions and activities are accomplished in and through talk-in-interaction. In face-to-face interaction, social actions and activities are accomplished through a variety of means, spoken, visual and tactile; in many cases, talk is inextricably embedded in the material environment and the bodily conduct of participants. So for example, gesture often works with and within particular utterances to accomplish a particular action, and turns at talk are delicately coordinated with the visual conduct, such as visual alignment, of the co-participant(s) (see e.g. Goodwin 1981; Heath 1986). Participants point, refer to and invoke objects in interaction, they use tools, artefacts and technologies, and the immediate environment provides resources for making sense of the actions of others (see e.g. Heath and Hindmarsh 2000; Heath and Luff 2000; Hindmarsh and Heath 2000). In face-to-face interaction therefore, bodily conduct and the material environment plays a critical part in the production and intelligibility of social action.

Unfortunately, research on non-verbal communication tends to separate conduct into different channels and to some extent disregard the ways in which talk and bodily conduct are interdependent in the practical accomplishment of social action. It also, like much sociological research, disregards the immediate environment, and the ways in which participants invoke and rely upon 'physical' features of the ecology to produce actions and make sense of each other's conduct. For example, an individual's shift in orientation may be sensible by virtue of the ways in which it is aligned towards an object such as a picture. So, it is somewhat surprising that in the social and cognitive sciences, research on communication and interaction, has largely disregarded the ways in which the immediate ecology features in the accomplishment of social actions and activities.

The actual significance or meaning of these objects and artefacts, which are seen, invoked, noticed and the like, is dependent upon the course of action in which they become relevant. Indeed, in recent years there has been a growing interest in what has become generally characterized as 'situated action'. This interest reflects a long-standing concern in the social sciences with context and the uniqueness of events and activities. There is a tendency, however, even among more radical analytic developments, to treat context as a framework in which action takes place. Features of particular context, including the physical environment and purpose of the occasion, are thought to bear upon the organization of the participants' conduct; in turn their actions and activities in part reproduce the characteristics associated with particular situations or contexts. Ethnomethodology and conversation analysis adopt a rather different approach. Rather than treating a particular situation as a framework in which conduct takes place, they treat context as the product of the participants' actions and activities. Participants constitute circumstances and situations, activities and events, 'in and through' their social actions and activities. Garfinkel (1967) suggests for example:

> in contrast to certain versions of Durkheim that teach that the objective reality of social facts is sociology's fundamental principle, the lesson is taken instead and used as a study policy, that the objective reality of social facts as an ongoing accomplishment of the concerted activities of daily life, with the ordinary artful ways of that accomplishment being by members known, used, and taken for granted, is for members doing sociology, a fundamental phenomenon. (Garfinkel 1967: vii)

With regard to context and situation it is critical to note the concern with the 'ongoing accomplishment of the activities of daily life'. Unlike other forms of qualitative inquiry, ethnomethodology and conversation analysis are concerned with the ways in which social actions and activities emerge moment by moment; situations and circumstances are ongoingly accomplished by participants themselves from 'within' those settings.

In interaction participants produce their actions with regard to the conduct of others, and in particular the immediately preceding action or activity. In turn, their action forms the framework to which subsequent action is oriented. So for example participants produce actions with regard to the prior action and the frame of relevancies that it establishes; moreover, it is understood by virtue of its location with regard to preceding action(s). Actions are also prospectively oriented, designed to encourage, engender, even elicit subsequent action, which in turn form the basis to the participants' assessment of each others' and their own conduct.

Within the unfolding course of sequences of interaction then, participants build an 'architecture of intersubjectivity' (Heritage 1984: 254) in which they display their ongoing orientations towards the business at hand and the emerging turns at talk. Heritage (1984) refers to the 'context sensitive–context renewing' character of action-in-interaction and points to the emergent, flexible and contingent organization of conduct. The sequential organization of action in interaction is a pervasive feature of the ways in which participants both produce and make sense of each other's conduct.

Particular actions establish the sequential import of specific actions by co-participants, actions which are relevant within particular locations, and which in some cases, if they do not occur, they are 'noticeably' or accountably absent. Consider for example the ways in which questions establish the sequential relevance of an answer, and how an answer is recognizable and acceptable by virtue of its juxtaposition with a question; or how, as in the example discussed later, close inspection of a patient's eye is sensible and legitimate by virtue of the patient pointing to the object and describing the difficulty. More generally, action within interaction provides opportunities for subsequent action, and is designed to build possibilities for conduct. The sequential location of action within the emerging course of interaction is critical to the production and intelligibility of conduct, and therefore to the analysis of social action and activity.

The analytic focus of these investigations is with the practices and reasoning, the methods, through which participants produce their own actions and make sense of the actions of others. As an approach, Sacks suggests that this stands in stark contrast to the majority of the social scientific endeavour:

> A curious fact becomes apparent if you look at the first paragraph – it may occur in the third paragraph – of reportedly revolutionary treatises back to the pre-Socratics and extending up to at least Freud. You find that they all begin by saying something like this: 'About what I am going to talk about, people think they know but they don't. Furthermore if you tell them it doesn't change anything. They still walk round like they know although they are walking around in a dream world.' ... What we are interested in is, what is it that people seem to know and use? Here what people know and use is not to be mapped for each area onto what it is that science turns out to know, but is to be investigated itself. (Sacks, verbal quote in Hill and Crittenden 1968: 13)

Through detailed scrutiny of particular cases, fragments of action and interaction, analysis is directed towards explicating the resources, the competencies, upon which people rely in participating in interaction. Interaction, the emergent and sequential character of conduct, provides unique opportunities to explicate these resources. We can examine subsequent action(s) and activities to examine how participants themselves are responding to each other's conduct, and in turn how participants respond to the responses of others. Each action displays an understanding of the prior, an understanding which is oriented to in subsequent action, and which may be subject to elaboration, clarification or repair. Interaction provides us with the resources with which to begin to systematically examine the participants' relevancies; the ways in which they deal with the actions of others and co-participants respond to their own actions. In this way, the sequential organization of interaction is both a topic and resource in these investigations (see e.g. Zimmerman and Pollner 1971; Sacks *et al.* 1974).

FIELDWORK AND VIDEO DATA

Although the primary data for analysis are video recordings of naturally occurring activities, it is critical that the researcher undertakes more conventional fieldwork. For example, research on interaction in complex organizational environments requires the researcher to become familiar with the setting. It is necessary to understand the sorts of activities in which people engage, the events with which they deal, and the sorts of tools and technologies they rely upon to do their work. Therefore, to become familiar with the setting it is often necessary to undertake extensive participant and non-participant-observation, and in many cases to have lengthy discussions with participants themselves.

Understanding the events and activities in medical settings, for example, includes developing an understanding of the technical medical jargon that is used and how it is deployed. It is also important to become familiar with the tools and technologies used by participants and the ways in which the various systems operate and are used within the setting. So for example documents, records, manuals and log books are a feature of many organizational environments and play a critical part in the ways in which participants organize and report activities and events. Without knowing how documents, such as a patient's medical record, are organized, the categories of information they provide, and the purposes to which they are put, the field researcher may find it difficult to understand a range of potentially relevant activities that feature on the recordings. In many settings therefore it is critical that video recording is coupled with extensive fieldwork in which the researcher becomes increasingly familiar with the characteristics of the environment unavailable through recordings alone.

In our own research, we conduct fieldwork before recording, and ordinarily undertake successive periods of fieldwork and recording over some period of time. It is necessary to undertake small amounts of fieldwork prior to recording in order to be able to decide where to place the camera and microphone so that the most relevant (views on) activities are

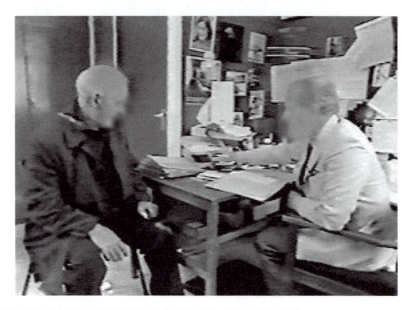

FIGURE 4.1   CAMERA ANGLE FOR THE MEDICAL CONSULTATION

captured. In the case of the medical consultation that we will discuss in detail later, our placement of the recording equipment was directed by specific concerns. Most notably, given our interest in bodily as well as spoken conduct, we positioned the camera in order to capture as much of the face and bodies of both participants as possible. The fairly standard positioning of the doctor and patient around the desk facilitated a relatively constant position. Additionally, we attempted to select an angle that enabled us to see clearly the objects on the desk in between the doctor and patient (Figure 4.1).

We routinely leave the camera running and therefore choose a wide enough angle to accommodate basic shifts in orientation and movement by the participants.[1] The main reasons for leaving the camera stationary in the setting are to allow the fieldworker to leave the consultation and to ensure that the participants are distracted as little as possible by the recording equipment. Goffman's powerful discussion of participation points to the inevitable significance of an individual within range of an event and in particular the person's contribution to the interaction (Goffman 1981). Both in undertaking field observation and video recording, we like other field researchers (see e.g. Goodwin 1981; Grimshaw 1982; Harper 1994; Prosser 1998) are sensitive to our part within and influence on the scene. Therefore we attempt to take precautions both to reduce 'reactivity' and to assess data for influence of the recording. Of course, the placement of the camera can help in this regard too. For ethical reasons, the patients are asked beforehand to participate in the study and thus they are aware that the camera is filming. However, the field researcher is able to assess where best to locate the camera so that participants are able to disregard the recording.

After an initial recording phase we often return to the setting for further fieldwork. For example, over the past few years we have undertaken a number of projects concerned with the control rooms and operation centres of London Underground. Following preliminary analysis, we returned to the control rooms to undertake more focused fieldwork and collect further video recordings (sometimes choosing different angles to provide access to different viewpoints on activities). This iterative characteristic of field studies is well known, and provides a critical resource not only for developing one's understanding of the setting, but also in refining analytic observations and insights. In certain cases, where we were puzzled by particular events we returned to the field with a small 'video Walkman' to play and discuss extracts from the video with the participants themselves; their observations not so much providing analytic resources but helping clarify understanding of particular incidents, specialized language or technologies.

ANALYSING CASES

Transcribing the data

Analysis of the video recordings involves the detailed scrutiny of particular fragments and we will consider one such fragment, a brief extract from the beginning of a medical consultation in this section. However, we will first consider how we initially approach the analysis of any fragment of data. One of the critical ways in which we can become familiar with a fragment and begin to explicate the arrangement and organization of the participants' actions is through the transcription of aspects of the interaction. To do this we draw on conventional orthographies used for the transcription of talk which provide a vehicle to begin to come to grips with the details of the talk and the ways in which it emerges. It allows us to clarify what's said, by whom and in what way, and to begin to explore potential relations between aspects of the interaction. The orthography used within conversation analysis was primarily devised by Gail Jefferson and we have summarized some of the symbols in the Appendix (see also Jefferson 1984). Transcription does not replace the video recording as data, but rather provides a resource through which the researcher can begin to become more familiar with details of the participants' conduct.

It is perhaps worthwhile introducing our example at this point. The fragment is drawn from a project concerned with medical practice in primary health care. It involved extensive fieldwork, discussions with practitioners and extensive video recording of actual consultations. The fragment involves the first few moments of a consultation. It gives a sense of how the consultation begins and the relevance of the various material sources to the interaction between patient and doctor.

Fragment 1   **Transcript 1**

                ((P. enters the surgery))

Dr: Do sit down::
             (5.5)
Dr: What's *up*?
             (4.8)
P: I've had a bad eye::: (.) °in there=
Dr: =Oh: yeah

Talk is laid out turn by turn, the length of silences and pauses measured in tenths of a second and captured in brackets, for example '(4.8)'. The colons, as in 'down::', indicate that the prior sound is stretched, the number of colons indicating the length of the sound. The underlinings, as in '*up*', indicate that the word, or part of the word, is emphasized. '°' indicates that the following word is said quietly, and '=' that the following utterance is latched to the prior. '(.)' indicates a mini-pause, a pause or silence of two-tenths of a second or less. Double brackets, '((P. enters the surgery))', house transcribers' descriptions of actions or events.

There is no general orthography used for the transcription of visual and tactile conduct, but over the years researchers have developed *ad-hoc* solutions to locating and characterizing action (see e.g. Goodwin 1981; Heath 1986; Kendon 1990). In our own studies we map fragments developing a characterization of at least the onset and completion of particular actions and their relations to each other. This often involves the use of graph paper, laying talk and silence horizontally across the page, and then mapping the details of the conduct in relation to each other. We also include notes on the use of various artefacts and significant changes in information displayed or documented within the environment (for example in records, on screens and display boards and the like). Consider the example shown in Figure 4.2. It is a version of one of the original 'maps' developed for the fragment under discussion. The transcript presents the participants' conduct horizontally, with dashes capturing the length of silences and pauses, one-tenth of a second indicated by one dash.

These more detailed transcriptions of a fragment are simply devices to enable the researcher to identify particular actions and to preserve a rough record of what has been found at some particular stage of the analysis. They are not designed to be read or used by others, or of course to provide a literal or true characterization of the events. However, they do provide a critical resource to help the researcher to establish the range and complexity of conduct within a particular fragment, and with which to begin to identify its character and location. Indeed, without logging the details of a fragment in this or a similar fashion, it is found that conduct is frequently mislocated, mischaracterized and in some cases missed all together. Transcription provides a vehicle for clarifying the location of actions and in exploring the potential relations between co-occurring and surrounding talk and bodily

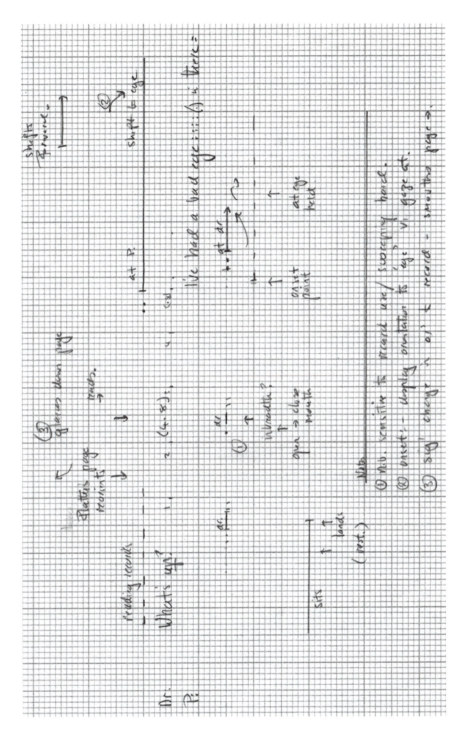

FIGURE 4.2 ORIGINAL DATA MAP FOR FRAGMENT 1

conduct. In particular, it is only through detailed investigation of the location and character of particular actions that we can begin to clarify their emergent and contingent relations between participants' conduct; the sequential character of action which is the pervasive organizational feature of human activity in social interaction.

The situated character of practical action, and the interest in the methodological resources used by the participants themselves, inevitably drives analytic attention towards the investigation of activities and events within the contexts in which they occur. Detailed and repeated inspection of the accomplishment of actual activities, coupled with the analytic orientations briefly discussed above, provide resources through which researchers can begin to identify the practices and reasoning through which particular events are produced and rendered intelligible.

In considering the fragment, for example, we would then want to develop a characterization of the activity which has evolved through our close looking in generating the transcript. To illustrate consider our description of this fragment.

Developing an analysis

As the patient enters the consulting room and walks towards the chair alongside the desk, the doctor utters 'What's *up*?' The utterance invites the patient to deliver his reason for seeking professional help. It projects a sequentially relevant action for the patient, and following a few seconds' silence, the patient does indeed deliver the appropriate response, 'I've had a bad eye::: (.)°in there.' The exchange involves the transition of the consultation from the 'preliminaries' to the 'business at hand', and the patient's response provides resources for subsequent enquiries, diagnosis and treatment. Progression into the business of the consultation is also dependent upon the bodily conduct of the participants and the use of particular tools and artefacts. It is worth noting at the outset for example that the patient's reply is delayed by four seconds or so, and is then accompanied by a gesture.

A second transcript, capturing particular aspects of their visual conduct, may be helpful. In this case the detailed 'map' depicted earlier has been pared down to leave those aspects most critical to the analysis. The transcript is accompanied by descriptions of particular actions or events (Figure 4.3).

The doctor produces the initiating utterance as the patient crosses the room. The patient sits down within a second or so, but remains silent. The doctor reads the medical records as the patient sits down. A few moments later, the doctor turns from the records to the patient. The patient immediately turns to the doctor and begins to reply. As he replies, he gestures towards his eye, and the doctor moves forward and inspects the difficulty.

The patient's reply is sensitive to the doctor's use of the medical record. He withholds his reply, the sequentially relevant response, until the doctor turns from the record to the patient and thereby visually completes the activity

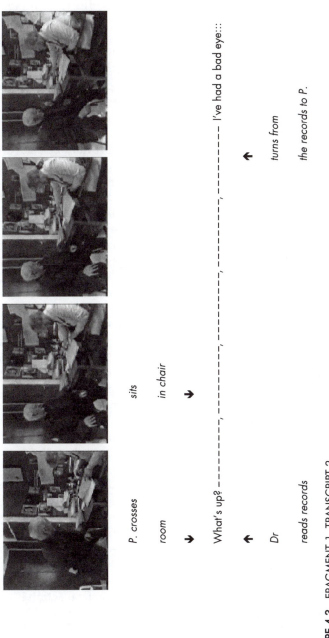

P. crosses   sits

room   in chair
  →   →

What's up? – – – – – – – – –, – – – – – – – – –, – – – – – – – – –, – – – – – – – – – I've had a bad eye:::

  ←   ←

Dr   turns from

reads records   the records to P.

FIGURE 4.3 FRAGMENT 1, TRANSCRIPT 2

in which he is engaged. The doctor's lack of orientation to the patient is legitimized by virtue of his reading the patient's medical record, as information gleaned from the record may be relevant to the subsequent proceedings. It should be added that glancing through the last few entries of a patient's record is a recurrent feature of the beginning of medical consultations at least in general practice. It provides information to enable the doctor to know, for example, whether the patient is returning to discuss a particular complaint, or whether the patient has suffered serious difficulties in the past which might be relevant to the presenting complaint.

There is further evidence to suggest that the patient's conduct is sensitive to the doctor's use of the medical record, and indeed, may encourage the doctor to bring the activity to a quick conclusion.

The patient glances at the doctor as he sits down, a juncture within the developing course of his own activity at which it may be relevant to reply and set the proceedings in motion. The doctor is reading the record. A moment later, the doctor raises his right hand and smoothes the page of the record. The gesture differentiates the doctor's activity. It displays a shift in alignment towards the document and potentially projects the possible completion of the reading activity by arranging the document as if in readiness for writing. As the hand presses the page, the patient turns to the doctor. He opens his mouth as if beginning to speak. As he opens his mouth, the doctor turns to another area of the page, while his hand moves forward to clasp a date stamp. The patient closes his mouth, turns away and licks his lips (Figure 4.4).

The patient therefore is sensitive to the ways in which the doctor reads and manipulates the medical records. The very lack of orientation by the doctor is accountable by virtue of his use of the record, and reading the record can be seen as relevant to the consultation and movement from the 'preliminaries' to the business at hand. Similarly, for the doctor, the patient's lack of immediate response, and his shifting orientation in the proceeding silence, is sensible by virtue of the patient's sensitivity to the use of the records. The medical records therefore are an integral feature of the participants' activities, both in the ways in which they produce their conduct, and in how they make sense of each other's actions.

One can also gain a feel for the emergent and contingent character of the participants' conduct. The patient's actions are sensitive to the emerging use of the record, they differentiate the actions of the doctor moment by moment within the developing course of the reading. Where the doctor looks, how he scans the page, his raising of the hand, the pressing of the page, inform the ongoing production of the patient's actions, just as the doctor himself is sensitive to the patient's shifting orientation to the activity. We can see therefore how the 'situated' and contingent character of practical action is shaped and created through the moment-by-moment production of the participants' actions. Each action is sensitive to the actions of the other, and provides the basis for subsequent conduct, as they emerge within the developing course of the activity.

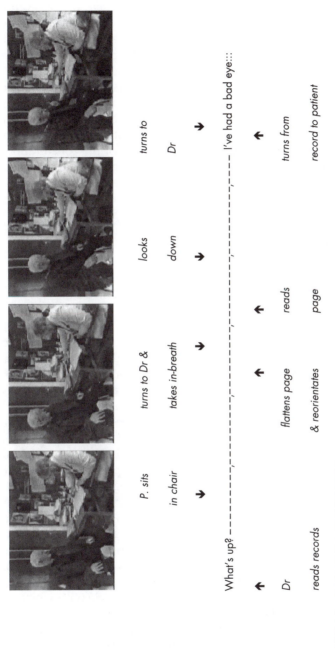

FIGURE 4.4 FRAGMENT 1, TRANSCRIPT 3

In this way therefore we can begin to disassemble aspects of the social and interactional organization which feature in the accomplishment of a particular event and provide for its character and uniqueness. Even this cursory glance at the fragment begins to reveal the complexity of the participants' activities and the resources which are brought to bear in the production and intelligibility of the beginning of the consultation. It reveals the emergent character of the participants' actions and the ways in which they are interactionally organized and accomplished. In the case at hand, it can be seen that while visual and tactile aspects of the participants' conduct are not organized on the turn-by-turn basis characteristic of talk, nonetheless the sequential character of conduct is a critical property of the production of action and its intelligibility. For example, the elicitation of the doctor's gaze is sequentially responsive to an action by the patient, and the doctor's reorientation forms the foundation to the beginning of the consultation. In turning to consider the methodological resources used by the participants in the activity's production and intelligibility therefore, attention inevitably turns to consider the ways in which actions are interactionally coordinated moment by moment, step by step. In this sense therefore context and intelligibility of the action is unavoidably and continuously emergent and assembled from within its production.

RECONSIDERING INTERACTION AND PHYSICAL SETTINGS

This analysis is designed to reveal how close looking at the details of interaction can be used to uncover critical resources used by participants in the organization of the medical encounter. As Hughes (1958) and many other ethnographers suggest, social interaction forms the foundation to the production of everyday activities, whether they involve a medical consultation, the operation of a control centre or a visit to museum or gallery (see e.g. Heath and Luff 2000; vom Lehn *et al.* 2001). Despite the recognition of the importance of interaction to everyday life and social organization within qualitative sociology, it has remained largely disregarded, 'noticed but not seen', remarked upon but to some extent unexplicated. It is not surprising however that ethnography, at least in sociology, has largely been unimpressed by the growing body of research concerned with language use and in particular talk in interaction. Such studies while providing impressive insight into the socially organized character of talk have seemed to disregard an array of considerations and concerns that form the focus of ethnographic inquiry. In this chapter, we wish to suggest that video-based field studies coupled with an appropriate analytic orientation, namely ethnomethodology and conversation analysis, can provide a vehicle with which to address one or two of the issues and substantive concerns that form part of more traditional ethnographic research, even though the phenomena of interest, the conceptual orientation and the ability to legitimize 'broader' contextual characteristics may seem somewhat over constrained.

Taking the example at hand, we can begin to examine the ways in which talk is inextricably embedded within the participants' visual and tactile conduct; their bodily conduct and the local ecology of objects and artefacts. Consider for example the patient's reply, his reason for seeking professional help. The response emerges in regard to the doctor's bodily conduct and in particular his visual realignment which enables him to see and look at the patient. The utterance is not only occasioned by the doctor's visual and vocal conduct, but also designed with regard to the accompanying bodily action, and in particular the ability of the doctor to see as well as hear about the source of the complaint. The patient's reply and gesture render the body relevant, in a particular way, then and there, and invite the doctor both to hear about and to inspect the complaint. The utterance, this single turn at talk, gains its sense and significance by virtue of the ways in which it invokes an aspect of the body, just as the visibility of a blemish in the eye provides sense to the utterance. In this, and a myriad of other ways, talk-in-interaction, and its significance then and there within the interaction, is accomplished through, and constitutes the relevance of the body and its conduct.

The spoken and bodily conduct of the participants is inseparable from, and reflexively constitutes, material features of the local environment, objects, artefacts and the like. For example, the initial delay in the patient's response is produced and accountable with regard to the patient sitting, the chair and its particular use marking the completion of a relevant course of action. The doctor's 'lack' of orientation towards the patient is not simply 'withholding gaze', but rather is sensible by virtue of his reading of the patient record and his use of the date stamp. As we have seen, the patient's own conduct is sensitive to the ways in which these artefacts are used, and even how the particular use of an artefact can prospectively display what it will take for it to be complete, and thereby serve to mark a potential turning point in the beginning of the consultation. These objects and artefacts come into play within the developing course of action. Not only is the participants' conduct oriented to these objects and artefacts in particular ways at particular moments, but also through the ways in which they are used, seen, noticed, disregarded and the like, the particular object gains a specific sense and relevance *from within the course of action*.

In undertaking video-based field studies of social interaction we have the opportunity of addressing characteristics of action and of settings which have formed a concern for more traditional ethnography. The physical environment, among other characteristics, is often treated as forming the framework for action and in various ways providing the resources including symbolic representations for organization and interpretation of action (see e.g. Blumer 1962). We too are keen to include the material environment, and of course bodily as well as spoken conduct, within the analytic scheme. Rather however than treating material realities as having an overarching influence on the field of conduct and thereby assuming that their sense and significance remains stable throughout the emerging course of events, such as a medical consultation, we need to examine the ways in which objects, artefacts and the like come to gain their particular significance at specific moments within courses of action. As we have seen, material features of the immediate setting are invoked, referred to, used, noticed, seen, at particular moments, for particular purposes, and they gain their sense or meaning at those moments from within the action in which they are momentarily rendered relevant. They feature both in the production of action and the ways in which the participants make sense of each other's conduct. The immediate ecology of objects and artefacts provides resources for the production of action, and in the ways in which participants themselves recognize and make sense of each other's conduct. The sense and determination of the material environments is *reflexively* constituted, in and through the participants' action and interaction (see also Wootton 1994; Goodwin 1995; Streeck 1996; Heath and Hindmarsh 2000; Hindmarsh and Heath 2000).

This concern with the ways in which the material environment features in practical action and interaction is reflected in the growing body of empirical research concerned with tools and technologies in complex organizational environments. This corpus of research, commonly known as 'workplace studies' (see for example Luff *et al.* 2000), consists of naturalistic studies of work, interaction and technology and provides programmatic examples of the ways in which video-based field studies of interaction can bear upon topic and concerns ordinarily associated with more traditional ethnography. These studies consist of analyses of work and interaction in settings such as control centres, news rooms, banks, and the like. Not only do they powerfully illustrate the importance of taking material features of the environment such as tools and artefacts seriously, but also, in addressing the ways in which such tools and the complex array of information they provide, feature in action and social interaction. In settings such as control rooms, there is a vast array of information provided in documents, on monitors, across diagrams at any one time, the critical issue is exploring and demonstrating what is relevant and how it is constituted as relevant, within action and interaction (see for example Heath and Luff 2000). If you like, such settings provide a substantive demonstration of the issues raised throughout this chapter; our problem is not simply taking the material environment seriously (like other potentially relevant features such as the organizational setting, participants' background and the like) but rather analytically demonstrating how such characteristics become relevant and reflexively constituted in action. Video recordings, often using multiple cameras, augmented by extensive fieldwork, provide unprecedented access to such complex tasks, and ethnomethodology and conversation analysis provide resources through which we can begin to unpack the interactional organization of activities and events in these complex technological settings and demonstrate the relevance of environment to actual courses of action. Such studies are not only beginning to provide a distinctive contribution to our understanding of organizational activities, but also changing the ways in which the social and cognitive scientists conceive of the interaction between human beings and technologies such as computers.

NOTE

1   We are currently using both analogue and digital video equipment. The analogue cameras are Sony Hi8 TRV65E, and digital, Sony TRV900E. We primarily use Sony EVC 500 machines for analysis; they have stable still frame and reasonable slow motion. It is normally necessary to use separate microphones and we mainly use a multi-directional microphone PZM, but in certain settings with significant background noise a mono-directional microphone such as a Sennheiser MKE300 is more successful. We always make and work on copies of the original data, as the repeated replaying necessary during transcription and analysis can severely damage tapes.

APPENDIX: CONVENTIONS FOR TRANSCRIBING TALK

The *Identity* of the speaker is indicated in the margin, sometimes alongside a line number. This example shows line 30 of a transcript, in which the patient is the speaker:

    30   P: in fact I'll do it right now.

(0.6)	A pause timed in tenths of a second
(.)	A pause which is noticeable but too short to measure
=	No discernible interval between adjacent utterances
erm:::	Elongated sounds – the longer the elongation, the more colons are added to the utterance or section of the utterance but- An abrupt cut-off of an utterance or part of an utterance is marked by a dash
under	Emphasized stretches of talk are underlined
>right<	Faster stretches of talk
°that°	Quieter stretches of talk
.	A stopping fall in tone, not necessarily the end of a sentence
,	Continuing intonation, not necessarily between clauses of sentences
?	Rising inflection, not necessarily a question
∧	Marked rising shift in intonation
∨	Marked falling shift in intonation
°hhh	In-breath
hhh	Out-breath

Overlapping utterances are marked by parallel square brackets:

    e.g.
    30 P: in fa [ct I'll do it right now.
    31 D: [oh right, okay

REFERENCES

Atkinson, P. (1995) *Medical Talk and Medical Work: The Liturgy of the Clinic*. London: Sage.

Becker, H. (1963) *The Outsiders*. New York: Free Press.

Bergmann, J.R. (1992) 'Veiled morality: notes on discretion in psychiatry', in P. Drew and J. Heritage (eds) *Talk at Work: Interaction in Institutional Settings*. Cambridge: Cambridge University Press.

Blumer, H. (1962) 'Society as symbolic interaction', in A. Rose (ed.) *Human Behaviour and Social Processes*, pp. 179–192. London: Routledge and Kegan Paul.

Boden, D. and Zimmerman, D.H. (eds) (1991) *Talk and Social Structure*. Oxford: Polity.

Davis, F. (1963) *Passage through Crisis: Polio Victims and their Families*. Indianapolis, IN: Bobbs-Merrill.

Drew, P. and Heritage, J. (eds) (1992) *Talk at Work*. Cambridge: Cambridge University Press.

Garfinkel, H. (1967) *Studies in Ethnomethodology*. Englewood Cliffs, NJ: Prentice-Hall.

Glaser, B. and Strauss, A. (1965) *Awareness of Dying*. Chicago: Aldine.

Goffman, E. (1961) *Asylums*. New York: Anchor.

Goffman, E. (1963) *Behaviour in Public Places: Notes on the Social Organization of Gatherings*. New York: Free Press.

Goffman, E. (1967) *Interaction Ritual*. New York: Doubleday.

Goffman, E. (1981) *Forms of Talk*. Oxford: Basil Blackwell.

Goffman, E. (1983) 'The interaction order: American Sociological Association, 1982 Presidential Address', *American Sociological Review* 48(1): 1–17.

Goodwin, C. (1981) *Conversational Organisation: Interaction between a Speaker and Hearer*. London: Academic Press.

Goodwin, C. (1995) 'Seeing in depth', *Social Studies of Science* 25(2): 237–274.

Grimshaw, A.D. (1982) 'Sound-image data records for research on social inter-action', *Sociological Methods and Research*, Special Issue on Sound-Image Records in Social Interaction Research 11(2): 121–144.

Harper, D. (1994) 'On the authority of the image: visual methods at the cross-roads', in N.K. Denzin and Y.S. Lincoln (eds) *Handbook of Qualitative Research*. Thousand Oaks, CA: Sage.

Have, P. ten (1991) 'Talk and institution: a reconsideration of the "asymmetry" of doctor–patient interaction', in D. Boden and D.H. Zimmerman (eds) *Talk and Social Structure: Studies in Ethnomethodology and Conversation Analysis*. Cambridge: Polity.

Heath, C.C. (1986) *Body Movement and Speech in Medical Interaction*. Cambridge: Cambridge University Press (Editions de la Maison des Science de l'Homme, Paris).

Heath, C. and Hindmarsh, J. (2000) 'Configuring action in objects: from mutual spaces to media spaces', *Mind, Culture and Activity* 7(1/2): 81–104.

Heath, C. and Luff, P. (2000) *Technology in Action*. Cambridge: Cambridge University Press.

Heritage, J. (1984) *Garfinkel and Ethnomethodology*. Cambridge: Polity.

Heritage, J. and Atkinson, P. (1984) 'Introduction', in P. Atkinson and J. Heritage (eds) *Structures of Social Action: Studies in Conversation Analysis*. Cambridge: Cambridge University Press.

Hill, R.J. and Crittenden, K.S. (eds) (1968) *Proceedings of the Purdue Symposium on Ethnomethodology*. Institute Monograph Series no. 1, Institute for the Study of Social Change, Purdue University.

Hindmarsh, J. and Heath, C. (2000) 'Sharing the tools of the trade: the interactional constitution of workplace objects', *Journal of Contemporary Ethnography* 29(5): 517–556.

Hughes, E.C. (1958) *Men and their Work*. Glencoe, IL: Free Press.

Hughes, E.C. (1971) *The Sociological Eye*. Chicago: Aldine.

Jefferson, G. (1984) 'Transcript notation', in J.M. Atkinson and J. Heritage (eds) *Structures of Social Action: Studies in Conversation Analysis*. Cambridge: Cambridge University Press.

Kendon, A. (1990) *Conducting Interaction: Patterns of Behaviour in Focussed Encounters*. Cambridge: Cambridge University Press.

Luff, P., Hindmarsh, J. and Heath, C. (2000) *Workplace Studies: Recovering Work Practice and Informing System Design*. Cambridge: Cambridge University Press.

Maynard, D.W. (1992) 'On clinicians co-implicating recipients' perspective in the delivery of diagnostic news', in P. Drew and J. Heritage (eds) *Talk at Work: Interaction in Institutional Settings*. Cambridge: Cambridge University Press.

Peräkylä, A. (1998) 'Authority and intersubjectivity: the delivery of diagnosis in primary health care', *Social Psychology Quarterly* 61: 301–320.

Pilnick, A. (1998) '"Why didn't you just say that?" Dealing with issues of asymmetry, knowledge and competence in the pharmacist/client encounter', *Sociology of Health and Illness* 20(1): 29–51.

Prosser, J. (ed.) (1998) *Image-based Research: A Sourcebook for Qualitative Researchers*. London: Falmer.

Roth, J. (1963) *Timetables: Structuring the Passage of Time in Hospital Treatment and Other Careers*. Indianapolis, IN: Bobbs-Merrill.

Sacks, H. (1992) *Lectures in Conversation, Volumes I and II*. Oxford: Blackwell.

Sacks, H., Schegloff, E.A. and Jefferson, G. (1974) 'A simplest systematics for the organization of turn-taking for conversation', *Language* 50(4): 696–735.

Schegloff, E.A. and Sacks, H. (1974) 'Opening up closings', in R. Turner (ed.) *Ethnomethodology: Selected Readings*. Harmondsworth: Penguin.

Silverman, D. (1999) 'Warriors or collaborators: reworking methodological controversies in the study of institutional interaction', in S. Sarangi and C. Roberts (eds) *Talk, Work and Institutional Order: Discourse in Medical, Mediation, and Management Settings*. Berlin: Mouton de Gruyter.

Simmel, G. (1950) *The Sociology of Georg Simmel*, edited by K. Wolff. Glencoe, IL: Free Press.

Strauss, A.L. (1964) *Psychiatric Institutions and Ideologies*. Glencoe, IL: Free Press.

Streeck, J. (1996) 'How to do things with things: objets trouvés and symbolization', *Human Studies* 19: 365–384.

Strong, P.M. (1979) *The Ceremonial Order of the Clinic*. London: Routledge and Kegan Paul.

vom Lehn, D., Heath, C. and Hindmarsh, J. (2001) 'Exhibiting interaction: conduct and collaboration in museums and galleries', *Symbolic Interaction* 24(2): 189–216.

Wootton, A.J. (1994) 'Object transfer, intersubjectivity and third position repair: early developmental observations of one child', *Journal of Child Language* 21: 543–564.

Zimmerman, D.H. and Pollner, M. (1971) 'The everyday world as phenomenon', in J.D. Douglas (ed.) *Understanding Everyday Life*. London: Routledge and Kegan Paul.

PART 2

GENERALIZATION, INTERPRETATION AND ANALYSIS

5 GENERALIZATION IN INTERPRETIVE RESEARCH

Malcolm Williams

In this chapter I will consider the question of whether it is possible to generalize from the results of interpretive research.[1] My argument will be that generalizations are legitimate if they are treated and made explicitly as (what I term) *moderatum* generalizations, within the context of a pluralistic approach to research. I will further argue that an affirmation of the possibility of generalization is an acknowledgement of the limits of interpretivism.

In sociology the question of generalization in interpretive research lies at the heart of an old debate about whether the discipline is nomothetic or ideographic in character – broadly speaking whether it is 'scientific' or 'humanistic'. If it is the former, then of course generalization, as part of an explanation–prediction schema in science, is permissible. Yet many of those working in the interpretivist tradition have often cast doubt upon whether this is the case and indeed the method itself is adopted because, it is said, the self-reflective, autonomous nature of human subjects produce states which are not amenable to the explanation–prediction schema of natural science.

This produces a problem for interpretive research. An ideographic discipline concerns itself with the understanding of an instance in a unique context. Analogously for the artist the appreciation and understanding of (say) Sisley's painting of the riverbank at St Mamnés cannot be extended to statements about the specifications of riverbanks elsewhere; it is intended as a unique appreciation of a moment. Likewise, for sociologists to interpret a set of biographical outcomes in a single agent, or the social milieu of group of agents, at a given time is a unique act. An ideographic account is an interpretation by a situated agent (the researcher) of a never to be repeated event or setting. It follows from this that the particulars of such accounts of the social world therefore cannot be used to generalize to other instances. Such a relativity of perspective is undoubtedly fruitful in a humanistic contemplation of the social world, where the aim is to produce the social equivalent of a Sisley painting, but it won't do in circumstances where decisions affecting the emotional and material existence of people are made on the basis of evidence produced. Increasingly interpretive research, in the form of focus groups or in-depth interviews, is called upon to provide just such evidence in the creation of local or national policy, or to evaluate existing programmes. Policy-makers need data they can rely on to reach their decisions. As Ray Rist (1998) put it:

What are the contours of the issue? Is the problem or condition one that is larger now than before, about the same, or smaller? Is anything known about whether the nature of the condition has changed? Do the same target populations, areas, or institutions experience this condition now as earlier? … What are the different understandings about the condition, its causes and effects? (Rist 1998: 406)

Now of course, some of the foregoing could be obtained through survey research, but by no means all. Sensitive topics or difficult to research populations (for example) can be known only through interpretive methods (see for example Renzetti and Lee 1993). Moreover survey research cannot usually provide the contextual detail necessary to interpret even its own results; we quite often need to know the ethnographic basis of the statistics produced by the survey (Gephart 1988).

If interpretivism is to be any use at all in social policy formulation or evaluation it must be able to say something authoritative about instances beyond the specific ones of the research. Moreover it is not just an issue for the pragmatic investigation of social problems or policy choices; the sociologist is interested in knowing something of the social world beyond isolated and fragmented accounts of interactions, or individual biographies. The sociologist wants to know about how social 'structures' are created, maintained or destroyed and must therefore look to evidence manifested in the specific features of the social world to do so. Such features are quite often at the level of micro-detail, but must be understood in such a way as to explain how they do, or do not, create, reproduce or destroy social structures. If one looks to the history of sociology, it is precisely at the level of micro-detail that researchers have claimed to find evidence of structure and indeed many of the classic interpretivist studies in sociology are attempts to explain particular forms of social structure.

In this chapter I will proceed as follows: first, I will provide some illustrations of the manifestation of generalization in interpretive research and the denial of its possibility by methodologists. This denial, I will suggest, is based on a narrow definition of what it means to generalize. Having outlined a possible form that generalization might take in interpretivism, in the second section of the chapter I discuss its limits and possibilities. Finally I will conclude that a recognition of such limits and possibilities entails the prospect of a reconciliation between the ideographic and nomothetic traditions.

DOING IT AND DENYING IT

Doing it

I offer two brief examples to illustrate the kinds of claims that are made in interpretive research. The first study, of children and fruit machine gambling (Fisher 1993), is a topic that is at least visually familiar to many of us in contemporary western societies. It can be seen as typical of the many projects aimed at testing or developing theoretical constructs that have potentially important sociological or policy implications. Indeed Sue Fisher's work, and a great many studies of this kind, has enormous importance in helping us to understand an actual or potential social problem. Her study was based upon an unobtrusive participant-observation of children in a gaming arcade (she worked as a part-time cashier in the arcade). Additionally she conducted ten in-depth interviews with young fruit machine players and four group interviews with secondary school children (Fisher 1993: 454). Fisher's observations led her to construct a typology of five categories of fruit machine player: Arcade Kings, Machine Beaters, Rent-a-Spacers, Action Seekers and Escape Artists (1993: 458). The typologies describe strategies of playing, the meanings that players attached to their activity, or the way in which individuals used the social space of the arcade. For example, Machine Beaters were individualists who liked to play alone with the aim of 'beating the machine' (1993: 462–463), Rent-a-Spacers primarily used the arcade as a meeting place, while Escape Artists gamble primarily to escape personal problems. Fisher concludes that while existing sociological explanations of gambling are heuristically useful, an examination of juvenile fruit machine gambling demonstrates 'the diversity of primary orientations which are intrinsic to gambling' (1993: 470). In a society where juvenile gambling is considered to be a social problem a study such as this allows us to see that gambling is not an homogeneous concept. The implication is that strategies to discourage such practices must arise from a consideration of its heterogeneity. Fisher's investigative strategy, if not the only one, was probably the best available in that micro-level detail was required to establish such heterogeneity.

Nevertheless she doesn't tell us why the particular arcade was chosen, why she conducted the number of interviews she did, nor the basis upon which respondents were selected. The 'typicality' of the location and the subsequent findings are simply assumed.

The second study is also about the social milieu of young people, but this time is concerned with youth style and musical taste. The author, Andy Bennett (1999), maintains that 'musical and stylistic sensibilities exhibited by the young people involved in the dance music scene are clear examples of a form of late modern "sociality" rather than a fixed subcultural group' (Bennett 1999: 599). The article itself uses a style of argument currently popular in interpretive sociology, whereby inductive support for one's argument is drawn variously from theoretical positions (in this case Maffesoli 1996), other interpretive studies (here Thornton 1995), second-order summaries of other studies (here Shields 1992),[2] as well as original research. The position Bennett advances is quite a plausible one, but the evidence itself has a differential status which is not discussed. Thornton (1995) herself claims to have conducted observations at over 200 discos, clubs, raves and concerts between 1988 and 1992 and maintains that 'I was unable to find a crowd I could comfortably identify as typical, average, ordinary, majority or mainstream' (1995: 106). Conversely Bennett claims that 'for many enthusiasts "clubbing" appears to be regarded less as a singular definable activity and more as a series of fragmented, temporal experiences' is 'clearly illustrated' (1999: 611) on the basis of one conversation with clubbers in Newcastle. Though the evidence in both cases supports Bennett's argument, the status of each set of evidence is at least quantitatively different. Of course it may be that Bennett's conclusion is based upon a great deal more observation than he reveals and it is also possible that his informants are very much more typical (in their untypicality) than many of Thornton's informers.

In each study the researcher attempts to interpret what is going on according to the subjective frame of reference of those observed, to capture the nuances and the singular characteristics of the social environment. In both they are inferring from specific instances to the characteristics of a wider social milieu. Both wished to use the evidence to support a sociological argument that the world is a particular way. Their work, metaphorically speaking, is not an appreciation of the riverbank at St Mamnés, but is a stronger claim about the way riverbanks are!

Of course their explanations may or may not be 'right' or 'correct' and indeed both researchers would probably stress the fallibility and incompleteness of the generalizations they make. Nevertheless to investigate is to ask 'why' questions, to seek explanations, however speculatively or tentatively held; in this respect there is no logical difference between the work of an interpretive researcher conducting detailed observations of a social setting and a large-scale national survey.

Denying it

Both Fisher and Bennett make generalizing claims, yet neither acknowledge nor deny they are doing so. Indeed this is not unusual; few interpretive accounts ever do discuss such things. The failure of a lot of empirical research to engage with these questions does not necessarily indicate poor quality research, but rather might itself be seen as an outcome of unfinished methodological business in interpretivism – specifically, whether it is, can or should be a nomothetic discipline.

Though the distinction and ensuing debate between the nomothetic and ideographic approach to studying the social world has its origins in the *methodenstreit* dispute of the nineteenth century, such debates have continued to preoccupy methodologists for much of the twentieth century. Many of the issues about the status of interpretivism can, as Martyn Hammersley (1989) documents, be found in the work of Herbert Blumer. This is not to suggest that Blumer is somehow the author of the present situation, but rather that his work typifies the longstanding angst in interpretivist methodology about the epistemological status of the method. Blumer's contradictory statements about the possibility of a social science, led him to both criticize and endorse scientific method, at the same time as advocating a 'naturalistic' approach to investigation.[3] While trying to bridge the gap between nomothetic and ideographic approaches, he alternately leaned toward each. Blumer, of course, was in the symbolic interactionist tradition, which while emphasizing the indeterminism of human action, nevertheless aimed to uncover processes in social life (Hammersley 1989: 162). Thus a requirement must be that the sociologist move from interpretations of specific agents' actions and situations, to social explanation.

Blumer's legacy, in interpretivism, is a fractured one. On the one hand there have been attempts to develop the kinds of non-statistical, yet rigorous scientific approach to the method Blumer favoured, in analytic induction (which I will discuss below) and grounded theory. On the other hand there has been a plethora of cross-influences with ethnomethodology, conflict theory, labelling theory, critical theory etc. The methodological priorities and messages were very different in each and often incompatible. While survey researchers could agree on a number of key tenets to the approach (e.g. the centrality of probability, reliability of instruments etc.) there was little the various strands of interpretivism could agree on, other than the importance of meaning, though even here this was a resource for most approaches, but became a topic itself for ethnomethodology (Williams and May 1996: 73–76).

It remains, however, that with a few honourable exceptions the methodological issues raised by Blumer's work, particularly that of the status of interpretive knowledge, have not been carried forward in a great deal of empirical research and as Hammersley (1989: 220) concludes, 'there has been a tendency in recent years to ignore the problems, and to forget the diversity of views adopted by both advocates and critics of qualitative method'. Indeed in the case of a great deal of interpretivism, Alan Bryman's (1988, 1998) contention that there is a disjunction between epistemology/methodology and method seems to be correct. One might argue, as I have elsewhere (Williams 2000: 87–103), that the adoption of interpretivist methods has quite often been the result more of adherence to an anti-science position than the utility of the method itself. The post-Kuhnian anti-positivist revolution of the 1960s and 1970s was not conducive to a fruitful discussion of issues such as generalization in interpretivism, because as Altheide and Johnson (1998) point out the 'traditional criteria of methodological adequacy were formulated and essentially "owned" by positivism' (1998: 286). To discuss generalization at all was to play by the positivists' rules. Instead methodological concerns have usually since translated into a search for 'interpretive validity' of one sort or another (validity as culture, as ideology, as gender, as language etc.) with concern more for the authenticity of contextual understanding.

Thus the possibility of generalization is rarely denied outright and where it is denied, caveats are often entered. In order to throw the issue into the sharpest light it is worth looking at two of the outright denials, the first from Norman Denzin (1983) and the second from Guba and Lincoln (1982).

Denzin (1983: 133), in claiming that 'the interpretivist rejects generalization as a goal and never aims to draw randomly selected samples of human experience', maintains that every instance of human interaction represents a 'slice from the lifeworld' (Denzin 1983: 134), carrying layered meanings which come in multiples and are often contradictory. The core of Denzin's argument can be summarized as individual consciousnesses are free to attach different meanings to the same actions or circumstances. Conversely different actions can arise out of similarly expressed meanings. Therefore there is an 'inherent indeterminateness in the lifeworld' (Denzin 1983: 133) which leads to too much variability to allow the possibility of generalization from a specific situation to others.

In rather similar vein Guba and Lincoln (1982) maintain that

> The aim of inquiry is to develop an ideographic body of knowledge. This knowledge is best encapsulated in a series of 'working hypotheses' that describe the individual case. Generalizations are impossible since phenomena are neither time- nor context-free. (Guba and Lincoln 1982: 238)

If the foregoing was right then generalization in interpretive research would indeed be impossible, but we have already seen that interpretivists do generalize. How can this be? The problem may well lie in what is meant by generalization.

Denzin attributes, to those he calls 'positivists', the following position:

> references to the social world that could not be verified under quantifiable, observable, scientifically controlled conditions must – following Wittgenstein's dictum – 'be passed over in silence'. (Denzin 1983: 132)

Such a position is probably one unrecognizable to even the most militant logical positivists and the generalizations that would emerge from the variant of 'positivist' sociology that Denzin paints could be made only in the 'closed' system of the laboratory. Open systems could not be studied and probabilistic conclusions would be invalid. If the conditions specified by Denzin are what are required for generalization, then I would have to agree with him that it is impossible in sociology and probably in quite a lot of the natural sciences too!

Guba and Lincoln (1982) similarly assert that 'Generalizations are impossible since phenomena are neither time- nor context-free'.[4] This would rule out generalization in complex biological systems, where for example the concept of 'fitness' or 'adaptability' can change over short spaces of time and between places (Kincaid 1996: 60).

One begins to get the impression that what Denzin (1983) and Guba and Lincoln (1982) mean by 'generalization' does not fully express all the available meanings. Let me suggest three possible meanings (there may be more):

Total generalizations: where situation S^1 is identical to S in every detail. Thus S^1 is not a copy of S but an instance of a general deterministic law that governs S also.[5] Such generalizations are in fact axioms and do no more than express instances of particular laws. Thus the rate of cooling of an electric element is an instance of (and calculable through) the second law of thermodynamics.

Statistical generalizations: where the probability of situation *S* occurring more widely can be estimated from instances of *s*. This is simply the relationship between sample and population and is the basis upon which most generalizations (other than some in physics and chemistry) in the natural sciences are made. It is, of course, the same basis upon which survey researchers in sociology generalize. The sociological survey usually depends upon some form of probability sampling, whereby within each stratum every case will have the same probability of selection. The survey researcher mostly depends upon the possibility of drawing the sample from a sampling frame, though sometimes (and this is more the case in the natural sciences) alternative means of inference and counting are used (see Bishop *et al.* 1975). Importantly however, the researcher is able to statistically express the level of confidence she has that her sample represents the population.

Moderatum generalizations: where aspects of *S* can be seen to be instances of a broader recognizable set of features. This is the form of generalization made in interpretive research, either knowingly or unknowingly. Bennett's assertion

> that such fluid and eclectic forms of music consumption, while they may assume particular forms of significance for clubbers, are not in fact restricted to urban dance music clubs but are also central to other aspects of youth and youth culture (Bennett 1999: 612)

is an example of such a general feature capable of reworking and enriching through specific instances of music consumption.

Outside of the axiomatic laws of nature specified in physics, chemistry and their cognate disciplines, total generalizations are impossible. Much of the world, natural and social, consists of complex phenomena, for which no laws (or at least only statistical laws) are available. But of course, even the complex phenomena of open systems lend themselves to statistical prediction to varying degrees of success (see for example Casti 1991). Finally *moderatum* generalizations in their simplest form are the basis of inductive reasoning in what Schutz (1972 [1932]) called 'the lifeworld', they are the generalizations of everyday life. Which of these does Denzin (1983) and Guba and Lincoln (1982) say are impossible? Well, it seems clear that the first is impossible in the social world and this seems to be trivially true. The second type of generalization, while possible in the social world, cannot usually be made from the kind of data generated by interpretive research. On the first two counts then, the generalization of interpretive findings is impossible, but what interpretivists do and I would suggest they are right to do, is make *moderatum* generalizations.

LIMITS AND POSSIBILITIES OF GENERALIZATION
IN INTERPRETIVIST RESEARCH

To disagree with the rather stark position of Denzin (1983) and Guba and Lincoln (1982) above is not to embrace one which denies the problems raised by attempts to generalize. It is however a position which rejects the suggestion that interpretations and explanation-generalization are logically incompatible. Their compatibility does, however, depend on recognizing the limits to generalization. In this section of the chapter I will discuss these limits and some of the attempts to address them before briefly setting out the case for *moderatum* generalizations.

The limits to which I refer are quite separate to the objections raised by Denzin (1983) and Guba and Lincoln (1982) and arise from problems in sampling, in the categories and representativeness of empirical generalizations and the wider theoretical inferences that might be made from such data.

Sampling

Once a research question is identified, a decision must be made in respect of who, or what, will be the focus of that investigation. Questions of generalization are tied to those of sampling because the sample is the bearer of those characteristics that it is wished to infer to a wider population. Survey researchers wishing to make inferences about a population will decide which are the appropriate sampling units and (as I noted above), wherever possible, will construct a probability sample. When this is not possible they will construct a non-probability sample (such as a quota sample) that emulates as accurately as possible a probability sample (Fink 1995: 19). Though such samples are not impossible in interpretive research, that interpretive methods are being used may be because the population in question is rare, elusive or the research must be covert (see for example studies by Fielding 1982; Holdaway 1982). Yet if it is accepted that generalization from interpretive data is a legitimate goal, then presumably interpretivists need a sample which will reflect the relevant characteristics of the wider group to which they wish to generalize. This is a matter that has been considered in some detail by Jennifer Mason (1996).

Mason (1996: 92–93) identifies four different sampling strategies in research. First, statistically representative samples (generally not possible or suitable in interpretivist research). Second, ad-hoc samples, where no selection categories are specified. This, as she points out, is often seen as the only alternative to the first strategy and advises against this approach because it limits the 'analytic potential of the study' (1996: 92). Such a sample never is truly ad hoc, because the researcher must inevitably use some criteria of selection. Third, a sample designed to provide a detailed, close-up or meticulous view of cases. The case, or unit, here may be a single individual, location language, document, conversation etc. Her fourth type of sample is that based upon a relevant range of units, related to a 'wider universe', but not representing it directly. The range referred to here might incorporate a range of experiences, characteristics, processes, types, categories, cases or examples, and so on (Mason 1996: 92).

The last two strategies may well be the best available, but in each a decision must be made as to what will count as representative cases, or relevant units. Of course both the interpretivist and the survey researcher, or experimenter, must decide the population about which inferences are to be made and this and the inferences themselves may not be right, but at least the survey researcher knows probabilistically how widely the identified sample characteristics can be inferred to the population (this of course assumes an adequate sampling frame). The survey researcher, for example, may hypothesize that there is a relationship between class and educational attainment. The hypothesis might have been wrong and it might have been the wrong hypothesis, but at least the existence (positive or negative) or non-existence of a relationship can be shown. No probability can be attached to any characteristic confirming or disconfirming the interpretivist's hypothesis.

For many interpretivists the last point constitutes a logical mistake – as Mason (1996: 91) claims, 'qualitative research uses a different analytical logic'.[6] This different 'logic' was perhaps most clearly expressed in Znaniecki's (1934) claims for analytic induction, which somewhat ironically makes generalizing claims very much stronger than most in survey research.

Znaniecki's method of analytic induction implicitly side-steps the sampling issue by first testing a hypothesis on a single or limited range of cases and continuing to do this until a disconfirming case is found, or until the point is reached when further study will tell us nothing new (1934: 249). Disconfirming cases lead to a revision of the hypothesis and the same procedure is followed until further disconfirmation, or again, until nothing new can be said. Znaniecki contrasts analytic induction with, what he calls, enumerative induction (statistical probability) and maintains that the former is the true method of science (1934: 236–237). It is also (he says) the superior method because it allows us to establish causal relationships (rather than probabilistic ones) by identifying the essential characteristics of the phenomena under study.

The sampling problem, as defined previously, is indeed avoided because every case selected is part of the sample until found to be otherwise. However, the assumptions made about the 'sample' then obtained do not hold and this was noted as early as 1951 by Robinson. According to the latter, Znaniecki's claim to be able to establish causal relationships by identifying essential characteristics, is unjustified (Robinson 1951: 817–818). What the method actually leads us to is the identification of the necessary conditions that must have been in place for the phenomenon to occur. Analytic induction studies only those cases in which the phenomenon occurs, while enumerative induction, the method of survey research, studies both those where it does and where it does not occur. Therefore, Robinson maintains, analytic induction cannot discover the sufficient conditions for the phenomenon to be explained. For example unemployment might be a necessary condition to bring about poverty in identified cases, but by studying only cases of unemployment it cannot be identified as a sufficient condition because we do not know whether it is present in the unexamined cases. Analytic induction was developed further by Cressey (1950) and Lindesmith (1968 [1947]), but these versions (and later ones) still do not overcome the inductive problem of inferring from a small number of known cases to those which are unknown. Other equally rigorous approaches based on grounded theory (Glaser and Strauss 1967) or case study research (see Gomm *et al.* 2000 for a discussion of this) must still encounter a variant of the inductive problem.

Categories

The identification of the essential characteristics, either in choosing or rejecting cases in analytic induction, or in sampling in interpretive research more generally, is a problem of decisions about categories. The categories come in many types: people, physical settings, cultural artefacts, language. Moreover the researcher may rely on these empirical characteristics to make theoretical claims (Hammersley 1992). The category problem takes two forms: first, that of the ontological status of categories, and second, the non-equivalence of categories in respect of their relationship to each other.

Generalizations have very different ontological statuses. Fisher (1993: 454), for example, tells us that most fruit machines have the same basic design. Likewise the physical description of the amusement arcade in which she made her observations, is a familiar one, even to non-aficionados. Thus not only will these characteristics constrain or enable their users in particular ways, but also an approximately similar environment will enable and constrain arcade users in other places. Generalizations made to other places will be of the *moderatum* kind, but they will have a validity greater than other kinds of categories that might derive from cultural characteristics. Fruit machines and gaming arcades are socially constructed, but they also have physical characteristics that are less transient, and therefore more easily verifiable in other instances, than those which attach to people.

Second, while we can talk of (for example) generalizations about parts of the physical environment having a greater validity than those about cultural characteristics, how do we measure that validity? Is a generalization about a fruit machine in Devon twice as likely to be right than one about a gambling strategy – or three times as likely, or equal? The problem is that the meanings of the actors can be of very different kinds. Kincaid (1996: 192), for example, lists five different uses of the term (Perceptual, Doxastic, Intentional, Linguistic, Symbolic, Normative). The nature of a generalizing claim about intentional meaning (of the kind made by Bennett 1999) or of normative meaning (of the kind made by Fisher 1993) – what norms the behaviour of the individual reflects or embodies, are then quite different to each other.

Third, as Martín Sánchez-Jankowski describes in Chapter 6 in this volume, the success of representing any setting will be strongly influenced by the resources available to the researcher. The researcher's ability to interpret sense data and to avoid reading too much or not enough into a situation will depend on personal experiences. Cultural consistency may be the basis for generalization, but one has to be able to recognize that cultural consistency.

In this respect the relationship of the researcher to the researched becomes important. As Jankowski points out, this doesn't mean that only insider accounts are admissible, but that one needs experiential knowledge to know what to look for. This might be a mixture of professional skills (e.g. note taking or ability to ask the right questions) and knowing something of the setting and the people in it. The latter is perhaps less of a problem for sociologists such as Bennett (1999) and Fisher (1993), who begin their research with a lot of tacit knowledge, but it may be more difficult for anthropologists working in non-western cultures. As Todd Jones (1998) asks (in respect of Geertz's interpretation of the Balinese Cockfight) how do we know that the interpretations made are the right ones, what alternatives might be available? In other words before we can say anything of Balinese cockfights, youth music, or gaming arcades in general, we have to know that the particular instances were reliably represented.

Theoretical inference

Interpretivists often maintain that rather than making empirical generalizations, they are making 'theoretical inferences', that is they draw conclusions from their data about the necessary relationships that exist among categories of phenomena. Hammersley describes three types of justification for theoretical inference:

(a) the claim that ethnographic work produces theoretical insights whose validity and value are to be judged by the reader;
(b) the idea that theories are universal claims that can be derived from the study of a single case which exemplifies a type;
(c) the argument that by studying critical cases we can, on the basis of the hypothetico-deductive method, draw inferences about the truth or falsity of universal laws. (Hammersley 1992: 91)

Hammersley is sceptical of all three justifications. I think he is right about the first and third, but I believe that the second may be permissible under certain circumstances. He dismisses the first justification on the grounds that there is nothing to help the reader to decide what is of value in the situation, what they will find insightful, or on what basis they might do this. Such claims, as Clive Seale (1999: 109–110) points out, need ultimately to reside in further empirical confirmation anyway, otherwise this implies a relativism about findings that puts them on a par with fiction.

The third justification is that of the kind employed in analytic induction and amounts to (what I described above) as a 'total generalization'; that is that the analysis of individual cases can lead to the discovery of a general 'law'. This view is rarely upheld in social science these days and increasingly less so in the natural sciences.

Hammersley claims that the second type of justification (b)

assumes that in some, rather mysterious sense there are ideal types of phenomena that provide the basis for understanding any of their instances, however much these may deviate from type. (Hammersley 1992: 2)

Ideal types are logically equivalent to theories and posit an ideal type of phenomenon (similar to an 'ideal gas' in physics). Though it is unlikely that the phenomenon itself will entirely conform to the ideal as described it either will, or will not, have features resembling the type. Indeed as Weber noted, ideal types of laws, or certain types of rational action, can be formulated with clarity (Weber 1978: 23) and they can be turned into testable propositions. There seems to be no reason why ideal types cannot be proposed and evidence for the existence of characteristics resembling those of the ideal type sought, in much the same way as any theory is tested. Analogously a physicist can posit a hypothetical gas that obeys laws of temperature, pressure and volume, knowing that no naturally occurring gas will obey all of those laws at the same time. However, it *is* true to say that evidence for the existence of characteristics conforming to the ideal type in one case cannot lead us to any kind of deductive statement about the wider existence of such types and necessary relationships cannot be claimed. Fisher (1993), for example, might conclude from her observations that certain types of gambling behaviour are confirmed, or disconfirmed in this instance, but she cannot deduce that this would be the case elsewhere.

POSSIBILITY OF *MODERATUM* GENERALIZATIONS

The ontological justification for *moderatum* generalizations lies with the nature of interpretation itself, in spirit somewhat closer to Weber and (despite the limitations of analytic induction already described) Blumer and the Chicago School than the forms of interpretive research that have evolved more recently.

During the 1980s and 1990s there has been a shift from a hermeneutic form of inquiry, which sought to uncover underlying meanings, allowing the sociologist to construct a picture of reality as interpreted by agents themselves, to interpretation as text centred (Denzin *et al.* 1998: 19–22). In the latter there is no reality to be uncovered, but a series of interpretations to be read as a text, a story or a travelogue. The change from the first to the second, though in general terms a consequence of the aforementioned 'anti-positivist' movement was, specifically in anthropology, the result of a dissatisfaction with a form of investigation which sought to establish an authentic account (of the kind found in the 'classical' anthropology of Radcliffe-Brown or Malinowski). Prominent in this view is Clifford Geertz (1971, 1984), but its influence has gone far beyond anthropology and reached its apotheosis in the fragmentation of postmodernism.

The move toward 'reflexivity' anthropology is an instance of a wider 'linguistic turn' in the humanities and social sciences. Seminal in this movement was Peter Winch's Wittgensteinian influenced work of the late 1950s and early 1960s (Winch 1990 [1958]). For him rule following was linguistic practice and as language is subject to variation (and shapes culture accordingly), then to know a culture one must come to know the language of that culture (1990 [1958]: 40–65). Such knowledge must necessarily be partial for the outsider and filtered through his or her own perspective. A further influence, though like Winch often an unwitting one, has been Jacques Derrida (1978). His deconstructionism, though emphasizing the separation of text as created from its creator, has been (mis)read as advocating a free play of subjective interpretation. Like Chinese whispers, the work of Winch, Derrida and other thinkers such as Charles Taylor and Jean François Lyotard, have been mobilized to justify a relativist interpretivism.

This, however, ignores an important characteristic of the social world, its cultural consistency. It is an unwarranted move from what is true that, first, there is cultural variation, much of which is mediated through language, and second, external interpretations will be mediated through the norms and values of the interpreter, to first, cultural variation and its linguistic expression/ motivation leads to an inherent indeterminateness which in turn produces too much variability to allow the possibility of generalization from a specific situation to others. Second, the external norms and values of the interpreter render impossible any reciprocity of perspective between the interpreter and the interpreted and consequently any objective account. In other words difficulty has been rendered as impossibility.

Let us concede that cultural incommensurability may well have prevailed in the Trobriand islands, when Malinowski did his fieldwork in the early part of the twentieth century. Moreover his accounts may be so distorted by his own positioning as to be of little value as an accurate account of life in the islands.[7] It may also be true that Geertz's (1971) account of the Balinese Cockfight suffered from the same problems of perspective (though he partially recognizes this), but such cultural incommensurability and distortion is surely much less likely in a British gaming arcade or music club! That is not to claim cultural homogeneity, but rather that the existence of some shared norms, a common language and physical referents can allow at least some reciprocity of perspective between researcher and researched, as well as viable comparisons between places. Moreover, even within settings, it is possible to differentiate between the validity of statements. For example, those of the kind Fisher makes about the design of fruit machines are more dependable than a statement about the players' strategies, which in its turn is more dependable than (say) statements about 'trust regarding money' among the players (Fisher 1993: 459).[8]

INTERPRETATIONS AND REALITY

To claim the existence of cultural consistency commits one to at least a minimal form of realism of the kind advocated by Blumer, whereby our accounts of the world are regarded as substantially reliable, yet incomplete and erroneous (Hammersley 1989: 125). We are attempting to describe the reality of the people we investigate. That the accounts produced are more than a 'story' or a 'text' is verifiable by those investigated, but it is more than this. Those 'realities' as experienced are often the outcomes of processes, the evidence of structures existing beyond the individuals investigated.[9] The heterogeneous identities of Bennett's (1999) youth music culture may seem fragmented and point to difference and individuality, but could not exist at all without a catalogue of pre-existing cultural icons for the club goers to call upon to create their identities. Even if the products of the fashion or music industry are more diverse than ever, the ownership and control of the production are not. Consequently even diversity of identity creation will have its antecedents in structural homogeneity.

If characteristics point to particular structures in one situation, then one can hypothesize that the existence of such structures in a further situation will lead to at least some similar characteristics. When they do not, this may be evidence of other mediating structural factors. In generalizing from one context to another we can carry with us hypothetical notions of structure or outcome. When either is present, in further situations, then it is reasonable to seek the other. However success in this quest cannot be seen as a firm deduction, but merely a weak inductive confirmation of one's hypothesis. Though there may be evidence of a shared reality as experienced, or shared underlying structures, the complexity of these structures and the possibility of agency to transform them, means that generalizations can be only moderate ones.

CONCLUSION: TOWARD METHODOLOGICAL PLURALISM

In this chapter I have tried to show that generalization is both necessary and inevitable in interpretive research. Without it interpretivism is art and while art is a laudable activity, it is inadequate as a basis for policy action and for claims about what the wider social world is like. Indeed generalization is commonplace in interpretive research and denials of its possibility arise from a misunderstanding of what can be meant by the term. It is a denial that has its origins in the anti-positivist revolution and the consequent abandonment of hermeneutics for the linguistic turn and text-centred approaches. These denied, or ignored, the cultural consistency necessary for agents to go about their daily lives. *Moderatum* generalizations arise from that cultural consistency and are the basis of inductive reasoning in the lifeworld.

There is then nothing special about *moderatum* generalizations and they are not just the preserve of the social scientist, but instead the means by which we are able to be social. However, they can also form the basis of testable social scientific evidence. If one is producing research which will lead to action that will change the world, then it surely incumbent upon the researcher to produce the best evidence possible. This I believe is something Weber recognized, in his plea for adequacy at the level of cause and meaning, the social world is such that in social science, one needs both the richness of interpretation and the ability to move beyond this to make claims about processes and structures. The interpretations one makes of any given situation have an ideographic character, a picture that has not only blurred edges, but also sharp features. It is these which we pick out, either as a result of striking characteristics we had not anticipated, or (more likely) as a result of some previous informal conceptual schema or more formally held theory. Described in this way, it is not so different from what a biologist or a geologist might do.

Indeed Weber (1975) speaks of nomothetic and ideographic approaches, not as scientific versus non-scientific modes of inquiry, but *both* as forms of scientific inquiry. The nomothetic Weber equates with the *abstract* generalizable law like statements,[10] whereas the ideographic he regards as the science of a *concrete* reality, of specific instances. Moreover he expressed the view that with the exception of pure mechanics and certain forms of historical inquiry all 'science' requires each mode of inquiry (Weber 1975: 57–58).[11] The view that sociology (or any social science) can be only ideographic would therefore be antipathetic to Weber (and of course the opposite would be true). While Weber did not go on to recommend methodological pluralism, this seems to be an inevitable conclusion if we accept that sociology has a nomothetic and an ideographic dimension.

The *moderatum* generalizations I advocate are, then, the bridge between the ideographic and the nomothetic. Such generalizations can be only moderate, but need only to be so. They can provide testable evidence of structure and outcomes of structure. Their limits lie in the logical problem of inductive inference and in the ontological problem of categorical equivalence. These problems cannot be transcended from within interpretivism and generalizations that go beyond the moderate are objectively unjustified. Somewhat ironically we end up with something like the working hypotheses of Guba and Lincoln (1982)[12] (suggested in the quote on page 130), but of course these are generalizations and as such we have to do something with them. We can let them stand (and in some instances this may be sufficient)[13] or we will want to develop them further. This development implies other methods (such as the survey or experiment) that can specifically address the weaknesses of interpretivism, such as category inequivalence and lack of representativeness in sampling.[14] The converse is of course true, whereby the weaknesses and limitations of surveys and experiments are the strengths and possibilities of interpretive approaches.

NOTES

1   Interpretivism and qualitative research are sometimes used interchangeably. For some the former term is often taken to mean all of those approaches in the human sciences that do not take a hypothetico-deductive approach to investigation, while others maintain more narrowly that qualitative research is itself characterized by an interpretive approach (Denzin and Lincoln 1994: 2). Nevertheless

even within survey or experimental research one can speak of variables having a qualitative dimension, but of course in these approaches to research generalization is advocated. Likewise those who regard themselves as interpretivists often differ in what counts as an interpretation, or how one should go about it (Kincaid 1996: 205–210). Neither qualitative research or interpretivism are precise or agreed terms.

2 What I have called 'second-order summaries' is evidence at third hand. Its authenticity and reliability is not discussed.

3 The appropriation of the term naturalism by interpretivists leaves a linguistic lacuna for the latter when they wish to describe social scientists who believe an ontological natural continuum is capable of methodological translation into scientific method to study the social world (the original use of the term). Thus everyone who isn't an interpretivist must be described as a 'positivist' . There is no collective term then available to describe positivists, realists, critical rationalists, scientific pragmatists etc.

4 Kincheloe and McLaren (1994: 151) express a similar view referring to the 'traditional' view of external validity as 'The ability to make pristine generalizations from one research study to another'.

5 It is possible to specify a number of different kinds of 'law' in natural science, but usually the term is taken to refer to a principle of nature that holds in all circumstances covered by the wording of the law. Certain statistical laws would allow for case exceptions and may be possible in social science (see Kincaid 1996: 63–90), however in this case the generalizations implied would be subsumed under my second category, or possibly a new category between the first and second. Interpretive methodologists often conflate these different kinds of laws, seeing them all as deterministic (see for example Altheide and Johnson 1998).

6 It is not clear what is meant by a 'different logic' here, but I take this to mean that there is an emphasis on inductive, rather than deductive logic.

7 Paul Theroux (1992), in his travelogue of Oceania, found that the inhabitants knew of Malinowski. They believed he had taken particular aspects of uninhibited celebration in the annual Yam Festival and generalized this as typical behaviour. Nevertheless his observations about the greeting of strangers and the dislike of obesity were found by Theroux (who is not a trained anthropologist) over half a century later, suggesting that in generalizing, Malinowski got some things right and some wrong (Theroux 1992: Chapter 6).

8 The difference between a concept of 'strategy' and that of 'trust' might be that the first could be treated as an observable in the context of the arcades, whereas the second is probably more likely to be known linguistically.

9 See Sam Porter, Chapter 2 in this volume, for a realist account of ethnography. I believe my argument here to be largely compatible with this view.

10 Strictly speaking the term nomothetic refers to the proposal or prescription of a law, but this is too harsh and a relic of positivistic determinism. It is more usefully employed (as I do here) to mean the proposal or prescription of regularities, which might be logically expressed in the same way as law like statements.

11 More recently this point has been made by Bruno Latour (1987) who suggests that quantification is just one manifestation of providing comparative and coherent descriptions in science.

12 Indeed Lincoln and Guba though denying the possibility of generalization in their 1982 work later come close to adopting this position; however, their route to so doing is littered with misconceptions about generalization (Lincoln and

Guba 1985). After Schwartz and Ogilvy they conclude that perfect samples or 'blurred' information need not be obstacles to what they term 'holographic' generalizations (they use the metaphor of the holograph to suggest that information about an object of study and the means to clarify it are each contained in unclarified versions). Of course 'deterministic generalization' has not been claimed, even by survey researchers for much of the twentieth century and for something to be a probabilistic generalization the odds of the sample characteristic being found in the population must be known, nevertheless they seem here to be moving toward accepting the possibility of *moderatum* generalization.

13   Of course some studies, such as an evaluation of a particular programme, may not imply generalization at all (Seale 1999: 107). However if the programme is to be generalized then so must the evaluation.

14   See for example Wainwright and Forbes (2000) for a discussion of the possibility of a methodological 'third way' in nursing research.

REFERENCES

Altheide, D. and Johnson, J. (1998) 'Criteria for assessing interpretive validity in qualitative research', in N. Denzin and Y. Lincoln (eds) *Collecting and Interpreting Qualitative Materials*. Thousand Oaks, CA: Sage.

Bennett, A. (1999) 'Subcultures or neo-tribes? Rethinking the relationship between youth, style and musical taste', *Sociology* 33(3): 599–617.

Bishop, Y.M., Fineburg, S. and Holland, P. (1975) *Discrete Multivariate Analysis*. Cambridge, MA: MIT Press.

Bryman, A. (1988) *Quantity and Quality in Social Research*. London: Routledge.

Bryman, A. (1998) 'Quantitative and qualitative research strategies', in May, T. and Williams, M. (eds) *Knowing the Social World*. Buckingham: Open University Press.

Casti, J. (1991) *Searching for Certainty: What Scientists Can Know about the Future*. London: Abacus.

Cressey, D. (1950) 'Criminal violation of financial trust', *American Sociological Review* 15: 738–743.

Denzin, N. (1983) 'Interpretive interactionism', in G. Morgan (ed.) *Beyond Method: Strategies for Social Research*. Beverly Hills, CA: Sage.

Denzin, N. and Lincoln, Y. (eds) (1994) *Handbook of Qualitative Research*. London: Sage.

Denzin, N. and Lincoln, Y. (eds) (1998) Collecting and interpreting qualitative materials. London: Sage.

Derrida, J. (1978) *Writing and Difference*, translated by A. Bass. London: Routledge and Kegan Paul.

Fielding, N. (1982) 'Observational research on the National Front', in M. Bulmer (ed.) *Social Research Ethics*. London: Macmillan.

Fink, A. (1995) *How to Sample in Surveys*. Thousand Oaks, CA: Sage.

Fisher, S. (1993) 'The pull of the fruit machine: a sociological typology of young players', *Sociological Review* 41(3): 41.

Geertz, C. (1971) *The Interpretation of Cultures*. New York: Basic Books.

Geertz, C. (1984) 'Thick description: toward an interpretive theory of culture', in M. Martin and L. McIntyre (eds) *Readings in the Philosophy of Social Science*. Cambridge, MA: MIT Press.

Gephart, R. (1988) *Ethnostatistics: Qualitative Foundations for Quantitative Research.* Newbury Park, CA: Sage.

Glaser, B. and Strauss, A. (1967) *The Discovery of Grounded Theory.* Chicago: Aldine.

Gomm, R., Hammersley, M. and Foster, P. (2000) *Case Study Method: Divergent Interpretations.* London: Sage.

Guba, E. and Lincoln, Y. (1982) 'Epistemological and methodological bases of naturalistic enquiry', *Education Communication and Technology Journal* 30: 233–252.

Guba, E. and Lincoln, Y. (1994) 'Competing paradigms in qualitative research', in N. Denzin and S. Lincoln (eds) *Handbook of Qualitative Research.* London: Sage.

Hammersley, M. (1989) *The Dilemma of Qualitative Method: Herbert Blumer and the Chicago Tradition.* London: Routledge.

Hammersley, M. (1992) *What's Wrong with Ethnography?* London: Routledge.

Holdaway, S. (1982) 'An inside job: a case study of covert research on the police', in M. Bulmer (ed.) *Social Research Ethics.* London: Macmillan.

Jones, T. (1998) 'Interpretive social science and the "Native's" point of view', *Philosophy of the Social Sciences* 28(1): 32–68.

Kincaid, H. (1996) *Philosophical Foundations of the Social Sciences: Analyzing Controversies in Social Research.* Cambridge: Cambridge University Press.

Kincheloe, J. and McLaren, P. (1994) 'Rethinking critical theory and qualitative research', in N. Denzin and S. Lincoln (eds) *Handbook of Qualitative Research.* London: Sage.

Latour, B. (1987) *Science in Action.* Milton Keynes: Open University Press.

Lincoln, Y. and Guba, E. (1985) *Naturalistic Inquiry.* Beverly Hills, CA: Sage.

Lindesmith, A. (1968 [1947]) *Addiction and Opiates.* Chicago: Aldine.

Maffesoli, M. (1996) *The Time of the Tribes: The Decline of Individualism in Mass Society.* London: Sage.

Mason, J. (1996) *Qualitative Researching.* Thousand Oaks, CA: Sage.

Renzetti, C.M. and Lee, R. (eds) (1993) *Researching Sensitive Topics.* London: Sage.

Rist, R. (1998) 'Influencing the policy process with qualitative research', in N. Denzin and Y. Lincoln (eds) *Collecting and Interpreting Qualitative Materials.* Thousand Oaks, CA: Sage.

Robinson, W. (1951) 'The logical structure of analytic induction', *American Sociological Review* 16: 812–818.

Schutz, A. (1972 [1932]) *The Phenomenology of the Social World.* London: Heinemann.

Schwartz, P. and Ogilvy, J. (1979) The emergent paradigm: changing patterns of thought and belief. Memlo Park CA: SRE International.

Seale, C. (1999) *The Quality of Qualitative Research.* London: Sage.

Shields, R. (1992) 'Spaces for the subject of consumption', in R. Shields (ed.) *Lifestyle Shopping.* London: Routledge.

Theroux, P. (1992) *The Happy Isles of Oceania.* Harmondsworth: Penguin.

Thornton, S. (1995) *Club Cultures: Music, Media and Subcultural Capital.* Cambridge: Polity.

Wainwright, S. and Forbes, A. (2000) 'Philosophical problems with social research on health inequalities', *Health Care Analysis* 8(3): 259–277.

Weber, M. (1975) *Roscher and Knies.* New York: Free Press.

Weber, M. (1978) 'The nature of social action', in W. Runciman (ed.) *Weber: Selections in Translation.* Cambridge: Cambridge University Press.

Williams, M. (2000) *Science and Social Science: An Introduction*. London: Routledge.
Williams, M. and May, T. (1996) *Introduction to Philosophy of Social Research*. London: Routledge.
Winch, P. (1990 [1958]) *The Idea of a Social Science and its Relation to Philosophy*, 2nd edn. London: Routledge.
Znaniecki, F. (1934) *The Method of Sociology*. New York: Farrar and Rinehart.

6 REPRESENTATION, RESPONSIBILITY AND RELIABILITY IN PARTICIPANT-OBSERVATION

Martín Sánchez-Jankowski

Sociologists and anthropologists have had a long and prominent history of using participation-observation methodology in addressing a full range of research questions. The primary concern of most of the participant-observation studies was to document the everyday activities of the societies, or sub-societies, they were observing. Endemic within this approach was the act of representation because the societies and sub-societies studied had to be formally represented to both other researchers and the general public. How this was to be done was left in the hands of the researcher(s) who were directly on the scene. Given that a significant amount of money and effort was required to undertake this research, there were generally few opportunities to replicate the study with the same group of people. Therefore, researchers using participant-observation as a method were entrusted with a considerable amount of responsibility. Thus, there is not a participant-observation study that has not involved the concepts of 'representation' and 'responsibility'. This chapter, in a very quick and skeletal way, identifies some of the tensions that exist for the researcher when dealing with representation and responsibility, the methodological problems that such tensions provide for the researcher in carrying out their study, the subsequent problems associated with the evaluation of evidence emerging from these studies, and some of the cues that should be utilized to determine the level of internal and external validity present in the study.

Before continuing, I want to make clear that this chapter is not about ethnography; it is about research that utilizes participant-observation methodology. I have avoided the word ethnography because the word has come to engulf a number of different kinds of studies, many of which have not done and are not interested in using participant-observation methodology (Gans 1999). Herbert Gans (1999) has observed that many researchers have utilized the word 'ethnography' to include a variety of conceptual and methodological approaches. For example, some position ethnography as an expression of writing (Clifford and Marcus 1986), or as part of the postmodern effort to deconstruct abstract categories by constructing alternative abstractions (Tyler 1986), or as a political activity (Marcus 1988). This chapter on the other hand is about the methodology that has data gathered by the researcher being present, and participating in the activities of the subjects under investigation; directly observing them and the other social phenomena relevant to the research question, i.e. participant-observation.

OBSERVATION, REPRESENTATION AND VALIDITY

Participation-observation has the advantage of being able to directly observe the behaviour of those who the researcher is interested in studying. It is precisely this ability that has often allowed ethnographers to believe that internal and external validity are integrated into the method of data collection itself.[1] That is to say, the data analysis is occurring at the same time that the data gathering is taking place, giving the participant-observer 'face validity'. However, this apparent advantage is not something that can be automatically taken for granted because 'face validity' is dependent on a number of contingent factors related to the observation of phenomena and its representation. It is the relationship between observation and representation that I first want to turn my attention to. In this regard, I will be addressing the broad question of how observed events *will* be represented?

The relationship between observation and representation seems to be quite straightforward. A field researcher observes and then records what he or she sees, thereby representing a particular object of study. It is this directness that is the basis for the claim that participant-observation has 'face validity' built into it. Yet the simple sequence of observation and recording are filled with critical conceptual and analytic junctures that require close scrutiny on the part of the researcher. In observing a certain object (a setting, person, thing) there exists certain points where interaction forms what I have called a 'critical conceptual and analytic juncture'.

The first of these critical junctures has to do with the interaction of the observer and the observed, and the filtering system employed to gather the data. This filtering system will determine not simply what will be seen and not seen, but how it will be seen. Just how the filtering system will represent the observed phenomena will depend on the content of the system's apparatus itself. For all participant-observers the filtering system is composed of the eyes, ears and smell associated with the sensory system of the body, as well as the knowledge-bank that is used to identify, catalogue and categorize. This knowledge-bank is of course the information and the apriority conceptualized schema that individuals have accumulated and developed to make sense of the constant stream of everyday information that must be quickly (sometimes instantly) arranged in a manner that allows a field researcher (actually any person) to decide what the most appropriate and/or necessary behaviours for a particular situation are. For any person (and in particular the subjects of research) it is the development of a given list of appropriate and necessary behaviours for various situations that provides the methodological problem for participant-observation researchers because they are dependent on their library of behaviours to determine what should, and should not, be included in the field notes. The fact that the researcher's technical capabilities (i.e. knowledge base and conceptual propensity) are one aspect of the first critical juncture of representation in participant-observation research is not intended to minimize the issue of values in research. The fact-value issue is one that confronts all social research, but it presents an ever-present danger for the participant-observer because he or she is the data-gathering instrument. Thus, participant-observers must remind themselves while they are observing and recording the data, as well as remind the reader once they are reporting their findings, that they were aware of this methodological issue and took steps to reduce errors associated with it. Without a public acknowledgement of the problem and some discussion as to the strategy employed to deal with it, the findings are subject to questions concerning the probability of 'type I and type II' errors.

The second obstacle associated with the researcher's filtering system has to do with the researcher's library of cues that help him or her determine what is going on in a particular social environment or interaction. The more cues researchers have in their library, the higher the probability that they will recognize important conditions in the social environment that are vital in answering their research questions. However, the library of cues not only must be extensive, but also must be varied. By varied, I am suggesting that the cues accumulated must not be of the same kind. That is to say, they must not come from simply one experience, because if they do, there will be the tendency to miss either important data or interpret the observations they have made inaccurately. This is not to suggest that it is only possible for someone who has experienced the same environment through the same lenses can study that environment. However, if a person has no experiential knowledge of the environment it increases the probability that the data collected may, and the emphasis here is on 'may', increase the possibility of committing a type I or type II error.[2]

The types of experiences, and the concomitant cues that emerge from them, can be related to any number of categories. The most basic examples are associated with class, gender and race. What I am suggesting is that just because a scholar is trained and has familiarity with what the literature says about a particular area of study, there is no guarantee that he or she will avoid committing errors of commission and/or omission. This is because the participant-observation researcher is the instrument for data-gathering, and thus the responsibility associated with gathering all relevant data is placed solely on the researcher. Therefore, like any instrument (e.g. a survey questionnaire), the researcher's personal and field-research background is very important because the information accumulated during this process will have provided him or her with the cues to more accurately decipher what is important data to record and what is not (Jackson 1987: 107). As I have said, there are no guarantees of course, and it is not my intent to argue that scholars can study only the group from which they have come, but rather to draw attention to the fact that researchers who study a group in which they have spent a good deal of time with, and therefore have become increasingly familiar with, there is a higher probability for them to see and record data 'relevant' to the research question than those with less familiarity (Emerson *et al.* 1995: 108–112). More specifically, knowing what it is that one is seeing is terribly important in determining whether such an event should be included in the notes and how it should be coded. The accuracy of such decisions will increase proportional to the amount of time spent by the researcher interacting with, and formally observing the subjects of study (Emerson *et al.* 1995).

The act of representation presents three rather major obstacles for the researcher. First, are all the actors, if actors are the primary observational objects, acting in a way that accurately represents: who they are personally; who they are in the particular situation under investigation; or who they are as a proxy for a particular general group? This problem always presents itself in the beginning of the fieldwork because the researcher is, to varying degrees, an alien in the environment. There is the tendency on the part of the subjects to act in a way that minimizes who they think they are. That is to say, to minimize what they believe are their negative attributes and accentuate their perceived positive ones. Or they may simply try to be, or avoid being, someone they think the researcher believes they are. Thus, in studies where the researcher has spent very little time in the field, there is a higher probability that the researcher has committed a type I or type II error (Leidner 1993).

The second major obstacle is to determine who saw what, when and how. Sometimes this is associated with research projects in which there have been more than one field-researcher gathering data. When there are two or more independent observations and there is conflict in the content of the field observations there is the need to reconcile the conflict because determining how to represent an object is dependent on a consistent pattern. The problem is to decide whether there is a substantive difference in observed behaviour, or a difference in each researcher's filtering system (May *et al.* 2000). If the differences remain random (i.e. no pattern) then it is very difficult to identify the exact origin of the problem. On the other hand, one might assume that if the differences were constant that it would be clear that a problem resonated with how the researchers were 'observing' people, places and events. Yet such an assumption would be premature because it is possible that each of the researchers were observing substantively different phenomena, or phenomena that presented itself in substantively different ways (Goffman 1959). This presents a dilemma as to how the object of study will be represented because what observations will take precedence and why determines the substance of representation; but it does not necessarily produce an accurate representation of the substance.

The sequencing of observations is also a factor in how the object of study will be represented. Here, I am referring to researchers who are both interacting, and thus observing and conversing, with one or more of the subjects under investigation. On the one hand, this is the substance of participant-observation research; on the other, it presents the researcher with another dilemma. Suppose the researcher is talking to one or more subjects, who recount an event that just occurred to them. The researcher observes their present state and has confirmation from all, or most, of those involved in a particular event that the event indeed occurred. Recording the data requires that the researcher note down what one or more of those involved in the event observed occurring. This event will be composed of both verbal and physical behaviour, and in listening to the subjects recount the event, there is a trail of verbal reflections on who said and did what, where and how. The substance of how this event will be represented is predicated on the observations of the participants and not that of the researcher since the researcher was not present at this time. In this instance, the validity of the representation can be increased if the researcher is using the news-media protocol of having three independent sources verify the action, but it cannot be authenticated. For example, recently there have been a number of investigative journalists who have written books representing the lives of African Americans living in poor and high-crime neighbourhoods. When reading these books, it is easy to be gripped by the events as they are recounted, but there are times when one wonders, 'how does the author/researcher know that?' This is particularly true when an event is being recounted and dialogue is present (Kotlowitz 1991: 127; Dash 1997: 26–27). In those cases, the representation of the event, or the event's representation of a larger object or condition, is predicated on unobserved phenomena, or at least unobserved by the researcher. Thus, the question of the observational accuracy, or its inexactness, remains an embedded feature in the researcher's representation of the participants' representations.

The means, or manner, of data collection is another factor in the representational process. It matters how notes are taken. There is no paucity of books describing the 'how to' of note taking, but the exact mechanism utilized has not been rationalized to the point that it is uniformed across research projects and disciplines (Jackson 1987; Sanjek 1990; Emerson *et al.* 1995). The question of what is the proper way to take notes is most likely to produce a vague answer like 'whatever you find useful for both documenting what you observed; and writing up the results at a later time' (Emerson *et al.* 1995: 13–16). An answer like this will allow researchers a great deal of flexibility for unique situations, but unlike other methods (e.g. survey questionnaires), it presents an irrational system full of ambiguity for systematic comparability and replication.

There are a variety of simple questions that have an impact on how systematically comparable and replicable the data will be such as: Are notes taken by longhand, shorthand, or tape recording? Do the notes that are taken need to be reinterpreted and/or rewritten at some later point in time? Are they stored in notebooks, on tapes, or computer files? Obviously, to address each of these questions adequately and consider their implications would require a separate chapter; however, to mention them raises the issue of whether the use of a computer file with its own structure and logic, might provide a means to log, classify, code and scale data in a way that allows some rationality to pervade the note-taking process (Dohan and Sánchez-Jankowski 1998). For example, if data (field notes) were made available in a systematically uniformed way, it would help to determine whether the account used in a paper, report or monograph was based on a single observation or some longitudinal pattern (Johnson and Johnson 1990). Without such a logical system, anarchistic data collection procedures will create ambiguous findings, which in turn will create strains in evaluating validity and reliability of representations within and across studies. In particular, there is the evaluative question of whether an author's sociological (or anthropological, economic and political) insight is based on a single observation, albeit interesting, or patterned behaviour (i.e. multiple observations). Obviously the difference is substantively significant because there is a greater chance of a type II error in the first instance than there is in the second.

MEANING AND REPRESENTATION

The representation of phenomena presents another challenge and that has to do with establishing the 'meaning' of an observed event or pattern of events. This constitutes the second critical juncture for the researcher. There are two broad aspects to the concept of 'meaning' that have implications for the participant-observer. The first has to do with establishing, where appropriate to the research, the meaning of certain actions to the subjects observed. This can take the form of determining what meaning the subjects gave to their own action, or it can be the meaning they gave to other actors' activities. In both cases, the primary effort is to understand how the subjects interpret their own and others' motives and behaviours. This is a problem that anthropology has confronted, and continues to confront, when studying divergent peoples and cultures (Geertz 1983). In essence, to penetrate accurately the subjects' understandings of reality, these researchers must put themselves in the minds of the subjects they are studying. Is this possible? Must a researcher become the subject they are researching? In Geertz's (1983: 58) judgement this is neither required nor possible, but for many other investigators the research question requires precisely this. In fact, participant-observers employing the ethnomethodological approach to their field of study believe not only that the researcher should be engaged in such questions (subjective meaning for the subjects), but also that with sustained training it is possible (Garfinkel 1967). Within this phenomenological-oriented tradition, the effort is to become the actor in order to go beyond empathy and establish understanding of the meanings that the actors of a given encounter gave to the encounter while it was occurring (Cicourel 1974; Schutz 1982). Thus, representation of the 'native's point of view' involved the interpretation of the native's interpretation of the physical, metaphysical, and symbolic world (Geertz 1974; Wacquant 1995). This reincarnates the basic question of whether it is possible to interpret the words and linguistic symbols of communicative behaviour as an accurate representation of an actor(s) meaning of an event(s). It also presents significant challenges to validating the meaning of the representations. If a follow-up study is not able to determine that the same meanings were in use as were found in a previous study, does this invalidate the meanings that were recorded in the prior study? Does it nullify the meanings found in the present study? Regardless of the epistemological orientation, with such a situation, the clouds of both a type I and type II error remain settled into an evaluative inversion. It is for this reason that ethnomethodology relinquished the quest for an answer to such a question and argued that social meaning is time, place and situation dependent. It is not something that is reproducible. Thus, representation in this context has qualities that are both dynamic and static in nature. The irony is that what the researcher sees is not what the reader gets, but rather what the reader gets is what the researcher sees through the act of transference that accompanies their (the researcher's) penetration of the subject's subjective vision and its meaning (Emerson 1970).

Similar to the concerns of the ethnomethodologists, the ethnographic studies that emerge from a symbolic interactionist conceptual framework also attempt to represent the meanings that individuals bring to their social world (Blumer 1969; Cicourel 1971). Here, however, the empirical representations are products of the researcher's understanding of the meanings that the subjects bring to, and get from, their social interactions (Morris 1962). This would also include two rather important factors. The first being recognizing and interpreting the symbols through which meaning is communicated, while the second has to do with determining the significance of the researcher (him/herself) to the subjects within their (the subjects') social milieu. Therefore, the representations generated from this research are built on the social meanings of behaviour as defined by the actors in relation to their interactions with each other and the researcher. Thus, instead of considering the researcher as an object of bias, as a participant-observer doing ethnography from a logical positivist tradition might, the symbolic interactionist simply considers it a part of the social environment that must be considered when trying to understand the social world (i.e. society) of the subjects (Horowitz 1995). In both the ethnomethodologist and symbolic-interactionist tradition, the representation of everyday life becomes first and foremost interpretively descriptive. Representing the 'common sense' through which people play out their ordinariness is the product of this research. Because there are so many individuals involved in the study, each with their own meanings for the interactional situations they find themselves, the researcher 'interprets' what he or she believes is the subject's own interpretive meaning for specific situations (Fine 1996, 1998). This produces 'rules' (Goffman 1963) or 'interpretative processes' (Blumer 1969) through which actors navigate their social world. The result of these approaches is that what the reader gets is not what the researcher sees, but rather, what the reader gets is what the researcher sees the subject(s) see (Wellman 1988).

RESPONSIBILITY AND REPRESENTATION

The concerns about representation are not simply limited to how social, political and economic phenomena will be depicted, but *how they should* be represented. It is here that the issues surrounding the concept of responsibility penetrate participant-observation studies. Stated more simply: once the data have been gathered and analysed, what is the proper way that they should be represented? It is at this juncture that the fact–value issue arises again and it does so in a way that Weber (1949) did not write on. In the instance that I am now referring to, the fact–value dilemma presents itself in ethical garb; however, it is the researcher's values that are standing nakedly before the reader.

There is no place where values plays a more prominent role than in the determination of what to include in the public version of a report. Although many considerations are present, there are three that are quite prominent. First, there are considerations as to whether the researcher ought to expose the faults of those he or she studies (Scheper-Hughes 1979). If they do, is it a violation of the ethics surrounding the social agreement made between researchers and subjects through the use of a formal protocol, or through the process of the researcher presenting him or herself as a close friend and confidant? Of course, this is a key issue to all research, but it is particularly present in participant-observation research because of the closeness (both physically and emotionally) that must be obtained between researchers and subjects. No doubt, there will be differences of opinion concerning the proper ethical position to be assumed, but the question itself conjures up the issue of 'responsibility' and its relation to 'representation'. For example, at one time the dominant position among many researchers studying the poor or underprivileged in a particular country was that the final report should not include negative, or self-destructive beliefs and/or behaviours that were observed during the research. The arguments for this were centred on two separate propositions that were often working simultaneously with each other. The first of these was that since the condition of the poor was assumed to be caused by structural problems, researchers who did expose negative beliefs and behaviours about socio-economically vulnerable populations were in effect blaming the victim for their present condition (Ryan 1971). The work of anthropologist Oscar Lewis (1961, 1964, 1966, 1975) was a primary target for this criticism because he described many negative personal attributes of the poor he studied.

The second proposition was that even if the researcher was not blaming the victim for their present condition, the evidence presented in the work could be used by politically sinister parties to carry out, or rationalize, actions that would hurt the population depicted in the study. This criticism was often utilized against scholars doing studies on racialized minorities (Frazier 1957; Horowitz 1984; Anderson 1990). Although the criticisms were not always issued in print, they existed in both the formal and informal conversations at professional conferences. The quality of the work was not the primary focus, even though some did try to undermine the arguments using methodological criticisms. The primary impetus for such criticisms was that the work could be detrimental to certain racial/ethnic minorities that were already the object of socio-economic and political discrimination.

Reflecting on such criticism there was a tendency to see that the responsible thing to do under such circumstances was to avoid describing the negative behaviour that was observed, even if this was a contributing factor to the subjects' place in life. Hence, responsibility for some researchers seemed to dictate that what they publicly reported was only part of what they saw. Thus, what the broader research community confronted was partial evidence with very high probabilities of type I and type II errors.

Yet, there is another fear faced by researchers that affects the 'quality' of the data that are ultimately presented. This fear is again associated with the subjects, but its primary focus is on what the subjects think of what the researcher has observed. In a sense it is the fear that what they (the researchers) have seen will, when described in the report, be offensive to the subjects. The full extent of this fear is that it will be offensive to subjects who have been very cooperative in letting the researcher carry out his or her work. This fear is based on some level of guilt that the researcher broke the social contract that had been entered into with the subjects. In fact, there may well be an even greater feeling of guilt centred on the question of whether the research has exploited the subjects by merely treating them as tools for the researcher's professional advancement (Scheper-Hughes 2000).

A far more intense fear is that if the subjects do not like what was said, they would go before the public and declare that what the researcher reported was not the truth. This occurred in a criticism of Whyte (1993 [1943]) and his *Street Corner Society*. In a follow-up study Boelen (1992) interviewed a number of the subjects that Whyte had identified in his study. She reported that most people refuted much of Whyte's account of the area. This type of follow-up study cannot act as an adequate replication because the mere rejection of Whyte's analysis on the basis of the subjects' response to it is not valid. What would be necessary is for Boelen (or some other researcher) to study a sociological area that could be defined as a 'slum' and empirically demonstrate that Whyte's findings about such areas were inaccurate. While Boelen's approach was not valid, the use of negative evaluations of a participant-observation analysis by the subjects can have devastating effects on the validity of the entire research project, as well as the researcher's career, so protecting against such an event is something that most researchers give some thought to.[3] The upshot of this fear is to influence researchers to be very careful about what they report. Responsibility assumes a variety of characters in this context. One way that responsibility plays itself out is to have the researcher offer the subjects the opportunity to review what has been written about them. This strategy has the advantage of informing the subjects what the researcher has seen and thinks about the observations. The hope is that this will reduce the subject's surprise, public embarrassment and humiliation, feelings of betrayal and outrage, and eliminate retaliation. Thus, responsibility is associated with letting the subjects read the report in an effort to elicit their responses, make the appropriate revisions, and ultimately secure their approval. The problem is what if the researcher removes some very important data that might be useful to other researchers. Or even more important, what if, to satisfy the opinions of the subjects, the researcher makes changes that compromise the accuracy of the account? It is difficult at best for everyday people to be trained anthropologists and sociologists; thus what the subjects understand as occurring is not necessarily what is occurring. This is not to suggest that what the trained anthropologist and sociologist observe is the only truth, but if professional training is to have authenticity, as it should, it needs to identify the general dynamics associated with the observed situations which the average person's everyday 'local knowledge' is not aware of (Emerson and Pollner 1988, 1992).

The issue of being responsible must not be trivialized. It is important that researchers assume responsibility for honouring the agreement that they established with their subjects when they began the research. Whatever the specifics of the agreement, it is important that participant-observation research protect the subjects' anonymity and confidentiality. Even in those cases where the subjects say they don't care about either, or they request that their names be made public in the report, both anonymity and confidentiality must not be compromised. If they are compromised, then there exists the potential for increased feelings of internal conflict about what the 'proper' position of responsibility should be. Such conflict can lead only to confusing issues concerning loyalty to informants for aiding them in their research with loyalty to the data themselves. This has often been called the problem of invoking one's values into the research process, but it is more than that. It goes beyond values; it is about understanding what is being seen for itself, of itself, and by itself.

Responsibility is also an issue when the researcher is observing behaviour that is illegal. This is a particularly acute problem when researchers go into a study already knowing that they will observe illegal behaviour. The law in the United States governing researcher–subject relations in this context does not allow for researcher–subject privilege. US law treats social scientists differently from journalists, doctors and lawyers where professional–client privilege is protected. As far as the law is concerned, social scientists must obey all the laws that every other citizen is required to obey. Therefore, if they see, or hear of a crime, they are obligated to inform law enforcement officials. This would also include testifying before a grand jury or in a court of law. Failure to obey these laws subjects the researcher to criminal charges ranging from conspiracy to contempt of court. However, at the same time the US federal laws pertaining to research (and monitored by each university's committee for protection of human subjects) require that researchers protect their subjects from physical, psychological and legal risks. Now if researchers see, hear or in fact participate (not knowing what was going on with their subjects until it was in progress) in some illegal activity, how should they behave? What is responsible behaviour? Is responsible behaviour turning in the subjects or protecting them? This ethical predicament has an impact on the issues of validity and reliability (Venkatesh 1999).

RELIABILITY AND REPRESENTATION

The last issue that I want to address is associated with the question of reliability and generalization. Another way of putting this is that in the previous sections I discussed issues about what participation-observation studies *will* (representation) and *should* (responsibility) represent, and in this section I will discuss what they *can* more generally represent.

Not all the researchers who utilize participant-observation methodology are interested in the issues of reliability and generalization. Certainly ethnomethodologists are not concerned with it since they believe that observable social phenomena are too tied to a specific time, place and circumstance to be generalizable. Even though some, not all, researchers operating under the symbolic-interaction tradition would not be wedded to the importance of reliability, there would be a desire on the part of most symbolic interactionist researchers to have their findings generalizable to other populations.

The ability to generalize to other populations is dependent on a number of factors related to the design, execution and content of each study. In the space provided for this chapter, it is not possible to discuss every issue that affects the ability to generalize, so I will simply concentrate on a few of the more important ones.

One of the most important factors determining the strength of a study to generalize has to do with whether the sample population is an accurate representation of other populations in society. This means that the first line of representation has to do with selecting a group of people that represents other populations that the researcher wants to say something about. Thus, selecting a sample is necessary and the strategy employed in doing so will affect the degree of reliability in findings. If researchers have chosen their site (sample) carefully to match other like sites, then one requirement affecting reliability has been satisfied. However, if the researcher has chosen poorly, then reliability has been compromised and generalization is problematic. Studies can be of physical areas like communities (Lynd and Lynd 1929; Warner 1963), ethnic groups (Liebow 1967; Horowitz 1984), social class groups (Burawoy 1979; Halle 1984; Burawoy and Krotov 1992), genders (Thorne 1993; Hagdagneu-Sotelo 1994), or some discrete category of groups of individuals in society (Goffman 1961; Fine 1978). When there is a mismatch it simply means that the researcher has chosen a person, place, time or group that do not represent other persons, places, periods and groups that the researcher made claims about, and thus he/she has fallen victim to a potential type I or type II error (Duneier 1992; Thorne 1993). In essence, there must be a match between the entity studied and the entity generalized about. For example, Duneier (1992) studied a cafeteria on the African American-dominated south side of Chicago. From this study, he argued that the claims made in much of the other research depicting African American men as irresponsible were inaccurate. The problem here was that while the argument that he was advancing was socially appealing, and there was an intuitive feeling within the broader research community that the argument was probably correct, the study itself was very vulnerable to a type I error. This is because the sample he chose was not able to reject the argument of the other contending studies. Observing people's behaviour in a cafeteria cannot tell the research how they behave (responsibly or not) in environments like work or the family. Such a sample can only tell you how they behave in a cafeteria like the one they are in.[4]

The study by Thorne (1993) is another example of a potential type I error. Her study looks at the issue of gender formation in children. She studied children at play in a school playground. Her argument is that gender is developed socially and as such is more socially determined than the counter-psychoanalytic theory of being biologically determined. While this may be true, we are here again faced with a potential type I error. Since Thorne studied children who were already in school, they had already passed the time when the counter-theory says that gender identity has been established. Thus, there is no way to rule out the claims of the contending theory unless a longitudinal study following very young children through the ages when the psychoanalytic theory would have predicted that gender identity would occur is done.

The length of time that researchers spend in the field will have a direct impact on the ability to generalize their representations to other populations or situations. When researchers spend small amounts of time doing field-work (weeks or a few months) there is the question of whether the actions being observed are representative of some general pattern or are idiosyncratic to the person, time or event observed. Without significant amounts of field time, it is unlikely that a sufficient amount of data will have been accumulated to establish a pattern. Incomplete patterns are simply that. They can be suggestive, but they cannot, and they should not, be represented as an empirical consistency (Leidner 1993). One of the most troubling aspects to evaluating participant-observation research has to do with whether the researcher is presenting a finding that has come from an established pattern in the data or simply an observation that is the most interesting. There is a great deal of pressure from researchers utilizing other methods of social inquiry to have participant-observers find something unique and different. For example, during a participant-observation session at the 1991 annual meeting of the American Sociological Association a discussant rose and addressed a member of the panel saying 'What is the point of using ethnography rather than other established methods like survey research if you can't tell us something we didn't already know?' The rationale was that participant-observers are so close to those they are observing that they should be able to come up with some finding or interpretation that is unique and insightful (Suttles 1976). Thus, for the participant-observer, finding one interesting observation and building it into a generalization is very tempting indeed. Yet, with limited numbers of observations, reliability becomes more tenuous and so does the ability to generalize.

The final element impacting generalizations (i.e. representations) has to do with the access of the researcher to those he/she is observing. There is an assumption that all participant-observers are by definition close, both physically and communicatively, to the subjects they are studying. This assumption is unfounded because there is a great deal of variation in the level of closeness between researchers and those they are observing. There are times when the researcher conducting the analysis part of a study was not the person who collected the data (Sullivan 1989). Often this situation is created when a team of researchers is utilized to collect the data. This occurs for a number of reasons, but two of the more significant ones are, first, the principal investigator has designed a comparative project and does not think that he or she can do all the sites in the time desired, and second, the principal investigator does not, because of a mismatch between his or her physical or social characteristics and those of the subjects, feel that he or she can gain the closeness necessary to execute the research properly (Moore 1978; Sullivan 1989). Whatever the reason, when teams are used there is an increased risk that the data are unreliable. Although a full elaboration of the problem cannot be done here, in brief the problem is that there is no way to judge the inter-researcher consistency in what each independent researcher observed. This situation produces problems in internal validity that has a direct impact on reliability, and this in turn impedes the researcher's effort to generalize (May *et al.* 2000).

Finally, there is a problem when the primary interpreter of what the principal investigator is representing as his or her own direct observation of behaviour is in fact not that of the researcher, but that of a key informant. This informant usually has been with the researcher from the start of the study, and is usually responsible for the researcher having obtained access to the subjects (Whyte 1993). The obvious problem is that the informer is not trained in one of the social sciences and this raises a question as to whether the informer's interpretation of behaviour is accurate. It could very well be accurate, but there is also a chance, and not an insignificant chance, that it is not accurate. Here again, the potential for a type I or type II error is great enough to make reliability tenuous at best. Ultimately a number of issues related to the investigator's observations influence how the subject matter can be represented, and this influences how other objects of like, or similar, composition can, and are, generalized to.

CONCLUSIONS: THE THREE Rs IN PARTICIPANT-OBSERVATION

One of the prevailing beliefs about participant-observation research is that it provides a clear and vivid picture of everyday life. In fact, it is this ability that has often been utilized by both participant-observers and survey researchers to justify the very use of this, as opposed to some other methodological approaches. Much of this justification is based on the belief that ethnographers simply detail life as it is. In other words, 'what they see as researchers is what readers get.' Yet, as I have argued in this chapter, this is an assumption that cannot be accepted in an unqualified way. Like any other method, there are a significant number of technical methodological issues that permeate the findings of each participant-observation study and many of the published participant-observation studies have serious problems that require reservation in fully accepting their findings.

One of the primary points that I want to make in this chapter is that an ethnographic piece of research should not be accepted or rejected merely on face value. Rather, it must be evaluated systematically. In this way, an assessment can be made as to whether the entire study is reliable, some parts are and others are not, or the entire study is compromised because of some endemic methodological flaw. When both quantitative and qualitative researchers utilize such evaluative care, ethnography will move beyond the novel, interesting and anecdotal and assume the ranks of the rigorous, systematic and generalizable. At the present time, participant-observation studies are generally not considered capable of proving or disproving a study that has utilized survey data with large samples in generating a set of findings and conclusions. This prejudice comes from both survey researchers' belief that large samples, standardized questions asked in systematic ways, and statistical techniques of analysis are the only reliable means to research a question, as well as from the failure of ethnographers to be careful in planning and executing their research. There is no question that anthropological and sociological ethnographers have contributed to that prejudicial argument. By not taking the proper care to eliminate potential type I and type II errors in participant-observation research a significant number of these studies remain confronted with the question: 'Is what we've got, what they saw?'

NOTES

1   Internal validity is the consistency between the operationalization of a concept at two or more points in the data analysis stage of the research. External validity is the consistency between the way that a particular concept or construct is defined for the study and the way that it is used in the standard literature.

2   A type I error is defined as accepting a research statement as being true when it is in fact false. A type II error is defined as rejecting a research statement as being false when it is in fact true (Blalock 1972).

3   William Foote Whyte was very upset by the Boelen (1992) piece because he thought it was a direct attack on his integrity as a researcher and a person. Thus, he felt compelled to defend himself at a session of the annual meeting of the American Sociological Association and in the fourth edition of his book (Whyte 1993: 360–371).

4   There was also the issue as to whether Duneier's choice of a cafeteria was typical of an African American eatery. The cafeteria was on the south side of Chicago, but

that part of the south side that is adjacent to the University of Chicago, which is an area that is wealthier and more racially integrated with white professors and students than nearly all the other areas on the south side. Thus, the issue of generalizing about how African Americans behave in a typical African American eatery is also vulnerable to a type I error.

REFERENCES

Anderson, E. (1990) *Streetwise: Race and Urban Change*. Chicago: University of Chicago Press.

Blalock, H.M. (1972) *Social Statistics*. New York: McGraw-Hill.

Blumer, H. (1969) *Symbolic Interaction*. Englewood Cliffs, NJ: Prentice-Hall.

Boelen, W.A.M. (1992) 'Cornerville revisited', *Journal of Contemporary Ethnography* 21(1): 11–51.

Burawoy, M. (1979) *Manufacturing Consent: Changes in the Labor Process under Monopoly Capital*. Chicago: University of Chicago Press.

Burawoy, M. and Krotov, P. (1992) 'The Soviet transition from socialism to capitalism: worker control and economic bargaining in the wood industry', *American Sociological Review* 57: 16–38.

Cicourel, A.V. (1971) 'Basic and normative rules in the negotiation of status and role', in D. Sudnow (ed.) *Studies in Interaction*. New York: Free Press.

Cicourel, A.V. (1974) *Language and Meaning in Social Interaction*. New York: Free Press.

Clifford, J. and Marcus, G.E. (eds) (1986) *Writing Culture: The Poetics and Politics of Ethnography*. Berkeley, CA: University of California Press.

Dash, L. (1997) *Rosa Lee: A Mother and her Family in Urban America*. New York: Plume.

Dohan, D. and Sánchez-Jankowski, M. (1998) 'Using computers to analyze ethnographic field data: theoetical and practical considerations', in J. Hagan (ed.) *Annual Review of Sociology*, vol. 24. Palo Alto, CA: Annual Reviews.

Duneier, M. (1992) *Slim's Table: Race, Respectability, and Masculinity*. Chicago: University of Chicago Press.

Emerson, J. (1970) 'Behavior in private places: sustaining definitions of reality in gynaecological examinations', in H.P. Dreitzel (ed.) *Recent Sociology No. 2: Patterns of Communicative Behavior*. New York: Macmillan.

Emerson, R.M. and Pollner, M. (1988) 'On the uses of members' reponses to researchers' accounts', *Human Organization* 47: 189–198.

Emerson, R.M. and Pollner, M. (1992) 'Difference and dialogue: members' readings of ethnographic texts', in G. Miller and J.A. Holstein (eds) *Perspectives on Social Problems: A Research Annual*, vol. 3. Greenwich, CT: JAI Press.

Emerson, R.M., Fretz, R.I. and Shaw, L.L. (1995) *Writing Ethnographic Fieldnotes*. Chicago: University of Chicago Press.

Fine, G.A. (1978) *With the Boys: Little League Baseball and Preadolescent Culture*. Chicago: University of Chicago Press.

Fine, G.A. (1996) *Kitchens: The Culture of Restaurant Work*. Berkeley, CA: University of California Press.

Fine, G.A. (1998) *Morel Tales: The Culture of Mushrooming*. Cambridge, MA: Harvard University Press.

Frazier, E.F. (1957) *Black Bourgeoisie: The Rise of the New Middle Class in the United States*. New York: Free Press.

Gans, H.J. (1999) 'Participant observation in the era of "ethnography"', *Journal of Contemporary Ethnography* 28: 540–548.

Garfinkel, H. (1967) *Studies in Ethnomethodology*. Englewood Cliffs, NJ: Prentice-Hall.

Geertz, C. (1974) '"From the native's point of view": on the nature of anthropological understanding', *Bulletin of the American Academy of Arts and Sciences* 28.

Geertz, C. (1983) *Local Knowledge: Further Essays in Interpretive Anthropology*. New York: Basic Books.

Goffman, E. (1959) *Presentation of Self in Everyday Life*. New York: Anchor.

Goffman, E. (1961) *Asylums*. Garden City, NY: Doubleday.

Goffman, E. (1963) *Behavior in Public Places: Notes on the Social Organization of Gatherings*. New York: Free Press.

Hagdagneu-Sotelo, P. (1994) *Gendered Transitions: Mexican Experiences of Immigration*. Berkeley, CA: University of California Press.

Halle, D. (1984) *America's Working Man: Work, Home, and Politics among Blue-Collar Property Owners*. Chicago: University of Chicago Press.

Horowitz, R. (1984) *Honor and the American Dream: Identity and in a Mexican American Community*. New Brunswick, NJ: Rutgers University Press.

Horowitz, R. (1995) *Teen Mothers: Citizens or Dependents?* Chicago: University of Chicago Press.

Jackson, B. (1987) *Fieldwork*. Urbana, IL: University of Illinois Press.

Johnson, A. and Johnson, O.R. (1990) 'Quality into quantity: on the measurement potential of ethnographic fieldnotes', in R. Sanjek (ed.) *Fieldnotes: The Making of Anthropology*. Ithaca, NY: Cornell University Press.

Kotlowitz, A. (1991) *There Are No Children Here: The Story of Two Boys Growing Up in the Other America*. New York: Anchor.

Leidner, R. (1993) *Fast Food, Fast Talk: Service Work and Routinization of Everyday Life*. Berkeley, CA: University of California Press.

Lewis, O. (1961) *Children of Sanchez*. New York: Random House.

Lewis, O. (1964) *Pedro Martinez: A Mexican Peasant and his Family*. New York: Random House.

Lewis, O. (1966) *La Vida: A Puerto Rican Family in the Culture of Poverty – San Juan and New York*. New York: Random House.

Lewis, O. (1975) *Five Families: Mexican Case Studies in the Culture of Poverty*. New York: Random House.

Liebow, E. (1967) *Tally's Corner: A Study of Negro Street Corner Men*. Boston, MA: Little, Brown.

Lynd, R.S. and Lynd, H.M. (1929) *Middletown: A Study of Contemporary American Culture*. New York: Harcourt Brace.

Marcus, G.E. (1988) *Ethnography through Thick and Thin*. Princeton, NJ: Princeton University Press.

May, R., Buford, A. and Pattillo-McCoy, M. (2000) 'Do you see what I see? Examining a collaborative ethnography', *Qualitative Inquiry* 6: 65–87.

Moore, J. (1978) *Homeboys: Gangs, Drugs and Prisons in the Barrios of Los Angeles*. Philadelphia, PA: Temple University Press.

Morris, C.W. (1962) *George Herbert Mead: Mind, Self, and Society From the Standpoint of a Social Behavioralist*. Chicago: University of Chicago Press.

Ryan, W. (1971) *Blaming the Victim*. New York: Pantheon.

Sanjek, R. (1990) *Fieldnotes: The Making of Anthropology*. Ithaca, NY: Cornell University Press.

Scheper-Hughes, N. (1979) *Saints, Scholars and Schizophrenics: Mental Health in Rural Ireland*. Berkeley, CA: University of California Press.

Scheper-Hughes, N. (2000) 'Ire in Ireland', *Ethnography* 1: 117–140.

Schutz, A. (1982) *Life Forms and Meaning Structures*, translated by H.R. Wagner. London: Routledge.

Sullivan, M.L. (1989) *'Getting Paid': Youth Crime and Work in the Inner City*. Ithaca, NY: Cornell University Press.

Suttles, G.D. (1976) 'Urban ethnography: situational and normative accounts', *Annual Review of Sociology* 2: 1–18.

Thorne, B. (1993) *Gender at Play: Girls and Boys in School*. New Brunswick, NJ: Rutgers University Press.

Tyler, S.A. (1986) 'Post-modern ethnography: from document of the occult to occult document', in J. Clifford and G.E. Marcus (eds) *Writing Culture: The Poetics and Politics of Ethnography*. Berkeley, CA: University of California Press.

Venkatesh, S. (1999) 'The promise of ethnographic research: the researcher's dilemma', *Law and Social Inquiry* 24: 987–991.

Wacquant, L. (1995) 'The pugilistic point of view: how boxers think and feel about their trade', *Theory and Society* 24(4): 489–535.

Warner, W.L. (1963) *Yankee City*. New Haven, CT: Yale University Press.

Weber, M. (1949) *The Methodology of the Social Sciences*, translated and edited by E.A. Shils and H.A. Finch. New York: Free Press.

Wellman, D. (1988) 'The politics of Herbert Blumer's sociological method', *Symbolic Interaction* 11: 59–68.

Whyte, W.F. (1993 [1943]) *Street Corner Society: The Social Structure of an Italian Slum*, 4th edn. Chicago: University of Chicago Press.

7 AUTOMATING THE INEFFABLE:

Qualitative software and the meaning of qualitative research

Nigel G. Fielding

Computers have been used for half a century in research using textual data but the introduction of software to support qualitative analysis has proven controversial in a way that it never was in the field of content analysis. To understand this controversy, and its implications for qualitative research, we begin with a description of qualitative software. We note that for most users the story of qualitative software is the story of the analytic procedure called 'code-and-retrieve'. But we will also sketch in other promising applications of qualitative software, including approaches to data analysis which are implicitly numerical or are based on formal logic.

The chapter moves on to explore how people actually use qualitative software, demystifying what sometimes seems a technical 'black art'. The point will be made that patterns of use are as apt to reflect the research environment as the technology. But we will also observe that software could play a significant part in changing the workings of the qualitative research community. However, the epistemological implications of qualitative software do not mirror the extent of its technical, practical and research environment implications. Epistemological preoccupations are more enduring than any technology.

WHAT IS COMPUTER ANALYSIS OF QUALITATIVE DATA?

Computers have already established a considerable presence in qualitative research, despite its self-image as a craft. Computers are routinely used at each stage of qualitative projects, from data collection through analysis to presentation (Weitzman and Miles 1995). Yet the information technologies which now support our writing, data collection and literature searches have attracted little comment, in contrast to the debates prompted by the emergence of software to support qualitative data analysis. It may not be coincidental that, in a field which has been slow to document and codify its procedures, the last practice to attract such attention has been that of data analysis. Indeed, even those indifferent to qualitative software may concede that its emergence has benefited the field by obliging us to be more explicit about how we manage, analyse and interpret qualitative data.

A dominant concern about qualitative software is that it may somehow 'take over' the analysis, imposing a standard approach and employing concealed assumptions, the so-called 'Frankenstein's monster' debate (Lee and Fielding 1991; Kelle 1995). It is sometimes forgotten that the monster was a threat only because he was abused by humankind. Qualitative software is, even now, quite limited in the kinds of support it offers for analysis, and there is no prospect that it will ever excuse the need for researchers to think. There is another kind of rebuttal to the take-over fear, though. The imposition of a standard approach is obviated by the sheer variety of packages, each displaying considerable distinctiveness. Each has merits and deficiencies which suit it better for particular kinds of work. Researchers need to determine which best fits the kind of work they do, both practically and analytically.

Software for computer-assisted qualitative data analysis (CAQDAS) seeks to facilitate data management chores which are tedious and subject to error when done manually, make the analytic process more 'transparent' and accountable, and support analytic approaches which would otherwise be cumbersome. From the late 1970s, when the first packages emerged for use on mainframe computers, the notable thing about qualitative software was that it was developed by social scientists, not computer scientists. Development was often in response to data management or analysis requirements on specific projects. The prototypes may have suffered bugs and forbidding interfaces but they were closely informed by what researchers regarded as essential to support qualitative data analysis. Although commercial pressures inevitably intrude as the software becomes more professional, developers still exchange ideas via conferences and publications, and most remain social scientists as well as developers. This makes for close awareness of developments with other packages and responsiveness to the needs of users.

The earliest computer application to textual data was content analysis, which pursues 'objective, systematic and quantitative description of the manifest content of communication' (Berelson 1952: 489). Programs had to store extensive documentary data, address text units as 'variables', produce 'concordances' (organized lists of words and phrases) and quickly access the context of particular text segments. The mode of analysis meant programs required statistical features or to allow data to be exported to statistical packages. These requirements produced software of limited use to qualitative researchers.

To marshal the variety of data that qualitative researchers use, software must be able to store data in different formats and enable researchers to annotate it so as to track the effects of field relations on it. Researchers need to move around the corpus looking at the relevance of specific analytic ideas to different segments, so they require a means to 'navigate' the database.

They must also be able to retrace their steps in these operations. 'Coding' is fundamental to qualitative data analysis. The corpus has to be divided into segments and these segments assigned codes (or categories) which relate to the analytic themes being developed (similarly, ethnomethodologists and conversation analysts need to assign to segments a term for routines which recur in behaviour/talk). Researchers aim for codes which capture some essential quality of the segment, and which apply to other segments too. Otherwise every segment would be a code and we would get nowhere; data analysis is a process of data reduction. During this process we sometimes need to revise codes, either globally or in application to particular segments. When data are coded we can retrieve them selectively using various analytic strategies. Researchers also need to be able to write 'analytic memos', for example, giving the reasons why they assigned a given code to a segment or part containing the germ of an analytic point they want to develop.

A TYPOLOGY OF QUALITATIVE SOFTWARE

Coding and retrieval of coded segments informs all three basic types of qualitative software: *text retrievers, code-and-retrieve* packages and *theory-building* software (Weitzman and Miles 1995). *Text retrievers*, such as Metamorph, WordCruncher, ZyINDEX and Sonar Professional, let users recover the data pertaining to each category where keywords appear in the data. For example, you may have a category called 'social class'. When you search for 'social class', wherever these words appear in the text the software will extract it. If the respondent did not use the keyword it must be added to the data so the segment can be retrieved.

Words, other character strings and combinations of these, in one or many files, can be retrieved, along with things that sound alike, mean the same thing, or have patterns like the sequences of letters and numbers in social security records. Retrieved text can be sorted into new files, and analytic memos can be linked to the data. Content-analysis capabilities are often provided, including facilities to handle quantitative data. Sophisticated variants like askSam and FolioVIEWS have more ways to organize text and make subsets. Some deal with highly structured text organized into 'records' (specific cases) and 'fields' (numerical or text information appearing for each case). Text retrievers are fast at retrieval. Their forte is information management where basic data is held on large numbers of people.

Code-and-retrieve packages, including HyperQual, Kwalitan, WinMAX and The Ethnograph support the division of text into segments, attaching codes to the segments, and retrieving segments by code (or combination of codes). A 'single sort' retrieves all the data pertaining to one code. 'Multiple sort' retrievals handle cases where one category is considered in relation to another, for example where data coded 'age' coincides with data coded 'social class'. Users may also do searches which recover only data where two particular characteristics apply but not a third; for instance, data from MALE

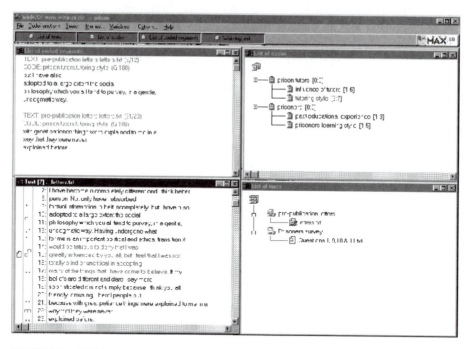

FIGURE 7.1　EXAMPLE OF CODE AND RETRIEVE SOFTWARE

respondents living in URBAN areas who are NOT married. Such strategies are called Boolean retrievals (following the 'and', 'or' and 'not' relations of Boolean mathematics). Various types of Boolean retrieval are supported.

Code-and-retrieve packages approach the writing of memos in different ways. Ideally the software reminds users that an analytic memo pertains to a segment every time it is inspected and displays the memo instantly if desired. Researchers sometimes need to retrace their interpretive work, particularly in team research, for example, to check coding has been consistent. Hypertext features allow users to move quickly around (navigate) the database.

WinMAX offers an example of contemporary code-and-retrieve software (Figure 7.1). The window at top right lists codewords hierarchically, with main codes followed by sub-codes; 'tutoring style' is highlighted as it is the code currently being considered. The bottom right window is a hierarchical list of the texts being analysed. At bottom left is the window containing the raw data currently being worked on, an extract from correspondence with a prisoner about the prison education programme. Note the icon in the extreme left margin; it indicates a memo has been written relating to a segment of the extract; to see it, the user clicks on the icon. In the next margin are markers indicating the extent of segments of the extract to which codes have been applied. The top left window lists the segments pertaining to the 'tutoring style' code, retrieved so the user can compare them.

Such software focuses analytic attention on relationships between codes (or categories) and data. *Theory-building software*, such as Atlas/ti, HyperRESEARCH, NUD*IST4, and N-vivo, emphasizes relationships between the categories, although code-and-retrieve support is also offered. These packages help users develop higher-order classifications and categories than those derived directly from data, formulate propositions which fit the data and test their applicability, or visualise connections between categories as an aid to conceptualization. Full Boolean searching and the ability to 'test' hypotheses may be offered. Some can show code names (or other objects, like memos) as nodes in a graphic display and users can link them to other nodes by specified relationships like 'leads to', 'is a kind of' and so on.

Such software can facilitate formal approaches to qualitative data analysis. A controversial example is the 'hypothesis test feature' in HyperRESEARCH. Users hypothesize a relationship between the occurrence of a particular statement in the data and the occurrence of another (*if* 'this' *then* 'that'). When the two occurrences are found together, this can be made part of another hypothetical relationship. To construct a testable hypothesis users may need several 'if' and 'then' rules, each using codewords assigned to the data. The hypothesis test searches for cases where the particular codewords occur in the particular combinations the proposition requires. If these are present that case supports the proposition.

Clearly such procedures take us some way from working with the data itself. Users have to assume that the data supporting these hypothetical relationships is comparable and that coding has been done in a commensurate fashion, because they are working 'one level up', with relationships between the categories/codes. Yet the comparability of qualitative data is problematic. Rapport with respondents may vary, respondents may talk with different degrees of specificity, and so on. Hypothesis-testing will be discussed further, after considering another formal approach.

Work with codes is not the only approach to qualitative data analysis. There is a fundamental distinction between analysis based on *codes* and analysis based on *cases*. Case-oriented approaches, the basis of analytic induction, suit some analytic purposes. Analytic induction considers instances where some phenomenon of interest is present, on the basis that it occurs only when particular conditions apply. The idea is to isolate the essential conditions determining the phenomenon. In fact, analytic induction also needs to consider cases where the phenomenon is *not* present, to be certain there are no cases where the conditions postulated for the phenomenon to occur appear in the absence of the phenomenon (Hicks 1994 called this 'neo-analytic induction'). Neo-analytic induction is useful in analysing dynamic processes, especially where there is an interest in causality. The approach called Qualitative Comparative Analysis (Ragin 1987) thinks in terms of outcomes, comparing outcomes across multiple cases. Cases are literally recognized as such from the different outcomes they display. Cases are differentiated by the relationship between their outcomes and the components they share with other cases having different outcomes. Qualitative Comparative Analysis (QCA) uses logic and mathematics to identify systematically 'universal conditions' which are always present in particular combinations when the phenomenon occurs. The 'QCA' software analyses conjunctures of particular elements of cases which bear on the outcome of a process.

We should note a further formal analytic approach using qualitative data. Event Structure Analysis represents series of events derived from fieldwork as logical structures, comprising elements and their connections. Like QCA it seeks explanatory models for interpreting sequences of events (Heise and Lewis 1988), having a chronological (process) orientation and concern with causal explanation. Its basic logic is that in each situation social actors have limited choices, and certain events cannot occur before their prerequisites. Based on these premises abstract logical structures of events are generated, and compared to actual event sequences. Event Structure Analysis is supported by a program called 'Ethno' (Heise 1991). The program enables users to model narrative accounts of event sequences and produce mathematically based causal accounts.

Like the hypothesis-testing approach of HyperRESEARCH, Qualitative Comparative Analysis and Event Structure Analysis involve high-level coding, but, unlike HyperRESEARCH, they also require extensive data reduction prior to analysis. Although the data that Qualitative Comparative Analysis and Event Structure Analysis use are qualitative, some do not regard these approaches as qualitative analysis at all. Their concern is that the analysis proceeds at a level too far removed from the original data and the context in which they were collected. They suggest that, if the data are going to be so stringently 'reduced', there is little point in collecting qualitatively 'rich' data in the first place. The status of these formal approaches is an important issue to which I will return.

There is a further formal approach that should be mentioned because it strongly embraces concerns about the importance of context. This approach is Formal Concept Analysis (FCA: Mackensen and Wille 1998) and, although it is mathematically based (on set theory), it supports the iterative process of formulating codes/categories familiar from grounded theory and which lies behind the code-and-retrieve packages. The prototype application is based on the TOSCANA data management system. FCA construes concepts as constituted by their 'extension' – all objects belonging to the concept – and 'intension' – all attributes valid for those objects. A concept can be graphically displayed in a line diagram or 'concept lattice' consisting of nodes, lines and labels. The extensions of the concept consist of all objects whose labels are attached to the node or to a node derivable by a descending path from the node, and its 'intensions' consist of all attributes whose names are attached to the node or to a node derivable by an ascending path from the node. The descending/ascending element reflects the hierarchy or 'levels' of data and concept. Analysis proceeds by traversing these paths from objects to attributes, investigating the concepts by 'zooming in' from a more abstract level to the data, or by following links from items of data to categories linked at several progressive levels of abstraction.

FCA offers a means to represent conceptual systems graphically while being able to return at any time to the data. The representation alerts users to concepts which are thinly supported (have few links to data), to empirical examples which contradict elements of postulated concepts, and to dependencies among categories. For example, research on the emergence of the notion of 'simplicity' as a criterion in classical music drew on a set of published sources in which the term was used, and various facets of these sources, including their date of publication. The pattern of diffusion of the 'simplicity' idea could be traced and key sources identified (as nodes with many links), allowing inferences about the degree of authority contemporaries accorded each source. The FCA approach uses mathematical techniques of conceptual and logical scaling to produce its concept lattices, but is more in line with the premises of qualitative research than the other formal approaches.

The three-fold typology of qualitative software can be regarded as successive generations (Kelle 1996). The first generation were word-processor and database management systems, which supported techniques like cut-and-paste but did not exceed the most basic requirements of data management. Specialized code-and-retrieve programs developed in the early 1980s contributed the ability to manage unstructured textual data and sophisticated cut-and-paste, indexing and memoing techniques. Most importantly, the second generation made coding and retrieval processes transparent. The third generation, with the ability to search for co-occurring codes, and methods to construct complex networks linking categories, codes, memos and text segments, provided facilities to support theory building and hypothesis testing. Mangabeira (1995) identifies the distinctive element of this third generation as being the model-building capabilities of the software.

The generational perspective has an important implication. As development proceeds and packages become more fully featured, a measure of convergence occurs. Exchanges between users and developers motivated many changes, others were imposed, the main example being the Windows operating system. Consequently the typology becomes less rigid; for example, one might regard WinMAX, the Windows release of the first generation package 'MAX', as a code-based theory builder rather than a code-and-retrieve package.

When qualitative software first emerged, it was informed by prevailing approaches to analysis. The main analytic metaphor was code-and-retrieve, and few looked to software to inspire new approaches to analysis. However, packages increasingly support procedures which are new or impractical without the computer. We can no longer argue that the software is simply an aid to code-and-retrieve or that code-and-retrieve is the essence of qualitative analysis. The question is, have users' practices changed accordingly?

WILL QUALITATIVE SOFTWARE KILL OFF MANUAL METHODS?

Many qualitative researchers remain committed to manual methods and, for certain purposes, manual methods have advantages over software, for example, where setting up the data in the required format would take a disproportionate time relative to the scope of the analysis. No one should feel guilty about not using software or pressured into adopting it. However, a major benefit of qualitative software is that it obliges researchers to be clearer about their reasoning, and enables the analytic process to be more transparent and therefore accountable. These characteristics will shift community standards of analytic quality over time, and those relying on manual methods may find themselves having to invest inordinate effort in the paper-based equivalents of procedures which are done in seconds using software.

It is important to repeat that simply using CAQDAS does not mean the whole analytic process takes place 'within' the software. It is true that prototype 'expert systems' have emerged, which, for example, prompt users to consider whether the data with which they have supported an inference is adequate. Such prompts are only as good as the criteria 'wired into' the program; expert system software has a potential role in teaching, but the prototypes encourage users to override program advice if they wish.

It is pedagogically desirable that those new to qualitative methods should have their initial experiences using manual approaches, to gain a firm grounding in procedures that they may later automate. This also avoids conflict between learning the rudiments of method and learning the procedures of software use; the consensus is that people should have a reasonable grasp of the foundations of qualitative research first (Allatt and Benson 1991; Fielding and Lee 1996).

CAQDAS IN THE RESEARCH ENVIRONMENT

Sales data for one of the longest established packages, The Ethnograph, suggests that early users featured in applied fields such as social research in medical settings rather than in discipline-based academic research. This may relate to the hope that CAQDAS can resolve time pressure, although such hopes appear to be false (Lee and Fielding 1995). Research suggests this pattern of adoption may also account for the typical mode of use, which tends to exploit data management rather than conceptualizing or analytic features (Fielding and Lee 1998).

One might assume that research on CAQDAS users would be dominated by reports of bugs, crashes, program architecture and so on – that is, technical and practical issues. However, the focus groups and individual interviews that Ray Lee and I conducted with about 60 CAQDAS users in Britain (Fielding and Lee 1998) revealed that the issues preoccupying users were not simply technical but matters of the 'research environment'. Tangled up with software use were fundamentals of the social context of research – sponsors' demands, deadline pressures, power relations in research teams and with research subjects, and so on. Accounting for respondents' experiences means exploring how 'software issues' impact on 'research environment issues', and vice versa.

Take, for example, the apparently banal matter of availability. Originally users found product information elusive and distribution amateur. Academics who sought advice from their university's computing centre almost invariably reported that staff had never heard of CAQDAS. Social science computing began and ended with statistics packages. Graduate students were particularly likely to be referred back to their own department but regardless of status the general response was that no one had requested such software before and resources were not available. The same story generally prevailed when requesters approached their own departments for help, except, in some cases, ignorance was compounded by hostility to the idea of 'mechanizing' the craft of qualitative analysis. We documented cases where users faced opposition to CAQDAS from senior project staff or doctoral supervisors.

Would-be users who finally got the software they wanted did not usually do so by comparative evaluation and discriminating choice, but because someone in their social network had details of a particular package. Computing centres remained unwilling to help with support and training, because staff would have to be found to evaluate and then support the new software. Training is, even now, largely ad hoc and patchily distributed; for example, in an exchange on the email list for Atlas/ti users a would-be user in Texas appealed for training, which elicited an offer if the individual could get to Santa Barbara. It is a long way from Texas to California. Thus, the seemingly straightforward matter of obtaining a package ready for use on one's own machine invokes issues concerning the status of qualitative research, computing centre resources, the organization of the software market, and training.

I noted that choice is often ad hoc. Yet packages vary and users need to choose carefully, taking account of not only cost and the availability of support but also the nature of the analytic project(s) for which the software is needed, the type of work they are likely to do in future (applied/academic, policy-related/conceptualizing, solo/team and so on), the balance between ease-of-use and availability of sophisticated features, and other factors (for full discussion of 'choice' issues, see Weitzman and Miles 1995). While applied researchers faced fewer problems justifying acquisition, and research sponsors appear to favour CAQDAS for reasons of legitimation, applied researchers face their own problems. Applied research features tight deadlines and has relatively straightforward analytic requirements. Users complained that data entry and setting-up occupied a disproportionate time relative to the analysis the sponsor wanted, and some felt they were under-utilizing the package.

Users expected three main things from CAQDAS: that it would save time, make analysis more thorough, and support analytic procedures that were impractical manually. However, we found no case where users reported CAQDAS saved on analysis time. This is probably not susceptible to a technological fix. Coding and analysis are (and should be) intrinsically time-consuming. Not only have developers not claimed that using CAQDAS is quicker, several emphasize the need for thoroughness in the coding process and reflect this in program design (this is not to say procedures for applying codes should not be simple and quick). What about the expectation that analysis would be more thorough? Users gave abundant testimony to this. Computers do not forget or mislay things, they always do the same procedure the same way, and, if users need reminding of how they have carried out some operation, the software can often help retrace steps. Users were in no doubt that CAQDAS can manage voluminous data more effectively than can paper-based methods.

But evidence was mixed on the support for sophisticated conceptual work. I already noted that some applied researchers found the pace of their work denied them time for creative play with advanced features; sometimes they simply did not have time to code all the data, seriously limiting the kind of analytic work possible. The value of CAQDAS to them was as an electronic filing cabinet, though some appeared to ease their frustration by promising themselves they would use the more advanced analytic features in their own time at some future point. Academic users were, generally, enthusiastic about the conceptualizing features, but reported problems learning how to use them. Graduate students were most enthusiastic about the conceptualizing features, perhaps suggesting a more open mind and fewer preconceptions.

Thoughts on the use of CAQDAS in the analytic process prompted reflections beyond technical, computing issues. Users tended initially to declare affiliation to a particular analytic approach, most often 'grounded theory', citing the appeal of rigorous analysis without quantification, the elevation of 'closeness to the data', and conceptualization emergent from the data rather than from formal theory. However, when we invited users to connect the elements of grounded theory procedure to the support offered by particular packages, accounts were seldom based on direct adherence to grounded theory procedures. It seems that users did not expect CAQDAS to support each element of grounded theory; they wanted something more flexible than that. Nor is the software as closely informed by grounded theory as the developers' early claims suggested. It goes little further than that CAQDAS packages are based on coding data segments and writing analytic memos. Thus, asserted affiliation to grounded theory should not determine our view of how qualitative software supports qualitative analysis. To suggest that CAQDAS particularly supports grounded theory work is as plausible as suggesting that all qualitative research is grounded theory. Indeed research can be both rigorous and illuminating without using a 'standard' approach at all (Weaver and Atkinson 1994).

Recent versions of qualitative software offer features which enable kinds of work which were not previously supported. It is particularly intriguing whether these features are being exploited, in light of the limited use of the more sophisticated analytic features noted in our research. Similarly, the extent of use of QCA and FCA would be of great interest, as these are associated with more formal approaches to qualitative data analysis, which are of considerable interest to researchers well outside the qualitative camp (Lindenberg 1998).

NEW TECHNOLOGIES = NEW ANALYSES?

While developers foresee an increasing integration of software tools this is unlikely to result in a 'superpackage' having every feature offered by any package. Instead, users will increasingly be able to transfer projects between packages, with coding done in one package, conceptual mapping in another, and so on. To enable this, there will be some standardization of procedures, a trend encouraged by operation under Windows. There is also a tendency to more visually based analytic and data presentation strategies. Current examples include the tree diagrams of NUD*IST4, N-vivo's visual approach to modelling, and the 'network views' of Atlas/ti. The latter also supports coding of graphic images. Packages also increasingly provide facilities to export worked projects to websites for joint work and dissemination. Other changes include more automated coding, the general move to provide full suites of Boolean operators, and better-designed interfaces with increased use of 'drag and drop' functionality. Several developers are adding format-ted text features, to preserve the cues to context these can offer, allow code assignments to stay linked to text as projects are moved between packages, and accommodate accents and non-standard symbols.

Adjacent technological developments also have implications for qualita-tive research. Data transcription is laborious, prone to error, expensive and subject to the sensibilities of transcriptionists. Voice recognition software, which converts speech to text, is improving. Software like DragonDictate, VoiceType, and Kurzweil Voice still pose considerable requirements in train-ing the recognition facility to the user's voice and checking output for accu-racy, nor are they cheap. But improvements are continual and prices should be set against the cost of transcription services. An alternative is 'direct tran-scription software', where speech is recorded on a CD-ROM and codes are applied not to text but to the sound segments themselves (e.g. *Code-A-Text, C-I-SAID, Qualitative Media Analyzer*). During retrieval the researcher can lis-ten to the actual data as well as read them as text. Pitch, modulation and other sound features can be monitored, allowing inferences from tone of voice as well as the words uttered. It is worth noting that the developer of *Code-A-Text* uses it in analysis of clinical/therapeutic interviews and in con-versation analysis. Such software may also be useful in market research, where time does not permit transcription, or in making a first high-level pass through the data to identify broad themes.

While technological developments contribute to change in approaches to analysis, they are but one influence among many. The new technologies available to qualitative researchers cannot but make for innovation and experiment (and an accompanying degree of confusion), but their transfor-mative potential (Lee 1995) is not so strong as to change the external forces which shape the qualitative research world or the internal variety which makes qualitative work so interestingly diverse. However, if we narrow our attention from the macro level, qualitative software and other IT, notably the Internet, does allow those who are so inclined to further develop the progress qualitative research shows toward greater formalization, and to help those who are so inclined to seek new community standards of participation in the products of qualitative research (see Mann and Stewart 2000). These themes are pursued below.

THE POTENTIAL TO GENERALIZE AND
THE INCLINATION TO PARTICULARIZE

Critics of qualitative research cite its lack of formality and cumulativeness. Until recently, this has been amplified by inattention to analytic principles and procedures in the qualitative methods literature. These traits compare unfavourably with the formal and systematic character of statistical analysis and survey methods. While analysing words is different from analysing numbers this is not a warrant to be evasive or mystical about our analytic procedures. Both formalism, the drive to construct algebraic expressions of axiomatic knowledge, and formalization, the effort to codify methodological procedures, are relevant here. As statistics has developed new tools, it has prompted more stringent criteria and procedures of quantitative analysis. In qualitative research, formalizing influences have concentrated on principles for data collection. The network of developers, users and methodologists associated with qualitative software has provided an impetus to formalization of analytic procedure. Further, some methodologists have sought to make the object of qualitative analysis the identification of formal conditions which capture, for example, cause and effect relationships. One might cite work by mathematical sociologists in modelling behaviour using ethnographic data (Abell 1988); such an orientation influenced the work in Event Structure Analysis (Heise 1991). Technology increasingly facilitates that kind of analysis. Yet, perhaps because such work is more keenly attended-to outside qualitative research (for example, in rational choice theory and social simulation), it attracts less notice than the more vocal analytic orientation which celebrates relativism and repudiates the search for formal knowledge and generalization.

The point about these ruptures relevant to qualitative software is that, while these commitments colour our attitudes to new technology, they have not come from technological developments but from adherence to intellectual traditions which have grown up in the theory and practice of qualitative research. The relativist and postmodern positions are products of the Romantic tradition in philosophy (Strong and Dingwall 1997), and one impetus to 'emotionalism' came from applied studies in medical settings. The new research technologies are not the source of new analyses, though they may be their vehicle. We might take for example the 'QCA' software developed by Drass (1989) and the hypertext-linking approach Weaver and Atkinson (1994) document in their writings on the use of GUIDE. The former addresses causal analysis, the latter celebrates chance discovery and the multiple meanings any text can support. The QCA approach is directed to formalism and a positivist understanding of data as facts that can be abstracted. Weaver and Atkinson (1994) pursue an ever-changing, suggestive analysis and a postmodern conception of data as infinitely contested interpretations. These approaches share no ground. Yet both have been operationalized by qualitative software in a way that would not otherwise be possible.

In fact, self-conscious 'landmark' texts, like Denzin and Lincoln's (2001) handbook, make it apparent that the growth and subdivision of schools of analytic thought has proceeded quite independently of IT developments. If we accept Denzin and Lincoln's classifications, we have several postmodern approaches to analysis, along with post-positivism and the evergreen interactionism. The liberal use of the prefix 'post' suggests that these are rebrandings of familiar branches of qualitative analysis. It is most unlikely that qualitative software will, in itself, prompt the invention of new methods or schools of thought. So far, at least, where technology transforms social science, it transforms procedure. An interview administered by Netcam allows a researcher in Guildford to do 'fieldwork' in Melbourne but the researcher will still have to wrestle with rapport, or its lack, when interpreting the data. There will be a difference of degree but not of kind.

The kudos associated with discovery of the 'new' encourages authors, editors and publishers readily to assign self-labelled new approaches to a new category. Notice, for instance, that, like the Denzin and Lincoln (2001) handbook, the volume you are reading has one, standalone chapter on 'software'. Why, one wonders, are software implications not discussed in relation to each of the fieldwork topics and analytic procedures? Instead, software is depicted as 'an approach' in itself (in the original Denzin and Lincoln volume (1994), it is a 'method of analysis': see Table 1.1, p. 12). No wonder those unacquainted with CAQDAS think it is a new and technicist approach, to put alongside critical theory, feminism and the rest.

It should therefore be said that there is little at the level of epistemology or approach to analysis in qualitative software which is not derivative of thinking that existed before a mouse was anything but an animal that squeaks. This is not to say that CAQDAS does nothing new. It allows us to operationalize procedures and approaches to analysis whose logical possibility was identified but whose demands were entirely impractical before the computer. An example might be the 'system closure' concept in NUD*IST4 and N-vivo (for a good practical account of using the latter, see Bryman 2001). Any 'transformation' that emerges will come as a result of being able now to test the consequences of procedures like QCA which, if its proponents are right, may enable credible claims to derive causal explanation inductively from non-numerical data. That would undeniably be a big thing, even a transformation, but it would not represent a new logic. We still confront the obstacles that were apparent to Weber. New technologies even mean we have to negotiate new ramifications of those problems; for instance, the Netcam example suggests that, in assessing context effects, we will have to make inferences about the effects of not being physically co-present. Software will enable us to tag and recover instances where those effects intrude on our analysis, though, and to retrace our analytic steps using 'audit trails', which may help us weigh up their impact. With technology we can do more, but we also have more to do.

FACILITATING TEAMWORK, ENABLING DEBATE, ENCOURAGING REFLEXIVITY

It takes time for markets to understand technologies, and what may eventually be prevalent uses may not be the obvious or the intended (e.g. the telephone was originally envisaged as a broadcast medium). One non-obvious use of qualitative software that could be very significant is in facilitating working cooperatively. CAQDAS packages offer a number of features to support joint work. In some cases, such as that of FCA, the idea of collaborative interrogation of the data is the essence of the software design. A virtue of team research is that it forces individuals to be more explicit about their reasoning. Software which enables individual inputs to be traced via 'audit trails' and work to be exported to websites for comment by dispersed team members can encourage sharper thinking and more clarity about how and why a particular analytic decision has been made. Where such features are used to encourage participation in analysis by interested outsiders they can enable debate which enhances the analysis and brings the findings to wider audiences. If the research subjects are encouraged to use these means to participate in the stages of inquiry subsequent to data collection we might even see a change in community understandings of research and what it is for. There is a particular potential for hypertext-based projects here, where outsiders might use the technology to construct their own interpretations of the data (Weaver and Atkinson 1994). The strong recent emphasis on relativism has given matters to do with reflexivity extra prominence; we increasingly recognize the need to track the effects of our own subjectivity and bring it to bear in our analysis. Again, CAQDAS can play a part, because it makes it easy to review the effects of sequences of program operations and to recast elements of the analysis to gauge their effects.

Qualitative software appears to have contributed to the rehabilitation and wider use of qualitative methods, by affording the technical appearance of formality that computer procedures have long lent to statistical research (Agar 1991). This helps establish credibility with research sponsors, be they government funding agencies, public service organizations or the private sector. Like the date with an old beau, qualitative research has also enjoyed new relationships on the rebound, as these selfsame funding bodies recognize the failures and limits of quantitative research. The analogy contains a warning. New enthusiasms are volatile. Qualitative research may enjoy a new vogue but it is conditional. The old prejudices remain. If the practice of qualitative research confirms that it is akin to writing fiction or dogma, betrays an inability to decide what the data mean, or the techniques are 'non-transferable' (cannot be taught), qualitative research will be back out in the cold. Technology does not obscure sloppy thinking, it exposes it.

These views are, of course, informed by a particular view of what research is for. Research produces knowledge. It may be knowledge for-its-own-sake or it may be applied, but our audience is the research community, including those who use research to make policy decisions which affect the community. In this context, both the appearance and the reality of formalization, of which research technology is a part, are important features of the qualitative scene. We can contrast this with another view, where we seek new audiences by moving away from conventional forms of research writing (Richardson 1994). This approach also often sees qualitative research as a means of empowerment of research subjects.

But regardless of our conception of research, qualitative software can change our relation to our audiences. The transparency of the analytic process, where software allows users to recover and display the steps in their reasoning, opens our work to discussion with others. For example, the user experiences research documented cases where these features encouraged applied research sponsors to play a part in the analysis. The ability to export parts of our data, or our write-up, to a website means that others can play a part. At minimum, research subjects and other participants are enabled to comment on the data and/or the analysis. This may make inquiry more open-ended, give voice to those whose account is normally silenced, and make researchers more accountable. Such possibilities do seem to address the business of 'empowerment'.

AUTOMATING THE INEFFABLE?

Qualitative software has contributed greatly to the research community. For methodologists, its real significance does not lie in technology or technique but in exposing areas in which accustomed reasoning is muddy, and enabling experiment with approaches which looked promising but whose resource requirements exceeded the capacities of manual methods. CAQDAS has stimulated a reappraisal of qualitative methodology. It has prompted us to reassess accepted epistemological canons (such as the role of hypothesis-testing in qualitative work), provoked new methodological debates (such as those over the status of coding or grounded theory) and tested new analytic approaches (such as qualitative comparative analysis or using hypertext as a freeform method of discovery). For researchers its benefits include data management capacities unquestionably superior to paper-based systems, facilitation of the orderly and accountable practice of analysis, and features which invite us to extract the maximum from our data. For research audiences, qualitative software augments the claim of qualitative research to legitimacy, but, more interestingly, beckons them to get more involved in the research rather than regarding it as a product they simply consume.

There are demerits too. For example, early users endured endless bugs, crashes and quirks, and even now the chance to make an informed choice and/or to gain access to systematic training is available to few. Opening up our texts via hypertext-based projects allows untutored use, which could result in serious disputes with research subjects and the misrepresentation of project findings. Automating code assignment allows blanket recoding rather than careful inspection of each segment before a code is assigned. Program complexity means that sometimes users have only a vague idea of what particular operations have actually done. Neo-quantification of program output may encourage inappropriate but apparently precise numerical analyses. These and other demerits may be regarded as elements of the one great problem, that qualitative researchers will claim for their findings, analyses and interpretations more than they should. So what's new? The field will respond to such problems as it always has, not by embracing articulated standardized criteria of validity, but by critical peer review, liberally interpreted community standards of analytic adequacy, and learning from experience (Altheide and Johnson 1994).

Qualitative research survived its years as the poor cousin of quantitative social science by creativity. It was 'a method of discovery'. It had a place even in survey research as a method to use at the pilot stage, because it was a source of ideas, hunches and hypotheses. Those who use qualitative software testify both that they get ideas from working with the software and that they get ideas in the traditional ways, in the bath, in the middle of a conversation, while landing at night. Using software won't prevent the 'eureka' effect but it won't guarantee it either.

REFERENCES

Abell, P. (1988) 'The "structuration" of action: inference and comparative narratives', in N. Fielding (ed.) *Actions and Structure*. London: Sage.

Agar, M. (1991) 'The right brain strikes back', in N. Fielding and R. Lee (eds) *Using Computers in Qualitative Research*. London: Sage.

Allatt, P. and Benson, L. (1991) 'Computing and qualitative analysis: issues in research methods teaching', in N. Fielding and R. Lee (eds) *Using Computers in Qualitative Research*. London: Sage.

Altheide, D. and Johnson, J. (1994) 'Criteria for assessing interpretive validity in qualitative research', in N. Denzin and Y. Lincoln (eds) *Handbook of Qualitative Research*, 1st edn. London: Sage.

Berelson, B. (1952) *Content Analysis in Communications Research*. New York: Free Press.

Bryman, A. (2001) *Social Research Methods*. Oxford: Oxford University Press.

Denzin, N. and Lincoln, Y. (eds) (2001) *Handbook of Qualitative Research,* 1st edn. Thousand Oaks, CA: Sage.

Drass, K. (1989) 'Text analysis and text analysis software: a comparison of assumptions', in G. Blank *et al.* (eds) *New Technology in Sociology: Practical Applications in Research and Work.* New Brunswick, NJ: Transaction.

Fielding, N. and Lee, R. (1996) 'Diffusion of a methodological innovation: computer-assisted qualitative data analysis in the UK', *Current Sociology* 44(3): 242–258.

Fielding, N. and Lee, R. (1998) *Computer Analysis and Qualitative Research.* London: Sage.

Heise, D. (1991) 'Event structure analysis: a qualitative model of quantitative research', in N. Fielding and R. Lee (eds) *Using Computers in Qualitative Research.* London: Sage.

Heise, D. and Lewis, E. (1988) *Introduction to ETHNO: Version 2.* Raleigh, NC: National Collegiate Software Clearinghouse.

Hicks, A. (1994) 'Qualitative comparative analysis and analytic induction: the case for the emergence of the social security state', *Sociological Methods and Research* 23: 86–113.

Kelle, U. (1996) 'Computer-aided qualitative data analysis: an overview', in C. Zull, J. Harkness and J. Hoffmeyer-Zlotnik (eds) *Text Analysis and Computers.* Mannheim: ZUMA.

Kelle, U. (1997) 'Theory building in qualitative research and computer programs for the management of textual data', *Sociological Research Online* 2(2).

Lee, R. (ed.) (1995) *Information Technology for the Social Scientist.* London: UCL Press.

Lee, R. and Fielding, N. (1991) 'Computing for qualitative research: options, problems and potential', in N. Fielding and R. Lee (eds) *Using Computers in Qualitative Research.* London: Sage.

Lee, R. and Fielding, N. (1995) 'Confronting CAQDAS: choice and contingency', in R. Burgess (ed.) *Studies in Qualitative Methodology.* New York: JAI Press.

Lindenberg, S. (1998) 'The influence of simplification on explananda: phenomenon-centred versus choice-centred theories in the social sciences', in H-P. Blossfeld and G. Prein (eds) *Rational Choice Theory and Large-scale Data Analysis.* Boulder, CO: Westview.

Mackensen, K. and Wille, U. (1998) 'Qualitative text analysis supported by conceptual data system', unpublished working paper, Mannheim: ZUMA.

Mangabeira, W. (1995) 'Computer assistance, qualitative analysis and model building', in R.M. Lee (ed.) *Information Technology for the Social Scientist.* London: UCL Press.

Mann, C. and Stewart, F. (2000) *Internet Communication and Qualitative Research: A Handbook for Researching Online.* London: Sage.

Ragin, C. (1987) *The Comparative Method: Beyond Qualitative and Quantitative Strategies.* Berkeley, CA: University of California Press.

Richardson, L. (1994) 'Writing: a method of inquiry', in N. Denzin and Y. Lincoln (eds) *Handbook of Qualitative Research,* 1st edn. London: Sage.

Strong, P. and Dingwall, R. (1997) 'Romantics and Stoics', in G. Miller and R. Dingwall (eds) *Context and Method in Qualitative Research.* London: Sage.

Weaver, A. and Atkinson, P. (1994) *Microcomputing and Qualitative Data Analysis.* Aldershot: Avebury.

Weitzman, E. and Miles, M. (1995) *Computer Programs for Qualitative Data Analysis.* Thousand Oaks, CA: Sage.

8 SUBJECTIVITY AND QUALITATIVE METHOD

*Valerie Walkerdine, Helen Lucey
and June Melody*

This chapter deals with the intersection of two issues which are central for any research in the social sciences – the issue of the place of our own subjectivity in the research process and, inside that, the issue of emotion and unconscious processes. It attempts to engage with the place of emotions in the construction of research accounts through our understanding of issues concerned with surveillance, truth, fictions and fantasies in the research process. The tricky issue of the place of one's own subjectivity is not new and has been a central issue for feminist research. Other chapters in this book raise important issues about the problems of reflexivity. In particular, we want to draw attention to Beverley Skeggs' discussion in Chapter 17 of the way in which the reflexive self is formed through the technology of the bourgeois self in which self-narration becomes confession. It is often seen as enough for researchers to assert their own subjectivity without also understanding the production of that subjectivity itself. This authorial self is not a core self which somehow shores up the possibility of the account. That self, like those of the research participants, is created as both fiction (in the Foucauldian sense) and fantasy. How then can we take the issue of subjectivity in research seriously? If research and subjectivity are produced through fictions and fantasies, then the issue of the narratives of the researcher and participants becomes more complex than the telling of different stories. Nor is it helped very much by a simple reference to Foucault's notion of the confessional, important as that is, as though that somehow obviated the necessity to engage with how the intersections of competing fictions and fantasies are lived by the subject. However reflexive researchers might be about their complex relation to the Other, trying to tell a story about themselves as part of the research, in order to avoid problems of speaking for those Others, nevertheless, issues of subjectivity do not disappear. We want to explore how we might begin to work with the multiple constitution of those discourses through which the subject is produced, to examine how this works emotionally, that is, how the intersection of fiction and fantasy is lived for both participants and researchers and how, out of the intersection of these, certain research stories get to be told. There is a level at which the practice of data collection suggests that we are seeking a truth about our research participants and that further, the deeper and more delving our questioning, the more profound that truth of the subject will be. This idea is seriously disturbed by Foucault's writings on the confessional and the idea that such an approach could be part of a will to tell the truth about the human subject – a desire to 'know' them psychologically rather than an understanding of the way in which they are produced as subjects by the very narratives and discourses that position them in the social world. However, subjectivity is not simply about being the 'sum total of positions in discourse since birth' (Henriques *et al.* 1998), but rather a complex understanding both of discursive constitution and the ways in which the relations between positionings are held together by and for the subject in ways which can be quite contradictory and conflictual. This works both for the researcher in the unsteady task of uncovering discourses and narratives and for the research subject and indeed for the dance between them which produces the stories told within the research. Understanding subjectivity therefore demands an understanding of emotions not because it seeks to uncover an essentialist depth psychology but because the fictions of subject positions are not linked by rational connections, but by fantasy, by defences which prevent one position from spilling into another.

POSTMODERN PSYCHOANALYSIS

Elliot and Spezzano (1999) specify this in relation to what they take to be the building blocks of a postmodern psychoanalysis:

> The development of a postmodern orientation to psychoanalysis is intended to draw attention to the decline of traditionalist, modernist approaches to knowledge and experience. Such a decline, however, is not coterminous with its disintegration. On the contrary, we argue that what is emerging today is a kind of *psychoanalysis of psychoanalysis*: a running together of modernist and postmodernist psychoanalytical currents, the rediscovery or invention of psychoanalysis as a vibrant theory and practice, the sharpening and differentiation of models of mind, the restructuring of methodology, and the rethinking of interactional configurations in which the self is understood in relation to others. (Elliot and Spezzano 1999: 28, original emphasis)

They go on to argue that there are three key points. First, that the linear model of the subject is challenged by notions of multiplicity and fracturing, which has effects in an approach to intersubjectivity which emphasizes the link between unconscious desire and otherness. Second, while traditionally, psychoanalysis aims for the translation of unconscious fantasy into rational understanding, the postmodern version 'underscores the centrality of imagination, desire and affect' (1999: 28) and intersubjectivity. Third, postmodern approaches internally critique the desire of psychoanalysis to be scientific and relate that critique to issues of epistemology and interpretation within the social and human sciences, aiming for a model of interpretation which is at once historical and personal. We would add to this one that is at once social, cultural and psychic. Hence our attempt to produce a new methodological turn, one which recognizes the critiques of psychoanalysis, of empirical work, of interpretation in the social sciences and tries to find a way forward. This is akin to the 'third space' which Cohen and Ainley (2000) characterize for youth research, in which the social, cultural and psychic are researched together and ways found to develop methodologies which respond to the demand for inseparability at the level of explanation.

Of course, many would argue that even keeping a notion of the unconscious and working with psychoanalysis, albeit in a postmodern fashion, uses a mode of explanation which removes historicity from the account. It is important therefore to recognize the way in which psychoanalysis is being used here and what psychoanalytic concepts are referred to. The central issue is to understand the way in which historically specific subject positions are held in place and the relations, conflicts and contradictions between them experienced both by the subject and as producing the subject. Our argument is that postmodern psychoanalysis potentially provides one way of understanding these issues by reference to concepts of fantasy, desire, anxiety, affect, defences, in short, to unconscious processes, and attempts to move away from any simple depth concept of a 'self' (Henriques *et al.* 1998). We would argue that such an approach is perfectly compatible with narrative and discourse approaches to the understanding of subjectivity and considerably adds to them (Frosh 2001). Moreover, if we understand the research process itself as the construction of its own fiction, the storying into being of an account, then the researcher is both written into and writes that story. The researcher's own fantasies become singularly important. So how can we explore the implications for method of taking account of both the subjectivity of the researcher(s) and the subjectivity of the participants as constituted through fiction and fantasy?

RESEARCH AS SURVEILLANCE

The background to this chapter is a long trajectory of work which attempted to make sense of the relationship between the work of one of us, Valerie, as an academic who grew up in the British working class, and working-class families who were the object of her research, who were both the object of a surveillant research gaze and the object of her own fantasies about their relation to her. When she was conducting some research on young girls at home and at school for a project in the early 1980s, she became aware of the ways in which the families she was working with might 'read' her as a middle-class researcher, while she, in fact, wanted them to be able to see the very part which was painfully invisible, indeed well hidden, that is the working-class child, who she imagined to be more like them and who, of course, did not want to look on them with a surveillant gaze. This work was subsequently written up as 'Video replay: families, films and fantasy' (Walkerdine 1985) and has been much discussed, debated and critiqued (see Walkerdine 1997 for a review). In particular, we want to dwell on the issue of the way in which we tried to understand the research process as surveillant – what is it that social and psychological research wants to know about the Other and why, what does this mean for the place of one's own subjectivity in the research process? If the issue of her own class background was such a potent emotional issue for Valerie in conducting the fieldwork, what place did it have in understanding the data? In the 1985 chapter, she speculated about meanings made by the working-class participants on the basis of her own fantasies, associations and identifications with them. But, as one critic clearly argued, how on earth could he know that she was not just projecting onto her research participants her own fantasies that in fact had nothing to do with them? Of course, he was quite right. How could she know and yet how could she not take account of both her own fantasies and those of the participants as these were so highly significant if we were attempting to understand not just subjectification (the discursive production of subject positions) but subjectivity? Since then the three of us have attempted to develop this line of thinking more systematically, to think about both the tricky surveillance of the research endeavour, our impossible desire to know what is *really* going on, to get up close and the importance of understanding our own place in research. The discussion which follows forms an attempt to begin to take seriously what it might mean to use psychoanalysis to understand the subjectivity of the researcher as it intersects with the participants and to argue for taking the fantasies and defences of participants seriously. In particular, we discuss the issues of transference and defences as they relate to attempts to take the place of subjectivity seriously in a systematic way.

THE SUBJECTIVITY OF THE PARTICIPANTS

We want to begin by making reference to a body of work contained in our study of transition to womanhood in Britain (Walkerdine, Lucey and Melody 2001). Here is one of the participants, 18-year-old Sharon, who did poorly at school, but harboured the ambition to be a judge, an ambition her working-class family knows about and endorses. Sharon has tried to undertake a BTEC (an alternative to A levels in Britain leading to university entrance). She has not been very successful and in fact dropped out of one course, but has begun another and met a sympathetic lecturer who is trying to help her in her ambition. This ambition is at one level obviously a laudable post-feminist one, but she is a very long way from achieving or even knowing how to achieve university entrance to an undergraduate degree. What we are interested in here is the way in which this expressed ambition sits alongside the following extract from an interview conducted by June Melody when she (June) was heavily pregnant. The conversation in the interview turns to relationships, sex and pregnancy. Sharon has begun a new relationship with an older man with whom she is having sex without contraception. June and Sharon are discussing the possibility of becoming pregnant as a result of unprotected sex.

Sharon:	It's the chance that you take though in't it. Really
J.M.:	Yeah sure, but so I mean you don't – if it happened it happened kind of thing, it doesn't cause you any anxiety –
Sharon:	I – me and my mum said to me if it happens, it happens. Just cross that bridge when we come to it.
J.M.:	Right. And you what – do you use contraceptives?
Sharon:	No
J.M.:	You don't – not at all?
Sharon:	No
J.M.:	So it's possible that you might get pregnant?
Sharon:	Yeah
J.M.:	And are you hoping that you will?
Sharon:	No not really. Hope in a couple of years I will but not yet.
J.M.:	Right – so it's quite likely that you will, if you're not using any contraceptive.
Sharon:	That's the chance innit.
J.M.:	Right. Um
Sharon:	S'pose I'd be scared if I didn't have my mum and dad's backing.
J.M.:	Right – so do you think you're trying to get pregnant?
Sharon:	No
J.M.:	On some level.
Sharon:	(*untrans.*)
J.M.:	But if you're not using contraceptives then it's very likely that you will.
Sharon:	Yeah it's likely that I will but I'm not like going out of my way to get pregnant or nothing like that.
J.M.:	Right. But you're not avoiding it so – um and is your boyfriend quite happy about that possibility?
Sharon:	Oh he don't he don't want me to get pregnant.
J.M.:	So what – he doesn't use any contraceptives?
Sharon:	No

Here June is finding it incredibly difficult to come to terms with the idea that at some level Sharon is not trying to get pregnant. We want to discuss this extract in two ways. First, it is possible to understand the probable yet unplanned pregnancy as being produced at the intersection of two competing positions – the post-feminist judge and the working-class young mother. If Sharon retains the fantasy of becoming a judge, a fantasy so very hard to live out, the unplanned pregnancy could be understood as offering a way out to another known and sanctioned position, the mother, a position so much easier to deal with for her family and well known and trodden (as her mother admits), without ever having to apparently give up on the ambition to be a judge. This interpretation demands an understanding not only of the contradictions between multiple subject positions but also of unconscious processes as a place where such conflicts and contradictions can be apparently worked on, resolved or kept at bay. This relates to the issue of how subjectivity is lived that we mentioned at the beginning of the chapter. However, the second and related issue is that the research participant is one part of the production of this in terms of a research narrative. The researcher has also to make sense of this conflict. For June, as interviewer, Sharon's response brought up some very difficult feelings, in this case, feelings of anger and irritation, which she expresses in her field notes:

> I felt incredibly irritated with her. I wanted to tell her how bloody stupid she was. It was nothing to do with morality. I don't have any strong feelings about whether she gets pregnant or not. I felt she was being quite hostile towards me (or was I feeling hostile towards her?) and was very ambivalent about being interviewed. In fact I really don't think she wanted to be interviewed at all. It seemed that she would do anything rather than give me a straightforward answer and that she was hoping to give me as little information about herself as she could get away with. Possibly in the hope that I would not be able to build up an accurate picture of her.

Of course, June's desire to 'build up an accurate picture' of Sharon can be counterpointed by what June projects onto Sharon as a desire to avoid this. In many ways, we can understand this dance as a classic relation of research desire – the desire to reveal counterpointed by the desire to conceal – on both the part of the researcher and the researched, in many ways the classic aspect of research as surveillance. And indeed, the copious discussions of ethnographers' differential treatment of their own field notes and their formal production of an account makes that ambivalent desire very clear. In that sense then, the idea of multiple subjectivity does not simply reside with the participant. We need to take account of the fantasies of the researchers and subjects in producing any account. How might we then make use of this multiplicity of both participant and researcher in the production of the research story?

We want to suggest that this takes us beyond a notion of reflexivity and towards this place in which the conflicts and contradictions of a multiple subjectivity are held in place.

While research in the social sciences is overwhelmingly premised on the notion of a rational, calculating subject, the subject of our discourse is altogether more irrational, anxious and 'defended' (Hollway and Jefferson 1997). Most qualitative research, including ethnographic research, is infused with a realism, with claims to an authenticity which purports to 'tell life how it really is'. Adding the researcher's voice in most cases is designed to fill some of the absences which 'difference' produces in order to construct a more complete, more 'real' ethnographic picture or which turns to the researcher because of the problems of Other discussed earlier. However, when attempting to take account of unconscious processes which are set in motion by all kinds of anxieties and fantasies, any notion of what constitutes the 'real' is seriously challenged. As Cohen (1999) argues:

> the relation between the real and the imaginary is not fixed, but tactically determined. By the same token the imaginary is not a distorted reflection of the real, nor is the real simply a site for a projection of fantasy. We are always dealing with a process of *double inscription* whose articulation varies according to a range of social circumstances. (Cohen 1999: 11, original emphasis)

The use of psychoanalytic concepts to theorize social phenomena and processes is growing in a number of disciplines. While the overwhelming majority of educational research is concerned with conscious processes, there is a growing and significant body of empirical work which is concerned to explore individual and institutional patterns of investment and disavowal which enter in the formation of pedagogic identities (Britzman 1995; Raphael Reed 1995; Shaw 1995; Pitt 1998). Oral historians have combined the techniques of life story research with insights from family therapy in order to explore the 'mixture of conscious and unconscious models, myths and material inheritance' (Bertaux and Thompson 1993) which combine to shape individual and family narratives (Ginzburg 1990; Thompson and Samuel 1990). In the field of urban sociology and cultural geography, researchers and writers are drawing in particular on the work of the object relations theorists in order to explore the relationship between subjectivity, society and space (Pajaczkowska and Young 1992; Rose 1993; Pile 1996; Aitken 1998; Cohen 1999). In psychology, a number of researchers have begun using psychoanalysis (for example, Sayers 1995; Frosh 2001).

However, with notably few exceptions (Raphael Reed 1995; Kvale 1999; Hollway and Jefferson 2000) there is little sociological engagement with the intrapsychic dimensions of research methodologies. In the volume *Psychoanalytic Aspects of Fieldwork*, Jennifer Hunt (1989) examines the methodological implications of a psychoanalytic perspective for ethnographic fieldwork. She pays particular attention to the psychodynamic dimension of the research encounter, pointing to the issue of transference and counter-transference in fieldwork, by examining the issue of projection of the subjects onto the researcher and vice versa. The essential feature of using psychoanalysis as a research tool is that the researcher is the primary instrument of inquiry. Using psychoanalytic techniques and theory in research involves using ideas that have been developed in the context of individual analysis and applied to something that is not taking place in the analytic context. While we would not dispute the undoubted and well-rehearsed problems with the universalism of psychoanalytic theory, we suggest that social and cultural analysis desperately needs an understanding of emotional processes presented in a way which does not reduce the psychic to the social and cultural and vice versa, but recognizes their mutual imbrication.

DETACHMENT AND DEFENCE

Usually the researcher listens to a story or makes an account but has no place to intervene or do anything with the account except to produce an academic narrative. This can be both comforting and distressing to researcher and researched alike. However, creating boundaries is quite different from being a detached observer. Detachment is often a form of defence. What is being defended against are intrusive feelings about the research process, the subjects, and the relationship between the two, including issues of transference and counter-transference (Walkerdine 1997). We want to argue that transferences, identifications and fantasies do not disappear when we are engaged in research; indeed, as Elliot and Spezzano (1999) state, research as an activity of Cartesian rationalism is itself to be critiqued. It is therefore crucial to acknowledge and attempt to understand what transferences and counter-transferences might be telling us as researchers. When Valerie did that early research in the 1980s, she was trying to sit at the difficult place of an academic who had grown up in the working class researching a working-class family who correctly understood research as surveillant. Her own attempt to deal with this was to write about her own fantasies that they could recognize her as the working class girl who was just like them and in turn that she could recognize them by being able to identify with them. Telling her own story therefore became an important way of explaining why she made a particular interpretation. But as we said, the critic correctly asked how indeed she would know that her interpretations were not simply projections of her own fantasies onto the family. But, more than this, it now seems to Valerie that in fact her own desire to identify herself as like them and them as like her was a painful defence against the recognition that she was indeed not like them at all, but had moved to a different social location and could no longer be recognized as that subject. Within psychoanalytic theory, identification or its absence can signal a defence against its opposite. The feeling that I am like my mother can signal a covering over of the painful differences between us, or my feeling that I am nothing like her can defend against feelings that I am far too like her for comfort. In this case then, instead of dealing with the complex and ambivalent position of her own fantasies and their relation to those of the participants, she simply used her own conscious identifications with the material they gave her. But what would it mean to be able to separate out the fantasies of the researcher and those of the researched? Do the issues of transference and counter-transference have anything to offer in storying subjects into being? It is all very well to speak of the 'defended subject' (Hollway and Jefferson 2000) but what of the defended researcher? The story Valerie told in the 1985 chapter about the working-class family and their watching a video of *Rocky II* was a romantic narrative in the sense that it tried to make an uneasy case for speaking about her instead of trying to speak for them. Of course, one irony of this was that she could speak of her own working-class childhood only as an academic who now had the legitimate space in which to speak. That which was gone forever, except in fantasy, was the object of a painful recognition. When Helen and Valerie researched middle-class families in the 1980s we became aware of our own envy of them and indeed what we saw as our hatred and contempt for them. This emerged because they seemed to have so much freedom of choice and both of us found that we felt particularly angry and envious of the way in which middle-class mothers would ask their 4-year-old daughters what they wanted to eat. We had not been offered a choice of meals as children! That something so apparently trivial can invoke such intense feelings must be a commonplace feature of the research encounter, and produce fantasies on both sides. Both researcher and researched can then use these fantasies to position each other within discourse. The issue here then is when those positionings are sedimented in the account as fact rather than as shot through with fantasy.

In the transition to womanhood research Helen felt positioned by working-class Mr and Mrs Cole initially as if she were a welfare agency 'snooper', while June felt positioned by Mrs Falmer, a professional middle-class mother, as if she were a therapist. It could be argued that these positionings have multiple effects. It is difficult to tell whether the researchers projected these positionings onto the participants, whether the participants projected them onto the researchers or whether they were mutually created. Perhaps what is important is that it is these positionings through which the subsequent interview is conducted and understood. The researchers and researched may like or resist their positionings. There is not just a simple story to be told. The story is created in and through these dynamics and so it seems important to understand what the dynamics are – and not only for the subjects of research. This is a long way from the presentation of an autobiographical account or of a reflexive account as some-how true because aspects of the researcher's narrative have been included. However, neither does this suggest that the subjectivity of the researcher is unimportant – far from it. In the case of Mrs Falmer, who cried during the interview, June felt at first comforted by the therapist positioning and then suspicious of her own desire to inhabit that position, for the interview to be therapeutic, not intrusive. June felt trapped between being an 'observer' and not getting involved and wanting to comfort and reassure Mrs Falmer. But she was also worried that the interview might be abandoned and was relieved that Mrs Falmer wanted to carry on, relieved that she was accepted as someone who would be 'safe' to cry in front of. In order to interpret these feelings, we need to make some connections with the sub-jectivity of the researcher. At this time June was taking steps to begin a psychotherapy training and fairly spontaneously took up the role of thera-pist, not saying too much, giving Mrs Falmer space to cry. However, June was very worried that things might become more difficult for Mrs Falmer after the interview and that a 'can of worms' had been opened and she was partly responsible for doing this. In her field notes she wrote: 'I imagined that having a good cry was what she needed, that it was good for her and was probably healing in some way.' The researcher can then feel some grati-fication about having something to do with this process as well as having her fantasy of being a therapist partially fulfilled. In this sense then, we can understand that the positions of, for example, 'benefits officer'/'welfare snooper' or 'therapist' are both created in discourse and work because the fantasy life of the subjects, researcher and researched, allows them to be mobilized as ways of coping with the encounter and defending against difficult feelings.

TRANSFERENCE AND COUNTER-TRANSFERENCE

Because of the complex nature of fieldwork and the fact that it does not take place in a clinical setting, transference and counter-transference are not literally translatable to the interaction with the researcher and subject. However, the research team found the concepts immensely useful. In the clinical setting transference is generally defined as unconscious archaic images, usually from the patient's childhood, that the patient imposes on the analyst. Counter-transference can refer to an analyst's unconscious response to the patient or to significant people in the patient's life, or to the patient's transferences. In the transition to womanhood research, for instance, interviewers were occasionally left feeling depressed after an interview even when the interviewees presented themselves as happy, cheerful and always positive. Psychoanalysts understand these emotions, when experienced as those of the analyst rather than the patient, as sometimes indicating the presence of emotions which have to be projected outwards by the patient onto the analyst because they are too painful or difficult to be experienced by the patient. We may feel a strong emotion when we hear a story but the participant may not seem to react in this way at all, or vice versa.

BEYOND CONSCIOUS IDENTIFICATION

The following example of one family with two sisters presents for us a way of understanding a possible way beyond the issue of conscious identifications with the participants by the researcher which we mentioned earlier. Angela is a middle-class 21-year-old high achiever who went to a prestigious private girls' school where she obtained ten grade A GCSEs, and three As and one B at A level. She went on to Oxford to study medicine. Angela has a younger sister, Heather, who 'only' obtained eight GCSEs and two A levels (all at grades A to C). Heather is also a gifted musician and has won much praise for her musicianship. Although not as outstanding as Angela's, Heather's exam results nevertheless placed her within the top 10 per cent of the 18-year-old national cohort at that time. However, within the family, the difference between the sisters is exaggerated into a huge gulf. Angela is seen as the success of the family while Heather, despite the reality of her achievements, is viewed as a 'failure' by her sister and both parents. They variously describe her as 'not very bright', 'not very academic' and a 'slow learner'. She will not be going to university, even though her grades would allow her to, but to a catering college to do a diploma in hotel management. We learn from her mother that Heather's identity as not very bright had germinated from the moment of her difficult birth. Her mother has carried extreme feelings of anxiety about Heather's intellect since this time, when she was convinced that Heather had suffered brain damage through oxygen deprivation, though there was no medical evidence for this.

However, the family narrative was very persuasive and June, who interviewed the family members, came away from the interview, at that point without the knowledge of her academic achievements, with the impression that Heather, whom she did not meet, was indeed an academic failure and possibly had learning difficulties. It was only when we analysed the data that the complexities in the family narrative were noticed. 'Triangulation' is a method developed within mainstream qualitative sociological research for dealing with problems of validity (Denzin 1978) and refers to the injunction to check pieces of information against at least one other independent source before regarding them as 'credible' (Lincoln and Guba 1985). Using this method in the case of Heather and Angela, information on Heather's educational failure would have been amply 'triangulated' by the testimonies of three members of her family. Regardless of the question whether members of the same family can be regarded as independent sources of data for the purposes of arriving at some 'truth', we wanted to use the insights of post-structuralism and psychoanalysis to go beyond this mainstream notion of truth. The issue is not whether 'Heather was slow' is true, but how is it produced as true, what does it mean, and to whom.

Our starting point is an apparently unproblematic description by some family members of Angela as bright and Heather as slow. But to take this description at face value would be to miss the complex dynamics that are going on, not only within this particular family but also across all the middle-class families. This family, like other middle-class families, are positioned as needing success to ensure the continuity of middle-class life. The desire and need for success within this framework defends against its opposite – the fear of failure. We could argue that it is partly this fear that has produced 'Heather as slow' as a fiction: Angela's brightness is intricately linked to Heather's slowness. Of course, it is crucial to acknowledge that in the circles in which only the top performance is considered good enough, Heather has indeed failed (cf. Walkerdine, Lucey and Melody 2001). The fiction, created out of the unconscious fears and fantasies of the family, thus becomes self-fulfilling.

Common to much qualitative analysis (Strauss and Corbin 1990; Silverman 1993) we can look at the face value of the individual narratives, listening and later reading for the overall plot, the 'story' that is being told, one containing events, characters and numerous subplots. Angela and Heather's case provides a stark example of how particular subject positions can be formed in relation to other family members. However, we can problematize the family narrative through an exploration of the unconscious projections, introjections and transferences that are in play. We pay close attention to words, images and metaphors, their occurrence and recurrence. Where in this narrative are there inconsistencies and contradictions; where do different parts of the narrative begin, stop, fade out, connect and disconnect; what are the absences in the narrative and where are the silences; what tone and register of voice is used and how does this change? These observations may prompt us to ask, 'Who is it that is speaking and who is being spoken to?' Although initially persuaded by the family narrative, June had a strong feeling that there was something wrong, that the narrative didn't quite fit. In this case, June felt very uncomfortable and discussed her feelings with the team. It was later when she reread her interview notes and listened to the taped interviews that she decided to get a copy of Heather's exam results. These clearly exposed the notion that Heather was an academic failure as a fantasy. For all of the working-class girls in our study to get eight GCSEs and two A levels grades A–C would be a cause for celebration.

In our analysis we attempted to understand the relation between the fiction of positioning and the fantasy. In order to do that we interrogated our own fantasies. In this case, instead of simply identifying or not with the participants, June asked what narratives, positions and fantasies were addressed by the family narrative. We asked, to which part or parts of me is the subject speaking? Which part of me is responding? In other words, who do I represent for the subject, and who do they represent for me? Parent, sister, social worker, teacher, child? It is by being aware of and listening to the different parts of our own fantasies, and to the place in us that responds to any given message, that allows us to tune in to the different meanings of our subjects. This gives us an important step beyond Foucault's subjects as fictions. We can be discursively positioned as, say, social worker, but the defences and fantasies embedded in that positioning are crucial for understanding the production of subjectivities.

In relation to the Angela and Heather example, it was June's relationship with her younger sister that helped us to explore the research encounter at this level. In her field notes she wrote:

> Although Angela and Heather come from an entirely different social class background from me there are very similar dynamics between the siblings. I, also the eldest, was always seen as the clever one in the family, very much like my father, as Angela was described, and was always given the message that I could achieve whatever I set out to. Whereas my younger sister was not seen as particularly bright and has spent most of her life feeling inadequate especially in relation to her elder sister.

Although the circumstances of Angela's family and June's family were quite different, there was enough in June's history for her to tune into some of the fantasies described by the different members of Angela's family. Of course, what we tune into in our own histories may be a projection onto the research subjects. This is where we need to check out our own story and be aware of its place. In clinical situations, analysts always check their interpretations against the progress of the analysis. For them, a good interpretation is one which produces some change or shift, has some effect on the progress of the analysis. Of course, it is much more difficult to do this in research, where it is often not possible to return nor to simply present our interpretation to the participants, as is proposed by some feminist attempts to counter power differentials by taking all work back to be checked by the participants themselves.

We are working with the premise that our experience of the dynamic at this time can tell us something important about this persons' relationship to the wider social world. So for instance, June's hunch that there was something that didn't 'fit' in this family narrative threw much light on other feelings that were coming up for all of the research team in relation to the middle-class girls. Most importantly, it told us something crucial about the anxieties which underpin the middle-class girls' success but also how this is masked by a hyper-rationalism that will always construct and promote a rational story. Heather's 'failure', then, is not only a projection within that particular family but also an effect of the relationship between specific social and cultural norms, discourses and family processes. This is neither a simply social nor a simply psychic process but has to be understood as working in a complex psychosocial manner.

It is not just the interviewee who puts up resistances to difficult feelings. As we will see with the examples of Anna and of Mr Cole, it was the researcher who was trying to defend against difficult feelings. Also we found that some of our participants (mostly middle-class men) felt uncomfortable with the 'power' dynamics of the research encounter. It seemed that in some cases the researcher was perceived as having the more powerful role and the participant attempted to have an effect on the dynamic. In one instance a middle-class father who was financially and professionally very successful and who had spoken at length about his own religious interests wanted to know about the researcher's religious views. Another Asian middle-class father, who was a highly educated professional, questioned the young Asian woman interviewer about her family and her language, speaking to her in Urdu. It could be argued that they were both trying to establish rapport, but this, and cultural norms in the case of the Asian father notwithstanding, the regularity with which professional, middle-class fathers attempted to 'interview' the female interviewer suggested that they were feeling vulnerable and their defence against this was to put themselves into a position that they perceived as more familiar, thereby reducing their vulnerability. A view which postulates that it is possible for researchers and subjects to be equal, becomes a fantasy. Looking at who reveals what to whom involves complicated plays of power.

WORKING WITH DIFFERENT INTERPRETATIONS

As we mentioned earlier in the chapter, qualitative approaches have often attempted to copy quantitative methods by finding a way to agree on the 'truth' of an interpretation. But what happens if we explore disagreements about interpretation in terms of the unconscious dynamics created within the research encounter? When June interviewed Jacky, a 21-year-old working-class woman, she felt that the interview was a struggle, that Jacky wasn't 'giving' her much, and felt extremely irritated by this young women. Margaret, our transcriber, talked about how angry she was with Jacky for feeling proud of 'pathetic achievements' such as passing her driving test, finding a boyfriend and getting a job. She couldn't wait to finish transcribing her tapes. Helen on the other hand liked Jacky, 'thought she was articulate and interesting and more giving than June had perceived'. These very different interpretations of the same data can be traced back to the differing histories of the research team. This example shows us quite clearly the need for the researchers to be able to distinguish what is their material from that of the subject. When we analysed the responses of the research team it became clear that when Margaret was 21, her life was not so different from Jacky's. June saw Jacky's lack of vision and ambition and her minor 'achievements' as being similar to those of her mother and sister, with whom she has difficult relations. Since her teenage years she has tried as much as she could to ensure that her life was as different from theirs as possible. This itself can be understood as a defence against the fear that they are too alike and that importantly, upward mobility has not completely erased the marks of working-class subjectivity. The transferences that took place during this interview made June aware of how afraid she was of ending up like them; their lives as she saw them had no sense of purpose or ambition, the very things that were both essential and crucial to her own identity. Deeply rooted conflicts about the researcher's sense of being were mobilized in this research encounter. This example also shows the importance of acknowledging and examining our feelings, which were clearly connected to the unconscious fantasies of the researchers. It needs to be emphasized that there were many disagreements in interpretation between members of the research team and often a lot of discussion about our different responses and interpretations. This usually involved recognizing aspects of our own subjectivity and the way in which our own histories influenced our interpretations. Thus, unlike most other approaches we did not prioritize the pursuit of agreement among ourselves, because we were specifically interested in the interpretative processes through which a particular reading is made. It would have been a nonsense to simply stifle that aim for the sake of agreement.

The researcher's defence mechanisms sometimes meant that she changed the subject or pushed the interviewee into another direction when what she found was too uncomfortable for her to deal with. Consider the following example in which Helen interviewed Mr Cole, Sharon's father. Mr Cole was so angry with his eldest son (who was, as it transpired in the interview, in fact his stepson) that when he stole jewellery and money from Mrs Cole, Mr Cole threw him out of the house. Mr Cole's feelings of betrayal went deep, as did his reluctance to 'forgive' his stepson. He said: 'You can trust a thief, but not a liar. As far as the family is concerned the boy doesn't exist'. Of course, the boy's existence was living proof for Mr Cole that his wife had not always been with him, that something intruded into the family dynamic. Treating him as if he didn't exist may have been a relief for Mr Cole, defending against difficult emotions like jealousy that he would rather not have felt. During the early part of the interview Helen felt that she had to struggle to get any rapport with him. Indeed, Helen's consistent impression of the whole interview, at the time and throughout subsequent case discussions was that Mr Cole resisted going into any detail with her about what had happened with this son. It was during one of these discussions that it was noticed that, at one point in the interview, Mr Cole had asked Helen whether she had any brothers or sisters. This question proved to be a crucial moment in the interview, because it was clear that when she replied that she was one of eight children (he was one of seven) his attitude changed noticeably and he became much more forthcoming with information about his relationship with his stepson.

However, it was at this point that Helen suddenly stopped Mr Cole in his tracks and changed the subject! How do we make sense of this interaction? It is important to note that establishing rapport in this particular interview was very important, as Helen had literally had the door shut in her face, and when she was finally let in the house by Mrs Cole she was left standing in the hallway while they sat in the living room and ignored her. She felt extremely uncomfortable and was very pleased that he said anything at all at the beginning. She wanted to answer his questions and wanted him to be able to identify with and feel safe with her. Analysis of the transcript shows that it was his knowledge of her as coming from a large family that allowed him to project some of his own fantasies onto her and make her a 'safe' person to whom to reveal some of his history. Simultaneously however, events within her own family which resonated strongly with what Mr Cole was now telling her, meant that she actually didn't want to hear any more of this painful story and changed the subject.

In this scenario, what can be seen as counter-transference is the subsequent shift from not revealing things about herself and being an anonymous interviewer to temporarily losing her identity as a researcher. What seemed to happen is that having slipped into a temporary identification with the Cole family, she suddenly felt very uncomfortable and reacted by abruptly breaking the rapport. The fact that she didn't want to continue the conversation suggests that counter-transference took place and this family represented someone else for her. It was difficult for her to keep the Cole and Lucey families separate. It is because it leapt over the boundary for her that it became uncomfortable. In an attempt to move away from these difficult feelings and to hold onto her researcher role she changed the subject. We spent a long time as a team exploring why Helen changed the subject. Because of some of the painful things that have happened to her family, she felt uncomfortable when invited to discuss them by 'outsiders', and wanted to relieve her anxiety and pain around these issues by changing the subject. Ironically, while this particular interaction created more empathy between the interviewer and interviewee, psychically, all Helen wanted to do was get out of the door that was previously shut in her face.

CONCLUSION: FANTASIZING SUBJECTIVITY

We suggest that far from opening up the simple confessional, an engagement with emotions and unconscious processes is absolutely crucial for understanding not only how multiple subjectivities are held together, but also the tricky place of emotions, ours and the participants', within the research process. This is not simply about the production of narratives even if some of those narratives are reflexively about ourselves. The approach potentially is just as deconstructive of the fantasies of the researcher and which bolster our own narratives of our subjectivity. Without this, we would argue that discursive and post-structuralist approaches have no way of understanding how subjects live the contradictions of positioning, the demands of imposed fictions or the exigencies of everyday life. It is for this reason that we felt and still feel that we need an approach which can examine how those contradictions and conflicts work to produce subjectivity in a way which takes us beyond the notion of simple narratives or discourses without ditching the lessons learnt from those approaches. Moreover, such a method needs to go beyond surveillance by interrogating the unconscious phantasies and conscious fantasies of the researcher and their place in the research narrative. This approach takes us away from an agreed version of events and towards an account which is always necessarily ruptured, fractured, partial. On one level it would be easy to say that we should simply incorporate the insights of psychoanalysis into qualitative methods. However, as we have argued, postmodern and post-structuralist critiques of truth make this at best a shaky exercise because it does not make sense to argue that depth methods simply get us closer to the 'truth', nor that psychoanalytic interpretations work on their own without their incorporation into a wider social and cultural framework. Indeed, doing just that fundamentally critiques psychoanalysis and takes us into the terrain that Elliot and Spezzano (1999) begin to map in relation to a postmodern turn which takes fantasies as a basic building block. Rather, we understand this work as dealing with the impossibility of detachment through methodological guarantees and have tried to find some way to take seriously a subjectivity that always intrudes, no matter what one's best intentions. This is not, and can never be, bias. Instead, it is part of a fundamental critique of methodology in the social sciences. It both challenges the possibility of social inquiry, demands to know what we really want to know and what we want to know it for, makes us look to our work as fictions not truths. And yet, at the same time, there are things that we cannot remain silent about, cannot ignore. This work is part of a struggle to do research differently, but would never be part of a model which sees research as unnecessary. Nevertheless, just as Beverley Skeggs (Chapter 17 in this volume) points to the reflexive self as being formed through the technology of the bourgeois self, we are confronted with the inevitability of the place of power within the account and the way in which our own inscription as researchers produces a deeply uncomfortable gulf between ourselves and our participants. This gulf produces an anxiety which is hard for the researcher to live with and hence the many ways of attempting to reduce that anxiety, such as co-authoring with the participants, writing a postmodern reflexive account which claims that the research is more about the self than the subjects of the research, using standpoint approaches to side with the subjects and so forth. The issue then is at least twofold. The anxiety and the practices which defend against it can be understood not as telling us anything fundamental about human subjectivity or psychological processes but about power, social distance and the place of 'truth' within the effectivity of the social sciences. Our surveillant and authoritative position makes us correctly anxious. But that does not mean that we should give up research because some things are important politically to be said even if their telling is so full of contradictions.

REFERENCES

Aitken, S.C. (1998) *Family Fantasies and Community Space*. New Brunswick, NJ: Rutgers University Press.

Bertaux, D. and Thompson, P. (eds) (1993) *Between Generations: Family Models, Myths and Memories*. Oxford: Oxford University Press.

Britzman, D. (1995) 'The question of belief: writing post-structural ethnography', *Qualitative Studies in Education* 8(3): 229–238.

Cohen, P. (1999) *Strange Encounters: Adolescent Geographies of Risk and the Urban Uncanny*, Centre for New Ethnicities Research, Finding the Way Home Working Papers no. 3. London: University of East London.

Cohen, P. and Ainley, P. (2000) 'In the country of the blind? Youth studies and cultural studies in Britain', *Journal of Youth Studies* 3(1): 79–95.

Denzin, N.K. (1978) *Sociological Methods*. New York: McGraw-Hill.

Elliot, A. and Spezzano, C. (1999) *Psychoanalysis at its Limits*. London: Free Association Books.

Frosh, S. (2001) 'Things that can't be said: psychoanalysis and the limits of language', *International Journal of Critical Psychology* 1: 28–46.

Ginzburg, C. (1990) *Myths, Emblems, Clues*. London: Hutchinson.

Henriques, J., Hollway, W., Urwin, C., Venn, C. and Walkerdine, V. (1998) *Changing the Subject: Psychology, Social Regulation and Subjectivity*, 2nd edn. London: Routledge.

Hollway, W. and Jefferson, T. (1997) 'Eliciting narrative through the in-depth interview', *Qualitative Enquiry* 3(1): 53–70.

Hollway, W. and Jefferson, T. (2000) *Doing Qualitative Research Differently: Free Associations, Narrative and the Interview Method*. London: Sage.

Hunt, J. (1989) *Psychoanalytic Aspects of Fieldwork*. London: Sage.

Kvale, S. (1999) 'The psychoanalytic interview as qualitative research', *Qualitative Inquiry* 5(1): 87–113.

Lincoln, Y.S. and Guba, E.G. (1985) *Naturalistic Inquiry*. Thousand Oaks, CA: Sage.

Pajaczkowska, C. and Young, L. (1992) 'Racism, representation, psychoanalysis', in J. Donald and A. Rattansi (eds) *'Race', Culture and Difference*. London: Sage.

Pile, S. (1996) *The Body in the City: Psychoanalysis Space and Subjectivity*. London: Routledge.

Pile, S. and Thrift, N. (1995) *Mapping the Subject: Geographies of Cultural Transformation*. London: Routledge.

Pitt, A. (1998) 'Qualifying resistance: some comments on methodological dilemmas', *Qualitative Studies in Education* 11(4): 535–553.

Raphael Reed, L. (1995) 'Reconceptualising equal opportunities in the 1990's: a study of radical teacher culture in transition', in M. Griffiths and B. Troyna (eds) *Anti-racism, Culture and Social Justice in Education*. Stoke-on-Trent: Trentham.

Rose, G. (1993) *Feminism and Geography: The Limits of Geographical Knowledge*. Cambridge: Polity.

Sayers, J. (1995) *The Man Who Never Was: Freudian Tales*. London: Chatto and Windus.

Shaw, J. (1995) *Education, Gender and Anxiety*. London: Taylor and Francis.

Silverman, D. (1993) *Interpreting Qualitative Data: Methods for Analysing Talk, Text and Interaction*. London: Sage.

Strauss, A.L. and Corbin, J. (1990) *Basics of Qualitative Research: Grounded Theory Procedures and Techniques*. London: Sage.

Thompson, P. and Samuel, R. (eds) (1990) *Myths We Live By*. London: Routledge.

Walkerdine, V. (1985) 'Video replay: families, films and fantasy', in J. Donald, C. Kaplan and V. Burgin (eds) *Formations of Fantasy*. London: Routledge.

Walkerdine, V. (1997) *Daddy's Girl: Young Girls and Popular Culture*. London: Macmillan.

Walkerdine, V. and Lucey, H. (1989) *Democracy in the Kitchen: Regulating Mothers and Socialising Daughters*. London: Virago.

Walkerdine, V., Lucey, H. and Melody, J. (2001) *Growing Up Girl: Psychosocial Explorations of Gender and Class*. London: Palgrave and New York: New York University Press.

PART 3

CHOICES IN CONTEXT

9 OBSERVATION AND INTERVIEWING:

Options and choices in qualitative research

Kathleen Gerson and Ruth Horowitz

Contemporary debates about the practice of social research have focused on distinctions between qualitative and quantitative approaches, often implying that qualitative approaches share a unified set of assumptions and methodological principles. In basic ways, this is so. Qualitative research always involves some kind of direct encounter with 'the world', whether it takes the form of ongoing daily life or interactions with a selected group. Qualitative researchers are also routinely concerned not only with objectively measurable 'facts' or 'events', but also with the ways that people construct, interpret and give meaning to these experiences. Qualitative approaches typically include attention to dynamic processes rather than (or in addition to) static categories, and they aim to discover or develop new concepts rather than imposing preconceived categories on the people and events they observe. These commitments form the common ground on which qualitative approaches are built.

Yet qualitative methodologies offer more than a set of shared epistemological assumptions. They actually encompass several distinct approaches, the most prominent of which are participant-observation and in-depth interviewing. At each stage in the research process, from formulating a problem to drawing conclusions, interviewing and observational techniques offer contrasting ways to approach the social world. This variety adds to the power and utility of qualitative approaches, but it also poses choices about how to study the social world. Since these choices arise at each stage of the research process, we will consider how qualitative researchers may resolve them in different ways.

The contrasts we consider involve fundamental differences in the way that qualitative research is conceived and conducted. In-depth interviewing, the method Kathleen Gerson uses to investigate how personal biographies interact with social institutions and structures, requires a more deductive approach to research design and theory building. Participant-observation, which Ruth Horowitz relies on for ethnographic fieldwork, is more likely to proceed inductively. Similarly, the unfolding of a life history cannot be directly 'observed', while ongoing interactions within and among groups cannot be ascertained by posing questions to individuals. Yet neither interviewers nor observers approach their work in a uniform way, and the choice to interview individuals or observe ongoing group processes reflects stylistic preferences as well as theoretical and substantive concerns. Reliance on an inductive or deductive approach also stems as much from differences in cognitive styles as from the demands of different methodological strategies. Whatever the reason for choosing to emphasize interviewing or observation (and any thorough qualitative researcher will use a little of both), there are nevertheless important differences in how the research process unfolds.

Drawing on our experiences in the field as well as our conversations about those experiences, we explore both the similarities and differences in the research issues that confront in-depth interviewers and participant-observers.[1] We present these experiences in the form of a dialogue and divide the research experience into a series of stages, such as 'formulating a problem', 'designing a strategy', 'life in the field', and so forth. In practice, processes such as data collection and analysis are rarely distinct or sequential tasks. The actual research process typically involves facing problems 'out of order' and coping simultaneously with a variety of methodological and theoretical conundrums. Indeed, a significant advantage of the qualitative approach is its flexibility in allowing the researcher to move back and forth in a cyclical way as the discovery of theoretical insights prompts adjustments in the research design. Despite the interactive and interwoven nature of qualitative strategies, our discussion uses a stage model as a heuristic device to isolate the distinct analytic challenges posed by different research tasks.

If our presentation takes the form of a dialogue, and even a debate between us as individuals, it is not meant to present an overly dichotomous or antagonistic picture of the differences between observation and interviewing (see Becker and Geer 1957; Kleinman 1994). To the contrary, these methods share a core of epistemological assumptions that make them complementary and interconnected. In the end, a good qualitative study requires some of both approaches. The choice is not which method to use, but rather which forms the foreground and which the background. While focusing on the distinct strengths and challenges of each approach, we are the first to recognize that the relationship between observation and interviewing is intertwined and mutually supportive. Neither of us would wish to proceed without the tools and insights of each.

FORMULATING A PROBLEM

Formulating a research problem is the most important and potentially most difficult task any researcher faces. It requires not simply choosing a topic, but approaching it strategically. The problem can arise in several ways – by locating an unresolved theoretical puzzle, by observing an empirical paradox, or simply by asking how some apparently understood slice of social experience or organization really works. The disparate ways in which research problems arise have implications for how they can be studied. When a project begins with an interesting or strategically located research site, participant-observation is the more obvious methodological choice. Starting with an empirical or theoretical puzzle, in contrast, often implies in-depth interviewing. While these are not rigid rules, and exceptions can always be found, it is a principle that clearly distinguishes our methodological choices.[2]

Interviewing

Although in-depth interviewing allows researchers to formulate their research problems in a variety of ways, my research always begins with a set of theoretical and historical questions about the nature, causes and consequences of some important but poorly understood large-scale social or demographic transformation. *Hard Choices* (Gerson 1985), for example, asks how, why and in what ways women negotiate commitments to family and work amid the new contingencies of post-industrial society. *No Man's Land* (Gerson 1993) follows a similar logic, but focuses instead on how men respond to changes in women's lives as they endeavour to carve a place for themselves in a social order no longer defined by male breadwinning. My current project, not surprisingly, investigates how the 'children of the gender revolution' have experienced growing up in the nontraditional arrangements pioneered by their parents and how they, in turn, are crafting new work and family strategies in a post-gendered age (Gerson 2001).

The focus on processes of change, both social and individual, is not accidental. Periods of rapid historical change provide ideal laboratories for uncovering the social bases of relationships and institutions that may remain hidden or seem given during relatively stable historical periods. Gender relations and hierarchies thus appear natural and inherent when hegemonic family structures marked by women's homemaking and men's breadwinning predominate. Questions about the social construction of gender inevitably arise, however, when households begin to diversify and women no longer consistently conform to gendered rules and expectations. At these points in history, the structural forms and cultural processes that either support or undermine the social organization of gender become more visible.

To unravel the complexities of large-scale social change, it is necessary to examine the intricacies of individual lives. Individual interviews provide the opportunity to examine how large-scale social transformations are experienced, interpreted, and ultimately shaped by the responses of strategic social actors. Macro-social trends thus provide the starting point for formulating a research problem. The empirical puzzles they raise, however, can be solved only by examining micro-social processes as they unfold in the lives of individuals.

Observation

Participant-observation studies can begin by choosing a site that helps explore gaps in theory (Burawoy *et al.* 1991) or choosing a site that offers the chance to observe groups or organizations of specific substantive interest. Whatever the impetus, the first need is to find a group or place to study and to pose a theoretically interesting problem. If interviewing emerges from a theoretical or empirical puzzle, participant-observation often relies more on the continuous development of questions during the research process.

Each of my projects has developed out of a general interest in groups located on the margins of society, whose members tend to be left out of active participation in 'mainstream' social and democratic processes. Examples of questions I ask upon entering the field are: 'What is really going on' in such groups or communities? How do people make sense of their social worlds? How do they strike a balance between group membership and wider social participation? And, finally, what limits and what helps to create the social worlds of the people?

My first project, *Honor and the American Dream* (Horowitz 1983) required locating a community in which I could study young people who were marginal to the economic and cultural mainstream. Since poverty and low levels of education were essential for my purposes, I chose the fifth poorest area in the city.[3] The preponderance of Mexican immigrants in this neighbourhood allowed me to study a group about which little was known at the time, especially in the context of a large, Midwestern American city. Finally, recent sojourns in Spain and Mexico left me well prepared to communicate in Spanish. While my choice to study a Chicano community was in part driven by the research question, it was also based on my fascination with Hispanic cultures.[4] This choice of a study site thus emerged not just because of its theoretically strategic location, but also because of its availability and my personal interests.

While this community fitted in with my general interests, I began to focus on specifying the sociological issues only after some time in the field. After several months, it became clear that young people held many different orientations and expressed them in a variety of ways. Some were heavily involved in street life, and some of those were members of street gangs. Others dreamed of attending college and were trying to do what seemed necessary to attain this goal. The young men and women, moreover, had different interactional patterns, and even members of the same family were pursuing different paths. Finally, the same young people acted differently in different settings. These findings made little sense from the perspective of the two prevailing models claiming to explain the lives of the poor. Both the culture of poverty and structural strain models failed to account for young people's creativity or for the struggles they mounted and the choices that they made in the face of great obstacles.[5] This insight produced a new focus, which then prompted me to formulate the next stage of the project.

My next study, *Teen Mothers: Citizens or Dependents?* (Horowitz 1995), also began with a concern for issues of marginality. In this case, government-funded welfare programmes were being blamed for contributing to the creation and dependency of unmarried teenage mothers. Despite the potentially large scope of this project, I wished to focus on the face-to-face interactions among these teen mothers and their programme supervisors. Fortuitously, several work-readiness programmes for teen mothers were being launched just as I began to formulate this project. A colleague, who had been asked to evaluate several programmes using survey instruments, thought it would be interesting to observe one programme on a regular basis. Taking advantage of this opportunity, I found a programme that invited me to participate (primarily because one of its designers had a master's in sociology and had studied qualitative methods). While my initial question, 'What happened in the "black box" of service delivery?', was vague, it became both broader and more specific as the research progressed. How did government policies translate from national mandates to local programmes and to the delivery of services within programmes? Why do liberal national policies sometimes further dependency and other times promote independence? These questions emerged as I became involved in the organization and familiar with the challenges it faced.

The process of formulating a problem thus differs for participant-observation and interview studies. In an observation-based project, a general question may orient the choice of field site, but more specific questions can only be developed as involvement in the field proceeds. Of course, the choice of a site is critical for it will set the boundaries within which questions and theoretical issues can emerge. Sites are usually chosen for a variety of reasons, including its convenience as well as its substantive interest or theoretical relevance. This choice does not obviate the need for developing an interesting, focused set of sociological questions.

Conclusion

These contrasts make it clear that research problems can arise in diverse ways. Whether questions are posed prior to or during the data collection stage, the challenge is to pose questions that illuminate larger theoretical and social concerns and to craft research problems that are theoretically central and empirically focused. Moreover, all qualitative research lends itself to viewing socially situated actions and their consequences. Whether the method is interviewing or observation, direct engagement in the social world focuses the sociological eye on the interaction between structure and action – on how people are embedded in larger social and cultural contexts and how, in turn, they actively participate in shaping the worlds they inhabit. Sooner or later, all qualitative strategies tend to expose the weaknesses of homogenizing or overdetermined frameworks and to replace them with theoretical approaches that focus on the social contexts that enable or constrain action and the individual actions that shape the organization of social life.

DESIGNING A RESEARCH STRATEGY

The techniques of interviewing and observation imply different types and degrees of preparation before entering the field. Interviewing cannot begin until decisions are made about who to interview and what questions to ask. Long before the first 'official' respondent is interviewed, theoretical analysis and pretesting are needed to guide the selection of a sample and the construction of an interview schedule (or open-ended questionnaire).[6] Participant-observers, in contrast, can enter the field as soon as a research site is chosen. The research questions can then emerge as field experiences uncover the central issues and problems. In developing a research design, interview studies must thus follow a more deductive logic, while observation studies can proceed more inductively.

Interviewing

For better or worse, an interview study requires substantial forethought and advance planning. It might appear easier, at least in the short run, simply to choose people at one's convenience and engage them in an unstructured conversation. In the long run, however, this strategy creates more problems than it solves. First, a theoretically focused study needs to choose a carefully targeted sample that is well situated to illumine the issues under analysis. The sampling strategy must provide an efficient way to answer large questions with a comparatively small group of people. In addition, effective interviews need to guide respondents through a maze of life experiences in an orderly fashion and within a limited period of time. It is thus necessary to decide in advance which slices of potentially infinite 'reality' are crucial and which are interesting, but nevertheless, less important for answering the research questions and resolving the relevant theoretical debates. A carefully constructed interview guide is also needed to collect information in a manageable form for later analysis. In-depth interviews should, of course, always leave room to discover the unexpected and uncover the unknown. Ironically, this is more easily accomplished by choosing a theoretically focused sample and developing an incisive and probing interview schedule.

In choosing a sample, the goal is to select a group of respondents who are strategically located to shed light on the larger forces and processes under investigation. My research, for example, draws its inspiration from Norman Ryder's classic insight that young adult cohorts occupy a strategic social-historical location that allows them to reveal and enact processes of social change (Ryder 1965). Ryder argued that young adults both reflect and enact new social forms because they are old enough to be making relatively autonomous decisions but young enough to be influenced by basic social shifts and to take advantage of new opportunities wrought by social change. My research focuses on this age group in order to examine how individuals on the cutting edge of social change contend with and respond to unexpected contingencies as they face crucial choice points in their lives. The coping strategies they develop in response to new social opportunities and constraints, in turn, shape the future direction of change.

Within a specified group (in my case, usually an age group or cohort), it is nevertheless important to interview people who vary in their social resources and in their responses to change. After focusing on a set of social experiences as they are embodied in cohort membership, the challenge is to choose a sample that can expose how different social locations (such as gender, race, and class position) pose different dilemmas, offer unequal resources, and create divergent options. By choosing a sample that controls for one consequential aspect of lived experience (e.g. age or generation), but varies on others deemed important in the theoretical literature (e.g. gender, race, class), the aim is to discover how similar social changes are experienced by different social groups. While this sampling approach may not yield a strictly representative sample, it provides a research strategy for discovering the ways that social circumstances shape individual experiences and choices.

Although the sampling procedure need not be strictly random, it is important to choose a sample carefully and with as little bias as possible. Readers and researchers alike need to be confident that the findings reflect larger trends and not just the idiosyncracies of a narrow or self-selected group. When possible, techniques especially likely to produce self-selection, such as snow-balling or advertising, should be avoided. When the contours or location of a particular group cannot be known in advance, strategies that rely on some form of self-selection may be the only way to find a sample.[7] In most cases, however, selecting a sample randomly from a larger group that shares a set of theoretically relevant characteristics is preferable. In the case of a cohort study, where the need to find people within a specified age range makes random sampling inefficient, it is more appropriate to use lists that not only can be sifted by age or birth date (e.g. college alumni lists or union rolls) but also contain variation in the important social factors under study, such as class, race and gender diversity.

A successful interview study also depends on the prior construction of a theoretically informed and user-friendly interview schedule (or questionnaire). First, the researcher needs to know what kind of information to gather. As important, those who have offered to give their time and share the intimate details of their lives also have the right to expect a clear, understandable, and supportive guide though a process that can be confusing and unsettling. One of the first phases of an interview study, therefore, involves the development and pretesting of a theoretically informed and effective interview guide.

In my research, these theoretical and practical concerns mesh in the form of the life history interview. The life history format draws theoretical attention to what C. Wright Mills, in *The Sociological Imagination* (1959), called the orienting framework of social science – the intersection of biography, history and social structure. Using this approach not only helps elicit theoretically relevant information but also helps create a comfortable, comprehensible structure within which participants can discuss their lives.

Sociological theories aside, people experience their lives not as a set of factors or variables, but rather as the unfolding of events, perceptions and feelings over time. Chronologically ordered questions thus provide a structure for recounting a coherent narrative and for remembering potentially important, but easily overlooked events and experiences. When the interview moves through a series of experiences, from past to present to imagined future, people are able to recall the unfolding of a specified set of occurrences (for example, family, work or relationship histories) and to place these histories in a social and perceptual context. Indeed, in formulating a depth interview, it is important to include probes that distinguish among the various dimensions of lived experience – including the actual event, the social context in which an event or experience takes place, the person's behavioural response, the person's feelings, perceptions and beliefs before, during and immediately following the experience, and the person's evolving and current interpretations of the experience. In this way, a well-constructed in-depth interview goes well beyond the more structured survey to explore a range of theoretically important dimensions, including pre-existing beliefs and outlooks, events and situations that trigger or prevent action, the social contexts in which choices are made, the social and psychological consequences of contextually embedded choices, and the longer-term interpretations that people develop as their lives proceed.

The life history approach offers powerful analytic tools for developing and using theory. By framing questions in terms of baselines and trajectories of change or persistence, it becomes possible to uncover the social, structural, and cultural bases of choices and actions that might appear natural or predetermined. By focusing on the events, factors, or circumstances that transform a person's life path, ideological outlook and sense of self, this framework draws the analyst's attention to processes of change over time. Comparing processes of change and stability highlights the ways that social arrangements can either reproduce pre-existing relations or prompt the emergence of new social and behavioural patterns. Finally, the focus on unfolding action strategies over time and within a social context helps to untangle causes and effects. (In my work, I investigate how beliefs, preferences, and choices, such as child-bearing and child-rearing decisions, change in response to structural and cultural opportunities and constraints. I also examine how people cope creatively with structural dilemmas and, in the process, develop new beliefs and ideologies about how to live and rear their children.)

While life course analysis offers a framework for discovering theory, it is not a theory in itself. Rather, it provides a powerful method for assessing the usefulness of prevailing theories and developing new theoretical perspectives.

My work is specifically concerned with comparing the power of individualist theories, which tend to posit unchanging psychological and even biological causes of behaviour, with social construction and developmental theories, which posit that human actions are embedded in social arrangements, emerge in different ways over time, and have consequences for the form social structures take. These theoretical concerns provide the direction for developing an interview schedule, for they point toward the critical factors (or range of important independent variables) and the critical outcomes (or dependent variables) that the interviews need to explore. Since my research is concerned with how and why people make their work and family choices and travel different pathways, my open-ended questionnaire (or interview schedule) must focus on measuring the shape of work and family trajectories (from early childhood expectations to current situations and outlooks to future plans and aspirations) as well as the childhood experiences and adult opportunities that might influence these diverse outcomes. In this way, the interview schedule can direct people to focus on the research's central theoretical concerns. It measures both the things to be explained and the full range of potential explanations.

Observation

After a research site is chosen and a general question is posed, a participant-observation study can proceed in a variety of ways. The first step, however, must be to gain access to the study site or group. While specifying the sociological problem must continue as well, this task must proceed alongside tackling the more practical challenges of gaining access and settling in at the research site. Problems of access can vary depending on the type of setting (formal or informal), the degree of control exercised by the participants, the politics of the group, the cultural and historical context, and the perceived social distance between the participants and the researcher.

Constraints on access to particular sites or groups are typical, and the political environment can make access especially problematic. My study of Chicago Chicano youth took place during the 1970s, when class and ethnic tensions and antagonisms made it difficult for university researchers to study poor, minority communities. Despite the dearth of community research being conducted at the time, I was able to overcome the resistance and become an accepted part of the daily landscape. To be sure, a number of politically active community members interviewed, investigated and challenged me. Gang members tested me on several occasions over the three years in the field. And while no one had the formal authority to keep me out, there were other means to do so. A month before I entered the community, for example, a camera was taken from a newspaper photographer and destroyed. Yet, amid the suspicions that I might be a prostitute, a narcotics agent and a social worker, I was able to develop close, ongoing and continually evolving relationships with many in the community. A careful, respectful and determined approach can overcome the obstacles set by initially mistrustful people.

When powerful people control access to a research site, the obstacles may be more daunting. Entry to controlled spaces, such as prisons, businesses and schools, are protected by powerful groups and individuals, and studying organizations of this type may pose considerable obstacles. For example, I was recently denied access to a professional organization despite their interest in my research and my own position as a group member. Worried about legal questions and vulnerabilities, powerful members rejected my entreaties to observe closed meetings. A fortuitous encounter nine months later, however, provided entry into a similar organization. The research could continue, but the research strategy was altered and the research questions reformulated. This is a particularly telling example of how the choice of – and access to – a site shapes the kinds of questions that can be posed and the kinds of answers that can be found. In the end, designing and carrying out a project may depend as much on fortuity, politics, networks and personal assets as on theoretical and substantive interests.

Once in the field, the data-gathering strategy may also need to change. Observational techniques involve a continuous process of observing, analysing, developing categories or classes of phenomena and their links, and searching for new data to explore the new categories. Starting with a general question renders everything potentially interesting and important. Since any observation can ultimately become sociologically relevant, it is necessary to observe and record almost everything in the beginning. As Becker (1998) suggests, one enters the field with concepts and ideas that direct our gaze and need to be recorded as fully as possible, as well as small, seemingly unimportant actions or words that can become critical.

Upon entering the field for my first project, the strategy was to locate a variety of groups and follow them as they traversed different settings. I attuned myself to all activities. After about five months, for example, a gang member took my arm as we crossed an icy street on our way to the corner store. Unused to such gallantry, I blurted out, 'Why did you do that?' He responded, 'My mother taught me to take a lady's arm when crossing the street.' Although a seemingly innocuous exchange, this conversation took on a deeper meaning in the context of theories about the social disabilities of delinquents. As I began to follow gang members to weddings, quinceañeras, and restaurants,[8] I found many additional incidents that cast doubt on these theories. My attention to that one small event thus triggered a focus on how gang members were able to adjust their behaviour from setting to setting and to make choices that reflected the needs of different situations. This insight, in turn, enabled me to dispute the validity of social disability delinquency theories. Without constant observation of the smallest interactional details, it would not have been possible to develop and test sociological categories and their links. In this way, life in the field consists of a continuously evolving research strategy.

Conclusion

Interviewing and observation typically involve (and often require) divergent research strategies. Interviewing depends on developing a research design from more general empirical and theoretical concerns and thus relies on a more deductive approach. An observation study can begin as soon as a research site is chosen and then proceed more inductively as what is really going on becomes clearer and a set of more specific questions and insights begin to emerge. Not all interview and observation studies need to diverge so starkly, but some differences in analytic technique are bound to emerge from these differences in data-gathering strategies. Both nevertheless aim to expand or transform common understandings of social processes and problems. The key is to choose the method that fits the problem.

LIFE IN THE FIELD: ENCOUNTERING THE SOCIAL WORLD

While life in the field can begin almost immediately for the participant-observer, the in-depth interviewer must spend more time and forethought preparing for field encounters. Whatever the degree of advance preparation, it is both exhilarating and frightening to begin the process of directly engaging ordinary people as they go about their daily lives or reflect upon where they have been and where they are going. The exhilaration stems from putting a plan into practice and *doing* sociology rather than just consuming the ideas and findings of others. Yet the prospect of entering unknown situations, meeting countless strangers, and putting one's most cherished ideas and perspectives to the test also tends to provoke anxiety, fear, and resistance. At this stage, fieldwork becomes as much an art as a science. And whether the method is interviewing or observation, it poses emotional as well as analytic challenges.

Interviewing

An interview study involves a series of discrete but demanding forays into the lives of strangers. Over and over again, the interviewer must contact and secure the help of others, travel to unknown places, engage in an intensive process whose goal is to reveal the intricacies of other lives, and then say 'good-bye'. Repeating this process dozens and even hundreds of times requires energy, courage, persistence, confidence and unassailable commitment.

Securing the help of strangers is, in some respects, the most anxiety-provoking task of the interviewer. It takes a strong belief in the value of one's project and a certain amount of chutzpah to ask others to share their most personal, intimate stories for no other reasons than the advancement of knowledge and the possibility of increased personal awareness. Even though most agree to help, the possibility of rejection arises anew each time a new batch of letters is sent and a new set of phone calls made. Convincing others to contribute to a project that must necessarily be a collective endeavour depends on having a strong belief in the value of the study and a warm but persistent approach. If these initial contacts secure a high level of participation, it becomes easier to keep spirits high when the inevitable, if rare, rejection occurs.

If making initial contact is the most uncertain part of the process, then conducting the interview is the most important and uplifting. Its success depends on mustering a range of emotional as well as analytic skills, including sympathy, support and intense concentration. The interview process also demands a willingness to put moral judgement aside, at least temporarily, in order to take on the perspective or role of the other. Indeed, the intensive, in-depth interview more closely resembles the therapeutic interview of clinical practice than the tightly controlled, closed-ended questionnaire used in social surveys. In-depth interviews may follow an organized set of ordered questions, but the purpose is to enhance full disclosure in order to get to know the person as a unified whole (rather than to retrieve a series of answers from a predetermined set of responses). The best interviews become a conversation between two engaged people, both of whom are searching to unravel the mysteries and meanings of a life.

Unlike therapy, however, the sociological interview spans one or two meetings and is not explicitly aimed at helping the respondent. Relationships must be forged (and ended) quickly, and they must be constantly re-established with new participants as the study proceeds. In-depth interviewing thus depends on creating trust, rapport and mutual commitment within a short time period.

Although it may seem paradoxical, the bounded nature of the interview and the professionally neutral stance of the interviewer make the process of disclosure possible. The structure of this situation, with its guarantees of confidentiality, creates a space outside the 'real' world in which disclosure and insight can proceed. Like strangers on a train, respondents gain the ear of a sympathetic but disinterested person who is not part of their social world. The implicit promise is to listen carefully and supportively, to refrain from drawing judgemental conclusions, to leave at the appropriate time, and to offer support and follow-up information if desired.[9] By creating an impartial emotional space, the interviewer provides the opportunity for people to step back from their ordinary routines and reflect upon their lives.[10] When these ideals are achieved, most are grateful for the attention of a supportive listener and energized by the insights they have gained.

Because depth interviews, unlike surveys, are conducted by one or, at most, a few persons, they take place slowly over an extended period of time. This process creates its own rhythm, serving as a check and balance for the imperfections of any one interview and allowing flexibility and change. Early interviews provide the occasion for discovering unanticipated insights, which can then be used to inform successive ones. Indeed, although interviewing cannot begin without a specified sample and a well-developed, if open-ended, questionnaire, the goal of early interviews is to search for unexpected findings in order to make adjustments and, if necessary, paradigmatic shifts. For example, I began my study of women's work and family choices assuming only married women could meaningfully discuss child-bearing decisions, but altered my sampling strategy when an early interview made it clear that single women were theoretically important and just as able to discuss the issues. By carefully listening to each interview, one at a time, unexpected findings can thus spark theoretical insights that lead to crucial methodological adjustments. While it can be difficult to let early preconceptions go, qualitative research depends on being open to the possibility of change. Indeed, it is good news when findings from the empirical world prompt to theoretical and methodological shifts. There is no reason to conduct a study if the answers are known from the start.

Of course, there is no perfect interview that can provide the whole story or the real 'truth'.[11] The interview method necessarily depends on people's varying abilities to recall the past, comprehend the present and consider the future. Some participants are able to offer great detail and insight, while others find it difficult to recollect past circumstances or contemplate future possibilities. Accordingly, some interviews will seem unsurprising and uninteresting, while others will prompt a new way of seeing concepts and organizing principles. This 'aha' experience is especially likely to happen when people offer answers that do not fit the study's presuppositions or the prevailing theoretical debates. Early in my research on the consequences of changing family forms, I interviewed a young man who described growing up in an outwardly traditional household that actually changed dramatically throughout his childhood. This surprising interview prompted me to shift from focusing on family structures, which are highlighted in the theoretical debate over family values, to examine family processes and trajectories (Gerson 2001).

Inevitably, some interviews will provide more useful information than others. No single interview, however revealing, can offer more than limited insight into general social forces and processes. Only by comparing a series of interviews can the significance of any one of them be fully understood. And, in the long run, each interview will add to the final story.

Over time, as the number of interviews grows, general patterns should begin to take shape out of what once appeared to be unique stories. Collective experiences begin to stand out from interesting but idiosyncratic anecdotes. And it becomes possible to anticipate the answers before the questions are asked. When new interviews are more likely to confirm earlier insights than to spark new discoveries, there is a good chance that theoretical saturation has been reached. When enough interviews have been conducted to reach and support theoretical conclusions, there is also good reason to conclude that a persuasive case can be made to others. No bell will sound or gun go off, but these experiences signal that the time has arrived to begin wrapping up the data collection process and disengaging from the field.

Leaving the field can be as difficult as entering it and, to some extent, it remains an arbitrary decision. There will always be another letter to send, another number to call, another person to meet, another life to explore. Yet, there also comes a time when more information yields little additional insight and, instead, simply makes the data less manageable.[12] At this point, it is time to shift from conducting interviews to concentrating on analyzing them.

Observation

By the time the interviewer enters the field officially, the participant-observer should be established in the field site. Issues, nevertheless, arise in the field that are similar to those faced by an interviewer as each strives to develop relationships of trust and goodwill, on which all qualitative techniques depend. For participant-observers, however, the research challenge is to focus on events as they unfold and relationships as they evolve. While observations occur in the present, the observer generally stays in the field for a considerable time period and must thus maintain relationships with people as they move into the future together. While introspective accounts add to the picture, the meat of fieldwork and analysis is the long-term observation of relationships and events – some routine, some not – as they develop, evolve, and sometimes change dramatically over time.[13]

Since the fieldworker must spend a substantial period of time in a 'natural' setting doing something that is decidedly not natural (that is, conducting research), the issue of one's role as a researcher, including matters of trust and confidentiality, inevitably arises. While some have argued that the researcher should disguise that role and simply join the setting, this strategy is both ethically questionable and frequently impossible. The social characteristics of the observer are often too different to offer any chance to disguise one's status or purposes. Fortunately, it is often more useful to be a bit of an outsider (Horowitz 1986). The outsider status of the observer, like that of the interviewer, makes it possible to ask probing and even silly or stupid questions, to remain in places from which insiders would be excluded, to violate rules that insiders could not violate, and to cross social lines between groups who may be in conflict or out of contact. Thus, in each of my projects, I have been able to study people who are different from me in obvious ways. Whether as a woman in a man's world or an older white woman in a world of minority teen mothers, my social identity as a person outside the usual social order may have posed a challenge, but it also provided an opportunity to gain a unique perspective.

To enter a world in which one is not naturally a part, a researcher needs to present an identity that permits relationships to develop. These relationships are often complex, are always changing, and will vary among the people and groups within the setting. In the Chicano community, which contained gang members, upwardly mobile college-bound youth, parents of varying outlooks, and political activists, I needed to develop different types of relationships with different people. Each of these bonds also changed over the course of more than three years, as some relationships grew stronger, others collapsed, and all needed constant work.

If the interview situation involves discrete encounters, usually with unconnected individuals, participant-observation involves immersion in a community or organizational setting where people are interacting regularly. They must, therefore, feel confident that the information they provide will not be shared with others. About six weeks after I began 'hanging' regularly with one of the gangs, I began to hear 'confidential' stories, which I later learned were fictional. These stories were purposely concocted to test my ability to keep a secret. At about the same time, gang members also increased the amount of illegal activities conducted in my presence in order to test my trustworthiness amid rumours that I might be a new type of narcotics agent. Although these tests posed dangers, they provided the means by which those involved in illicit activities were able to accept me as a confidante.

As time in the field unfolds, personal feelings also evolve. Strong emotional ties are not unusual, although they can be positive or negative. They can also interfere with the research process or make leaving difficult. While I developed strong, long-term bonds with many of the people in the Chicano community, I became disenchanted with a number of the staff running the social service programme in the teen mothers project. Indeed, as I invested more time in the research, I began to wish I could avoid many of the social workers and even remove the programme from their grasp. As I left the building each day, I began to feel the same relief expressed by the teens enrolled in the programme. When the programme ended, and my research was, of necessity, over, a sense of relief swept over me. At least, in this case, exit was relatively easy.

Every field setting will involve some demands on the researcher, whether it is to express one's views, to account for one's presence, or to take sides. It is not possible to remain continually neutral over a period of several years. Nor can one entirely succeed at consistently expressing the 'right' view to the 'right' group, especially since expressing contradictory views will generally become known as people talk among themselves. In my community research, for example, a central challenge emerged from others' demands that I become a member of the community and abide by the local rules for women. The gendered norms of the community circumscribed my options and required I spend less time with gang members. In contrast, my current project on professions has placed me in a setting in which I am considered an expert. Continual interest in my opinions and advice makes it difficult to ask naive questions that might uncover how others account for particular events or actions.

Unlike interviews, which are short term and private, participant-observation involves a web of relationships that, like any set of relationships, involves negotiation and change. Over time, it becomes increasingly difficult to avoid getting lost in the setting, to avoid feeling part of the community, and to avoid taking sides. It can also be difficult to know when and how to leave.

A project can end because the field site changes or disappears or because someone else (perhaps a publisher or dissertation supervisor) says it is time to stop. Most often, however, the decision to leave the field is based on an assessment that enough has been uncovered and the time has come to move to a new stage of analysis. Such a pragmatic approach cannot, however, provide much guidance about the future of field relationships. These decisions require personal discretion and are likely to vary with the field experience. Even though I left the field in Chicago in order to finish my degree, I returned to conduct a follow-up prior to writing *Honor and the American Dream* (Horowitz 1983) and I continue to see some of the people who became friends.

There is rarely a clear or consistent deadline for ending a project or severing the relationships it created. In the absence of a faculty adviser, publishing deadline or fortuitous end-of-the-field situation, the decision to leave needs to emerge from the research process itself. While each event may seem new, and people's lives continue to change, there comes a time when these new occurrences offer little that is new sociologically. Do I have enough evidence to persuade audiences? Have I developed my concepts, categories and theories, and am I satisfied with my evidence? Can I tell a reasonably complete sociological story? When the answer to these questions is 'yes', it is time to leave.

Conclusion

The choice to interview or observe depends on the personal preferences and styles of the researcher, the question, and the logical demands of the project.[14] Personal interests and varying attractions to particular research strategies surely influence the kinds of questions we ask. Once the questions are posed in a particular way, however, the choice of a research strategy becomes clear.

If the prospect of joining a community, becoming immersed in the lives of its members, and negotiating ongoing relationships over a period of years is appealing, participant-observation is likely to be the method of choice. The bounded yet intense nature of the in-depth interview creates a different set of contingencies. Like the therapeutic process, the sociological interview requires forging a close bond in a short and bounded time period and then letting go. The process of developing many intense but circumscribed relationships draws on different personal resources than does the process of maintaining a small number of multi-stranded relationships over an extended period of time. Yet, one cannot choose a method without making sure that the question to be answered is tightly connected to that method.

The different nature of the methods also poses different obstacles. Participant-observers must justify and explain their presence to those being studied. They must be prepared to share their views and make personal disclosures. Their own social experiences and statuses matter. The interviewer, in contrast, needs to offer support and sympathy while also withholding information that might influence a respondent's answers. Understanding and encouragement are essential aspects of an interview, but this must be balanced with a certain degree of circumspection. The challenge is to create an environment in which the participant feels accepted and thus free to disclose and reflect honestly on controversial personal and political issues. (Over the years, for example, Kathleen's interviews have delved into such highly charged experiences as sexual infidelity, criminal activity and wife battering.) A sympathetic and encouraging ear is not only helpful but also necessary. Such feedback, however, needs to be socially and politically neutral so that the respondent does not feel judged or tempted to say only what he or she imagines the interviewer wishes to hear. While a degree of withholding is needed during the interview, a fuller and more open exchange of personal opinions and experiences can take place when it is over.

Observation and interviewing also focus on different levels of analysis and tend to produce different types of findings. Observation necessarily attends to interactions, group processes, talk and evolving situations. Interviewing provides a way to uncover the motives, meanings and conflicts experienced by individuals as they respond to social and interpersonal situations and conflicts. To discern patterns and links, observers must spend a long time in a few settings, while interviewers must traverse a wide area in order to meet a large number of people. Similarly, observation takes place in natural social settings, which are embedded in ongoing daily patterns, while interviews ask people to take time out from the 'actually occurring world' to contemplate from a distance the trajectory of their lives from past to present to imagined future.

Despite the stylistic and analytic differences, both methods offer the chance to peer beyond the surface into the inner workings of other social worlds and to see the larger world from others' perspectives (see Mead 1964 [1934]; Berger and Luckmann 1967). The distinctions between interviewing and fieldwork, moreover, are never clear cut. Fieldwork can involve studying settings for which the researcher possesses advanced knowledge and familiarity, and interviewing can extend well beyond short-term meetings to encompass multiple interviews with the same person over an extended period of time. Both methods typically involve intense physical and emotional immersion, even in the short run. The thin line between insider and outsider status is one that must always be negotiated. In the end, the success of any qualitative approach requires creating bonds across the researcher–respondent divide. These relationships may emerge in different ways and take different forms, but they share the common goal of transforming strangers into confidants.

ANALYSING FINDINGS AND DEVELOPING THEORY

Qualitative techniques offer a way to confront the messy 'facts' of social life directly, unmediated by survey instruments, hired interviewers, or secondary, archival sources. Yet the hard work would not be worth the effort if it failed to generate new ways of making sense of social arrangements and processes. The purpose of good research design is to create the optimal conditions for making a theoretical contribution, and the work remains unfinished until this is accomplished.

Interviewing and observation share a set of conceptual and practical tools for arriving at theoretical conclusions. The careful attention to data collection produces material that is reliable and believable. The tight control and personal scale of qualitative projects engenders material appropriate for answering the questions posed. And the vision imposed by one person or, at most a small group of people, generates a focused analysis in a unified, coherent voice.

Interviewing and observation, nevertheless, employ different approaches to analysing data and reaching theoretical conclusions. Interviews focus attention on individual biographies, which become a lens through which to view social contexts and arrangements. Individual lives are seen to embody larger structural and cultural formations. Participant-observation, in contrast, generally focuses analysis on groups, collectivities and interaction patterns. Interactions among individuals, not individual characteristics, are more likely to form the basic units of analysis. These are just some of the differences in how interviewers and participant-observers may analyse their material in the search for theoretical discoveries.

Interviewing

Although analysis begins the first time an interviewer sits down with a participant, it takes a new and more directed form after all interviews have been collected and transcribed. At this point, it becomes both possible and necessary to step back and seek the shape of the forest amid the trees. The time has come to transform a series of individual interviews into a coherent and theoretically trenchant argument about group structures and processes.

In the absence of careful forethought, consolidating new discoveries into innovative explanations would depend on either luck or intuitive genius. Certainly, it never hurts to have a bit of both. Fortunately, brilliant insight need not be accidental. Carefully designed and implemented research sets the stage for theoretical breakthroughs, and hard work in the earlier phases reaps immense rewards at the end. In research as in baseball, as Branch Rickey famously argued, 'Luck is the residue of design'.

While never relinquishing the inspiration of a sociological imagination, there are nevertheless some identifiable steps to follow in the analytic process. The first involves a careful reading of all interview transcripts. Even interviews whose meaning seemed straightforward when conducted can take on a new resonance in the context of all the others. This is the time to ask a set of crucial questions about each respondent and about the group as a whole: what general shape does each person's life take? What general paths have people followed? Considering the group as a whole, what are the range of important outcomes? How does the sample divide into groups, and what general form does each group take? Which interviews seem interesting, and which seem obvious? What makes one interview more interesting than another?

By subjecting each interview to close scrutiny, and by comparing it to the others, a set of categories for organizing analysis will begin to emerge. If all goes well, these categories will be quite different than the ones that seemed obvious before the study began. In my research on women's choices, I set out to compare women who chose to become full-time mothers with those who preferred to work, either by combining it with motherhood or choosing to remain childless. As I immersed myself in the interviews, however, I began to realize that, regardless of the ultimate choice, some biographies were more complicated, more intensely experienced, and more compelling than others. Slowly, as I reread and rearranged the interviews into shifting groups, I realized that the more interesting interviews revealed personal biographies marked by significant and unexpected change while the less intense interviews involved lives that followed anticipated and relatively predictable paths. As I solved this puzzle, a new set of categories emerged. The study shifted from the analysis of static choices to a focus on pathways of change and stability. And as I began to look for the unexpected experiences and turning points that marked change in the lives of my respondents, I began to appreciate the importance of searching for the unexpected in my own data as well.

After, and only after, careful reading has created a feel for the interviews as a whole, it is time to begin the more formal process of creating analytic categories and concepts. This step must necessarily be more systematic. Indeed, I approach it in ways that resemble the logic of survey research: first, identify the phenomenon to be explained (or the dependent variable) and, then, identify the range of factors and processes that may or may not contribute to its explanation (the independent variables). By moving back and forth between data and concepts, an interactive and iterative process helps define an emerging set of categories or 'ideal types' that become the project's explanatory foci. The dimensions of importance and the boundaries between categories become clearer as decisions are made about where each interview belongs in the overall scheme. Inevitably, some cases will provide the purest examples of each type, and others will seem ambiguous and hard to place. The ambiguous cases point the way toward more sophisticated categories that can do a better job of capturing the complexity of social experience. In the end, all ambiguity cannot be resolved, but it should become increasingly easier to organize each interview's facts within a larger analytic scheme.

Once the categories that provide an explanatory focus are clarified, the interview material can be organized into analytic groupings. If the first task involves clarifying outcome categories, this stage involves identifying and measuring the factors and processes that help account for these outcomes. Here, it is helpful to ask how and to what extent prevailing theories are either supported or undermined. Which findings suggest that earlier theoretical assumptions are inadequate or incomplete? In what direction do these findings point for a more powerful explanation? In my research on men's fathering patterns, I discovered that early childhood models did not explain adult choices. Most changed their outlooks over time and then reinterpreted the past in light of newly emerging perspectives. Men who grew up to be distant from their own children pointed to the example of their own distant fathers as an important cause, but those who became deeply involved in rearing their children pointed to their equally distant fathers as negative influences and examples of what to avoid. As my analysis revealed the malleability of early childhood experiences, I began to search for other factors to explain why some men become involved fathers while others confined their parental involvement to breadwinning and still others abandoned their offspring. When I compared socialization experiences with other factors, such as work histories and relationships with women, I discovered that adult opportunities and contexts served to either reinforce or undermine earlier outlooks and orientations. In this way, a new framework took shape that moved beyond the prevailing focus on gendered personalities instilled in childhood to focus on how institutional arrangements, in the form of opportunities and constraints, shape adult pathways and strategies and allow people to use their childhood experiences in diverse and innovative ways.

These findings also prompted me to focus on the turning points in people's lives and on the events that trigger change. Such situations illumine the social conditions that encourage or even require change, and they suggest that stability results from the convergence of institutional forces which make change difficult or impossible. Looking at critical choice points also draws attention to the active and creative ways that people respond to unexpected circumstances. Instead of passively accepting the injunction not to work when their children were young, for example, women were more likely to change their child-rearing beliefs in order to justify combining work and motherhood.

The long-term shape of social change thus depends on the innovative strategies that people develop in the face of unavoidable but socially constructed dilemmas. The systematic, comparative analysis of interview biographies provides a method to clarify the interaction between structure and action. It draws attention to the role of institutional arrangements in creating or preventing personal change and also to the role of creative human action in shaping the contours of institutional change.

Observation

In participant-observation, analysis and data collection are inseparably intertwined. First, the categories are constructed and tested in the field, and connections between categories explored – always with an eye toward where the observer was, what was seen, and how it was seen. Much of the theory is developed from observations as they are gathered. Then, as

Becker (1958, 1998) and Glaser and Strauss (1967) argued, it is essential to revise, retest and revise again in the process of moving back and forth between data and theory, until they mesh.

Participant-observation is often used to understand a particular place, group, organization or substantive problem rather than to demonstrate the relationship between abstract categories of values, attitudes and behaviour (Becker 1958, 1998). While much of the work of discovering 'what is going on here?' occurs during the data collection stage, there typically remains more to do after leaving the field. Like in-depth interviews, all field notes must be read several times to develop more refined categories and connections among the categories. The major story may not become clear until all the minor themes and concepts have been developed.

Projects sometimes begin with the goal of understanding what is going on, but the analysis cannot end there. In *Teen Mothers* (Horowitz 1995), I wanted to understand what happened in programmes that delivered services to teen mothers who were welfare recipients. Prevailing accounts offered mixed observations about why some programmes succeeded and others did not. In addition to the amount of time or the kinds of services provided, did success or failure depend on the structure of the programme itself? Studying one programme could not uncover the relationship between time spent on activities or the kinds of services provided and various outcomes. As the programme developed, however, I noticed that the young mothers became involved and interested in some classes but uninterested and occasionally angry during others. This observation led me to focus on how the social service providers interacted with the teens. Some told the teens what to do and how to do it; they stressed that there were right and wrong answers to everything; and they compared their own 'successful' lives with the 'wasted' lives of their students. Other providers raised problems and issues and asked the teens to resolve them, suggesting possible choices that the teens may not have envisioned.

To see if these patterns were organized and recurring or merely a reflection of particular staff and groups of young women, I observed these processes over time as a second session began with a new group of teens and some new staff as well. The same patterns quickly emerged among these new groups, establishing the organized nature of the relationships. From these early insights, I developed categories of providers, including the 'arbiters' (who stressed a rigid worldview based on rules and strict hierarchies) and 'mediators' (who stressed change based on learning how to face barriers and resolve difficult situations). The arbiters defined their job as helping only the most successful to leave their pasts behind. The mediators, in contrast, endeavoured to provide the skills that young mothers needed to envision and choose the lives they wished to lead.

My notes revealed that social workers treated the teens in different ways and used different interactional strategies. It also became clear that the staff targeted different types of teens and used their power in different ways. With a larger sample of providers, the study could have explored why the social workers developed such opposing views. (In that event, in-depth interviewing using a life course approach could have expanded the range of study questions.) With so few cases, however, I could only suggest how the providers' worldviews were reflected in their experiences outside the pro-gramme. Their interactional patterns in the programme were consistent with the ways they had talked about their experiences and organized their lives outside of it.

Analysing daily, micro-level interactions has implications for the study of power. Interaction patterns can also be used to contribute to the under-standing of the outcomes of national-level policies. My findings demonstrate how policies developed at the national level were translated, interpreted and implemented as they made their way to state-level programmes and then to local staff and, finally, to clients. While national and state policies were con-sistent with the notion that teen mothers were (and should be treated as) independent agents, the way in which arbiters delivered services increased teen dependency and confirmed their identities as failures on the periphery of society. Ironically, these findings provide support for both the conserva-tive perspective, which argues that welfare permits and increases the depen-dency of the poor, and the left's critique of the welfare state, which argues that welfare prevents the poor from demanding more broad-based legal and social rights of citizenship. The mediators' stress on teen involvement and decision-making, however, provides an alternative social policy approach that encourages teen mothers to become independent, active citizens. By offering an interesting story about what is going on, participant-observation can and should provide insights about how organizations, policies, and large scale social processes work in daily life.

Conclusion

Whether the findings take the form of thick description or explanatory analysis, the ultimate goal is theoretical insight. Qualitative techniques pro-vide a set of analytic tools to discover, understand and explain the forms that social organizations take and the paths socially embedded actors follow. Qualitative researchers are able to step outside the normal categories of social experience, to view the whole terrain comparatively, and to develop concepts and categories that could not be discovered from the vantage point of social actors (much as fish remain unaware of the water in which they swim).

There can be many paths to the same destination, and different qualitative strategies should ultimately yield complementary theoretical insights. Despite our contrasting empirical and analytic styles, we have both became attuned to the theoretical importance of processes of change and the critical turning points that marked significant choices and changes in people's lives. We have also discovered the innovative strategies that emerge as social actors cope with contextual constraints, socially structured conflicts and unexpected opportunities. We have discovered, in different ways, how turning points and triggering situations illumine the organizational or structural factors that normally remain hidden and may produce outcomes that appear preordained. Finally, in addition to using empirical findings to advance sociological understanding, we also endeavoured to use sociological analysis to understand and benefit human society.

BEYOND DICHOTOMOUS DISTINCTIONS

Although we have highlighted the distinctions between interviewing and observation, simple dichotomies are misleading and inaccurate. If each approach offers its own distinct view of social reality and its own method for discovering the unexpected, careful fieldwork inevitably involves both observation and interviewing. Observational techniques provide a way to collect direct information about how individuals, groups and organizations behave in a range of settings as well as a way to observe how people explain their behaviour to each other. Interviews offer a systematic way to uncover people's experiences over time as well as their perceptions, motives and accounts of these experiences and actions. Yet interviewers also observe and use their observations to gather supporting information about the lives of participants. And participant-observers must inquire about the reasons for actions that others in the setting take for granted as well as actions that take place away from the researcher's presence. Each method thus relies on strategies that are central to the other. Even if the epistemological assumptions on which each approach is based differ in theory, they often converge in practice. Good interviewers rely on observation to confirm, cast doubt on, enrich, and make unexpected discoveries, and ethnographers often find themselves probing for the significance of observed actions and interactions through conversations. Some projects explicitly combine the two. Each approach permits the researcher to formulate new strategies as the data collection develops. An interviewer may discover in the interviews a place where participant-observation may be useful to add dimension to a particular aspect of the project. A participant-observer may decide that interviews may illuminate a particular issue. Taken together, both methods provide a richer, more complete, and more complex view of social life than either can offer on its own.

Ultimately, both approaches aim to uncover the unexpected, to make sense of puzzling or paradoxical phenomena, and to discover new ways of understanding taken-for-granted or apparently well-understood social arrangements and processes. It is surely counterproductive to try to assess which method is 'better'. The pertinent questions always remain: which approach is most appropriate to answer the questions being posed? And how best can the chosen method be carried out? Qualitative researchers should choose the method that best fits their theoretical concerns and personal strengths and then strive to enact it as carefully and thoroughly as possible. Their work will be enriched by eschewing rigid or invidious distinctions and using as many research strategies as needed. There can be, and often are, several paths to the same end. The 'best' method is the one that is well conceived and carefully executed. The qualitative findings and analysis will then be rich in theoretical potential.

ACKNOWLEDGEMENTS

Our thanks to Amanda Coffey for insightful and helpful comments on an earlier draft of this chapter.

NOTES

1   This dialogue has developed not only out of our personal research experiences (in which Gerson relies on in-depth interviewing and Horowitz on participant-observation), but also in the process of co-teaching a graduate course on the full range of qualitative methods.
2   Burawoy *et al.* (1991), for example, argue that a participant-observation study should begin with a specified theoretical problem.
3   I found this neighbourhood in the 1970 *Chicago Fact Book*, which utilized Burgess's original social areas and provided census statistics and a short history of the area.
4   I use the designation Chicano because the young people preferred it, though many of the older residents at the time would have preferred Mexican American. As a political statement, it meant that those who were Chicano would actively choose between aspects of the United States culture and that of Mexico.
5   At the time, there was a prolonged debate about the extent to which poverty was a result of structural inequalities (Gans 1962; Liebow 1967) or a culture of poverty (Miller 1958; Lewis 1966).
6   The terms 'interview schedule' and 'questionnaire' are used interchangeably to refer to the open-ended, but structured set of questions that are used to guide an in-depth interview. An instrument of this kind is needed to provide an orderly experience to the respondent and to insure that each person is asked a comparable set of questions. Most interviews take between 2 and 4 hours. Any period longer than that will tire both the interviewer and respondent. Unlike the focus group where the participants respond to each other in addition to the researcher, during an interview, the respondent focuses only on the interviewer.
7   People involved in the underground economy or delinquents not in jail are examples of groups who can be found only by voluntary selection procedures such as snowballing or advertising (Inciardi *et al.* 1993).
8   Quinceaneras are parties with communions given for 15-year-old girls to mark the transition from childhood to young adulthood (Horowitz 1993).
9   The first obligation of the interviewer, like that of the physician, is to 'do no harm'.
10 Homes provide the greatest opportunity to observe people in a naturalistic setting. Whether the interview location is a home, an office, or a public place, the choice should be left to the respondent. What matters most is to find a place that affords the time and space to relax. Privacy is the most important condition for self-disclosure. It is best to arrange a time and place to meet without interruption

or observation by parents, friends, lovers or co-workers. The arrival of others is not ideal, but it does provide an opportunity to observe interactions and follow up on information gleaned in the interview.

11 Both Jennifer Mason and Steph Lawler (Chapters 10 and 11 in this volume) are concerned with the construction and interpretation of the interview. We agree with Mason that it is important to explore the context surrounding and running through the interviews. We emphasize the importance of using participant-observation as well as seeking patterns both within and across interviews to help contextualize our findings.

12 In the case of 2–4-hour interviews, my rule of thumb it that fewer than 60 interviews cannot support convincing conclusions and more than 150 produce too much material to analyse effectively and expeditiously.

13 There are many studies that focus on discrete time units. In studies of meetings where decisions are made, for example, data is collected at many meetings. In such a case, change might occur either within the span of a meeting or across a number of meetings.

14 We are more sanguine than Tracey Reynolds (Chapter 14 in this volume) about the ability of researchers to bridge the power difference between the researcher and the informant. Such differences should never be ignored in either the data-gathering or the analytic process. Yet neither of us has experienced significant problems gaining access to informants, and both of us are always mindful of how our position as a researcher might affect our research and analysis. Needless to say, we take all possible measures to minimize both the existence and perception of a power imbalance. Horowitz (1983, 1995) discusses these issues.

REFERENCES

Becker, H. (1958) 'Problems of inference and proof in participant observation', *American Sociological Review* 23: 652–660.

Becker, H. (1998) *Tricks of the Trade*. Chicago: University of Chicago Press.

Becker, H. and Geer, B. (1957) 'Participant observation and interviewing', *Human Organization* 16: 28–32.

Berger, P. and Luckmann, T. (1967) *The Social Construction of Reality*. New York: Anchor.

Burawoy, M. *et al.* (1991) *Ethnography Unbound*. Berkeley, CA: University of California Press.

Gans, H. (1962) *The Urban Villagers*. New York: Free Press.

Gerson, K. (1985) *Hard Choices: How Women Decide about Work, Career, and Motherhood*. Berkeley, CA: University of California Press.

Gerson, K. (1993) *No Man's Land: Men's Changing Commitments to Family and Work*. New York: Basic Books.

Gerson, K. (2001) 'Children of the gender revolution: some theoretical questions and findings from the field', in V.W. Marshall, W.R. Heinz, H. Krueger and A. Verma (eds) *Restructuring Work and the Life Course*. Toronto: University of Toronto Press.

Glaser, B. and Strauss, A. (1967) *The Discovery of Grounded Theory*. Chicago: Aldine.

Horowitz, R. (1983) *Honor and the American Dream: Culture and Identity in a Chicano Community*. New Brunswick, NJ: Rutgers University Press.

Horowitz, R. (1986) 'Remaining an outsider: membership as a threat to research rapport', *Urban Life* 14: 409–430.

Horowitz, R. (1993) 'The power of ritual in a Chicano community', *Marriage and Family Review* 19: 257–280.

Horowitz, R. (1995) *Teen Mothers: Citizens or Dependents?* Chicago: University of Chicago Press.

Inciardi, J., Horowitz, R. and Pottieger, A. (1993) *Street Kids, Street Drugs and Street Crime*. Belmont, CA: Wadsworth.

Kleinman, S., with Stenross, B. and McMahon, M. (1994) 'Privileging fieldwork over interviews, consequences for identity and practice', *Symbolic Interaction* 17: 37–50.

Lewis, O. (1966) *La Vida*. New York: Random House.

Liebow, E. (1967) *Tally's Corner*. Boston, MA: Little, Brown.

Mead, G.H. (1964 [1934]) *On Social Psychology*. Chicago: University of Chicago Press.

Miller, W. (1958) 'Lower class culture as a generating milieu for gang delinquency', *Journal of Social Issues* 14: 3–14.

Mills, C.W. (1959) *The Sociological Imagination*. New York: Oxford University Press.

Ryder, N.B. (1965) 'The cohort as a concept in the study of social change', *American Sociological Review* 30 (Dec.): 843–861.

10 QUALITATIVE INTERVIEWING:

Asking, listening and interpreting

Jennifer Mason

In qualitative research, interviews are usually taken to involve some form of 'conversation with a purpose' (Burgess 1984: 102). The style is conversational, flexible and fluid, and the purpose is achieved through active engagement by interviewer and interviewee around relevant issues, topics and experiences during the interview itself. This interactive, situational and generative approach to the acquisition of data is usually contrasted with the more structured composition and uniform style of a survey interview. It has its roots in a range of theoretical and epistemological traditions, all of which give some privilege to the accounts of social actors, agents, individuals, or subjects, as data sources, and which assume or emphasize the centrality of talk and text in our ways of knowing about the social world. There is less consensus about what kinds of data such accounts, talk and text constitute, or which layers or elements of 'the social' they illuminate, and perhaps most importantly about how well (or badly) they do what they say they do. Yet the popularity of interview methods among qualitative researchers is striking, to the point where they are commonly taken to be 'the gold standard of qualitative research' (Silverman 2000: 291–292). But the elevation of just one humble research method to such heights, as Silverman has warned, is not without its costs. In this chapter I shall examine some of the issues and challenges raised by the use of interview methods in qualitative research.

Interview methodology begins from the assumption that it is possible to investigate elements of the social by asking people to talk, and to gather or construct knowledge by listening to and interpreting what they say and to how they say it. Good interviewing is clearly in no small part about an interviewer's skills in asking, listening and interpretation (Mason 1996), but these are more than skills which can simply be acquired and deployed. Asking, listening and interpretation are *theoretical projects* in the sense that how we ask questions, what we assume is possible from asking questions and from listening to answers, and what kind of knowledge we hear answers to be, are all ways in which we express, pursue and satisfy our theoretical orientations in our research. It is these issues, rather than questions about skill and technique in interviewing, which I want to focus on here. I shall discuss some of the key questions with which researchers have to deal in the process

of asking, listening and interpretation, and illustrate how decisions which
are made about each of these constitute the theoretical project. Finally, I shall
consider some of the limitations of the interview method's reliance on talk
and text.

EXCAVATION OR CONSTRUCTION?

Interviews involve dialogue between two or more people, but how should a
researcher direct or drive the conversation to ensure that the interview generates data appropriate to their research questions or their 'intellectual puzzle' (Mason 1996)? Two key issues to work out here are first, where is the
social phenomenon or process which is being investigated thought to be
located (the location question)? And second, on what basis can the interviewee and the interview illuminate it? Is the interviewee a straightforward
informant, and the interview an information-gathering exercise? Or is the
relationship of interviewee and interview to knowledge construction more
complex than this?

Let us take an example to help establish some of the possibilities here.
Suppose a researcher is interested in questions about contemporary parenting, and specifically in ideas about how parenting should be done, what is
good parenting and what is bad.[1] One possible orientation to the 'location
question' is that ideas and values about parenting exist 'out there' – in the
social world in the form perhaps of ideologies – or 'in there' – in people's
attitudes and beliefs. In this version, ideas and values have a tangible and
static existence on particular planes of the social. This orientation to the location question casts the interviewee as informant – on the social world, or on
themselves – and the job of the interview is to unearth the relevant information. Thus interviewing becomes the art of knowledge excavation and the
task is to enable the interviewee to give the relevant information in as accurate and complete a manner as possible. Kvale describes something similar
and uses the metaphor of 'interviewer as miner' (Kvale 1996: 3). This is one
type of theoretical project, but it is clearly based on a fairly simplistic ontology (theory of what the social is) and epistemology (theory of how the social
can be known).

Alternatively, the researcher may suspect that values and moralities of
parenting are less like tangible things existing out there or in there whose
nature and shape can be charted, and instead they are processes of social
construction and practices which are fluid, negotiated and contextual. Thus,
instead of moralities of good parenting existing in clear and discoverable
attitudes, morality might be a form of practice such as for example where
people try to do, feel or say what seems best or the 'right thing' through the
way they parent in specific circumstances. If moralities take shape, or operate, only through practices, negotiations and people's contextual reasoning
processes – in other words if they *are* the processes – then asking about 'good
parenting' in a decontextual way is unlikely to produce meaningful data.

This means that the interview method is up against some major challenges. It cannot *unearth* the relevant data, using the interviewee as informant, because the phenomenon under research does not have a static decontextual and therefore uncoverable existence. Yet the interview, or the interviewer cannot be in all of the relevant contexts to witness the operation of practices and processes, which in any case may not be observable in the conventional sense. One way to attempt to resolve this dilemma is to treat the interview as a site of knowledge construction, and the interviewee and interviewer as co-participants in the process. This, then, is a different type of theoretical project and one which I would argue is based on a more sophisticated, and more satisfactory, ontology and epistemology.

GENERALITIES OR SPECIFICS?

If interviewing – and asking, listening and interpretation as theoretical projects – is the art of construction rather than excavation, then the task is to work out how to organize the asking and the listening so as to create the best conditions for the construction of meaningful knowledge (about moralities of parenting, or whatever). One way is to ask the interviewee to recount or narrate relevant situations, contexts and events so they can effectively construct or reconstruct (to continue with the same example) moralities of parenting in the interview setting. The assumption here is that by grounding the interview dialogue in relevant contexts, knowledge about moralities practised outside the interview setting can be constructed on the basis of interactions within it because the operation of morality as process or practice becomes more possible to articulate through the specifics of the narrative. Knowledge gained in this way is a co-production since it is dependent upon the combined efforts of interviewer and interviewee in conjuring up the relevant contexts from which they think, talk, act and interpret (see also Holstein and Gubrium 1995).

In practical terms, this means that instead of starting from interview questions which invite generalities or abstractions like 'What is good parenting?', the researcher needs to devise questions and modes of asking which both anticipate and discover the range of contexts in which moralities of parenting get done by or in relation to their interviewee. Questions, therefore, might focus upon the detail of how they 'do parenting' on an everyday basis or at 'definitive moments' by asking, for example, how they organize various aspects of their relationships with their children and *what matters* to them (and conversely what does not) in the different contexts raised. Questions may have a biographical or life story orientation, particularly if the researcher suspects that moralities of parenting are processual over time and lifetimes.

In this type of theoretical project, then, questions should be couched in specifics rather than generalities. The practice of asking about the everyday has a long established pedigree in qualitative research, and is based on the idea that the way people make sense of the social is grounded in their everyday – even routine – experiences. Similarly, the practice of focusing on definitive moments or points of renegotiation or change is well established. But does this mean that it is never useful or productive to ask interviewees for generalities or abstractions?

It may of course be interesting to see whether people are prepared to answer these kinds of questions. If, for example, an interviewee is prepared to say, in response to the 'What is a good parent?' question, that 'A good parent is one who is caring but also exercises discipline', then surely the very fact that they dealt with the question and devised an answer must mean something? The difficulty lies in working out what it does mean, that is in the interpretation. If we assume that moralities are processes and practices, then an abstracted or generalized answer cannot make any sense without some knowledge of how it relates to the individual's practices and experiences, since individuals do not inhabit abstract and generalized social worlds (even when they are being interviewed). That an interviewee would make a statement like this in an interview context *might* tell us something about the sense of a moral self which they were creating in that setting, but we would not have the tools or materials to fashion this into a generalization of our own about how that related to other contexts.

In fact, my own research into family and kinship suggests that interviewees often ask for clarification of abstract and generalized questions because these kinds of questions do not make immediate sense and people find it difficult to formulate an answer (see especially Finch and Mason 1993, 2000; Mason 2000). Where they do, the answers often appear very cliched and empty of any grounded meaning. Hollway and Jefferson (2000) report similar difficulties in their research into fear of crime. This is a problem, because if further clarification and possibly contextualization is required for the question to make sense and for an answer to seem possible, then it seems likely that there is no level of the social which corresponds to the abstract version of the question, and that the theoretical project is flawed. It may, however, be useful to track the kinds of clarifications that interviewees seek – what kinds of contextual or other information do people require in order to formulate a response? Or, if they answer the question by relating it to their own or someone else's circumstances, how are these connections between the abstract and the situated made? This might yield knowledge about relevant contexts and forms of morality. However, this way of situating interviewees' responses is likely to be a rather hit-and-miss affair, and is much inferior to the strategy of beginning with contexts relevant to the interviewee, given that it is ultimately based on the same assumption that moralities are contextual.

Of course this raises the question of whether *everything* about moralities of parenting is contextual. Do people never look outside the parochial boundaries of their own situation to more abstract notions of right and wrong and, if they do, can specific rather than abstract questions really illuminate this? One response to this question is to ask whether interviews can ever tell us everything we want to know about our research problem – in this case moralities of parenting – and that is an issue to which I shall return shortly. But the other response is that yes, specific questions about people's own experiences can make a much better job of enabling us to analyse whether and how people *use* abstractions (in this case abstract moral principles of right and wrong) in their practices, than can abstract questions themselves. Take the following example of an excerpt from one of my recent research projects on the topic of how families handle inheritance.[2] This interviewee, like many others, is conveying a great deal about moralities of parenting, but what he says is a response to questions about his specific circumstances – in this case as a member of the first generation in his own family to be a home-owner – and about his own bequeathing intentions.

> I still think that it would be good for my children to make their own way. They shouldn't be helped too much, shouldn't expect too much. … It sounds a bit reactionary, this. But it does build your character. I think that they shouldn't have things too easily … I don't really assume that I've got to hand on the wealth that we will have to the children … it's probably better for me if I use some of it before I go, and probably better for them in some way that they should make their own way. (Finch and Mason 2000: 125–126)

For this interviewee, good parenting involves not passing on too much in a material sense to one's children. He articulates that very clearly, using a moral discourse, without being asked 'What is good parenting?' His account blends the general (they shouldn't have things too easily) with the particular ('good for my children to make their own way', 'I don't really assume that I've got to hand on the wealth that we will have to the children') and is articulated through – because it is located within – a particular context or set of circumstances. In analysing the very many moral accounts which that research project generated from its specific and contextual questions, we are able to get a better sense of how moralities of parenting are used or operate, in their abstract and their particular guises, than had we simply asked about the rights and wrongs of inheritance and parenting in abstract ways. In writing our analysis from that particular project, Janet Finch and I developed the analytical and methodological device of 'the narrative' in a rather specific way to help us to engage with these relationships between the general and the particular. We derived 'composite' moral narratives from our interviewees' many personal stories, and from what they told us of their hopes and fears about inheritance. We explain the logic of this as follows:

> We have used the concept of narrative as a methodological and analytical device to illustrate some of the consistencies in our interview data but, more than that, to communicate accounts and scenarios which people recognise and, most notably, which they fear. In this sense, the narrative is an expression of people's attempts to connect up their own experiences and reasoning with something which they perceive to be more generalised, and the significant point is that many people do this. The narratives we have used tend to be expressions of what people think should

not happen, or what they do *not* want for their own families, and are scenarios which they actively try to avoid. This means that the stories which the narratives contain do not in and of themselves represent an empirical and generalisable reality of kinship. They do not describe what people generally do, nor do they represent moral rules about what they should do. However, we learn about people's practices and moral reasoning through them because many people use narratives like those we have sketched out to locate and make sense of their own (usually oppositional) practices. This means that the construction of generalising narratives, as a way of contextualising their own practice, is an important element in the way in which people *do* kinship and inheritance. (Finch and Mason 2000: 165, original emphasis)

One way to try to shortcut this process is to ask about generalities and abstractions in the first place rather than to derive them from interviewees' accounts, but to do it in a situated way through the use of vignettes – hypothetical scenarios concocted by the researcher in advance of the interviews, possible on the basis of existing interview data (for example, it would be possible to use composite narratives of the kind discussed above). The vignette is presented to the interviewee, who then is asked to say what the people involved in the scenario should do, or what they themselves would do in that situation (Finch 1987). This may be a particularly useful way of asking questions in ethically and morally sensitive situations, because in theory in word it allows the interviewee to discuss their own moral reasoning without having to (publicly) locate what they say in the detail of what may be difficult or private experiences. The logic is that interviewees are asked to do moral reasoning on the spot, but are given contextual information – albeit hypothetical – with which to do this. Also, if used flexibly in qualitative interviews, vignettes can allow the researcher to track in a much more contextual and sensitive way any further clarifications which interviewees require, and hence what contextual knowledge is relevant to the reasoning process (for examples of this see Finch and Mason 1993; Smart and Neale 1999).

This seems a more satisfactory way of asking abstract questions because although not directly situated in the interviewees' own experiences, it does use notions of situatedness and context in strategic ways as part of a theoretical project. We are left, however, with the question of what the data might mean. Their connection to contexts other than the interview itself may be tangential at best, and they could not therefore be used as knowledge about the interviewee's own situated moral practices, or their own situated moral reasoning, unless the vignettes had been used as vehicles to get the interview to produce dialogue about these directly.

To sum up, one good reason to avoid questions which seek or encourage generalities and abstractions is that the knowledge which we produce from these may not be quite what we think it is, and what it is may be quite limited when seen in the context of the overall theoretical project we are pursuing. Another more practical reason is that once an interview takes on that kind of abstract discursive style it may be difficult to regain the contextuality so central to the construction of situated knowledge. In part, this is because the construction and reconstruction of relevant contexts in an interview is probably only possible in a sustained way – it is not an activity which can be dipped into and out of. I shall expand on this point in the next section. It seems sensible, therefore, to avoid abstractions and generalities in qualitative interviews unless we are very sure we have a use for them.

STRUCTURED OR 'STRUCTURE-FREE'?

The types of questions an interviewer asks, and the way they listen to and interpret the answers they are given, undoubtedly help to shape the nature of the knowledge produced. However, interviews are not just about the asking of questions and the proffering of answers to those questions, and to argue that they are would be to cast the role of the researcher too deterministically, among other things. Indeed, in interpreting data, it is very important for researchers to see that sometimes what an interviewee says is not the straightforward answer to the interviewer's question that it is presumed to be. For example, if an interviewer asks whether an interviewee's father treats her and her sister equally and she answers that yes, he loves them both, we cannot assume on the basis of this answer that the concept of *equality* itself figures in that interviewee's family practices, experiences and reasoning.

The idea that interviewees may be 'answering' questions other than those we are asking them, and making sense of the social world in ways we had not thought of, lies behind many qualitative interview strategies. The logic that we should be receptive to what interviewees say, and to *their* ways of understanding, underpins much of the 'qualitative' critique of structured survey interview methods. The problem is not only about how questions are asked (for example in abstract or specific terms), but also about the structure or framework for the dialogue. A structure or sequence of questions which is rigid, and which is devised in advance by the interviewer, by definition lacks the flexibility and sensitivity to context and particularity required if we are to listen to our interviewees' ways of interpreting and experiencing the social world.

However, this raises a problem, because despite the use of the term 'unstructured interview' in some methodological discourses, it is not possible to conduct a structure-free interview not least because the agendas and assumptions of both interviewer and interviewee will inevitably impose frameworks for meaningful interaction. The question to be addressed by the researcher is instead how to, and how far to, structure an interview, and the answers once again depend upon their theoretical orientations. Most qualitative researchers try to structure interviews in ways which are meaningful to interviewees (and relevant to the research), and many try to minimize their own role in the process of structuring and in the sequencing of the dialogue.

One example of this is life history or biographical interviewing. Here, the structuring principle – interviewees' own life story – is considered to be meaningful to them, and the sequence is taken from that story, rather than from a pre-devised list of questions. Many life history interviewers will try to facilitate the telling of the story more than to direct it. This approach is based on the logic that the significance of social experience will be revealed through contextual data, and that the way to achieve this is to ask interviewees to structure their own life story narrative, sometimes according to specified principles (for example, family biography, work biography, educational biography) and to follow their own cues.

The point is that the structure offered – the telling of a life – allows interviewees to craft their own narrative around their own concerns, experience and perspectives (Miller 2000). Even so, it is important to appreciate that the narrative itself is a cultural form or genre with its own structural conventions, rather than a neutral medium for the simple excavation of facts (Chamberlain and Thompson 1997). Thus although this approach may feel more 'hands off' from the interviewer's point of view, the imperative toward a particular kind of structuring on the interviewee's part may nevertheless be quite strong. The narrative form shapes what is being told in certain ways, providing coherence, sequentiality, a sense of progression, a purpose or a plot, and an author. Narratives encourage the construction of a beginning, a middle and an end.

For some, like Chamberlain and Thompson (1997), the analysis of narrative and discursive conventions and their relationship to social practices and experiences *is* the theoretical project, the object of study, and finding ways to elicit narratives from interviewees is a crucial part of that. From this perspective, the structural tendencies imposed by the narrative form are of interest in themselves and thus are far from being a problem. For others, however, they are a problem, because they tidy up and sanitize what are often messy social processes and experiences, yet these – in all their messiness – are the objects of study.

Hollway and Jefferson (2000), for example, argue that a preoccupation with the biographical or other coherence of the narrative, and the emphasis this places on the capacity of the narrator to know and tell their story, leads the researcher to miss highly significant and less formally structured elements of social experience. Instead, they advocate the 'free association narrative'. This method is based on psychoanalytic principles, and in particular on the idea that an interview should find ways to tap those elements of the subject's experience which are not recountable or explainable by themselves – elements which are not authored. They argue that:

> by asking the patient to say whatever comes to mind, the psychoanalyst is eliciting the kind of narrative that is not structured according to conscious logic, but according to unconscious logic; that is, the associations follow pathways defined by emotional motivations, rather than rational intentions. According to psychoanalysis, unconscious dynamics are a product of attempts to avoid or master anxiety. This suggests that anxieties and attempts to defend against them, including the identity investments these give rise to, provide the key to a person's Gestalt. By eliciting a

narrative structured according to the principles of free association, therefore, we secure access to a person's concerns which would probably not be visible using a more traditional method. While a common concern of both approaches is to elicit detail, narrative analysis has a preoccupation with coherence which we do not share. Free associations defy narrative conventions and enable the analyst to pick up on incoherences (for example, contradictions, elisions, avoidances) and accord them due significance. (Hollway and Jefferson 2000: 37)

Allowing interviewees to 'free associate', for Hollway and Jefferson (2000), gives researchers using psychoanalytic principles a way into the unconscious because it allows them to spot and make sense of connections, schisms and defence mechanisms within the narrative, whether or not the interviewee is aware of them. Hollway and Jefferson achieved this by training themselves to be the 'almost invisible, facilitating catalyst to their [interviewees'] stories. Being "almost invisible" ... means not imposing a structure on the narrative' (Hollway and Jefferson 2000: 36). The *Gestalt* in which Hollway and Jefferson are interested is not a consciously constructed life narrative, nor is it an understanding of the place and use of narratives in social practice. Instead, it is a psychosocial subject, which is not consciously authored and cannot be articulated in conventional narrative form.

This kind of theoretical project demands that the interview 'structure' allows spaces for free association, for example through allowing interviewees to develop points and stories in depth and return to them at will even though their relevance to the substantive concerns of the research may not be evident, and certainly through not enforcing a particular sequence of questions. The irony, of course, is that even free-association narratives require some kind of structure to make the telling of them possible; indeed Hollway and Jefferson developed seven standard starter questions around which they encouraged the development of the narratives. It demands an act of faith (in psychoanalytic principles) to believe that it is the unconscious rather than something more social or cultural which consequently does the structuring of free association. Nevertheless Hollway and Jefferson's work demonstrates par excellence, as does that of Chamberlain and Thompson (1997), what is more often unrecognized: that how a researcher deals with issues of interview structure and sequence is always part of their theoretical project, whether or not they acknowledge it.

CHALLENGING OUR THEORETICAL ORIENTATIONS?

My argument so far – that how we ask and listen are theoretical enactments of our assumptions around where the phenomena we are interested in are located, and how the interviewee and interview can illuminate the issues – has rested on the assumption that we know what it is we are looking for, be that contextual moral practices, a psychosocial subject, or the use and operation of narratives. My critique of general and abstract interview questions is based on the argument not only that these direct attention to wrong or 'non-existent' locations (for example, abstract attitudes and values), but also that they miss the point about morality in that they assume it is a thing rather than a process or practice. I take the view that all research has some kind of theoretical orientation, as do all forms of asking, listening and interpretation, whether or not this is articulated, and therefore there is always some sense in which researchers know what they are looking for, ontologically speaking. But how far should we use our interviews to view the social world in different ways, and to see things we are *not* looking for, as well as those we are?

Let us continue to explore this question in relation to my moralities of parenting example. The version of morality which I have set out has its own set of theoretical underpinnings. Could they, should they, be challenged or tested through interview methodology? My answer is a qualified yes, but we need to explore what is involved to work out how this might feasibly be done. First, we need to establish the social-theoretical context which makes possible the formulation I have offered that moralities of parenting are contextual.

The 'postmodern turn' in social theory has helped to throw issues about morality into the limelight because it questions the degree to which moral absolutes, created by higher-order experts and institutions, continue to hold any sway in what is seen as the new, fragmented and fluid social order. The apparent lack of a coherent and uniform moral order or clear sets of rules about what is right and what is wrong are seen as part of far-reaching social changes involving the demise of social structures, traditions and institutions as organizing principles of the social world. For some, this means that the capacities for individual action, agency, choice and reflexivity are increased while simultaneously people develop a lack of trust in familiar institutions and universal truths (see e.g. Giddens 1991). For others, the retheorization and exploration of morality and ethics, as forms of agency practised by individuals and in relationships and interactions (rather than as truths dictated from on high) take centre stage (Bauman 1993; Finch and Mason 1993, 2000; Sevenhuijsen 1998; Smart and Neale 1999). A form of ethics derived from the 'concrete' rather than the 'generalized other' underpins this (Benhabib 1992: 9–10). Perhaps for the first time in the history of sociology, the intimate relationships people have with one another are therefore no longer seen as side issues in social science, but are considered absolutely central to these new forms of agency and practice, and as a lens for understanding social change and the social world more generally (Giddens 1992; Beck and Beck-Gernsheim 1995).

As a consequence of these changes in the way we theorize the social world, and the changes we consider to be taking place in that world, the question of how morality works in personal relationships has begun to occupy the imaginations of many researchers. If it cannot be said simply that people follow the rules created for them by religious and other institutions, then how do people work out what is right and what is wrong in their relationships with others (if they do not simply follow moral rules and codes)?

Have people dispensed with morality altogether? Are questions of right and wrong, or 'the proper thing to do' of any concern or consequence in personal relationships? What forms do they take? How are they expressed or practised? How and when do they change?

The language used to frame these kinds of questions – moral practices, moral agency – itself stands in marked contrast to earlier (even interactionist) social scientific concerns with moral rules, norms and codes. It also seems highly consistent with an actor/agent-centred form of social inquiry such as the qualitative interview.

But there are other ways of looking at these issues. One has already been alluded to throughout, and is the antithesis, namely that morality is a framework, or a set of rules, norms and traditions. According to this approach, detraditionalization and fragmentation plus the potential for human agency and interaction have been overstated. Another sees human agency not so much as overstated, but as missing the point altogether, and proposes a project of 'decentring the subject'.

The 'discursive turn' in social theory has claimed the death of the subject, and especially of the rational, unitary, self-governing subject who can account for their practices and reveal the logic of those practices in a research interview. Instead, the concern is with multiple subject positions created through, for example, moral discourses, and the centrality of text, language and practice in those discursive processes. Agency, and a concern with the agent, are not part of the epistemological vocabulary here, yet how morality works or, more accurately, how morality is constructed discursively, might very well be.

To return to the point about seeing what we are *not* looking for, the key question is, then: if we are looking for moral practices and agency, could we see moral *norms, rules, traditions* or *discourses*? Does the orientation to moralities of parenting and to the process of construction in the interview setting overemphasize the individual, and human agency? Does an emphasis on interviewees' narratives produce an oversanitized, overcoherent story which again has the effect of overplaying agency and rationality? As well as questioning the form which morality takes, we might also question the idea of morality itself. Is the concept of morality the right one? Does morality have anything to do with parenting? Or is parenting more about practical (and impractical) actions, power relations and so on? Similarly, what theoretical baggage does the concept of 'parenting' carry – with its implication that this is a skill or a project practised on or 'done-to' children, rather than a two (or more) directional relationship extending beyond childhood?

Clearly, it is possible to generate a long list of alternative conceptual and theoretical orientations and, in and of itself, that might feel like rather a meaningless task. The point here is, however, to advocate that researchers develop enough of a sense of alternative conceptualizations of their research problem, and the different types of theoretical project that they might involve, in the ways I have suggested, to enable them to devise ways of testing their own approach both within and beyond interview methodology.

So, for example, to try to avoid an overemphasis on the individual and on agency, we might consider gaining other forms of data which are less reliant on the mechanism of self-report, and which reflect on other levels or dimensions of the social (such as observation, demographic data analysis). We might seek out inconsistencies just as much as consistencies in our interview questions to try to avoid oversanitizing our data. We might focus less on our key concepts and more on wider or looser ones – even oppositional ones – which give us the possibility of seeing other things as well. In the example I have been using that might involve seeking out 'what matters' in parent–child relationships rather than the narrower concept of morality specifically. Finally, we might focus on relationships between people, without presupposing anything directional about these, rather than treating 'parenting' as a practice done to children, or a set of skills possessed by parents. This inevitably raises the question of *who* has the knowledge, the experience, the defended self, or whatever, that we are interested in. If we see our focus as *relationships* (parent–child) rather than individualized practices or skills possessed (parenting), then parents' perspectives can provide data on only part of this. We need to interview children too, at the very least.

In the process of challenging our theoretical orientations, we need also to ask a more fundamental question about interview methodology, and that is, are talk and text enough? Do interviews give too much epistemological privilege to the idea of the individual, articulate, rational actor? Can interviews, whether with carefully selected ranges of individuals, or with groups, ever tell us about those elements of the social which appear to go beyond or operate outside individuals – whether these be discourses, or institutions, or systems? Can they tell us about elements of the social which are not accessible through talk? While we cannot expect interviews to be able to do everything for us, I want to conclude with a consideration of some of the limitations imposed by an emphasis on talk and text.

CONCLUSION: BEYOND TALK AND TEXT?

So far in my discussion I have argued that the way we ask questions, listen to and interpret talk, all constitute theoretical projects. Underpinning the kind of theoretical project I have outlined is the assumption that talk and text are central in our ways of knowing the social world. In qualitative interviewing, 'talk' means interactive talk, and some of the enthusiasm for the method which has emerged in recent years is undoubtedly a reaction against the asking of questions in less interactive ways, for example through postal questionnaires and structured questionnaire surveys. Many qualitative researchers would probably agree with Fontana and Frey (1998) that

> as long as many researchers continue to treat respondents as unimportant, faceless individuals whose only contribution is to fill one more boxed response, the answers we, as researchers will get will be commensurable with the questions we

ask and with the way we ask them. ... The question must be asked person-to-person if we want it to be answered fully. (Fontana and Frey 1998: 73)

Even Hollway and Jefferson's (2000) psychosocial subject and intersubjectivity, which operate in part through the unconscious and through feelings (as well as through talk and conscious interaction, discourses and so on) can best be known according to them through interview talk, albeit they propose a focus on the spaces and schisms within dialogue. Although what they are interested in operates at a level or in ways which cannot be reasoned or explained (they argue that people are not 'their own best explainers'), they nevertheless argue that we can construct knowledge of it by listening to people's free associations, connected and disconnected narratives, and interpreting them through a psychoanalytic frame. This does of course raise some political problems around the issue of claims to truth.

The privileging of talk is understandable in the climate described by Fontana and Frey (1998), yet we should not allow our enthusiasm for the rich and fascinating data which can be generated in interviews to stop us seeing some of the limitations of using talk and text to construct knowledge, and to contemplate ways of overcoming these.

Criticisms of interview and biographical methods have for a long time pointed to the vagaries of memory, selectivity and deception in interviewees' accounts (see Chamberlayne *et al.* 2000 for a useful review) and also to issues around fluency and divergent linguistic codes. Furthermore, it is important to engage with the 'politics of talk', and to recognize that what counts as language, who uses it, what is its nature, what it can mean and do, are not merely part of a neutral and given reality, but are products of power relations and struggles (O'Brien and Harris 1999). All of these factors indicate, with different implications, that we should not read interviewees' accounts as straightforward descriptions of social experience.

But the points I want to make move beyond the question of whether or not we can take interviewees' accounts at face value, towards questions about those elements of the social which cannot be expressed through talk, and which are not situated in talk. Of course the idea that individuals cannot express everything in which we might be interested in words has long underpinned observational methods, but there may be elements of social experience which cannot readily be observed either.

I am referring to processes of thought, feeling, emotion, sentiment and so on. These may be rather significant and, certainly, one can readily see that my example of moralities of parenting may be closely bound up with these or, to put it another way, such moralities may be played out or practised in those unspoken social locations. There is a danger first that an emphasis on what can be articulated verbally obscures these and, second, that the 'discursive turn' in social science, with its emphasis on text and the discursive construction of subject positions, rules these out of the frame altogether.

Yet researching these elements of the unspoken is inherently problematic, and we may need to find ways of encouraging non-verbal expression to explore dimensions which people find difficult or impossible to express in words because, to reiterate an earlier point, we need to create the best contextual conditions for the construction of meaningful knowledge. Methods which encourage non-verbal expression are increasingly deployed in research with children. For example, play and drawing are now commonly used as research tools with children, because it is recognized that they may find certain ideas and experiences difficult to express in words, and also because key elements of their social experiences, practices and relations may not occur or be manifest in dialogic form in their everyday lives in the first place. Yet it is strange, as well as patronizing to children, that such considerations are so rarely applied to adults also (see Solberg 1996). Furthermore, even in research with children there is probably some way to go in working out how non-verbal products and processes should be interpreted and expressed.

It is of course possible to treat non-verbal products and processes as *texts* which represent unspoken dimensions of the social world or through which those dimensions are constituted. This involves a generous definition of 'text' but as Devine and Heath point out in their discussion of postmodernism and empirical research, 'a text can be anything from a literary text, an official document, or an interview transcript through to a photograph, a movie or a building' (Devine and Heath 1999: 207). Yet constituting non-verbal products and processes as texts may miss the point about what they are and what they are meant to be, and may obscure their processual, agentic and non-discursive nature.

That suggestion is supported by experience of family and kinship research, where fairly frequent use is made of various different ways of diagrammatically mapping and charting the 'closeness' or the 'supportiveness' of people's relationships, but where what seems most important is not the chart or family tree which is produced – the 'text' – so much as the sometimes agonized processes which people are observed to go through in trying to decide which relative or friend goes where in it (Finch and Mason 1993; Flowerdew 1999). It is interesting that the act of placing a relative in a chart often is treated by the person doing it as highly significant in itself: something is being done more than said, and something non-verbal is being expressed. Incorporating this kind of activity into an interview thus helps to create a rather different context for the construction of a more non-verbal kind of knowledge.

Using non- (or semi-) verbal techniques such as these, or photography or video recording, which consciously and conscientiously move beyond a preoccupation with talk or with text, is clearly an important way in which we might explore non-verbal elements of the social. Although they are often accompanied by talk, and sometimes used within an interview context, these methods draw heavily on observational techniques developed by social anthropologists and ethnographers. We must, however, be mindful of the epistemological assumptions we make when we employ this kind of methodology, and when we attempt to interpret our data. In particular, we should not assume that visual methods, for example, produce knowledge which is somehow less constructed or more directly representational than verbal interview methods. The critique of the idea of excavation of data which I outlined earlier applies with equal force in relation to visual artefacts and products. Instead the point is to evoke or construct knowledge about non-discursive experience, and the argument is that using non-verbal methods should help to create conditions appropriate for the generation of such knowledge.

Examining the role of non-verbal elements in social relations, and of objects and artefacts – again not just as texts or representations – is important here. To explore moralities of parenting, for example, one might use people's personal photographs, objects and possessions as starting points for discussion and observation, as well as for analysis in their own right. In a recent study of inheritance, my colleagues and I looked at (often literally) objects people had inherited and investigated what kinds of objects they were, where people kept them, considered what their role was in kin relationships, what they symbolized or expressed, what was their 'lifespan' and the changing nature of their ownership, and so on (see Finch and Mason 2000).

Methods which seek to explore the non-verbal *non-verbally* can of course be complemented by more traditional approaches, such as making inferences about, for example, emotions and feelings on the basis of what people say, how they say it, and what they do not say. We can sometimes discern whether someone is used to thinking in a particular way by what they say, and we can infer that something is taken for granted if they do not see it necessary to mention it. We can sometimes infer how emotionally engaged they are with a particular issue by how they talk about it, and we can get a sense of what matters emotionally by observing their demeanour as they speak. We can ask people to try to articulate elements of the non-verbal, to tell us how they feel, and what makes them angry or sad.

It is clear that there is a great deal of scope for developing methods which loosen the grip of talk and text on our research imaginations, and this might be done under the auspices of a range of different types of theoretical project, within and outside of interview methods. At the very least, researchers using interview methodology should consider carefully whether strategies which prioritize talk and text can deliver the required goods.

NOTES

1   Investigation into 'moralities of parenting' is one of the key interests of the ESRC Research Group for the study of Care, Values and the Future of Welfare (CAVA) at Leeds University, of which I am a member. Further information is available from the website: www.leeds.ac.uk/cava

2   This project, 'Inheritance, Property and Family Relationships', was funded by ESRC, grant no. R000232035. It was directed by Janet Finch, Jennifer Mason and Judith Masson, and the research officers were Lynn Hayes and Lorraine Wallis.

REFERENCES

Bauman, Z. (1993) *Postmodern Ethics*. Oxford: Blackwell.

Beck, U. and Beck-Gernsheim, E. (1995) *The Normal Chaos of Love*. Cambridge: Polity.

Benhabib, S. (1992) *Situating the Self: Gender, Community and Postmodernism in Contemporary Ethics*. Cambridge: Polity.

Burgess, R.G. (1984) *In the Field: An Introduction to Field Research*. London: Allen & Unwin.

Chamberlain, M. and Thompson, P. (1997) 'Genre and narrative in life stories', in M. Chamberlain and P. Thompson (eds) *Narrative and Genre*. London: Routledge.

Chamberlayne, P., Bornat, J. and Wengraf, T. (2000) *The Turn to Biographical Methods in Social Science*. London: Routledge.

Devine, F. and Heath, S. (1999) *Sociological Research Methods in Context*. London: Macmillan.

Finch, J. (1987) 'The vignette technique in survey research', *Sociology* 21(1): 105–114.

Finch, J. and Mason, J. (1993) *Negotiating Family Responsibilities*. London: Routledge.

Finch, J. and Mason, J. (2000) *Passing On: Kinship and Inheritance in England*. London: Routledge.

Flowerdew, J. (1999) 'Reformulating familiar concerns: parents in stepfamilies', unpublished PhD thesis, University of Leeds.

Fontana, A. and Frey, J.H. (1998) 'Interviewing: the art of science', in N.K. Denzin and Y.S. Lincoln (eds) *Collecting and Interpreting Qualitative Materials*. London: Sage.

Giddens, A. (1991) *Modernity and Self-Identity: Self and Society in the Late Modern Age*. Cambridge: Polity.

Giddens, A. (1992) *The Transformation of Intimacy: Sexuality, Love and Eroticism in Modern Societies*. Cambridge: Polity.

Hollway, W. and Jefferson, T. (2000) *Doing Qualitative Research Differently: Free Association, Narrative and the Interview Method*. London: Sage.

Holstein, J. and Gubrium, J. (1995) *The Active Interview*. Thousand Oaks, CA: Sage.

Kvale, S. (1996) *InterViews: An Introduction to Qualitative Research Interviewing*. London: Sage.

Mason, J. (1996) *Qualitative Researching*. London: Sage.

Mason, J. (2000) 'Deciding where to live: relational reasoning and narratives of the self', working paper no. 19, Centre for Research on Family, Kinship and Childhood, University of Leeds.

Miller, R.L. (2000) *Researching Life Stories and Family Histories*. London: Sage.

O'Brien, M. and Harris, J. (1999) 'Modernity and the politics of identity', in M. O'Brien, S. Penna and C. Hay (eds) *Theorising Modernity: Reflexivity, Environment and Identity in Giddens' Social Theory*. London: Longman.

Sevenhuijsen, S. (1998) *Citizenship and the Ethics of Care: Feminist Considerations on Justice, Morality and Politics*. London: Routledge.

Silverman, D. (2000) *Doing Qualitative Research: A Practical Handbook*. London: Sage.

Smart, C. and Neale, B. (1999) *Family Fragments?* Cambridge: Polity.
Solberg, A. (1996) 'The challenge in child research: from "being" to "doing"', in
  J. Brannen and M. O'Brien (eds) *Children in Families*. London: Falmer.

11 NARRATIVE IN SOCIAL RESEARCH

Steph Lawler

Our own most cherished conceits, stubborn evasions or persistent illusions are all fashioned by a growing stock of cultural narratives, as we try to make sense of the past and its connections to our lives in the present. This ... is what we need to study, not seek to evade. (Lynne Segal, Why Feminism?, p. 118)

Within social research, one compelling reason for carrying out qualitative interviews is that they offer a means of exploring the ways in which social actors interpret the world, and their place within it. These interpretations are often extremely complex and nuanced, and would be difficult to access through other means. This chapter is about one way in which such interpretation can be conceptualized. It deals with the 'narrative' dimensions of people's accounts within qualitative research – the ways in which people make and use stories to interpret the world. I want to emphasize, however, that I am not using 'narrative' here to indicate a 'story' that simply 'carries' a set of 'facts'. Rather, I see narratives as *social products* produced by people within the context of specific social, historical and cultural locations. They are related to the experience that people have of their lives, but they are not transparent carriers of that experience. Rather, they are interpretive devices, through which people represent themselves, both to themselves and to others. Further, narratives do not originate with the individual: rather, they circulate culturally to provide a repertoire (though not an infinite one) from which people can produce their own stories.

In other words, my argument here is that, not only do people often produce 'storied' accounts of themselves and their relation to the social world (within and outside of the research setting), but also the social world is itself 'storied'. That is, stories circulate culturally, providing a means of making sense of that world, and also providing the materials with which people construct personal narratives as a means of constructing personal identities. I argue within this chapter that narratives – which I define briefly here (though I return to the question of definition later) as accounts which contain transformation (change over time), some kind of 'action' and characters, all of which are brought together within an overall 'plot' – are a central means with which people connect together past and present, self and other. They do so within the context of cultural narratives which delimit what can be said, what stories can be told, what will count as meaningful, and what will seem to be nonsensical.

Although narratives are most closely associated with life history research, I want to suggest here that attention to narrative can be an extremely useful way of conceptualizing the kinds of accounts people produce in qualitative interviews more generally. Narratives, whether personal or 'public', neither begin nor end in the research setting: they are part of the fabric of the social world. Nevertheless, the research setting is one arena within which narratives can be elicited and explored. If research participants are given sufficient space within research based on interviews, it is likely that they will produce narratives if asked about their lives (Riessman 1993). These narratives may be fragmentary and partial – indeed, it is likely that they will be – but can nevertheless tell us a great deal about the person and the social world she or he inhabits. As always, the kind of knowledge we produce through research will depend on what we set out to find. So, research which explores the narratives people produce will necessarily be interpretivist in nature: it will work from the basic premise that individuals and groups interpret the social world and their place within it. The question is less 'What happened?' than 'What is the significance of this event?' (White 1996).

From this perspective, conceptualizing interview accounts in terms of narrative – what Somers and Gibson (1994) call 'conceptual narrativity' – can be seen as a means of confounding the false dichotomy by which an interviewee's account is conceptualized *either* as an unproblematic reflection of lived experience *or* as 'a distorting screen that always projects experience out of its own categories' (Ezzy 2001: 24). It is not that 'the facts do not matter': nor is it the case that '*only* the facts matter'.[1] Rather, facts (or experience) and the interpretation of those facts (or that experience) are envisaged as necessarily entwined.

SOME BACKGROUND

Conventionally, the study of narrative has been associated with literary texts, in which context the study has largely centred on the technical components of the narratives themselves. However, recent social-scientific work has drawn attention to the significance of narratives for a study of the social world. In this respect, this recent work is drawing on a relatively long tradition in social science, from the call for a 'sociology of biography' made by the nineteenth-century philosopher Wilhelm Dilthey (1976), through the ethnographic work of the Chicago School (which elicited individual biographical accounts) and life history work to contemporary qualitative research which draws on fragments of narrative (see e.g. Simonds 1992, 1996; Rickard 2001). From the start, such work, although disparate in many ways, has been in marked contradistinction to positivism, which would hold that the only social facts worth consideration are those phenomena which are directly observable and (in some sense) measurable.[2] From the perspective of narrative inquiry, what is apparent – what can be seen and observed – is not all there is to say: a much more interesting issue is that of interpretation – how social actors interpret the social world, and their place within it. Without a consideration of this interpretivism, what is apparent may be not simply inadequate but misleading. Consider, for example, an action as simple as that of raising an arm. This same act could be understood in a variety of ways, depending on the context: it can, variously mean, for example, hailing a taxi, greeting a friend, or voting (Ricoeur 1991a). As Lois McNay argues, 'Meaning is not inherent to action but is the product of interpretative strategies amongst which narrative is central' (McNay 2000: 95).

It is this anti-positivism which leads Somers and Gibson (1994) to characterize narrative as the 'epistemological other' of sociology. They argue, in other words, that the entire project of sociological theorizing and research has been premised on a disavowal of narrative. They suggest two principal reasons for this disavowal, both connected with the 'self-identity project' of the social sciences: first, because social scientists have tended to limit their definition of 'narrative' to that of merely a representation. In other words, narratives have conventionally been treated merely as (more or less transparent) 'carriers' of a set of 'facts': they have not in themselves been seen as social products. Second, Somers and Gibson (1994) argue, the issues with which studies of narrative are typically concerned – issues of ontology and identity – have been defined as outside of the remit of sociological concern.

Against this position, Somers and Gibson (1994), following Paul Ricoeur, suggest that researchers and theorists adopt what they call 'conceptual narrativity'. This is, in brief, a position which postulates

> that social life is itself *storied* and that narrative is an *ontological condition of social life* … that stories guide action; that people construct identities (however multiple and changing) by locating themselves or being located within a repertoire of emplotted stories; that 'experience' is constituted through narratives; that people make sense of what has happened and is happening to them by attempting to assemble or in some way to integrate these happenings within one or more narratives; and that people are guided to act in certain ways, and not others, on the basis of the projections, expectations, and memories derived from a multiplicity but ultimately linked repertoire of available social, public and cultural narratives. (Somers and Gibson 1994: 38–39, original emphasis)

Somers and Gibson point up some important issues in relation to the study of the social world, even if, as I think, they rather overstate their case that sociology is premised on *not* being narrative. The study of narratives may have been peripheral in sociological research, but it has managed to exist within it. It is fair to say, however, that recent developments within sociological work have made the study of narrative both more pressing and more central. These developments include, for example, an increasing attention to 'textuality': to the ways in which written (or spoken) texts are not simply unproblematic 'reflections' of some pre-existing reality, but work to *produce* (what we count as) social reality. Further, if narratives are *not* merely carriers of something else (something more important) then they must be subject to scrutiny, rather than simply taken as given. Also relevant here is an increasing attention to issues of selfhood, subjectivity and identity, including an overturning of conventional modernist assumptions about the self. Increasingly, selves are acknowledged as neither entirely unique, asocial beings, nor as entirely determined by social structures. This leads to a radical questioning of the conventional binarisms of sociology: structure and agency, individual and society, self and other (Stanley and Morgan 1993). In later sections, I address these issues: first, though, I consider how narratives work through processes of emplotment.

EMPLOTMENT

I have already given a brief definition of narrative – of what makes an account a narrative (as opposed, for example, to a chronicle, an archive, or a set of questions and answers) and here I want to expand on this definition. I am following the work of Paul Ricoeur (and later writers who have followed his conceptualization of narrative) who, more than anyone else, has considered narrative as a category by which people make an identity. Building on his argument, I will argue that this identity is not isolated from the social world: rather, it is intimately bound up with the social world.

To recapitulate, narrative must contain transformation, plot line and characters. But these components must be brought together within an overall plot. For Ricoeur, the central element of a narrative is its plot. Plots are not selected a priori, but are produced through the process of *emplotment*. Ricoeur defines emplotment, at its most basic, as 'a synthesis of heterogeneous elements' (1991a: 21). He elaborates three main (and overlapping) forms of synthesis at work in emplotment:

> **1. the synthesis between many events and one story**. In this context, an event is more than simply something that happens: it must have a part in the story, contributing to the progress of the narrative. It must contribute to the coherence and intelligibility of the narrative.
> **2. the synthesis between discordance and concordance**. In other words, the plot *both* incorporates quite disparate events and episodes, unintended consequences, and so on, *and* functions as a totality: one story.
> **3. the synthesis between two different senses of time**. Time, on the one hand, as open and indefinite, embedded in a series of successive incidents (so that we ask of a story, 'and then? and then?') and time as something closed and 'over with'. As Ricoeur puts it, 'time is both what passes and flows away and, on the other hand, what endures and remains'. (Ricoeur 1991a: 22, original emphasis)

Although Ricoeur's definition of emplotment may seem pitched at a rather high level of abstraction, the main point is relatively straightforward: that it is emplotment which makes an account a narrative. It is emplotment which turns disparate events into 'episodes' (Somers and Gibson 1994) which have a part in the beginning, the end and the movement of a plot. Even if the events seem unrelated they will be brought together through the overall coherence of the plot. Conversely, it is the absence of emplotment which means that archives, questions and answers and so on, are not narratives. These forms do not incorporate the important element of time, in which time passing structures the narrative and earlier events are seen to cause later ones, nor do they hinge on an overall 'plot'.

Within narratives, and through processes of emplotment, prior events seem *inevitably* to lead to later ones, and the end of the story is understood as the culmination and actualization of prior events. Significance is conferred on earlier events by what comes later. In this sense, narratives become naturalized as the episodes which make up the 'plot' appear inevitable, and even universal. The end of a story does not have to be predictable, but it must be meaningful. In short, a narrative must have a *point*: as both Paul Ricoeur (1980) and Carolyn Steedman (1986) have pointed out, the question every narrator tries to fend off is, 'So what?' And for narratives to have a point, they must incorporate this important element of bringing together disparate elements into a single plot:

> The connectivity of parts is precisely why narrativity turns 'events' into episodes, whether the sequence of episodes is presented or experienced in anything resembling chronological or categorical order. And it is emplotment which translates events into episodes. As a mode of explanation, causal emplotment is an accounting (however fantastic or implicit) of why a narrative has the story line it does. (Somers and Gibson 1994: 58)

The significance of events is, inevitably, rooted in personal and social histories, and in social 'intelligibility norms' (Gergen and Gergen 1986) – in what gets to count, socially, as significant. Later sections will explore these issues, as they consider the usefulness of narrative inquiry for connecting the past and present of the social actor, and for connecting those two apparently ever-divorced categories – 'the individual' and 'the social'. Before this, though, I want to try to make the issues more concrete by introducing a fragment of a narrative.

NARRATIVITY: A CASE STUDY

The narrative I discuss here is taken from my research with mothers of daughters (Lawler 2000a). It is part of a set of three interviews with one woman, Barbara,[3] and is taken from a much longer dialogue throughout which Barbara narrates her class movement. I want to emphasize that this is a specific type of narrative (a narrative about self-development, self-actualization and movement, not only through time, but also through space and through social categories) and I do not intend it to stand for all narratives. Rather, my intention is to use this extract as an illustrative device.

Barbara grew up in a working-class family, and considers herself to have now become middle class, largely through marriage to a middle-class man. Her account generally unsettles many conventional notions of 'class identity': although she considers herself middle class, Barbara related many expressions of pain and inadequacy at lacking a *history* of being middle class. It would be impossible to read off Barbara's own (narrativized) identity simply from the 'external' markers conventionally used – for example, her house, her job, her income. This is part of Barbara's account of her classed movement.[4]

Barbara:	You know, this idea of ketchup on the table. All that sort of thing I did away with immediately [when she got married]. I always wanted – er, I don't know – [*long pause*]
S.L.:	Tablecloths? [*laughs*]
Barbara:	Tablecloths, yes! [*laughs*]. And my husband, well he accepted it, but now he's beginning to think, well, you know, why? Like eating fish and chips on the prom sort of thing. I didn't want anything to do with that and he's got a habit of doing that and [her daughter] Julia's got a habit of doing that, and I feel – hmmm. I enjoy being ...... middle class. Yeah, I do. I'd hate to ...... to go back. It's not back – there's no back and forward, is there? To not have the ...... – I've changed so much. My lifestyle's so different. You know, the sort of house I have, the way I decorate it. The activities I have, my pastimes, are all – I suppose could be classed as middle class. And I love it, *that's what I am.* As a little girl, everybody else had these plastic eggcups. I always had the one that wasn't broken when we were bombed out [in the Second World War]. It was china, and it was decorated. And it was always Barbara's, and Barbara always had to have the same spoon. But *that was me*, from, you know, knee high. I always wanted to get out. There were fine things in life that I wanted to appreciate [*laughs*]. Does that sound dreadful?
S.L.:	No. I identify with that, actually.
Barbara:	Oh good. 'Cause I just feel dreadful sometimes saying it. (added emphasis)

There are several ways in which this extract could be interpreted: Barbara's words could, for example, be seen as 'innocent' purveyors of some prior truth. Alternatively, her post-hoc version of events could be seen as 'biasing' her account, making it one characterized by *un*truth.[5] Yet what, for me at least, is more interesting, is the issue of interpretation – the ways in which Barbara uses (culturally circulating) stories to interpret her life.

The extract, though very brief, has the components of a narrative: it has transformation (change over time), as Barbara's identity (and her 'lifestyle') is changed – even though, as we will see, the change is to something she considers herself to already have been. Action and characters are minimal, but nevertheless present. And a range of disparate elements is brought together within an overall plot – one which, in this case, centres on a transformation through class movement. The plot incorporates Ricoeur's concept of synthesis, as it synthesizes many disparate events (eating fish and chips on the prom, the change in how meals were served when Barbara got married, her childhood attachment to an eggcup and a spoon) into one overall story, one totality (the story of what Barbara is like and of how she came to be how she is). It does this within a synthesis of two different aspects of time, so that Barbara's early life, for example, is *both* closed and 'over with' *and* enduring into the present. Time seems to move forward through the story, although the story is not, in fact, narrated in a linear way.[6] Most Euroamerican readers will read linear progression *into* narratives (especially life narratives), not least because Euroamericans tend to conceptualize adult traits, circumstances and characteristics as rooted in childhood events. Events come to seem 'logically' related to each other through time. But Ricoeur's insight is to argue that the logic which relates these elements to each other is not that of nature, or of individual psychology, but of narrative itself.

THE SIGNIFICANCE OF NARRATIVE: LINKING PAST AND PRESENT

> Memory is not like a video record. It does not need images, and images are never enough: moreover, our memories shade and patch and combine and delete. ... the best analogy to remembering is storytelling. ... We constitute our souls by making up our lives, that is, by weaving stories about our past, by what we call memories. The tales we tell of ourselves and to ourselves are not a matter of recording what we have done and how we have felt. They must mesh with the rest of the world and with other people's stories, at least in externals, but their real role is the creation of a life, a character. (Hacking 1995: 250–251)

Any research which aims for more than a snapshot of the social world must be able to somehow account for the relationship between the present and the past. For example, in asking people to recount (whole or partial) stories, some attention must be given to the epistemological status of such stories: what kind of knowledge do they represent? What kind of knowledge is being produced when conceptual narrativity is used? Memory is notoriously unreliable, but the issue here is one of more than faulty versus accurate memory. Carolyn Steedman (1996) points out the obvious, but little-noted, fact that the past is no longer here: in searching for the past, '[t]he search is for a lost object, which really cannot be found, for the object is altered and changed by the very search for it, into something quite different and strange' (Steedman 1996: 103). We must constantly engage in recall, retelling, interpretation, in order to conjure up the past: we must engage in what Ian Hacking (1994, 1995) has called 'memero-politics' – a process by which the past is interpreted in light of the knowledge and understanding of the subject's 'present'.[7] As Steedman puts it:

> We all return to memories and dreams ... again and again; the story we tell of our life is reshaped around them. But the point doesn't lie there, back in the past, back in the lost time at which they happened; the only point lies in interpretation. The

past is re-used through the agency of social information, and that interpretation of it can only be made with what people know of a social world and their place within it. (Steedman 1986: 5)

There is no unmediated access to the 'facts of the matter', nor to a straight-forward and unmediated 'experience', either for the researcher, or indeed for the research subject. As the past is remembered, it is interpreted and reinter-preted in the light of the person's knowledge and understanding. Liz Stanley (1992) points up this gap between past and present in her analysis of auto/biography: she argues:

> the 'self who writes' has no more direct and unproblematic access to the 'self who was' than does the reader; and anyway 'the autobiographical past' is actually peopled by a succession of selves as the writer grows, develops and changes. (Stanley 1992: 61)

So too with other forms of research: neither researcher nor researched can fully access or inhabit a past which is inevitably gone.

So, my argument here is that attention to narrative provides a way of con-ceptualizing links between past and present (rather than seeing such links as unproblematic and straightforward). Conventionally, the problem of 'stories' is seen to centre on 'bias': is the subject misremembering, misrepresenting or simply lying about earlier events? But this accent misses the point: there is *no* 'unbiased' access to the past. Indeed, the past is constantly worked and reworked to provide a coherent sense of the subject's identity. Ricoeur (1991b) calls this 'narrative identity' and Somers and Gibson (1994), 'ontological nar-rativity'. Both are referring to processes by which people construct identities that are relatively coherent and stable through using stories.

The argument being made here is that we all tell stories about our lives, both to ourselves and to others; and it is through such stories that we make sense of the world, of our relationship to that world, and of the relationship between ourselves and other selves. Further, it is through such stories that we produce identities. Every time we write a CV, or give an account of ourselves to a friend or an acquaintance, or explain inherited characteristics, we are engaged in story-telling, and producing an identity which is relatively stable across time. Stories, or narratives, are a means by which people make sense of, understand, and live their lives. Henrietta Moore argues, 'narrative is a strategy for placing us within a historically constituted world. … If narrative makes the world intel-ligible, it also makes ourselves intelligible' (Moore 1994: 119).

For Ricoeur, identity is something which is *produced* through narrative. A complete life story characterizes the interval between birth and death. Partial life stories will capture some part of that interval. But, as Ricoeur notes, assimilating a *life* into a *story* is not so natural or so obvious as it might appear; this process should be subject to scrutiny. So what is the relationship between living and narrating? Between a life and a life story?

Through process of emplotment, social actors constitute a life, and in the process, constitute an identity. Identity is not a pre-given entity, on to which narrative structures are (more or less violently) imposed. Rather, the very constitution of an identity is configured over time and through narrative. What the plot configures is how the person comes to be who he or she is (as in Barbara's narrative). Emplotment configures a self which appears as the inevitable outcome and actualization of the episodes which constitute a life. The self is understood as unfolding through episodes which both express and constitute that self.

In Ricoeur's formulation, then, the self, itself – that apparently most natural and asocial of phenomena – is profoundly social, and is always-already interpreted. He writes:

> the self does not know itself immediately but only indirectly by the detour of the cultural signs of all sorts which are articulated on the symbolic mediations which always already articulate action and, among them, the narratives of everyday life. Narrative mediation underlines this remarkable characteristic of self-knowledge – that it is self-interpretation. (Ricoeur 1991b: 198)

Identity, then, is not something foundational and essential, but something *produced* through the narratives people use to explain and understand their lives. Gayatri Spivak puts it neatly: 'We "write" a running biography with life-language rather than word-language in order to "be". Call this identity!' (Spivak 1997: 359).[8]

In narrating a story, social actors organize events into 'episodes' which make up the plot. What we make of 'experience' depends on what we know about the ways in which those experiences relate to the wider social circumstances of our lives. Although this is, inevitably, a post-hoc treatment, the events of a life come to appear as though naturally and inevitably leading to their specific conclusion. We 'read time backwards', as Ricoeur puts it, 'reading the end into the beginning and the beginning into the end' (Ricoeur 1980: 183), interpreting later events in the light of earlier ones, and interpreting the self in terms of the emplotment of events:

> Memory … is itself the spiral movement that, through anecdotes and episodes, brings us back to the almost motionless constellation of potentialities that the narrative retrieves. The end of the story is what equates the present with the past, the actual with the potential. The hero *is* who he [*sic*] *was*. (Ricoeur 1980: 186, original emphasis)

Narrative, then, both connotes and constitutes movement – the movement from the potential to the actual, from what could be to what is, from past to present, from present to future. In the process, it works to *naturalize* the plot, making later events seem the natural and inevitable culmination of earlier ones. But what looks like a natural, causal relationship is, according to Ricoeur, a teleological one: that is, the episodes which make up the plot are there because of the purpose they serve (which is, *producing* a coherent plot): 'Looking back from the conclusion to the episodes leading up to it, we have to be able to say that this ending required these sorts of events and this chain of actions' (Ricoeur 1980: 174).

In this sense, we can perhaps rework Kierkegaard's famous pronouncement that 'Life is lived forward but understood backwards' (quoted in Geertz 1995: 166), as we envisage life as something both lived and understood forward *and* backward in a 'spiral movement' of constant interpretation and reinterpretation. People constantly produce and reproduce life stories on the basis of memories; interpreting the past through the lens of social information, and using this information to formulate present and future life stories. Narrative provides a means of conceptualizing people in the context of history: if the past is always interpreted through the present, then equally, this (interpreted) past informs the present.

If we return to the extract from Barbara's account, above, it is clear that Barbara is producing this narrative, not from the past, but out of the *present*. She is interpreting her earlier life in the light of what she now knows. Indeed, earlier events gain significance only through events that come later. Through narrative Barbara is able to constitute a more or less coherent self:[9] one which, in this case, is marked as always-already middle class. Despite expressions of change, the movement of the plot leads to her *becoming* what she *is* ('that was me'; 'that's what I am'). Hence, 'the end is read into the beginning and the beginning into the end' (Ricoeur 1980: 183) as Barbara narrates an identity that is stable across time. Emplotment brings together past and present events in (what is understood to be) a logical, coherent and meaningful overall 'story'.

THE SIGNIFICANCE OF NARRATIVE: LINKING THE INDIVIDUAL AND THE COLLECTIVE

So far, I have argued that people use narratives to interpret the social world and their place within it, and, further, to constitute an identity. However, people are not free to fabricate narratives 'at will' (Somers and Gibson 1994; Ewick and Silbey 1995; McNay 2000). The stories produced by individual social actors would make no sense if they did not accord, however obliquely, with broader social narratives.

Narrative links together the individual and collective in two ways: first, because narratives of individual lives must always incorporate other life narratives: hence the myth of the 'atomized individual' is immediately exploded, as the connectivity of personal narratives comes to the fore (Stanley 1992; Miller 1999). Second, and as I have indicated, narratives are not only produced by individuals, but also circulate socially. Somers and Gibson (1994) refer to such narratives as 'public narratives' – narratives which are 'attached to cultural and institutional formations rather than the single individual' (Somers and Gibson 1994: 62). They might also be seen as 'traditions' (Taylor 1989), although they do not have to be particularly ancient. These narratives include stories produced to explain scientific 'discovery' (Myers 1990), the rise of disciplinary frameworks (Somers and Gibson 1994) and stories produced within and about legal frameworks

(Ewick and Silbey 1995). Paul Ricoeur argues that the kinds of public narratives on which people draw to frame their personal narratives are largely those of the literary tradition. However, this perspective tends to underplay the workings of power in the social world: it is important to stress that public narratives are powerful in structuring the kinds of things which can be said (and, conversely, foreclosing certain kinds of story). Ewick and Silbey (1995) write: 'Consent rules, as they operate within different cultural and institutional settings, define *what* constitutes an appropriate or successful narrative' (Ewick and Silbey 1995: 207, original emphasis).

For most contemporary Euroamericans, for example, any (personal or public) story which used genetic explanations as a means of causal explanation would be likely to be accepted far more readily than one which relied on, say, witchcraft as a means of structuring events – not necessarily because the hearer (or reader) has first-hand evidence either way, but because the former explanation accords with what Gergen and Gergen (1986) call the 'intelligibility norms' of this particular culture.

One particularly compelling public narrative for contemporary Euroamericans is that of childhood 'development', in which later (adult) psychologies are inevitably rooted in earlier (childhood) events. Euroamericans almost inevitably look to childhood as the grounds of adulthood, and, for this reason, childhood is ascribed a 'special' status. It is scarcely possible to formulate a coherent life story without using, in some ways, narratives of development. Similarly, the narrative of heterosexual romance and marriage remains compelling even in the face of rising divorce.

The point about public narratives is not their facticity or otherwise. It is not, for example, that the narrative of childhood development is 'true' while that of heterosexual romance is 'false'. The point, rather, is that they *become* 'truths' through their frequent repetition across a range of sites and, in many cases, through their association with 'expert' disciplines (such as psychology). Both types of narrative can incorporate different kinds of interpretation, but, equally, both must rely on certain assumptions about what is to count as 'true' and 'reasonable'. Narrative is frequently linked with authoritative, expert knowledges, but this link is obscured through narrative's use of the inclusive voice of the story-teller, rather than the authoritative voice of the expert (Franklin 1990). Hence 'we' can be drawn in to the story, using its framework as a schema of self-understanding.

Barbara's narrative illustrates this link between personal and public narratives. Her story is coherent precisely because it resonates with broader public narratives and symbolic systems. She takes several mundane items of everyday life – tablecloths, eggcups, spoons, ketchup on the table – and constructs a story around them. The story she constructs is one about class and, more specifically, class movement and class desires. Barbara uses her desire for 'fine things' to mark out the distinctiveness of her childhood self, and also to mark out that self's trajectory from childhood to her present age.

She is able to do this because these items are not only 'things' but also saturated with meaning. They become symbols within her story, becoming meaningful precisely *through* their part in a narrative. She is able to use these symbols because both she and I inhabit a culture in which they are saturated with classed meanings. Her individual story is narrated within a *collective* set of meanings. In other words, the symbolic meaning of these things does not originate with Barbara: rather, they circulate culturally to signify class. I shall not go into the cultural configurations of class here: the point is that Barbara uses widely circulating cultural symbols to produce her own narrative. (But see e.g. Bourdieu 1984, 1993, 1999; Skeggs 1997; Walkerdine 1997; Reay 1998; Lawler 1999, 2000a, 2000b.) 'Ketchup on the table' and 'eating fish and chips on the prom' signify much more than types of food and where they are eaten. They signify a specific kind of classed location, from which Barbara wants to distance herself.

Social location is significant here. Not only is there a limited range of stories which can be told, but differential social positioning is reflected in the kinds of stories people tell. If people interpret the past 'through the agency of social information', as Steedman (1986) argues, then that social information is going to be, to some degree at least, contingent on their social positioning. 'What people know of the world' is not free floating: it is a product of their specific social location. Some narratives will not easily 'fit': not all will afford an easy recognition. So Steedman (1986) presents her working-class childhood as one which did not readily accord with hegemonic narratives of 'normal' (middle-class) family life.

Barbara, similarly, is located within a classed system within which *both* her working-class background *and* her desire to become more middle class are frequently marked as pathological (Walkerdine 1990, 1997; Skeggs 1997). Further, there are few narratives which are available to Barbara, as a woman, to narrate her classed movement. There is, for example, no readily available female equivalent of 'the working-class boy made good' narratives popularized in the post-war period (Steedman 1986; Walkerdine 1997). This is especially so for women whose 'upward' class mobility has been effected through marriage to middle-class men. Hence, any kind of narrative around class is difficult for her and always risks the opprobrium of being labelled 'pretentious' (Bourdieu 1984). This, I think, is why Barbara (very reasonably) looks for reassurance at the end of the extract above. Both she and I are aware that we can easily be labelled pretentious. But it is important to ask what kinds of power are working through rendering some kinds of narrative 'noble' and others 'trivial' or 'petty' (or indeed, pretentious). Whose lives are given worth through these processes? Whose lives, conversely, are not?[10]

USING NARRATIVITY

The task of researchers using conceptual narrativity is multilayered: first, they must set in place the conditions in which people are likely to produce narratives. A structured questionnaire, for example, is unlikely to do this, and clearly straightforward observation will not do it either. Second, researchers have to analyse those accounts in terms of narrative. Narratives do not have to be lengthy or full accounts of a life: they simply have to incorporate the processes of emplotment outlined above. Third, researchers need to consider the kinds of publicly circulating narratives on which social actors draw, and which operate as constraints on the kinds of narrative they can produce. And fourth, they have to consider the relationship between these public narratives and the personal narratives produced. This relationship need not be harmonious or smooth: the process of constructing a personal narrative is creative work (even if it is not self-consciously so) and people may well use public narratives only to oppose them. Further, people frequently combine fairly contradictory forms of narrative in producing their personal narratives. So, for example, people may postulate a self which is the product of genetic inheritance at the same time as postulating a self which is the product of social shaping. In this, they are drawing on competing narratives, yet combining them in a new narrative form.

Above all, the researcher must consider the processes of interpretation going on, both personally and publicly. But research, of course, introduces another level of interpretation – that of the researcher. It is important to reiterate here my earlier suggestion that narratives are not produced, *ab initio*, in the research setting. However, this does not mean, either, that narratives are simply 'imported' more or less wholesale into the research setting. Rather, if narratives are constantly worked and reworked, then they are also being reworked in the research itself. In this sense, they are co-produced between the researcher and the research subject (see Jennifer Mason, Chapter 10 in this volume). In Barbara's narrative, my own intervention, although fairly minimal in this extract, does, to some extent, move the narrative along. The kinds of questions asked, the whole direction of the research, will to some extent influence the kinds of narrative research subjects produce in the research itself, as will the location of the researchers themselves.[11] Again, the issue here is *not* one of 'bias' or 'distortion', but one of the *inevitability* of interpretation and reinterpretation.

CONCLUSION

I have argued in this chapter that conceptual narrativity offers a way of considering the kinds of stories which people tell without considering such stories as *either* expressions of an 'authentic' identity, *or* as ideological 'traps'. Rather, stories are actively worked up by social actors, though not, of course, from an endless repertoire of social narratives: only some things can be said at all; and only some things can be said from any specific social and historical location. The 'truths' people produce through such stories are not 'truths' as conventionally understood in positivist social science: nevertheless, they do speak certain 'truths' about people's (socially located) lives and identities.

Through such narratives (and within social and institutional constraints) people produce identities (however fragmented, multiple and contingent). Thus, from this perspective 'identity' is not something which can be read off from an externally imposed schema. People may well belong, relatively unproblematically, to groups designated 'working class', 'women' and so on (although, of course, they may not); but this in itself does not tell us about the kinds of identities they build. Although the identities people hold are certainly related to the social context they inhabit, the process of *being* anything is, it seems to me, more complicated than simply an identification with single, externally imposed, categories.[12] What is more, people's interpretation of the world cannot be assumed from these categories. And if this is the case, then the doing of qualitative research becomes pressing indeed. If we want to find out how people make identities, make sense of the world and of their place within it – if we want to find out how they interpret the world and themselves – we will have to attend to the stories they tell.

ACKNOWLEDGEMENTS

My thanks to Steve Fuller and to Paul Johnson for comments on earlier drafts of this chapter.

NOTES

1 Narratives have been approached in many different ways in social research – often precisely as either simply 'reflecting' events, or as independent of events. For a good overview, see Ezzy (2001). My aim here is to consider the process as much more entangled than either of these polarities allow.

2 Although, as Michael Erben (1993) rightly notes, Paul Ricoeur, despite his hermeneutical stance 'is entirely willing to accept the products of positivism' (Erben 1993: 17), I doubt that many positivists would accept a narrative interpretation of events.

3 'Barbara' is a pseudonym. A full account of the methodology can be found in Lawler (2000a).

4 In the extract that follows, six dots (……) indicate a pause.

5 The dichotomy to which I referred in the Introduction at the beginning of the chapter.

6 Indeed, Barbara's own problematizing of a linear model of time ('It's not back – there's no back and forward, is there?') highlights this point – neither lives nor stories, she suggests, are as linear as we might assume.

7 See also J-B. Pontalis, who argues, 'Any story, however truthful it aims to be, is a reconstruction from the vantage-point of the *present*' (Pontalis 1993: xv).

8 Although 'word language' is also necessary, of course, in order to represent this running biography to ourselves and to others.

9 The whole, unified and coherent self may be a fiction, but it is one with which many people – perhaps most of us – work. At the same time, however, people may well be able to accommodate levels of non-coherence within their self-narratives. This is why I characterize the self which is constituted here as *more or less* coherent. In many ways, the narrative Barbara presents unsettles the idea of a coherent self: elsewhere, she talks of her classed identity as 'two aspects of your life, which you try to juggle' (Lawler 2000a: 109).

10   Although this is not the place to explore the subject in detail, it is worth noting that 'resistance narratives' may themselves be extremely restrictive, working to approve some types of action and diminish others. Pamela Fox (1994), for example argues that notions of resistance tend to approve only behaviour approved by the bourgeois observer – behaviour which 'not only resist[s] domination but [does] so for decidedly progressive aims' (Fox 1994: 8). This may be why narratives of (for example) 'the heroic male worker' can seem so attractive (signalling, at least in a more optimistic time, the demise of capitalism). But it must be asked what happens to those whose narratives cannot easily fit this template. Are they condemned to being characterized as 'reactionary' (as, indeed, working-class women often have been)? Ironically, the 'respectability' espoused by many working-class women (Skeggs 1997) may be held in contempt precisely by those who have the cultural capital to shrug off respectability.

11   Barbara was embarrassed to tell me some of these things, and only did so after a long discussion of classed position and classed movement. My own located-ness is, I think, important here. Barbara and I share a similar class background, and similar feelings of occupying a class 'hinterland'.

12   For example, the working-class women in Beverley Skeggs' (1997) study frequently *dis*identified from the category 'working class'. In my own work (see Lawler 2000a) I found that the mothers I interviewed often disidentified from the category 'mother'.

REFERENCES

Bourdieu, P. (1984) *Distinction*, translated by R. Nice. London: Routledge and Kegan Paul.

Bourdieu, P. (1993) *The Field of Cultural Production: Essays on Art and Literature*, edited and introduced by R. Johnson. Cambridge: Polity.

Bourdieu, P. (1999) *The Weight of the World: Social Suffering in Contemporary Society*. Cambridge: Polity.

Dilthey, W. (1976) *Selected Writings*. Cambridge: Cambridge University Press.

Erben, M. (1993) 'The problem of other lives: social perspectives on written biography', *Sociology* 27(1): 15–25.

Ewick, P. and Silbey, S. (1995) 'Subversive stories and hegemonic tales: toward a sociology of narrative', *Law and Society Review* 29(2): 197–226.

Ezzy, D. (2001) *Qualitative Analysis: Thinking, Doing, Writing*. St Leonards, NSW: Allen and Unwin.

Fox, P. (1994) *Class Fictions: Shame and Resistance in the British Working-Class Novel 1890–1945*. Durham, NC: Duke University Press.

Franklin, S. (1990) 'Deconstructing "desperateness": the social construction of infertility in popular representations of New Reproductive Technologies', in M. McNeil, I. Varloe and S. Yearley (eds) *The New Reproductive Technologies*. London: Macmillan.

Geertz, C. (1995) *After the Fact: Two Countries, Four Decades, One Anthropologist*. Cambridge, MA: Harvard University Press.

Gergen, K.J. and Gergen, M.M. (1986) 'Narrative form and the construction of psychological science', in T.R. Sarbin (ed.) *Narrative Psychology: The Storied Nature of Human Conduct*. New York: Praeger.

Hacking, I. (1994) 'Memero-politics, trauma and the soul', *History of the Human Sciences* 7(2): 29–52.

Hacking, I. (1995) *Rewriting the Soul: Multiple Personality and the Sciences of Memory.* Princeton, NJ: Princeton University Press.

Lawler, S. (1999) 'Getting out and getting away: women's narratives of class mobility', *Feminist Review* 63: 3–24.

Lawler, S. (2000a) *Mothering the Self: Mothers, Daughters, Subjects.* London: Routledge.

Lawler, S. (2000b) 'Escape and escapism: representing working-class women', in S. Munt (ed.) *Subject to Change: Cultural Studies and the Working Class.* London: Cassell.

McNay, L. (2000) *Gender and Agency: Reconfiguring the Subject in Feminist and Social Theory.* Cambridge: Polity.

Miller, R.L. (1999) *Researching Life Stories and Family Histories.* London: Sage.

Moore, H. (1994) *A Passion for Difference: Essays in Anthropology and Gender.* Cambridge: Polity.

Myers, G. (1990) 'Making a discovery: narratives of split genes', in C. Nash (ed.) *Narrative in Culture: The Uses of Storytelling in the Sciences, Philosophy and Literature.* London: Routledge.

Plummer, K. (1995) *Telling Sexual Stories: Power, Change and Social Worlds.* London: Routledge.

Pontalis, J-B. (1993) *Love of Beginnings.* London: Free Association Press.

Reay, D. (1998) *Class Work: Mothers' Involvement in their Children's Primary Schooling.* London: UCL Press.

Rickard, W. (2001) '"Been there, seen it, done it, I've got the t-shirt": British sex workers reflect on jobs, hopes, the future and retirement', *Feminist Review* 67: 111–132.

Ricoeur, P. (1980) 'Narrative and time', *Critical Inquiry* 7(1): 169–190.

Ricoeur, P. (1991a) 'Life in quest of narrative', in D. Wood (ed.) *On Paul Ricoeur: Narrative and Interpretation.* London: Routledge.

Ricoeur, P. (1991b) 'Narrative identity', translated by D. Wood, in D. Wood (ed.) *On Paul Ricoeur: Narrative and Interpretation.* London: Routledge.

Riessman, C.K. (1993) *Narrative Analysis.* London: Sage.

Segal, L. (1999) *Why Feminism? Gender, Psychology, Politics.* Cambridge: Polity.

Simonds, W. (1992) *Women and Self-Help Culture: Reading between the Lines.* New Brunswick, NJ: Rutgers University Press.

Simonds, W. (1996) 'Consuming selves: self-help literature and women's identities', in D. Grodin and T.R. Lindlof (eds) *Constructing the Self in a Mediated World.* Thousand Oaks, CA: Sage.

Skeggs, B. (1997) *Formations of Class and Gender: Becoming Respectable.* London: Sage.

Somers, M.R. and Gibson, G.D. (1994) 'Reclaiming the epistemological "Other": narrative and the social constitution of identity', in C. Calhoun (ed.) *Social Theory and the Politics of Identity.* Cambridge, MA: Blackwell.

Spivak, G.S. (with E. Rooney) (1997) 'In a word: interview', in L. Nicholson (ed.) *The Second Wave: A Reader in Feminist Theory.* New York: Routledge.

Stanley, L. (1992) *The Auto/biographical I.* Manchester: Manchester University Press.

Stanley, L. and Morgan, D. (1993) 'Editorial introduction', *Sociology* 27(1): 1–4.

Steedman, C. (1986) *Landscape for a Good Woman: A Story of Two Lives.* London: Virago.

Steedman, C. (1996) 'About ends: on the ways in which the end is different from an ending', *History of the Human Sciences* 9(4): 99–114.

Taylor, C. (1989) *Sources of the Self*. Cambridge, MA: Harvard University Press.

Walkerdine, V. (1990) *Schoolgirl Fictions*. London: Verso.

Walkerdine, V. (1997) *Daddy's Girl: Young Girls and Popular Culture*. London: Macmillan.

White, H. (1996) 'Commentary', *History of the Human Sciences* 9(4): 123–138.

PART 4

POWER, PARTICIPATION AND EXPERTISE

12 ENGAGEMENT AND EVALUATION IN QUALITATIVE INQUIRY

Linda McKie

Increasingly, social scientists are working with community groups and policy-makers to undertake and support the evaluation of a range of community-based projects (Connell *et al*. 1995; Voyle and Simmons 1999; Wallerstein 1999). These developments are part of a more general trend to evaluate complex social interventions and community work as a means of informing policy and practice. In many of these projects there has been a consideration, if not the actual conduct, of qualitative evaluation (Chelimsky 1997; Shaw 1999). The overall aim of this chapter is to assess the potential for qualitative research to address critically issues around power and participation in evaluation. It is the relationship between qualitative methodology and evaluation, and the implications of this for the actual conduct of an evaluation, that is the focus of this chapter.

There is often a presumption among many researchers that choosing qualitative methods will enhance the potential for participants' own voices and values to inform the research process and thus illuminate in a grounded fashion the evaluation of a project or policy. Underpinning this presumption is a view that qualitative research can provide a more informative picture of culturally based processes and practices and a depth to context-based explanations of events, processes, outcomes and ultimately future policy and practice. Certainly a qualitative approach can focus on accounts of the origins and progress of events, and thus the complexity and multidimensionality of the local contexts and relationships. In this way it is argued that a qualitative approach ensures a degree of participation not possible with a quantitative perspective. Yet these claims can raise expectations among research participants about the conduct of an evaluation that cannot or may not be met. Crucial to these expectations is competing perspectives on power and the potential for an evaluation to truly engage with communities and other stakeholders.

To illustrate and illuminate debates on qualitative methodology and evaluation I draw upon my experiences of and data from two qualitative evaluations:

- *SONAS Community Health Project*. Sonas is the Gaelic word for 'good fortune, happiness and well-being' and the project is located in five of the islands in the Western Isles of Scotland. The project commenced in 1993 and until 1996 was funded by the Health Education Board for Scotland (HEBS), which also funded an evaluation of the first three years' work. During this period the project provided a range of health activities ranging from group work, the provision of one-to-one counselling work, and workshops and conferences (SONAS 1996).

- *Women, Low Income and Smoking Project.* Nineteen community-based initiatives across Scotland were funded to explore new ways of working on smoking reduction among women living on low income. This Action on Smoking and Health (ASH) Scotland project was funded by HEBS and operated between 1996 and 1999. There were nineteen community-based projects funded in two waves to explore new ways of reducing smoking among women on low incomes.

In the former I was commissioned by the funding body to coordinate the evaluation and in the latter project I was a member of the evaluation advisory group.

Both of these projects are evaluations of community health projects. Community health work describes processes by which a group in a given locality (or organized around a specific topic) defines its health needs, considers how those needs can be met and decides collectively on priorities for action (Connell *et al.* 1995). Invariably, the type of community health work undertaken dictates the evaluation approach and methods. Communities are complex entities and are comprised of heterogeneous groups and stakeholders. Illumination of the processes by which the various constituencies in communities negotiate and refine agendas on health and how these are implemented in related activities tends to lead to the adoption of qualitative methods.

The chapter opens with a brief discussion of definitions of evaluation and qualitative evaluation, and revisits some of the 'basic set[s] of beliefs that guides action' (Guba 1990: 17). Subsequently, data from the two evaluations are presented to inform a critical discussion of qualitative methodology and evaluation. In the final section the ideas and practice of qualitative evaluation are considered with specific reference to the relationship between the evaluator and stakeholders and recipients of the programme.

EVALUATION, RESEARCH AND QUALITATIVE EVALUATION

At a fundamental level the evaluation of social interventions is concerned with making an assessment; of judging the merit of an activity or programme and assessing it against the goals that were established at the outset (Barlow *et al.* 2001). In a broader sense evaluation seeks to address practical problems and make judgements of merit or worth so as to provide recommendations and outcomes that may inform future activities (Connor 1993). More than ever before community groups, voluntary sector organizations, local authorities, and the UK National Health Service are being required to build in evaluation from the outset of projects or policies in order to gain reliable information about activities as well as evaluating processes and outcomes (Wimbush and Watson 2000). Nevertheless, many evaluations commence well into the implementation of a project or policy and thus leave limited time and space for the stakeholders and recipients to take part in the design or conduct of the research and evaluation. However, in both of the projects discussed in this chapter evaluation was built in from the beginning and active participation of the various groups in setting both the research and practice agendas was promoted. Thus these are useful examples to explore the ways that commissioners, evaluators and project participants recognized and struggled with issues of power, ownership and participation.

Contemporary evaluation research has its origins in the push to develop evidence-based action in educational and social policies during the 1960s. Controlled evaluations of projects or policies were often assessed against behavioural and other measurable outcome criteria, for example evaluations of penal, educational and community policies. These assessments were thought to provide the opportunity to verify what worked, or otherwise, and to ensure accountability. Quantitative methods are often used in the belief that these could provide practitioners and professionals with clear-cut, valid and reliable easy-to-follow results and implications for future work. Yet many of these evaluations have been criticized for failing to bring to life not only the everyday workings of policies or projects but also the lessons that might be gained from reflecting upon processes, for example, working with a range of groups and professionals to establish a project or implement a policy. Shaw (1999) comments:

> quantitative evaluations, outcome-orientated measures of accountability, are typically bereft of the intensity, subtlety, particularity, ethical judgement and relevance that potentially characterize evaluation born of ethnography. (Shaw 1999: 1)

While a qualitative approach has become increasingly popular in the evaluation of a range of activities, not least of which is the evaluation of community-based projects and policies, many policy-makers and practitioners continue to favour quantitative approaches. Some commentators and researchers suggest that qualitative evaluation should be used only when quasi-experimental quantitative designs will not work (Chelimsky 1997). Many are uneasy with the ambiguities posed by qualitative data especially in the context of the subjective relationship between evaluator and those participating in the project and hence evaluation research. But for the proponents of qualitative evaluation it is the 'particular challenges and constraints facing evaluation [that] usually require qualitative evaluation as a methodology of choice' (Shaw 1999: 5). Qualitative methodology affords a means of providing distinct data and qualitative evaluation of theorizing problems and approaches. It enables stakeholders and project recipients to highlight and reflect upon what worked and how this came about, and affords an opportunity to chart and reconcile multiple stories of a project. Nevertheless it would be naive to presume that the adoption of qualitative methodology necessarily enhances participation. Not all qualitative methods promote participation to the same degree. For example, nominal group processes such as the Delphi technique (Grbich 1999: 116) may actually diminish a sense of participation or ownership of the research process. As a first stage this technique involves a panel's identification of a range of issues on a topic and from that a series of questionnaires are sent out to panel members to further consider their opinions on issues raised. This process is repeated until areas of consensus, divergence and minority arguments become evident. However, the Delphi technique has been criticized for creating a notion of 'experts' and often involving those who developed a project or policy in a process that aims to consider and influence change. These concerns further raise the need for the application of qualitative methods in a fashion that reflects upon and seeks active inclusion, dialogue and deliberation in all stages of planning, data collection and analysis and consideration of outcomes and recommendations.

Crucial to qualitative evaluation research is an appreciation of the distinct nature of evaluation and of research. There are differences between the two that emerge with reflection upon the purposes of each (Shaw 1999: 11). Most significantly, there is a general agreement that evaluation makes judgements on the merits of specific policies or programmes (although there is a lot of debate on approaches to evaluation) while research is concerned to theorize and describe issues or problems. Debates abound on the epistemological underpinnings of qualitative research that range from an emphasis on methods and techniques to paradigmatic perspectives (Grbich 1999). Qualitative research can 'provide important insights into different perceptions of "reality" although debates continue as to whether the researcher should view "reality" from the outside or appreciate their role in the construction of social meaning' (Guba 1990: 27).

Qualitative methodology offers opportunities for evaluation research that it would be useful to outline. Drawing upon Miles and Huberman (1994) and Shaw (1999) there are a number of opportunities and characteristics to consider:

- contact with participants is possible at various levels in a manner likely to provide a depth, as well as breadth, to accounts of events, and to provide a spatio-temporal context to these (Bryman 2001: 277).
- there are opportunities to gain a holistic overview by locating accounts in a context of a social intervention and wider social, political and economic structures (Bryman 2001: 278).
- it is possible to develop a relationship between data at various levels from the 'on the ground' participants to policy-makers and funding bodies (Shaw 1999: 90).
- qualitative approaches 'can effectively give voice to the normally silenced and can poignantly illuminate what is typically masked' (Greene 1994: 541).
- analysis and writing up is represented in words and based upon judgement. Thus conclusions can be open to challenge as subjective (Shaw 1999: 179).

Qualitative evaluation is appropriate where potential outcomes are not clear in advance, for example, where a project may involve numerous groups or issues, where commissioners are interested in appreciating and understanding social processes and processes of participation in the project, and diverse data sources are available. Time and resources must be available to explore a range of data sources and not just the most obvious. Finally, there must be agreement among the commissioners of the evaluation, practitioners and participants with the approach and methods. Crucial to the design and conduct of qualitative and participatory evaluation is transparency and negotiation; not every researcher nor commissioning body is comfortable with ongoing review and renegotiation of data sources, data analysis and the evaluation process.

Without a consideration of the role of power differentials in establishing agendas for a project and an evaluation, qualitative evaluation can appear transparent but will merely reinforce inequities in decision-making and project activities. Denzin and Lincoln (1994) argue that only since the mid-1970s have notions of objectivity and value-free research been challenged by postmodern and cultural studies (Lincoln 1994). Within contemporary debates researchers can propose a reconceptualization of evaluation research and produce research designs and processes that challenge the maldistribution of resources and power between researcher and researched. This can involve both qualitative and qualitative methodologies. However, while qualitative evaluation may be perceived as producing material that can be useful and potentially powerful in giving voice to the concerns and ideas of a range of people and groups, in the policy arena its value continues to be questioned and muted. Not only is its value questioned, often in comparison to quantitative work, but also it has been criticized as reflecting the views of the researcher/evaluator who may be driven by idealism or realism borne out of the aesthetics of pervasive accounts of groups or individuals.

POTENTIAL AND PITFALLS FOR A PARTICIPATORY EVALUATION

Qualitative research may involve a greater commitment from the researched in that data collection frequently requires an infinite and in-depth relationship to be developed between themselves and the researcher. Add to this the critical assessment element of evaluation and the relationship between the people who are giving their time to provide data and the evaluator of that time becomes imbued with the differential operation of power. As Tracey Reynolds (Chapter 14) demonstrates, power in social research is 'multifaceted, relational and interactional and is constantly shifting and renegotiating itself between the researcher and the research participants according to different contexts and their differing structural locations'.

Lofland and Lofland (1995) note the ethical dimensions to qualitative research, not least of which, and of great relevance to evaluation, is the question 'is it ethical to take sides or to avoid taking sides in a factionalized situation?' While authors have sought to address ethical issues in qualitative evaluation it is essential for the evaluator to state clearly where they stand on issues such as participation in the design and conduct of the project; the ownership of data, input and responses to data analysis; ongoing feedback on the final report and dissemination (Shaw 1999; Wallerstein 1999).

Concerns about participation in evaluation raise specific issues for qualitative evaluations. While community-based qualitative research and evaluation may seek to generate information and knowledge, there are instrumental goals of evaluation that pose particular ethical and practical problems. A major issue is the multiplicity of definitions of 'community' and the voices within spatial or interest based definitions of community (Peterson and Lupton 1996). There are myriad interpretations and workings of any community-based project; the breadth of groups and coalitions mean that there is no one single project to evaluate. As Wallerstein (1999: 42) argues, 'with increasing participatory evaluations, community members have raised ethical challenges, wanting evaluations to be useable and accountable to the community, instead of abstract reports, token feedback, or summative information that is received too late to be useful'. Changing social, economic and political environments also present additional challenges to the evaluator as these will impact on the project and shift the content and context of community health work.

Shaw (1999: 140) notes that participation in an evaluation requires a clarity and mutual agreement on a number of matters such as the purpose of the participation; a recognition of the varying interests of participants; mechanisms for exchange and communication, and an appreciation of the benefits or potential drawbacks of involving people in the evaluation. On this last point participation can place a further burden on people whose perceptions of evaluation may be that of a judgement on their work or lives, and can further complicate the effort of general input to a project. Participation in qualitative evaluation is critically explored in the action research evaluation undertaken of the SONAS Community Health Project.

Raising expectations of evaluation, particularly the potential to participate in dynamic contexts, makes it difficult to develop a clear purpose and evident participation in evaluation while avoiding fears that qualitative evaluation is an opaque way of making a judgement on local input and involvement. In the second example, the evaluation of the Women, Low Income and Smoking Project, I consider the dilemmas posed when the evaluator and project team sought to actively tackle notions of 'power over' through supporting initiatives to undertake evaluation themselves. Huberman (1991) has suggested that there is a 'two community' problem with the researcher and the researched community having differing norms, values and expectations. Huberman (1991) proposes three types of relationships that can provide barriers to participation and collaboration:

- 'Hello–goodbye' where researchers and communities meet, dance together, then wander off.

- 'Two planets' where neither group has much contact with each other.
- 'Stand-off' where there is little agreement and some resentment between communities and researchers.

The type of relationship that will develop in any evaluation is dependent upon a range of factors including the abilities, capabilities and character of the evaluator, commissioners and participants (factors we often try to dismiss from academic debate on research and evaluation), resources, aims and objectives of the evaluation, and geography and locality. Postmodern research proposes a dialogue and praxis between researchers and participants to question issues of power and reciprocity (Wallerstein 1999). In practical terms the negotiation of agendas to establish a qualitative evaluation may be characterized by opposing and conflicting ideas on methods and approach. Therefore establishing and reviewing the aims of and format for an evaluation is an ongoing and necessary process for mutual appreciation of the possible benefits of qualitative evaluation.

As researchers we may locate ourselves in terms of gender, race, class and status in relation to others. Yet we cannot anticipate how those involved in the research and evaluation may perceive the role, authority and ultimately the power of the evaluator. Communities may seek to establish their power and knowledge bases and struggle with evaluators and commissioning bodies to tackle those who appear to exert 'power-over' them and strive for notions of 'power-with' (Wallerstein 1999). There are those in projects (stakeholders and recipients) who may know about certain kinds of research and thus gain a power base in negotiations of agendas. By contrast, those for whom evaluation is a relatively unfamiliar activity may recognize the potential to draw a critical assessment from the research and consider resisting or posing barriers to further involvement in the project or the evaluation. Heron (1996: 27) asserts that cooperative inquiry may not achieve participation and that 'qualitative research about people is a half-way house between exclusive, controlling research on people and fully participatory research with people'. Further he criticizes what he perceives as an emphasis in qualitative research as 'empowerment under the aegis of subtle benign oppression' and 'luring gatekeepers and informants into being studied by a design in which they are not invited to collaborate, and to which, at best, they are only invited to give informed consent' (Heron 1996: 28). Lynne Haney (Chapter 13) calls for feminist scholars to think more seriously about 'the politics of reflexivity in different research settings'. In her exploration of two ethnographic studies she outlines how she opted to conduct her research not from an inward perspective of autobiography but instead to turn outward establishing and assessing the impact of the wider social world on the participants and issues more generally. Acknowledging our position as social scientists and our potentially unique broad perspective on social life, Haney argues for a more contextual approach to reflexivity that considers, amongst other contexts, institutional structures, community life and historical legacies. These are major challenges to the power/knowledge and relationships between the researcher and evaluator. However, advocating power analysis, reflexivity and dialectic between researcher and researched are starting points in revealing the dynamics of power and participation in qualitative evaluation.

In the evaluations discussed below action research and case study approaches were adopted. Action research is a means of gathering data about a project, and reflecting on this material across different levels of participation in the project. The overall aim of this approach is to generate knowledge and, on the basis of this, to adapt or change the project on an ongoing basis (Hart and Bond 1995). It is an approach that emphasizes collaboration and participation. These aims sound worthy but are not without debate and controversy as discussed below. Case studies 'examine the bounded system of a program, an institution, or a population' (Marshall and Rossman 1989: 44) with the purpose being 'to reveal the properties of the class to which the instance being studied belongs' (Guba and Lincoln 1981: 371). For Atkinson and Delamont (1993) the issue of what counts as a 'case' is potentially problematic. Stake (1995: 133) proposes that 'the case to be studied probably has problems and relationships, and the report of the case is likely to have a theme, but the case is an entity. The case, in some ways, has a unique life.' Marshall and Rossman (1989) go on to detail the purpose of the case study being to chart, depict and characterize events and activities. In the second evaluation discussed in this chapter, the Women, Low Income and Smoking Project, the decision to adopt this approach and its implications for qualitative evaluation are considered.

EXPLORING PARTICIPATION AND POWER IN QUALITATIVE EVALUATION

The findings and outcomes of the evaluations are detailed elsewhere (ASH Scotland and HEBS 1999; McKie 2000) and brief descriptions of the projects and evaluations are presented here. While both evaluations were of projects premised upon a community development approach to health work, issues arose which were of relevance to the various localities and the respective projects. Projects were established in communities undergoing a series of economic and social shifts and with cultural and religious histories. These contexts and shifts necessitated an appreciation of tensions within communities, between agencies and issues of communication and power between evaluators, facilitators and participants. These issues are first explored through experiences and data derived from *SONAS: Community Health Work in the Western Isles* (McKie 2000). In this account of an evaluation I highlight the classic dilemma for the qualitative evaluator. In my role as coordinator for the evaluation I created concerns among the funding body and management groups about the objectivity of the evaluation research and content of the final report. These concerns arose from my attempts to address notions of 'power-over' the community in the evaluation, believing I might promote the potential to develop 'power-with' communities, so recipients and stakeholders might use the evaluation to inform future work.

SONAS Community Health Project

The islands on which the project is located cover an area of approximately 70 square miles and the distance between South Uist and Stornoway (the administrative centre for the Western Isles) is 120 miles. These islands are situated to the west of mainland Scotland and are the last landmass before Newfoundland. Roads, causeways and ferry and air services interconnect the islands. It is costly to travel between the islands and within the islands bus services are extremely limited. As a result a car is a necessity to access most local services. The remoteness of the islands is exaggerated in the winter months with less frequent transport services and poor weather. Yet the long winter months are characterized by many social and cultural activities. This pattern of life provides mechanisms through which the loneliness and boredom of the winter may be addressed. The extra daylight of the summer months is maximized for family and home-based activities, and work in tourism and related services.

Employment is either related to the landscape and sea – crofting, tourism and fishing – or derived from public sector bodies – health services, education, regional council and army. Private sector employment is minimal and often linked to sole or joint trading in crafts (predominately jewellery manufacture), fish farming or building. Unemployment is evident across all the islands. Also many men and women work on a seasonal and part-time basis; a sizeable minority have two or more jobs which vary according to the seasons. In addition, there are tensions between so-called 'incomers' and locals. Being an incomer suggests a person or family who have settled in the islands to take up employment (often professional and better paid jobs) or to retire. These tensions reflect economic and cultural differences.

The SONAS Community Health Project commenced in 1993 and was funded by HEBS for three years to April 1996 (£40,000 per annum was allocated for each of the three years); subsequently the Western Isles Health Board took over funding. The overall aims of the project were to

- identify the health education needs of populations in remote and rural areas, specifically the Western Isles communities
- develop and pilot innovative methods of health education and promotion, based on the concept of community health volunteers
- devise and set up, where possible, mechanisms and structures to facilitate the involvement of local communities in assessing and tackling health education priorities
- make recommendations for future health and social policies
- develop resource materials and guidelines for use by other agencies or organizations wishing to learn from the project and devise similar schemes
- evaluate and disseminate the work of the project.

HEBS funded the project under its 'demonstration' project scheme to explore the potential to learn from the community development approach to health work as applied in rural areas. A partners group was set up to act as an advisory and steering group and this comprised a representative from HEBS, Western Isles Health Board and the Scottish Community Development Centre. A project coordinator and a part-time administrator were appointed.

The project spent the first two years of funding developing a community agenda for health work and existing groups and activities combined with newly formed groups to consider a range of health issues from men's health, to chronic illness and mental health. A major aim in these early years was to gain as much involvement from various dimensions of the island communities as possible. A range of access points were developed from one-to-one counselling, workshops, conferences, open meetings and group work. In addition, the project became active in local economic and planning debates on the sustainability of these remote and rural communities. However, putting the abstract notion of community development principles into concrete action as a health project began to mirror tensions within the islands, as well as creating further problems.

As coordinator of the evaluation for the project I took up my role in late 1993. By this time the evaluation had been put in place and initial research work undertaken by Lisa Curtice and Andrew MacGregor. The overall aim of the evaluation was to provide a critical assessment of the work, management structure and organization of the SONAS project. The evaluation was a formative and summative one, employing an action research approach. As a result the process and outcomes of the project were examined on an ongoing basis and on the analysis of data the evaluation team undertook regular feedback. Qualitative methods were used: focus groups, semi-structured interviews and questionnaires comprising open-ended questions. Small area census data were also utilized to provide a socio-economic profile of island life (McKie 1996). Participants in the project were encouraged to take an active involvement in the monitoring, reflection and resultant change processes. Drafts of data analysis were returned to many respondents and data regularly discussed with the project advisory and partners groups. In addition, project participants were encouraged to record activities, interviewing each other, making videos of activities and taking photographs, and sharing this material with the evaluation team (McKie 2000).

In 1996 the Western Isles Health Board took over funding for the project and this decision was based upon the outcomes of the evaluation. The project continues but has become more focused upon major health themes of cancer, coronary heart disease and stroke and mental health. Whenever possible the project coordinator continues to develop work with a community development ethos.

Objectivity and power: perceptions of and dilemmas for the evaluator

The SONAS project and evaluation were set up in the first three months of 1993 as the funding body, HEBS, wished to ensure that monies were allocated by the end of a given financial year. The speed with which the project was set up had repercussions for communication and for dialogues between groups that impacted on much of the first two years of the project and the evaluation. For example, prior to the launch of the project there was no time for consultation with local people on either the content of the project or methodology of the evaluation. Nor was there time to consider the local cultural and socio-economic contexts. While local activists expressed an early interest in the project, local people were unsure what the project was about and initially concerned about becoming too involved. The coordinator of the first year of the evaluation did make contact with many local groups and people but most were hesitant about involvement early on, instead preferring to 'wait and see what takes off'. In addition, given the geographical location of the project, initially there was little contact between the commissioners, funders, project coordinator (newly in post), the evaluation team and local people. All the key players in funding, monitoring and evaluating the project were based in a range of organizations in mainland Scotland or in the island's administrative centre 120 miles away.

The project was launched in the summer of 1993 at a public meeting held at a local hotel. Invitations were sent to local organizations and the event was well attended. However, the meeting proved to be tense, with local people unsure what was expected of them at either the meeting or in the project and the evaluation. In subsequent research for the evaluation local people commented that the launch meeting was 'very much run by outsiders' (identified as the partners' representatives) and did not provide clear guidance on developing project work. These views were further complicated by a sense among many local people that the project designers and the evaluation team had failed to appreciate:

- *Previous experiences of community development projects.* In the 1980s a number of community development projects had been located in the islands on such topics as economic regeneration and childcare. Many appreciated the ethos of the approach but had witnessed these projects come and go; once funding ceased there was little left behind despite the rhetoric of ownership by the community. So while assuming knowledge of the approach among local people the partners had failed to consider how previous projects had actually worked. In addition, the SONAS project was to recruit community health volunteers. The role of these volunteers was unclear and many local people described this idea as 'cheap labour' and a possible 'cost-cutting' approach by the health board.
- *Local debates on the role of the Western Isles Health Board.* Many spoke of staff from the administrative centre in Stornoway 'jetting in and out'. The community hospital in one of the islands was being considered for closure and this reinforced a sense of outsiders failing to consider local agendas and the potential role of local community decision-making. These views were further complicated by an admission on the part of HEBS that SONAS was a mechanism for delivering health promotion in remote and

sparsely populated localities; some felt that the project would prioritize health board interests rather than those of local people.

- *Economic concerns.* With rising unemployment rates and the contraction of an army base on one of the islands there were major concerns about the economic fortunes of the islands. As a consequence some questioned the need for a health project as opposed to economic regeneration work.

- *Diversity in and between islands.* There are religious and cultural differences between the islands in the north of the Western Isles. The islands in the north are predominately Protestant in religious and cultural make-up, and the administrative services are located on one of these islands, while the islands in the south are largely Catholic in religious outlook and attitudes. Communities are heterogeneous and tensions evident between those who have come to the islands to take up employment (often better paid professional jobs) and local families who have had to adapt to changing economic opportunities of the islands. Some expressed concerns that 'outsiders', including the partners' group, held inappropriate notions of a rural idyll with close-knit communities and that these views had led to inadequate preparation for the project and evaluation.

While the partners' group agreed that the project should be led by a community agenda and ultimately 'owned' by local people, the speed with which the project had been set up had not allowed for local consultation or reflection on the social and economic contexts. In many ways the community development ethos provided a strength of approach to the project. Yet ironically, at the earliest stages of the project, local people questioned the community development ethos of the partners and the evaluation. There was a sense, strongly vocalized by local people, that the project and evaluation were being imposed on communities and that this was unlikely to promote participation in either the project or the research.

Issues raised about the role of the evaluator

Much of the first year of the evaluation was spent winning local people over to the approach and methods – convincing them that their voice could have an equal weight with others. The qualitative approach to collecting and recording information on the cultural and local contexts was emphasized, as was transparency over data analysis and the process of regular feedback. A local health survey was suggested and local work on this was conducted but funded from other sources. Yet it was difficult to deal with the community's direct criticisms of the early stages of the project and evaluation. Even at this stage changes had taken place in key members of local groups, the partners' group and in the evaluation team. Certainly the evaluation was shifting in response to changes in the project and personnel. While these views and changes were recorded and fed back to the partners' group and local people they illuminated the reality that the evaluator represented and mediated several power bases.

First, as the evaluator I had the authority of the partners' group, especially the funding body, HEBS. Many local people perceived the evaluation team and the process of the evaluation as another means of collecting information from 'insiders' to judge the project and to promote decisions by 'outsiders' on the future of the work and the extension of the three-year post of project coordinator. I emphasized my own position as a researcher, employed at a university and commissioned as an independent evaluator. While many appreciated I was not working for the funding body, not everyone shared perceptions of my role as independent and separate. Initially I used academic terms to describe the evaluation and this appeared to illuminate notions of evaluation as a critical assessment. This prompted me to talk instead of recording a history of the project and of local responses to it. While this made some aspects of the evaluation work and processes more accessible, I was never fully able to overcome the sense that I was part of a critical and potentially negative decision-making process rather than an evaluator informing the future of the project. This was brought home to me after completing an interview with an active participant in the project who commented, 'Was that OK? What I said won't lose anyone their job will it?' Similar comments were addressed to me after two focus groups conducted with local health groups. For the duration of the evaluation some participants were extremely cautious in their interaction with me. One local woman said this 'was nothing personal. We just don't want to run the risk of losing anything that brings something to these islands.' After this comment I began to feel a sense of responsibility for the future of the project and the need to make sure any decision to change or end the project was firmly grounded in research evidence. One means of addressing these concerns was to ensure transparency in the process of data analysis and involve as many participants as possible as well as members of the partners' group.

I also had the authority of being an academic working from a university on the mainland. I came into the island communities for a week at a time but went home to a somewhat more secure economic situation than most of those from whom I was collecting information. My pattern of working was at odds with the seasonal nature of local life. Early on I recognized that island life was organized around the weather in a way that challenged my assumptions that the best time for me to collect data would be the spring and summer months. I was told in no uncertain terms that little would happen with the project over the summer but rather that a whole raft of cultural and social activities would start in the autumn and run over the winter. Involvement in these various groups and meetings gave people a reason to socialize and tackle the potential isolation of the long winter months. If I wanted people to speak to me then I would have to adapt to this cycle of local activities and so I changed the schedule for the research and the evaluation. However, I had demonstrated a lack of knowledge and awareness of local culture and patterns of activities.

Yet I did have several factors in my favour. Being Irish, and having moved a number of times to study and to work in islands proud of their Celtic traditions and from which many migrated, did provide some common ground. I was also working at a university located in the north of Scotland, with all the travel difficulties associated with that, and this ensured that I visited the islands for at least a week at a time. To a degree I avoided the tag of 'jetting in and out'. Also being female and a mother gave other avenues to relate to some of the project participants. Nevertheless, it was difficult to overcome the sense that the evaluation was imposed, and that while ongoing attempts were made to renegotiate the content and schedule of the research, in that negotiation I demonstrated a lack of knowledge on local culture and concerns. I was never able to overcome contradictory perceptions of local people and partners. Local people tended to see me as generally supportive of the project but part of a decision-making process on the future of the project in which they had little say. In contrast, the partners expressed concern that I might be too involved in local matters and thus less objective. For example, a member of the partners' group was concerned with the number of interviews and focus groups conducted with local people. This member of the group regularly queried the health knowledge and skills of local people and their ability to comment upon the content of the project and thus suggested that too many data were collected from sources less well informed than others.

Women, Low Income and Smoking Project

In this, the second of the qualitative evaluations, I consider the dilemmas posed by actively seeking to tackle notions of 'power-over' and propose ways to develop 'power-with' community-based initiatives in evaluation. Funded by HEBS and run by ASH Scotland, the Women, Low Income and Smoking Project aimed to explore new ways of working with a community development approach to address smoking reduction among women living on low income (Gaunt-Richardson et al. 1998). The project also sought to gain new insights into appropriate ways of evaluation by drawing upon the skills and experiences of funded initiatives, participants and the commissioning groups. Distributing a total of £37,000, nineteen initiatives were awarded grants of between £500 and £3,000 to undertake work that would operate for a maximum of a year and provide a final report on evaluation.

A variety of methods were used by the initiatives to provide an opportunity for participants to address their smoking behaviour while developing new skills and interests and raising their confidence and self-esteem. Though some initiatives tackled smoking using direct methods, focusing on cessation, the majority used a variety of indirect methods such as poetry and video work, drama, exercise and diversionary activities, as a means of engaging with women to tackle the issues around smoking. Approaches to evaluation by the respective initiatives also demonstrated a diversity of methods and resources (Amos et al. 1999; Barlow et al. 1999; McKie et al. 1999).

Those funded agreed to record their work and produce a final report that would also form an evaluation of the initiative. Although 20 per cent of the grant award was withheld until submission of the final report, where cash flow was found to be a problem it was agreed to review individual cases. The final report was to be as short or as long as initiatives wished but did have to provide a full report of activities and the views of participants. It was hoped that reports might also consider such issues as planning, participation, sustainability, and working across groups and organizations. Further it was anticipated that initiatives would come to a critical self-assessment of their work.

A project manager and administrator were appointed, a management group established to oversee the project work and an evaluation advisory group set up to support the evaluation work of the initiatives. Two information days, a seminar day and an end of project conference were organized to bring initiatives together at different stages of the small grant funding process so as to enhance opportunities for initiatives to share their work plans, methods and learning. A database detailing information from all the small grant applications was set up to provide general information and data for the evaluation. Four project bulletins were produced to disseminate information about the funded initiatives to groups and organizations throughout Scotland and a final report circulated nationally and internationally (Gaunt-Richardson *et al*. 1998; ASH Scotland and HEBS 1999).

The potential for 'power-with' in qualitative evaluation

Given that the Women, Low Income and Smoking Project adopted a community development ethos it was anticipated by ASH and HEBS that the evaluations undertaken by the initiatives would be pluralistic in nature and probably utilize qualitative methods. The evaluation advisory group was established early in the life of the project to provide general support and advice both to the project manager and to the facilitators of individual initiatives. Its role was not to undertake evaluation research *per se* but to work towards extracting overall conclusions from the final reports of the initiatives.

This group was appointed after the project format and content had been agreed and a number of assumptions about evaluation had already been made by HEBS and ASH, namely, first, that most community groups would have previously acquired skills in evaluation, especially given the increasing trend to accountability in the voluntary and public sectors. It was felt that working with initiatives and drawing upon their strengths, while recognizing that limited support may be required, would be an approach sympathetic to the community development ethos of the project.

Second, given the above it was further presumed that the evaluation advisory group would compile the evaluation of the overall project as final reports were submitted. The skills of the advisory group were to be accessible to initiatives at the information days and accessed at other times through the project manager. These arrangements were publicized in the project newsletter and by the project administrator and manager. Thus limited resources and time were allocated in the initial project budget and timetable to support evaluation.

Third, ASH Scotland had little prior experience in evaluation and no experience of community development work and the evaluation of such projects. Therefore advice was sought from national and local bodies such as HEBS; this further reinforced the assumption that skills, resources and experiences in the community could and should be drawn upon.

At its first meeting the members of the evaluation advisory group agreed that they were keen to achieve a balance between securing meaningful information and evaluations, and asking too much of initiatives that had day-to-day community work to develop on relatively small sums of money. Yet in the early months of the project it became evident that to assume that past skills and experiences would equip initiatives to undertake a relatively independent evaluation of innovative community-based work was placing too much pressure upon many of the facilitators and indeed participants. In addition, the project was designed more than a year prior to its launch and in the intervening period senior personnel at ASH and HEBS had changed.

An information day was held in the first months of the project and brought together the funded initiatives, the project management and evaluation advisory groups to consider, among other issues, the evaluation. The information day started with a number of presentations on the ethos of the project, tobacco control and evaluation. Over coffee a number of facilitators expressed concern at the time and skills they felt were required to fulfil the evaluation requirements. As initiatives got underway some realized that their experience in group work and community development did not necessarily equip them for evaluation. During small group discussions specifically on recording and evaluation, the variation in skills and experiences became apparent. One initiative questioned the relevance of the whole idea of evaluation. Later it transpired that this community group secured two to three grants per year from a range of funding bodies and had never submitted a final report. This success in acquiring grants was linked to the high levels of deprivation in their locality and the community group being the only one in the area. Hence the facilitators failed to appreciate the relevance of evaluation work and actively questioned what they considered to be 'a lot of fuss'.

Others asked for practical guidance on research methods. Recording work through the minutes of meetings, attendance records at sessions, and designing and administrating the occasional short questionnaire were the levels of experience in most of the community groups. The idea of exploring the place of smoking in women's lives, the processes of establishing and sustaining a group and working with other organizations left many feeling distinctly uneasy. Even those working in an organizational context that might have staff who were trained in evaluation and who actively supported this dimension of an initiative's work began to express concerns. More worryingly, as the project manager visited initiatives it became evident that some were struggling with evaluation work but were trying to hide this for fear of calling into question the release of the final 20 per cent of the grant. Nevertheless the majority of Wave 1 initiatives started recording work and used a range of methods to do so.

In reflecting upon these concerns, the evaluation advisory group and project manager agreed to provide specific support for several groups, for example, one initiative received input from a consultant researcher. Further, we explored the availability and relevance of resource materials on evaluation aimed specifically at community groups. Most resources, however, were aimed at health promotion or community education officers and assumed a good level of knowledge of research methods. The project manager and administrator spent an increasing amount of time on supporting recording work and the evaluation advisory group began to meet more often.

By early 1997 a new problem was emerging, namely, the analysis of material, especially the analysis of qualitative data from interviews and focus groups. One initiative asked the project manager to look through twelve large files of material and notes on interviews, and advise on what could be derived from this for the final report! Others also began to ask for detailed advice on analysis and what should go into the final report. In conjunction with the advisory group, the project manager designed a series of evaluation questions that initiatives could consider when compiling their final report; a number of the initiatives found these extremely useful in providing a format for decisions on information to include and dimensions of their work that required reflection and critical assessment.

Change and evaluation research

In the light of these events Wave 2 applicants were asked to provide further detail on their evaluation plans and encouraged by the project manager to spend time planning recording and evaluation work in the early stages of activities. Yet the project manager and evaluation advisory group began to feel increasing responsibility to relieve the pressures felt by many facilitators, to support those who could do this work but might have lacked confidence, and to ensure a level of quality in final reports that would allow overall conclusions to be drawn. At the same time the project as a whole was gaining publicity in Scotland and across the rest of the UK and Europe, and was receiving numerous requests for further information and for detail on the outcomes and recommendations when these became available.

As a result the evaluation advisory group proposed a change to the evaluation approach. We had reached a point where the idea of 'power-with' initiatives had been challenged. Our adherence to the notion of supporting a community development approach to evaluation and support for independent evaluations by the respective initiatives had led to a series of concerns that might have been avoided with some early work on mapping the skills and experiences of facilitators. Luckily the evaluation advisory group and project manager had a high level of commitment to the project and additional time available to undertake a change of role. So after two lengthy meetings, one with the project management group, it was agreed to undertake five in-depth case studies of selected initiatives. These were chosen to reflect the range of settings, methods and content of the project.

The evaluation advisory group now had to negotiate this shift in over-all approach to the evaluation while not diminishing the potential impact of the final reports of the initiatives. On seeking agreement from five initiatives to undertake a case study it became evident that some of these initiatives had begun to find evaluation so time-consuming or problematic that the idea of a case study undertaken by someone experienced in research was received as welcome support. In the case of one initiative the case study formed the only evaluation as participants and facilitators just did not know how they would or could undertake this element of their work.

The three members of the evaluation advisory group, a member of the project management group and the project manager agreed to undertake the research for the case studies and so roles changed from that of advisers to researchers. The case study methods included:

- a review of relevant documentation from the application form, to planning documents, other records, and if available, the final report
- interviews with facilitators
- when possible, group interviews with participants
- a review of presentations made at the information days and final project conference.

Data collection was undertaken in 1998 and early 1999. By this time several of the case study initiatives had completed their work. However, it was possible to interview the majority of facilitators and in every case meet some participants. It was recognized that while case studies might provide some depth to identifying and exploring issues relevant to the given 'case initiative', it would be difficult to draw overall conclusions on the project. For the end of project report, key learning from a review of reports from the initiatives was reported alongside themes emerging from the five case studies. We were careful not to diminish the evaluation work of the initiatives in the dissemination of the findings from the project.

The Evaluation Journey: An Evaluation Resource Pack

In a final review meeting of the Women, Low Income and Smoking Project, initiatives praised the level and quality of support received from ASH

Scotland. Facilitators commented that they had gained so much in the development of their skills, and a number have gone on to achieve further grant awards and to undertake appropriate evaluation work. Not every organization can provide this level of support, and a major recommendation to emerge from the meeting was the need for resource materials and for related ongoing general and specialist advice services for evaluation.

A major theme to emerge from the project as a whole was the need for resource materials on recording and evaluation that were both informative and accessible to community groups. *The Evaluation Journey: An Evaluation Resource Pack for Community Groups* (Barlow *et al.* 2001) was developed from the learning from the project and from further interviews with facilitators. The pack provides information on the rationale for evaluation; planning and participation; collecting information using conventional and unconventional methods; analysis; report writing and dissemination. The pack is being piloted and once revisions are made publication will follow.[1]

The hope by the project management and evaluation advisory groups to create qualitative evaluations that reflected notions of 'power-with' the funded initiatives had proved extremely difficult to realize. Their assumptions about skills and resources were ill founded, and further, suggest that a number of national and local organizations may also be overestimating the skills available. In addition, the analysis of qualitative data, and the level of support required to undertake evaluation work at a community level were also underestimated. On reflection we recognized that the theory of seeking to work in an egalitarian manner may sometimes pose problems and issues for those less confident and experienced in research. The evaluation of the ASH Scotland Tobacco and Inequality project has drawn upon this learning.[2] An independent evaluator has been appointed, in addition to the provision of materials and support from an evaluation advisory group (Barlow *et al.* 2001).

CONCLUSIONS: THE IMPLICATIONS FOR QUALITATIVE EVALUATION

In the 1990s the growth in demands for accountability and the evaluation of community-based work placed a number of pressures upon researchers and communities. Ultimately, evaluation involves making an assessment, both judging the merit of an activity or programme and assessing outcomes against potentially shifting aims and objectives. Qualitative evaluation has been conceived of as one means of addressing the potentially problematic issues of how to make evaluation a participatory activity and thus enhance the potential for reflexivity.

The epistemological underpinnings of qualitative research are often cited as promoting the potential for participation and tackling notions of power and authority between researcher and the researched. As illustrated in the qualitative evaluations considered above, these claims must be set within the everyday context of the origins of a project, and the realities facing those who commission, implement and participate in a project. Most evaluators develop what Huberman (1991) has described (as we have seen) as a 'hello–goodbye' relationship with communities, that is researchers and communities meet, dance together, then wander off. This is perhaps the best to hope for as the researcher will almost always leave, and, even if honest about the power basis to evaluation will be considered to have exercised their subjectivity on data and any final report.

In a review of the evaluation of the SONAS Project it was evident that an involvement in and commitment to evaluation must be established in the design stage and regularly reviewed. The relevance of community health work to the accountability procedures of organizations varies, as does the appreciation of process evaluation. In its earliest days this evaluation suffered from a failure to undertake consultation prior to the start of data collection or to situate the evaluation in local socio-economic and political debates. Despite the wish to make the evaluation as transparent as possible there was a sense of the exercise of 'power-over' the community among many local people. Ironically, in attempting to address potential concerns about 'power-over' and ensure recognition of skills and experiences in the community the evaluation of the Women, Low Income and Smoking Project caused concerns among community groups who felt pressured by the demands of an independent evaluation.

Community-based evaluation does not take place in a vacuum. Yet all too often researchers presume that by adopting qualitative methodology they have addressed the potential concerns of communities about power, authority and participation. Drawing upon the two qualitative evaluations discussed in this chapter there are a number of implications I will discuss under three headings: inclusion, dialogue and deliberation.

Inclusion

While qualitative research may, as Heron (1996) asserts, be considered as 'a halfway house' between controlling research on people and achieving participation, the epistemic basis to qualitative evaluation does afford the potential to develop a dialogue and praxis. Identification of the groups and individuals participating in an evaluation and clarification of their respective positions on a project and evaluation must be a starting point for evaluation work. Crucial to this is a consideration of understandings and values on participation, inclusion, change and proposed content and potential outcomes from the research and evaluation (Barnes and Wistow 1992).

Regardless of the methodology considered for the evaluation, a profile of communities and localities should be undertaken prior to the project or policy and evaluation commencing. If self-assessment is proposed the skills of those involved should be ascertained and support made available as mutually agreed. The profiling work should include detail of social, economic and political factors and set these in an historical context (Scottish Poverty Information Unit 1999). Profiling is likely to illuminate pertinent issues; for example, debates about a possible hospital closure can alert evaluators to issues that may impact on the design and conduct of the evaluation. Most importantly the process will identify groups and individuals who should be included in the research and evaluation.

Dialogue

Creating a dialogue between participants, funders and project facilitators requires a reflexive stance on the role of researcher and researched. A series of questions arise which include, among others:

- Where did the original idea emerge from?
- Was consultation undertaken or is the policy or project being imposed in a top-down fashion?
- How much say do the community and researcher have in the design, conduct and analysis of the research data?
- Are there plans for community input to the final report? If not, might this be possible?
- Are there mechanisms for community members or commissioners to comment upon the conduct and outcomes of the research and evaluation activities?

It is all too easy to accept a commission for an evaluation, especially in the current climate that values the award of external research grants, but the responsibilities and ethical issues can change a seemingly straightforward project into a highly problematic and stressful one.

Deliberation

In the analysis of data and consideration of outcomes and recommendations it is imperative to appreciate that a multiplicity of definitions of community exist and will give rise to a range of voices and opinions. These may also give rise to potentially competing interpretations of events and data and place the evaluator in the difficult situation of having to decide on a final version of events and analysis of data. Researchers must be honest about their power/knowledge bases and address the ethics of research and evaluation. Just adopting qualitative methodology is only part of the answer to ensuring a multiplicity of voices can be heard through qualitative evaluation. As Heron (1996) argues participation may not be feasible or obtainable, especially where there are external researchers or evaluators, but there are dangers in asserting that participation is either not possible or that qualitative methodology will provide the appropriate context:

[providers] should be sensitive to the demands they are placing on people whose lives are already complex and demanding. They should be ready to ensure that people derive some direct benefits from participation, as well as ensuring that ... participation is justified by the outcomes it achieves. (Barnes and Wistow 1994: 91)

The discussion in this chapter has used data drawn from two community health projects to demonstrate the values and pitfalls of engaging in evaluation research. The evaluations and projects themselves achieved a number of successes in policy and practice terms, for example they provided an evidence base on the opportunities for and barriers to community health work through the consideration of the dynamic nature of participation in community projects and evaluation. The communities provided their own determination of 'success' by reflecting on the content and processes of the project and had a direct input to the research as well as the final report. Lastly, through the process of qualitative evaluation the commissioners accepted that community involvement in the various stages of the evaluation and project was an imperative to both the development and assessment of the project.

As noted earlier the evaluation of the SONAS Project assisted in the decision to retain the project. Although it has been adapted to reflect specific health issues the project continues to work with a community development ethos and this approach has been accepted by a majority of health board members and health care professionals. Recommendations from the Women, Low Income and Smoking Project have led to ongoing work to promote community-based evaluation work and community development work on tobacco issues through the Inequality and Tobacco Project. The projects and evaluations have also provided further input to a number of theoretical debates concerning community development and community health work which have been discussed elsewhere (McKie 1996, 2000; ASH Scotland and Health Education Board for Scotland 1999).

SUMMARY

The overall aim of this chapter was to assess the potential for qualitative research to address critically issues around power and participation in evaluation, particularly between the researcher and researched. As asserted earlier in the chapter there has been presumption that qualitative research can provide a more informative picture of culturally based processes and practices in a manner that enhances the potential for a more equal relationship between the researcher and researched. However, as Tracey Reynolds (Chapter 14) contends, 'power in social research is not a fixed and unitary construct' and the realities of the shifting nature of power are evident in the evaluations discussed above.

Several key issues were considered in this chapter:

- Evaluation is about making an assessment and this process and outcome will raise concerns and may cause sensitivities (Wallerstein 1999).
- Researchers cannot presume that the adoption of qualitative research will necessarily tackle issues such as power differentials and participation. They must consider the politics of reflexivity in different research settings (Lynne Haney, Chapter 13).
- When evaluating or researching community-based work researchers must appreciate the multiplicity of definitions of community and power differential within communities (Connell *et al.* 1995).
- So as to illuminate local issues and structures researchers must also extend 'outward to look more broadly at the social world' through perspectives on 'institutional structures, community life and historical legacies' (Lynne Haney, Chapter 13).
- Researchers must appreciate the role of subjectivity in the analysis and writing up and thus the need to ground assertions in various forms of evidence and reflection (Shaw 1999).

ACKNOWLEDGEMENTS

I would like to thank all those who participated in the two evaluations considered in this chapter, namely SONAS Community Health Project and Women, Low Income and Smoking Project. In developing my ideas on, and work in, qualitative evaluation I would like to acknowledge the ongoing support and advice of Kathryn Backett-Milburn, Joy Barlow, Paula Gaunt-Richardson, Maureen Moore, Norma Neill, Emma Witney and Daniel Wybrow. Many thanks to Susan Gregory, Paula Gaunt-Richardson, Kathryn Backett-Milburn, Margaret Black and Emma Witney for comments on earlier versions of the chapter and to Tim May and the anonymous reader for editorial advice.

NOTES

1   *The Evaluation Journey. An Evaluation Resource Pack for Community Groups* can be obtained from ASH Scotland, 8 Frederick Street, Edinburgh EH2 2HB, Scotland. Email: ashscotland@ashscotland.org.uk. Web page: http://www.ashscotland.org.uk
2   The Tobacco and Inequality Project commenced in 2000 and runs for three years with the overall aim of developing community-based services to support the reduction of smoking among those living on low income; to develop further approaches to community-based evaluation, and to support national, regional and local responses to the White Paper on tobacco *Smoking Kills* and the White Paper on health, *Towards a Healthier Scotland*. As part of this project six community-based initiatives have been funded for one year, with a grant of £10,000 to investigate new ways of working and offer new services to individuals and groups and improve and develop the way existing services are offered. Further information can be obtained from ASH Scotland.

REFERENCES

Amos, A., Gaunt-Richardson, P., McKie, L. and Barlow, J. (1999) 'Addressing smoking and health among women living on low income III: Ayr Barnardo's Homeless Service and Dundee Women's Aid', *Health Education Journal* 58: 329–340.

ASH Scotland and Health Education Board for Scotland (1999) *Breaking Down the Barriers: Women, Low Income and Smoking, Final Report*. Edinburgh: ASH Scotland.

Atkinson, P. and Delamont, S. (1993) 'Bread and dreams or bread and circuses? A critique of case study research in evaluation', in M. Hammersley (ed.) *Controversies in the Classroom*. Buckingham: Open University Press.

Barlow, J., Gaunt-Richardson, P., Amos, A. and McKie, L. (1999) 'Addressing smoking and health among women living on low income II: TAPS Tiree – a dance and drama group for rural community development', *Health Education Journal* 58: 321–328.

Barlow, J., McKie, L. and Gaunt-Richardson, P. (2001) *The Evaluation Journey: An Evaluation Resource Pack for Community Groups*. Edinburgh: ASH Scotland.

Barnes, M. and Wistow, G. (eds) (1992) *Researching User Involvement*. Leeds: Nuffield Institute for Health Service Studies, University of Leeds.

Bryman, A. (2001) *Social Research Methods*. Oxford: Oxford University Press.

Chelimsky, E. (1997) 'Thoughts for a new evaluation society', *Evaluation* 3(1): 97–104.

Connell, J., Kubisch, A., Schorr, L. and Weiss, C. (eds) (1995) *New Approaches to Evaluating Community Initiatives: Concepts, Methods and Contexts*. New York: Aspen Institute.

Connor, A. (1993) *Monitoring and Evaluation Made Easy: A Handbook for Voluntary Organisations*. Edinburgh: HMSO.

Denzin, N. and Lincoln, Y. (eds) (1994) *Handbook of Qualitative Research*. Thousand Oaks, CA: Sage.

Gaunt-Richardson, P., Amos, A. and Moore, M. (1998) 'Women, low income and smoking: developing community-based initiatives', *Health Education Journal* 57 (4): 303–313.

Grbich, C. (1999) *Qualitative Research in Health*. London: Sage.

Greene, J. (1994) 'Qualitative program evaluation: practice and promise', in N. Denzin and Y. Lincoln (eds) *Handbook of Qualitative Research*. Thousand Oaks, CA: Sage.

Guba, E. (1990) 'The alternative paradigm dialog', in E. Guba (ed.) *The Paradigm Dialog*. Newbury Park, CA: Sage.

Guba, E. and Lincoln, Y. (1981) *Effective Evaluation*. San Francisco, CA: Jossey-Bass.

Hart, E. and Bond, M. (1995) *Action Research for Health and Social Care*. Buckingham: Open University Press.

Heron, J. (1996) *Co-operative Inquiry: Research into the Human Condition*. London: Sage.

Huberman, M. (1991) 'Linkage between researchers and practitioners: a qualitative study', *American Educational Research Journal* 27: 363–393.

Lincoln, Y. (1994) 'Tracks toward a postmodern politics of evaluation', *Evaluation Practice* 15(3): 299–309.

Lofland, J. and Lofland, L. (1995) *Analysing Social Settings*. Belmont, CA: Wadsworth.

McKie, L. (1996) *SONAS: An Evaluation of the Second Year of the Project*. Edinburgh: Health Education Board for Scotland.

McKie, L. (2000) *SONAS: Community Health Work in the Western Isles*. Edinburgh: Health Education Board for Scotland.

McKie, L., Gaunt-Richardson, P., Barlow, J. and Amos, A. (1999) 'Addressing smoking and health among women living on low income I: Dean's Community Club – a mental-health project', *Health Education Journal* 58: 311–320.

Marshall, C. and Rossman, G. (1989) *Designing Qualitative Research*. London: Sage.

Miles, M. and Huberman, A. (1994) *Qualitative Data Analysis: An Expanded Source Book*. Thousand Oaks, CA: Sage.

Peterson, A. and Lupton, D. (1996) *The New Public Health: Health and Self in the Age of Risk*. Thousand Oaks, CA: Sage.

Scottish Poverty Information Unit (1999) *Community Profiling Resource Pack*. Glasgow: Glasgow Caledonian University.

Shaw, I. (1999) *Qualitative Evaluation*. London: Sage.

SONAS (1996) *People, Community and Health: A Hebridean Conference*. Benbecula: SONAS Western Isles Community Health Project.

Stake, R. (1995) *The Art of Case Study Research*. Thousand Oaks, CA: Sage.

Voyle, J. and Simmons, D. (1999) 'Community development through partnership: promoting health in an urban indigenous community in New Zealand', *Social Science and Medicine* 49: 1,035–1,050.

Wallerstein, N. (1999) 'Power between evaluator and community: research relationships within New Mexico's healthier communities', *Social Science and Medicine* 49: 39–53.

Wimbush, E. and Watson, J. (2000) 'An evaluation framework for health promotion: theory, quality and effectiveness', *Evaluation* 6(3): 301–321.

13 NEGOTIATING POWER AND EXPERTISE IN THE FIELD

Lynne Haney

It was in the late 1970s that feminist scholars began to critique many of the assumptions underlying social scientific research and to develop their own methodological approaches. Much of this early work was influenced by traditional standpoint theory and its recognition of the social origins of knowledge. Feminist scholars used these insights to argue for the existence of a 'women's standpoint' – a perspective on the social world that was grounded in women's shared social locations (Hartsock 1987; Smith 1987). The logic was clear: by beginning their inquiries from the standpoint of women, feminist social scientists would arrive at a clearer, more lucid understanding of power relations (Harding 1991). Our research methods would then reflect this approach. Instead of insisting on a separation between the 'knower' and the 'known', feminist social scientists would enjoin them. They would transform the research experience into a dialogue and a shared project of illumination. In effect, feminist methodology would give rise to alternative research practices, thus disrupting the androcentric bias that seemed to plague so much traditional social science.

Such arguments were clearly a sign of the times, symptomatic of larger trends in feminist theory. Yet as feminists began to construct more nuanced theories of gender, this methodological paradigm was challenged. In particular, as feminist theorists became more attentive to the intersection of race, class and gender and of the 'serial' quality of gender, they began to question the existence of a women's standpoint (Harding 1998; Young 1995). This led to the recognition that women were themselves situated differently, in ways that both allied and divided them. Thus, feminist scholars began to advance methodological approaches that took into account the similarities and differences among women (Harding 1998; Collins 2000). This implied the development of 'mixed' standpoints, 'flexible' standpoints, and 'partial' perspectives (Haraway 1991; Sandoval 1991; Collins 2000). Whatever their specific approach, most scholars agreed on the need for increased 'reflexivity' in feminist research. In fact, the call for reflexivity has become almost a catch phrase used to denote many different practices. As a research strategy, reflexivity can imply addressing the power embedded in the researcher/researched relationship and sharing this interpretive power with those being studied. As an analytical tool, reflexivity can mean recognizing researchers' own social locations and disentangling how they might shape the empirical analysis (Stacey 1988; Fonow and Cook 1991; Reinharz 1992).

As a graduate student in the early 1990s, I followed these feminist methodological debates closely. In its many incarnations, feminist methodology spoke to my academic concerns and desire to do social science in a different way. Dorothy Smith's (1987) theory of the 'everyday world as problematic' exerted a particularly strong influence on my development as a social researcher. Her work addressed my sociological 'problem with no name' by pointing out that traditional sociology tended to take its questions from an 'administrator's world'. It also provided an alternative way to do social science: by beginning our investigations from the standpoint of the everyday, Smith argued that sociologists would be better able to unearth 'relations of the ruling' and to trace 'lineaments of oppression' (Smith 1987: 154). This approach appeared to turn traditional sociology on its head; it implied listening to women's voices and transforming what they find problematic into sociological inquiry.

Smith's sociological approach has been used with great success in a variety of empirical studies on education and work, as Chapter 1 in this volume outlines. In my own research, I transported the model to another social arena – the state. Initially, this seemed like quite a stretch; both feminist and non-feminist scholars had tended to view the state from above, as a strictly macro-level entity (MacKinnon 1989; Orloff 1993; Pateman 1988). Nevertheless, I set out to conduct a series of feminist ethnographies of the state. I first attempted this in a study that examined the concrete interactions in a probation office and a group home for incarcerated teen mothers in California. My second ethnography of the state was conducted as part of a larger project on the development of the Hungarian welfare system. This study analysed shifts in the operation of Hungarian welfare through an examination of its national-level policies and local-level practices. In both studies, the goal was to construct a view of the state from below, from the perspective of those caught in these systems.

While this methodological approach sounded promising in the abstract, a plethora of unexpected issues surfaced during the research process. Within these settings, 'relations of the ruling' were enacted among women. These were cases where some women (as state actors) wielded power over other women (as clients). In effect, the 'lineaments of oppression' ran through and among women. Those attributes that some women deemed problematic were considered unproblematic by other women. In fact, power was exercised through this labelling process and subsequent determinations of what was un/problematic in everyday life. At the centre of these conflicting definitions of the situation were struggles over power and expertise: who knew what was best for women? What was their knowledge based on? How was it legitimized?

In this chapter, I discuss the practical exigencies I encountered while conducting two ethnographies of the state and how they complicated my ideas about 'reflexive' research practices. How does a feminist scholar analyse 'relations of the ruling' when they occur among women? How does a feminist sociologist adjudicate among women's conflicting views of what is problematic in everyday life? And how does a feminist researcher cope with situations in which listening to women's voices places her on competing sides of institutional divides? Other researchers have grappled with similar dilemmas through an inward approach to reflexivity – by turning the analytical focus onto themselves and interrogating their own positionality. In this chapter, I argue for the opposite approach. Instead of turning inward, I grappled with the politics of ethnographic practice by turning outward. In the first study, this implied moving beyond the confines of my specific field sites to expose the structural forces that impinged on their institutional relations. In the second study, it meant pulling back from the ethnographic present and moving toward ethnohistory. In both studies, the extension beyond the local enabled me to unearth the broader social forces that worked to pit women against one another in the everyday life of the state.

POLITICS OF PATRIARCHY IN THE EVERYDAY LIFE OF THE STATE

In early 1992, I began my first ethnography of the state in the California juvenile justice system.[1] My goals were lofty: I set out to study the state in a way that took feminist methodological and theoretical principles seriously. Instead of formulating my questions from an administrative angle, or from the policies and laws dictated from above, my inquiries would be grounded in the everyday lives of women in the juvenile justice system. Thus, I imagined that the research would centre on the lives and experiences of female clients. As I conceptualized it at the time, the research was to examine female clients' understanding of the power exerted over them, the modes of control they were subjected to, and the standards of appropriate behaviour used to evaluate them. To do this, I grounded the research in two institutions – a county Probation Department and a group home for incarcerated teen mothers.[2]

Everyday relations of the ruling

The initial phase of the research project involved interviewing those in charge of both institutions. It was here, in those early interviews, that the theoretical and methodological complications began to surface. Almost without exception, those in charge of these institutions were women: the overwhelming majority of probation officers (POs) were women of colour, while the entire group home staff was female. In and of itself, this was not surprising; historically, social welfare occupations have been predominately female. Far more surprising were these women's representations of their positions in the justice system. Most of them denied being part of this system altogether; they spoke in 'us versus them' terms as a way of distancing themselves from what occurred in other justice institutions. POs frequently opposed their work to that of the courts and juvenile hall. While the latter were punitive and coercive, POs presented their work as protective and just. They saw it as their job to keep young women out of other parts of the system and to serve as a buffer against its brutality. The group home staff articulated a similar distrust of the system. For them, this meant the youth prison, the California Youth Authority. The staff also believed it was their responsibility to protect young women from the punishment of this other institution. In both cases, female state actors claimed to work in opposition to the punitive practices of the system.

Perhaps even more surprising were these women's agendas for their female clientele – agendas that appeared to be quite feminist in orientation. The main PO that I worked with, Carol Jackson, was an African American woman in her early fifties. Her primary agenda for the more than 100 young women under her supervision was to enhance their independence. For Carol, this meant one main thing: to make her female clients less dependent on men. Over and over again, Carol instructed her clients that a reliance on men would bring them down; not only were men unreliable and irresponsible, but also they would squash women's strength and drive them to crime. Her arguments could have been taken from an introductory textbook discussion of 'private' patriarchy and its dangers for women (see McIntosh 1978; Zaretsky 1982; Abramovitz 1988).

The group home staff worked with similar ideas about the importance of female independence and autonomy. For them, the main threat to young women was not men but the government. They were concerned about how the teen mothers under their supervision seemed reliant on state pro- grammes and assistance. According to them, such reliance endangered women: it created a 'cycle of institutional dependency' that undercut women's initiative, self-confidence and motivation. Their arguments could also have been taken from an introductory textbook discussion, this time of 'public' patriarchy and its threat to women's well-being (see Brown 1981; Boris and Bardaglio 1983; Burnstyn 1983).

These arguments about the source of and solution to women's problems were not simply rhetorical. After spending months observing interactions among these women, it became clear that these facilities were organized to reflect these messages. POs continually lectured their clients about the dan- gers of men; they sought to instill self-esteem in their female charges by crea- ting a buffer between them and their boyfriends (or homeboys) and by steering these young women toward their female networks and kin. The group home staff was equally inventive. They constantly lectured the girls about the limitations of government and state assistance; they established house rules geared toward the demonstration of autonomy and they manipu- lated the girls' relationship to their own babies (who also lived in the house) so as to convince them that one had to be self-sufficient to mother properly. In short, these facilities problematized female dependency and set out to socialize their clients against the currents of private and public patriarchy. As I wrote in an early set of field notes: 'Could these be feminist institutions? ... Could I have stumbled on a feminist arm of the state?'

Had I listened only to the women in charge of these facilities, I might have answered such questions in the affirmative. But there was another set of women's voices struggling to be heard. And when I listened to them, the picture became far more complex. Female clients in both facilities saw nothing emancipatory about the discourses or the practices of the women supervising them. The young women under Carol's control found their relationships with men to be unproblematic: some of them looked to men for protection in their violent neighbourhoods; others turned to men as an important source of financial support in their impoverished communities; still others viewed men as a source of pleasure in an otherwise painful existence. The teen mothers in the group home were also troubled by the staff's preoccupation with self-sufficiency. They saw nothing wrong with the use of government assistance: many of them interpreted state support as critical for those without the skills to make it on their own, while others appropriated state support to counter a series of institutional injustices and inequalities.

Clients' views about what they needed to survive in everyday life prompted them to resist. In fact, they began to behave in precisely those ways that the women in charge of them found so problematic; they accentuated exactly those attributes that the women supervising them were so troubled by. The young women under Carol's supervision reaffirmed what they believed to be the benefits of their heterosexual relationships: they became more steadfast in their defence of their homeboys; they highlighted their femininity to demonstrate what they accrued from it in everyday life. Similarly, the teen mothers in the group home protested the staff's attempts to make them self-sufficient: they mobilized state actors from other facilities to exert power over the staff; they even established a welfare club to contest what they considered the staff's condescending attitude about public assistance. In doing so, these young women ended up reinforcing precisely what the POs and the group home staff sought to undercut.

These institutional patterns of control and resistance presented me with a series of research dilemmas. Both sites were comprised of diverse groups of women who were allied and divided in complex ways; even their understandings of these alliances and divisions varied. As a feminist researcher, I was pulled in competing directions. My insistence on listening to women's voices placed me on both sides of the institutional divide. On the one hand, I understood the concerns of POs and the group home staff. Indeed, they were different from those working in other parts of the system; they were deeply committed to the girls they supervised; and they struggled to develop an analysis of what could help these young women. On the other hand, female clients presented a serious challenge to this definition of the situation. Their resistance also had to be taken seriously, particularly given the ingenuity, passion and feistiness with which they waged it. As a feminist scholar, how was I to make sense of these competing perspectives? And how was I to evaluate the outcomes of these battles, as young women frequently ended up more committed to relationships that may have undercut their well-being in the long run?

Moving beyond the everyday

For a variety of reasons, I could not grapple with these research dilemmas by using reflexivity as either a research strategy or an analytical tool. As a research strategy, reflexivity seemed to be of little help: it was just not viable to turn the research into a collective project of understanding or dialogue. In these deeply divided institutions, it would have been nearly impossible to control the social power that my analysis could have wielded. My analysis may have had unintended effects on the POs and group home staff, exposing them to their clients' mockery and leaving them vulnerable to attack. Or it could have had adverse effects on the young women, informing the staff of their survival strategies and thus teaching them how to control the girls more effectively. And I shudder to think of the politics involved in bringing these sides together to listen to one another. Nor could I imagine using reflexivity as an analytical tool by turning inward and socially locating my own knowledge claims. As I have discussed elsewhere, my position in the field was so variable that it was nearly impossible to determine how who I am shaped my definition of the situation (Haney 1996). It also felt like an escape, a way of retreating from a complex social reality into the subjective realm of autobiography.

Hence, instead of turning inward, I grappled with these dilemmas by extending the research outward. This extension implied two moves. First, I broadened my analysis to encompass the structural context within which these institutional battles occurred. It would have been quite easy for me to deem female state actors as out of touch with the plight of their clients. But that would have ignored the larger context in which they worked. Indeed, these women were situated in a bifurcated juvenile justice system, largely borne out of the deinsitutionalization movement of the 1970s. They knew quite well that their girls would suffer if channelled into other parts of the system. Their agendas for their clients then reflected this institutional reality. In effect, their institutional positions provided them with particular views of what threatened their clients, leading POs to attack private patriarchy and the group home staff to target public patriarchy. For their part, clients were not as aware of this broader institutional context; they had relatively limited experience in the system. Instead, their agendas were rooted in their need to survive in everyday life. And this frequently pushed them to defend their relationships with men and/or public assistance programmes.

This leads to the second way that I extended the research beyond the confines of these institutional interactions. In addition to contextualizing these interactions in the structure of the justice system, I connected them to the surrounding inner-city community. This enabled me to understand further these women's competing definitions of the situation. In short, I began to see their contrasting agendas as rooted in very different views of inner-city life. POs looked at these communities and saw men as the biggest threat to their girls' well-being, while the group home staff saw danger in their girls' reliance on public assistance. Yet the girls' experiences in these communities taught them about the usefulness of heterosexual relationships and of access to state support. Hence, these women's institutional interactions were propelled by different positions in and evaluations of the broader urban context.

In this way, moving beyond the local world of juvenile justice offices enabled me to resist choosing sides in their institutional divides. It permitted me to take different women's voices seriously. And it allowed me to understand where each side was coming from and the social factors that shaped their perspectives. Had I turned inward or remained at the local level, I would not have captured such complex relations. Nor would I have grasped the complicated 'lineaments of oppression', especially those emanating from the structure of the justice system and of inner-city communities. In Dorothy Smith's terms, it was necessary for me to leave the realm of the everyday in order to problematize its relations of the ruling. As Smith put it in Chapter 1 in this volume: 'The work of the sociologist is to discover these relations and to map them so that people can begin to see how their own lives and work are hooked into the lives and work of others in relations of which most of us are not aware.' I learned a similar lesson about the practical limitations of reflexivity in my second ethnography of the state.

POLITICS OF EXPERTISE IN THE EVERYDAY LIFE OF THE STATE

Shortly after I completed my research on the California juvenile justice system, I embarked on a study of the Hungarian welfare state.[3] I had been preparing for this latter research for some time; from the onset of my graduate studies, I had planned to locate my dissertation project in Hungary. It was in this area of the world that my interest in gender and the state first emerged: as an exchange student in Hungary in the mid-1980s, I first became aware of the important role of the state in the constitution of gender relations. Yet, by the mid-1990s, my understanding of the relationship between gender and the state had been complicated. My California research had sensitized me to the macro- and micro-level embodiments of the state and the possible disjunctures in their gender regimes. Thus, I weaved these lessons into my Hungarian study, setting out to examine the state's gender regimes as articulated in both its national policies and institutional practices. The goal was to analyse the Hungarian welfare state as a layered entity comprised of multiple apparatuses and gender regimes. For all of the reasons discussed above, I also embarked on this study with a far more cautious attitude toward 'reflexivity' as a research practice and an analytical tool.

Transitional relations of the ruling

I began this project by locating two Budapest locales within which to ground the research. In the end, I chose two districts with demographic parallels to larger Hungarian trends, thus ensuring that my findings were as generalizable as possible. Within these locales, I arranged to conduct ethnographic work in three key welfare institutions: child protective services (*Gyámhatóságok*), child guidance centres (*Nevelési Tanácsadók*) and family support services (*Család Segítö Szolgálatok*). Hence, this research project had a far broader scope than my California study. In this work, I mediated among a total of six institutions in two locales.

Despite the differences in size, scope and context, I was immediately struck by the similarities between the issues plaguing the Hungarian and California state institutions. As in the California study, I uncovered extreme divisions within and among Hungarian welfare institutions. Here, too, state actors differentiated themselves from one another, which led to all sorts of institutional battles and struggles. Moreover, in Hungarian welfare institutions, these conflicts were also motivated by competing definitions of the situation and ideas about what clients needed. And here, too, relations of the ruling were worked out among women, creating complex alliances and divisions between female state actors and their female clientele.

At the same time as these institutional dynamics resembled those I encountered in California, they also had a particularly Hungarian flavour. The discourse of these state actors was not even remotely feminist. Hungarian welfare workers rarely even acknowledged that close to all of their clients were women. Thus, their definition of the situation did not involve analyses of the dangers of female dependency. In fact, as the research progressed, I began to see this denial of clients' gender positions and identifications as a central thread that ran through all of these institutions (Haney 1997). State actors in the six facilities I studied adhered to a strikingly similar material reductionism, a conception of need that reduced their clients' problems to material deprivation. Their institutional battles then centred on who was better able to assess and remedy this deprivation. Some of them turned to their institutional experiences to argue that they had the know-how to address clients' material problems. Others pointed to their education and training as social workers to proclaim that they were best equipped to combat client poverty. Still others claimed that their access to state resources put them in the position to alleviate client deprivation. In effect, underlying welfare workers' institutional battles were conflicts over expertise: who had the knowledge and the legitimacy to target and treat client poverty?

In Hungary, this discourse of expertise was highly politicized. Unlike other cases in which expert discourses served to depoliticize welfare work, Hungarian welfare workers framed their expertise as resistive (Kunzel 1993; Gordon 1994). They represented their expertise as a corrective to the orientation of the socialist state, which they believed had failed to recognize poverty, individual deprivation, and social problems. Thus, many of them described their work as socially transformative. As caseworkers administered means tests and distributed poor relief, they thought they were protecting their clients' well-being. As social workers interpreted everything from domestic violence to alcoholism to depression as outgrowths of financial hardship, they believed they were working in their clients' best interest. For them, proclaiming expertise was a definitively political act; in the seemingly chaotic post-socialist world of displacement, it was a way of formulating rational analyses of social problems.

Yet given the lessons I learned in my California study, I knew that there might be another side of the story. As it turned out, Hungarian clients did indeed have a very different definition of the situation. For some, material problems were not the main threat to their well-being. While these women were in relatively stable economic positions, they had other needs as mothers, wives and women – needs that remained unaddressed by welfare workers. They often viewed welfare workers' material reductionism as a way to silence them and to channel them out of the welfare system altogether. More common were clients with material problems who accepted the available poor relief while voicing a series of additional needs. As they interacted with welfare workers, these women frequently demanded more comprehensive and less fleeting assistance – help with their abusive husbands, their rebellious children, their limited work opportunities, and their emotional turmoil. They viewed welfare workers' expert discourse as a new form of power, as a way of maintaining distance from them. They saw the resulting institutional practices as mechanisms to segment them into specialized categories and to ignore the complexity of their dislocation (Haney 2002).

Clients' alternative definition of the situation then prompted them to resist. Some did this by challenging the means tests that formed the basis of welfare work; they argued that such tests ignored the many issues impinging on their everyday lives. Others resisted by drawing into view additional parts of their lives; they linked their material deprivation to deeper social and psychological problems. Still others personalized their relationships with welfare workers; they struggled to force welfare workers to see them as multifaceted people whose lives were not dissimilar from their own. In short, through their strategizing, clients tried to complicate welfare workers' constructions of them as simply materially needy. They contested the expert discourse of poverty regulation by mobilizing other social identities, contributions, and needs.

As I observed these institutional interactions, I found myself confronted with research dilemmas similar to those I faced in the California study. Hungarian institutions were also fraught with conflicts and struggles among women. Here the battles were less about the politics of patriarchy and more about the politics of expertise. Yet this difference did not make these struggles any easier to analyse. On the one side were welfare workers, many of whom I had formed close connections to. I knew they were not mean-spirited women; most of them did their best to cope with the difficult conditions surrounding them. On the other side were clients, who were themselves facing severe material, familial, social and personal problems. Their definition of the situation could not be ignored; their strategies of resistance were an index of the form of power they felt subjected to. Hence, I was in a familiar position: once again, my commitment to listening to women's voices put me on opposite sides of an institutional divide. How was I to arbitrate among these perspectives and to make sense of these power relations?

Moving beyond the ethnographic present

As in the California study, a move toward reflexivity – in both senses of the term – was not a viable way to resolve these research dilemmas. Perhaps even more than in the previous study, I was acutely aware of my social location from the start of the Hungarian research, especially of my role as an American researcher. During the early 1990s, Hungary was inundated with western researchers who saw the country as a social laboratory in which to study the dynamics of social change. As a result, many Hungarians began to feel like laboratory animals, constantly under the gaze of western social scientists. To some extent, my knowledge of Hungarian and focus on under-studied social groups differentiated me from these researchers. But my identity as an American sociologist did follow me wherever I went, producing a combination of intrigue, weariness, appreciation and fear in those I studied.

Acknowledging my social position was one thing, but inserting it into the research process or data analysis was quite another. In this context, it did not seem feasible or responsible to try to turn the research into a collective project of dialogue. The social power implied by such an intervention was clear: it would have been akin to what was being done by countless western experts deployed to teach Hungarians about democratization and marketization. This was especially true given what was at issue in these welfare institutions – expertise and the legitimization of knowledge. Similarly, using my social location as an analytical tool seemed equally irresponsible. Among other things, it felt like a self-indulgent way of appropriating the exotic other to learn more about myself.

Thus, instead of entering into these battles over expertise or using them to question my own position in the field, I once again extended the research outward. This involved two moves. First, I broadened the research to uncover the origins of this expert discourse, a move that took me back in time. More specifically, I supplemented the ethnographic work with an analysis of historical documents and with interviews with government officials and welfare professionals. Through this work, I discovered that the ubiquitous discourse of poverty regulation arose in the early 1980s as a critique of socialist welfare. It had been part of the emergent democratic opposition, a way for social scientists and activists to critique the seemingly discretionary character of state socialist policies and to argue for a welfare system more sensitive to the needs of the impoverished (Haney 2000).

In this way, welfare workers accurately portrayed their expertise as socially transformative; historically, it had been part of a social democratic critique of actually existing state socialism. Yet my historical work also uncovered that, by the late 1980s, this expert discourse was co-opted by another set of actors: global police officers from the International Monetary Fund and World Bank who used it to bolster their neo-liberal welfare agenda (Haney 2000). In effect, these agencies drew on a discourse of poverty regulation to justify the scaling back of the welfare state and the emergence of a system based exclusively on poor relief. So when clients argued that this discourse was a threat to their well-being, they were also correct; indeed, it had become a way to legitimize state retrenchment. Hence, by extending beyond the contemporary world of welfare, I was able to provide a context for and an explanation of the institutional politics of expertise.

The second way I extended the research outward took me even further back in time. As I continued to observe the conflicts between welfare workers and clients, it became increasingly clear that they were propelled by competing definitions not only of the present, but also of the past. While the California institutional conflicts had been motivated by alternative views of the community and what was possible within it, the Hungarian battles were shaped by different understandings of the socialist welfare system and what had been possible within it. Hence, to analyse these battles fully, I had to unearth what the Hungarian world of welfare looked like prior to the rise of an expert discourse of poverty regulation. This pushed the research into the realm of ethnohistory. It also added over a year to the data collection. To construct a view of the socialist welfare system from below, I systematically analysed over 1,200 case files from the welfare institutions included in my study, many of which stretched back to the inception of state socialism.

All of this historical work paid off. On the one hand, I began to see welfare workers' claims about their distinctive approach as historically accurate. Indeed, under state socialism, welfare work had been far less specialized and more discretionary. And, indeed, early welfare workers rarely recognized client poverty, preferring instead to intervene into clients' lives to resolve other familial problems. On the other hand, clients' demands for fuller, more comprehensive assistance also became more understandable. Having been socialized in the previous system, which had accorded them considerable practical and discursive resources, they rightfully expected broader forms of social protection from the state. Thus, when seen from a historical perspective, these institutional battles began to make sense: they were struggles over changes in the meaning and connotations of state assistance (Haney 2002).

None of these insights would have surfaced had I confined my research to the ethnographic present. By extending the research outward and into the realm of ethnohistory, I was able to take women's competing definitions of the situation seriously. In short, my Hungarian research exposed how 'relations of the ruling' often must be historicized. It also illuminated how 'lineaments of oppression' can have historical roots and how researchers often must move backwards in time to capture them fully. In Smith's (1987) terms, it was necessary for me to leave the everyday world of the present before I could fully problematize it.

POLITICS OF REFLEXIVITY IN FEMINIST SOCIAL SCIENCE

In their methodological writings, feminist social scientists have made a number of convincing arguments about the importance of reflexive research.

For many of them, reflexivity has served as a powerful methodological and analytical tool. As a research strategy, reflexivity enabled them to become more sensitive to the power relations embedded in the research process (Krieger 1983; Stacey 1990). As an analytical tool, reflexivity allowed them to interrogate their own social location and to disentangle how it shaped their definition of the situation (Behar 1993, 1996). As a result, feminist scholars have produced new interpretations of the forms of power embedded in everyday life (Smith 1990). In its many incarnations, reflexivity permitted feminist scholars to investigate social relations of gender in an increasingly responsible and responsive way.

None of the reservations expressed in this chapter were meant to negate these contributions. Instead, they suggest that when it comes to research practices, scholars might want to think more seriously about the politics of reflexivity in different settings. Given the particularities of my ethnographic sites, turning the research into a collective dialogue or becoming more auto-biographical did not seem like a viable or desirable way to address the research challenges I confronted. Perhaps they would have seemed more viable in a setting where power relations were not enacted among women. Perhaps they would have seemed more desirable in a less divided setting where I was not pulled in conflicting directions. Thus, perhaps reflexivity should be understood in relationship to what is possible in different research contexts and environments. Just as gender itself is increasingly conceptual-ized as contextually and historically variable, so too should our methodo-logical approaches to studying it (Marshall 2000).

In an ironic twist, my struggles with conceptualizations of reflexivity actually reaffirmed my commitment to a key principle underlying the concept – doing social science in a way that does not harm the women I study. They also gave me new ways to transform my research practices to reflect this principle. Indeed, it is irresponsible to deny the power relations inherent in the researcher–researched relationship. Yet sometimes taking this seriously means that researchers should refrain from exposing their subjects to the social power of their analyses and texts. And sometimes this means resisting the temptation of turning the research into a shared dialogue or a method of collective understanding. It is understandable that many researchers choose to share their analyses with those they study, but it is also understandable why others opt not to. In my California and Hungarian research, this way of diffusing the power relations in my research could have had the opposite effect; it could have left the women I studied more vulner-able and exposed. A more contextual approach to reflexivity would therefore disentangle the *principle* from the *practice* – valuing our desire to be intellec-tually democratic, while acknowledging the multiple ways we can reach this end in our research practices.

Yet another principle was reaffirmed through my struggles with reflexivity: I became increasingly aware of how social research can help those we study. When confronted with the complex politics of ethnographic practice, I opted not to turn inward, to the realm of autobiography. Instead, I extended outward to look more broadly at the social world. This enabled me to keep sight of one of the main goals of feminist social science: to illuminate the gendered relations of the ruling. There is an undeniable politics to feminist social science, one that cannot be reduced to our own biographies or to our relationship to the groups we study. This politics stretches into institutional structures, community life and historical legacies. My struggles with reflexivity in both the California and Hungarian projects highlighted this larger context and how, in order to capture it, I had to extend outward in time and space. Once again, a more contextual approach to reflexivity would encompass this recognition. Such an approach would prompt us to acknowledge how our positions as social scientists accord us a uniquely broad perspective on social life. And it would accentuate how we can and should use these positions to extend beyond the ethnographic present, thus exposing the structural and historical forces that work to constrain and enable women in everyday life.

NOTES

1 See Haney (1996) for a full explication of my empirical findings in this study, as well as an abridged discussion of many of the methodological issues raised in this chapter.
2 For a more detailed discussion of how and why I selected these particular field sites, see Haney (1996).
3 See Haney (2002) for an extensive discussion of this study's empirical findings as well as the methodological issues I confronted while I conducted the research.

REFERENCES

Abramovitz, M. (1988) *Regulating the Lives of Women: Social Welfare Policy from Colonial Times to the Present*. Boston, MA: South End.

Behar, R. (1993) *Translated Woman: Crossing the Border with Esperanza's Story*. Boston, MA: Beacon.

Behar, R. (1996) *The Vulnerable Observer: Anthropology that Breaks your Heart*. Boston, MA: Beacon.

Boris, E. and Bardaglio, P. (1983) 'The transformation of patriarchy: the historic role of the state', in I. Diamond (ed.) *Families, Politics and Public Policy*. New York: Longman.

Brown, C. (1981) 'Mothers, fathers and children: from private to public patriarchy', in L. Sargent (ed.) *Women and Revolution*. Boston, MA: South End.

Burnstyn, V. (1983) 'Masculine dominance and the state', in R. Miliband and J. Saville (eds) *The Socialist Register*. London: Merlin.

Collins, P.H. (2000) *Black Feminist Thought: Knowledge, Consciousness, and the Politics of Empowerment*. New York: Routledge.

Fonow, M. and Cook, J. (1991) *Beyond Methodology*. Bloomington, IN: Indiana University Press.

Gordon, L. (1994) *Pitied but not Entitled: Single Mothers and the History of Welfare*. Cambridge, MA: Harvard University Press.

Haney, L. (1996) 'Homeboys, babies, men in suits: the state and the reproduction of male dominance', *American Sociological Review* 61(5): 759–778.

Haney, L. (1997) '"But we are still mothers": gender and the construction of need in postsocialist Hungary', *Social Politics* 4(2): 208–244.

Haney, L. (2000) 'Global discourses of need: mythologizing and pathologizing welfare in Hungary', in M. Burawoy *et al.*, *Global Ethnography: Forces, Connections, and Imaginations in a Postmodern World*. Berkeley, CA: University of California Press.

Haney, L. (2002) *Inventing the Needy: Gender and the Politics of Welfare in Hungary*. Berkeley, CA: University of California Press.

Haraway, D. (1991) *Simians, Cyborgs, and Women*. New York: Routledge.

Harding, S. (1991) *Whose Science? Whose Knowledge?* Bloomington, IN: Indiana University Press.

Harding, S. (1998) *Is Science Multicultural?* Bloomington, IN: Indiana University Press.

Hartsock, N. (1987) 'The feminist standpoint: developing the ground for specifically feminist historical materialism', in S. Harding (ed.) *Feminism and Methodology*. Bloomington, IN: Indiana University Press.

Krieger, S. (1983) *The Mirror Dance: Identity in a Women's Community*. Philadelphia, PA: Temple University Press.

Kunzel, R. (1993) *Fallen Women, Problem Girls: Unmarried Mothers and the Professionalization of Social Work, 1890–1945*. New Haven, CT: Yale University Press.

McIntosh, M. (1978) 'The state and the oppression of women', in A. Kuhn and A. Wolpe (eds) *Feminism and Materialism*. London: Routledge.

MacKinnon, C. (1989) *Toward a Feminist Theory of the State*. Cambridge, MA: Harvard University Press.

Marshall, B. (2000) *Configuring Gender: Explorations in Theory and Practice*. Peterborough: Broadview.

Orloff, A. (1993) 'Gender and the social rights of citizenship', *American Sociological Review* 58: 303–328.

Pateman, C. (1988) *The Sexual Contract*. Stanford, CA: Stanford University Press.

Reinharz, S. (1992) *Feminist Methods in Social Research*. New York: Oxford University Press.

Sandoval, C. (1991) 'U.S. Third World feminism: the theory and method of oppositional consciousness in the postmodern world', *Genders* 10: 2–24.

Smith, D. (1987) *The Everyday World as Problematic: A Sociology for Women*. Boston, MA: Northeastern University Press.

Smith, D. (1990) *The Conceptual Practices of Power: A Feminist Sociology of Knowledge*. Boston, MA: Northeastern University Press.

Stacey, J. (1988) 'Can there be a feminist ethnography?', *Women's Studies International Forum* 11: 21–28.

Stacey, J. (1990) *Brave New Families*. New York: Basic Books.

Young, I.M. (1995) 'Gender as seriality: thinking about women as a social collective', in L. Nicholson and S. Seidman (eds) *Social Postmodernism*. Cambridge: Cambridge University Press.

Zaretsky, E. (1982) 'The place of the family in the origins of the welfare state', in B. Thorne and M. Yalom (eds) *Rethinking the Family*. New York: Longman.

14 ON RELATIONS BETWEEN BLACK FEMALE RESEARCHERS AND PARTICIPANTS

Tracey Reynolds

A traditional claim within social research is that the interview process produces an unequal exchange between the 'powerful researcher' and the 'powerless research participant' (Katz 1996). A key factor underpinning such a claim is the idea that interviews actively encourage research participants to disclose what is often very personal and intimate detail of their lives, only then to have these accounts objectified, dissected and scrutinized. In contrast researchers reveal little personal information about their own lives and furthermore control the research process through, for example, the selection and analysis of the research data (Holland and Ramazanoglu 1994). Feminist researchers, among others, have long challenged claims of the 'objective' researchers who remain detached from and in control of their subject of inquiry. Despite these claims there still persists an understanding of the research relationship determined by the 'powerful researcher' and 'power-less research participant'. Power within such a context is constructed as one-directional and unitary, stemming from a single source: flowing from the researcher down to the research participant. Furthermore, it negates the multiple and complex ways in which power is understood and exercised by the researcher and research participant.

This chapter explores the interactional, contextual and transitory nature of power relations between the researcher and research participant within the research process. I suggest that structural divisions in society, such as race, class and gender divisions, and in particular the differing class, race and gender status of the researcher and research participant directly influences power relations in this research relationship.

TELLING MY STORY: A PERSONAL PERSPECTIVE OF A BLACK FEMALE RESEARCHER INTERVIEWING BLACK WOMEN

My thinking concerning the problematical and shifting position of power relations within the research first emerged as a result of my own experiences interviewing other Black women.[1] During 1996, as part of my PhD thesis, I conducted in-depth qualitative interviews with twenty Black mothers, living in London. The study set out to investigate the mothering experiences of Black women, and in particular the effects of race, racism and cultural identity in structuring their mothering identity (see Reynolds 1999). A key idea of the study was to position Black women as active and participatory subjects of social research. Consequently the mothers in the study assumed a central role in constructing and 'giving voice' to their multiple and diverse experiences. Their central role within the interview process support the view promoted by Black feminist standpoint theory that Black women need to take up a central position in (re)naming and (re)defining their own lives (Hill-Collins 1991; Afshar and Maynard 1994). In terms of the actual interview, each of the women was interviewed by myself on a single occasion, with each interview lasting three to four hours on average. The age range of the mothers that participated in the study was very wide (from 18 to 81 years) and encompassed women who were not only mothers but also grandmothers and great-grandmothers (five in total). This wide age range was beneficial to the study because it allowed an understanding of how age and generation difference between myself, as researcher, and the mothers, as research participants, can influence power relations during the research process.

From the very onset when I was thinking about the issue of sample size and data collection, my assumption that it would be easy for me as a Black woman to find other Black women willing to participate in the study was immediately challenged. My initial request for interview met with an ambivalent response by the mothers. The mothers' ages were a particular factor to these varying responses. The (relationally) younger Black mothers (what I term in the study 'second' and 'third' generation mothers)[2] openly welcomed my request to be interviewed for the study.[3] In contrast the vast majority of older mothers (age 50 years or more and 'first' generation mothers) viewed my request for interview with a greater sense of unease, suspicion and mistrust. I had to work hard to overcome this initial resistance by these women. In order to do so I turned to people who were well liked, trusted and respected within the local Black community, for example Black community workers and senior members of the Black church, as my first points of access to these mothers. After explaining the purpose of the study and my exact role within this, I was given the names of women who might be willing to take part in the study. The actions of these community members can be likened to that of a 'gatekeeper' (Walsh 1998; de Vaus 2001), controlling my access to the older mothers. Traditionally used in professional and organizational settings, gatekeepers work to protect the interests of their particular organization, professional body or in other instances the vulnerable groups in society (for example, children and mentally ill people). However, as David Walsh (1998) notes, unofficial 'gatekeepers' also exist in various group settings to ensure that their particular group or community is being represented in the best light. In my study the 'gatekeepers' wanted to make sure the research would not be used to further pathologize Black mothers and the wider Black community. Therefore the fact that I was a Black woman myself counted for little in terms of securing access to these Black mothers.

Angela McRobbie (1982) states that 'no research can be understood in a vacuum' and the Black mothers and the gatekeepers' responses to the study and towards me must be understood within this wider social context. Black women in Britain have historically occupied a problematic position within social research. With some notable exceptions, and primarily as a result of the work developed under Black feminist theory (see e.g. Bryan *et al.* 1985; Mirza 1997; Sudbury 1998; Lewis 2000), there has been a tendency for social research in Britain to identify Black women either as marginal to the debate or as occupying a pathological and problematical position in society. For example, social research has been used to apportion blame to Black women for many of the social problems existing within the Black community (i.e. poverty, unemployment, the educational underachievement of Black children) and identify them as responsible for the so-called breakdown of the Black family (Dench 1996; Berthoud 2001). So pervasive are these negative images of Black women across post-industrial western societies such as the UK and the USA that there was a feeling among the mothers that social research has contributed towards reinforcing such images. This in turn also influenced the mothers' willingness to participate in the study. As one mother explained to me:

> I'm always careful when people say that they doing research on us Black people. They take our stories and try to twist things so that we look bad. They have all of these professionals asking questions about how we live and our lifestyles and then they say that it's all our own faults because we don't have proper families, we don't have discipline, we don't know how to bring our children up properly. That's why I'm very careful what I say to people because they can turn around and use it against me. (Pearl, age 69, first generation Black mother)

As Pearl's quotation indicates, this reluctance by many of the older mothers to take part in the study represents a wider suspicion that their personal accounts and that of other Black women could unintentionally contribute towards this negative portrayal of Black women. Tellingly, the mothers also understood that despite my position as academic researcher, as a Black woman I was still subject to similar structural constraints as them on account of sharing the same race and gender location. As a consequence the mothers were highly aware that my role as interviewer did not automatically translate into me having power and control of the analysis and reporting of the data. There was no guarantee that others would not use their accounts to represent them negatively. I was frequently asked at the start of each interview who was I doing the research for? Was anyone else involved in the project? Would I be involved in the finally writing up of the study? Underpinning these questions was an implicit assumption and concern by the mothers that my role as researcher would be strictly limited to conducting the interviews. Another more powerful person (such as a white male academic) would have the responsibility for analysing and reporting the data.

Recent findings concerning Black women in academia would certainly support the Black mothers' concerns. Two articles that appeared in the *Times*

Higher Educational Supplement (2000) suggested that Black women in academia still continue to face sexual and racial discrimination and that Black female academics are overwhelmingly concentrated in short-term research posts. Similar studies by Haideh Moghissi (1994) and Penny Rhodes (1994) also report that a disproportionate number of Black female researchers are employed only in the fieldwork stages, and lack overall control of the research project.

IMPLICATIONS OF RACE, CLASS AND GENDER DIFFERENCE IN RETHINKING POWER RELATIONS

Power relations that exist between the researcher and the research partici- pant are in a constant state of flux because each of them moves to occupy a position of power and authority during the interview. At a very basic level, power may be vested with the researcher in terms of the design, implemen- tation and the final reporting of the data. However, the research participant also exercises power in terms of actively selecting the information they will make available to the researcher during the interviews. This is particularly true of research where there are limited research data available and the researcher is motivated to establish new ideas, generate new knowledge or gain new insight into social groups where little is known about them (Gilbert 1993; see also Kathleen Gerson and Ruth Horowitz, Chapter 9 in this volume). In terms of my own study the limited amount of literature concerning Black mothers in Britain meant that I had to depend heavily on the mothers' accounts of their experiences to generate a theory of Black mothering in Britain (see Reynolds 1999).[4] The limited options for me in turning to alter- native sources (i.e. related literature and policy reports) in which to gain information meant that in one sense the mothers exercised power and authority over me. However, in another way power and authority rested with me because I had ultimate control over the selection, interpretation and analysis of the information that they provided. Therefore the power relations between the mothers and myself, as researcher, involved a dynamic, fluid and two-way interactive process.

A reflexive understanding of power relations between the researcher and research participant in social research is inextricably linked to wider race, class and gender divisions in society. Diane Wolf (1996) suggests that domi- nant groups in society generally conduct research and more often than not their research focus is on groups and individuals who are less privileged than they are. For instance it is common practice for researchers of middle-class backgrounds to study working-class groups. Similarly, the research relation- ship of white female researchers and Black female research participants exists in a far greater proportion than Black female researchers who research white women's lives or indeed other Black women. In fact, one of the challenges within Black feminism has been to encourage more Black feminist researchers to undertake research addressing Black women's experiences (see Mirza 1992,

1997). This does not mean, however, that research undertaken by white female researchers among other groups on Black women is of little value and offers limited contribution to the debate. In addition to providing useful analysis, such research can also be viewed as a conscious attempt by white female researchers to understand the complexities of Black women lives, previously ignored, so that they can construct an inclusive model of womanhood that takes accounts of racial difference and diversity (for example, see Skeggs 1994).

Nonetheless, the research (im)balance between white female researcher and Black female research participant prevalent in much of social research points to the particular way that race, class and gender intersect and directly impact on research relationships. The commonly held research position of the white female researcher and Black female research participant is indicative of the racial privilege and power that white women possess in relation to Black women at societal level. Philomena Essed notes that their relational dominant position is sustained by 'cognitions, actions and procedures that contribute to the development and perpetuation of a system in which white dominate Blacks' (Essed 1991: 39). Therefore, even in instances whereby white women choose not to exercise power on an individual basis, the system is set up to benefit their interests and reinforce their structurally dominant position. Within the research process this often manifests itself in the way that white feminist researchers sometimes adopt a 'colour blind' approach to their study, or the way that they do not adequately consider the implications of race difference on power relations within research (Bhopal 1995).

In contrast, Black feminist researchers have little choice but to develop a reflexive understanding of the implications of their racialized and gendered status on the research process, and the way that this may inform power relations. Kum Kum Bhavnani's (1993) discussion concerning her interviews with a group of adolescents about their schooling is particularly useful in demonstrating how societal structural divisions directly impact on and transform power relations between the researcher and research participant. In her study Bhavnani, a female Asian researcher, interviewed a group of Asian schoolgirls and a group of white schoolboys of similar age and class background within a large multi-ethnic school. She reflects that during interviews with the group of white schoolboys power rested with the boys. It was the boys who dictated the format of the interviews and they also controlled the pace and style of questioning. In contrast, in her interviews with the Asian schoolgirls Bhavnani felt that she assumed the power in this relationship as a result of her being older than the girls and from an educated middle-class background. Interestingly, the Asian schoolgirls also perceived her as a figure of power and authority in a way that the white schoolboys did not. In attempting to theorize these changing power relations, Bhavnani comments:

> my age, and my assumed class affiliation may have been taken as sources of potential domination. However, my racialised and gender ascription suggested the opposite. That is, in this instance, the interviewees and myself were inscribed

within multi-faceted power relations which had structural dominance and structural subordination in play on both sides. (Bhavnani 1993: 101)

As this quotation indicates, Bhavnani's 'Asian-ness' and 'female-ness', two fundamental aspects of her personal identity, inscribed her a structurally subordinate status in relation to the white boys whose 'whiteness' and 'maleness' placed them in a structurally dominant location. Both Bhavnani and the schoolboys themselves recognized this factor and as a result she was not recognized by them as a figure of power and authority despite being older than the boys, educated and middle class compared to their working-class status. In essence Bhavnani's structurally subordinate gendered and racialized status prevented her from actively assuming power and authority at this small-scale and localized level of research.

I did not confront this issue of 'race' and gender difference on power relation in my own research because I share the same gender and racial status as the women I interviewed. In the absence of race and gender divisions, however, social class became an important factor in structuring power relations between the mothers and myself. Age and generation difference emerged as secondary concern. The mothers' understanding of their social class location and their perceptions of my own social class status in relation to themselves influenced their behaviour towards me (see also Steph Lawler, Chapter 11 in this volume). This understanding was based on a combination of objective (such as the Registrar-General and income levels) and subjective definitions of social class (access to cultural, social, economic and symbolic capital) (see also Reay 1998). Those mothers who viewed themselves as middle class generally did so on the grounds that they had greater access to economic (e.g. professional jobs with relatively high salaries) and cultural capital (e.g. academic and professional qualifications; professional networks etc.) than other Black women. In contrast those mothers who saw themselves as working class did so as a result of their limited access to such resources.

Based on the mothers' own individual assessments of social class difference during the interviews I alternated between being perceived by these women as occupying either a working-class or a middle-class status. Their perceptions directly influence their responses towards me and created a shifting power dynamic between us. Denise, a mother who defined herself as working class, offers a clear illustration of this. When I initially approached her for interview she commented:

Denise: Are you sure that you want to interview me?
T.R.:   Yes, why wouldn't I want to interview you?
Denise: I'm not educated like you. You're a *professional middle-class Black woman*. I'm just a hairdresser, a *working-class girl* and I don't know if I'll say the right things. I bet you never have that problem because you've got the same background with doctors and lawyers, people like that. (Denise, age 21, working-class mother, added emphasis)

Within the context of our research relationship it is clear that Denise perceives me as an educated professional middle-class woman. Rightly or wrongly she employs this assessment of my class location to make assumptions about me having what she associates as middle-class skills and attributes. Moreover, she does not see herself as possessing these same skills and attributes in equal measure as a result of her working-class location. Not explicitly revealed in this quotation, but nonetheless significant, is that Denise's positioning of me as middle class and a 'professional educated Black woman' enabled me to assume relative power and authority in my interview with her. From the very onset, she saw me as an authority figure and she allowed me to control the style and pace of the interview. Denise also organized her daily activities to fit around my time schedule (instead of vice versa) and during our interview she constantly sought reassurance from me that she was correctly answering the questions that I asked concerning her own mothering experiences.

This middle-class status I was given by Denise (as well as by some of the other working-class mothers) also created a taken-for-granted assumption that I had access to certain information and resources that they, as working-class women, would be restricted from accessing. Some of the working-class mothers, in particular those who had low educational attainment, would ask my opinion about the social and educational aspects of higher education. In addition they would ask my advice on career and housing matters and requested my help in obtaining information for them from officials because of a feeling that I would receive a more positive response than themselves. For example, Joy, a working-class mother, asked me to speak to her housing officer about an error made concerning an unpaid bill:

> I keep calling them and they just keep pushing from one person to another. Could you come with me when I go up there again next week? If you explain things, it'll sound better coming from you? I bet they'll listen to you. They'll take you more seriously. (Joy)

Both Denise's and Joy's quotations demonstrate that not only was I considered as the 'powerful researcher' within the interview context but also I was viewed as having a more powerful status than these mothers in wider society as a consequence of my assumed middle-class location.[5]

The research relationship was somewhat different in the interviews with the Black mothers who viewed themselves as middle class. It quickly became apparent that these mothers were keen to establish power and control of the interviews. In contrast to some of the working-class mothers who were intimidated by my researcher status, and flattered that I was interested in what they had to say about their lives, many of these mothers considered themselves equal to or of a higher status to me, the researcher. As a consequence, in all but two interviews I was informed in advance of the amount of time that I would be allocated for interview and in each instance the mothers were keen that I establish my academic credentials and research knowledge.

The mothers working in the high-status professional occupations (e.g. solicitor, chief executive of a mental health trust, doctor and senior lecturer) also requested copies of the full interview transcripts and they asked to see my research findings before they were published. Another striking aspect when comparing my interview experiences was the way that these mothers talked in more generalized terms about Black mothers in Britain and discussed in less detail their personal and individual experiences. The research relationship between these women and myself involved more negotiation around trading information – each question that I asked is followed by a question from the mothers about my own personal experiences – than the working-class mothers. This treatment of the interviews marked a significant departure from the usual understanding of the interview process where it is the role of the researcher to explicate information from the research participant and it is the role of the research participant to offer up the necessary information.

Alongside the class difference, the wide generation difference between myself and four of the older mothers (aged 81, 76, 65 and 61 respectively) also dramatically impacted on challenging the notion of the 'powerful researcher'. Yet, with notable exceptions (see e.g. Titley and Chasey 1996), age and generation difference as a factor in altering power relations between the researcher and research participant has received limited critical attention. During these interviews I felt intimidated by the wide age difference and the fact that these mothers possess a wealth of experience. My own cultural background also meant that I was raised to respect my elders and not question them on matters that would prove to be embarrassing or intrusive for fear of appearing disrespectful. As a consequence I felt reluctant in posing questions to these mothers that I had no problems asking the younger Black women, such as the discussion areas that centred on constructions of Black female sexuality and sexual identity. In this instance, I felt once again that power and authority rested with the research participants, contradicting the traditional viewpoint of the 'powerful researcher'.

CONCLUSION

In conclusion I would say that my position as a Black female researcher interviewing Black women provided an interesting challenge to the notion of the 'powerful researcher' who exercises power and authority over the 'powerless researcher'. The research revealed that 'powerful researcher' is not a given aspect of social research and that this is very much contingent upon structural differences such as race, class and gender divisions. As this chapter vividly illustrates, racial and gender privilege and dominance of certain groups in society can, in interviews, translate into power and dominance over social groups subordinated to them, irrespective of whether they are the researcher or research participant. Where the researcher and research participant share the same racial and gender position, such as a Black female researcher interviewing Black women, power between the two groups is primarily negotiated through other factors such as social class and age difference. This interaction between race, class and gender suggest that power in social research is not a fixed and unitary construct, exercised by the researcher over the research participant. Instead, as I attempt to highlight in this chapter, power is multifaceted, relational and interactional and is constantly shifting and renegotiating itself between the researcher and the research participant according to differing contexts and their differing structural locations. Consequently, any understanding of Black women's experiences within social research needs to be viewed in the context of their wider structural location in society.

NOTES

1   The Black mothers and myself are all of African Caribbean origin.
2   The 'second' and 'third' generation mothers are those women who were born in Britain from the 1960s onwards. In contrast 'first' generation mothers refers to those women who were born in the Caribbean and migrated to Britain as adult women or young girls during the period of mass migration of Caribbean people as a result of the rebuilding programme in Britain during the post-war years.
3   The main reason for this was that I had been personally recommended to them by a mutual friend. There is also the belief that because I am closer in age to these women they could relate to me better but I concede that this view is largely unsubstantiated.
4   After the fieldwork stage of the research a major study by Goulbourne and Chamberlain (1999) investigated Caribbean families in Britain.
5   There was also the other ethical issue here concerning research boundaries. It was difficult to maintain these boundaries at times and keep solely to my role as researcher but I sought to overcome by acting as a 'referral agent', passing the mothers on to agencies who would be able to directly assist them.

REFERENCES

Afshar, S. and Maynard, M. (eds) (1994) *The Dynamics of Race and Gender: Some Feminist Interventions*. London: Taylor and Francis.

Berthoud, R. (2001) 'Family formation in multi-cultural Britain', paper presented at one day conference, Changing Family Patterns in Multi-Cultural Britain, National Parenting and Family Institute, London.

Bhavnani, K. (1993) 'Tracing the contours: feminist research and feminist objectivity', *Women's Study International Forum* 16(2): 95–104.

Bhopal, K. (1995) 'Women and feminism as subjects as Black Study: the difficulties and dilemmas of doing fieldwork', *Journal of Gender Studies* 4(2): 153–168.

Bryan, B., Dadzie, S. and Scafe, S. (1985) *The Heart of the Race: Black Women's Lives in Britain*. London: Virago.

Dench, G. (1996) *The Changing Place of Men in Family Cultures*. London: Institute of Community Studies.

De Vaus, D. (2001) *Research Design in Social Research*. London: Sage.

Essed, P. (1991) *Understanding Everyday Racism*. Newbury Park, CA: Sage.

Gilbert, N. (1993) *Researching Social Life*. London: Sage.

Goulbourne, H. and Chamberlain, M. (1999) *The Caribbean Family and Living Arrangements in the Trans-Atlantic World*. London: Macmillan.

Hill-Collins, P. (1991) 'Learning from the outsider within: the sociological significance of Black feminist thought', in M. Fonow and J. Cook (eds) *Beyond Methodology: Feminist Scholarship as Lived Research*. Bloomington, IN: Indiana University Press.

Holland, J. and Ramazanoglu, C. (1994) 'Coming to conclusions: interpretation in researching young women's sexuality', in M. Maynard and J. Purvis (eds) *Researching Women's Lives from a Feminist Perspective*. London: Taylor and Francis.

Katz, C. (1996) 'The expeditions of conjurers: ethnography, power and pretense', in D. Wolf (ed.) *Feminist Dilemmas in Fieldwork*. Boulder, CO: Westview.

Lewis, G. (2000) *Race, Gender and Social Welfare*. London: Polity.

McRobbie, A. (1982) 'The politics of feminist research: between talk, text and action', *Feminist Review* 12: 46–57.

Mama, A. (1993) 'Women's abuse in London's Black communities', in W. James and C. Harris (eds) *Inside Babylon: The Caribbean Diaspora in Britain*. London: Verso.

Mirza, H. (1992) *Young, Female and Black*. London: Routledge.

Mirza, H. (ed.) (1997) *Black British Feminism*. London: Routledge.

Moghissi, H. (1994) 'Sexism and racism in academic practice', in S. Afshar and M. Maynard (eds) *The Dynamics of Race and Gender: Some Feminist Interventions*. London: Taylor and Francis.

Reay, D. (1998) *Class Work: Mothers' Involvement in their Children's Primary Schooling*. London: Taylor and Francis.

Reynolds, T. (1999) 'African-Caribbean mothering: reconstructing a "new" identity', unpublished PhD thesis, South Bank University, London.

Rhodes, P. (1994) 'Race-of-interviewer effects in qualitative research', *Sociology* 28(2): 547–558.

Skeggs, B. (1994) 'Refusing to be civilised; "race", sexuality and power', in S. Afshar and M. Maynard (eds) *The Dynamics of Race and Gender: Some Feminist Interventions*. London: Taylor and Francis.

Sudbury, J. (1998) *Other Kinds of Dreams: Black Women's Organisations and the Politics of Transformations*. London: Routledge.

Times Higher Educational Supplement (2000) '2.3% and 9.8%...', 7 April: 18–19; 'Stopped by the unsound barrier', 14 April: 22–23.

Titley, M. and Chasey, B. (1996) 'Across difference of age: young women speaking of and with old women', in S. Wilkinson and C. Kitizinger (eds) *Representing the Other: A Feminist and Psychology Reader*. London: Sage.

Walsh, D. (1998) 'Doing ethnography', in C. Seale (ed.) *Researching Society and Culture*. London: Sage.

Wolf, D. (ed.) (1996) *Feminist Dilemmas in Fieldwork*. Boulder, CO: Westview.

PART 5

REFLEXIVITY, THE SELF AND POSITIONING

15 ETHNOGRAPHY AND SELF:

Reflections and representations

Amanda Coffey

The relationships between researcher and researched have always been the subject of debate and scrutiny in qualitative research. Qualitative methods texts, for example, have always, as a matter of course, offered comment and advice on personal field roles and managing relationships in the field. Often this has focused on pragmatic issues such as guarding against over-familiarity and the effects of context on the relationships that are formed in the field. The general emphasis has conventionally been on the negotiation and craft-ing of personal and social 'research' relationships in order to facilitate the expedient collection of data. But increasingly, attention has been paid to the range of experiences and emotions that are part and parcel of undertaking (qualitative) research. Here, the researcher-self has become a source of reflec-tion and re-examination; to be written about, challenged and, in some instances celebrated. In more general terms, the personal narrative has developed as a significant preoccupation for many of those who espouse qualitative research strategies (Atkinson and Silverman 1997). There is an increasingly widespread assumption that personal narratives offer uniquely privileged data of the social world; personal narratives (re)present data that are grounded in both social contexts and biographical experiences. The per-sonal narratives of the *researcher* have formed part of this movement, to be told, collected and (re)presented in the research and writing processes. In the course of these developments the auto/biographical *work* of utilizing quali-tative research strategies has been centrally located.

It has long been recognized that ethnographic or qualitative fieldwork has a biographical dimension. Ethnographers are, after all, concerned with observing, (re)constructing and writing lives and experiences of *Others*. In writing and representing the social world they are primarily analysing and reproducing lives (Stanley 1993) and in this context the researcher serves as a biographer of *Others*.

> While disclosure of intimate details of the lives of those typically under the ethno-graphic gaze (the informants) has long been an acceptable and expected aspect of ethnographic research and writing self-disclosure among ethnographers

themselves has been less acceptable and much less common. (Reed-Danahay 2001: 407)

But the qualitative researcher or ethnographer are simultaneously involved in auto/biographical work of their own. The personal approach is certainly not a new direction for ethnography (see Reed-Danahay 2001 for a useful summary), although personal narratives of fieldwork have often been positioned as a parallel trope (to the more formal ethnographic text or monograph). Field notes and research journals have long been used to record the feelings, emotions and personal identity work that can come with prolonged research engagement (see Sanjek 1990). Indeed there are a variety of ways in which qualitative researchers (authors) have reflected upon and written about the self in *or* as texts of the field. These range from personal accounts of the research process, through 'confessional tales' of fieldwork (cf. Van Maanen 1988), to autoethnography (Ellis and Bochner 2000). Some position the self as an integral part of the broader research process; some pay particular attention to the ethnographer-as-author; others centre the researcher's life as subject as well as the researcher and producer of the text.

This chapter explores these relations between qualitative research, representation and self. The chapter locates 'writing the self' within contemporary ethnography, and seeks to explore the intertextuality of, and the boundaries between, ethnography and autobiography. The chapter documents some of the ways in which the self has been revealed in qualitative writing, and considers recent (though thus far marginal) moves toward autoethnography. The chapter has four main sections. First, I locate issues of self and representation within an historical narrative of ethnography and qualitative methods more generally. Second, I consider the ways in which the self has been positioned and (re)presented in conventional ethnographic texts. Third, I explore contemporary ethnographic representations and the ways in which these evoke the intertextuality of ethnography and (auto)-biography. Finally I discuss the rise of autoethnography. The autobiographical turn with/in ethnography can be seen, in part, as a response to the sustained and valid critiques of ethnographic texts, and has much to commend it. However, the counterclaims of overindulgence and narcissism demand that the (re)production of the self with/in the text is critically examined, and (perhaps) approached with caution.

CRISIS, CREATIVITY AND FUTURES

The historical framework of qualitative research developed by Denzin and Lincoln (1994, 2000), captures the sense of diversity in qualitative work, as well as locating the (auto)biographical turn. In their original schema Denzin and Lincoln (1994) identified 'five moments' of qualitative research. The first moment was identified as part of a positivist programme, and was sustained by the myth of the heroic, lone fieldworker. This moment, the time of 'traditional' qualitative research, spanned 1900 to the Second World War, and was concerned with 'offering valid, reliable, and objective interpretations' of the social world (Denzin and Lincoln 1994: 7). The second moment (from 1950 to 1970) is located within modernism, and marked by both enhanced creativity and attempts to formalize qualitative research methods. This moment built upon the 'canonical works of the traditional period', marked the beginnings of the qualitative methods text, and was a 'moment of creative ferment', whereby 'the modernist ethnographer and sociological participant observer attempted rigorous qualitative studies of important social processes, including deviance and social control in the classroom and society' (Denzin and Lincoln 2000: 14).

The third moment, that of 'blurred genres', was marked by a new multiplicity of theoretical orientations and alternative paradigms, alongside the development of new strategies for data collection and analysis. This era (from 1970 to 1986) saw the publication of what came to be definitive texts on qualitative methods, for example Lofland (1971) in the USA; Hammersley and Atkinson (1983) and Burgess (1984) in the UK; as well as the establishment of a range of qualitative journals. Geertz (1973, 1983) called for 'thick description', and opened up debates about the nature of cultural representation. It is during this era that the author's presence in the text came to be increasingly recognized and visible. These themes are followed through into the 1990s and the fourth moment, where qualitative methods experienced crises, consolidation and experimentation.

The fourth moment coincides with the so-called crises of legitimation and representation in ethnographic research (Atkinson and Coffey 1995). Here the received canons of truth and method were challenged, not least through the critical examination of textual practices. This moment was signalled by the publication of *Writing Culture* (Clifford and Marcus 1986) and placed in hazard both the textual products of qualitative work, and the authority of the researcher. One of the main consequences of the fourth moment has been variously termed the linguistic turn, the interpretative turn and the rhetorical turn, and an enhanced awareness of ethnographic writing (and indeed representation). Hence the revisiting of qualitative accounts and analyses has taken place, in order to grapple with issues of legitimacy, authority and the conventionality of texts. This has heralded the movement of qualitative research into new directions and representational territories.

The fifth moment – 'the postmodern period of experimental ethnographic writing' (Denzin and Lincoln 2000: 17) – characterizes contemporary ethnography of the mid-1990s through diversity and a continuing series of tensions. It aims to make sense of crises of legitimation, representation and praxis, and to respond to postmodernism and the interpretive turn. In their earlier developed account of this moment Lincoln and Denzin (1994) observed that

> Qualitative research embraces two tensions at the same time. On the one hand, it is drawn to a broad, interpretative, postmodern, feminist, and critical sensibility.

On the other hand, it can also be drawn to a more narrowly defined positivist, postpositivist, humanistic and naturalistic conceptions of human experience and its analysis. (Lincoln and Denzin 1994: 576)

Denzin and Lincoln identify a sixth 'messy' moment (see Denzin 1997) that captures the discourses of the late 1990s. This notes the emergence of 'a cacophony of voices speaking with various agendas' (Lincoln and Denzin 1998: 409) and is characterized by reflexive, experimental texts, multiple stories, styles and futures (Atkinson *et al.* 1999). There is little doubt as to the general existence of this multiplicity that Denzin and Lincoln identify, and their characterization of contemporary ethnography identifies and captures the diversity of contemporary ethnography. While this kind of periodization is a useful means of attempting to document historical and contemporary developments (especially so in terms of representation), it can be criticized as presenting an overly rigid characterization (see Atkinson *et al.* 1999; Coffey 1999; Delamont *et al.* 2000). Denzin and Lincoln's 'moments', certainly the earlier ones, are perhaps too neatly packaged, and the contrasts too heavily drawn between earlier and later eras. This perhaps does a disservice to earlier generations of qualitative scholars, while at the same time implying that *all* contemporary qualitative research takes place in an intellectual field teeming with contested ideas and set against a backdrop of a carnivalesque diversity of standpoints, methods and representations. It is misleading to limit variety and diversity to more recent times, as ethnographic research has always contained within it a variety of perspectives and many contemporary ethnographers continue to draw on classic (formalist) modes of field research (and representational styles). However, the general developmental thrust and identification of tensions and shifts contained in the moments model are useful for examining the relationships between ethnography, representation and self.

The researcher self is most visible in the latter moments of the Denzin and Lincoln model. That is not to say that past generations of researchers have failed to experience fieldwork in emotional, subjective and personal ways. But recent articulations provide a more recognizable and acceptable environment in which to confront and represent the (auto)biographical. The literary or interpretive turn has made it easier to utilize (auto)biographical and personal narrative genres. In addition, the significant contributions of postmodernism and feminism have encouraged views of the social world in terms of multiple voices and perspectives. Denzin and Lincoln's sixth moment, for example, points to experimental representational styles that disrupt and recentre the self. And in Lincoln and Denzin's (2000) vision of the future of qualitative research – the seventh moment – these themes are recurrent and consolidated. The seventh moment 'connects the past with the present and the future' and qualitative inquiry is imagined in the twenty-first century as 'simultaneously minimal, existential, autoethnographic, vulnerable, performative and critical' (Lincoln and Denzin 2000: 1,048). Selves, autobiographical ethnography, representation and performance are all part of an envisaged future of qualitative work. There is an emphasis on 'making ourselves visible in our texts' (2000: 1,053); and on not one future but many, not

> one 'moment', but rather many; not one 'voice', but polyvocality; not one story, but many tales, dramas, pieces of fiction, fables, memories, histories, autobiographies, poems and other texts to inform our sense of lifeways, to extend our understandings of the Other, to provide us with the material for 'cultural critique'. (Lincoln and Denzin 2000: 1,060)

Qualitative research then in the twenty-first century is drawing upon earlier moments, crises and critiques in order to take stock and move forward. Emergent in this is the consolidation of the personal and ethnographic self, and the continuing development of strategies to return the ethnographer/researcher/author/self to the qualitative text.

REVEALING/RETURNING THE ETHNOGRAPHER

In recent articulations of the presents and futures of qualitative inquiry it is easy to assume that the self in the text is a relatively recent phenomenon. And to some extent this assumption has merit. In Denzin and Lincoln's analysis the self is most clearly revealed from the mid-1980s – the fourth moment – and the crises of legitimation and representation. As part of the rethinking of ethnographic and qualitative texts, authorship, authenticity and voice have all been repositioned (see Chapters 8, 16 and 17 by Walkerdine et al. Adkins and Skeggs in this volume) and innovative ways adopted as mechanisms for writing the self into the text. But it is worth acknowledging that there are a range of examples of those engaged in ethnographic or qualitative research reflecting upon and rewriting the self into research texts and representations. These are not all new, or necessarily innovative. They include field notes and research diaries, personal narratives of the research process and confessional tales, as well as tales of the self, which treat the self as the unit of analysis and/or subject of representation. All of these recognize, though to differing degrees, the authorship of research texts and the positionality of the self within both the research and representational processes.

Field notes and journals are an obvious and longstanding form of embracing the self in the products of qualitative research, though they are often overlooked as such. These are the building blocks of qualitative research, a place for the accumulation of data and reflections. Field journals, personified in the diaries of the social anthropologist Malinowski (1967), serve as classic examples of these (textual) products. Field journals and diaries provide textual, though often private, space for the recording of research experiences, feelings and emotions. These kinds of texts are usually kept separate from 'data' field notes of the research setting, people, places and events. While personal, autobiographical narratives may form part of field-note writing, this does not necessarily imply any kind of public reflection or reclaiming of the self. Field notes are private texts and are rarely shared in their raw form. Quoted field-note extracts are usually tidied up or edited, and relatively few researchers choose to share their personal 'sacred' diaries of the field (Lederman 1990). Yet while there is now a greater tolerance or expectation of a revealing of the self in the ethnographic text, the personal has never been subordinate in the private world of field notes. It is the textual *visibility* of the self that has undergone transformation.

It has become an increasingly common feature of qualitative research, certainly since the mid-1970s or so, to produce personal narratives of the qualitative research process. However, it is still relatively common practice to separate these personal accounts from the data or analysis proper. Confessional tales of the field (cf. Van Mannen 1988) or 'fables of rapport' (Clifford 1983) are still more usually written as parallel adjuncts to the research monograph. Indeed conventions of writing about the self in the research process continue to reinforce the ethnographer as split personality – the authorial monograph writer and the personal self. So while it is increasingly construed as acceptable, and even desirable, to (re)construct and (re)write the self, there is still ambivalence about how far such practices and texts should be part of, or divert us from, 'telling the story of the field'. Collections such as Hobbs and May (1992) and Lareau and Shultz (1996) recapitulate some of the general themes of this genre of confessional tale – revealing some of the personal sides of fieldwork and dealing with problematics such as access, immersion, departure, field roles and so on. Senior anthropologists in *Others Knowing Others* (Fowler and Hardesty 1994) provide further exemplification. Here personal portraits are painted of the discipline, long-term fieldwork and reformulations of the self through time and place. The conceptualization of ethnographer as voyager is a common theme of these confessional tales or personal fieldwork stories (Atkinson 1990, 1996). The researcher is (re)presented as a naive explorer or social intruder who learns to live on the margins, engaging in a quest of discovery, and maybe learning something about themselves along the way. The confessional allows for self-revelation and indiscretion, but within a recognizable and acceptable format. Whyte's semi-autobiographical account of the evolution of fieldwork for *Street Corner Society* (Whyte 1981) is a classic example of this kind. He admits to a lack of confidence, to incompetence and ignorance. He presents a narrative of learning by trial-and-error, getting by, of mistakes and survival. He presents himself as human, fallible and with no exceptional powers. As such confessional tales

> provide clarity of how methodological goals such as building rapport are translated into action. They provide insight into the kinds of factors other researchers considered when they stumbled into difficulty and the strategies – for example, of reflection and data analysis – that researchers used to extract themselves from their temporary woes. More to the point, they highlight the uncertainty and confusion that inevitably accompany field research. (Lareau and Shultz 1996: 2–3)

Despite their increasing acceptance as part of the research endeavour, these personal tales of qualitative inquiry are still cautious in the ways in which they approach the subject of self. Usually located alongside the ethnographic text proper, these accounts may actually serve to isolate, rather than integrate, the self. The confessional genre is one of description rather than analysis, presenting a version of the self as mediating, consequential or problematic – and hence revealing only a semi-detached or partial self.

Some authors have chosen to take the relationship between research, the text and the self to different dimensions; locating the self more centrally in the contexts and products of qualitative inquiry. These have taken a number of forms. For example research monographs such as Kondo's *Crafting Selves* (1990) and Fordham's *Blacked Out* (1996) present multilayered texts that challenge the dichotomy between researcher and researched, author and Other. These authors frame their accounts with personal reflexive views of the self. Their accounts are situated with/in their personal experiences and sense making. The authors form part of the representational processes in which they are engaging. Thus the 'story' of (in these instances) the Japanese workplace and the African American School are interwoven with personal journeys and narrations. In other instances the autobiographical has been used more substantively as a basis for data collection, analysis and understanding. Early versions of this approach utilized personal life experiences as the basis for modest fieldwork, (re)presented in conventional ways. For example Delamont (1987) and Beynon (1987) chose to write ethnographic accounts about hospital stays, although both were keen to play down the scholarly contributions of their pieces. Neither used them as reflexive writings on the relationships between the self, the field and the text. Indeed the self is distanced and even apologized for. Both used the collection of field notes as mechanisms for getting through and understanding personal medical events, and did not undertake to claim more than that. To some extent the distinction can be implicitly drawn here between therapy (using field notes as a means of getting through and understanding periods of illness) and ethnography (Ellis and Bochner 2000) – a point to which I return later in this chapter.

Contemporary ethnographic writing on illness and the body further blurs boundaries between ethnography and autobiography. For example Sparkes's (1996) ethnographic body narrative is personal and highly reflexive. Using extended diary entries and personal conversations, Sparkes reconstructs his failing body-self over his biographical career. His body-self is centrally positioned in his text and analysis. This gives a performative quality to the piece, and positions it in terms of autobiographical writing and reflection. The following extract is illustrative of this.

Spotting for a rest I turn toward Kitty, my wife, who is 6 months pregnant. 'Déjà vu' I say to her, 'It's happening again.' The tears well up in her eyes and we hold each other close in the corridor. I kiss her on the cheeks. I kiss her eyes. As the roundness of her stomach presses against me a wave of guilt washes over me. Kitty is pregnant, so tired, caring for Jessica our daughter (3 years old at the time) and now having to worry and cope with the stress of me and my body failure. My uselessness makes me angry with my body. At the moment I *hate* it intensely. (Sparkes 1996: 468, original emphasis)

Sparkes's text presents a rather different relationship between ethnography and the self. The personal and the ethnographic are interwoven and over-lapping. It can be located within a wave of autobiographical-ethnographic writing that has taken the self as the focus of inquiry. Much of this writing has focused on issues of illness and the body. For example Paget (1990, 1993) provides moving ethnographic accounts of living (and dying) with cancer, Kolker (1996) reflects upon battles with breast cancer and Tillmann-Healy (1996) has written evocative text on her ongoing relationship with the eating disorder bulimia:

In the spring of 1986, at the age of 15, I invited bulimia to come to live with me. She never moved out. Sometimes I tuck her deep in my closet behind forgotten dresses and old shoes. Then one day, I'll come across her – as if by accident – and experi-ence genuine surprise that she remains with me. Other times, for a few days or perhaps a week or month, she'll emerge from that closet to sleep at my side, closer than a sister or lover would. This is our story. (Tillmann-Healy 1996: 76)

These ethnographic texts are not, then, tales of the naive incompetent, over-coming adversity and difficulty in the quest for data. They are not simply providing personalized accounts of fieldwork or the research process. Rather, the self and the field become one – ethnography and autobiography are symbiotic. In these instances writing and representing reveals, consoli-dates and disrupts the self (or selves). In the next section of this chapter I turn to these (new) relations between the self and the (textual) products of ethnography.

PERFORMANCE, POETICS AND AUTOETHNOGRAPHY

Representation has become both contested and innovative in contemporary qualitative research practice. Qualitative writing has always reflected variety – of disciplinary styles, genres, textual conventions and subject matter. Yet in recent years, representation and authorship have been especially dynamic. This has in part been due to temporal and critical movements such as postmodernism and (post)feminism; also to the attendant crises of legiti-mation and representation of qualitative texts. The authoritative status of the conventional monograph has been questioned and reassessed. The diversifi-cation of representation styles has also been influenced by the calls to alter-native genres and (non)textual styles, and not least by the rise in ethnographic autobiography.

Despite a recognition that the production of qualitative or ethnographic texts has never been especially static or monolithic, it has been only since the mid-1980s (Denzin and Lincoln's fourth moment) that the production and reading of these texts have been subjected to detailed and critical scrutiny. These critical (re)readings have formed part of more general debates about the (textual) representation of culture and reality (Atkinson 1990, 1996). The authority of the text has been addressed and questioned by, for example, feminism, postcolonial/critical race theory, queer theory and postmodernist arguments – all of whom have challenged the taken-for-granted assumption that the researcher can be speaker for the *Other* (see Lather 2001; Skeggs 2001). From Said's (1978) sustained commentary on the orientalism of western observation, which casts observer as privileged and the observed as subjugated and muted subjects of dominating discourse (Ardener 1975), through to contemporary ethnographic work in racialized contexts by authors such as Stack (1996) and Fordham (1996), the privileging and power of texts have been acknowledged and critiqued. Fordham (1996) summarizes this potential power:

> Those empowered to use one of society's most powerful weapons – the pen – can permanently shape or transform our thinking. If this premise is accurate, our perceptions of an entire generation could be permanently altered as a result of these ethnographic images. (Fordham 1996: 341)

Issues of representation have formed part of the sustained dialogue between feminism and ethnography (Skeggs 2001). The feminist critique of ethnographic texts has gone beyond simple considerations of gender at the level of social actor and/or author – to issues of voice, exploitation and power (Mascia-Lees *et al.* 1989; Clough 1992; Wolf 1992; Olesen 2000; also see Lisa Adkins, Chapter 16 in this volume). Feminist qualitative research praxis has brought to the fore relationships between the personal, the biographical and the social. Indeed, as Jennaway (1990) has argued, many of the developments embedded in a postmodern ethnography have a basis in feminist ethnographic discourse.

> The move towards egalitarian relations of textual production, dialogic and polyphonic cultural scripts, collaborative authorship, the decentering of self and disalienation of the ethnographic other, the move away from systems of representation which objectify and silence the ethnographic other, i.e. the general reflexive stance, are things to which feminist theory ... has long been adverting. (Jennaway 1990: 171)

The critical attention that has been paid to the processes and products of qualitative research writing has led to a more self-conscious approach to authorship and audience. The impersonal all-but-invisible narrator status of the author has been questioned, alongside a critical appreciation of the power relations of textual production and representation of the social world. In placing the observable into recognizable textual formats, the opportunity to make the social world 'readable' has now been located alongside issues of authorship, authenticity and responsibility. Moreover, conventional ethnographic texts, such as the research monograph, have been criticized for failing to do adequate justice to the polyvocality of social life and the complexity of social forms, experiences and biographies. These sustained critiques have prompted, and can be framed within, the articulation, practice and evaluation of other representational forms. Often referred to as alternative or experimental (though they adopt conventional genres found in the worlds of literature, theatre and biographical practice), these forms of representation could be viewed as part of an avant-garde (or postmodern) spirit of experimentation. They are innovative and creative responses, presenting new ways of seeing and representing. They also reflect a more general (postmodernist/feminist/critical race theory) agenda of addressing how research is translated into representational and knowledge forms. Conventional scholarly texts have been held up as embodying an essentially modernist set of assumptions – predicated on a discovery of social reality, through selective, unproblematized and scientific acts of engagement, inspection and notation (and told through a realist, narrated genre). Postmodern agendas treat the status of texts in different ways, as *representations* or interpretations of social reality. This allows for the transgression of literary boundaries, and calls for an aesthetic that does not necessarily celebrate a consistency of form. The *Writing Culture* anthology (Clifford and Marcus 1986) heralded this new realization, asserting the need for more dialogic and reflexive approaches, and recognizing the politics and poetics of research writing. The feminist critique of this collection – for a lack of engagement with feminist writing and scholarship (see Gordon 1988; Wolf 1992; Babcock 1993), and consequent collection *Women Writing Culture* (Behar and Gordon 1995) – adds further dimensions to these realizations, and fuels the desire to seek alternative scholarly narratives and representation forms.

There are a number of ways in which the qualitative researcher's position of privilege has been transformed through representation diversification. However as Lather (1991) has argued, these alternative representational modes do not necessarily remove issues of power from ethnographic production, and are at risk of falling into 'static claims' of authenticity (Lather 2001). Nevertheless the textual formats of ethnographic representation have been challenged, and a more self-conscious approach has been prompted. Significantly these calls to 'new' forms of representation have signified a return of the author to the text (Lincoln and Denzin 2000). Drawing on a dialogic approach to text (Holquist 1990; Allan 1994), many of these 'alternative' representational forms actually exploit the conventions of naturalistic conversation or theatre or literature, in order to draw out the poetical and performative qualities of everyday life. Ethnodrama or ethnographic theatre is one articulation of this approach – producing scripts, or even live performances of social events. Mienczakowski (1995, 1996) has used ethnodrama extensively to 'performance' the experiences of people undergoing processes of detoxification (see also Mienczakowski 2001 for a critical review of performed ethnography). Paget (1990) adopted a perfomative or dramaturgical approach to give ethnographic representation to experiences of cancer (see also Bluebond-Langer 1980, who used a similar approach to explore the social worlds of dying children). Multivoiced (or split-screen) texts have also been used to represent the polyvocality, or multivocality, of social life and research endeavours. For example Lather and Smithies (1997) used split-text formats to give layers of voices (their own and their respondents') in their representation of women living with HIV/AIDS. Fox (1996) experiments with multivoiced texts to (re)present contested voices and give subversive readings of child sexual abuse.

Ethno-poetry is a further example of a literary form utilized to ethnographic ends. The use of poetry in ethnographic representation can offer a means of capturing the pauses, rhymes and rhythms of everyday life, enabling the social world to be seen, heard and felt in new dimensions (Richardson 1994).

> Writing 'data' as poetic representations reveals the constraining belief that the purpose of a social science text is to convey information as facts of themes or notions existing independent of the contexts in which they were found or produced – as if the story we have recorded, transcribed, edited and written up in prose snippets is the one and only true one: a 'science' story. Standard prose writing conceals the handprint of the sociologist who produced the final written text. (Richardson 2000: 933)

Richardson's story of the life of Louisa May (Richardson 1992) is one of the most cited of the ethnographic poems. Richardson represents her informant's life in poetic form, using Louisa May's 'voice, diction, hill-southern rhythms and tone' (Richardson 2000: 933). The result is a striking, historically situated, poetic narrative. Like McCoy's (1997) poetry exploring pre-service teacher discourses, Richardson's poetry provides a mode of evocative representation which disrupts the conventional, and undertakes new understandings.

Alternative forms of representation have been particularly well utilized as mechanisms for representing deeply personal (or sensitive) events, emotive voices and stories, and for making the author a visible presence in the text. Moreover, and especially relevant in the context of this chapter, they have been used as representation devices for (re)writing the self (see Ellis and Flaherty 1992). As has already been noted, authors have given ethnographic purchase to their experiences of illness and the body (Paget 1993; Kolker 1996; Sparkes 1996; Tillman-Healy 1996). They have also been used to explore personal experiences and relationships (Ellis and Bochner 1992; Ellis 1995; Fox 1996; Quinney 1996; Ronai 1996), as well as the experiences and processes of writing (Richardson and Lockeridge 1991; Bochner and Ellis 1996; Ely et al. 1997). These personal autobiographical narratives can be located within a broader genre of autoethnography (Ellis and Bochner 2000). This term encapsulates many variants on a theme – such as autobiographical ethnography, ethnobiography and personal ethnography (see Reed-Danahay 1997).

> Autoethnography is an autobiographical genre of writing and research that displays multiple layers of consciousness, connecting the personal to the cultural. Back and forth autobiographers gaze, first through an ethnographic wide-angle lens, focusing outward on social and cultural aspects of their personal experience; then, they look inward, exposing a vulnerable self that is moved by and may move through, refract, and resist cultural interpretations. (Ellis and Bochner 2000: 739)

These autoethnographic texts are first person accounts, drawing on personal experiences of the author. They are autobiographical ethnographic 'essays' that can take different representational forms, for example dialogues, scripts, stories, poems, diaries and journals, photographic essays, biographical reflections and multilayered writing. Autoethnography relates the research process to both the social world and the self, draws on personal stories and narratives and consolidates intertextuality between ethnography and autobiography. In their chapter for the *Handbook of Qualitative Research* (Denzin and Lincoln 2000) Ellis and Bochner take their readers on a number of journeys in order to trace the history of, explain and give meaning to autoethnography. Through conversations, social science prose, student supervision, and department colloquia, Ellis and Bochner (2000) defend and expand autoethnographic praxis and writing. They argue for personally meaningful ethnography and the working of the spaces between social science prose and other genres.

VOCAL TEXTS AND SHARING LIVES

If weaving the self into the ethnography is a journey, then autoethnographies represent possible destinations. We do not have to travel there in order to acknowledge that the personal self, the ethnographic self and the author self are interwoven in complex ways. The myth of the silent author has been exposed. The position adopted by Charmaz and Mitchell (1997: 194) occupies a middle ground here. They argue that just as there is merit in humility and deference to the views of Others, and to reasoned, systematic discourse, so too is there merit in 'a visible authorship'. While the words of ethnographers are neither magical nor authoritative, neither is the author's voice a biased irrelevancy. They advocate vocal texts where the author is an active and visible participant. This highlights the understanding of voice articulated by Hertz (1997), and the dilemma of presenting the author self while simultaneously writing and representing the voices and selves of Others.

> We do ourselves and our disciplines no service by telling half tales, by only reporting finished analyses in temperate voice, by suppressing wonder or perplexity or dread. Alternatively, writing tricks and data transformations may distract us, but they do not guarantee a clearer tale or a greater truth. Turning Henry and Ric into iotas of a path model, or changing John and Patricia into stanzas of a song will not make their lives more vivid or true than candid description. Henry and Ric and John and Patricia have every right to expect us to represent their lives as something

more than scientific artefacts or art objects. In ethnography, the emergent self is acculturated; it learns the limits of its own power. Fieldwork leavens immodesty but it does so imperfectly. And that is good. (Charmaz and Mitchell 1997: 212–213)

As one moves along the road toward autoethnography the issue of representing the Other is both revealed and complicated – as subject and author entwine or merge (Richardson 2000). Some of the criticisms that have been levelled at ethnography, and qualitative research more generally, are crystallized in considerations of autobiographical ethnographic practice. For example the reliance on memory, issues of reliability and validity, and generalization. Ethnography is about experiencing, remembering and sharing lives through the act of memory, and as such autoethnography is no different from this. Memories are personal and biographical but are organized through culturally shared, socially situated and temporal resources. Memories draw on cultural meanings and language that are biographical and collective. As we are only too aware, reliability and validity are vexed questions in qualitative research generally (see Hammersley 1991), although as Ellis and Bochner (2000) stress there are differing and contested definitions of both concepts. There is no reason why autoethnography cannot seek verisimilitude, and reliability checks attempted. Likewise the generalizability claims of ethnography are well rehearsed (see Coffey and Atkinson 1996) and can hold fast for autoethnography – observing that all lives are particular, local, temporal, culturally and historically situated.

A more particular criticism levelled at autobiographical ethnography writing, drawing on the personal narrative, is the potential for romanitizing the self (Atkinson 1997; Atkinson and Silverman 1997) or of engaging in gross self-indulgence. Here the argument is surely one of balance; between on the one hand the visible authorship of the text, and, on the other hand, texts that engage in personal narratives and experiences of the author. Lather's essay for the *Handbook of Ethnography* (Atkinson *et al.* 2001) warns that 'at risk is a romance of the speaking subject and a metaphysics of presence complicated by the identity and experience claims of insider/outsider tensions' (Lather 2001: 483). Hence sentiments of authenticity and voice should not be used to 'appropriate the lives of others into consumption, a too-easy, too familiar eating of the other' (Lather 2001: 484). Mykhalovskiy (1997) has argued that autobiographical sociology *per se* is not necessarily narcissistic or self-indulgent, and that such a charge can actually be perceived as ironic. For it inevitably gives support for 'a solitary, authorial voice who writes a text disembodied from the individuals involved in its production' (Mykhalovskiy 1997: 246). Mykhalovskiy argues that personal experience and autobiographical text can be sources of insightful analysis, reacting against the (perceived and real) insularity of academic writing. However, there are those who remain highly sceptical of autobiographical ethnography (see Atkinson 1997) dismissing its claims to be social science, and using its potential therapeutic consequences to undermine it (see Bochner 2001 for a critique of this position). Ellis and Bochner (2000) address the issues raised about autoethnography, as supporters of the genre(s). They call for 'evocative' social science that recognizes the centrality of personal stories:

> A text that functions as an agent of self-discovery or self-creation, for the author as well as for those who read and engage the text, is only threatening under a narrow definition of social inquiry, one that eschews a social science with a moral center and a heart. Why should caring and empathy be secondary to controlling and knowing? Why must academics be conditioned to believe that a text is important only to the extent it moves beyond the merely personal? (Ellis and Bochner 2000: 746)

ENDINGS OR BEGINNINGS?

Conclusion 1: (auto)-biographical work	Conclusion 2: new ethnography	Conclusion 3: beyond ethnography?
It is not necessary to render the self as the explicit focus of qualitative inquiry in order to recognize the (auto)biographical work that is routinely accomplished. Detailed or prolonged fieldwork inevitably involves the researcher in various kinds of autobiographical practice and rightly so. The self is shaped by relationships and experiences that are not suspended for the duration of a	Autoethnography widens/blurs/ disrupts the boundaries of qualitative research. It interweaves the personal and the social, moving back and forth between the two. It links pasts, presents and futures of qualitative inquiry. It redefines old spaces and opens up new spaces. It reworks dichotomies between subjectivity and objectivity, autobiography and culture, the social and the self. It provides a mechanism for extending ethnography	What we are witnessing may be a new form of ethnographic practice, or it may not be ethnography at all. Autoethnography could be accused of producing self indulgent writings, published under the guise of social research. There is a danger here of providing ample ammunition for critics of qualitative inquiry. It is uncertain whether there are any long-term

research project. The personal self cannot, nor should not, be separated from the practical, intellectual and social processes of qualitative research. This is not advocating that a/the primary aim of qualitative research is a better or more complex understanding of self. Nor is this a case for purely self-referential or autobiographical fieldwork. But in recognizing the 'self-work' that is part of both research and representational processes, there is greater scope for understanding and making sense of social settings and cultural processes. This does not imply an uncritical celebration of the self. But it does imply recognition that the self is part of the field and beyond the academy and encourages 'writers to make ethnography readable, evocative, engaging and personally meaningful' (Ellis and Bochner 2000: 761). Autoethnography draws on the therapeutic and analytical value of personal narratives and self-stories, and makes visible that which is often dismissed or rendered invisible in qualitative inquiry. The practice of autoethnography is still relatively marginal to the mainstream of qualitative research – and only time will tell what place it holds in ethnographic futures. But we ignore what it has to teach us at our peril. benefits for the development of ethnographic research and text, beyond the centralizing of the self as omnipresent. In responding to calls for polyvocality and the recognition of multiple voices, there is a danger of creating mono-vocal and self-indulgent texts. Autobiographical ethnography (Reed-Danahay 1997) has much to commend it, not least in rendering the self a visible and vocal presence. However, it is debatable as to whether utilizing ethnographical strategies to write autobiography really counts as ethnography at all. This may be especially the case where the only 'field' researched and represented is the self. Utilizing part of the text. It promotes the intertextuality of biography and ethnography. It argues for vocal texts and a diversity of representational forms, visible authorship and a reflexive approach.

ethnographic devices to work through life events can have therapeutic and analytical value, but should not detract from the work of qualitative inquiry in observing and understanding the social world. That is, autoethnography can be a beginning of the journey but should not be the final destination.

REFERENCES

Allan, S. (1994) '"When discourse is torn from reality": Bakhtin and the principle of chronotopicity', *Time and Society* 3: 193–218.

Ardener, S. (ed.) (1975) *Perceiving Women*. London: J.M. Dent.

Atkinson, P. (1990) *The Ethnographic Imagination*. London: Routledge.

Atkinson, P. (1996) *Sociological Readings and Re-readings*. Aldershot: Avebury.

Atkinson, P. (1997) 'Narrative turn in a blind alley?', *Qualitative Health Research* 7: 325–344.

Atkinson, P. and Coffey, A. (1995) 'Realism and its discontents: on the crisis of cultural representation in ethnographic texts', in B. Adam and S. Allan (eds) *Theorizing Culture: An Interdisciplinary Critique after Post-Modernism*. London: UCL Press.

Atkinson, P. and Silverman, D. (1997) 'Kundera's *Immortality*: the interview society and the invention of the self', *Qualitative Inquiry* 3(3): 304–325.

Atkinson, P., Coffey, A. and Delamont, S. (1999) 'Ethnography: post, past and present', *Journal of Contempoary Ethnography* 28(5): 460–471.

Atkinson, P., Coffey, A., Delamont, S., Lofland, J. and Lofland, L. (eds) (2001) *Handbook of Ethnography*. London: Sage.

Babcock, B. (1993) 'Feminism/pretexts: fragments, questions and reflections', *Anthropological Quarterly* 66(2): 59–66.

Behar, R. and Gordon, D.A. (eds) (1995) *Women Writing Culture*. Berkeley, CA: University of California Press.

Beynon, J. (1987) 'Zombies in dressing gowns', in N.P. McKeganey and S. Cunningham-Burley (eds) *Enter the Sociologist*. Aldershot: Avebury.

Bluebond-Langer, M. (1980) *The Private Worlds of Dying Children*. Princeton, NJ: Princeton University Press.

Bochner, A.P. (2001) 'Narratives virtues', *Qualitative Inquiry* 7(2): 131–157.

Bochner, A.P. and Ellis, C. (1996) 'Talking over ethnography', in C. Ellis and A.P. Bochner (eds) *Composing Ethnography: Alternative Forms of Qualitative Writing*. Walnut Creek, CA: Altamira.

Burgess, R.G. (1984) *In the Field*. London: Allen and Unwin.

Charmaz, K. and Mitchell, R.G. Jr (1997) 'The myth of silent authorship: self, substance and style in ethnographic writing', in R. Hertz (ed.) *Reflexivity and Voice*. Thousand Oaks, CA: Sage.

Clifford, J. (1983) 'On ethnographic authority', *Representations* 2: 118–146.

Clifford, J. and Marcus, G.E. (eds) (1986) *Writing Culture: The Poetics and Politics of Ethnography*. Berkeley, CA: University of California Press.

Clough, P.T. (1992) *The End(s) of Ethnography*. Newbury Park, CA: Sage.

Coffey, A. (1999) *The Ethnographic Self*. London: Sage.

Coffey, A. and Atkinson, P. (1996) *Making Sense of Qualitative Data*. Thousand Oaks, CA: Sage.

Delamont, S. (1987) 'Clean baths and dirty women', in N.P. McKeganey and S. Cunningham-Burley (eds) *Enter the Sociologist*. Aldershot: Avebury.

Delamont, S., Coffey, A. and Atkinson, P. (2000) 'The twilight years? Educational ethnography and the five moments model', *Qualitative Studies in Education* 13(3): 223–238.

Denzin, N.K. (1997) *Interpretive Ethnography*. Thousand Oaks, CA: Sage.

Denzin, N.K. and Lincoln, Y.S. (eds) (1994) *Handbook of Qualitative Research*. Thousand Oaks, CA: Sage.

Denzin, N.K. and Lincoln, Y.S. (eds) (2000) *Handbook of Qualitative Research*, 2nd edn. Thousand Oaks, CA: Sage.

Ellis, C. (1995) *Final Negotiations: A Story of Love, Loss and Chronic Illness*. Philadelphia, PA: Temple University Press.

Ellis, C. and Bochner, A.P. (1992) 'Telling and performing personal stories: the constraints of choice in abortion', in C. Ellis and M.G. Flaherty (eds) *Investigating Subjectivity: Research on Lived Experience*. Newbury Park, CA: Sage.

Ellis, C. and Bochner, A.P. (2000) 'Autoethnography, personal narrative, reflexivity: researcher as subject', in N.K. Denzin and Y.S. Lincoln (eds) *Handbook of Qualitative Research*, 2nd edn. Thousand Oaks, CA: Sage.

Ellis, C. and Flaherty, M.G. (eds) (1992) *Investigating Subjectivity: Research on Lived Experience*. Newbury Park, CA: Sage.

Ely, M., Vinz, R., Downing, M. and Anzul, M. (1997) *On Writing Qualitative Research: Living by Words*. London: Falmer.

Fordham, S. (1996) *Blacked Out: Dilemmas of Race, Identity and Success at Capital High*. Chicago: University of Chicago Press.

Fowler, D.D. and Hardesty, D.L. (eds) (1994) *Others Knowing Others: Perspectives on Ethnographic Careers*. Washington, DC and London: Smithsonian Institution Press.

Fox, K.V. (1996) 'Silent voices: a subversive reading of child sexual abuse', in C. Ellis and A.P. Bochner (eds) *Composing Ethnography: Alternative Forms of Qualitative Writing*. Walnut Creek, CA: Altamira.

Geertz, C. (1973) *The Interpretation of Cultures*. New York: Basic Books.

Geertz, C. (1983) *Local Knowledge: Further Essays in Interpretive Anthropology*. New York: Basic Books.

Gordon, D.A. (1988) 'Writing culture: writing feminism – the poetics and politics of experimental ethnography', *Inscriptions* 3(4): 7–24.

Hammersley, M. (1991) *Reading Ethnographic Research*. London: Longman.

Hammersley, M. and Atkinson, P. (1983) *Ethnography: Principles in Practice*. London: Tavistock.

Hertz, R. (ed.) (1997) *Reflexivity and Voice*. Thousand Oaks, CA: Sage.

Hobbs, D. and May, M. (eds) (1992) *Interpreting the Field*. Oxford: Clarendon.

Holquist, M. (1990) *Dialogism*. London: Routledge.

Jennaway, M. (1990) 'Paradigms, postmodern epistemologies and paradox: the place of feminism in anthropology', *Anthropological Forum* 6(2): 167–189.

Kolker, A. (1996) 'Thrown overboard: the human costs of health care rationing', in C. Ellis and A.P. Bochner (eds) *Composing Ethnography: Alternative Forms of Qualitative Writing*. Walnut Creek, CA: Altamira.

Kondo, D.K. (1990) *Crafting Selves: Power, Gender and Discourses of Identity in a Japanese Workplace*. Chicago: University of Chicago Press.

Lareau, A. and Shultz, J. (eds) (1996) *Journeys through Fieldwork*. Boulder, CO: Westview.

Lather, P. (1991) *Getting Smart: Feminist Research and Pedagogy with/in the Postmodern*. New York: Routledge.

Lather, P. (2001) 'Postmodernism, post-structuralism and post(critical) ethnography: of ruins, aporias and angels', in P. Atkinson, A. Coffey, S. Delamont, J. Lofland and L. Lofland (eds) *Handbook of Ethnography*. London: Sage.

Lather, P. and Smithies, C. (1997) *Troubling the Angels: Women Living with HIV/AIDS*. Boulder, CO: Westview.

Lederman, R. (1990) 'Pretexts for ethnography: on reading fieldnotes', in R. Sanjek (ed.) *Fieldnotes*. Ithaca, NY and London: Cornell University Press.

Lincoln, Y.S. and Denzin, N.K. (1994) 'The fifth moment', in N.K. Denzin and Y.S. Lincoln (eds) *Handbook of Qualitative Research*. Thousand Oaks, CA: Sage.

Lincoln, Y.S. and Denzin, N.K. (1998) 'The fifth moment', in N.K. Denzin and Y.S. Lincoln (eds) *The Landscape of Qualitative Research*. Thousand Oaks, CA: Sage.

Lincoln, Y.S. and Denzin, N.K. (2000) 'The seventh moment: out of the past', in N.K. Denzin and Y.S. Lincoln (eds) *Handbook of Qualitative Research*, 2nd edn. Thousand Oaks, CA: Sage.

Lofland, J. (1971) *Analyzing Social Settings*. Belmont, CA: Sage.

McCoy, K. (1997) 'White noise – the sound of epidemic: reading/writing a climate of intelligibility around the "crisis" of difference', *Qualitative Studies in Education* 10(3): 333–348.

Malinowski, B. (1967) *A Diary in the Strict Sense of the Term*. London: Routledge and Kegan Paul.

Mascia-Lees, F.E., Sharpe, P. and Cohen, C.B. (1989) 'The postmodernist turn in anthropology: cautions from a feminist perspective', *Signs* 15: 7–33.

Mienczakowski, J. (1995) 'The theatre of ethnography: the reconstruction of ethnography in theatre with emancipatory potential', *Qualitative Inquiry* 1: 360–375.

Mienczakowski, J. (1996) 'The ethnographic act: the construction of consensual theatre', in C. Ellis and A.P. Bochner (eds) *Composing Ethnography: Alternative Forms of Qualitative Writing*. Walnut Creek, CA: Altamira.

Mienczakowski, J. (2001) 'Ethnodrama: performed research – limitations and potential', in P. Atkinson, A. Coffey, S. Delamont, J. Lofland and L. Lofland (eds) *Handbook of Ethnography*. London: Sage.

Mykhalovskiy, E. (1997) 'Reconsidering "table talk": critical thoughts on the relationship between sociology, autobiography and self-indulgence', in R. Hertz (ed.) *Reflexivity and Voice*. Thousand Oaks, CA: Sage.

Olesen, V. (2000) 'Feminisms and qualitative research at and into the Millennium', in N.K. Denzin and Y.S. Lincoln (eds) *Handbook of Qualitative Research*, 2nd edn. Thousand Oaks, CA: Sage.

Paget, M.A. (1990) 'Performing the text', *Journal of Contemporary Ethnography* 19: 136–155.

Paget, M.A. (1993) *A Complex Sorrow: Reflections on Cancer and an Abbreviated Life*. Philadelphia, PA: Temple University Press.

Quinney, R. (1996) 'Once my father travelled west to California', in C. Ellis and A.P. Bochner (eds) *Composing Ethnography: Alternative Forms of Qualitative Writing*. Walnut Creek, CA: Altamira.

Reed-Danahay, D. (1997) *Auto/Ethnography: Rewriting the Self and the Social*. Oxford and New York: Berg.

Reed-Danahay, D. (2001) 'Autobiography, intimacy and ethnography', in P. Atkinson, A. Coffey, S. Delamont, J. Lofland and L. Lofland (eds) *Handbook of Ethnography*. London: Sage.

Richardson, L. (1992) 'The consequences of poetic representation: writing the other, writing the self', in C. Ellis and M.G. Flaherty (eds) *Investigating Subjectivity: Research on Lived Experience*. Newbury Park, CA: Sage.

Richardson, L. (1994) 'Writing: a method of inquiry', in N.K. Denzin and Y.S. Lincoln (eds) *Handbook of Qualitative Research*. Thousand Oaks, CA: Sage.

Richardson, L. (2000) 'Writing: a method of inquiry', in N.K. Denzin and Y.S. Lincoln (eds) *Handbook of Qualitative Research*, 2nd edn. Thousand Oaks, CA: Sage.

Richardson, L. and Lockeridge, E. (1991) 'The sea-monster: an "ethnographic drama"', *Symbolic Interaction* 13: 77–83.

Ronai, C.R. (1996) 'My mother is mentally retarded', in C. Ellis and A.P. Bochner (eds) *Composing Ethnography: Alternative Forms of Qualitative Writing*. Walnut Creek, CA: Altamira.

Said, E. (1978) *Orientalism*. London: Routledge and Kegan Paul.

Sanjek, R. (ed.) (1990) *Fieldnotes*. Ithaca, NY and London: Cornell University Press.

Skeggs, B. (2001) 'Feminist ethnography', in P. Atkinson, A. Coffey, S. Delamont, J. Lofland and L. Lofland (eds) *Handbook of Ethnography*. London: Sage.

Sparkes, A. (1996) 'The fatal flaw: a narrative of the fragile body-self', *Qualitative Inquiry* 2(4): 463–494.

Stack, C.B. (1996) 'Writing ethnography: feminist critical practice', in D.L. Wolf (ed.) *Feminist Dilemmas in Fieldwork*. Boulder, CO: Westview.

Stanley, L. (1993) 'On auto/biography in sociology', *Sociology* 27(1): 41–52.

Tillman-Healy, L.M. (1996) 'A secret life in a culture of thinness: reflections on body, food and bulimia', in C. Ellis and A.P. Bochner (eds) *Composing Ethnography: Alternative Forms of Qualitative Writing*. Walnut Creek, CA: Altamira.

Van Mannen, J. (1988) *Tales of the Field*. Chicago: University of Chicago Press.

Whyte, W.F. (1981) *Street Corner Society*, 3rd edn. Chicago: University of Chicago Press.

Wolf, M. (1992) *A Thrice Told Tale: Feminism, Postmodernism and Ethnographic Responsibility*. Stanford, CA: Stanford University Press.

16 REFLEXIVITY AND THE POLITICS OF QUALITATIVE RESEARCH

Lisa Adkins

In writing this chapter I have recalled Probyn's (1993: 2) question which she posed in her introduction to *Sexing the Self*: 'who speaks for whom, why, how and when?' Probyn's question concerned the stakes involved in speaking the self in cultural studies. I recall it here as it is my contention that this kind of question, and much of the work which has allowed such a question to be asked, including the making transparent of who is speaking in the social sciences, risks being disallowed by the current emphasis in much social research on reflexivity. Specifically, in this chapter I shall argue that the current turn to reflexivity in social research, or at least, a particular version of reflexivity, concerns a configuration of the relation between subjectivity and knowledge or knower and known which allows only certain subjects to speak. Thus I shall suggest that reflexivity inscribes a hierarchy of speaking positions in social research. What is particularly ironic regarding this inscription is that reflexivity is widely understood to make visible the relations between knower and known and hence redress the problem of the concealment of normatively constituted speaking positions. For example, reflexivity is very often represented as the critical opposite of universalist and objectivist social research where the very practices of that research constitute such speaking positions (see e.g. Pels 2000). Yet I shall argue in this chapter that reflexivity privileges a particular relation between knower and known even as it ostensibly appears to challenge – indeed undo – such forms of privileging. In particular, I shall highlight how in current social research practice reflexivity is attributed to some positions and analysts and not to others and moreover how (for some) reflexivity is serving as an index for judgements regarding 'good' and 'bad' social research. To address these points I discuss aspects of my qualitative research regarding sexuality and labour markets, and especially sexuality and service labour (see e.g. Adkins 1995, 2000). What I draw attention to particularly is a review of some of my research in this area, especially some of the points of critique raised in this review. I do so not because I want to take this opportunity to mount some kind of defence of my research. Rather, I do so because these points of critique highlight for me some of the issues at stake in current disputes over reflexivity, and in particular highlight the limits of a form of reflexivity which is currently being encouraged in social research.

To begin to lay out these limits I turn first to some recent discussions of reflexivity in relation to social research.

REFLEXIVITY AND SOCIAL RESEARCH

Reflexivity continues to be recommended as a critical practice for social research (see e.g. Steier 1991; Woolgar 1991a; Alvesson and Skoldberg 2000; Pels 2000), especially as it is often understood as an antidote to the problems of realism. For example, reflexivity has been recommended as a response to and indeed is often represented as an answer to the crises of representation and legitimation in social research associated with postmodernism and post-structuralism (Denzin and Lincoln 1994: 10–11). These crises have concerned making problematic a number of central assumptions of qualitative research. Thus the idea that researchers can somehow directly capture lived experience has been troubled by the argument that experience is created in the social texts written by researchers. In addition, the criteria for evaluating and interpreting social research have been problematized. Thus terms such as reliability, generalizability and validity have come into scrutiny in terms of what totalizing and universalizing assumptions they make regarding the social, knowledge and ways of knowing. Denzin and Lincoln (1994) suggest that the result of these crises is that 'any representation must now legitimate itself in terms of some set of criteria that allows the author (and the reader) to make connections between the text and the world written about' (Denzin and Lincoln 1994: 11). And one way in which social researchers have attempted to perform such legitimization is through a turn to reflexive practice (Game 1991), including new forms of textual expression and analysis.

This turn to reflexivity is clearly visible in the social studies of science where one consequence of applying the argument that 'natural' scientific knowledge is a social construct to the knowledge generated by the social sciences has been a turn to reflexivity. Thus in their introduction to 'the reflexive project' in regard to the social studies of science, Woolgar and Ashmore (1991) have posited reflexivity as a kind of antidote to the problems of both realism and relativism. They discuss the ways in which, as they see it, the conventions of realism constrain explorations of knowledge practices and inhibit the development of reflexive practice in the social sciences. Such practice is itself illustrated by the self-conscious, reflexive style of the introduction to the collection. Here, Woolgar and Ashmore explicitly give presence to more than one textual voice in dialogic form to remind the reader:

> that interpretation goes on all the time, that the idea of one reading – a singular correspondence between text and meaning – is illusory. In particular, the dialogue is one way of introducing some instability into the presumed relationship between text and reader. (Woolgar and Ashmore 1991: 4)

Thus such forms of textual expression are located as potentially overcoming the problems of realism in social research through a self-consciousness regarding the role of the author in producing accounts of the social world. Such self-reflexivity is understood to destabilize the relations between text and reader, author and text, researcher and social life. In short, such practices are understood to destabilize all that realism held in place. Consider, for example, the following (abridged) section of dialogue in which such a self-consciousness is enacted to both take account of its own production and to illustrate the ways in which realist conventions inhibit the development of reflexive practice (I shall return to this dialogue in a later section of this chapter):

REITERATING THE TIRED OLD PLATITUDE THAT ALL TEXTS ARE MULTIVOCAL ...?
Certainly not.
... TRYING TO FIND A NEW WAY OF SUPPLYING REFERENCES THAT HAVE USED OR DISCUSSED THE SECOND VOICE DEVICE ...?
Look, it's your intervention. I don't see why you're asking me. ... And while you're thinking about that you might explain why you appear in UPPER CASE this time?
WHAT DO YOU MEAN?
... the use of UPPER CASE makes it seem like you're shouting!
... YOUR MONOPOLY OF THE CONVENTIONAL IDIOGRAPH MAKES ME SEEM LIKE THE ODDBALL. BESIDES I THOUGHT WE'D BOTH AGREED THAT THERE WAS NO REAL DIFFERENCE BETWEEN US: THAT WHEN ALL WAS SAID AND DONE WE ARE NOT TWO VOICES BUT TWO SETS OF INTER-CHANGEABLE SCRIPTED REMARKS; THAT OUR ORIGINS SHOULD NOT BE HELD AGAINST US AS SOURCES OF SANCTIONABLE CONSISTENCY, AS LABELS TO WHICH OUR REMARKS ARE HELD ACCOUNTABLE, AS ...
... Why don't you just say that actors' voices can emanate from quite different and interchangeable identities, and that this can be done without any evident contradiction on the part of actors themselves?
YOU THINK THAT'S LESS OBSCURE
Not very.
BUT THE BASIC POINT IS THAT WE COULD SWITCH ROLES WITHOUT ANY-ONE NOTICING?
Yes.
AND THAT WE COULD DROP THIS UPPER CASE/lower case DISTINCTION IN ORDER TO DELIBERATELY CONFUSE OUR SUPPOSEDLY SEPARATE IDENTITIES?
Right. (Woolgar and Ashmore 1991: 3)

Such textual self-consciousness is understood however to overcome the problems of not only realism, but also relativism. Woolgar and Ashmore discuss how in the relativist (or constructivist) social study of science, while the topic of investigation – science – is relativized, a realist methodology is maintained. The consequence of this adherence to a realist methodology is the construction of a new metascientific reality – that 'scientific knowledge is built in such and such a way and has such and such a character' (Woolgar and Ashmore 1991: 4). But within such relativist approaches the nature of the reflexive similarity between findings and methods is itself not an issue: 'reflexivity is either treated as an inherent but uninteresting charac- teristic of such work … or, by contrast, is actively opposed' (Woolgar and Ashmore 1991: 8). Thus Woolgar and Ashmore point to a lack of reflexivity regarding the effectivity of method in regard to social world construction in such approaches. In short, such approaches do not problematize the role of the author in producing social worlds. And as an escape from such problems the abandoning of the commitment to realist methods is recommended along with a take-up of the reflexive project, a project described as concern- ing 'some of the most exciting intellectual work currently being undertaken anywhere' (Woolgar and Ashmore 1991: 9).

REFLEXIVITY AND ITS LIMITS

May (1998) has, however, noted a number of limitations of such reflexivity for social research. He distinguishes two dimensions of reflexivity: endoge- nous and referential. By endogenous reflexivity he refers to the ways in which the actions of members of a given community are seen to contribute to the constitution of social reality itself. This dimension of reflexivity includes not only 'the methods of people within lifeworlds who are the sub- jects of social investigation but also those within social scientific communi- ties in terms of how they construct the topics of their inquiries and conduct their investigations' (May 1998: 8). By referential reflexivity May refers to 'the consequences that arise from a meeting between the reflexivity exhibi- ted by actors as part of a lifeworld and that exhibited by the researcher as part of a social scientific community' (May 1998: 8). Through a review of reflexivity in the social sciences in relation to social research – from Weber, through the ethnomethodologists, to the methodological changes brought about by post-structuralist and postmodern arguments – May shows how in all of these different traditions there is a tendency to bracket referential reflexivity. He argues that this has the effect of producing an inward-looking practice that results in a failure to adequately understand the role and place of the social sciences in the study of social life (May 1998: 18). The methodological implications of 'postmodernism' for social research[1] – including the critique of the idea that the relation between research produc- tion and the representation of the social world may take place according to universal concepts of reliability and validity – are, for example, understood to have resulted in such a bracketing of referential reflexivity and a focus on endogenous reflexivity alone. For instance, May notes a tendency 'to take the words that are written about social life as *the* central topics for the social con- struction of reality' (May 1998: 17, original emphasis) with the consequence that the authority of the author often becomes an important focus. Indeed, cer- tain critiques of the authority of the author have led 'to research accounts that reproduce ego-identity!' (May 1998: 18). Thus May sees the problematization of social science methodology – especially the techniques of representation of the social world – to have led in some quarters to a (rather ironic) privileging of a new form of authority – that of the author. Instead of turning inwards in this way and relieving social science of engagement with the social world, May suggests the social sciences need also embrace referential reflexivity. Quoting Fay (1996), he agrees that the worth of social science should be judged in terms of 'what it tells us about those under study, not just what it reveals about the social scientist' (quoted in May 1998: 20).

May's distinction between endogenous and referential reflexivity and his claims regarding the limits of reflexivity for social research may be paralleled to Latour's (1991) arguments regarding the problems of reflexivity in regard to the social studies of science. Latour distinguishes between what he terms meta- and infra-reflexivity. By meta-reflexivity he refers to 'the attempt to avoid a text being believed by its readers' (Latour 1991: 166), while infra-reflexivity concerns the 'attempt to avoid a text *not* being believed by its readers' (Latour 1991: 166, original emphasis). Latour's meta-reflexivity is similar to May's endogenous reflexivity. It is based on the idea that 'the most deleterious effect of a text is to be naively believed by the reader as in some way relating to a referent out there. Reflexivity is supposed to counteract this effect by rendering the text unfit for normal consumption' (Latour 1991: 168).

Latour argues that this position makes a number of assumptions, including that people easily believe what they read, and that believing always involves relating an account to some referent 'out there'. Yet the most bizarre assumption involved in meta-reflexivity, Latour suggests, inheres in arguments regarding self-reference. Here Latour refers to Woolgar's (1991b) discussion of reflexivity, where there is an assumption that an ethnographic text which discusses the ways in which ethnography is produced, is more reflexive than an ethnographic text which talks, say, about the Balinese. But Woolgar goes further, to suggest that such a reflexive account could be replaced by another account (or layer of reflexivity), since the reflexivity concerned in discussing the ways in which ethnography is produced could be a naive way of telling a true story about ethnographic production. But still more, this third layer may not be reflexive, and thus Woolgar imagines 'many other rungs on this Jacob's ladder' (Latour 1991: 168). The problem Latour has here is that an nth degree account is no more and no less reflexive than any of the others in the chain:

> A text about … [a] way of writing about the Balinese is no more and no less reflexive than … [a] text about the Balinese and this is no less and no more reflexive than what the Balinese themselves say. (Latour 1991: 168)

The whole vertigo regarding self-reference, Latour argues, stems from a very naive belief that the same actor appears in the first and last text, while at the same time believing that when a text does not have an author as one of its characters it is less reflexive than when it does, 'as if these were not, in semiotic terms, two similar ways of building the enunciation' (Latour 1991: 169).

In place of piling layer upon layer of self-consciousness to no end and holding on to the possibility of reaching a meta-language – searching for a meta-meta-language that would judge all others – Latour asks, why not just have one layer, the story, and obtain the necessary amount of reflexivity from somewhere else? This strategy concerns what Latour refers to as infra-reflexivity and is close to May's notion of referential reflexivity. Instead of focusing on the knower, infra-reflexivity concerns both the knower and the known, 'displaying the knower and the known and the work needed to interrupt or create connections between A and B [elements to provide explanations and elements to be explained]' (Latour 1991: 172). This he says is a non-scientific way of studying the natural and social sciences. Instead of turning to the word, Latour urges let us go back to the world. He considers, for example, completely 'unreflexive', 'journalistic' accounts of the world in which it is things – such as computers – which appear as reflexive, active, full of life, and ready to take part in dramatic stories, and thus are not objects in the way that empiricists would have them. Latour proclaims: 'there is more reflexivity in one account that makes the world alive than in one hundred self-reflexive loops that return the boring thinking mind to the stage' (Latour 1991: 173). Thus while Latour agrees that the problems located by the reflexivists are correct, and that the reflexive trend is inescapable ('otherwise our field would … be self-contradictory': Latour 1991: 176), like May, Latour also agrees that meta- or endogenous reflexivity is too limited as an alternative, especially since in the end it endorses a scientistic agenda by believing that there is no other way out of empiricism than language and self-reference. For Latour, a better strategy is to search for non-scientific and weaker explanations, and to look for reflexivity not 'in' the author but in the world.[2]

REFLEXIVITY 'IN THE WORLD'

But are these problems at issue only in regard to textual self-consciousness or to endogenous or meta-reflexivity? In what follows I suggest that many of the same points – especially the location of reflexivity 'in' the self – may be made in relation to the research practices that social researchers have taken up in relation to 'the world', that is, in regard to the kind of research which both May (1998) and Latour (1991) suggest is the domain of referential or infra-reflexivity, that is, of the kind of reflexivity which is about the knower and the known. To do so, and with May and Latour's distinctions between endogenous and referential or meta- and infra-reflexivity in mind, I want to now turn to a review (Williams 1997) of some of my research regarding sexuality and labour markets (Adkins 1995). Here the reviewer compares aspects of my research account with a research project on masculinity in British corporate culture (Roper 1994). The latter involved life histories conducted with twenty-five men and five women executive managers, while my own research involved two case studies of service (tourist) organizations in the UK (a hotel and a theme park) and a study of the organization of the occupation of public house management.[3] Like some other commentators on organizations, Roper foregrounds the operation of homosocial relations between men in organizations, while in my own account I stress that in service organizations a heterosexual imperative may be central to understanding the organization of service labour. Here then we have two accounts that are squarely in the world, yet, as we shall see, the reviewer attributes referential reflexivity to Roper's account (and to Roper himself) and discounts it from my own. The grounds on which the reviewer makes this move I believe may tell us much about the limits of reflexivity as a critical practice for social research.

The reviewer describes my own and Roper's (1994) study, charts out her points of contention, and then makes what for me are some interesting moves in terms of the current debates regarding reflexivity. She says that reading these two books together made her 'ponder some epistemological issues involved in gender research on organizations when it is conducted either by a man or a woman' (Williams 1997: 519). In particular, she was 'struck by the different depictions of male sexuality in the two studies' (Williams 1997: 519). She describes a portrayal of men as hostile to women in my study, and in Roper's study a 'much more humane and sympathetic view of his subjects' (Williams 1997: 519). Williams is anxious to get to grips with these differences, and on this she has two proposals. The first concerns empathy, which she understands to be an effect of the social characteristics of the researchers. She suggests:

> Part of the difference may stem from empathy: as a young woman, Adkins no doubt had difficulty seeing the world from the vantage point of the sexist managers and ride operators she interviewed. In contrast, Roper admits to experiencing countertransference in his interviews: he describes tensions he felt 'between affection and criticism, sympathy for the organization man's masculinity, and an often uncomfortable identification with it' (p. 40). (Williams 1997: 519)

The second proposal, which Williams suspects is more important than the first – indeed, she says 'something more than differences in empathy may be going on here' (Williams 1997: 519) – concerns the relations between researchers and research subjects. To illustrate this issue, Williams turns to Roper's study. In particular, she discusses how Roper's study points to the importance of the business world as an arena for intimacy among men. Summarizing this aspect of Roper's research Williams writes:

> Men are drawn into the competition, aggression, and risk of business because it is one of the only avenues available to them to establish close, personal, emotional bonds with other men. Women represent a threat to this homosocial world. In fact, Roper found that men were much more inhibited with their emotional expressiveness with women than with other men. Career women provoked fears in the men about the security of the gender order and their own masculinity. (Williams 1997: 519)

Crucially for Williams, it is this aspect of Roper's study which is held to explain the differences in the 'depictions of male sexuality in the two studies'. On Roper's research regarding homosociabilty in organizations she says, 'If this finding is correct – *and I believe that it is* – this could help to explain the different depictions of men in the two works' (Williams 1997: 519, added emphasis). In short, Williams argues in effect that my research was an outcome of the kind of homosocial logic identified by Roper. In Williams's view, I was positioned by such a logic in that my experiences in the two tourist organizations were mediated by organizational homosociability, and hence, as a consequence, my research was a direct effect of this logic. She suggests:

> Adkins's male respondents may have seen her as an intruder and an interloper – a challenge to their masculinity and to their authority over women – and treated her accordingly. Roper's male respondents, in contrast, clearly saw him as 'one of them' or at least a younger version of themselves: many projected their own values and ambitions onto him, offering him unsolicited advice about his career and giving him business contacts. (Williams 1997: 519–520)

Roper's account of homosociability in organizations is therefore held by Williams to be correct ('if this finding is correct – and I believe that it is') and is mobilized to position my research as the effect of this logic. Moreover, according to Williams, unlike Roper, I could neither escape nor be aware of this logic as a result of certain social characteristics: 'as a young woman, Adkins no doubt had difficulty seeing the world from the vantage point of the sexist managers and ride operators she interviewed'. In effect, Williams is claiming that certain immanent characteristics (in this case age and sex) on the part of the knower meant that a 'meeting of the reflexivity exhibited by actors as part of a lifeworld and that exhibited by the researcher as part of social scientific community' (May 1998: 8) was not possible in my research. Thus for Williams age and sex ensured that this research could not involve referential or infra-reflexivity, including the various forms of identification between knower and known described by Roper in regard to his research project. Indeed, Williams goes on to write that it is unfortunate that I have not provided any information about how I was treated or how I felt doing the study (Williams 1997: 520), that is, that I did not provide a more self-conscious account of fieldwork of the sort given by Roper. In making these claims however, Williams assumes or reads in an antagonism between myself and the various men I interviewed in the course of this research project. Yet in assuming such an antagonism, Williams ignores the accounts provided by the men and women interviewed of their experiences of work in tourist organizations and their explanations of aspects of service work organization including selection criteria, rules and regulations and the specifics of service work, especially the significance of issues of self-presentation in relation to customers. Williams therefore discounts referential reflexivity from this research not only on the grounds of age and sex on the part of the knower, but also on the grounds of an assumed antagonism and hostility in relation to the knower on the side of known.

What interests me about Williams's review is the kind of politics around reflexivity in regard to social research being enacted here, about who and who is not recognized as capable of being both self and referentially reflexive in regard to social research *in the world*, that is reflexive in terms of the knower and the known. Let me pose a number of questions to get at this politics. Why is Roper's account read as concerning self and referential reflexivity but reflexivity discounted in my own on the grounds of age and sex on the side of the knower and antagonism on the side of the known? Why is my research discounted on the grounds of a logic which my own positioning did not allow me to 'see', while Roper's positioning is understood to be constitutive of both self-reflexivity and the kind of reflexivity between knower and known (referential or infra-reflexivity) which writers such as May and Latour suggest the social sciences need to embrace? Why does the reviewer foreground the relationships between the researchers and the men interviewed in Roper's and my own study and ignore the relationships between the researchers and the women interviewed in the respective studies? Why doesn't the reviewer see similar problems in Roper's research with respect to his relationship with the women executive managers he interviewed to those she accredits to mine in relation to interviewing men? In short why does my sex (and age) matter while Roper's does not? My answer to these questions is that it has something to do with the concept of reflexivity, and in particular that reflexivity concerns a particular figuring of the relationship between the knower and the known, not only in regard to textual and other forms of endogenous reflexivity, but also in regard to social research 'in the world'. Specifically, and in the section which follows I will suggest that reflexivity in regard to social research concerns a form of relationship between the knower and the known which positions the researcher as able to 'speak' (and be viewed as 'correct') via a particular figuring of identity. However, I suggest that this speaking position does not concern a claim of a transcendental positioning as in realism, but rather that in reflexive social science practice such a speaking position is constituted in terms of a vision of a *mobile relation to identity* on the side of the knower in relation to the known. In short, I shall argue that calls for reflexivity in social research concern this kind of vision of mobility in regard to identity. One implication of this argument is that the kinds of problems located by May and Latour in regard to reflexivity are not simply confined to meta- or endogenous reflexivity but also to the reflexivity associated with being in the world. Another however, and as I shall make clear, is that there are a number of exclusions from reflexivity. To make this argument I turn to Felski's (1995) analysis of the emergence of self-conscious textualism in the writings of the literary avant-garde. I do so because Felski's analysis highlights the kinds of politics in regard to reflexivity which I want to suggest are at issue in relation to contemporary calls for reflexivity in relation to social research. If my turn here to textual reflexivity seems odd in the light of the way May and Latour tend to associate textual reflexivity with endogenous or meta-reflexivity and their distinctions between endogenous/meta-reflexivity and referential/infra-reflexivity, I hope it will become clear that part of my argument is that I am not sure if these distinctions can be so easily drawn.

SELF-REFLEXIVITY AND THE POLITICS OF SUBVERSION

In *The Gender of Modernity* Felski (1995) discusses how during the late nineteenth century the literary avant-garde pursued a self-consciousness textualism as a strategy of subverting sexual and textual norms. Such a strategy was deployed in the context of the emergence and rise of consumerism for the middle classes, particularly for middle-class women. This 'feminization' and aestheticization of the public sphere, Felski suggests, was threatening to bourgeois men whose social identity had been formed 'through an ethos of self-restraint and a repudiation of womanly feelings' (Felski 1995: 90). Yet for men who were disaffected from the dominant norms of middle-class masculinity, Felski argues the emergence of an aestheticized and feminized modernity offered hope of an alternative to the forces of positivism, progress ideology, and the sovereignty of the reality principle. And it was this alternative that offered the literary avant-garde a ground to challenge traditional models of masculinity via an imaginary identification with the feminine (Felski 1995: 91). This took the form of a self-conscious textualism which

> Defined itself in opposition to the prevailing conventions of realist representation, turning to a decadent aesthetic of surface, style and parody that was explicitly coded as both 'feminine' and 'modern'. (Felski 1995: 91)

While as Felski points out these practices were limited to a small, if influential group, nevertheless in questioning dominant ideals of masculinity this group aimed at 'the heart of bourgeois modes of self-understanding' (Felski 1995: 92), in particular, these practices denaturalized masculinity. Thus masculinity could no longer be assumed to be fixed, unitary and stable. But Felski argues it is a mistake to understand the feminization of texts as simply undoing gender, since the appropriation of an aesthetic of parody and performance 'reinscribes more insistently those gender hierarchies which are ostensibly being called into question' (Felski 1995: 92). This, she argues, is the case as the transgressive power of the feminine in such texts is predicated on a 'radical disavowal of and dissociation from the "natural" body of woman' (Felski 1995: 92).

Felski considers a number of avant-garde texts to give flesh to this proposal. Here, she draws attention to the ways in which femininity was crucial to the self-reflexivity of such texts. She considers, for example, how the trope of femininity is mobilized to epitomize artifice rather than authenticity and acts 'as a cipher for the very self-reflexivity of poetic language itself' (Felski 1995: 94). The key precondition of this move was the aestheticization of woman in relation to consumerism, and in particular how the everyday practice of femininity gradually came to concern practices of adornment and self-presentation. This aestheticization of woman decoupled femininity from the natural body, and as a set of signs femininity lent itself to appropriation. Through this very artificiality 'femininity was to become the privileged marker of the instability and mobility of modern gender identity' (Felski 1995: 95). For example, in avant-garde texts the 'modernness' and supposed transgressiveness of the male protagonists in regard to gender is portrayed in terms of femininity. Thus the protagonists possess traits usually associated with women such as a love of fashion, sensitivity and vanity and they spend much time in private space codified as feminine rather than in the public sphere of work and politics, often locked into practices of self-reflection and self-contemplation in regard to their aesthetic practices. In addition, language itself in such texts is an object of display, with description taking priority over narrative, form over substance, style over history, characteristics which the protagonists also share. This abandonment of realist conventions in such texts leads, Felski argues, to a self-conscious preoccupation with the surface of language, a self-consciousness which is evident in the use of techniques of cliché, stereotype and paradox which undermine any referential dimensions. Thus in these texts the transgressiveness of the protagonists (their mobility in terms of gender) and the challenges to realism and to conventional codes of masculinity all converged on the appropriation of the trope of femininity, whose very stylization, denaturalization and artificiality provided the grounds for such moves.

But while Felski draws attention to the ways in which the trope of femininity is central to such moves she also highlights a number of key exclusions from this textual strategy. For example, while women's bodies in such texts are often portrayed as aestheticized – for instance, through portrayals of women as actresses, performers, images and works of art – nevertheless women are denied mobility in regard to gender and an ironic self-consciousness in relation to this aestheticization. Indeed, women are portrayed as embodying 'artifice naively ... without being able to raise it to the level of philosophical reflection' (Felski 1995: 110). The subversion of gender norms is therefore not available to women 'whose nature renders them incapable of this kind of free-floating semiotic mobility and aesthetic sophistication' (Felski 1995: 106). For example, Felski points to Huysman's text *Against the Grain* (1884), where after fantasizing about the possibility of erotic perversity with a masculine female athlete, the male protagonist is dismayed to find that she is 'unable to transgress the limits of her own gender' (Felski 1995: 111) and possesses 'all the childish weaknesses of a woman' (Huysman, in Felski 1995: 111). In avant-garde texts women are thus excluded from a self-conscious transcendence of corporeality and identity. And in this context Felski draws attention to how the very strategy of subversion deployed in such texts is constitutive of new boundaries and gender hierarchies, as well as to the similarities between self-conscious literary texts and modern rationalism. In particular, the latter share a vision of overcoming the constraints of psychological determination and dissolving the power of sexual difference. Reducing the body to a free floating play of signs and codes, aestheticism, like science, positions itself as being against (female) nature. (Felski 1995: 112)

But Felski also notes the similarities between the early modernist concerns to overcome gender via the feminine, and more recent concerns with destabilizing power of feminine textuality, especially in the 'deployment of the motif of "Becoming woman" as a trope for the crisis of Western philosophical thought' (Felski 1995: 113). Felski argues that in such contemporary strategies the fantasy of becoming woman is often defined in opposition to the naivety of feminists' struggles for social change which are read as either essentialist or as concerning phallic identification. On such strategies she writes:

> Without wishing to exaggerate the similarities between very different intellectual and political contexts, one might note that this strategy appears to enact an uncanny repetition of the dandy's affirmation of his own 'feminine' semiotic at the expense of women. (Felski 1995: 113)

For the purposes of this chapter what I take from Felski's analysis of literary avant-garde texts is that self-reflexivity has an important – yet often hidden – effectivity in regard to gender, even as it appears to challenge or subvert gender norms. Indeed, a similar logic is also located by Ahmed (1998) in her analysis of the postmodern genre of meta-fiction – a genre of writing which is often understood to concern an extreme form of self-reflexivity and as overcoming the conventions of realism. Ahmed (1998) notes that while often fascinated with sexual difference and sexuality, nevertheless this genre is not read as being about such differences. Indeed they are often read as overcoming such differences (see e.g. Kaufmann 1998). But she argues while postmodern fictions are often read as such, they 'may re-constitute those differences differently, through the very experimentations with literary form' (Ahmed 1998: 150). Via a detailed analysis of meta-fictional stories, Ahmed suggests that such a reconstitution may take place through the way in which the self-reflexivity of such narratives concerns a masculine mode of enunciation. For example, she draws attention to how the self-reflexivity of such narratives often concerns a liberal and masculinist freedom to create woman, as well as phantasies of 'over-coming gendered and generic limits as an aspect of a masculine mode of enunciation' (Ahmed 1998: 158).

REFLEXIVITY AND THE POLITICS OF MOBILITY

With similar caveats as Felski's in mind in regard to issues of historical, intellectual and political specificity, what I want to draw attention to is the affinity between the kinds of politics of reflexivity in regard to gender at issue in relation to the self-consciousness of the literary avant-garde and postmodern fictions located by Felski (1995) and Ahmed (1998) respectively, and the politics of reflexivity at issue in regard to social research 'in the world'. Consider, for example, the disembodied textual mobility enacted by Woolgar and Ashmore (1991) in their self-conscious dialogue above ('BUT THE BASIC POINT IS THAT WE COULD SWITCH ROLES WITHOUT ANYONE NOTICING? Yes. AND THAT WE COULD DROP THIS UPPER CASE/ lower case DISTINCTION IN ORDER TO DELIBERATELY CONFUSE OUR SUPPOSEDLY SEPARATE IDENTITIES? Right'). Thus, as Felski argues in relation to the literary avant-garde the apparent transgressiveness of such self-reflexivity – indeed the speaking position of such self-reflexive texts – is constituted through a vision of a self-conscious transcendence of corporeality and identity. But consider also the non-textual, non-endogenous, referential, *'in-the-world' mobility* accredited to Roper (1994) by Williams (1997) in terms of the relationship between knower and known. Specifically, Williams accredits Roper's research with referential or infra-reflexivity (and his account is understood to be 'correct') on the grounds of an account of a recursive identification between knower and known, that is, on the grounds of Roper's identification with the male organizational executive managers he interviewed, and an account of the latter's identification with Roper, evidenced in offers of career advice and business contacts. Thus what constitutes Roper's account as reflexive for Williams is a vision of mobility in regard to identity on the side of the knower in relation to the known, that is a mobility both in terms of identity and identification (in this case a mobility in terms of different forms of masculinity) as well as a self-consciousness regarding this mobility.[4] For example, according to Williams, such mobility ensured that Roper's research involved the kind of challenge to subject–object relations in relation to the knower and the known which a more reflexive social research reaches towards. By contrast, in regard to my research (Adkins 1995) Williams disallows such a reflexive dimension by attributing a *lack* of mobility in regard to identity and identification to the knower in relation to the known. In short, Williams suggests that the problems of my particular research project related to the inability to overcome identity – age and sex – and that this fixity in turn led to a lack of reflexivity – referential and endogenous – and to problematic research. Hence her claim that I 'had difficulty seeing the world from the vantage point' of those I interviewed and her assumption of hostility between those interviewed and myself.[5] It seems therefore that the capacity for reflexive social research, and in particular the precondition of referential reflexivity (for example, claims of a recursive identification between knower and known), is an issue of overcoming fixity on the part of the knower through a vision of a mobile relation to identity in relation to the known.

While for the literary avant-garde and for the contemporary textual self-reflexivists reflexivity is constituted through a vision of a self-conscious transcendence of corporeality and identity, it seems that reflexivity 'in the world' is constituted through a similar vision of mobility in regard to identity. As we have seen, Felski has shown how the reflexivity of the literary avant-garde was constituted through a mobility in regard to gender, yet this mobility was predicated on a 'radical disavowal and dissociation from the "natural" body of the woman' (Felski 1995: 11). Hence in avant-garde texts women are denied mobility in regard to gender identity 'whose nature renders them incapable of this kind of free-floating semiotic mobility' (Felski 1995: 12). And so too it seems that a similar politics of exclusion is at issue in regard to reflexive social research. Thus according to Williams (1997), age and sex may render women incapable of mobility 'in the world' and hence referential and self-reflexivity in regard to the social research process. In this context, and along the lines of Felski's questioning of the subversiveness of the literary avant-garde, the progressiveness so often ascribed to reflexive social research – not only endogenous, but also referential – must surely be questioned. Indeed, reflexivity as a critical practice may be far from neutral and in particular may have a hidden politics of gender. Specifically, if reflexivity between knower and known is constituted via a vision of a mobile relation to identity on the part of the knower in relation to the known, and women are excluded from such mobility on the grounds of their 'nature', then much like the self-reflexivity of the literary avant-garde such strategies 'in the world' may also concern the inscription of new gender hierarchies. Here the issue concerns who can speak 'for whom, why, how and when' in the age of reflexive social science. For as I hope to have illustrated through the example of two research projects, reflexivity in terms of the knower and the known may inscribe a hierarchy of speaking positions in relation to gender (for a further example of such an inscription see Barnes *et al.* 2000). The inscription of this hierarchy is however hidden by claims that reflexivity is a 'good' and 'progressive' thing in regard to the gender politics of social research. Indeed, what is ironic regarding this inscription is that reflexivity is often understood in part to concern a response and antidote to feminist critiques of universalism in regard to social research (see e.g. Gergen and Gergen 1991). Thus a more reflexive politics of location in regard to both the knower and the known in social research developed in part due to feminist critiques of universalism in social research. Yet while reflexivity ostensibly calls into question such universalism, and in particular appears to call into question assumptions of a masculine speaking position and the normalization of masculine experiences, at the same time reflexivity may be constitutive of new hierarchies in social research, particularly if reflexivity is attributed to certain selves and not to others.

CONCLUSIONS: SITUATING REFLEXIVITY 'IN THE WORLD'

In a critique of the reflexive ethnographic turn in anthropology, and in particular a turn to self-reflexivity (where 'the reflexive gaze stops at the author': Probyn 1993: 80) Probyn has drawn attention to the ways in which self-consciousness on the part of reflexive ethnographers often relies on making respondents as well as 'the field' stationary. What I am suggesting is that in regard to referential reflexivity a similar logic is also at issue regarding speaking positions on the side of the knower. Thus while some social scientists are deemed mobile (and their research hence reflexive and sound), others are deemed fixed (their research unreflexive and hence questionable).[6] Discussing self-reflexivity further, Probyn (1993) has argued that the problem in regard to reflexivity is not that there should not be reflexivity regarding one's research practices, but rather that it 'is the conception of the self at work within this reflexivity that is at fault' (Probyn 1993: 80), a conception which she characterizes as concerning an ontological egotism. Against this conception of the self, Probyn insists that it is vital always to ask 'what had to be held in place in order for this self to appear at all' (Probyn 1993: 80). Thus, she posits an understanding of the self as a speaking position based on a questioning 'of how it is that I am speaking' (Probyn 1993: 80; see also Skeggs 1995). It is precisely this kind of questioning which I am suggesting may be disallowed in reflexive social science through a *normalization* of a speaking position based on a vision of a mobile relation to identity, a normalization which makes invisible exclusions from this vision. Thus while Probyn, along with writers such as May (1998) and Latour (1991), has questioned the version of the ego-centred self posited in regard to endogenous and self-reflexivity, I would suggest that this questioning also needs to be extended to referential or infra-reflexivity, particularly if, as I have suggested, the politics of reflexivity allows only some people to speak.

Felski denaturalized the speaking position of the avant-garde and called into question the apparent transgressiveness of their textual strategies by showing how a self-conscious speaking position relied on an appropriation of femininity, an appropriation made possible by the emergence of consumerism for the middle classes. Following this strategy, alongside Probyn's suggestions regarding the importance of historically situating speaking selves and questioning conceptions of selfhood at work in social research, we might ask how it is that the referentially orientated social researchers are speaking? What has to be held in place in order for vision of the self with a mobile relation to identity to appear? We do not have to look far in the social sciences to find arguments regarding an increasing reflexivity of social life (see e.g. Beck *et al.* 1994). Nor do we have to look far regarding arguments about an uneven distribution of reflexivity in regard to class, gender and other contemporary axes of difference such as sexuality, indeed to find arguments that reflexivity may be an important constituent of such differences (see e.g. Lash 1994; Illouz 1997; McNay 1999; Adkins 1999, 2001). Lash (1994), for example has considered how distributions of reflexivity are central to new axes of class formation (see also Illouz 1997), and I have considered how categories of sexuality and in particular heterosexuality are increasingly defined in terms of self-reflexivity (Adkins 2001). What such analyses suggest is that the version of the self at issue on the side of the knower in relation to reflexivity 'in the world' – that is, a vision of the self with a mobile relation to identity – may be the ideal self of late modernity. Reflexivity may then be far from the critical practice it is often understood to be for social research. Indeed while reflexive social research practice ostensibly aims to redress the normalization of particular privileged speaking positions both in relation to the knower and the known it seems, as Haraway has argued, that 'reflexivity, like reflection, only displaces the same elsewhere' (Haraway 1997: 16).

NOTES

1 May (1998) recognizes that a set of diverse thinkers are classified under the term 'postmodernism'.
2 See also Lash (1994), who makes a similar point in regard to cognitive understandings of reflexivity in regard to social theory.
3 The case studies looked at governance in tourist organizations including the regulation of employee behaviour and appearance and interactions with customers. This involved non-participant observation of employee and customer interactions and training sessions, semi-structured interviews with managers, supervisors and employees, and documentary research on the changing formal organizational policies regarding governance in these areas. The study of the occupation of public house management involved interviews with public house managers (husband and wife teams), interviews with company (brewery) personnel managers and documentary research regarding the shifting organization of this occupation. The latter primarily concerned analysis of company records and policy documents.
4 Indeed, it has been suggested that reflexivity is constituted through mobility within and across fields in the context of intensified social differentiation (McNay 1999).
5 In so doing Williams disputes my account of the significance of heterosexuality as an organizing principle of service labour. This raises interesting – if complicated – issues regarding the politics of reflexivity in regard to sexuality.
6 See also Lynch (2000), who likewise argues that in contemporary social research reflexivity is being used as the basis for such judgements.

REFERENCES

Adkins, L. (1995) *Gendered Work: Sexuality, Family and the Labour Market.* Buckingham: Open University Press.

Adkins, L. (1999) 'Community and economy: a re-traditionalization of gender?', *Theory, Culture and Society* 16(1): 119–139.

Adkins, L. (2000) 'Mobile desire: aesthetics, sexuality and the "lesbian" at work', *Sexualities* 3(2): 201–218.

Adkins, L. (2001) 'Risk culture, reflexivity and the making of sexual hierarchies', *Body and Society* 7(1): 35–55.

Ahmed, S. (1998) *Differences that Matter: Feminist Theory and Postmodernism.* Cambridge: Cambridge University Press.

Alvesson, M. and Skoldberg, K. (2000) *Reflexive Methodology: New Vistas for Qualitative Research.* London: Sage.

Barnes, T., Horner, G., Murphy, A., Pang, X., Powell, R., Rempel, G., Richardson, K., Vasudevan, A. and Winders, J. (2000) 'Capital culture: a review essay', *Environment and Planning D: Society and Space* 18: 275–278.

Beck, U., Giddens, A. and Lash, S. (1994) *Reflexive Modernization: Politics, Tradition and Aesthetics in the Modern Social Order*. Cambridge: Polity.

Denzin, N. and Lincoln, Y. (1994) 'Entering the field of qualitative research', in N. Denzin and Y. Lincoln (eds) *Handbook of Qualitative Research*. London: Sage.

Fay, B. (1996) *Contemporary Philosophy of Social Science: A Multicultural Analysis*. Oxford: Blackwell.

Felski, R. (1995) *The Gender of Modernity*. Cambridge, MA: Harvard University Press.

Game, A. (1991) *Undoing the Social: Towards a Deconstructive Sociology*. Toronto: University of Toronto Press.

Gergen, K. and Gergen, M. (1991) 'From theory to reflexivity in research practice', in F. Steier (ed.) *Research and Reflexivity*. London: Sage.

Haraway, D. (1997) *Modest_Witness@Second_Millennium.FemaleMan_Meets_ OncoMouse: Feminism and Technoscience*. New York and London: Routledge.

Huysman, K. (1926 [1884]) *Against the Grain [A Rebours]*. Paris: Groves and Michaux.

Illouz, E. (1997) 'Who will care for the caretaker's daughter? Towards a sociology of happiness in the era of reflexive modernity', *Theory, Culture and Society* 14(4): 31–66.

Kaufmann, L. (1998) *Bad Girls and Sick Boys: Fantasies in Contemporary Art and Culture*. Berkeley, CA: University of California Press.

Lash, S. (1994) 'Reflexivity and its doubles: structure, aesthetics, community', in U. Beck, A. Giddens and S. Lash, *Reflexive Modernization: Politics, Tradition and Aesthetics in the Modern Social Order*. Cambridge: Polity.

Latour, B. (1991) 'The politics of explanation: an alternative', in S. Woolgar (ed.) *Knowledge and Reflexivity: New Frontiers in the Sociology of Knowledge*. London: Sage.

Lynch, M. (2000) 'Against reflexivity as an academic virtue and source of privileged knowledge', *Theory, Culture and Society* 17(3): 26–54.

McNay, L. (1999) 'Gender, habitus and the field: Pierre Bourdieu and the limits of reflexivity', *Theory, Culture and Society* 16(1): 95–117.

May, T. (1998) 'Reflexivity in the age of reconstructive social science', *International Journal of Social Research Methodology* 1(1): 7–24.

Pels, D. (2000) 'Reflexivity one step up', *Theory, Culture and Society* 17(3): 1–25.

Probyn, E. (1993) *Sexing the Self: Gendered Positions in Cultural Studies*. London and New York: Routledge.

Roper, M. (1994) *Masculinity and the British Organization Man since 1945*. Oxford: Oxford University Press.

Skeggs, B. (1995) 'Introduction', in B. Skeggs (ed.) *Feminist Cultural Theory: Process and Production*. Manchester: Manchester University Press.

Steier, F. (ed.) (1991) *Research and Reflexivity*. London: Sage.

Williams, L. (1997) 'Review essay', *Journal of Contemporary Ethnography* 25(4): 516–520.

Woolgar, S. (ed.) (1991a) *Knowledge and Reflexivity: New Frontiers in the Sociology of Knowledge*. London: Sage.

Woolgar, S. (1991b) 'Reflexivity is the ethnographer of the text', in S. Woolgar (ed.) *Knowledge and Reflexivity: New Frontiers in the Sociology of Knowledge*. London: Sage.

Woolgar, S. and Ashmore, M. (1991) 'The next step: an introduction to the reflexive project', in S. Woolgar (ed.) *Knowledge and Reflexivity: New Frontiers in the Sociology of Knowledge*. London: Sage.

17 TECHNIQUES FOR TELLING
THE REFLEXIVE SELF

Beverley Skeggs

Debates about reflexivity rely upon a concept of a self. Most recent debates on reflexivity have focused upon how this reflexive self can be known through particular methodological techniques, such as confessions, auto-biographies, experimental writing, autoethnography, etc. (see Amanda Coffey, Chapter 15 in this volume). In this chapter I make an argument for a turn away from this self-telling to paying attention to research practice and research participants. In order to make this argument I show how the concept of the self (in particular the reflexive, knowing, inner self) was a specific historical production that was produced through particular methodologies: forced telling for welfare for the working class and authorial exhibitionism for the middle classes. However, this is not a straightforward story as feminism and gay and lesbian politics used similar methods of telling in order to make political claims. Notwithstanding this dissident divergence, I show how the techniques of telling also rely on accruing the stories of others in order to make them into property for oneself. It is therefore the method that is constitutive of the self, not the self of the researcher that always/already exists and can be assumed in research.[1]

To make my argument the chapter is divided into four sections. The first explores the historical conditions of possibility for the production of particular 'selves', paying close attention to the development of the confessional as a method that can be used in the contemporary. The second section brings this method up to date with a discussion about recent forms of testimony, showing how gender is produced through this process and how it has been utilized for dissident stories. The third section then explores Strathern's theories of attachment and detachment to show how reflexivity, as a particular methodological technique, became a mechanism of self-possession. This leads into a debate in the fourth section that explores the costs involved in becoming a flexible, reflexive knowing self, showing that in order for some people to move, to be reflexive, others must be fixed in place. Here I draw on two research projects in which I have been involved to explore the earlier debates in practical detail, drawing attention to the difference between claiming reflexivity as a resource for authorizing oneself (*being*) and *doing* reflexivity in practice.

TECHNIQUES FOR TELLING: FORCING THE WORKING-CLASS SELF INTO EXISTENCE

This section begins with a brief analysis of the conditions of possibility for contemporary telling enabled by the confessional. Stanley (2000) has argued that the emphasis placed on the self and its mediation by discursive practices results in the social being collapsed into interior processes. On the contrary, I hope to show how it is precisely through the telling of the self that the social processes (of positioning, of value, of moral attribution) are put into effect. The telling of the self becomes a manifestation and maintenance of difference and distinction. Berlant (2000) would go even further and argue that the telling of the self through particular techniques is now enabling the re-formation of the nation in the USA, and you cannot get much more social than that.

Abercrombie *et al.* (1986) argue that the confessional, like Christianity as a whole, preceded the emergence of feudalism, having its modern origins in the thirteenth century. It survived the onslaught of competitive capitalism to flourish in a capitalist system. The confessional played an important role in the historic emergence of the individual, self-conscious person equipped with subjectivity and moral standards. They distinguish between the role of the confessional in guilt cultures and shame cultures. In guilt cultures social control is exercised as if it were internally in the conscience of the individual and behaviour is monitored by these forms of guilt reaction. By contrast, in shame cultures, social control is exercised through mechanisms such as public confrontation of the sinner, gossip and more public and overt forms of moral restraint. The institution of confession presupposes the existence of a doctrine of personal guilt, a moral order against which an individual can sin, with a variety of techniques for speaking about and hearing confessional statements.

They argue that there are strong reasons for believing that a system of control by the inner cause of conscience was a very peculiar development in western society, which led to a uniqueness in the development of the modern personality. It is the private and interior nature that distinguishes it from other forms of confessional, in particular in the emergence of the concept of conscience. The confession was part of a new logic of *personhood,* organized around the key concepts of conscience, consciousness, feeling and sentiment (Huff 1981).

While feminist theorists have drawn attention to the impossibility of women becoming persons of conscience (e.g. Pateman 1988), Goody (1983) argues that the influence of Christianity did actually enable some women to be seen as worthy of personhood. He argues that because the Church needed converts and bequests, upper-class women could be part of the property settlement of families, they were treated as individuals endowed with reason, will and independence. It was a tiny group, but one which, he argues, had some influence at court. As social control became a significant social issue in the eighteenth and nineteenth centuries, the attribution of moral worth to some women (not just upper class) was enabled through the representations of the 'angel at the hearth' and the 'recuperable working-class woman'. As

David (1980) and Donzelot (1979) illustrate, working-class women were recruited by the state to take control and responsibility of their potentially disruptive and disreputable men-folk and children.

Foucault (1976) notes how the confessional became employed in a variety of different forms for social control, including the intimate with the legislative, practices which always express power and knowledge:

> It plays a part in justice, medicine, education, family relationships and love relations, in the most ordinary affairs of everyday life, and in most solemn rites; one confesses one's crimes, one's sins, one's thoughts and desires, one's illnesses and troubles; one goes about telling, with the greatest precision, whatever is most difficult to tell. (Foucault 1976: 59)

In Foucault's work the confessional shifts from what people consciously hide from themselves and becomes concerned with what is disguised from them in the unconscious. Foucault's interest in confession is in the impersonality of the scene by which personal subjectivities become formed, of how taxonomies become rationalized to mark the subject's place within a categorical typification. Abercrombie *et al.* (1986) show how the traditional Catholic confessional was appropriated by Protestant biography, then redeployed in the modern psychoanalytic confessional and finally reconstituted in bureaucratic forms of inquiry. The confessional mode becomes part of the bureaucratic apparatus of the modern state. This is a story of a technique expanding and being deployed in different ways, but always in ways that produced distinction between groups. The form of individualism that developed from the confessional can be seen as a consequence of discursive struggles. This discursive development, they argue, was the outcome of intellectual conflicts, competition between groups and classes, and of institutional changes.[2]

The discursive struggle has a long and dispersed history intricately tied up with relations of classification, namely who could be a self. The self that could be told also had to *be seen* to be known fully. The struggle around representations became a significant arena for struggle in which different technologies (such as printing press, art, and eventually TV and Internet) enable different forms of narration and visuality.

Abercrombie *et al.* (1986) show how the self become a resource that could be mobilized for the display of cleverness, as a form of intellectual property. For instance, in a study of the formation of the individual, they show how particular techniques were deployed for displaying the characteristics of the self. They point out that in representations of the face in the pre-modern period, the artist's purpose was not to convey a likeness of the individual but to show their status and authority (e.g. depiction of office, patriarchal and religious status, etc.).

Hunter (1992) argues that the self-reflexive person became consolidated in the nineteenth century as a principle of romantic aesthetics, namely that of overcoming incompleteness and aspiring to full humanity by using techniques of self-cultivation which aimed to harmonize and reconcile the different, fractured, divisive aspects of personhood. The introduction and repetition of the chronological form is linked to this desire (Evans 1999).

Bennett (1998) takes this a step further by showing how certain intellectual agendas such as the aspiration to reflexivity translate the dialectical technique of person formation into a dialectical-historical method. This process enables the intellectual call to self-reflexivity to become translated as a normative requirement of rigorous methodology, when really it is merely a mechanism by which the romantic aesthetics of the whole and coherent self are put into place in the name of intellectual practice. He also points out how the concern with the technique of the coherent self as methodological practice always produces a present 'self'. That is, a self that is always reliant on history and memory.

If we think of this process as a form of self-technology we direct our attention to the ways in which the relations between persons and cultural resources are organized by particular cultural technologies, and to the variable forms of work on the self, or practices of subjectification, which such relations support. These practices display not so much a particular form of (self) consciousness or interiority but the cultural resources and the social positions on which the person/researcher can draw and by which they are located. It is therefore a matter of positioning and access to the means of telling. It is also about the ability to be heard.

Steedman (1998) shows how histories of the modern self are inextricably bound up with techniques of writing and telling the self, more specifically with histories of narrative. Giddens (1991) for instance, notes how through a three hundred year development period in the west personhood and self-identity have come to be understood as 'the self ... reflexively understood by the person in terms of his or her biography' (Giddens 1991: 52–54). He understands the telling of the self not so much as a form of writing, rather as a form of cognition 'the core of self-identity in modern life' (1991: 53).

Taylor (1989), surveying the whole of western philosophy, shows that the significant feature in regard to the self is the movement of the self from *outside to inside*. The self gained an interiority that could be told through particular techniques.[3] Like Bennett (1998), he also adds memory to the self-formulae, whereby remembering the self is a necessary requirement to telling and writing the interiority. The method of telling was always significant in the formation of the knowing-self.

Steedman (2000) develops this further. She points to the significance of the tradition of the 'great European novel' to show how what we tell and how we tell it was part of the technique of literary production. That is, certain forms of subjectivity, 'the knowing self', were always attributed to the bourgeois subject. The working class, she argues, were offered the position of subjectivity to occupy only if they could fit into a particular mode of telling. Both her detailed historical studies of the concept of childhood and the development of 'creative writing' as a form of educational practice show how the concept of a recuperative self was developed in working-class children. Different techniques of telling enable the attribution of the 'self' to different groups.

Significant to the distinction between different types of individuals being produced by different technologies is the attribution of moral value that was enabled through particular forms of telling. Steedman shows how certain forms of subjectivity became related through self-narration to the administration and distribution of poor relief. Thereby subjectivity became related to legal decisions about social worthiness. The most well known of these is the narrative of the deserving poor, in particular the gendered variant of the recuperable fallen woman, who reiterates the story of seduction and betrayal.[4] In these characterizations legally required questions structure the forms of telling and thereby the conditions of possibility for the narration of the self. The accounts produced and recorded are forms in which the interlocutor has been removed and are structured through answers. She argues:

> By these means, multitudes of labouring men and women surveyed a life from a fixed standpoint, told it in chronological sequence, gave an account of what it was that brought them to this place, this circumstance now, telling the familiar tale for the justices clerk to transcribe. (Steedman 1998: 17–18)

She also lists other forms of enforced self-narration: literary Grub Street; philanthropic societies; criminal tales; working-class histories. In particular 'the plebeian, subaltern and female' were particular sources of interest.[5] In most of these the life of these preconstituted selves are structured in a way in which events *happen to* the protagonist. Vincent (1991) argues that families came to be seen as poor when they could no longer keep their stories private. The state, he argues, had the most sophisticated repertoire of devices from reading the marks of poverty inscribed on bodies, on clothes, on moving through the streets. All these mechanisms, Steedman (1998) argues, assumed that the subaltern *could* speak, and that the dispossessed could come to an understanding of their own story. Svensson (1997) in a contemporary study shows how this model of forced telling is employed in Swedish prisons. She shows how the biographical project of the state frames prisoner identity and the morality that is attached to it via the distinction between good and bad selves. She argues that this is a form of symbolic violence that seems to almost erase the possibilities for any form of radical autoethnography. How can you be radical if your self is named and organized for you?

This forced telling is in contrast to the stories of the 'great individuals' who were agents of their own subjectivity, who produced themselves. They were not positioned by the law or circumstance. Rather, they conducted their selves through their own narration. Ricoeur (1990) argues that the process of fictionalizing enables a permanence of the self. It is marked, he argues, by key phrases such as 'I had to', 'I did', 'I refused'. The significant difference between those whose key phrases were given to them to tell and those who produced their own is the marking of the class difference of telling. Interestingly, Chanfrault-Duchet (2000) argues that this process is not marked by gender.

Robbins (1986) argues that self-narration was also strongly related to the construction of 'character' and 'personhood' whereby only the bourgeoisie were seen to be capable of being individuals. Character, he argues, was the 'mask that people were expected to don in the face of power' or 'character was a statement in which one employer described to another ... the habits and qualities of a servant' (Robbins 1986: 35). Stanley (2000) draws attention to the 'currency' of character so that domestic servants needed a 'character statement' to show what kind of person they were as well as what sort of labour they could sell:

> The 'character' was not only a moral statement but also a highly constitutive practice that could and did have repercussions for people's places within the labour market, within 'respectable society' and also as moral beings: it indicated what someone's status and worth should be taken to be, and the giving and withholding of 'characters' [sic] was highly consequential for people's positions within class, status and other hierarchies. (Stanley 2000: 42)

The contemporary link that is now being made between appearance and character as a requirement of the middle-class service sector of the labour market (e.g. du Gay 1996), therefore can be seen not as a new phenomenon but a new way in which the surveillance of labour is moving into the middle classes.

The other significant feature of this process is that the working class did *not* write themselves; they told the story as proscribed and were transcribed. So access to the self is limited by the means and techniques of telling and knowing. Marcus (1994) argues that the autobiographical form historically came to mark and be marked by the privilege of self-possession. Being the author of one's life rather than the respondent to another's interlocutions generated different sorts of personhood; a class difference that is being reproduced in contemporary forms of telling.

The class divided techniques for telling the self: the legislated, often invisible interlocutor who framed particular ways of producing the working-class self and the individualized unique self of the bourgeoisie informed the generation of ways of telling and hearing the self that are now incorporated into a variety of contemporary sites, as we shall see in the next section which explores the gendering of the testimonial self (a more contemporary form of reflexivity).

The centrality of legislation for the materialization of the self can be seen in the recent moves towards telling as testimony. The concept of testimony comes from, first, a legal framework whereby witnesses in court bear testimony. As Cosslett *et al.* (2000) show, testimony connects the first-person narrative to truth-telling. Second, testimony has a religious connotation, closely related to the confessional whereby testifiers bear witness to their conversion or beliefs. In both these senses, they point out, the term has important resonances for feminism, which begins with women speaking out about their hitherto unheard experiences and testifying to their 'new' feminist beliefs. The proliferation of testimonial forms involves an extension of the legal domain into other realms of politics and culture.

Testimony, they note is an occurrence in the present to do with the meaning of the past now, facilitated by specific situations and interchanges. The testimonial also demands a witness. Ahmed and Stacey (2001) argue that recent testimonial moves, such as the South African Truth and Reconciliation Commission and the Stolen Generation testimony in Australia, enable the position of the witness and the victim to become aligned because both are presented as the site from which justice can be delivered (see Probyn 2000). But, they argue, if testimony is bound up with truth and justice, then its coming into being also registers the crisis in both of these concepts; for one testifies when the truth is in doubt. Therefore 'truth' can be seen to be subject to appeal, the result of political claims, the result of political struggle between competing groups. Who can tell and how becomes central to this process (as Lynne Haney explores in Chapter 13 in this volume).

Berlant (2001) argues that contemporary expressions of self-expressivity and self-reflexive personhood link norms of expressive denegation to genres that conventionalize and make *false equivalents* among diverse traumatic consequences. She shows how the appropriation of legal rhetoric in tales of testimony aim to claim the authority of self-evidence (as opposed to authority bequeathed by institutions).

This, argue Cosslett *et al.* (2000), shows that the telling of the self is neither simply externally required or internally generated, that subjectivity is an effect produced by forms of autobiographical practice and does not precede it. They argue that this means that gender itself is therefore also produced in autobiographical practice. It is the method that reproduces the performative power of the categories that are brought into effect.

Paradoxically, it was dissident movements that argued for the contemporary telling of oneself as a public gesture of personhood. It was feminists who insisted on putting one's self into the research process. This methodological technique often merged with confessional and testimonial techniques used to make political and moral claims on the dominant order (the specificity of these techniques will be developed later). The demand to put one's self in the research was ironically a technique to expose the power, positioning, privilege and complacency of those (usually male) researchers who claimed objectivity, and played the 'God Trick' of evading responsibility for their work (Haraway 1991).[6] Specifically, its aim was to question the exchange system by which women could and were put to use for voyeurism, surveillance and appropriation in research (see Valerie Walkerdine *et al.*, Chapter 8 in this volume).

Mary Evans (1999) also shows how testimonial practices associated with bourgeois individualism were used to tell 'sexual stories' in which the 'coming out' narrative operates almost as a form of redemption. This should not surprise us as David Evans (1993) shows how central individualism was to the formation of dissident sexual movements that developed in the 1960s.

Mary Evans (1999) also shows how the telling of the self became explicitly gendered from the early 1960s: women's autobiography became more prolific, more radical and more innovative while men's reproduced the traditional definition between the public and the private but declare itself as male. However, by the 1990s she notes that accounts by men were beginning to identify their vulnerability (the men's magazine *Achilles Heel* in the 1980s could be seen as a significant primary influence in this trend). As could the stories by Gay men who were beginning to become more public with their sexual stories. The confessional guilt scenario has been repeatedly reproduced and also repudiated by popular male self-telling – Hollywood films such as *American Beauty* (1999) and *Falling Down* (1993) – which can be seen to be representative of male revenge stories in which women are pathologized as the emasculating force.[7]

Dissident stories tried to produce their own identities, rather than those imposed upon them, or they resignified positions already offered (such as queer, Black). Plummer (1996) argues this identity formation can only take place after the process of imagining, visualizing, articulating, vocalizing and becoming story-tellers. The story will take the form of a recognizable identity (it needs to be repeated with symbolic value for it to become known) with a sense of past, present, future, history, difference, anticipation (Plummer 1996: 43). The next stages he identifies are creating communities of support and creating a culture of public problems.

However, all these stories need to attribute to themselves moral value or worth. Brown (1995) for instance, has shown how the 'wounded attachment' was the foundational force of feminism, enabling women to claim the moral value of suffering, pain, wound and oppression. To challenge the power of normative masculinity feminists established a popular and research agenda through the sharing of experiences (often through the method of 'consciousness raising'). The intensity and presence of these stories did impact upon the political agenda (e.g. rape, domestic violence and child abuse are issues that are now heard and taken seriously). However, as feminism's range increased fragmentation and struggle occurred between groups and these were often formulated through identity politics. What Plummer (1996) identifies as an essential process to establishing the tales of the subaltern on the public agenda came to result in competition for authority and moral high ground.

This is why stories of identity (I am a man/woman/lesbian/gay/disabled researcher) may replace critical interrogation into the intricate composites and reifications of the positions we inhabit and the resources to which we have access. Being positioned by structural relations (sexuality, gender, race, class) does not necessarily give access to ways of knowing (although some standpoint theorists would argue that it helps: see Skeggs 1995; Maynard 1998).[8] As Haraway argues:

> Location is not a listing of adjectives or assigning of labels such as race, sex and class. Location is not the concrete to the abstract of decontextualisation. Location is the always partial, always finite, always fraught play of foreground and background. Text and context, that constitutes critical inquiry. Above all, location is not

self-evident or transparent. ... Location is also partial in the sense of being *for* some worlds and not others. (Haraway 1997: 37, original emphasis)

The 'self' became implicated through debates on identity in which political claims were made for superior epistemological authority on the basis of where one was located within categorical positions (Bar On 1993). The debates over identity and epistemological justification were not about research practice but about the claim and *right to know.* It was a naive formulation of 'position must thereby equal truth must thereby produce authority and legitimation.' Identity politics have created particular problems in *claims* for authority as a property relation.

Following the feminist analysis of power relations in the research process began the anthropological questioning of colonial authority and authorial responsibility. This has often been called a crisis of representation but as Strathern (1987) argues, it is more of a crisis in authority in which representation is the technology that shapes the formation of the crisis. These calls for more ethical and responsible research involved an interrogation of one's location, positioning and cultural resources, *but not* of the *self.* Otherwise identity becomes the effect of feminist rhetoric, tactics and strategies in which the most powerful are able to mobilize their cultural resources against others. The morality of marginality becomes a card to be played in a game of identity politics in which political claims are made.

Having established the terrain by which the self can be known and told, but also used to articulate dissident categorizations and claim moral authority, the next section explores how the self is extended through the telling of the stories of others for further self-fashioning.

SELF-EXTENSION/SELF-AUTHORIZING

The process of telling the stories of the subaltern has been institutionalized in anthropology and sociology as a mechanism by which the self of the writer, researcher is known. So those excluded from selfhood, personhood, individuality, become the object (often objectified) by those who have access to the subject positions of researcher/writer which they use to constitute themselves as interlocutors. The lives of others can be used as extensions of the self – a temporary possession – in which they are brought into self-reflection and then discarded when unnecessary. The use of 'others' to know and constitute the self has a long history in colonialism (Ahmed 2000). Ethnography has been one of the main methodologies by which the possessive individual could be constituted. The possessive individual has the relational capacity to draw to her or himself objects waiting to be personalized through acts of appropriation or consumption (Foster 1995; Strathern 1999).

Yet, as Strathern (1991) points out in her study of extension, it is not just the putting on of parts but the notion of part *as dramatic* that elicits the opportunity for another form of extension, that of *performance* (Munro 1996).

The addition of a part (object) extends the possibilities for cultural performance as 'part' (subject). Objects and subjects thus move hand in hand. Strathern's point is that we move (as researchers) from figure to figure, attaching and detaching are part of the researcher performance, and crucially, as Munro points out, seeing the second figure involves forgetting parts of the first figure. This is always a system of exchange in which the field of exchange is premised on the establishment of prior values. Use values and exchange values thereby move hand in hand. Some objects are seen as more valuable and useful in the performance of self.

Callon (1986) calls this process 'interressments' – the devices by which researchers detach others from elsewhere in order to attach them to themselves. The effect of this passive reflection is highly limiting:

> What is lost are the embodied and spatialised political relations that produce, erode, support, subtend, and surround the mirror. What remains is an overly narcissistic, voluntaristic, and materially stable view of subjectivity and social relations. ... Such theorising additionally depends upon a very particular viewing context, one that speaks of privilege and bodily/spatial control. (Callon 1986)

Strathern keeps together the dual meaning of attachment; as Munro points out:

> first as movement to and from something and second as attachment, feelings of belonging to something. By keeping both meanings of attachment alongside each other, Strathern prevents the latter experience being made disjunct as (merely) subjective, or rejected as emotion. (Munro 1996: 262)

However, Munro warns against reading this in a realist way as if a core self appropriates a range of identities. This is to assume that there is a true self to which one can return. He argues that in the process of extension one is never travelling out of place (that is the core self) rather the only movement is circular, from one figure to another. One figure picks up on what the other excludes. Moreover, appropriation does not necessarily assume magnification and expansion. We can also shrink, hide, become anonymous. Both processes accomplish extension through artefacts. He argues that we are always in extension: '*Indeed extension is all we are ever in*' (Munro 1996: 264, original emphasis) because there is no core self. But the whole process is predicated on the power and ability to move,[9] on access to others and the ability to mobilize resources.

Lury (1998) develops this idea further through the concept of prosthetic culture. She argues that we are now in a period of self-refashioning in which two central processes – indifferentiation and out-contextualization – enable the '*thought*' of reflexivity to become objectified in itself. She argues:

> The previously naturally or socially determined aspects of self-identity are taken out of context and refashioned. This is not simply a process of de- and re-contextualisation, but a reconstitution or regrouping in order to make visible *the ability of a thing, an object, a part to be taken out of context*. ... As a consequence,

individuals, if they are acknowledged as units of analysis at all, are seen not as wholes but as the sum of diverse factors amenable to analysis and manipulation by specialists. They have been outcontextualised. (Lury 1998: 19, original emphasis)

It is this fragmentation and out-contextualization that can be constituted as the 'thought' of reflexivity. This should alert us to the different ways in which reflexivity can be used: as attachment; as out-contextualized object; as reification; as game-play. But also what are the categorizations available, the social relations and constituents of power that enable some to participate in exchange in the formation of themselves? We need to question who is available as a part/object and how they are being used in the constitution of self-extension, detachment or shrinking. We need to think about the economy of exchange, which as Edward Said (1978) pointed out some time ago, is always uneven in the trading of culture. Papastergiadis (1999) describes these forms of exchange as a multidirectional circuit board, where connections and short-circuiting may occur. For instance, in the space of colonial encounters, Pratt (1992) shows how forms of uneven exchange bristle with conflicts and contradictions. The taking on of attachments and detachments is fraught with power and struggle.

Nast (1998) uses the metaphor of the mirror to draw attention to specific techniques in the process of exchange, namely, how others are appropriated through mirror imagery, by which the image of oneself is seen through the mirror relief of the other.[10] In this imagery the reflecting surface is passive, it is 'out there' in texts, notes, memories, to be taken and reflected upon inside human heads:

> understanding difference through mirroring depends on a dichotomy that reduces otherness to a singular distinction: me (here)/not me (there). The me-centred process tames 'otherness', making it something one ably decides upon and crafts and something one *chooses* to learn about or reject. (Nast 1998: 95, original emphasis)

Nast (1998) explores how this privileged self-concern has been used in anthropology to *define* difference, to *make* difference, this is in contrast to earlier definitions whereby being reflexive was about comparatively reflecting upon one's cultural practice in relation to others', so as to recognize and come to some understanding of difference (Nast 1998: 94). The central point in all these accounts is how reflexivity becomes a property of the researcher's self *not* of the practice of the participants. Rendering of difference becomes translated into properties of the self (or in the case of copyright, properties of the self – writing the self – become properties of multinational publishing companies). So the possibilities for the reflexive self is framed by these different processes of exchange (attachment and detachment) and techniques of telling and knowing. These have to be legitimized and authorized.

This is why those who advocate the telling of the self are not always those whose research is informed by reflexive practice (i.e. an understanding of the positions and locations of power of others). Rather they are making direct claims to know via their own positioning (and/or more recently their textual style). I would even argue that the centring of the self is a particular technique of eclipsing and de-authorizing the articulations of others. It is all a matter of whom the researcher thinks is important. So the dictum to be reflexive has become interpreted in a banal way, whereby the experience of the research is one of the researcher-only and their story. Their story is based on their identity, which is usually articulated as a singularity and takes no account of movement in and out of space, cultural resources, place, bodies and others but nonetheless authorizes its self to speak. As Probyn (1993: 80) argues, 'It is not the process of being reflexive about one's research practices that is the problem. ... it is the conception of the self at work within this reflexivity that is at fault.' It is the tendency to think that the problems of power, privilege and perspective can be dissolved by inserting one's self into the account and proclaiming that reflexivity has occurred in practice. Telling and doing are two very different forms of activity.

Strathern (1999) shows how not only is the self crafted from reified, objectified relations but also property claims are then made from these. She argues that where things already appear to exist in the world then establishing 'property' is a question of creating personal claims in them:

> When the 'thing' that becomes property through the claims that people make on it is then perceived as the product of social relations in the first place, that fresh perception may itself be perceived as a product of social effort for it requires and constitutes knowledge. (Strathern 1999: 18)

The claims people make through relations with others is imagined and framed as relations of body substance and property relations (Strathern 1999: 21). For instance in a book on *Rethinking Social Research*, one of the editors notes:

> In exploring the social relations of the research process, researchers need to interrogate *their own* relationships to the research context and to research participants. In part this leads to questions of *identity* and the *rights* of the researcher to be involved in certain areas of research. (Truman in Humphries and Truman 1994, added emphasis)

In this proscriptive statement Truman frames the research relations in terms of self-ownership (identity) and the property rights of access to other bodies. The groups Truman describes in her research become the 'things' identified by Strathern (1999) as products of the social relations 'in the first place'. This enables researchers to foreground their sensitivity as a product of ethical knowledge, while what it hides is the property relations of object and subject for which responsibility is evaded, although claimed. The lack of attention to reification and the reproduction of classification systems is how reflexivity gets invoked in a naive attempt to shore up the researcher's claim to authority. Bizarrely reflexivity becomes detached from practice and attached to self.

By reflexivity Bourdieu (1992) does not mean direct self-examination. As Griller (1996) notes, he is particularly disdainful: 'Objectivation of any cultural producer involves more than pointing to – and-bemoaning – his [*sic*] class background and location, his race or his gender' (Waquant 1989). One of these resources is not our own self or other authorization that has hitherto been discussed, but access to institutional or legitimate authority. This is why Bourdieu (1992: 111) argues we need to explore 'the relationship between the properties of discourses, the properties of the person who pronounces them and the properties of the institution which authorises him [*sic*] to pronounce them'.

Just as the middle class has always been able to use and access the bodies of the working class for labour, now knowledge of and from others is used to shore up the composite of the academic reflexive self. The skills which are accessed through research, produced through reflexivity and authorized through writing are the means by which the research self comes to be formed and known. Strathern (1999) takes this one stage further, arguing the logic is manifest through intellectual property rights in which property is culturally validated as extensions of person in the appeal to the moral right of creators to their creations. But the creation has come out of the attachment of others who are given no property right at all. So the use of others as resources through the reflexive writing self becomes the means by which political claims are made and authority transferred; hooks (1990) contemplates the continued use of other people's suffering to make the modern suffering, reflexive, bourgeois self:

> No need to heed your voice when I can talk about you better than you can speak about yourself. No need to hear your voice. Only tell me about your pain. I want to know your story. And then I will tell it back to you in a new way. Tell it back to you in such a way that it has become my own. Rewriting you I rewrite myself anew. I am still author, authority. I am still coloniser, the speaking subject, and you are now at the centre of my tale. (hooks 1990: 345)

The ability to be reflexive via the experience of others is a privilege, a position of mobility and power, a mobilization of cultural resources. Rabinow (1977) in reflections on his fieldwork in Morocco explicitly defines his goal in the interpretation of his fieldwork as 'the comprehension of the self by the detour of the comprehension of the other' (Rabinow 1977: 5). But he also argues that this is unavoidable as some form of symbolic violence is always inherent in the structure of the situation (see Killick 1995).

What is at stake in the translation/interpretation of the experiences of 'others' by ethnographers is made explicit in the 'Bell Debate'. This was generated after white feminist ethnographer Diane Bell and her 'collaborator', an Aboriginal woman, Topsy Nelson, published an article in *Women's Studies International Forum* on the rape of Aboriginal women by Aboriginal men (Bell and Nelson 1989). A letter to the journal in February 1990 accused Bell of creating divisions within the 'Aboriginal community', appropriating Topsy Nelson's voice by citing her as a co-author rather than as an 'informant', of exhibiting white imperialism, of exercising middle-class privilege. (Bell 1993: 108)

Ahmed (2000) argues that what is at stake in this debate is not just a question of who is speaking and who is being spoken for, rather it is about the relations of production that surround the text: how it was that Bell came close enough to Topsy Nelson to enable this debate to be aired in public. The ethical problems of ventriloquism (Visweswaran 1994), of producing the 'native' as authentic and truth (Spivak 1990; Narayan 1993), of spuriously 'giving voice', of accountability and responsibility and 'sheer arrogance' (Agar 1980), are all produced through postcolonial critique which forefronts the ethics of merging the voices of others.

Both Nelson and Bell argued that their article was produced as a result of friendship. Yet Bell constantly frames her work and her ethnography in an academic mode of production. Nelson was not passively appropriated in this situation and argues that she used Bell 'to write it all down for her'. Yet as Ahmed (2000) argues, their friendship was strategically framed; their friendship was a technique of knowledge. She argues that the need to make friends with strangers (the basis of most ethnography) works, in terms of relationality and dialogue, to conceal the operation of an epistemic division within the process of becoming more intimate with one who has already been designated as strange. Centuries of colonialism designate some people as knowers and some as strangers (sometimes with some stories worth telling, but only in particular ways, as Steedman earlier noted). We are positioned by these relations and techniques and therefore acknowledgement of the unequal forms of exchange they reproduce is *not* about telling the self but being aware of positioning and the limits on the mobility of some groups.

To support her argument Ahmed (2000) draws on Bell's (1983) earlier ethnography *Daughters of the Dreaming* to show how Bell again authorizes her ethnography. In other words, Ahmed (2000) argues, Aboriginal women are present in the ethnography only in so far as they establish a term in an argument that has its terms of reference in anthropology. They are authorized through the language of academic anthropology by which their words are translated and interpreted. It is these sorts of debates that have led to greater attention being paid to the issues of representation and the conditions of possibility that enable ethnographies to be produced at all.

We can ask, if the subaltern speaks, how is it that we can hear her? Can the subaltern authorize herself if she cannot speak or be heard only through the self/words of others? Spivak (2000) argues no. But unless researchers like Bell make subaltern stories available how would we know about the subaltern at all? If subaltern groups have no access to the mechanisms for telling and distribution of their knowledge, how do others even know that they exist? It is surely a matter of how we do the research rather than abdicating completely. It is interesting that Ahmed (2000), the vociferous critic of subaltern ventriloquism, is a literary textual critic who has not delved into the difficult, messy world of empirical work. How do textual critics access subaltern texts? Where do they come from? They are usually also a product of relations of appropriation (publishing is after all a capitalist industry designed for profit). As Rabinow (1977) earlier argued we are always implicated in the circuits of symbolic violence. It is how we play these circuits that counts, as Bourdieu (1993) would argue. Certainly it is not by reauthorizing our selves through telling and confession but through *practice*. This is practice that understands the relations of production, that is aware of the possibilities for appropriation, that knows about the constraints of disciplinary techniques and the power relations of location and position, and that does not reify and reproduce the categorization that enable exploitation and symbolic violence.

In Ahmed's arguments there is a risk of assuming that epistemological authority (e.g. inequality of knowledge about culture) must necessarily entail a social/moral inequality of worth between the researcher and researched. Yet I know some things about the women I studied that they don't know, just as they know things about me that I don't. Often other people know things about us that we do not see or understand. Also by virtue of my training, experience, ethnographic labours and time, I have access to explanations and interpretations that do offer some epistemological authority, but this need not contradict the moral equality between us.[11] It was the merging between my knowledge and the women's own knowledge that produced the explanations in my earlier *Formations* research (Skeggs 1997). Most of us do empirical research to learn from others, not to exploit and use them. It is therefore important not to confuse positioning with morality or we become complicit in the reproduction of passive pathologies.

MOBILE AND FIXED SELVES

Rather than explicitly telling the self, new forms of textual technique have been invented which de and re-centre the self simultaneously. These new techniques (such as those developed by Woolgar and Ashmore (1991) and named 'the reflexive project', critically exemplified in Lisa Adkins, Chapter 16 in this volume) decentre the singular voice while displaying the copious amounts of cultural capital that is necessary to be able to engage in textual play. Textual demonstration displays the cleverness of the writer while also supposedly decentring them at the same time. This is not just a matter of the powerful claiming marginality. Rather it is about the powerful showing how well they understand power by playing with it. It is a matter of having your authority and eating it. They authorize themselves through their own cultural resources. For as Rabinow (1986) notes, groups long excluded from positions of institutional power have less concrete freedom to engage in textual experimentation. And Strathern (1987) argues that a lot of the ironic re-readings of the 'new ethnographers' look remarkably self-referential and self-legitimizing.

Consider also which forms of research are open to reflexive techniques. Woolgar and Ashmore (1991) are playing with texts and scientific knowledge. They are not playing with subaltern research participants. They may have far less responsibility and accountability to those they are researching. They are not using the lives of others to shore up their displays of clever play with disciplinary technique. This is quite a different matter for ethnographers who do have research participants to whom they are (supposedly if they are ethical) answerable.

Yet these telling of personal stories and textual play can be seductive. They engage us in the game. The telling of personal stories operates as a form of rhetoric whereby we become seduced by the confession, the immediacy of the experience of being there and the personal information. The telling of research stories not only enables the researcher to be identified as 'real' but also grants the spurious authority of authenticity, as Atkinson (1990) documents so well. He shows how two techniques in particular, the interspersal of 'authentic' voices from research participants and the confessional account of the researcher operate as forms of textual seduction, leaving us less likely to question the authority of the researcher and likely to attribute value to the spatial 'being there' nature of their experience. Nobody can read Rosaldo's (1989) account of his partner's death and not be moved. However, this does not always work. The accounts of men's confessions of sexual relationships in the field can have the opposite effect. Rather than displaying their reflexive awareness of power relationships, they can betray their complete ignorance (see Warren 1988, and the collection by Kulick and Willson 1995). The ways in which the self is made reflexive in these accounts depends upon the ethics by which the self–other relationship is read and formed in practice.

So for instance Lisa Adkins shows in Chapter 16 how in a comparative review of her book *Gendered Work: Sexuality, Family and the Labour Market* (Adkins 1995) with that of Roper (1994) on *Masculinity and the British Organization Man since 1945*, Williams (1997) attributes more authority to the writing of the self-reflexive account which solidly places the male author at the centre of the research experience. Less authority is given to Adkins's reflexive practice that informed every stage of the research, because it is not told from the point of self-narration and confession. So the narration of the self in the experience is given more authority than reflexivity in the research practice itself. The researcher self becomes the site of authority, rather than the participants' accounts and explanations (as in Adkins's research project). It is as if the researcher is the only source of knowledge, hence the only source of self-reflection.

Tracing the development of the modernist literary avant-garde in the late nineteenth century through to the postmodern writings of the contemporary, Adkins shows how men have used a form of self-conscious textualism via an imaginary identification with femininity to produce a decadent aesthetic of surface, style and parody. It is the ability to use the '*imaginary feminine*' which has absolutely no bearing on the reality of women's lives that she argues is being reproduced today at the expense of women. This leads Adkins to argue that the technique of literary self-reflexivity may produce new gender hierarchies, in which those once marginalized by feminism in the academy reclaim their space through the imaginary positioning of themselves as sensitive textual and reflexive researcher. That they attribute reflexivity to themselves and not to the researched suggests that it is just another authority claim. She argues that it is no coincidence that the 'reflexive self' is promoted as the new ideal figure of late modernity (see Beck *et al.* 1994) because what it offers is a re-traditionalization of gender, class and sexual relations. We only need to ask who is representing themselves as reflexive, as having a self worth knowing, a voice worth hearing. Zizek (1997) argues that fixing, appropriation and refiguring are central to the constitution and development of late capitalism, embedding of gender in circuits and networks that provide advantages for certain groups of men. In earlier work, Adkins (2000) and Cronin (2000) have shown how new forms of de-traditionalization, the 'freeing of agency from structure' and the 'mobile self' (e.g. Urry 2000), are exactly that: they are mechanisms for re-traditionalization, the fixing of the feminine, authorizing masculine privilege and a distraction from pernicious and ubiquitous class and race inequalities.

Even Lash (1994), one of the main proponents of de-traditionalization and reflexivity draws attention to what he calls 'the structural conditions of reflexivity', especially 'reflexivity winners' and 'reflexivity losers'. Moreover, Spivak (2000) shows how subaltern knowledge can be converted into property and capital through processes of labour market reflexivity, in a way in which global feminism itself may be complicit in the transformation of indigenous women's knowledge into property. Lury (1998) suggests that where structural classifications have been abandoned because they are no longer seen to inhere in the individual, but are rather seen to be the effect of technical prosthesis, that what in fact may be happening is more intense forms of classification. These are the reflexivity losers who cannot access and utilize reflexivity as a cultural resource for either management strategy or narrating them-selves. So we have a distance drawn between the experimental individualism in which reflexivity is a tool by which the resource-ful self is produced. The logic of this experimental individualism for those who can tool themselves up via attachments and detachments is that disembedding, de-racination, de-gendering and de-classing is possible. This is at a time when such classifications are becoming even more acute for those at the extreme ends of the social scale.

However, many ethnographies have been an attempt to challenge the historical bourgeois classification and categorizations that render others as strangers, unworthy of knowing. Others and strangers can challenge the complacency of academic discourse and explanations (just as they did in the *Formations* research: Skeggs 1997). The women of my research did not need me to make their understandings, they had already arrived at them. They had their own reflexivity. Sometimes I did provide alternative (feminist) explanations and they grew into these at a later date.[12] Sometimes they rejected them entirely.

What I did was to provide a distribution network and translate their understandings into a way of challenging prior state, popular and academic discourse about them. The tautology of using categories (such as class, woman, race) that reproduce the history of classification is definitely problematic. However, they can be re-signified, modified and attention drawn to reification and their historical constitution. They do not have to be naively reified and reproduced. I tried to provide what Bourdieu (2000) identifies as a *negation of a denegation*. I showed how they knew they were being misrecognized by others and how this enabled them to know their value and position in an exchange rate mechanism. And for Bourdieu there is no worse dispossession, no worse privation, than that of the losers in the symbolic struggle for recognition. As he shows symbolic power relations are set up and perpetuated through knowledge and recognition.

May (2000) argues that the capacity of the individual to position himself or herself will relate to how they are accommodated within wider cultural views with respect to belonging. This, he argues, will then relate to the attributes the person possesses within the given constellations of social relations (or what Bourdieu names as fields, namely the structured space or positions whose properties depend on positions within those spaces: Bourdieu 1993: 72). My ethnographic research (Skeggs 1997) demonstrated the incongruence between dispositions and positions, showing that the positions on offer (available and known through historically generated symbolic representations) denied any sense of belonging with any value. The women of the research strived to be recognized and positioned as respectable, not as working-class women, which for them was loaded with judgements of inadequacy. In a similar way to Steedman's historical accounts above, the women of the research were expected to tell their lives to various local state authorities that confirmed what they considered to be negative evaluation. The women knew how they were being read and positioned, they knew the possibilities that this afforded and they resisted. They did not want to be fixed in place. They did not want to be rendered immobile.

In this sense their knowledge about their own situation meant that they moved between what May (2000) describes as endogenous reflexivity (the knowledge that is born, deployed and arises from the immediate social and cultural milieus) and referential reflexivity (the process of re-cognition in which the knowledge generated enables the agent to understand the conditions through which such practices are both enabled and constrained). They made reflexive movements, not just as research participants, but on a daily basis as part of how they lived their lives. They knew and experienced the difference between positioning, belonging and mis-recognition. They knew about being fixed in place. They knew how to dissimulate. Their referential reflexivity enabled them to understand their circumstances, what they did not have was access to the requisite resources to improve upon those circumstances.

Their reflexivity was entirely different to my own researcher reflexivity. I used the term at the time to mean the feminist reflection back upon power and practice which folds into thinking abut how social change can occur. In the process of my research this meant attention was given to power relationships, attention to the representation of research participants and attention to issues such as ethics, reciprocity and responsibility (see Skeggs 1997: ch 2). I did not interpret it to be about self-narration or putting myself in the research process. In fact when asked to write about the research, that is exactly what I did. I wrote about the research process, not about myself. I wrote about power, not me. But I was continually asked to put myself in the picture. I was there all the time of course in my body, I had conducted, interpreted, lived the research for eleven years, how could I not be? But I was not interested in self-narration or producing an autobiographical account of myself, although publishers, editors and audiences were. I was interested in interpretation, inequality and impact, not about how it influenced me but the research process itself. This is qualitatively different.

In fact when I did attempt to write my 'self' into the research after much persuasion I regretted it. I unwittingly (or stupidly) reproduced the fixity of my parents in a way they had spent all their lives – like the research participants – trying to avoid. To explicate I will reproduce what I wrote in *Formations*:

> I write this as my mum unpacks the crystal glasses she has bought me to mark my respectability. I have never achieved the respectability that my parents spent their lives desiring and struggling for (I am not married with children, supported and protected by an economically secure male, sexually contained, and my house is rarely immaculately hygienic – although to others my independence and my job may appear as highly respectable). If my parents surround me with the appropriate symbols they hope I may be marked. (Skeggs 1997: 14)

> The chapter on class was excruciating to write as I realised how I, too, had strongly invested in respectability when intimidated at University. I was forced to remember how I had lied about my mother and father's occupations because I was scared to be recognised as inferior. (Skeggs 1997: 15)

My parents were hurt and horrified when they read this.[13] Why I am ashamed of them so much? They wondered why they were positioned as inferior. Then I realized what I had done. Myself-telling had fixed them in order to explain my movement from them, the distance that I had drawn (I later write about the different capitals: economic, social, symbolic and cultural that I have accrued). My reflexivity, my mobility, my self-narration was based on them remaining in place. Steph Lawler (2000) explores concepts of escape and escapism and shows that while escape from the working class is read as heroic, escapism can be seen only as failure.

McNay (1999) argues that reflexivity is an irregular manifestation dependent on a particular configuration of power relations. This makes it possible to see how some forms of reflexivity are reproductive, repetitious and reinforce existing power relations, while others may be challenging and disruptive. But we will only know if we have some sense of the possibilities for action, access to resources and the fields, networks, or structural configurations in which the reflexivity takes place. For this we need to dislocate reflexivity from narrating the self, as a property of persons in the process of attachment and detachment. So we can see that there is a difference between the researcher and the research participant's reflexivity depending on their prior positioning and the resources on which they can draw. This difference builds on the earlier distinction between telling = being and doing = practice.

In a more recent project on Violence, Sexuality and Space, reflexivity was built into the design. It was not a matter of self-narration. We had fortnightly group meetings between the five researchers to discuss any issues that had arisen. The process is similar to that outlined by Valerie Walkerdine *et al.* in Chapter 8 in this volume, yet we used history, positioning and interest rather than psychoanalysis to understand the different investments the researchers made. All the researchers were schooled in the basics of feminist research (through previous research projects), so they were able to raise issues of reciprocity, ethics, representation and responsibility. This became particularly crucial on matters of collecting data on sexuality (and the Economic and Social Research Council remit to store data with the public service *Qualidata*). We had to think through how not to 'out' people, how to make sure they could not be identified in any way. We even had the most elaborate and lengthy discussion about how to make the bars anonymous for fear of 'outing' research participants. This became increasingly ridiculous as the TV programme *Queer as Folk* made most of the bars easily identifiable to a national audience. We did consider changing the very famous male leather bar The Rembrandt to the Van Dyke! These ethical issues informed our every movement, to the extent that at moments the entire research stopped while we collectively pondered, struggled and argued over the issues the research was raising. Reflexivity was about collective practice, thrashed out in discussion, always trying to be responsible, accountable and ethical with an awareness of our positioning and partialities. If we forgot these we were sure to be reminded by other members of the team. It would have also been difficult to narrate five different selves. What each researcher represented was a position, an investment, a habitus, a history and a politics. The significance of these depended on the issue and alignments changed throughout the research. How these were deployed in practice and analysis was monitored carefully.

CONCLUSION

I hope that I have shown how there is a significant difference between being reflexive and accruing reflexivity to oneself through a process of attachment and as a cultural resource to authorize the self and doing reflexivity: building sensitivity into research design and paying attention to practice, power and process. Understanding the historical development of the methods that were used to generate a self should alert us to how and who can mobilize the concept. And this is what is crucial. It is the use and interests to which methods (such as telling and testimony) are put that matters. Just as ethnography as a method has been used as a colonial form of control, used by the Central Intelligence Agency to collect 'intelligence' and used by radical working-class historians to challenge the violence of historical classifications, reflexivity as a method has similar disparate uses: for feminist and gay dissident stories, for the re-traditionalization of masculine academic authority, for the reconstruction of the US national formation. Within these different uses the self is given different amounts of significance, and this I would argue is a useful signal to be alert to when interpreting and reading qualitative research. When the self is made a significant focus we need to ask the classic sociological question 'in whose interests?'. We need to ask how is it that the earliest calls to examine power and responsibility have become calls to centre on the self. How did this happen?

We also need to be alert to the self being centralized through processes of attachment and detachment whereby others just become resources for self-formation. But again this is never a straightforward process (what in research ever is?). There is a danger (as in the Bell–Ahmed debate) to equate epistemological authority with moral inequality. Again this misses the power relations that inform the research process, failing to acknowledge the different resources to which we as researchers may have access. The earliest feminist researchers stressed that we need to pay attention to how we occupy positions of power, to accept that we do and to live these with responsibility and accountability. This means we have to acknowledge that as researchers we do inhabit positions of power, but these may shift and they are rarely easily known. Even the technique of 'telling one's story' may look like an innocent method, but as Steedman has shown, being forced to become public, may only reproduce histories of inequality.

What we need to do is to return to reflexivity as practice and process as a matter of resources and positioning; not a property of the self. We need to expose our desire for rhetorical reflexivity as a technique for seducing the reader into our authorial power. If we need to interrogate ourselves at all it is to stop us fixing others in place so that we can theorize the benefits of mobility. Rather than asking 'Can the subaltern speak?' we need to ask 'Can we hear?' Telling has always been moral. A call is made here for a movement from telling and confession to practice and positioning. This is a call for accountability and responsibility in research, not for self-formation and self-promotion.

NOTES

1   Here I distinguish between the concept of the self as a coherent unity, a category which has been developed in Western societies through the methods outlined in this chapter and through the 'psy' sciences (see Rose 1989) and the concept of subjectivity which is not coherent and which we all live with in ways we do not often know (see Skeggs 1997).

2   Individualism shapes capitalism in that it provides a particular type of economic subject, namely the individual and individual property ownership. Yet capitalism also influences individualism by confirming its discursive dominance and emphasizing the positive aspects of individualistic theory.

3   This may present particular problems for the use of Bourdieu's concept of habitus that in its formation is the 'internalization of externality'. This is how he holds together the objective social structure with the subjective world in which social relations become embedded social practices.

4   Although as Gilman (1990) shows, the undeserving poor, from which the recuperable were drawn, were made up of a variety of ethnicities.

5   Probably one of the most famous of these is the story of Hannah Cullwick, who kept diaries for her employer Arthur Munby, who had a fascination and fetish with the dark, dirty, strong bodies of working-class women (see McClintock 1995).

6   The desire to acknowledge the partiality and value-laden nature of research has a long history (see Weber 1949).

7   Rap music and White British film have reproduced this narrative of the emasculating woman for a long time who interferes in the real business of friendship between men (see Skeggs 1994a).

8   Just as standpoint was something the researcher used to take on behalf of others, which then became a means of asserting individual and self-authority (see Probyn 1993; Skeggs 1995), the concept of reflexivity has been involved in similar moves. Whereby authority shifts from one of taking a position in order to make a political claim for a structural grouping, to one of owning that position as an individual, as a form of subjectivity.

9   This is not dissimilar to the arguments surrounding the cultural omnivore who is of the middle-class and is able to appropriate working-class tastes in order to extend his/her cultural repertoire (see Erikson 1991; Peterson 1996).

10 This is beautifully visualized in the film *Fightclub*, where the Edward Norton character is exposed by the Helena Bonham Carter character (Mira) who mirrors and repeats his inauthenticity. Although, typically as a woman she comes to figure fixed authenticity by the end of the film.

11 Thanks to Andrew Sayer for clarifying this: see Skeggs (1994b) for a development of this argument.

12 This was particularly the case with domestic violence, which was initially seen as a demonstration of love but then later understood for the violent abuse that it was. Explanations need the right time and place to work.

13 I can reproduce this here as we have had some painful and productive debates about the issue, although my mother still thinks things all went wrong with her and my life when I went away to 'that bloody university' which filled my head with stupid ideas.

REFERENCES

Abercrombie, N., Hill, S. *et al.* (1986) *Sovereign Individuals of Capitalism*. London: Allen and Unwin.

Adkins, L. (1995) *Gendered Work: Sexuality, Family and the Labour Market*. Buckingham: Open University Press.

Adkins, L. (2000) 'Objects of innovation: post-occupational reflexivity and re-traditionalisation of gender', in S. Ahmed, J. Kilby, C. Lury, M. McNeil and B. Skeggs (eds) *Transformations: Thinking through Feminism*. London: Routledge.

Agar, M.H. (1980) *The Professional Stranger: An Informal Introduction to Ethnography*. New York: Academic Press.

Ahmed, S. (2000) *Strange Encounters: Embodied Others in Post Coloniality*. London: Routledge.

Ahmed, S. and Stacey, J. (2001) 'Testimonial cultures: an introduction', *Cultural Values* 5(1): 1–6.

Atkinson, P. (1990) *The Ethnographic Imagination*. London: Routledge.

Bar On, B-A. (1993) 'Marginality and epistemic privilege', in L. Alcoff and E. Potter (eds) *Feminist Epistemologies*. London: Routledge.

Beck, U., Giddens, A. and Lash, S. (1994) *Reflexive Modernization: Politics, Tradition and Aesthetics in the Modern Social Order*. Cambridge: Polity.

Bell, D. (1983) *Daughters of the Dreaming*. St Leonards, NSW: Allen and Unwin.

Bell, D. (1993) 'The context', in D. Bell, C. Caplan and W.J. Karim (eds) *Gendered Fields: Women, Men and Ethnography*. London: Routledge.

Bell, D. and Nelson, T. (1989) 'Speaking about rape is everybody's business', *Women's Studies International Forum* 12(4): 403–447.

Bennett, T. (1998) *Culture: A Reformer's Science*. London: Sage.

Berlant, L. (2000) 'The subject of true feeling: pain, privacy, politics', in S. Ahmed et al. (eds) *Transformations: Thinking through Feminism*. London: Routledge.

Berlant, L. (2001) 'Trauma and ineloquence', *Cultural Values* 5(1): 41–58.

Blackwood, E. (1995) 'Falling in love with an-other lesbian: reflections on identity in fieldwork', in D. Kulick and M. Willson (eds) *Taboo: Sex, Identity and Erotic Subjectivity in Anthropological Fieldwork*. London: Routledge.

Bourdieu, P. (1992) *Language and Symbolic Power*. Cambridge: Polity.

Bourdieu, P. (1993) *Sociology in Question*. London: Sage.

Bourdieu, P. (2000) *Pascalian Meditations*. Cambridge: Polity.

Brown, W. (1995) 'Wounded attachments: late modern oppositional political for-mations', in J. Rajchman (ed.) *The Identity in Question*. New York and London: Routledge.

Callon, M. (1986) 'Some elements of a sociology of translation: domestication of the scallops and the fishermen of St Brieuc Bay', in J. Law (ed.) *Power, Action and Belief: A New Sociology of Knowledge*. London: Routledge.

Callon, M. (ed.) (1986). *Some Elements of a Sociology of Translation: Domestication of the Scallopse and the Fishermen of St Brieuc Bay. Power, Action and Belief: A New Sociology of Knowledge*. London: Routledge.

Chanfrault-Duchet, M.-F. (2000) 'Textualisation of the self and gender identity in the life story', in T. Cosslett, C. Lury and P. Summerfield (eds) *Feminism and Autobiography*. London: Routledge: 61–76.

Cosslett, T., Lury, C. and Summerfield, P. (eds) (2000) *Feminism and Autobiography*. London: Routledge.

Cronin, A.M. (2000) 'Consumerism and "compulsory individuality": women, will and potential', in S. Ahmed, J. Kilby, C. Lury, M. McNeil and B. Skeggs (eds) *Transformations: Thinking through Feminism*. London: Routledge.

David, M. (1980) *The State, the Family and Education*. London: Routledge and Kegan Paul.

Donzelot, J. (1979) *The Policing of Families: Welfare versus the State*. London: Hutchinson.

du Gay, P. (1996) *Consumption and Identity at Work*. London: Sage.

Erickson, B. (1991) 'What is good taste for?', *Canadian Review of Sociology and Anthropology* 28: 255–278.

Evans, D. (1993) *Sexual Citizenship: The Material Construction of Sexualities*. London: Routledge.

Evans, M. (1999) *Missing Persons: The Impossibility of Autobiography*. London: Routledge.

Foster, R.J. (1995) 'Print advertisements and nation making in metropolitan Papua New Guinea', in R.J. Foster (ed.) *Nation Making: Emergent Identities in Postcolonial Melanesia*. Ann Arbor, MI: University of Michigan Press.

Foucault, M. (1976) *History of Sexuality, Volume I*. Harmondsworth: Penguin.

Foucault, M. (1977) *Discipline and Punish: The Birth of the Prison*. London: Allen Lane/Penguin.

Giddens, A. (1991) *Modernity and Self-Identity: Self and Society in the Late Modern Age*. Cambridge: Polity.

Gilman, S.L. (1990) 'I'm down on whores: race and gender in Victorian England', in D.T. Goldberg (ed) *Anatomy of Racism*. Minneapolis: University of Minnesota Press.

Goody, J. (1983) *The Development of Family and Marriage in Europe*. Cambridge: Cambridge University Press.

Haraway, D. (1991) *Simians, Cyborgs, and Women: The Reinvention of Nature*. London: Free Association Books.

Haraway, D. (1997) *Modest_Witness@Second_Millenium. FemaleMan c_Meets_ Onco_Mouse tm: Feminism and Technoscience*. London and New York: Routledge.

hooks, b. (1990) 'Marginalising a site of resistance', in R. Ferguson, M. Gever, T.T. Minh-ha and C. West (eds) *Out There; Marginalisation and Contemporary Culture*. New York and Cambridge, MA: New Museum of Contemporary Art and MIT Press.

Huff, T.E. (ed.) (1981) *On the Roads to Modernity, Conscience, Science and Civilisations: Selected Writings by Benjamin Nelson*. Totowa, NJ: Rowman and Littlefield.

Humphries, B. and Truman, C. (eds) (1994) *Rethinking Social Research: Anti-Discriminatory Approaches in Research Methodology*. Aldershot: Avebury.

Hunter, I. (1992) 'Aesthetics and cultural studies', in L. Grossberg, C. Nelson and P. Treichler (eds) *Cultural Studies*. London: Routledge.

Killick, A.P. (1995) 'The penetrating intellect: on being white, straight, and male in Korea', in D. Kulick and M. Willson (eds) *Taboo: Sex, Identity and Erotic Subjectivity in Anthropological Fieldwork*. London: Routledge.

Kulick, D. and Willson, M. (eds) (1995) *Taboo: Sex, Identity and Erotic Subjectivity in Anthropological Fieldwork*. London: Routledge.

Lash, S. (1994) 'Reflexivity and its doubles: structure, aesthetics, community', in U. Beck, A. Giddens and S. Lash (eds) *Reflexive Modernization: Politics, Tradition and Aesthetics in the Modern Social Order*. Cambridge: Polity.

Lawler, S. (2000) 'Escape and escapism: representing working class women', in S. Munt (ed.) *Cultural Studies and the Working Class: Subject to Change*. London: Cassell.

Lury, C. (1998) *Prosthetic Culture: Photography, Memory and Identity*. London: Routledge.

Marcus, L. (1994) *Auto/Biographical Discourse*. Manchester: Manchester University Press.

May, T. (2000) 'A future for critique? Positioning, belonging and reflexivity', *European Journal of Social Theory* 3(2): 157–173.

Maynard, M. (1998) 'Feminists' knowledge and the knowledge of feminisms: epistemology, theory, methodology and method', in T. May and M. Williams (eds) *Knowing the Social World*. Buckingham: Open University Press.

McClintock, A. (1995) *Imperial Leather: Race, Gender and Sexuality in the Colonial Context*. London: Routledge.

McNay, L. (1999) 'Gender, habitus and the field: Pierre Bourdieu and the limits of reflexivity', *Theory, Culture and Society* 16(1): 95–119.

Munro, R. (1996) 'The consumption view of self: extension, exchange and identity', in S. Edgell, K. Hetherington and A. Warde (eds) *Consumption Matters*. Cambridge: Blackwell.

Narayan, K. (1993) 'How native is the "Native" anthropologist?', *American Anthropologist* 95(3): 19–34.

Nast, H. (1998) 'The body as "Place": reflexivity and fieldwork in Kano', in H. Nast and S. Pile (eds) *Places through the Body*. London: Routledge.

Papastergiadis, N. (1999) *The Turbulence of Migration*. London: Routledge.

Pateman, C. (1988) *The Sexual Contract*. Cambridge: Polity.

Peterson, R. and Kern, R. (1996) 'Changing highbrow taste; from snob to omnivore', *American Sociological Review* 61: 900–907.

Plummer, K. (1996) 'Intimate citizenship and the culture of sexual storytelling', in J. Weeks and J. Holland (eds) *Communities, Values and Intimacy*. London: Macmillan.

Pratt, M.L. (1992) *Imperial Eyes: Travel Writing and Transculturation*. London: Routledge.

Probyn, E. (1993) *Sexing the Self: Gendered Positions in Cultural Studies*. London: Routledge.

Probyn, E. (2000) 'Shaming theory, thinking disconnections: feminism and reconciliation', in S. Ahmed, J. Kilby, C. Lury, M. McNeil and B. Skeggs (eds) *Transformations: Thinking through Feminism*. London: Routledge.

Rabinow, P. (1977) *Reflections on Fieldwork in Morocco*. Berkeley, CA: University of California Press.

Rabinow, P. (1986) 'Representations are social facts: modernity and post-modernity in anthropology', in J. Clifford and G.E. Marcus (eds) *Writing Culture: The Poetics and Politics of Ethnography*. Berkeley, CA: University of California Press.

Robbins, B. (1986) *The Servant's Hand: English Fiction from Below*. Durham, NC, and London: Duke University Press.

Ricoeur, P. (1990) *Soi-meme comme un autre*. Paris: Seuil.

Roper, M. (1994) *Masculinity and the British Organization Man since 1945*. Oxford: Oxford University Press.

Rosaldo, R.A. (ed.) (1989) *Culture and Truth: The Remaking of Social Analysis*. Boston, MA: Beacon.

Rose, N. (1989) *Governing the Soul: The Shaping of the Private Self*. London: Routledge.

Said, E. (1978) *Orientalism*. London: Routledge.

Skeggs, B. (1994a) 'Refusing to be civilized: "race", sexuality and power', in H. Afshar and M. Maynard (eds) *The Dynamics of Race and Gender*. London: Taylor and Francis.

Skeggs, B. (1994b) 'Situating the production of feminist ethnography', in M. Maynard and J. Purvis (eds) *Researching Women's Lives from a Feminist Perspective*. London: Taylor and Francis.

Skeggs, B. (ed.) (1995) *Feminist Cultural Theory: Process and Production*. Manchester: Manchester University Press.

Skeggs, B. (ed.) (1997) *Formations of Class and Gender: Becoming Respectable*. London: Sage.

Skeggs, B. (2001) 'The toilet paper: femininity, class and mis-recognition', *Women's Studies International Forum*, 24 (3/4): 295–307.

Spivak, G.C. (1990) *The Post-colonial Critic: Interviews, Strategies, Dialogues*. London: Routledge.

Spivak, G.C. (2000) 'Claiming transformation: travel notes with pictures', in S. Ahmed, J. Kilby, C. Lury, M. McNeil and B. Skeggs (eds) *Transformations: Thinking through Feminism*. London: Routledge.

Stanley, L. (2000) 'From "self-made woman" to "women's made selves"? Audit selves, simulation and surveillance in the rise of public woman', in T. Cosslett, C. Lury and P. Summerfield (eds) *Feminism and Autobiography*. London: Routledge.

Steedman, C. (1990) *Childhood, Culture and Class in Britain*. New Brunswick, NJ: Rutgers University Press.

Steedman, C. (1998) 'Enforced narratives: notes towards an alternative history of the self', paper presented at Autobiography: Writing the Social Self seminar, Lancaster University.

Steedman, C. (1999) 'State sponsored autobiography', in B. Conekin, F. Mort and C. Waters (eds) *Movements of Modernity: Reconstructing Britain 1945–1964*. London: Rivers Oram.

Steedman, C. (2000) 'Enforced narratives: stories of another self', in T. Cosslett, C. Lury and P. Summerfield (eds) *Feminism and Autobiography: Texts, Theories, Methods*. London: Routledge.

Strathern, M. (1987) 'Out of context: the persuasive fictions of anthropology', *Current Anthropology* 28(3): 251–281.

Strathern, M. (1991) *Partial Connections*. Maryland: Rowman and Little.

Strathern, M. (1999) *Property, Substance and Effect: Anthropological Essays on Persons and Things*. New Brunswick, NJ, and London: Athlone.

Svensson, B. (1997) 'Auto/ethnography', in D.E. Reed-Danahay (ed.) *Rewriting the Social Self*. Oxford: Berg.

Taylor, C. (1989) *Sources of the Self: The Making of the Modern Identity*. Cambridge: Cambridge University Press.

Urry, J. (2000) *Societies Beyond the Social: Mobilities for the Twenty First Century*. London: Routledge.

Vincent, D. (1991) *Poor Citizens: The State and the Poor in the Twentieth Century*. London: Longman.

Visweswaran, K. (1994) *Fictions of a Feminist Ethnography*. Minneapolis, MN: University of Minnesota Press.

Waquant, L. (1989) 'Towards a reflexive sociology: a workshop with Pierre Bourdieu', *Sociological Theory* 7: 26–63.

Warren, C.A.B. (1988) *Gender Issues in Field Research*. London: Sage.

Weber, M. (1949) *The Methodologies of the Social Science*. New York: The Free Press.

Williams, L. (1997) 'Review essay', *Journal of Contemporary Ethnography* 25(4): 516–520.

Woolgar, S. and Ashmore, M. (1991) 'The next step: an introduction to the reflexive project', in S. Woolgar (ed.) *Knowledge and Reflexivity: New Frontiers in the Sociology of Knowledge*. London: Sage.

Zizek, S. (1997) 'Multiculturalism, or, the cultural logic of multinational capitalism', *New Left Review* 225: 28–52.

18 EMOTIONS, FIELDWORK AND PROFESSIONAL LIVES

Sherryl Kleinman

The pain in my chest pushes me to the floor of my bleak apartment. I lie flat on my back, trying to catch my breath and recapture my life. I am 27 and accustomed to somatizing my stresses, but this pain is new and hurts more than anything I've experienced before. I write in the mornings and teach in the afternoons, and the pain conveniently stays away while I work. But knowing that the pain will return in the evening pulls at the edges of my mind, distracting me some place below consciousness. I am alone in my pain, though I talk about it sometimes with long-distance friends. They're still in graduate school, and I envy all the griping they do in the community I left behind in the bright light of finishing first. I dare not mention my pain to my mentors; I'm a grown-up now, a person with a real job. I don't want them to think they wasted their time on someone who is falling apart at the moment when she's supposed to have it together.

Or perhaps they'll think I'm an ingrate. I got a tenure-track job in a 'top department', the career equivalent of what my family calls a good catch. But I'm finding the workplace a disembodied space where no one has chest pains, menstrual cramps, loneliness, or doubt about their work. And I don't hear any self-deprecating humour in the hallways.

I must do my work without kindred spirits, produce through pain, and make plenty of individual achievements so that the elders will let me stay. Miserable as I am, I worry that I won't be able to make it. Is my negativity about being here really a way to protect myself from possible failure at tenure time? It's easier to leave a place you don't like. There's so little interaction with my colleagues that I don't often have to nod a well-adjusted face. But I have to live with myself and I'm still missing the valued selves I used to know.

RESISTING PROFESSING

The person in the vignette is who I was when I moved to the job I have now held for twenty years. Why did I feel alienated and experience such intense pain? Why had my experiences in graduate school (as a qualitative researcher and symbolic interactionist) felt so much better? And how did the organization I came to study help me understand myself and my relationship to academia? Through studying 'Renewal' (a holistic health centre) and learning to understand it through a *feminist* symbolic interactionist lens, I figured out the tale of Renewal and fashioned a less painful role for myself in academia.

I suspected that being a professor could be lonely, but my time in graduate school had kept me from seeing it clearly. Perhaps I had it too good as a student. Even as an undergraduate at McGill University (in Montreal, Quebec) I had had lively, ongoing talks with more than one professor about fieldwork projects I pursued as independent studies. At McMaster University (in Hamilton, Ontario) where I did my MA, there were several qualitative researchers on the faculty, and they treated me more as a colleague than a student. When I started the PhD programme at the University of Minnesota (in Minneapolis), Gary Fine found me and suggested we co-author papers. We met weekly, writing a few pages a week, exchanging our pages, revising each other's words so that it wasn't clear who wrote what by the time our articles made it into print. Then I was a visiting graduate student at Northwestern University, where I took courses with Howard Becker in qualitative methods and writing and collected the fieldwork data that became my dissertation and first book (Kleinman 1984). From Howie I learned that doing sociological work is always a collective process. He had successfully used that framework to analyse art, something conventionally regarded as a product of individual talent or genius (see Becker 1982). Certainly his analysis must be true of sociology, a field lacking an exotic aura. Thinking of sociological work as a social process demystified creativity and made it easier to be a student: you were part of something larger, you should share your work-in-progress, and making mistakes was necessary for learning.

In graduate school I learned the doing (and doings) of sociology in the context of a community of engagement. Howie also made you feel that your work wasn't done until it was out there for others to read and use. That was a moral obligation: you were part of a community where people learned from each other and you should participate. But that take on publishing is quite different from careerist productivity, where the main point of doing the work is to get a job, get tenure, get promoted, and get famous.

I admit it: I did not want to be a grown-up. I was already a responsible person who worked hard, but being a grown-up meant proving yourself to your colleagues and claiming to know more than students. As I understood it, professing meant posturing. I knew I had flourished in a context where I didn't have to be the expert and where I had had many people to talk to about work and everything else. I lived a life with little division between the personal and the professional in a community that provided a combination of challenge and succour.

Many graduate students feel infantilized by an educational system that keeps them proving themselves to advisers and committee members (Sanford 1976). And too many faculty members exploit students or ignore them. I was lucky – and the system should be changed so that students need not depend on luck. Other students say good riddance to graduate school and are relieved to do their work without having an adviser glaring over their shoulder or sitting too far away to care. But, I entered the life of the professional in a state of grief.

At my job I had to work without kindred spirits because I was the only fieldworker in a department whose reputation had become synonymous with quantitative work. I took on the burden of proving that a qualitative person (a member of the minority group I belonged to) could do the (almost) impossible: publish enough work of high quality to get tenure in a top-ranked US department. The 'US' part mattered; I grew up in Montreal at a time in Canada when American still meant better.

I felt ambivalent about the system itself, but mostly I was just a part of it – a system that makes prestige into currency and ranks quantitative work above qualitative. I knew that producing a lot was a surer way to stay in the system than producing a few pieces of high quality that might take a long time. I knew the system is a never-ending test: you're only as good as your *next* article or book. Co-authoring was acceptable, but ultimately others would want to know who did exactly what in the making of the product. I was becoming part of a system modelled after an individualist careerist model.

Within that model, seeking support becomes a sign of weakness. Even without any well-developed feminist analysis, I sensed that women (there was only one other woman in the department) had to be even more careful than men about asking for help of any kind. Would a man who had asked about 'how things work around here' have been seen – might still be seen – as a go-getter rather than as needy? I did not take that chance. I also knew, though I did not say this to myself, that as a *woman* using *soft* methods, I was doubly not-man (i.e. not legitimate). I remember thinking early on that I had better publish my dissertation with a high-status university press to make up for the conventional belief that qualitative work isn't serious, systematic or rigorous.

The model of the professional is that of 'rational man'. As Rosabeth Kanter found in her 1977 study of a corporation, managers at Indsco (whether male or female) were expected to live out the masculine ethic. This ethic

> elevates the traits assumed to belong to men with educational advantages to neces-
> sities for effective organizations: a tough-minded approach to problems; analytic
> abilities to abstract and plan; a capacity to set aside personal, emotional consider-
> ations in the interests of task accomplishment; a cognitive superiority in problem-
> solving and decision-making. (Kanter 1977: 22)

I found the same model in my department. Although no one talked about what they expected of me, I knew I was meant to put aside doubts and fears, have congenial but distant connections with colleagues, and temper my sense of humour. Kanter found that this masculine ethic did not translate into macho behaviour or temperament at Indsco. Rather, the atmosphere 'was rather bland and easygoing – even emotionless' (Kanter 1977: 41). This emotional culture had a purpose: it was meant to 'exemplify collaboration, agreement, consensus' (1977: 41). Jack Sattel (1998) makes a similar argument about the role of inexpressiveness among men. He writes:

> To effectively wield power, one must be able both to convince others of the right-
> ness of the decisions one makes and to guard against one's own emotional involve-
> ment in the consequences of that decision; that is, one has to show that decisions

are reached rationally and efficiently. One must also be able to close one's eyes to the potential pain one's decisions have for others and for oneself. ... A little boy must become inexpressive not simply because our culture expects boys to be inexpressive *but because our culture expects little boys to grow up to become decision makers and wielders of power.* (Sattel 1998: 425; original emphasis)

Women who enter positions of decision-making and power are expected to do the same. As Jane Roland Martin (2000: 50) put it: 'An educated woman in the public arena not only can be like a man, she must be. This is what the education–gender system mandates.'

The (inexpressive) culture of politeness in my department not only made life easy in some ways, but also masked potentially conflictual differences in perspectives, methods and politics. As a result, we had neither nasty factions nor passionate intellectual arguments. Politeness, I discovered, works better for those who have more power and who agree with each other than for those without power and who might want to stir things up. The guise of consensus created by the culture of politeness left me, the token qualitative person, both silent and lonely.

FINDING 'RENEWAL'

Given the distant (though pleasant) atmosphere in the department, the lack of intellectual kin, and the unspoken presence of performance pressures, my chest pains are not that surprising. Nor was my choice of a new fieldwork site, a holistic health centre. I hoped that members of Renewal would show emotional sensitivity, talk about their feelings, and connect those feelings to the body and the mind. I expected to find an atmosphere of informality and humour among people who had no investment in conventional legitimacy. Looking back, I wanted a haven away from the sociology department, a place where I could recapture my graduate student self.

At a health food restaurant I picked up a free newsletter that described Renewal's mission:

Our approach is 'holistic.' This means that we encourage the acceptance, nurturing and integration of all aspects of the individual: mental, physical, emotional, spiritual, and social. We believe that optimal health can be attained only by viewing the person as a whole and by emphasizing that the locus of responsibility for achieving such 'wholeness' lies with each individual.

On an October afternoon I found my way to an old, slightly rundown two-storey house. I was pleased that Renewal had the look of an alternative organization – homey and funky.

I met two participants that day, both of whom, I learned later, were central actors at Renewal. Carla, a staff member and volunteer, had just been appointed coordinator. She was in the 'office area' of the main floor, doing something with the membership list. Karen, who I learned later was a novice practitioner, emerged from the bathroom, towel-drying her hair. I had mixed reactions to the scene, an early ambivalence that resurfaced throughout the study. I enjoyed the casual atmosphere, away from the stuffy air of Hamilton Hall. But Karen's behaviour gave me a twinge: I found it *too* casual. I suppressed that thought; after all, I excelled in informality. I told myself she acted this way because no clients were around.

And where *were* the clients? That worried me, too. I didn't see anyone waiting for a practitioner. Perhaps a few clients were upstairs, I thought. (Carla had said that's where the practitioners treated clients.) But I didn't hear any rumblings above me.

I asked Carla and Karen how participants might feel about having a sociologist hanging around. Both of them said others would like the idea. Carla told me I'd need the approval of the board of directors and suggested I attend the board meeting that evening. At the mention of 'board meeting', Karen sighed and said, 'Oh, you might be bored. We talk so much about money!' Carla urged me to study Renewal, saying they needed someone 'who'd be objective' about the centre. That gave me a twinge: what an odd choice of words to describe what an alternative organization needed.

Later that evening I attended my first board meeting (these were held every other week for about three hours). All twelve members (six women and six men) showed up. They were white, mostly in their late twenties or early thirties. Some of the men had long hair and wore jeans and tie-dyed shirts. Some of the women wore peasant skirts. I felt pretty comfortable, though I had the vague sense that I was in another time. Yet the content of the meeting jarred with how members looked. Much of the talk was about budgets, money, fundraisers and the like (as Karen had warned). Would this study bore me? No one talked about holistic healing, countercultural ideals or relationships among members.

Board members' talk, though not their appearance, contradicted my assumptions about alternative organizations. I expected members to talk about the interesting stuff, not the kinds of things I imagined board members in conventional organizations talked about. At the same time I wondered if Renewal would stay in operation. Their references to being 'in the red' left me feeling anxious about whether Renewal would fold before I had a chance to study it.

By the end of the evening I felt ambivalent about the study, the organization and the participants. My reactions to Renewal alternated throughout the study. Sometimes I thought the organization wasn't alternative enough, a reaction I had after listening to hours of money-talk at that first meeting. Was members' idealism limited to their clothing? Other times I thought of members as disorganized or as acting inappropriately for a health centre (hence my discomfort at watching Karen towel-drying her hair). Renewal seemed neither a legitimate conventional organization nor a convincing alternative. As I wrote in my field notes, 'Renewal isn't even a legitimate illegitimate organization!'

I felt guilty about my conflicted feelings toward participants. Fieldworkers are supposed to like those who let us study them. The first lesson of fieldwork (perhaps the main one) is to develop empathy. But through the long process of this study I learned, then wrote about with Martha Copp (Kleinman and Copp 1993), a different methodological lesson: *what* researchers feel is much less important than *how we use those feelings* to understand the people we study. The complex feelings I experienced throughout the research and writing of *Opposing Ambitions* (Kleinman 1996) eventually became resources for analysing the data.

Examining my ambivalence about Renewal and about my first job gave me insights into *participants'* struggles. Like them, I was someone who had experienced the late 1960s and the 1970s as a period of self-transformation. Members of Renewal developed a moral identity (a valued identity central to their self-concept) based on the idea that they were alternative – 'doing something different', as they often put it. Yet, they also wanted to distance themselves from outsiders' views of a holistic centre (in the 1980s) as flaky. They, like me, wanted to have it both ways: get some conventional legitimacy while doing interesting, alternative work. I wanted to get 'fed' by an alternative place that I could study and then turn into publications. But it took me years to recognize these similarities.

I attended board meetings from October 1980 to December 1981. I arrived early to talk with board members before the meetings, and often stayed afterwards. I took detailed notes (as close to verbatim as possible), which I typed up the following day. I attended all retreats (the setting where participants *did* talk about their feelings), attended most of the practitioners' bi-weekly meetings, participated in fundraisers and took part in their workshops on holistic healing. I conducted two-hour, tape-recorded interviews from 1982 to 1985 with twelve central members. I also examined organizational documents, including minutes of board meetings, newsletters, membership bulletins, and financial and other committee reports.

A TASTE OF INEQUALITY

The structure of Renewal mirrored members' dual concerns with being both conventional and alternative. One part of Renewal was constituted by six private practitioners (four men, two women) who were paid by individual clients and then gave a portion of their earnings (determined by the board) to the organization. This payment was sometimes referred to as rent. The other, 'educational', part of Renewal was non-profit and was run by three or four staff members (all women) and several volunteers (almost all women). Low-cost classes and workshops were offered to the public through this part of Renewal. Staff did the office work for Renewal, ran the physical plant, and were responsible for putting the membership bulletin together. They also helped produce the newsletter that announced classes. Practitioners received about 30 dollars an hour for their services as psychotherapists, nutrition therapists, massage practitioners or stress managers. Given Renewal's financial problems, the staff were often unpaid, and received 4 dollars an hour when they did get paid. Overlap existed between the two parts; practitioners did some volunteer work, often headed major committees, and sometimes taught workshops. Staff, volunteers and practitioners were represented on the board.

I felt uneasy about the structure because it seemed inequitable and entirely conventional. Weren't members perpetuating a two-class system at Renewal? In addition to discrepancies in pay between staff and practitioners, staff members sometimes made appointments for the practitioners or gave them phone messages. Although staff were presumably working for the non-profit part of Renewal, they were, to some extent, working for the private practitioners, but not getting paid for their services.

There were also differences in power, prestige and respect. Two male practitioners, the only remaining founding members of Renewal, had the greatest influence, particularly at board meetings. (A third founding member, also a male practitioner, quit a few months after I arrived.) Jack was chair of the board of directors. Ron headed the committee that determined which classes and workshops were worthy of inclusion. Since the board made most of the decisions, from hiring and firing to approving all committee work, having influence on the board was no small matter. In addition, members accorded Ron and Jack the most respect, attention, nurturance and affection.

FEELINGS AS ANALYTIC TOOLS

The above synopsis makes discrepancies between members' ideals and reality clear, yet it was years before I felt confident that inequalities *existed* at Renewal and even longer before I committed myself to writing about them. Figuring out the story of Renewal took a long time: I did not complete the book until the mid-1990s (the book was published in 1996). Looking back, my discovery and participation in the sociology of emotions and in feminist theory brought me to a place that made it possible for me to finish the book and to create a less alienating academic role for myself.

I did not want to acknowledge the full force of my negative feelings, either about academia or participants at Renewal. I had wanted to get a 'good job', so how could I complain? Wasn't my unhappiness with the department a sign of my own incompetence? Similarly, if I had acknowledged my anger or disappointment with participants at Renewal, I would have had to face my fear of being unempathic and thus incompetent as a fieldworker. It was easier for me to ignore my 'inappropriate' feelings most of the time.

Even when I became convinced that inequalities existed at Renewal – with the key male practitioners at the top and the female staff and volunteer women at the bottom – I did not have complete empathy for the women. They did not seem to *mind* getting less pay or having less influence. At times I thought of them as spineless, failing to stand up for their rights. (I'll return to this later.)

My anger and disappointment made me uncomfortable. Some days I believed my anger was justified; other days I felt angry at myself for being angry at them. I knew something was wrong and that I needed to figure out why I felt so uncomfortable. But I kept putting aside my discomfort. Instead, I continued to collect data, leaving my feelings out of my field notes. Because I attended meetings at Renewal as an observer more than as a participant, I channelled my energy into a singular focus on note-taking.

Working as an automaton was new for me, but I could look at the growing pile of notes and tell myself I was being productive. Turning my dissertation into a book and writing other articles allowed me to compartmentalize my feelings. Surely my troubling feelings would disappear soon or at least by the time I stopped collecting the data. Denying these feelings left me with a spirit-sapping lethargy. The project became a job, an obligation rather than a choice. Because of my doubts about the project, I did not want to talk about it; I focused instead on feeling good about my other projects. But the malaise and nagging feelings of incompetence continued. So did the chest pains.

I found myself reproducing the very model of academia that I questioned: do your work no matter what, don't let feelings interfere, be productive for the sake of being productive ... and keeping your job. I had been educated in intellectual passion, but in the *job* I had quickly become the emotionless (repressed, perhaps) manager described by Kanter (1977).

The sociology of emotions helped me break through this self-distancing. In the early 1980s emotions were becoming legitimized as an area of study in sociology. As I look back, I think the emergence of that area also legitimized *my* having feelings. Emotions were no longer physiological impulses or weaknesses to be dismissed. Rather, emotions were both a social process and a social product. As Arlie Hochschild (1983: 211) put it, 'Social factors enter not simply before and after but interactively *during* the experience of emotion.' Hochschild underscored 'during', but the word 'interactively' was more important to me. If emotions were crucial for understanding how people interacted (the heart of symbolic interactionism) then researchers could not ignore them. Rather, leaving out emotions could now be considered a form of neglect. (To be fair, some symbolic interactionists had paid attention to emotions, but now we had a mandate systematically to analyse emotions as social phenomena.) Hochschild (1983: 17) further legitimized emotions by arguing that a feeling is a 'sense, like the sense of hearing or sight. In a general way, we experience it when bodily sensations are joined with what we see or imagine. Like the sense of hearing, emotion communicates information. ... From feeling we discover our own viewpoint on the world.'

Our feelings may be accurate or not; either way, they provide clues and hypotheses about ourselves and the world. Maybe my feelings about participants at Renewal could tell me something, could be a part of the process of understanding what was going on there. Maybe my ambivalence about academic culture could also tell me something.

Self- and other-awareness did not immediately follow my discovery of the sociology of emotions. And the path it opened up for me was difficult. But I now had some sociological tools, concepts like emotion work, emotional labour and feeling rules. I also had Hochschild's (1983) study of flight attendants and bill collectors to teach me about gendered patterns in emotional labour: who did which kinds of emotional work, at home and in the workplace, and who bore the brunt of others' emotional outbursts.

I started to see emotions as central to understanding a variety of situations. For example, in the early 1980s I was on a dissertation committee for Trudy Mills at the University of North Carolina. She was doing long interviews with women who had once used the services of a battered women's shelter. I came late to the work; Trudy was just about done when she asked me to serve on her committee. In her work, she described the stages the women went through, calling one of them 'numbing'. At her defence I told her that this stage intrigued me because it seemed to contradict George Herbert Mead's (1934) idea of the reflexive self. When the women acted like (self-described) zombies, they no longer saw themselves as objects to themselves (as Herbert Blumer 1969 would have put it). Trudy and I wrote an article (Mills and Kleinman 1988) that examined the relationships between cognitions and emotions, not just in theory, but in people's experiences of themselves in the world. Two of our ideas stuck with me. First, the women went numb when they saw themselves in a bad situation from which they could not imagine escaping. Second, although we at first thought of numbing as a cognitive state, a distancing from emotions, we eventually changed our minds. As we wrote, 'Numbness may protect the individual from experiencing particular feelings [but] numbness itself is an *overpowering* feeling-state' (Mills and Kleinman 1988: 1,012).

Similarly, when I tried to protect myself from what I considered to be inappropriate feelings about members of Renewal, I thought of myself as unemotional and perhaps objective (at times), but I was actually in a state that bracketed deep thought and thus analysis. As Martha Copp and I wrote in *Emotions and Fieldwork*:

> [Numbing] involves a reduction, not an enhancement, of our cognitive faculties. Ignoring and suppressing feelings are emotion work strategies that divert our attention from the cues that ultimately help us understand those we study. In the case of Renewal, I (Sherryl) should have asked myself, What kinds of assumptions about countercultural organizations, women's mobility, and paid work am I bringing to the study? What kinds of assumptions or ideas do the participants have that differ from mine? Because we are of similar age, class, and educational background, how have we come to hold different views (if indeed we do)? Do the women feel happy about their position or are they hiding their resentment? Do they recognize differences between themselves and the (better-paid, higher-status) male practitioners? Do they think of themselves as having less? What do they want? (Kleinman and Copp 1993: 33)

My anger toward, then distance from, the women led me to put off doing interviews with them for about a year. Yet the interviews (which I'll get to later) helped me piece together their stories, develop empathy for their actions, and at the same time see (from a sociological lens) what they did not.

I also wrote an article with Allen Smith, who was collecting data on medical students' emotion-management strategies (Smith and Kleinman 1989).

We analysed how students dealt with their feelings of desire and disgust for patients and their discomfort at dealing with cadavers. We showed how the professional culture, which disallowed talk about feelings toward patients, nevertheless provided students with ways to deal with their feelings (see Smith and Kleinman 1989). The ideal of doctors' 'detached concern' was tied to their authority; professionals, like the successful managers Kanter (1977) had described at Indsco, could be counted on as those who would 'set aside personal, emotional considerations in the interests of task accomplishment'. But what were the costs? As Allen Smith and I learned, medical students also became desensitized to patients, at times blaming patients for their own inappropriate feelings. At other times the students managed their discomfort by making jokes that their patients would not have liked to hear. Their compartmentalizing of patients into analytic pieces of anatomy and physiology spilled over into the medical students' personal lives, where they reduced lovers and partners to interesting body parts. Writing that article taught me connections between the culture of medical school and my own discomfort as a 'professional' who could not admit feelings of vulnerability. Like the medical students (and, I imagine, doctors as well) I learned not to talk about such things with my colleagues. Professors, like medical students, are expected to display a 'cloak of competence' (Haas and Shaffir 1977).

FEMINIST FIELDWORKER

Changes in my understanding of feminism also validated my emotions and helped me understand the interactional dynamics at Renewal. Recall that although I felt comfortable being around the staff women, they also struck me as weak. I knew I needed to talk to them to find out why they had so little resistance to their low position in the organization. When I interviewed them I used my fieldwork training to get them to tell me their story and to develop empathy. How did they come to participate at Renewal? What did they seek and did they feel they had found what they were looking for? I learned that the women had joined Renewal when they were at a low point in their lives and were searching for a community of sentiment – a place of like-minded people who would allow them to build their self-esteem through meaningful work and caring relationships. For example, one woman who had just recovered from what she saw as the isolation of being with her child, had this to say:

> When you have a baby it's really like being in isolation. It was for me for a while. It was like being in prison. Because there's so much work to be done, so much involvement, you know, hour after hour after hour. For me it was very difficult, very confining, and my husband was traveling a lot. So most of it was up to me. I think I was just ready to open up, meet new people. I wasn't aware of that then. I was getting my strength back physically and was ready to start doing something at the time. (quoted in Kleinman 1996: 90)

Other women had other stories: one woman had just moved to town and had no friends; another woman had recently gone through a divorce; others were in rocky relationships.

Around the time that I did some of the interviews I was reading Carol Gilligan's (1982) work on (alleged) differences in moral reasoning between women and men and Jean Baker Miller's (1976) work on the 'new' psychology of women. Both of these works validated the relational model, or what Gilligan called an 'ethic of care'. Miller argued that although caring for others was largely devalued by men (and some women) as 'unmasculine', it was central work for humankind. These books helped me appreciate the caring work that the women at Renewal did, work I had earlier questioned because of its association with devalued femininity. I began to think of the staff women as having worthy values. After all, they were willing to work for a cause (holistic health) for little or no pay, focus on the personal growth of themselves and others through relationships at Renewal, and do much of the emotional labour for the organization. For this stage of my analysis, they moved from weaklings to saints.

The male practitioners at Renewal also wanted a community of sentiment and participated in the circles and encounter-group style interactions at retreats (held every few months outside the work setting), but they mostly wanted a non-alienating place in which to ply their trade. To some extent, my own desires fit theirs: I would have liked a friendlier, more supportive environment in which to do sociology, one where it was OK to admit vulnerabilities some of the time.

From what I could tell, the staff women were searching for connection and trying to develop a sense of competence, and they largely got those needs met at Renewal; the male practitioners were searching for an unstuffy place in which to do their work and were also satisfied. So who was I to say that there was a problem? Was my gut sense that inequalities existed really a sign that I was a cynical sociologist? Did it mean that my analysis would not be appreciative enough of participants? An old favourite quotation from Herbert Blumer (1969) haunted me:

> To try and catch the interpretative process by remaining aloof as a so-called 'objective' observer and refusing to take the role of the acting unit is to risk the worst kind of subjectivism – the objective observer is likely to fill in the process of interpretation with his [or her] own surmises in place of catching the process as it occurs in the experience of the acting unit which uses it. (Blumer 1969: 86)

Had I committed the worst sin of fieldwork and substituted my own meanings for theirs?

Reading feminist theory brought me back, time and again, to my gut sense of the existence and playing out of inequalities at Renewal. Perhaps the data should have been enough for me to recognize the inequalities: the difference in pay between staff and practitioners alone was a blatant contradiction of anything anybody might call an alternative organization. The staff women were paid from The Center, while the practitioners were paid from clients individually. Only after getting paid from clients did the practitioners give money to the non-profit part, and this largely constituted cheap office rent. But even with hindsight it makes sense to me that I considered this material dimension only a part of the story; I knew I needed to give credence to the different meanings that the staff and practitioners gave to their participation. Eventually, paying attention to their meanings led me to see that salary inequities were tied to *other* inequalities, both insidious and subtle.

bell hooks' essays on gender and domination in *Talking Back* (1989) informed my analysis. She argued that gender oppression is the only form of inequality where the oppressed are meant to *love* their oppressors. And the female staff members did love the key male practitioners. Part of the staff women's inability to see the inequalities in pay, prestige, respect and affection came from their romantic relationships with the men. Following the conventional heterosexual model for middle-class white women, they fell in love with men who were taller, richer and had more credentials (in conventional *and* alternative terms) than they did. In short, the staff women believed that the men were superior. The two key practitioners had started Renewal, a fact that brought them the moral authority of pioneers. As Carla, a key staff member, put it:

> I can remember when I started volunteering, going to work on the Holistic Therapies Festival. I went in with some trepidation because it all seemed so new to me. They all seemed so intelligent and so educated, and I was feeling not so good about myself ... I was intimidated by people at Renewal. They seemed just more like what I wanted to be: progressive-minded, intelligent, motivated, and creative enough to take the initiative to create this place. (quoted in Kleinman 1996: 93)

The staff women felt grateful for the attention they received from the powerful men. It took them a long time to see that they were actually taking care of the men rather than the reverse: making appointments for the practitioners, doing the day-to-day work of the organization, and keeping the powerful happy.

Feminists' analyses of emotions challenged my earlier 'different-but-equal' story of staff–practitioner relations. Alison Jaggar's (1989) work on what she calls 'outlaw emotions' (conventionally unacceptable feelings) validated *my* gut feelings about inequalities at Renewal. As she argues, outlaw emotions

> may provide the first indications that something is wrong with the way alleged facts have been constructed, with accepted understandings of how things are. Conventionally unexpected or inappropriate emotions may precede our conscious recognition that accepted descriptions and justifications often conceal as much as reveal the prevailing state of affairs. Only when we reflect on our initially puzzling irritability, revulsion, anger, or fear may we bring to consciousness our 'gut level' awareness that we are in a situation of coercion, cruelty, injustice or danger. (Jaggar 1989: 161)

Yet I also learned from Jaggar that feelings are a resource, not the final authority. An uncritical feeling should not

> be substituted for supposedly dispassionate investigation. ... Like all our faculties, they may be misleading, and their data, like all data, are always subject to reinterpretation and revision. Because emotions are not presocial, physiological responses to unequivocal situations, they are open to challenge on various grounds. They may be dishonest or self-deceptive, they may incorporate inaccurate or partial perceptions, or they may be constituted by oppressive values. (Jaggar 1989: 163)

Emotions, then, are also 'a political terrain' (Boler 1999: 7).

My sense that oppression/inequality existed at Renewal had to be tested. Did the data I had on members' patterned actions and patterned silences fit a picture of inequality? I knew that if systematic inequalities existed, I would have to spell them out. And, *members'* equal-but-different story, which had also for a time been *my* story, would have to become data for me to analyse.

I learned that participants' notions of equality were individualistic and apolitical, almost antipolitical. For them, occupational status, gender, income and so on were unimportant; these social attributes constituted superficial differences among people. They believed that each individual is unique, special and worthy of equal respect. But my observations revealed that members gave each other *un*equal respect and that respect depended in large part on participants' social statuses. So they failed to live up to their own standards. As I put the story together, I came to see that members wanted to be an alternative organization that others would take seriously (an alternative organization with some conventional legitimacy). They knew that others (in the 1980s) thought of them as flaky and they found it exciting when they had access to conventional sources of legitimacy (for example, when a doctor of medicine joined the board and practised a few hours a week at the centre). Similarly, they liked having me (a faculty member at the University of North Carolina) as a 'consultant'. Members' concern with legitimacy also upped the male practitioners' status: members needed their status *as men* and as those with some credentials to legitimize the flaky (read: feminine) centre.

Male privilege operated in that the staff women (in particular) saw Ron and Jack (the key practitioners) as men who could have become doctors or acquired some other better-paying professional work. Hence, Ron and Jack received extra points for being at Renewal: they were seen as those who possessed something they could give up. The staff women, on the other hand, were not seen as heroic for voluntarily foregoing their (meagre) salary when money was needed for electricity. In fact, the male practitioners criticized them for paying themselves last. 'You have to learn to take better care of yourselves,' Jack said to Carla and Jane.

I came to think of the staff women as the 'housewives' for the organization ('the family') and for the key men in it (their 'husbands'). Like the housewives whom Viviana Zelizer (1989: 365) studied, the staff women's money 'retained a collective identity, while men's ... money was differentiated and individualized'. Since members expected the staff women, like good wives, to give without receiving individual payment, members didn't define the staff's unpaid work as a sacrifice. Yet, when practitioners said they'd pay more rent to Renewal, others expressed gratitude. Members' 'economy of gratitude' (Hochschild 1989) reflected conventional gender expectations. As Hochschild (1989: 95) has argued, 'the broader culture helps fix in the individual a mental baseline against which any action or object seems extra, and so, like a gift'. Only those who had privileges to sacrifice (the male practitioners) could get points for giving them up.

Members assumed that they had transcended the inequalities associated with status differences simply by being members of an organization called 'alternative'. Membership itself conferred alternative (and thus fair) status. As I learned at their retreats, the rules of conflict there ignored power differences between staff and practitioners and focused instead on what they called personal issues or personality differences. In addition, their rituals of solidarity (hugging, circles) masked inequalities.

I put together a story of Renewal that both appreciated the work the women did and yet acknowledged its costs (what might be called a critical appreciation). Jean Grimshaw's (1986) *Philosophy and Feminist Thinking* helped me out. She wrote: 'I believe it is wrong to present a conception of woman *merely* as victim; nevertheless I think it is crucial to recognize the ways in which women are sometimes disabled and oppressed by the very qualities which are also in a way their strength' (Grimshaw 1986: 202). That the staff women valued and enjoyed nurturing others did not cancel out the oppressive consequences of such acts. Nurturing was tied to inequalities at Renewal not only by the low pay the women received for it. That only staff women did the nurture-work reinforced the idea that nurturing is 'women's work', devalued work not expected of the men. Being a practitioner – doing instrumental, 'men's work' – was more valuable and deserving of remuneration. Nurture-work helped relations at Renewal and, in the larger scheme, helps humankind, but its exclusive practice by a less powerful group ensures its devaluation and deprives women of *others'* nurturing.

Sandra Bartky's (1990) analysis of women's nurturing of men as a false kind of power fits well with the staff women at Renewal:

> The *feeling* of out-flowing personal power so characteristic of the caregiving woman is quite different from the *having* of any actual power in the world. There is no doubt that this sense of personal efficacy provides some compensation for the extra-domestic power women are typically denied: If one cannot be a king oneself, being a confidante of kings may be the next best thing. But just as we make a bad bargain in accepting an occasional Valentine [in heterosexual relationships] in lieu of the sustained attention we deserve, we are ill advised to settle for a mere feeling of power, however heady and intoxicating it may be, in place of the effective power we have every right to exercise in the world. (Bartky 1990: 116)

What made it difficult for me to come to a feminist analysis? The emotional repression central to the role of the academic provided one barrier. Only by acknowledging my feelings about participants, the organization and the project was I able to get the clues that opened the door to sociological analysis. Even once I took on the sociology of emotions I still had difficulties moving toward a fully feminist analysis. Why? One of the tenets of field-work provided a barrier: don't have an agenda (see DeVault 1999: 5–19). Certainly feminism, with its feet firmly grounded in social change, had an agenda. Yet, I now believe that a feminist agenda would have helped me figure out the story sooner. I wish I had read Marilyn Frye's (1983) founda-tional feminist chapter, 'Oppression', before I entered Renewal. She makes an argument for the systematic wires in a birdcage that keep women oppressed, even as some of us also have privileges of class, race, sexuality and so on. As she put it:

> Consider a birdcage. If you look very closely at just one wire in the cage, you cannot see the other wires. If your conception of what is before you is determined by this myopic focus, you could look at that one wire, up and down the length of it, and be unable to see why a bird would not just fly around the wire any time it wanted to go somewhere. Furthermore, even if, one day at a time, you myopically inspected each wire, you still could not see why a bird would have trouble going past the wires to get anywhere. There is no physical property of any one wire, *nothing* that the closest scrutiny could discover, that will reveal how a bird could be inhibited or harmed by it except in the most accidental way. It is only when you step back, stop looking at the wires one by one, microscopically, and take a macro-scopic view of the whole cage, that you can see why the bird does not go anywhere; and then you see it in a moment. It is perfectly *obvious* that the bird is surrounded by a network of systematically related barriers, no one of which would be the least hindrance to its flight, but which, by their relations to each other, are as confining as the solid walls of a dungeon. (Frye 1983: 4)

Sociologists and other social scientists have, in fact, documented these wires: sexist language, the wage gap, men's violence against women, women's 'second shift' in the home, women's 'third shift' (taking care of relation-ships), the sexual double standard, women taking their husband's family name, the continual struggle for reproductive rights, and the list goes on. Should we ignore the abundant data and analyses of systematic gender inequality as we start a new project by calling it an agenda? Or should we call it professional negligence to disregard the information and analyses already out there?

Frye's metaphor and other feminist work provide a sensitizing frame for me for future projects. As with my pre-feminist fieldwork, I will take notes on what I see, find patterns in the setting, and analyse them sociologically. But I will begin with Joan Acker's (1991) idea that gender is not merely 'an addition to ongoing processes, conceived as gender neutral. Rather, it is an integral part of those processes, which cannot be understood without an analysis of gender' (Acker 1991: 167). For example, to understand Renewal, I had to see that the organization was typed as feminine even though no one said it, and that this unspoken typification gave more credit to the male practitioners. I also had to see that while the male practitioners could be valued by everyone as those who had given up potential class privilege to work there, the two female practitioners (who had little to 'give up') were seen as *seeking* privilege and hence distrusted for having questionable motives. And at retreats, members treated the male practitioner who consistently refused to talk about his feelings as emotionally deep, while they criticized the female staff member who occasionally withheld her feelings as 'pulling a power play'. Even when the staff women gained a quasi-sociological understanding of power relations at Renewal – after their romantic relationships with the key male practitioners ended – they continued to give the men points:

> I still think Ron and Jack are such wonderful people in many ways. Yet they had such blind spots. Real blind spots. You've got to understand that they are probably better than a lot of men. They're a lot more human than men on the outside. (quoted in Kleinman 1996: 119)

My feminism is grounded in symbolic interactionism in that it directs me towards the *how* of inequality. That I pay attention to inequalities and want to *change* them comes from my feminism. As a feminist symbolic interactionist, I seek to understand the reproduction of inequality and the consequences of that process for making social change. For example, in the study of Renewal I came to ask: how could a group of people so strongly committed to being alternative fail to recognize the blatant contradictions between their goals and practices? I concluded that members were so invested in their identity as alternative that they could not bear to see or deal with how their practices contradicted their ideals. Their retreats largely built solidarity and thus masked the unequal weight they gave to women and men, staff and practitioners.

I might have ended the book with generalizations about moral identities, but instead I used Renewal to provide a lesson for all of us who feel smug or self-congratulatory or merely comfortable in our own alternative identities:

> Whether we take on the identity of feminist, leftist, or antiracist we can do one of two things: don the identity and feel good about ourselves for having it [as members of Renewal did], or see it as a symbol of a lifetime commitment to critical self-reflection and radical action. … Without such self-examination we may think of ourselves as progressive, but fail to build a better alternative. (Kleinman 1996: 140)

BUILDING AN ALTERNATIVE

Without having taken the feminist turn, I doubt I would have written a book that focused on the reproduction of inequality and ended it with the lessons that story can teach us about working for social change. And without the qualitative-symbolic interactionist tools and training I acquired in graduate school, I doubt I would have figured out the intricacies of that reproduction.

How did my turn to a feminist symbolic interactionism inform my role as an academic? Seeing the academic role as a social construction with built-in distancing to others and to oneself freed me from an obligation to enact the masculine ethic that Kanter (1977) described. I could be a responsible person without the trappings of grown-ups ('professionals').

Providing a fully developed alternative model requires more than I can do here, but I'll briefly discuss one aspect of my role as an academic – a teacher of graduate seminars – that students experience as qualitatively different from the usual 'professorial' role. Much of what I do builds on the kinds of seminars I had with Howard Becker in graduate school (see also Kleinman *et al.* 1997). I've since learned that having students treat each other as colleagues rather than as competitors is less common than I'd thought, so I will provide some details.

I design my graduate seminars as cooperative rather than competitive arenas in which I encourage students to study what is meaningful to them rather than what they think they *should* study. For example, on the first day of each graduate seminar (whether in qualitative methods, feminist theory, symbolic interactionism or writing) I have students freewrite in class about the following: 'If I were to tell someone on the bus about my project, I'd say…'. This gets students to explain what they're doing in clear terms, without jargon. It also raises the question of whether what they're studying would be of interest to any individual or group outside the academy, itself a political and ethical issue. After about seven minutes of freewriting, I ask them to finish the sentence they're on, and then start another freewrite: 'The reason I care about this topic/question/project is …'. I make it clear that academic justifications (such as filling a gap in the literature) is not what I have in mind. I tell them to emphasize the 'I' in the 'why I care'. Many students have told me that this exercise gives them a needed reminder of why they came to graduate school in the first place, something they'd lost sight of while taking courses, preparing for exams, and jumping through other institutional hoops. Each student reads her/his freewrite aloud and we comment on them one at a time (see Peter Elbow's 1980 discussion of reader-based versus criterion-based feedback). Often it becomes clear that the writing in the first exercise is stilted, with lots of sentences that use the passive voice, and an absent author. The second freewrite is usually freer in tone and clearer than the first. Students recognize that they don't *have to* write in a distanced manner. We also discuss why (sociologically) academic writing often has this objective face (see Gusfield 1976; Becker 1986; DeVault 1999: 161–174).

We comment on a student's paper for one of the three hours of each weekly seminar. The student provides copies of her/his paper the week before and we read it and write comments on it for the following week. Then we discuss the paper in class. Students have told me that they knew little about what their colleagues were working on (except for the topic) before this class. By focusing on each other's work, the students are given the opportunity to build an intellectual community rather than remain an aggregate of classmates. (This model of scholarship as a joint venture, even in single-authored pieces, has led some students to develop ongoing writing/dissertation groups after the end of the seminar.) I make it clear that commenting is the time to provide constructive criticism rather than an opportunity to show (off) how smart they are. 'Leave your macho intellectualizing at the door,' I tell them. At the same time, I emphasize that hiding their criticisms is equally irresponsible: it's better for them to find out the problems with their work right now than to hear it from journal reviewers later on.

This past semester I had students write two-page reflection papers about the assigned readings that they then read aloud in class. I encouraged them to link the theories and studies we were reading to their own lives or to any happenings in the world. We took notes while each student read aloud and then discussed the comments after the readings were done. Each student felt vulnerable reading their words out loud. This shared vulnerability led students to give each other their full attention and a fair reading. In their course evaluations, students wrote uniformly positive comments about this assignment, and said they also learned a lot about each other from doing it. By sharing their two pages and reading and commenting on each other's longer work every week, students developed a sense of community in the classroom (and outside it).

I ask students to write a self- and course-evaluation at the end of the semester. One way to write it, I tell them, is to start with: 'If I were to tell someone about this class, I would say ...'. One student's writing (about my course in symbolic interactionism) captures the intersection of community-building, authenticity and intellectual passion that can happen in the classroom:

> It's a class that's about listening and paying attention to the small things, to all things. It's a class that helps you come to a real respect for who your classmates are, for their interests, for their lives and experiences. It helps you see your class-mates in new ways and you learn about their good humor, keen sense of obser-vation, and passions. It's a hard class for someone like me, who wants clear and fast answers. And for that reason it's a class that people who want the answers should take because I learned that answers don't come easily, and they're not neat and simple. Good theory embraces complexity and paradox. We took seriously the challenge of seeing what is – looking and scrutinizing and asking why is 'it' this way. This class teaches you not to take anything for granted. To talk openly about sexism, racism, discrimination, power, and violence. It's a class that has helped me find out who I am and what I want to be. To stop lying, to stop pre-tending to be who I am not (for others).

Other students commented on how the readings came alive for them through their writing. As one student put it, 'In other classes, what we've read for that day has been treated as an object and a clear boundary has been drawn between us (as a class) and *it*.' She then went on to describe how that boundary is analogous to the distance that researchers are supposed to have between themselves and those they study: 'I've got these latex gloves on, and everything can be abstracted and I – my past, present, my life – doesn't have to or need to be in the mix of it all.' She, along with other students, wrote about how, in our class, we learned to *shape* the materials we read and figure out what relevance they had to social patterns we too are caught up in. The theories were no longer objects out there, apart from us. Before this seminar began, I worried about whether I could make the core readings in symbolic interactionism live (for me, and consequently, for them). After all, I'd initially read them as an undergraduate, reread them for comprehensive exams in graduate school, and reread them again for seminars I've taught off and on since 1980. Hearing the students' two-page papers each week revived my own interest in the classic material on the self, identity, accounts, deviance, socialization and so on. Each week I looked forward to hearing what the students had *done* with the material; the students had the same anticipation.

I openly critique academic posturing and the productivity model in my seminars. I teach feminist theory, fieldwork and writing in ways that make us accountable to our readers and to those we study. I push students to think about the values implicit in the 'professional model', in making productivity the highest goal, in putting aside political engagement, and in neglecting our relationships inside and outside the academy.

Acknowledging that the academic-professional model has problems opens up the possibility for alternatives (see Roland Martin 2000). Let's use our sociological tools to build an academic culture that avoids the polite blandness found in some departments and the intellectual posturing found in others. Let's learn how to make challenging *and* caring classrooms and corridors, and develop more humane relationships with colleagues, students, staff, and the wider community. My hope is that a new model will help each of us move from day to evening without a tightness in the chest.

REFERENCES

Acker, J. (1991) 'Hierarchies, jobs, bodies: a theory of gendered organizations', in J. Lorber and S.A. Farrell (eds) *The Social Construction of Gender*. Newbury Park, CA: Sage.

Bartky, S.L. (1990) 'Feeding egos and tending wounds: deference and disaffection in women's emotional labor', in S.L. Bartky, *Femininity and Domination*. New York: Routledge.

Becker, H.S. (1982) *Art Worlds*. Berkeley, CA: University of California Press.

Becker, H.S. (1986) *Writing for Social Scientists*. Chicago: University of Chicago Press.

Blumer, H. (1969) *Symbolic Interactionism: Perspective and Method*. Englewood Cliffs, NJ: Prentice-Hall.

Boler, M. (1999) *Feeling Power: Emotions and Education*. New York: Routledge.

DeVault, M.L. (1999) *Liberating Method: Feminism and Social Research*. Philadelphia, PA: Temple University Press.

Elbow, P. (1980) *Writing with Power*. New York: Oxford University Press.

Frye, M. (1983) 'Oppression', in M. Frye, *The Politics of Reality*. New York: Crossing Press.

Gilligan, C. (1982) *In a Different Voice: Psychological Theory and Moral Development*. Cambridge, MA: Harvard University Press.

Grimshaw, J. (1986) *Philosophy and Feminist Thinking*. Minneapolis, MN: University of Minnesota Press.

Gusfield, J. (1976) 'The literary rhetoric of science: comedy and pathos in drinking driver research', *American Sociological Review* 42: 16–34.

Haas, J. and Shaffir, W. (1977) 'The professionalization of medical students: developing competence and a cloak of competence', *Symbolic Interaction* 1: 71–88.

Hochschild, A.R. (1983) *The Managed Heart: Commercialization of Human Feeling*. Berkeley, CA: University of California Press.

Hochschild, A.R. (1989) 'The economy of gratitude', in D.D. Franks and E.D. McCarthy (eds) *The Sociology of Emotions: Original Essays and Research Papers*. Greenwich, CT: JAI Press.

hooks, b. (1989) *Talking Back: Thinking Feminist, Thinking Black*. Boston, MA: South End Press.

Jaggar, A.M. (1989) 'Love and knowledge: emotion in feminist epistemology', in A.M. Jaggar and S.R. Bordo (eds) *Gender/Body/Knowledge: Feminist Reconstruction of Being and Knowing*. New Brunswick, NJ: Rutgers University Press.

Kanter, R.M. (1977) *Men and Women of the Corporation*. New York: Basic Books.

Kleinman, S. (1984) *Equals before God: Seminarians as Humanistic Professionals*. Chicago: University of Chicago Press.

Kleinman, S. (1996) *Opposing Ambitions: Gender and Identity in an Alternative Organization*. Chicago: University of Chicago Press.

Kleinman, S. and Copp, M.A. (1993) *Emotions and Fieldwork*. Newbury Park, CA: Sage.

Kleinman, S., Copp, M.A. and Henderson, K. (1997) 'Qualitatively different: teaching fieldwork to graduate students', *Journal of Contemporary Ethnography* 25: 469–499.

Mead, G.H. (1934) *Mind, Self, and Society*. Chicago: University of Chicago Press.

Miller, J.B. (1976) *Toward a New Psychology of Women*. Boston, MA: Beacon.

Mills, T. and Kleinman, S. (1988) 'Emotions, reflexivity, and action: an interactionist analysis', *Social Forces* 66: 1,009–1,027.

Roland Martin, J. (2000) *Coming of Age in Academia: Rekindling Women's Hopes and Reforming the Academy*. New York: Routledge.

Sanford, M. (1976) *Making it in Graduate School*. Berkeley, CA: Montaigne.

Sattel, J.W. (1998) 'The inexpressive male: tragedy or sexual politics?', in M.S. Kimmel and M.A. Messner (eds) *Men's Lives*. Boston, MA: Allyn and Bacon.

Smith, A.C. and Kleinman, S. (1989) 'Managing emotions in medical school: students' contacts with the living and the dead', *Social Psychology Quarterly* 52: 56–69.

Zelizer, V. (1989) 'The social meaning of money: "Special Monies"', *American Journal of Sociology* 95: 342–377.

INDEX

Abell, P. 172
Abercrombie, N. 350, 351
Abu-Lughod, L. 20
Acker, J. 389
Action-in-interaction 106
action research 268
  see also SONAS Community Health Project
Adkins, L. 337, 344, 346, 364, 365
Afsar, S. and Maynard, M. 301
Agar, M. 174, 362
age
  power relations 307
Ahmed, S. 343, 357, 362, 363
Ahmed, S. and Stacey, J. 355
Allan, S. 322
Allat, P. and Benson, L. 168
alternative identities 390
Altheide, D. and Johnson, J. 60, 176
analytic process 216, 220, 281
  interviewing 216–18
  participant observation 216, 218–20
  see also computer software
Anderson, E. 151
anonymity 153
Antonio, R. 74
Archer, M. 64
Ardener, S. 321
Arnup, K. 29
Atkinson, P. 318, 321, 325, 364
Atkinson, P. and Coffey, A. 315
Atkinson, P. and Delamont, S. 268
Atkinson, P. and Silverman, D. 313
attention frame 23
Audit Commission 84
autobiographical work 319, 320, 326–8
  see also autoethnography
autoethnography 314, 323–4, 325, 326, 327, 328
  memories 325
  self-indulgence 325
  see also autobiographical work

Bakhtin, M. 19, 20, 27, 42
Barlow, J. 262, 279, 283
Barnes, M. and Wistow, G. 280, 282
Bartky, S. 388
battered women study 35–9
Becker, H. 208, 219
Becker, H. and Geer, B. 200
Behar, R. 297
Bell, D. 362
Bell, D. and Nelson, T. 361
Benhabib, S. 234
Bennett, A. 127–8, 131, 138, 352
Berelson, B. 162

Berlant, L. 350, 355
Bertaux, D. and Thompson, P. 185
Berthoud, R. 302
Bhaskar, R. 61, 62, 63, 64–5
Bhavnani, K. 304–5
Bhopal, K. 304
Black mothers study 300–1
  assessment of social class differences 305, 306
  central role of mothers 301
  power relations 303, 305, 306, 307
  resistance to participation 301, 302
Black women
  identification in social research 302
  research undertaken by white females 304
  see also Black mothers study
Blumer, H. 128–9, 150, 383, 385
Boelen, W. 152
Boler, M. 387
Boolean retrievals 164
Bourdieu, P. 4, 21, 70, 79, 80, 253, 361, 363, 366
Bourdieu, P. and Wacquant, L. 4
Brewer, J. 60, 65
Brown, C. 68, 356
Bryant, C. 6
Bryman, A. 129, 173, 264
Burawoy, M. 202
Burawoy, M. and Krotov, P. 154
Bureau of Justice 84
Burgess, R. G. 225

California juvenile justice system study 288
  conflict of views 290
  extending the research outward 291–2
  female clients' views of men and state assistance 290
  staff agendas for clientele 289
  staff representations of position in justice system 288–9
Callon, M. 358
CAQDAS *see* computer software
case-oriented approaches 165–6
case studies 268
  see also Women, Low Income and Smoking Project
causal relationships 133
Chamberlain, M. and Thompson, P. 232, 233
Chanfrault-Duchet, M. 353
Charmaz, K. and Mitchell, R. 324–5
Chatterton, M. and Hougland, P. 91
Cheek, J. 58

Chelimsky, E. 263
Cheng, L. and Gereffi, G. 39
Cicourel, A. 149, 150
Cicourel, A. and Kitsuse, J. 94
class
    power relations 303, 304, 305, 306, 307
    reflexivity 346
    telling of the self 354–5
Clifford, J. 58
Clifford, J. and Marcus, G. 20, 144, 315, 322
Cohen, P. 184
Cohen, P. and Ainley, P. 181
collective entities
    concept of 55
Collier, A. 62
Collins, P. 286
community
    building 391, 392, 393
    power over 274
    power with 274, 275
computational narrativity 244
computer software 162, 167, 168
    adoption of 168
    analysis time 169–70
    availability of 169
    benefits of 168, 170, 175–6
    case-oriented approaches 165–6
    changing relationship with audiences 175
    choice of 169
    code-and-retrieve packages 163–5, 167
    coding 163
    content analysis 162
    developments in 171
    disadvantages of 167–8, 176
    event structure analysis 166
    formal concept analysis 166–7
    hypothesis test features 165
    impact on research environment 168–71, 172,
        173, 174
    teamwork, facilitating 174
    text retrievers 163
    theory-building software 165, 167
    training 169
Comte, A. 62
'conceptual narrativity' 244
confessional
    development of 350, 351
    guilt cultures 350
    origins of 350
    personhood 350
    role of 350, 351
    shame cultures 350
confidentiality 153
Connell, J. 262, 283
consciousness
    false 63
    modes of 17
conversational analysis 22, 104
Corsiaros, M. 84, 85, 86, 88, 90
Corwin, R. 87
Cosslett, T. 354, 355
counter-transference 188, 193, 338
Craib, I. 64
Crapanzano, V. 58
Cressey, D. 133
critical (re)reading of research texts 320, 321, 322
critical realism 53, 60, 61
    example research study 65–70

critical realism cont.
    rejection of individualist reductionism 61
    structures 60–1, 62, 63, 64
    use of 65
Cronin, A. 365
cultural consistency 137, 138
Currie, D. and Wickramasinghe, A. 39

Dash, L. 148
David, M. 351
De Vault, M. 26, 27, 46, 389
de Vaus, D. 301
Delphi technique 264
Dench, G. 302
Denscombe, M. 60
Denzin, N. 129, 130, 131, 136, 189
Denzin, N. and Lincoln, Y. 173, 265, 314–17,
    324, 333
Derrida, J. 3, 137
descriptions 19, 20
designing research strategy
    interviewing 204–7, 209
    participant observation 204, 207–8, 209
detachment 384
    as a form of defence 185, 186, 187
detective work 83, 93, 95–6
    aims of detectives 88
    bargaining 82, 83
    clearance rates 84, 85
    definition of a case 89
    effectiveness 88–9, 94
    field for 82, 92, 93, 94
    frame 83, 94
    indices of success 88
    knowledge 86–7
    motives and satisfaction 87–8
    occupational culture 89–92
    rationality 83, 92, 93, 94, 95, 96
    resources 86
    role of detectives 83–4
    salience of cases 89
    sequence of events 81
    skills 86
    surround of policing 81, 94
    working cases 82, 83, 84–5
    working style 87
    workloads 86, 89
Devine, F. and Heath, S. 238
dialogic relationships 20, 21
Dilthey, W. 243
direct transcription software 171
discourse 17, 26
    concept of 40–1
    'order of' 20
    see also mothering discourse
discursive turn 235
divergence 22
Dohan, D. and Sanchez-Jankowski, M. 149
domestic abuse study 35–9
domestic labour 46
Donzelot, J. 351
Drass, K. 173
duGay, P. 354
Duneier, M. 154
Durkheim, E. 54, 55, 57–8

Eco, U. 76
Elliot, A. and Spezzano, C. 180, 186

Ellis, C. and Bochner, A. 314, 319, 323, 324, 326
Elster, J. 77
Emerson, R. 21, 147, 148, 150
Emerson, R. and Pollner, M. 153
emotions
    'inappropriate' 386
    management of 383–4
    sociology of 382
    use as a resource 387, 388–9
empathy 338, 384, 385
emplotment 245–6
endogenous reflexivity 335
    see also reflexivity
Ericson, R. 83
errors
    type I 146, 154
    type II 146, 154
escapism 367
Espeland, W. 92
Espeland, W. and Stevens, M. 79
Essed, P. 304
ethic of care 385
ethics 154
ethno-poetry 323
ethnodrama 322, 323
ethnography
    and biography 313
    and critical realism 64
    concept of 41–2
    meta narrative of 58
    need to extend the research outward 297–8
    new forms of 326–8, 363
    role of 65
ethnomethodology 104
evaluation
    definition of 264
evaluation research 262–3
Evans, D. 355
Evans, M. 352, 355
event structure analysis 166, 172
everyday/everynight worlds
    18, 19, 42
evidence based action 263
Ewick, P. and Silbey, S. 252
experience
    concept of 42, 43
Ezzy, D. 243

Fabrega, H. 75
Fabrega, H. and Silver, D. 75
face validity 145
Fagan, J. and Davies, C. 81
false consciousness 63
fantasies of researchers 194
Fay, B. 336
Felski, R. 340, 341–3, 345, 346
femininity of texts 341–3, 364–5
feminist critique of ethnographic texts 321
feminist methodology 286, 287
    see also California juvenile justice system study;
        Hungarian welfare state study
field 80, 81
    detective work 82, 92, 93, 94
field notes and journals 317–18
    therapeutic use of 319–20
Fielding, N. and Lee, R. 168
fieldwork 209
    choice of strategy 214, 215

fieldwork cont.
    interviewing 209–12
    participant observation 212–14
Finch, J. 228, 229, 230, 234, 238, 239
Finch, J. and Mason, J. 229, 230
Fine, G. 150, 154
Fink, A. 132
Fisher, S. 126–7, 134, 137
Flowerdew, J. 238
Fontana, A. and Frey, J. 236, 237
Fordham, S. 321
formal concept analysis 166–7
formal rationality 75
    see also rationality
formulating research problems 200–1, 203–4
    interviewing 201
    participant observation 202, 203
Foster, R. 357
Foucault, M. 4, 20, 40, 41, 351
Fowler, D. and Hardesty, D. 318
frame 81
    analysis 80
    contents 83
    location of 94
Frazier, E. 151
free association narrative 232–3
Frosh, S. 181
fruit machine gambling study 126–7
Frye, M. 389

Gadamer, H.-G. 28, 58
gambling study 126–7
Game, A. 333
Gans, H. 144
Garfinkel, H. 5, 41, 103, 104, 105, 149
'gatekeepers' 301
Gaunt-Richardson, P. 274
Gee, J. 41
Geertz, C. 75, 149, 251
gender
    inequality 386, 387, 388, 389, 390
    power relations 303, 304, 305
    reflexivity 343, 346, 364–5
    telling of the self 355–6
generalization 59, 125, 126
    categories, problem of 134–5
    cultural consistency 137, 138
    denial 129, 130
    examples of 126–8
    fieldwork time 155, 156
    inter-researcher consistency 156
    justification for 136, 137, 138, 139
    meanings of 130–1
    participant observation studies 154–6
    sampling 132–4, 154–5
    theoretical inferences 135–6
generation differences
    power relations 307
Gephart, R. 126
Gergen, K. and Gergen, M. 246, 252
Gerson, K. 201, 211
Giddens, A. 57, 64, 79, 234, 352
Gilbert, N. 303
Ginzburg, C. 185
Glaser, B. and Strauss, A. 134, 219
glossing 103
Goffman, E. 67, 78–9, 80, 81, 100, 103,
    108, 150, 154

Gordon, L. 293
Grbich, C. 264
Greene, J. 264
Greenwood, P. 85, 90
Griffith, A. 23–4
Griffith, A. and Smith, D. 28, 34
Grimshaw, J. 388
Guba, E. 262, 264
Guba, E. and Lincoln, Y. 129, 130, 131, 268
Gulbenkian Commission 6

Haas, J. and Shaffir, W. 384
habitus 21
Hacking, I. 248
Hagdagneu-Sotelo, P. 154
Hammersley, M. 60, 129, 134, 135, 136, 138
Haney, L. 267, 283, 291, 293, 295, 296
Haraway, D. 347, 357
Harding, S. 286
Harding, S. and Hintikka, M. 4
Harré, R. 5
Harstock, N. 286
Hart, E. and Bond, M. 268
Heise, D. 166, 172
Heise, D. and Lewis, E. 166
Henriques, J. 180, 181
Heritage, J. 106
Heritage, J. and Atkinson, P. 103
Heron, J. 267, 280
Hertz, R. 324
Hicks, A. 165
Hill, R. and Crittenden, K. 106
Hill-Collins, P. 301
Hobbs, D. and May, M. 318
Hochschild, A. 382, 388
Hockey, J. 57
Holland, J. and Ramazanoglu, C. 300
Holloway, W. and Jefferson, T. 184, 186, 228,
    232–3, 237
Holquist, M. 322
homocide detectives *see* detective work
homosociability 338, 339
Hooks, B. 361
Horowitz, R. 150, 151, 154, 202, 203,
    212, 219
hospitals
    racism study 65–70
housework 46
Hoy, D. 4
Hoy, D. and McCarthy, T. 6
Huberman, M. 266
Huff, T. 350
Hughes, D. 66, 67, 68
Hughes, E. 99, 100, 101, 116
Humphries, B. and Truman, C. 360
Hungarian welfare state study 292, 293, 295
    clients' needs 294
    conflicts over expertise 293, 294
    divisions within and among welfare
        institutions 293
    extending the research outward 295–6
    resistance and conflict 294
Hunt, J. 185
Hunter, I. 351
Huysman, K. 342

identifying with participants 188–91, 192
    see also counter-transference

identity formation 356
illegal activities
    participant observation studies 153–4
inclusion in research
    consideration of 280, 281
induction
    analytic 133
    enumerative 133
infra-reflexivity 336, 337
    see also reflexivity
institutional ethnography 18–19, 26
    aims of 21, 39, 40
    alternative perspectives 30
    concept of 41–2
    direction, need for 23
    origins of 17
    social, the 21–2
    social relations 30
institutional interaction 101
institutional language 19
institutions 22, 23
    concept of 43
intelligibility norms 246, 252
inter-researcher consistency 156
interaction order 100
interpretations 3–4
interpretive processes 150
interressments 358
interviews 221, 225
    analytic process 216–18
    concepts to focus on 233–6
    designing research strategy 204–7, 209
    devising questions 227, 228, 229, 230
    directing 226, 227
    establishing rapport 192–3
    fieldwork 209–12, 214, 215
    formulating research problems 201
    free association narrative 232–3
    institutional discourse 26
    interepretation 228
    learning from 27, 28
    life history approach 206, 231–2
    limitations of 26, 237–8
    modes of asking questions 227, 228,
        229, 230
    non-verbal expression 238, 239
    structure of 231–3
    techniques used 227
investigation
    naturalistic approach to 128

Jackson, B. 146, 148
Jagger, A. 386–7
Jefferson, G. 109
Jennaway, M. 321
Johnson, A. and Johnson, O. 149
juvenile fruit machine gambling study 126–7
juvenile justice system *see* California juvenile
    justice system study

Kant, I. 60
Kanter, R. 377, 382, 391
Katz, C. 300
Kelle, U. 162, 167
key informants
    observations of 156
Kincaid, H. 130, 134
Kleinman, S. 200, 376, 380, 384, 386, 390, 391

Kleinman, S. and Copp, M. 380, 383
Kotlowitz, A. 148
Krieger, S. 297
Kulick, D. and Willson, M. 364
Kunzel, R. 293
Kvale, S. 226

LaCapra, D. 54
language and social organization 43–4
Lareau, A. and Shultz, J. 318
Lather, P. 322, 325
Latour, B. 336–7
Lawler, S. 246, 367
Lederman, R. 318
Lee, R. 171
Lee, R. and Fielding, N. 162, 168
Leidner, R. 147, 155
Lemert, C. 73
Lewis, O. 151
Liebow, E. 154
life history approach 206, 231–2
life story research 185
Lincoln, Y. 265
Lincoln, Y. and Denzin, N. 316, 317, 322
Lincoln, Y. and Guba, E. 189
Lindenberg, S. 171
Lindesmith, A. 133
lineament of oppression 287
local knowledge 153
location question 226
Lofland, J. and Lofland, L. 265
Lury, C. 359, 365
Lynd, R. and Lynd, H. 154
Lyotard, J.-F. 3, 58

Macdonnell, D. 40
Mackensen, K. and Wille, U. 166
MacKinnon, C. 287
Macpherson, Sir W. 87
Maffesoli, M. 127
Mangabeira, W. 167
Manicom, A. 23, 30, 31
    see also mothering for schooling project
Mann, C. and Stewart, F. 172
Marcus, G. 144, 354
Marshall, B. 297
Marshall, C. and Rossman, G. 268
Martin, J. 378
Martinez, R. 90
Marx, K. 62
Marx, K. and Engels, F. 63
masculinity in British corporate culture study
    337–40, 344
Mason, J. 132, 133, 225, 226
May, T. 1, 3, 4, 147, 156, 335–6, 339, 366
McConville, M. 83, 88
McCoy, L. 27
McKie, L. 268, 270
McNay, L. 244, 367
Mead, G. 76, 383
medical consultation study see video-based
    field studies
Meehan, A. 92
memero-politics 248
Merelman, R. 74
meta-reflexivity 336, 337, 341
    see also reflexivity
methodenstreit dispute 128

Mienczakowski, J. 322
Miles, M. and Huberman, A. 264
Miller, R. 232, 251, 385
Mills C. 2, 206
Mills, T. and Kleinman, S. 383
moderatum generalizations 125, 131, 132, 138
    justification for 136, 137, 138, 139
    see also generalization
Moore, J. 156
morality 233, 234, 235, 236
Morris, C. 150
mothering discourse 28, 29, 30, 31, 32
mothering for schooling project 24, 32
    interviews 24–5, 26–7
    learning from interviews 27, 28
    mothering discourse 28, 29, 30, 32
    scope of the project 25–6
    situating experiences 25
    social relations 27, 33–4
mothers
    teenage 203, 219–20
    see also Black mothers study; mothering
        discourse; mothering for schooling
        project; mothers of daughters study
mothers of daughters study 246–8, 251,
    252, 253
multiple subjectivity 184, 193–4
multivoiced texts 323
Munro, R. 357, 358
musical taste study 127–8
Myers, G. 251
Mykhalovskiy, E. 325

Narayan, K. 362
narratives 229, 242, 243, 244, 245
    analysis of 254
    components of 247–8
    composite moral 229
    'conceptual narrativity' 244
    effect of social positioning 253
    free association narrative 232–3
    illustrative example 246–8
    influence of researchers 254
    interpretation in 247
    linking past and present 248–51
    linking the individual and the collective 251–3
    personal 251, 252, 254, 313, 314, 318,
        319, 320
    plots 245–6
    producing an identity 245, 249–50
    public 251, 252, 254
    'resistance narratives' 253, 256
    setting conditions for 253
    social products, as 242
Nast, H. 359
negative reality 81
negotiation 265
neo analytic induction 165
non-verbal expression 105, 238, 239
Norris, C. 3
'numbing' 383

objectivity 20
O'Brien, M. and Harris, J. 237
occupational culture 84
occupational perspectives 91
ontological narrativity 249
oral historians 185

organic solidarity 54
Orloff, A. 287
outlaw emotions 386

Papastergiadis, N. 359
Parkin, F. 56
Parsons, T. 69, 73–4
participant observation studies 144, 145, 156–7,
  202, 215, 221
 access to sites/groups 207–8
 analytic process 216, 218–20
 anonymity 153
 confidentiality 153
 designing research strategy 204
  207–8, 209
 fieldwork 212–14
 formulating research problems 202, 203
 generalization and representation 154–6
 illegal activities 153–4
 meaning and representation 149–50
 observations of key informants 156
 responsibility and representation 151–4
 validity of representation 145–9
participation in research projects 263–4, 266, 279.
  280, 281–2
Pateman, C. 287
patriarchy
 private 289
 public 289
Pavis, S. 59
Pence, E. 33, 35–9, 40, 44
personal narratives 251, 252, 254, 313
  314, 320
 separating from main analysis 318, 319
Peterson, A. and Lupton, D. 266
phenomenological ethnography
  56–7, 59
Pierce, C. 76
Plummer, K. 356
poetic representations 323
police detectives see detective work
Porter, S. 57, 65
positionings
 researchers and participants 187
Poster, M. 73
postmodern turn 234
postmodernism 58, 59
power relations 68, 191, 267, 268, 279, 280, 294,
  297, 300, 303, 307
 age and generation differences 307
 exposing subjects to harm 297
 link to race, class and gender 303, 304, 305,
  306, 307
 professional power 69, 70
 reflexivity 367–8
primary reality 80
Probyn, E. 332, 345–6, 360
processing interchanges 36–7, 44
professional ideology 69
professional power 69, 70
profiling of communities
 need for 280, 281
psychoanalysis 180, 181, 185, 186

qualitative comparative analysis 165
qualitative evaluation research 283
 characteristics of 264
 developments in 314–17

qualitative evaluation research cont.
 dialogue, creating 281
 use of 263, 265
 value of 265
qualitative software see computer software
quantitative evaluations 263

Rabinow, P. 361, 363
race
 power relations 303, 304, 305
racism 302–3
 research project on 65–70
Ragin, C. 165
rapport
 interviews 192–3
rationality 73, 78, 79–80
 formal 75
 forms of 74
 frame, field and surround 80–1
 self-presentation 78, 79
 semiotics 75–6
 situational 76–7
 studies of 74, 75
 substantive 9, 75
 see also detective work
reactivity 108
realism
 analytical 60
 critical see critical realism
 subtle 60
reconstruction 4
Reed-Danahay, D. 314
reflexive anthropology 136
reflexivity 4–5, 340, 349
 accountability and responsibility, need
  for 369
 centring of the self 360, 363, 369
 class, gender and sexuality 343, 346, 364–5
 collective practice 368
 contextual approach to 297, 298
 development of self-reflexive person 351–2
 escapism 367
 importance of 296–7
 infra 337, 341
 limitations of 335, 336, 337
 meanings of 286–7, 297
 meta 336, 337, 341
 mobility in regard to identity 344, 345, 346
 participants 366
 power relations 367–8
 referential 335, 340
 self-extension 357–8, 359, 361
 self-refashioning 358–9
 structural conditions of 365
 support for 333, 334, 335
 textual 341
 thought of 359
 uses of 369
 see also autobiographical work;
  autoethnography; field notes and
  journals; personal narratives; telling
  of the self
relationships between researcher and researched
  266–7, 313, 338–9
 see also power relations
renewal 378–80
 developing empathy 384, 385
 gender inequality 386, 387, 388, 389, 390

renewal *cont.*
    legitimacy, concern with 387
    members' respect for each other 387
    scope of study 380
    structure of 380–1
representational forms 322, 323
research
    definition of 264
research desire 184
'resistance narratives' 253, 256
'reverse archaeology' 58
Rex, J. 66
Richardson, L. 175, 323
Ricoeur, P. 244, 245, 246, 249, 250, 353
Riessman, C. 243
Rist, R. 125, 126
Robbins, B. 354
Robinson, W. 133
Roper, M. 337, 338, 364
Roth, J. 100
ruling relations 19, 39, 40, 287
Ryan, A. 77, 151
Ryder, N. 204–5

Sacks, H. 104, 106
Said, E. 58, 359
sampling 132–4, 154–5, 204, 205
Sanford, M. 376
Sanjek, R. 148
Sattel, J. 377, 378
Schegloff, E. and Sacks, H. 104
Scheper-Hughes, N. 151, 152
Scheurich, J. 58
Schutz, A. 22, 56, 57, 131
Seale, C. 135
Segal, L. 242
self-assessment evaluations
    need for support 280
self-conscious textualism 341–3, 364–5
self-extension 357–8, 359, 361
self-presentation 78, 79
self-refashioning 358–9
self-reflexive person
    development of 351–2
semiotics 75–6
sexual discrimination 302–3
sexuality and labour markets study 337–41, 344
Shaw, I. 263, 264, 266, 284
Shields, R. 127
Sica, A. 75
Silverman, D. 102, 189, 225
Simmel, G. 99
Simon, D. 85, 86
situational rationality 76–7
    see also detective work; rationality
Skeggs, B. 363, 366, 367, 369
Smart, C. and Neale, B. 230
Smith, A. and Kleinman, S. 383, 384
Smith, D. 286, 287, 296, 297
Smith, D. E. 20, 24, 26, 33, 41–2, 43, 44, 45, 46
Smith, G. 26, 31, 35, 36, 37, 45
smoking project *see* Women, Low Income and
    Smoking Project
social interaction 100, 101, 117
    awareness of 102–3
    context and situation 104, 105
    effect on organizational life 99, 116
    material environment, effect of 118

social interaction *cont.*
    non-verbal expression 238, 239
    sequences of interaction 105, 106, 107
    talk and bodily conduct 104
    see also video-based field studies
social relations 27, 30–4, 40, 45
    see also social structures
social structures 53, 54, 59, 60, 61, 63, 64
    relationship with social actions 63, 64, 70
    see also social relations
software *see* computer software
Somers, M. and Gibson, G. 243, 244, 245, 249, 251
SONAS Community Health Project 261–2
    aim of the evaluation 270
    aims of the project 269, 270
    approach to evaluation 270
    background knowledge 269, 270
    consultation 271
    evaluation team, local people's perception of
        273, 274
    knowledge and awareness of local culture and
        activities 272, 273, 274
    local people's views of launch 271–2
    participants, involvement of 270
    power relations 272
    relating to participants 273–4
    value of 282
Sparkes, A. 319–20
speech genre 19
Spivak, G. 250, 362
split-screen texts 323
sponsors' interests 4, 5
Stacey, J. 297
Stack, C. 321
'Standard North American family' 24
standpoint
    flexible 286
    mixed 286
    women's 286
Stanley, L. 58, 251, 313, 350, 354
Stanley, L. and Morgan, D. 245
statistical generalizations 131
status characteristics 66
Steedman, C. 246, 248, 249, 253, 352, 353
Stock, A. 35
Strathern, M. 357–8, 360, 361
Strauss, A. 100
Strauss, A. and Corbin, J. 189
Strong, P. and Dingwall, R. 172
structuralism
    versions of 78
structures of relations 62
subjectivity
    multiple subjectivity 184, 193–4
    participants 182–3
    researchers 187
substantive rationality 76–7
    see also rationality
Sudnow, D. 83
Sullivan, M. 156
survey research 126
Suttles, G. 155
Svensson, B. 353
symbolic anthropology 75

Taylor, C. 352
teamwork
    use of qualitative software 174

teenage mothers study 203, 219–20
telling of the self 352–3
  class differences 354–5
  confessional 350–51
  forced telling 353
  gender influences 355–6
  moral value 356
  positioning 356–7
  public gestures of personhood 355
  testimonies 354–5
  see also personal narratives; reflexivity
testimonies 354–5
texts 22, 23
  co-ordinating sequences of action 35, 36–8
  concept of 45
  multivoiced 323
  processing interchanges 36–7, 44
  role of 34–5
  significance of 34, 35
  text-reader conversations 35
  vocal 324
theoretical inferences 135–6
theory of structuration 64
therapeutic use of field notes 319–20
Thompson, P. and Samuel, R. 185
Thorne, B. 154
Thornton, S. 127
Tillman-Healy, L. 320
total generalizations 130
transcription of talk 109–12
  conventions used 119
  direct transcription software 171
  example of 110, 111
transference 188
transition to womanhood study 182–4, 192–3
transparency 265
triangulation 189
Tyler, S. 144

unconscious fears and fantasies of participants
  188, 189, 190
Unger, R. 4

value free research
  challenges to 265
Venkatesh, S. 154
Verstehende sociology 55
  vagueness of 56
video-based field studies
  benefits of 103
  camera positioning 107, 108, 109
  developing an analysis 112–16
  influence of the recording 108, 109
  need for further recordings 109
  need for related studies 107, 108
  opportunities for 116, 117, 118
  transcription 109–12, 119

video-based field studies cont.
  use of 103–4
  see also social interaction
Vincent, D. 353
Visweswaran, K. 362
vocal texts 324
voice recognition software 171

Wacquant, L. 149
Waegel, W. 84, 85
Walker, G. 25
Walkerdine, V. 181, 182, 186, 189, 253
Wallerstein, N. 266, 267, 284
Walsh, D. 301
Waquant, L. 361
Warner, W. 154
Weaver, A. and Atkinson, P. 170, 173, 174
Weber, M. 55–6, 136, 139, 151
Weitzman, E. and Miles, M. 161, 169
Wellman, D. 150
White, H. 243
Whyte, W. 152, 156, 318
Williams, L. 129, 337–41, 344, 345
Williams, M. and May, T. 129
Wilson, J. 85
Wimbush, E. and Watson, J. 263
Winch, P. 62, 137
Wolf, D. 303
women
  Black see Black women
  exclusion of, in sociology 18
  nurturing of men 388
  see also gender; mothers; sexual discrimination
Women, Low Income and Smoking Project 262
  aims of project 274
  analysis of data 277
  background knowledge 275
  case studies 278
  community groups, skills of 276–7, 279
  evaluation advisory group, role of 275–6,
    277, 278
  final reports 275, 277
  final review meeting 278–9
  initiatives used 274
  value of 282
Woolgar, S. and Ashmore, M. 333, 334, 344
work
  concept of 46–7
workplace studies 118
wounded attachment 356

Young, I. 286
youth style and musical taste study 127–8

Zelizer, V. 387
Zizek, S. 365
Znaniecki, F. 133